ARCHAEOLOGICAL HERITAGE LAW

Neil Cookson, BA, PhD (Cantab), MIFA,
Solicitor
Lecturer at The College of Law, York

Barry Rose Law Publishers Ltd
Chichester

ISBN 1 872328 94 6

Printed in Great Britain by
Antony Rowe Ltd, Chippenham, Wiltshire

Barry Rose Law Publishers Ltd
Little London
Chichester

Mr Stevens:
"Two great white vans pull up at English Heritage every morning, one is from the Department of the Environment, one is from the Department of National Heritage -"
Mr Callaghan:
"Bringing money!"
Mr Stevens:
"- and call again in the evening, not bringing money, but bringing work".

(Third Report from the House of Commons National Heritage Committee, 1994, volume II, 159)

CONTENTS

Foreword   ix

Table of Cases   xiii

Table of Statutes   xxi

Statutory Instruments   xxxvii

European Legislation   xli

Abbreviations   xliii

Acknowledgement   xlix

Introduction   li

Chapter One:
Heritage Organisations and their Functions   1

Chapter Two:
Ancient Monuments and Archaeological Areas   63

Chapter Three:
Burials and Portable Antiquities   206

Chapter Four:
International and European Initiatives   257

Chapter Five:
Listed Buildings and Historic Landscapes   302

Chapter Six:
Archaeology and Planning Law 399

Appendix – Chapter 1 525

Appendix – Chapter 2 536

Appendix – Chapter 3 597

Appendix – Chapter 4 683

Appendix – Chapter 5 688

Appendix – Chapter 6 811

Bibliography 869

Index 871

FOREWORD

Colin Renfrew
(Professor Lord Renfrew of Kaimsthorn)

This important book is a significant testimony to the way the concept of 'Heritage' – which could be defined as that part of the nation's past which is of public interest and concern – has emerged in recent decades. Archaeology is no longer simply an interesting and perhaps romantic academic pursuit. It is now an area of considerable *public* concern. Neil Cookson's impressive volume offers a thorough and much-needed guide to the various and increasingly numerous areas of intersection between Archaeology and the Law, many of which are today subsumed under that rubric of Heritage.

Thirty years ago the overlap areas between Archaeology and the Law seemed few and relatively simple. Protection to important archaeological sites was afforded by 'scheduling' – that is to say by the decision of the relevant Secretary of State (acting under advice) to place them upon the schedule of ancient monuments. Particularly important sites could be brought under his 'Guardianship' – and they were then looked after by the staff of the Directorate of Ancient Monuments. Important finds of ancient gold and silver were dealt with by the law of Treasure Trove. And that was more or less that.

Today English Heritage, or to give that body its statutory title, the Historic Buildings and Monuments Commission for England, may lay claim to be the nation's leading Quasi-Autonomous Non-Governmental Organisation (QUANGO). The whole field of Rescue Archaeology has developed, co-ordinated at national level by the Archaeology Division of English Heritage, which works alongside the division responsible for Historic Buildings. Archaeology now plays a recognised role within the planning process, with the recognition that when a new development threatens the archaeological record of the past, it is the developer who must make provision for the protection of that record, or for its appropriate documentation, often through excavation.

The law sometimes works in mysterious ways, and in this area it was not the Ancient Monuments and Archaeological Areas Act of 1979 which proved especially influential, but a rather obscure document issued by the Department of the Environment 11 years later – 'Planning Policy Guidance Note 16: Archaeology and Planning' (PPG 16) – which has proved influential among local authorities and their planning departments, where many of the key decisions are taken on the ground.

It is one of the merits of *Archaeological Heritage Law* that it covers very effectively not only the legal aspect, the statutory framework, but also the way in which the law works in practice, through the numerous public bodies which have a hand in these matters. The planning departments of local authorities, at both district and county level are important here and so is English Heritage. But there are several other relevant organisations, as Dr. Cookson very clearly documents. Unfortunately government departments change even more frequently than governments. So what used to be called the 'Department of the Environment' has now changed its name to something more complicated, while the 'Department for National Heritage' now, at the time of writing, rejoices under the title of the 'Department for Culture, Media and Sport'. Moreover the Royal Commission on the Historical Monuments of England has just been amalgamated with English Heritage.

When such bureaucratic changes are a frequent occurrence one needs sure guidance such as Dr. Cookson provides. More significantly perhaps there have been some important changes in practice. The Treasure Act of 1996, as clearly explained here, has made important changes in the way 'portable antiquities' are dealt with. Moreover there is now in place a Voluntary Recording Scheme for Portable Antiquities, which may yet develop (as it certainly should) into a coherent national organisation for the recording of these small but significant components of the national heritage before they are dispersed.

There is an international dimension to these matters, discussed here in the chapter on 'International and European Initiatives'. At the time of writing the Government, which announced a review in June 1997, has still not decided whether or not Britain should ratify the 1970 UNESCO Convention on the 'Means of Prohibiting and Preventing the Illicit Import, Export and Transfer of Ownership of Cultural Property'. Yet it freely admits that it is not currently against the law in this country to offer publicly for sale antiquities which have been illicitly excavated overseas and illegally exported to Britain from their country of origin. There is today widespread disquiet on these issues, and recently the London auctioneers Sotheby's decided to bring to an end their auctions of antiquities, which had brought adverse comment in the media on essentially ethical grounds. These are all matters which fall – or which should fall – within the scope of archaeological heritage law, and it is one of the merits of Neil Cookson's book that he examines very carefully just how the current law works, in practice as well as in theory.

This is a book which will be found useful by lawyers,

who often understand little of archaeology, and by archaeologists, who generally know little of heritage law. I am impressed by how much ground today there is in this field, and by how thoroughly Neil Cookson has covered it. It is an area where the law is evolving quite rapidly and indeed needs to evolve further, along with developing archaeological practice. 'Heritage' is a concept that has had public currency only for about 15 years – I remember the early debates during 1984 and 1985 within the Historic Buildings and Monuments Commission for England, of which I was then a member, before it took the decision to call itself 'English Heritage', and to develop a suitable logo. Not everyone was in favour of what at that time seemed the rather trendy word 'heritage'. Yet Heritage Management Studies are now a component of degree courses in many Departments of Archaeology in this country. Heritage Law is thus itself a new concept although it embraces some of our earliest legal provisions, namely those relating to Treasure, which have their origins three-quarters of a millennium ago. It is becoming quite a complex story, and we are grateful to Neil Cookson for offering us so comprehensive a guide.

Cambridge,
March 1999

TABLE OF CASES

Amalgamated Investment and Property Company v. John
    Walker and Sons [1976] 3 ll ER 509 CA   335, 337
American Cyanamid v. Ethicon Limited [1975] AC 396   430
Anisminic Ltd v. Foreign and Commonwealth
    Compensation Commission [1969] 1 All ER 208, HL   149
Armory v. Delamirie [1558-1774] All ER Rep 121   239
Ashby Railway Carriage and Iron Company v. Riche LR 7 HL 653 41
Associated Provincial Picture Houses Ltd v.
    Wednesbury Corporation [1948] 1 KB 223 CA   107, 110, 143
Re Atkins [1989] 1 All ER 14 Cst Ct   209
Attorney-General v. Trustees of the British Museum
    [1903] 2 Ch 598   231, 240
Attorney-General v. Wiltshire United Dairies (1921) TLR 884   109
Attorney-General ex rel. Bedfordshire County Council v. Trustees
    of Howard United Reformed Church, Bedford [1976] AC 363 357
Attorney-General of the Duchy of Lancaster v.
    GE Overton (Farms) Ltd [1982] 1 All ER 524 CA   230, 237, 240, 241
Attorney-General ex rel. Sutcliffe, Rouse and Hughes v.
    Calderdale Metropolitan Borough Council (1983) 46 P & CR 399   317

Barratt Development (Eastern) Limited v. Secretary of
    State for the Environment and Oadby & Wigston
    Borough Council [1982] JPL 648   433
Barvis Limited v. Secretary of State for the
    Environment (1971) P & CR 710 CA   309
Bath City Council v. Secretary of State for the
    Environment [1983] JPL 737   374, 713, 801
Berkeley v. Poulett (1976) 241 EG 911; 242 EG, 32 CA   310-11
Bizony v. Secretary of State for the Environment [1976] JPL 306   112, 141
Bolton Metropolitan Borough Council v. Jolley [1989] 1 PLR 97   390
Bolton Metropolitan Borough Council and Others v. Secretary
    of State for the Environment [1995] The Times, May 25, HL   145
Bradford Metropolitan Borough Council v. Secretary of
    State for the Environment (1986) 278 EG 1473 CA   110
Brighton Borough Council v. Secretary of State for the
    Environment (1978) 39 P & CR 46   433
British Railways Board v. Secretary of State for the
    Environment and Hounslow London Borough Council
    [1994] JPL 32 HL   465

Buckinghamshire County Council v. Hall Aggregates
   (Thames Valley) Limited [1985] JPL 634 CA   108

Chorley and James et al v. Secretary of State for the Environment
   and Basingstoke and Dean Borough Council [1993] JPL 927 CA   457
Clarke v. Secretary of State for the Environment
   [1992] EGCS 42 CA   143
Coal Contractors Ltd v. Secretary of State for the
   Environment and Northumberland County Council
   (1994) 68 P & CR 285 QBD   258
Congreve v. Home Office [1976] QB 629 CA   108
Corthorn Land and Timber Co v. Minister of Housing
   and Local Government (1966) 17 P & CR 210   310
Corven's case (1612)   227
Crédit Suisse v. Allerdale Borough Council (1994) QBD   45
Crisp from the Fens Limited v. Rutland County Council
   (1950) 1 P & CR 48   110
Croydon London Borough Council v. Gladden [1994]
   1 PLR 30 CA   429
Currie's Executors v. Secretary of State for Scotland
   [1992] SLT 69   200

Daniel Davies & Co v. London Borough of Southwark
   [1994] JPL 1116 CA   510
Lady de Wyche's case (1469)   228
Debenhams plc v. Westminster City Council [1987] 1 AC 396   315
Dyer v. Dorset County Council [1988] 3 WLR 213 CA   316

Elitestone Ltd v. Morris and Another [1997] 2 All ER 513   310-11
Elwes v. Brigg Gas Company [1886-90] All ER Rep 562   237
Empress Car Company (Abertillery) Ltd v. National
   Rivers Authority [1997] JPL 908 DC   171

Fawcett Properties Ltd v. Buckingham County Council
   [1960] 3 All ER 503 HL   460
Fawcett Properties Ltd v. Buckingham County Council
   [1981] AC 578   109
Fratelli Costanzo v. Commune di Milano [1989]
   ECR 1839   262
Re Friends of the Earth [1988] JPL 93 CA   150

Gammon (Hong Kong) Ltd v. Attorney-General of Hong
    Kong [1985] AC 1 PC   381
Good v. Epping Forest District Council [1994] JPL 372 CA   508
Gouriet v. Union of Post Office Workers [1978] AC 435   157
Grampian Regional Council v. City of Aberdeen District
    Council [1984] JPL 590   111-12, 122, 465, 482

Hall & Co Ltd v. Shoreham-by-Sea Urban District
    Council [1964] 1 All ER 1 CA   110
Handoll and Others v. Warner Goodman and Streat (A Firm)
    and Others (1995) 25 EG 157; (1995) 70 P & CR 627 CA   463
Handyside's case (c1750)   226
Hayne's case (1613)   227
Hayns v. Secretary of State for the Environment
    (1977) 36 P & CR 317   111
Hazell v. Hammersmith and Fulham London Borough
    Council [1991] 1 All ER 545 HL   41
Heatherington (UK) Ltd v. Secretary of State for the
    Environment and Westminster City Council (1995)
    69 P & CR 374 QBD   457
Hitchcock v. Walter (1838)   228
Homebase Ltd v. Secretary of State for the Environment
    [1994] EGCS 17 CA   145
Hounslow London Borough Council v. Secretary of State
    and Lawson [1997] JPL 141 QBD   379
Hoveringham Gravels Ltd v. Secretary of State for the
    Environment [1975] 1 QB 754 CA   399, 435, 436
Hughes and Hughes v. Doncaster Borough Council
    (1990) 61 P & CR 355, HL   200

I.R.C. v. National Federation of Self-Employed and
    Small Businesses Ltd [1981] 2 All ER 93 HL   151

J Murphy & Sons Ltd v. Secretary of State for the
    Environment [1973] 2 All ER 26   433

Kaur v. Secretary of State for the Environment and
    Greenwich London Borough Council [1990] JPL 814   427
Michael Kemis v. Salisbury District Council (*Re* The
    Moot, Downton, Wiltshire) (1994) 34 RVR 172   180

Kent Messenger Ltd v. Secretary of State for the
  Environment (1976) JPL 372   347
Kirklees Metropolitan Borough Council v. Batchacre
  Ltd (1987) unreported   380
Kirklees Metropolitan Borough Council v. Wickes
  Building Supplies Ltd [1993] AC 220   430

Leigh v. Taylor [1902] AC 157   310
Leominster District Council v. British Historic
  Buildings and SPS Shipping [1987] JPL 350   380
Loup and Others v. Secretary of State for the
  Environment and Salisbury District Council [1996] JPL 22 CA   432
Low v. Secretary of States for Wales and Glyndwyr
  District Council [1994] JPL 41 CA   143

Marshall v. Southampton and South West Hampshire
  Health Authority [1986] 2 All ER 584 HL   261-2
Mid-Devon District Council v. Avery [1994] JPL 40 DC   375, 382

National Rivers Authority v. Alfred McAlpine Homes
  East Ltd (1994) *The Times*, February 3, DC   166-7
National Rivers Authority v. Yorkshire Water Services
  Ltd [1995] 1 All ER 225 HL   166
Newbury District Council v. Secretary of State for the
  Environment [1980] 1 All ER 731 HL; [1981] AC 578   460-1, 462, 509
North Wiltshire District Council v. Secretary of State
  for the Environment [1992] JPL 955 CA   144

Oldham Metropolitan Borough Council v. Attorney-General
  [1993] 2 All ER 432 CA   222

Padfield v. Minister of Agriculture Fisheries and Food
  [1969] AC 997   108
Paola Faccini Dori v. Recreb Srl (1994) *The Times*, August 4, ECJ   261
Parker v. British Airways Board [1982] 1 All ER 834 CA   238
Pilbrow v. St Leonard, Shoreditch Vestry [1895] 1 QB 433   316
Re Ponsford and Newport District School Board [1894] 1 Ch 454 CA   216
Pyx Granite Co Ltd v. Minister of Housing and
  Local Government [1958] 1 QB 554 CA; [1959]
  3 All ER 1 HL   112, 460

R. v. Bovis Construction Ltd [1994] Crim LR 938   75, 169
R. v. British Coal Corporation *ex parte* Ibstock
   Building Products Ltd [1995] JPL 836 QBD   297-8
R. v. Browning [1996] 1 PLR 61 CA   385, 428
R. v. Camden London Borough Council *ex parte* Comyn
   Ching (1984) 47 P & CR 417   390
R. v. Canterbury City Council *ex parte* David Halford
   February 1992; CO/2794/1991   717
R. v. Chambers [1989] JPL 229, Cambridge Cr Ct   384
R. v. Cotswold District Council *ex parte* Barrington
   Parish Council [1997] EGCS 66   150
R. v. CPC (UK) Ltd (1994) *The Times*,
   August 4, CA   166, 383
R. v. Cunningham [1958] 3 All ER 711 CA   172
R. v. Dacorum Borough Council and Another *ex parte*
   Cannon [1996] EGCS 97 DC   376
R. v. Elmbridge Borough Council *ex parte* Active
   Office (1997) *The Times*, Dec 29, QBD   374
R. v. Endersley Properties Ltd (1975) P & C R 399   384
R. v. Hancock [1990] 3 All ER 183 CA   232
R. v. Hancock and R. v. Strickland [1986] AC 455   172
R. v. H.M.I.P. *ex parte* Greenpeace Ltd (1993)
   The Independent, September 30; [1994] 4 All ER 329   152-3
R. v. Hertfordshire District Council *ex parte*
   Sullivan (1981) JPL 752   340
R. v. Hillingdon London Borough Council *ex parte*
   Royco Homes Ltd [1974] QB 720; (1974) 28 P & CR 251   148
R. v. Hope (1996) *The Times*, July 31   172
R. v. Kelly and Another (1998) *The Independent*,
   June 4 CA   226
R. v. Kerrier District Council *ex parte* Uzell
   [1996] 71 P & CR 566   425
R. v. Lawrence [1982] AC 510   172
R. v. Leeds City Council *ex parte* Hendry (1994)
   The Times, January 20 CA   148
R. v. Leominster District Council *ex parte* Antique Country
   Buildings Ltd and Others (1988) 56 P & CR 240, QBD   344, 370, 380
R. v. London Borough of Camden *ex parte* Bellamy
   [1991] JPL 255 CA   318

R. v. McCarthy & Stone (Developments) Ltd [1998] CLR 424,
    Newport Cr Ct   385
R. v. Nedrick [1986] 3 All ER 1 CA   172
R. v. North Devon District Council *ex parte* Tarn
    (1998) February 20 unreported   312
R. v. North Somerset District Council and Pioneer Aggregates
    (UK) Ltd *ex parte* Garnet and Piersenne [1997] JPL 1015   150
R. v. North Yorkshire County Council *ex parte* Brown
    and Cartwright (1999) *The Times*, February 12   262
R. v. Peach [1990] 2 All ER 966 CA   234
R. v. Poole Borough Council *ex parte* Beebee [1991] 2 PLR 27   279
R. v. Redditch Borough Council *ex parte* Albutt, Clews
    and Scott [1996] JPL B85 QBD   432
R. v. Richmond-upon-Thames LBC *ex parte* McCarthy
    and Stone (Developments) Ltd
    [1991] 3 WLR 941 HL   44, 45, 47, 109, 403
R. v. Sandhu (Major) [1997] JPL 853   382
R. v. Secretary of State for the Environment *ex parte*
    Johnson and Benn [1998] JPL B7   147
R. v. Secretary of State for the Environment *ex parte*
    Leicester City Council (1988) P & CR 364   393
R. v. Secretary of State for the Environment *ex parte*
    Marson (1998) *The Times*, May 18 CA   281
R. v. Secretary of State for the Environment *ex parte* Rose Theatre
    Trust Company (1990) 59 P & CR 257 QBD   67, 68, 152, 153, 154, 479
R. v. Secretary of State for National Heritage *ex parte*
    J Paul Getty Trust (1994) *The Independent*, November 7   256
R. v. Secretary of State for Wales *ex parte* Kennedy [1996] JPL 645   311
R. v. Secretary of State for Wales *ex parte* Swansea
    City Council (1998) December 14   391
R. v. Seymour [1989] CLR 360 CA   168
R. v. Simpson (1993) 14 Cr App R(S) 602   169
R. v. Sims (J.O.) Ltd (1993) 96 Cr App R 125; (1992)
    The Independent August 3; (1992) CB July 20   159, 168
R. v. Somerset County Council *ex parte* Dixon
    [1997] COD 325   154
R. v. South Hertfordshire District Council *ex parte*
    Felton [1990] EGCS 34 CA   320
R. v. Stroud District Council *ex parte* Goodenough
    [1982] JPL 246 DC   152, 397

R. v. Swale Borough Council and Medway Ports Authority
ex parte Royal Society for the Protection of Birds
[1991] JPL 39   274

R. v. Wells Street Metropolitan Stipendiary
Magistrates *ex parte* Westminster City Council
[1986] 3 All ER 4; (1987) 53 P & CR 421   381-2

R. v. West Dorset District Council *ex parte* Searle
(1998) unreported CA   348-9

R. v. West Oxford District Council *ex parte* Pearce
Homes [1986] JPL 523 QBD   510

R. v. Westminster City Council *ex parte* Monaghan
[1989] 2 All ER 74 CA   349, 434

Re Racal Communications Ltd [1981] AC 374   149

Robbins v. Secretary of State for the Environment
[1989] 1 All ER 878 HL   393, 750, 806

Rolf v. North Shropshire District Council (1988)
P & CR 242 CA   395

Roy v. Kensington & Chelsea and Westminster Family
Practitioner Committee [1992] 1 AC 624   147

Royal Borough of Windsor and Maidenhead v. Secretary
of State for the Environment and Others (1988)
56(3) PCR 427 QBD   339

Runnymede Borough Council v. Harwood [1994]
1 PLR 22 CA   429

St Albans District Council v. Secretary of State for the
Environment and Allied Breweries Ltd [1992] EGCS 147   432

Re St Barnabas' Church, Dulwich (1994) *The Times*,
January 20, Southwark Cst Ct   362

Re St Luke the Evangelist, Maidstone [1995]
1 All ER 321   361

Re St Mary's, Banbury [1987] 1 All ER 247   361-2

SAVE Britain's Heritage v. Secretary of State for the
Environment [1991] 2 All ER 10 HL   144, 349-50, 439

Seddon Properties Ltd v. Secretary of State for the
Environment (1978) 42 P & CR 26   101, 143

Shimizu (UK) Ltd v. Westminster City Council [1997]
1 All ER 481   340, 344, 350

South Hams District Council v. Halsey [1996]
JPL 761   429, 430

South Lakeland District Council v. Secretary of
    State for the Environment [1992] 2 WLR 204 HL   351, 722
South Staffordshire Water Company v. Sharman
    [1895-99] All ER Rep 259   237-8
Stringer v. Minister of Housing and Local Government
    [1971] 1 All ER 65   433, 439

Tesco Stores Ltd v. Secretary of State for the
    Environment and Others [1995] 2 All ER 636 HL   509, 513-14, 516
Till v. Market Weighton Parish Council [1961] 3 All ER 1022   216
Twyford Parish Council v. Secretary of State for the
    Environment and Transport [1992] Env.L.R. 37 QBD   262

Watson-Smyth v. Secretary of State for the Environment and
    Cherwell District Council (1992) 64 P & CR 156 QBD   311-12, 316
Watts v. Secretary of State for the Environment
    [1991] JPL 718 QBD   318
Waverley Borough Council v. Fletcher [1995]
    4 All ER 756   238, 240
Welwyn-Hatfield District Council v. Secretary of
    State for the Environment and Morgan Electronics
    Ltd [1991] JPL 1019   101-2
Westminster City Council v. Croyalgrange Ltd [1985] 1 All ER 740   171
Westminster City Council v. Portland Estates plc [1985] AC 661   145
Wimpey Homes Holdings Ltd v. Secretary of State for the
    Environment and Winchester City Council [1993] 2 PLR 54 QBD   511
Woodspring District Council v. Unit Construction
    South West and Accado (1989) 4 PAD 20   99
Worsted Investments Ltd v. Secretary of State for
    the Environment and Uttlesford District Council
    [1994] EGCS, 66 QBD; [1994] JPL B111-12   320
Wychavon District Council v. Secretary of State for
    the Environment and Another (1994) *The Times*,
    January 10 QBD   262

TABLE OF STATUTES

Acquisition of Land Act 1981	62, 179, 392, 751
Agriculture Act 1986	263
Ancient Monuments Act 1931	63, 192, 435-6, 536
Ancient Monuments and Archaeological Areas	
Act 1979 (AMAA)	4, 6, 17, 19-20, 22, 43, 63-4,
	109-10, 121, 293, 402, 530, 536-63, 843
Part I	201, 422, 429, 529
Part II	7, 23, 77, 80, 125, 127, 129, 133,
	136-8, 139, 141, 174, 202, 422
Part III	138
s.1	6, 23, 64, 329, 419, 479, 525, 536-9, 564
s.1A	23, 538-9, 549
s.1(1)	66
s.1(3)	67, 70
s.1(4)	72
s.1(6A)	76
s.1(7)	74
s.1(11)	66
s.2	6, 23, 81, 88, 91, 94, 105, 158, 159-70, 177, 196,
	201, 207, 387, 419, 525, 539-41, 564, 846
s.2(1)	81, 105, 159, 160, 166, 198
s.2(2)	81, 82-3, 90, 160, 163, 165, 167
s.2(3)	81, 105, 106, 159
s.2(4)	105, 113, 115
s.2(5)	97, 105, 113
s.2(6)	105, 106, 159, 160, 163
s.2(7)	163, 165, 167
s.2(8)	163, 164
s.2(9)	164, 165
s.3	26, 84, 201, 541-2
s.3(3)	93
s.4	124, 202, 542-3, 550
s.4(1)	106
s.4(3)	124
s.4(4)	124
s.5	5, 7, 78, 169-70
s.6	77, 80, 197, 203
s.6A	24, 77-8, 80, 197, 203

s.7	196, 197-8, 202, 205, 543-5, 577-8, 581-2
s.7(2)	197-200
s.7(3)	197
s.7(4)	198
s.7(6)	198
s.8	201
s.9	196, 201, 205, 577-8, 581-3
s.9(2)	201, 202
s.9(3)	201
s.9(4)	202
s.9(5)	202
s.10	15, 24, 77, 179, 196, 203
s.10(1)	178
s.10(4)	179, 203
s.11	15, 24, 35
s.11(1)	178
s.11(1A)	179
s.11(2)	179
s.11(3)	179
s.11(4)	179
s.12	15, 180-1
s.12(1)	181
s.12(1A)	181
s.12(7)	181
s.13	35, 79, 182
s.13(1)	181
s.13(2)	181
s.13(4)	182
s.14(1)	182, 183
s.14(2)	183
s.14(3)	182
s.15	183, 196, 203
s.15(1)	183
s.15(2)	183
s.15(5)	183
s.16	15, 183-4, 196, 203
s.16(1)	183-4
s.16(1A)	183
s.16(2)	183

s.16(4)	184
s.16(5)	184
s.16(6)	184
s.16(8)	184
s.17	25, 88, 90, 98, 123, 189, 190-3, 518, 545-7, 847
s.17(4)	191-2
s.17(5)	192
s.17(7)	193
s.17(8)	193
s.19	169, 173, 184-6
s.19(1)	184
s.19(2)	184-5
s.19(4)	185, 186
s.19(4A)	185
s.19(5)	186
s.19(6)	186
s.19(7)	158, 186
s.19(8)	185
s.19(9)	184
s.20	186, 188
s.20(3)	25
s.24	88-9, 90, 98, 190, 193, 847
s.24(1)	188
s.24(2)	188
s.24(3)	188
s.24(3A)	27
s.24(3B)	188
s.24(4)	188
s.25	25, 194
s.25(2)	190
s.25(3)	194
s.25(3A)	24
s.26	79, 80, 197, 204
s.26(1)	78
s.27	197, 200
s.28	66, 158, 159, 166, 169, 170-2, 174, 177, 207, 386, 387, 846
s.28(1)	172
s.28(2)	172

s.33	23
s.33(1)	127
s.33(2)	127
s.33(2A)	128
s.33(4)	128
s.33(5)	128
s.34	23, 592
s.34(1)	132
s.34(4)	23
s.34(5)	133
s.35	131-2, 137, 138, 140, 586-94, 595
s.35(1)	130, 137, 158
s.35(3)	129
s.35(4)	129
s.35(7)	134
s.35(8)	130, 137
s.35(10)	137, 156, 158
s.36	130
s.36(1)	130
s.36(2)	130
s.36(4)	130, 158, 174
s.37	137, 594
s.37(1)	131
s.37(2)	131
s.37(5)	137
s.37(6)	138
s.38	130, 135, 140, 197, 204
s.38(1)	133
s.38(3)	134, 592-4
s.38(4)	134, 135
s.38(5)	135
s.38(6)	135
s.38(7)	135, 137
s.38(8)	135
s.39	197, 204
s.40	136, 197, 204
s.40(6)	31
s.41(1)	129, 134, 589
s.42	25, 158, 174-5, 177, 233, 249, 547-8, 633, 847

s.42(1)	175
s.42(2)	174-5
s.42(3)	175-6
s.42(5)	175, 177
s.42(6)	176
s.42(7)	176
s.43	79, 197, 204
s.44	77, 78
s.44(8)	158, 174
s.45	20, 25, 26, 39, 44, 47, 74, 136, 190, 195-6, 513, 549, 848
s.45(1A)	20, 25
s.45(2)	42
s.45(3)	80
s.46	197, 203-4, 205, 577-8, 582
s.46(2)	204
s.46(3)	136
s.47	201, 203, 204, 583
s.50	26, 845
s.50(1)	73, 93
s.50(2)	93, 179
s.50(3)	130
s.53	73, 74, 549
s.53(1)	250
s.54	80, 136
s.54(3)	80, 643
s.55	100, 140, 141-6, 147, 149, 151, 549-51
s.55(1)	141, 142
s.55(2)	128, 142, 146
s.55(6)	142
s.55(7)	146, 149
s.56	76
s.57	25, 75, 173
s.57(2)	173
s.57(3)	158
s.58	167
s.61	20, 64, 160, 173, 551-5
s.61(1)	83, 129, 188, 589, 591
s.61(4)	42, 80, 194, 594

s.61(7)	65-6, 69, 73, 250, 305, 309
s.61(8)	73, 313, 363
s.61(9)	65
s.61(10)	321
s.61(12)	16, 66, 79, 175, 178, 180, 195, 549
s.61(13)	360
s.106	97, 292, 320
Sch. 1	23, 95, 98-9, 101, 105, 107, 124-5, 158, 174, 202, 543, 556-71, 845
Sch. 2	127-8, 142
Ancient Monuments Consolidation and Amendment Act 1913	11-12, 536
Ancient Monuments Protection Act 1882	63
Building Act 1984	397
Burial Act 1857	158, 207-14, 215-17, 223, 224-5, 600
Capital Transfer Tax Act 1984	17
Care of Cathedrals Measure 1990	7, 360-1
Care of Churches and Ecclesiastical Jurisdiction Measure 1991	360
Civil List Act 1952	639
Coal Industry Act 1994	87
Coal Industry Nationalisation Act 1946	87
Coast Protection Act 1949	419
Compulsory Purchase Act 1965	179, 590
Compulsory Purchase (Vesting Declarations) Act 1981	179
Copyright, Designs and Patents Act 1988	813
Coroners Act 1988	640, 642
s.13	627
s.30	640, 642
s.36	640
Coroners Act (Northern Ireland) 1959	642-3
Criminal Damage Act 1971	386
Criminal Justice Act 1982	547
Criminal Justice Act 1991	385, 428
Crown Proceedings Act 1947	3, 147
Customs and Excise Management Act 1979	253
Disability Discrimination Act 1995	802
Disused Burial Grounds Act 1884	211, 213, 214, 217, 223, 225, 600

Disused Burial Grounds (Amendment) Act 1981   213, 214-15,
216-24, 363, 597-9, 600
Electricity Act 1989   269, 415, 420
Environment Act 1995   10, 39, 127, 191, 331, 400, 421-2
  s.97   326-7
European Communities Act 1972   260, 268
Faculty Jurisdiction Measure 1964   359-60
Field Monuments Act 1972   64, 192
Finance Act 1983   16
Forestry Act 1967   419-20
Government Trading Funds Act 1973   3
Harbours Act 1964   270
Highways Act 1980   272, 399-400, 415, 596
Historic Buildings and Ancient Monuments
  Act 1953 (HBAMA)   12, 19-20, 22, 110, 64, 323,
530, 694, 787
  s.3A   27
  s.4   354, 785
  s.5   24, 35
  s.5(1)   16
  s.5A(1)   16
  s.5B   27
  s.8C   322
Historic Monuments (Northern Ireland) Act 1971   64
Housing Act 1985   397
Housing Act 1988   214, 215, 600, 773
Import and Export Control Act 1990   253
Import, Export and Customs Powers (Defence) Act 1939   253
Income and Corporation Taxes Act 1988   17, 34
Land Compensation Act 1961   179, 197, 200, 202, 394,
534, 582, 752, 807
Land Drainage Act 1991   419, 595
Law of Property Act 1925   193, 523, 547
Law of Property (Miscellaneous Provisions) Act 1994   252
Leasehold Reform Act 1967   62
Leasehold Reform, Housing and Urban Development
  Act 1993   529, 725
Local Authorities (Goods and Services) Act 1970   42
Local Authorities (Historic Buildings) Act 1962   43

Local Government Act 1972	42, 44, 47, 496
s.111	817
s.222	156
s.250	559, 563
Local Government Act 1985	47
Local Government (Contracts) Act 1997	43
Local Government (Miscellaneous Provisions) Act 1976	414, 424
Local Government (Miscellaneous Provisions) Act 1982	519, 817
Local Government, Planning and Land Act 1980	335, 600
Local Government (Records) Act 1962	330
Local Land Charges Act 1975	75, 192
London Buildings (Amendment) Act 1939	397
Merchant Shipping Act 1995	244, 251, 611, 639
Museum of London Act 1965	47
Museum of London Act 1986	47, 48
National Heritage Act 1980	33-8
National Heritage Act 1983	4, 22, 27, 64, 73-4, 147, 528-35
s.32	10, 11, 22, 528
s.33	10, 11, 17, 21-2, 67, 186, 190, 380, 528-31, 563
s.33(1)	17-19, 25-6, 66, 68
s.33(2)	15, 17-20, 25, 66, 79, 194, 322
s.33(2A)	157, 429
s.33(3)	17, 19-20
s.33(4)	17
s.33(5)	19, 20
s.33(6)	19, 20, 24
s.33(8)	15, 21, 79, 178
s.34	10, 17, 22, 190, 531-2
s.34(2)	14
s.35	10, 14-16, 21, 22, 66, 186, 532
s.35(2)	21
s.35(3)	21
s.35(5)	15
s.36	10, 22, 24, 78-9, 533-4, 578, 583-5
s.37	10, 11, 21, 22, 534-5
s.38	14, 19
s.39	12
Sch. 3	11-14

Sch. 4   19-20, 22, 563, 581-2
National Heritage Act 1997   34, 36-8
National Lottery etc Act 1993   36
National Trust Act 1907   62
New Roads and Street Works Act 1991   272, 733
New Towns Act 1981   213-14, 215, 600
Norfolk and Suffolk Broads Act 1988   127
Occupiers Liability Acts 1957 and 1984   187
Open Spaces Act 1887   214, 600
Open Spaces Act 1906   214, 216, 600
Pastoral Measure 1983   9, 214-15, 216-19, 223-4, 364,
526, 600, 758-9, 773

Pipelines Act 1962   269
Planning and Compensation Act 1991   23, 303, 375,
384, 404-5, 423, 430, 713, 801, 848
     s.12   508
     s.15   270
     s.26   431
     s.29(1)   529
Planning (Listed Buildings and Conservation Areas)
     Act 1990   6, 17, 22, 43, 158, 213, 303, 402, 418, 419
     Part I   224
     Part VIII   727
     s.1   23, 525, 699, 736, 777, 783, 844
     s.1(1)   305, 309, 311, 334
     s.1(3)   305, 321
     s.1(4)   334
     s.1(5)   309, 311, 314-15, 369, 709, 789
     s.2   525
     s.2(2)   338
     s.2(4)   338
     s.3   336, 525, 741, 780
     s.3(2)   336
     s.3(8)   24
     s.4   525
     s.5   525
     s.6   335, 525
     s.6(1)   335
     s.7   338, 366, 380, 381, 419, 699, 783

s.8	381, 796
s.8(1)	339
s.8(2)	31, 341, 367
s.8(3)	371, 713, 800-1
s.9	160, 357, 370, 380, 381-5, 387, 397, 714, 799-800
s.9(1)	377
s.9(2)	377
s.9(3)	802
s.10(2)	352, 796
s.12	353, 526, 787, 788
s.13	353, 355, 526, 785, 787
s.14	526
s.14(2)	24
s.15	526
s.15(1)	785
s.15(5)	785
s.16	526, 695, 765
s.16(1)	364
s.16(2)	319, 321, 342
s.16(3)	366
s.17	526, 797-8
s.17(1)	364
s.17(2)	365, 372
s.17(3)	365-6, 725, 774
s.18	366, 526, 797
s.19	526, 798
s.20	371, 526
s.21	526, 728
s.21(3)	372
s.21(4)	798
s.22	526
s.22(3)	373
s.24	9, 526, 799
s.25	9, 526, 799
s.26	9, 526, 799
s.28	526, 799
s.29	336, 525
s.30	525, 526
s.32	398, 799

s.32(2)	398
s.32(4)	398
s.33	799
s.34	9, 526, 799
s.35	9, 526, 799
s.36	799
s.37	799
s.38	370, 772, 801
s.38(2)	373-4, 378
s.38(4)	378
s.39	9, 370, 376, 526
s.39(1)	377
s.40	9, 526
s.41	9, 426
s.41(1)	377
s.42	377
s.42(1)	376
s.43	375-7
s.43(4)	375
s.44A	380, 429
s.45	24
s.46	9, 375, 526
s.47	203, 388, 391-7, 526, 802
s.47(4)	393, 395
s.48	24, 392-4, 526, 749, 802, 805
s.48(1)	392
s.49	394
s.50	203, 394, 526, 752, 807
s.52	7, 526, 752, 807
s.53	526
s.54	312, 388-91, 397, 526, 748, 752, 759, 802, 804
s.54A	691, 721
s.54(4)	389
s.54(5)	389
s.55	389-90, 526, 804
s.55(2)	389
s.55(3)	389
s.55(4)	389
s.56	397, 802

s.57	719
s.59	357, 383, 385-6, 387, 714, 742, 780, 800
s.60	7, 526, 808
s.60(1)	356, 357
s.60(3)	357, 753
s.60(5)	356, 753
s.60(7)	364, 758
s.61	82, 203, 312, 321, 352, 370, 387, 846
s.62(1)	373
s.63	373
s.64	376
s.66	321, 323, 332, 338, 363, 695, 765, 783
s.66(1)	319, 440, 694, 764
s.67	319, 696, 763-4
s.69	7, 526, 531, 715-16, 767
s.70	7, 526
s.71	693, 718
s.71(2)	770
s.72	363, 694, 720, 764
s.72(1)	351, 440
s.73	720, 763-4
s.74	9, 350, 526, 723, 725, 771-2
s.74(2)	788
s.74(3)	774
s.75	82, 526, 723, 771-2
s.75(1)	357
s.75(2)	756, 758
s.75(7)	753
s.76	526, 748-9, 804
s.83	389
s.83(1)	314
s.84	314
s.91(2)	309, 311
s.101(3)	389
s.107	723
s.108	723
s.211	776
s.336	724
Sch. 4	338

Protection of Military Remains Act 1986   251
Protection of Wrecks Act 1973   7, 72-3, 250-1, 526, 555
Public Libraries and Museums Act 1964   43, 47
Taxation of Chargeable Gains Act 1992   17, 34
Telecommunications Act 1984   416, 418
Territorial Waters Jurisdiction Act 1878   74
Theft Act 1968   158, 232
Town and Country Planning Act 1947   334
Town and Country Planning Act 1971   303, 435
  s.52   508, 523
  s.54A   335
  s.55   384
  s.115   393
Town and Country Planning Act 1990   94, 100, 121, 158, 209, 213, 214, 215, 218, 224-5, 278, 293, 303, 323, 330, 337-9, 352, 386, 399, 400-1, 413, 553, 816
  Part VIII   776
  s.36(3)   454
  s.54A   96, 286, 405, 431-2, 435, 442, 445, 456-7, 459, 472, 763, 771
  s.55(1)   199, 401-2, 411
  s.55(1A)   402, 411
  s.55(2)   269, 402
  s.57(1)   400
  s.70   96, 342, 772
  s.70(1)   458, 459
  s.70(2)   404, 431, 457, 459
  s.71   772
  s.71A   268, 270
  s.72   465
  s.72(1)   459
  s.77   416, 488
  s.78   401, 486-7, 489, 524
  s.78(2)   487
  ss.82-87   848
  s.90(1)   416
  s.90(2)   416
  s.90(2A)   415

s.91	458, 773
s.91(2)	106
s.91(3)	458
s.92	458
s.92(2)	106
s.97	479
s.102	772
s.103	772
s.106	113, 123, 417, 434, 497, 507, 508-23, 772, 817, 829, 841
s.171A	106, 424, 430
s.171B	426
s.171C	423
s.172	424, 772
s.173(4)	425
s.174	427
s.174(2)	428
s.175(4)	427
s.178	426
s.179	426
s.186	427
s.187	428
s.187A	430
s.187B	156-7, 429
s.196A	424
s.239	224, 600
s.240	224-5, 600
s.262	817
s.268	416
s.288	140, 147, 279, 524
s.289(4A)	427
s.299	417
s.299A	417
s.320	496
s.322A	496
s.330	423
s.336	321, 376, 774
s.336(1)	309
Sch. 6	496

Town and Country Planning (Scotland) Act 1972   553
Transport and Works Act 1992   269, 271, 275, 414-15,
                             556, 558, 571, 730-1
Treasure Act 1996   229, 231-2, 234, 235-6, 240-50,
                             297, 602, 637-43
    statutory code of practice   604-36
Tribunals and Inquiries Act 1992   142, 144, 551
Trustee Investment Act 1961   33
Value Added Tax Act 1994   189
Water Act 1989   166
Water Industry Act 1991   422
Water Resources Act 1991   10, 171, 419, 421
Wildlife and Countryside Act 1981   406

STATUTORY INSTRUMENTS

Ancient Monuments (Applications for Scheduled
Monument Consent) Regulations 1981
  (SI 1981, No.1301)   83, 564-71, 845
Ancient Monuments (Claims for Compensation) (England)
  Regulations 1991 (SI 1991, No.2512)   205, 577-85
Ancient Monuments (Claims for Compensation) (Wales)
  Regulations 1991 (SI 1991, No.2647)   205, 583
Ancient Monuments (Class Consents) Order 1981
  (SI 1981, No.1302)   84, 89, 91, 92
Ancient Monuments (Class Consents) Order 1984
  (SI 1984, No.222)   84
Ancient Monuments (Class Consents) Order 1994
  (SI 1994, No.1381)   83, 84, 85, 89-90, 93, 190, 193
Areas of Archaeological Importance (Notification of
  Operations) (Exemption) Order 1984
  (SI 1984, No.1286)   131, 409, 589, 595-6
Care of Cathedrals Rules 1990 (SI 1990, No.2335)   360-1
Ecclesiastical Exemption (Listed Building
  and Conservation Areas) Order 1994
  (SI 1994, No.1771)   357, 753, 808
Electricity and Pipeline Works (Assessment of
  Environmental Effects) Regulations 1990
  (SI 1990, No.442)   268, 269, 687
Electricity and Pipeline Works (Assessment of
  Environmental Effects) (Amendment) Regulations
  1996 (SI 1996, No.422)   687
Environmental Assessment (Forestry) Regulations
  1998 (SI 1998, No.1731)   686
Environmental Assessment (Salmon Farming in Marine
  Waters) Regulations 1988 (SI 1988, No.1218)   686
Environmental Information Regulations 1992
  (SI 1992, No.3240)   262
Export of Goods (Control) Order 1992 (SI 1992, No.3092)   253
Export of Goods (Control) Order 1994 (SI 1994, No.1191)   253
Faculty Jurisdiction Rules 1992 (SI 1992, No. 2882)   209, 224, 600
Harbour Works (Assessment of Environmental Effects)
  (No.2) Regulations 1989 (SI 1989, No.424)   686

Harbour Works (Assessment of Environmental Effects)
Regulations 1988 (SI 1988, No.1336)   686
Hedgerows Regulations 1997 (SI 1997, No.1160)   327-9, 331
Highways (Assessment of Environmental Effects)
Regulations 1988 (SI 1988, No.1241)   686
Highways (Assessment of Environmental Effects)
Regulations 1999 (SI 1999, No.369)   268, 271-2, 686
Highways (Traffic Calming) Regulations 1993   732
Historic Monuments and Archaeological Objects
(Northern Ireland) Order 1995   643
Human Remains Removal Licence (Prescribed Fees)
Order 1982 (SI 1982, No.364)   211, 600
Land Drainage Improvement Works (Assessment of
Environmental Effects) Regulations 1988
(SI 1988, No.1217)   686
Local Authorities (Capital Finance) Regulations 1990   395, 751
Operations in Areas of Archaeological Importance
(Forms of Notice etc.) Regulations 1984
(SI 1984, No.1285)   129, 586-94
Planning (Listed Buildings and Conservation Areas)
Regulations 1987   303
Planning (Listed Buildings and Conservation Areas)
Regulations 1990   303, 338, 342, 352-3, 372, 740
Return of Cultural Objects Regulations 1994
(SI 1994, No.501)   262
Rules of the Supreme Court Order 53   141, 146-8, 149, 151, 155
Order 94   141, 142, 143
Secretary of State for Culture, Media and Sport
Order 1997 (SI 1997, No.1744)   3
Secretary of State for the Environment, Transport and
the Regions Order 1997 (SI 1997, No.2971)   3
Stonehenge Regulations 1997 (SI 1997, No.2038)   173
Town and Country Planning Appeals (Determination
by Inspectors) (Inquiries Procedure) Rules 1992
(SI 1992, No.2039)   489
Town and Country Planning Appeals (Inquiries
Procedure) Rules 1992 (SI 1992, No.2038)   489
Town and Country Planning (Applications) Regulations
1988 (SI 1988, No.1812)   403, 438-9, 466, 827, 838

Town and Country Planning (Assessment of
   Environmental Effects) (Amendment) Regulations
   1994 (SI 1994, No.677)   270
Town and Country Planning (Assessment of
   Environmental Effects) Regulations 1988   686, 848
Town and Country Planning (Churches, Places of
   Religious Worship and Burial Grounds) Regulations
   1950 (SI 1950, No.792)   225, 600
Town and Country Planning (Consultation with the
   Garden History Society) Directions 1995   324
Town and Country Planning (Control of Advertisements)
   Regulations 1992   726-7, 775
Town and Country Planning (Development Plans)
   Regulations 1991   404, 690
Town and Country Planning (Enforcement) (Inquiries
   Procedure) Rules 1992   303
Town and Country Planning (Enforcement Notices and
   Appeals) Regulations 1991 (SI 1991, No.2804)   374, 429
Town and Country Planning (Environmental Assessment
   and Permitted Development) Regulations 1995
   (SI 1995, No.417)   268-9
Town and Country Planning (Environmental Assessment
   and Unauthorised Development) Regulations 1995
   (SI 1995, No.2258)   269, 686
Town and Country Planning (Environmental Impact
   Assessment) (England and Wales) Regulations 1999
   (SI 1999, No.293)   268, 272-86, 683-4, 686
Town and Country Planning Fees Order   403
Town and Country Planning General Development
   Order 1977   410
Town and Country Planning General Development
   Order 1988   410, 694, 697, 722-3, 773, 825, 828
   art.4   526, 697, 723
   art.18   284
   art.23   285
Town and Country Planning (General Development
   Procedure) Order 1995   123, 321, 458, 466, 487, 839
   art.1   478
   art.3   291

art.4   9
art.7   282
art.8   282, 405
art.10   7, 26, 199, 284, 324
art.20   285, 499
art.23   487
Town and Country Planning (General Permitted
  Development) Order 1995 (SI 1995, No.418)   91, 198, 339, 402-3,
                                    405-13, 414, 420, 426, 686, 837
art.1   405, 410
art.3   405, 407, 409, 411
art.4   412
art.5   412
art.7   408-9
art.10   268
art.26   26
Town and Country Planning (Modification and Discharge
  of Planning Obligations) Regulations 1992
  (SI 1992, No.2832)   520
Transfer of Functions (National Heritage) Order 1992
  (SI 1992, No.1311)   2
Transport and Works Applications (Listed Buildings,
  Conservation Areas and Ancient Monuments
  Procedure) Regulations 1992 (SI 1992, No.3138)   415, 559, 570, 731
Transport and Works (Applications and Objections)
  Procedure Rules 1992 (SI 1992, No.2902)   271, 272, 571
Transport and Works (Assessment of Environmental
  Effects) Regulations 1995 (SI 1995, No.1541)   271, 687
Transport and Works (Assessment of Environmental
  Effects) Regulations 1998 (SI 1998, No.2226)   271, 687

EUROPEAN AND OTHER LEGISLATION

Council Directive 85/337/EEC	261, 262, 266, 267, 268-9, 271, 275, 286-8
Council Directive 90/313/EEC	263
Council Directive 93/7/EEC	262, 295
Council Directive 96/61	278
Council Directive 97/11	262, 266, 267, 270, 275-6
Council Regulation 85/797	263
Maastricht Treaty	260
Treaty of Rome	260-1
Hague Convention (1954)	257
World Heritage Convention (1972)	258

ABBREVIATIONS

Statutes

AMAA	Ancient Monuments and Archaeological Areas Act 1979
HBAMA	Historic Buildings and Ancient Monuments Act 1953
NHA	National Heritage Act (1980, 1983 or 1997, as indicated)
PCA	Planning and Compensation Act 1991
P(LBCA)A	Planning (Listed Buildings and Conservation Areas) Act 1990
TA	Treasure Act 1996
TCPA	Town and Country Planning Act (1990 unless stated otherwise)
TWA	Transport and Works Act 1992

Statutory Instruments

GDO	Town and Country Planning General Development Order 1988
GD(P)O	Town and Country Planning (General Development Procedure) Order 1995
GPDO	Town and Country Planning (General Permitted Development) Order 1995
P(LBCA)R	Planning (Listed Buildings and Conservation Areas) Regulations 1990

Circulars and Guidance

DOE — Department of the Environment circular

Environment
  Circular — Circular of the DETR which covers environmental matters

PPG — Planning Policy Guidance Note

PG(W)PP — Planning Guidance (Wales) Planning Policy

WO — Welsh Office circular

Organisations and Offices

ACAO — Association of County Archaeological Officers

ADAO — Association of District Archaeological Officers

ALGAO — Association of Local Government Archaeological Officers

Cadw — Welsh Historic Monuments

CBA — Council for British Archaeology

CBI — Confederation of British Industry

CWGC — Commonwealth War Graves Commission

DAC — Diocesan Advisory Committee (of the Church of England)

DCMS — Department for Culture, Media and Sport

DETR — Department of the Environment, Transport and the Regions

DNH — Department of National Heritage

DOE — Department of the Environment

EH — English Heritage

HLF — Heritage Lottery Fund

HRP — Historic Royal Palaces

HSD	Heritage Sponsorship Division (of the DNH/DCMS)
ICE	Institute of Civil Engineers
ICOMOS	International Council on Monuments and Sites
IFA	Institute of Field Archaeologists
JCT	Joint Contracts Tribunal
NAR	National Archaeological Record
NHMF	National Heritage Memorial Fund
NMR	National Monuments Record
P.C.A.	Parliamentary Commissioner for Administration
RCAHM(w)	Royal Commission on the Ancient and Historical Monuments of Wales
RCHM(e)	Royal Commission on the Historical Monuments of England
SCAUM	Standing Conference of Archaeological Unit Managers
SMR	Sites and Monuments Record
SSCMS	Secretary of State for Culture, Media and Sport
SSETR	Secretary of State for the Environment, Transport and the Regions

Procedural

AAI	Area of archaeological importance
BPN	Building preservation notice
CA	Court of Appeal
CPO	Compulsory purchase order
Cr Ct	Crown Court
Cst Ct	Consistory Court

DC	Divisional Court
EIA	Environmental impact assessment
ESA	Environmentally sensitive area
EU	European Union
GV	Group value
HL	House of Lords
LBC	Listed building consent
MPP	Monuments protection programme
PC	Privy Council
QBD	Queen's Bench Division (of the High Court)
RSC	Rules of the Supreme Court
SMC	Scheduled monument consent
UDP	Unitary development plan

Bibliographical

A.C.	Appeal Cases (Law Reports)(HL)
All E.R.	All England Law Reports
BAN	British Archaeological News (now British Archaeology) (CBA)
CB	Conservation Bulletin (EH)
Ch	Chancery (Law Reports)
CLP	Conservation Issues in Local Plans (EH, 1996)
CLR	Current Law Review
COD	Crown Office Digest
Crim L R	Criminal Law Review
Cr. App. R.	Criminal Appeal Reports
DETR 1997	DETR Consultation paper on the implementation of EC Directive 97/11 on Environmental Assessment

DOE 1992	Environmental Assessment: A guide to the Procedures (6th impression). London, HMSO
DOE 1995	Preparation of Environmental Statements for Planning Projects that Require Environmental Assessment: A Good Practice Guide. London, HMSO
E.C.R.	European Court Reports
EFP	Encyclopaedia of Forms and Precedents, 5th edn. (Butterworths)
E.G.	Estates Gazette (Law Reports)
E.G.C.S.	Estates Gazette Case Summaries
EH 1992	Development Plan Policies for Archaeology
EH 1994	Proposed Amendments to Legislation (consultation paper)
EH 1995	Development in the historic environment (advice note)
Env. L.R.	Environmental Law Review
Halsbury	Halsbury's Laws, 4th edn. (Sweet and Maxwell)
HC 1987	First Report from the House of Commons Environment Committee, vols I-III, 146 of 1987
HC 1994	Third Report from the House of Commons National Heritage Committee, vols I & II, 139 of 1994
IFA OP	Occasional paper published by the IFA
IFA TP	Technical paper published by the IFA
J.P.L.	Journal of Planning and Environment Law
KB	King's Bench (Law Reports)
MAP	The Management of Archaeological Projects, 2nd edn. (EH, 1991)
M.L.R.	Modern Law Review
N.L.J.	New Law Journal

P.A.D.	Planning Appeal Decisions
P. & C.R.	Property and Compensation Reports
P.L.R.	Planning Law Reports
POH	Protecting Our Heritage (DNH/WO consultation paper, 1996)
PP(HL)	Parliamentary papers of the House of Lords
Q.B.	Queen's Bench (Law Reports)
R.V.R.	Rating and Valuation Reporter
SCP	The Supreme Court Practice, 1999 (Sweet and Maxwell)
S.L.T.	Scots Law Times
T.L.R.	Times Law Reports
W.L.R.	Weekly Law Reports
YDAS	York Development and Archaeological Study (Ove Arup & Partners, 1992)

ACKNOWLEDGEMENT

Over the years many people have stimulated my interest in archaeology and its relationship with the law. I owe a particular debt of gratitude to Dr Bob Yarwood (formerly of Leeds University and West Yorkshire Archaeology Service) and Professor Paul Mellars (Corpus Christi College, Cambridge). In legal practice I have had the good fortune to work with several colleagues who have been of invaluable assistance in broadening my understanding of planning and development law: Bill Marshall Smith and Stephen Turnbull (of Booth & Co, Leeds, as it then was); Peter Beales (of Oldham Metropolitan Borough Council); and Richard Frankland and Dr Joan Rees (Chief Solicitor and Chief Planning Officer, respectively, to Redcar and Cleveland Borough Council). A feature of research in archaeological practice and procedure is the willingness of staff at English Heritage, Cadw and the Royal Commissions to help out with repeated questions and points of clarification. I am indebted to them. When this work was in its early stages it was also of great benefit to have participated in the regional working parties supported by English Heritage (under the direction of Dr Bill Startin and Dr David Fraser). Dr Ian Goodall and Colum Giles (both of the RCHM(e)) have been helpful in clarifying the role of the RCHM(e). On the administrative front I thank Judith Rushton: large parts of the text would never have found their way from barely decipherable jottings to finished text without her apparently endless energy and resourcefulness. Finally, and continually, I am grateful for the insight and support of my wife, Dr Gill Cookson, and the patience and dedication of my publishers.

INTRODUCTION

The discovery of an archaeological site invariably arouses interest. A landowner may have mixed feelings, depending on the nature of the site. A property developer may meet the discovery with consternation, particularly if its location is set to have a major impact on his plans. The local archaeologist may be relieved that something of note is occurring in his area, although if he or she is academically inclined the discovery may be an unwelcome intrusion into a formerly seamless thesis. The treatment of an archaeological site, whether newly discovered or not, will arouse no less interest. Indeed, as a site's status is assessed and plans are discussed all interested parties will realise, if they did not do so beforehand, that from both the technical and legal perspective treatment of archaeological sites is a complicated matter. The technical expertise to deal with sites is spread thinly. The techniques themselves, like the law surrounding them, are unusually varied. And yet the successful treatment of such sites may be the difference between a feasible and a flawed development proposal, a viable and an unviable economic unit, a credible planning and conservation strategy or, in cases where the criminal law intervenes, reasonable behaviour and imprisonment.

The law of archaeological sites, even if limited to the conservation aspects, is a complicated matter not because of the depth or detail of any particular part of the law; there are few aspects of the law in this area which need to be interpreted with the attention required by the proverbial tax statute. It is complicated in the main because a number of usually distinct branches of the law converge. Typically there are questions about land ownership, statutory protection of land and buildings, planning law and authorisation of development, compensation, ownership of portable objects, copyright in drawings and archives, procurement contracts and grants, and ecclesiastical or burial law. Criminal and civil law, together, play a considerable part in the protection of land and buildings, planning law, ownership of portable objects and burial law. Planning law, compensation, portable objects and the protection of land and buildings are also the subject of different forms of quasi-judicial proceedings. In addition, as archaeological issues arise in relation to both buildings and sites it must be appreciated that protection may be afforded by at least two different codes, that is the listed buildings code and the ancient monuments code (although it is an over-simplification to equate monuments with sites and listed buildings with buildings!).

When most archaeological work took place within the public sector this complexity was less of a legal concern than today. Perhaps those nearest to the working of government had a ready grasp of the intricacies concerned; perhaps a more relaxed relationship between the parties involved at that time meant that a rigorous understanding of the legal issues was seldom called for. Recent years have certainly seen an increase in the number of independent archaeological consultants and contractors, carrying out a much greater proportion of the available archaeological work. The growth in the independent sector has been stimulated by the adoption by advisory agencies – English Heritage in particular – of something akin to the 'polluter pays principle', and an increasingly competition-orientated approach to archaeological funding; both of which have arrived at a time when central government is reluctant to see local authorities provide more of the services required. The influence of national agencies has not declined, however, and they are still very influential in the authorisation, programming and funding of archaeological work. Where before there were contracts of service there are now contracts for services; funding is more likely to be by way of loans than grants, with risks covered by private insurance, not taxation. Rather than dealing directly with the ministry, participants in the market for archaeological services will often rely on independent arrangements ordered according to ministerial guidance and other published advice. The situation now is as complicated as ever and, to judge from both the interest shown by archaeologists in 'law and archaeology' seminars, and the interest of lawyers and their clients in planning policy and archaeology, the legal issues related to archaeological sites are of general professional concern.

This Book and the Literature

The chapters below focus on conservation law and archaeology rather than procurement and construction law, that is the law of the protection of sites and buildings, planning law, burial, artefacts, environmental assessment and not the law relating to health and safety, employment or construction contracts.

There have been useful beginnings in this area, by Suddards (1988), and now Suddards and Hargreaves (1996); the latter has a chapter dealing with archaeology and planning. Ross (1991) looks at heritage law and procedures from an administrative perspective, part of which is devoted to conservation of the archaeological heritage. Mynors (1995) too gives a concise account of ancient monument law and archaeology. However, all of these works adopt a broad canvas, which usually covers listed buildings, conservation areas, tree preservation orders, ancient monuments and other related topics in equal measure; of necessity archaeology does not receive there the special attention which its particular nature demands, nor is the level of detail, especially in relation to statutory provisions and participating organisations, sufficient to make the works as helpful to archaeologists, or those considering archaeology, as they are to urban planners and historic buildings specialists. For a relatively comprehensive survey of the law as it relates to archaeological sites, especially from the planning law perspective, the most recent text is the most useful: Pugh-Smith and Samuels (1996) has a wide compass, bringing in topics such as ecclesiastical buildings, parks and gardens, and the function of heritage organisations, where these matters shed light on archaeological conservation. Unlike the other works mentioned in this paragraph and the encyclopaedias mentioned below, Pugh-Smith and Samuels is concerned almost exclusively with archaeology. This concern manifests itself in over 200 pages of appendices, a substantial proportion of which is given over to guidelines for archaeological projects issued by the IFA and other conservation bodies. This is in contrast to the present work, which has a more detailed treatment of the legal processes (including appeals, planning obligations, legal challenges and prosecutions), and annexes statutory and legal materials in preference to non-statutory codes of practice and technical advice.

An authoritative and practical guide to both the AMAA

1979 and the P(LBCA)A 1990 appears in the relevant chapters of Sweet and Maxwell's *The Encyclopedia of Planning Law and Practice*, where statutory provisions are set out and accompanied by extensive advisory notes. Butterworth's *Planning Law Service* also has useful sections dealing with archaeology, ancient monuments and archaeological areas but has a more limited coverage of statutory materials. However, both encyclopedias cover the complete range of planning law, and include volumes of work on matters as diverse as hazardous substances legislation and advertisements, hardly relevant to archaeological conservation.

Although not specifically a law text, Hunter and Ralston (1993) is another book of which readers need to be aware. This is a collection of papers on 'archaeological resource management'; part two, entitled 'Frameworks', has particularly useful chapters on the law relating to portable antiquities (Longworth), ancient monuments (Breeze), ecclesiastical buildings (Bianco), archaeology underwater (Firth) and the international context (Cleere). Another book, McGill (1995), provides an extended guide to the intricacies of project planning, implementation and finance. Like Hunter and Ralston, McGill is not primarily a legal work but covers specific areas of law, for example construction contracts, within the field of project management. McGill has been criticised for an obsolete philosophical perspective and a superficial treatment of archaeological matters (Darvill: 1996), but there is useful material here for anybody considering archaeology in the construction context.

The Institute of Field Archaeologists (IFA) has published technical and occasional papers, especially works on burial law, environmental assessment and archaeological contracts. However, neither the IFA, the Council for British

Archaeology nor English Heritage has yet produced a comprehensive manual of archaeological law.

In this book the law is divided into six subjects, most of them of relevance to the conservation of any significant archaeological site in England and Wales. Chapter one places considerable emphasis on the functions of heritage organisations. Chapter two deals at length with the statutory basis of ancient monuments law, local and national procedures and the relevant judicial remedies. The new and old law relating to treasure is discussed at chapter three, together with other provisions affecting the treatment of buried remains. In chapter four the effects of European and international codes and conventions are summarised, as a context for national measures. Chapter five briefly discusses listed buildings law and related topics as they most often influence the treatment of archaeological sites and structures. Chapter six considers the nature of planning law and its impact on archaeological sites.

Practitioners will be aware of the difficulties in obtaining workable subject divisions in the area of archaeology law. As a word of warning, but also as a guide, therefore, it should be mentioned that 'archaeological sites in the countryside' is not dealt with as a distinct topic, nor are contracts or insurance. The latter are considered briefly in the context of archaeology and planning in chapter six; the former is only part of the discussion in chapters two, four and six. Compensation under the AMAA 1979 is dealt with in chapter two, but compensation under the TCPA 1990 is not covered. The law of chattels forms part of the discussion in chapter three and, to a lesser extent, in chapter six. Ecclesiastical law features in chapter five; constitutional law is a significant ingredient of chapters one, two, three and four; and the law of the sea is briefly referred to in chapter six. Local inquiries are considered in relation to scheduled monuments, listed buildings and planning applications but detailed discussion of inquiries procedure is limited to the treatment of archaeological issues within the planning system, and not the minutiae of inquiry rules and procedures. Anyone engaging in a planning inquiry should consult *The Encyclopedia of Planning Law and Practice* already referred to, or a similar work, in which the regulations, guidance notes and statutory provisions relating to conduct, costs and timetables are set-out. Health and safety at work is not covered in detail: there is already an accessible summary of the issues as they relate to archaeological sites in Health and Safety in Field Archaeology (1991, revised 1993 and subsequently), published by the Standing Conference of Archaeological Unit Managers.

Changes in Law and Guidance

It is hoped that this book will draw together many of the disparate strands of law affecting archaeological sites and monuments. However, even in an area which is sometimes perceived as dusty and peripheral, the law is subject to frequent changes and amendments, sometimes all the more difficult to track and to gauge because of their laconic treatment by the legislature or ministry, and their lack of publicity.

Welsh planning guidance has recently undergone extensive revision and, although substantially the same as its English equivalents, may be amended further now that heritage responsibilities have been transferred to the Welsh Assembly. In England, PPG 1 and PPG 7 were revised and reissued in 1997, and there was a new circular on planning obligations. Earlier this year new regulations were made in relation to environmental impact assessment, the changes now being incorporated into chapter four of this work. There have been no proposals published for the revision of PPG 16, although the document, published in 1990, is now ripe for amendment and has already been cancelled in Wales.

There are signs that the archaeological heritage is about to benefit from a systematic - though not fundamental – legislative review. In May 1996 the Department of National Heritage and the Welsh Office published jointly a consultation document entitled *Protecting our Heritage* ('POH'), which invited responses to suggestions for legislative reform. One suggestion in POH was to introduce new legislation to give the National Heritage Memorial Fund trustees wider powers, so that proceeds allocated from the National Lottery to the Fund could be applied for a wider range of projects. The NHA 1997 now contains the new powers and refers specifically to archaeological purposes.

In relation to listed buildings POH contemplates the introduction of a system of 'provisional listing'; automatic issuing of 'certificates of immunity from listing' where a building has been rejected as unworthy of listing (instead of on specific application as at present); the possibility that factors such as economic, financial and personal considerations should be taken into account when listing a building; and special procedures for the listing of modern buildings.

The most pertinent changes as far as the archaeological heritage is concerned are those in section 4 of POH. Section

4 considers a large number of changes to ancient monuments law, including: creating an offence of removing finds from scheduled sites without consent; an express requirement for scheduled monument consent for any 'disturbance' of a scheduled monument; removal of the 'ignorance defence' from section 2 of the AMAA; rationalisation of the definition of the term 'ancient monument' in the NHA 1983 and the AMAA; raising the maximum fine, on summary conviction, to £20,000 for offences under section 2 or section 28 of the AMAA; introducing into scheduled monument law a procedure similar to the listed building enforcement notice; repealing part II of the AMAA (and so scrapping Areas of Archaeological Importance); devolving the determination of scheduled monument consent applications to local authorities, along listed building consent lines; the introduction, in England only, of a statutory duty for relevant local authorities to maintain a Sites and Monuments Record; introducing a statutory duty under the TCPA 1990 to have regard to ancient monuments and their settings when determining planning applications; and extension of English Heritage's powers in relation to maritime archaeology, in particular a power to act in territorial waters beyond England.

Section 5 of POH proposes a rationalisation of the confusing statement of English Heritage's duties and functions contained in section 33 of the NHA 1983. There are also proposals to confer power on English Heritage (a) to participate in or form any company whose objects fall within English Heritage's statutory functions (in contrast to the limited powers currently contained in section 35 of the NHA 1983); (b) to give advice outside the United Kingdom; and (c) a general power to charge for services where a person or body has requested the services in question.

These suggestions and proposals must be borne in mind, especially in relation to statements about the current powers of English Heritage (chapter one) and the provisions of the AMAA 1979 (chapter two). Some proposals, such as the devolution of scheduled monument consent determinations, seem unlikely to be enacted in the foreseeable future. Others, such as the extension of English Heritage's powers and amendments to section 2 of the AMAA are more likely to occur within this Parliament, perhaps as an adjunct to the merger of the RCHM(e) with English Heritage (see chapter 1). The likelihood of repeal of part II of the AMAA is more difficult to assess, although English Heritage is in favour of repeal. Repeal of part II is unlikely to occur without the comfort - especially in historic cities - of new statutory duties to maintain SMRs and to take account of scheduled and unscheduled monuments when making planning decisions.

The Law stated is that of England and Wales.

York
June, 1999

CHAPTER ONE

HERITAGE ORGANISATIONS AND THEIR FUNCTIONS

U nderstanding heritage law requires consideration of the legal and administrative basis of those organisations instrumental in formulating and operating heritage policy. This is not an easy task. In 1992 a series of complex arrangements resulted from the transfer of most (but not all) ministerial functions in this area from the Department of the Environment to the newly created Department of National Heritage; in England the sophisticated relationship of the Historic Buildings and Monuments Commission ('English Heritage') with both ministries is an additional, complicating factor. Archaeological policy and practice in England and Wales is also the product of many, contrasting organisations, both public and private. Indeed, although acronyms abound – HBMC, Cadw, HRP, RCHM(e), IFA or CBA, for example – there is often a minimal understanding of the legal status and functions of heritage organisations, even amongst archaeologists.

This chapter considers the most important bodies involved with conservation of the archaeological heritage:

Secretary of State for Culture, Media and Sport (formerly the Secretary of State for National Heritage);
Secretary of State for the Environment, Transport and the

1

Regions
Historic Royal Palaces;
English Heritage (and Cadw);
Royal Commission on the Historical Monuments of England (and its sister organisation in Wales);
National Heritage Memorial Fund (and the National Heritage Lottery Fund);
'Units' within local authorities, museums and universities;
National museums and national archaeological societies;
Archaeological trusts;
Independent consultants and commercial contractors;
Institute of Field Archaeologists;
Council for British Archaeology; and
National Trust for Places of Historic Interest or Natural Beauty.

(The planning functions of local planning authorities and national parks are considered in chapter six).

The Secretary of State for Culture, Media and Sport and The Secretary of State for the Environment, Transport and the Regions

1.01 The Secretary of State for Culture, Media and Sport (SSCMS) is a corporation sole, that is a corporation consisting of only one member at a time. The corporation, i.e. the office, was constituted under article 2(1) of The Transfer of Functions (National Heritage) Order 1992 (S.I. 1992, No.1311) as the Secretary of State for National Heritage but is now renamed, pursuant to the Secretary of

State for Culture, Media and Sport Order (S.I. 1997, No.1744). The Secretary of State for the Environment, Transport and the Regions (SSETR) is another corporation sole, in this case constituted by the Secretary of State for the Environment, Transport and the Regions Order (S.I. 1997, No.2971). The Order provides for the retention of distinct reference to 'Environment' guidance and circulars. In the sphere of archaeological policy reference will usually be to the SSETR's environmental functions and the abbreviations 'DETR' or 'SSETR' should be considered accordingly.

Both the SSCMS and the SSETR are ministers in the sense that they head one or more of the ministries by which all acts of the Crown must be undertaken. They are responsible as servants of the Crown for the acts of their ministries and may in appropriate circumstances claim privileges and rights generally afforded the Crown (as amended by the Crown Proceedings Act 1947), including Crown immunity and prerogative powers. Ministers do not have any general authority to trade their departmental functions for profit, nor can surpluses of a Department be carried forward from one year to the next unless express authority provides otherwise (under the Government Trading Funds Act 1973, for example).

1.02 Before the creation of the Department of National Heritage (DNH) in 1992, most ministerial functions relating to the 'built heritage' were carried out in England by the Secretary of State for the Environment (in consultation with English Heritage), and in Wales by the Secretary of State for Wales. In Wales the situation remains as it was before 1992, with the Secretary of State for Wales (and now the Welsh Assembly) continuing to be responsible for listed building and ancient monument administration (as far as archaeology is concerned through the executive agency known as Welsh Historic Monuments (Cadw)).

In England the situation is very different. Until 1992 the Secretary of State for the Environment (which ministry is now combined with Transport) had responsibility for all decisions in listed building and ancient monument matters, maintenance of the historic royal palaces, as well as the policy aspects of heritage conservation. Most inspectors and caseworkers employed by the Department of Environment (DOE) had transferred to English Heritage, a separate statutory corporation, when the latter was formed in 1984, but throughout the 1980s the DoE retained a 'Directorate of Ancient Monuments and Historic Buildings', consisting of about 1000 staff, most of whom were employed in the Department's historic royal palaces function. The historic royal palaces were transferred to a distinct (but still departmental) agency in 1989 – the Historic Royal Palaces Agency (HRPA). After this only about 50 staff were involved in what is known as the Department's 'Heritage Sponsorship' function, which included residual ancient monument casework; Heritage Sponsorship remained entirely a departmental function, as it comprised all of those statutory decision making responsibilities which vest in the Secretary of State under the AMAA 1979 and the NHA 1983, for which the Government has said accountability to Parliament should be retained. 'Heritage Sponsorship' also included the monitoring and/or funding of all 'independent' agencies, most notably English Heritage, the National Heritage Memorial Fund and the Royal Armouries. The Heritage Sponsorship Division of the DOE transferred to the newly created DNH in 1992.

1.03 By 1992, ministerial functions relating to archaeology and the built heritage in England, though important, were limited in scope. The DNH inherited the bulk of the DOE's functions in this area, but the DNH (like its successor, the DCMS) does not carry out archaeological work in the field and, in conservation matters generally, Secretaries of State appear content to stand behind English Heritage. Since English Heritage assumed its full functions in April 1984 neither the DOE nor the DNH/DCMS has been responsible for the inspection of or professional advice on historic buildings, ancient monuments or archaeological sites. Nor have the Secretaries of State been responsible – at least, not directly – for the management or marketing of the 400 or so 'properties in care' (now referred to by English Heritage as 'historic properties'), or for the making of grants for heritage purposes, except under special programmes or to the public bodies which they sponsor. The general principle adopted by the Secretaries of State, both before and after the creation of the Department of National Heritage, seems to be that a relevant function will be delegated to English Heritage if both the function can be lawfully delegated and it is politically acceptable to do so. This means that the lion's share of archaeological expertise, both at the operational and administrative level, has for some years been with English Heritage.

1.04 The residual but important functions of the Secretaries of State in archaeological and related matters were summarised in *Responsibilities for Conservation Policy and Casework* (joint Department of the Environment/Department of National Heritage Circular 20/92;1/92, reproduced at appendix 1A of this work).

The DCMS as successor to the DNH has responsibility for:

(a)   all policy relating to archaeology (including marine archaeology) and conservation of the built heritage;

(b)   the funding and control of English Heritage, the National Heritage Memorial Fund, the Royal Commission on the Historical Monuments of England (RCHM(e)) and other public heritage bodies (the *Third Report of the House of Commons National Heritage Committee* lists a total of 36 such bodies for which the former Secretary of State for National Heritage was responsible (HC 1994, 139-II, 34));

(c)   listing of buildings under sections 1-6 of the P(LBCA)A 1990 (but not the determination of those applications for listed building consents referable to the Secretary of State – which is still a function of the Secretary of State for the Environment, Transport and the Regions);

(d)   scheduling ancient monuments (after consultation with English Heritage) and maintaining the relevant schedules under section 1 of the AMAA 1979;

(e)   the determination of applications for scheduled monument consent under section 2 of the AMAA 1979, and the processing of scheduled monument consent inquiries/hearings before the same are conducted by an inspector from the Planning Inspectorate;

(f)   confirming compulsory purchase orders for the acquisition of historic buildings, or itself compulsorily acquiring listed buildings (after consultation with English Heritage);

(g)   acquiring land by agreement for the purposes of section 52 of the P(LBCA)A 1990;

(h)   authorising English Heritage to effect urgent works to preserve a listed building (in Wales, but not in England, the appropriate Secretary of State may execute such works himself; contrast the position under section 5 of the AMAA 1979, where the Secretary of State is empowered to carry out emergency repairs to ancient monuments);

(i)   procedures and reserve powers relating to the designation of conservation areas (under sections 69-70 of the P(LBCA)A 1990);

(j)   the protection of wrecks under section 1 of the Protection of Wrecks Act 1973; and

(k)   directions relating to the operation of the exemption for ecclesiastical buildings under section 60 of the P(LBCA)A 1990, and directions relating to the exclusion of certain buildings from the requirement to obtain consent to the demolition of unlisted buildings in conservation areas.

This list, like the ministerial guidance, is not exhaustive. Certificates of 'immunity from listing' are now dealt with by the DCMS, as is the administration of Areas of Archaeological Importance (under part II of the AMAA 1979). The SSCMS also performs ministerial functions under the Care of Cathedrals Measure 1990 and under art.10(1)(l) of the GD(P)O.

1.05 The DCMS works closely with the DETR on many matters which fall partly within the remit of both ministries. This is most apparent perhaps in relation to listed buildings and conservation areas, where there is a substantial overlap of functions between the Departments, as recognised in the joint PPG 15 (*Planning and the Historic Environment*).

The DETR retains responsibility for all town and country planning matters, including development plan policy, planning call-ins and appeals. Any revision of PPG 16 (Planning and Archaeology) would doubtless be another collaborative effort.

As a general rule, unless an archaeological matter falls within the remit of English Heritage or the limited conservation responsibilities of the DETR (see paragraph 1.07), it will be the responsibility of the DCMS.

1.06 An area in which the SSCMS has sole and extensive responsibility is in the funding and monitoring of public heritage bodies. Depending on the nature of the body, the Secretary of State's approval may be required for budgets, a corporate plan or staffing levels. The Secretary of State must also usually consent to the appointment of 'board members' and may appoint the chairman. (In some instances these powers of appointment vest in the Prime Minister or The Queen). A clearer idea of the Secretary of State's control is gained when looking at the position of English Heritage, a body constituted under separate Act of Parliament and therefore one of the more independent of these organisations (see pararaphs 1.11-1.13 below).

1.07 Circular 20/92 includes amongst the responsibilities of the Department of the Environment [*Transport and the*

Regions]:

(a)   ministerial decisions to call-in listed building and conservation area applications (together with decisions on these applications);

(b)   determination of statutory appeals against a refusal by the relevant authority of listed building consent or conservation area consent;

(c)   determination of non-statutory, Crown applications, under DOE Circular 18/84;

(d)   ministerial functions under sections 24-26 (revocation of listed building consent), 34-35 (listed building purchase notices), 39-41 and 46 (listed building enforcement notices) and 74 (demolition of unlisted building in conservation areas) of the P(LBCA)A 1990, together with ministerial decisions on listed building compensation cases;

(e)   confirmation or otherwise of directions affecting conservation areas made by planning authorities under article 4 of the GPDO.

(f)   consideration of proposals submitted by the Church Commissioners, pursuant to the Pastoral Measure, for the demolition of a listed church or a church situated in a conservation area.

Historical Royal Palaces ('HRP')

1.08 The five unoccupied royal palaces, the Tower of London, Kew Palace, Hampton Court, Kensington Palace and the Banqueting House were retained within the care of the Secretary of State for the Environment when most other historic properties were transferred to English Heritage in the mid-1980s. For five years following the establishment of English Heritage these properties were managed directly by the Department of the Environment until a separate agency – HRPA – was constituted in 1989.

The palaces are some of the leading historic properties in England, especially in terms of income generation. Exploitation of their importance by HRP made the palaces nearly financially self-sufficient in revenue terms (HC 1994, paragraph 416). The agency is now constituted as a distinct charitable trust, by Royal Charter. Beyond the five palaces the HRP does not have a significant archaeological role, and concentrates more on the development of its specialist skills in maintaining historic furnishings and building fabric.

The Historic Buildings and Monuments Commission (English Heritage)
(Sections 32-37 of the NHA 1983, which constitute English Heritage, are reproduced at appendix 1B of this work)

1.09 English Heritage is seen increasingly as the main guardian of archaeology and the built heritage in England; it is popularly, if mistakenly, seen as an arm of central government, possessing almost unlimited powers in conservation matters. It will be interesting to see if Parliament does eventually vest in English Heritage such extensive decision-making functions as were, for example, vested in the National Rivers Authority, under the Water Resources Act 1991, or in the Environment Agency under the Environment Act 1995. There is certainly a desire amongst some archaeologists for the transfer of the Secretary of State's functions relating to the scheduling of monuments to English Heritage. Currently, however, English Heritage's responsibilities and powers are limited to the role of adviser and manager.

1.10 English Heritage is a statutory corporation established under section 32 of the National Heritage Act 1983. Its activities are expressly limited to England and land immediately bordering England (sections 33 and 37, NHA 1983) (contrast the positions of 'Historic Scotland' and Cadw which, respectively, as a directorate of the Scottish Office and an executive agency of the Welsh Office, are limited only by the Crown functions of their ministries).

The board of management of English Heritage is composed of between 8 and 17 commissioners. Commissioners are appointed by the SSCMS, who must have regard to the specific suitability of each commissioner bearing in mind the balance of skills available to the Commission as a result of all such appointments (NHA 1983, schedule 3, paragraph 3). Commissioners may be removed from office if the Secretary of State is satisfied that for reason of absence, bankruptcy, incapacity through physical or mental illness or other inability, or unfitness to discharge his functions, a commissioner should be removed (NHA 1983, schedule 3, paragraph 3(7)).

1.11 The NHA 1983 requires the appointment of two advisory committees, one for historic buildings and one for ancient monuments (schedule 3, paragraph 9; the Ancient Monuments Board for England and the Historic Buildings Council for England established, respectively, under the Ancient Monuments Consolidation and Amendment Act

1913 and the HBAMA 1953, as advisors to the Secretary of State, were abolished under section 39 of the Act). The commissioners have appointed other, non-statutory committees to advise on tax, historic areas, and conservation in London.

The public have little or no contact with the commissioners or the advisory committees. The public will deal mainly with the chief officer and other staff appointed by the Commission. The power to appoint staff is contained in schedule 3, paragraph 4 of the NHA 1983. The SSCMS must approve the appointment of the chief officer (schedule 3, paragraph 4(1)); otherwise the commissioners are empowered to determine all staffing levels, staff salaries, conditions of service and pensions. The commissioners themselves are entitled to such remuneration and allowances as the SSCMS agrees with the Treasury (schedule 3, paragraph 11).

The commissioners must at their meetings disclose any interest which they have in a contract with English Heritage, and must not take part in any decision or deliberation in relation to such a contract (NHA 1983, schedule 3, paragraph 7)); in any other case commissioners must disclose their interest and the meeting will decide if the matters disclosed could be prejudicial.

1.12 Control of English Heritage by the Secretary of State was one of the subjects addressed by both the House of Commons National Heritage Committee (HC 1994) and the House of Commons Environment Committee (HC 1987). The main control is financial, as approximately 90% of the funding of English Heritage comes in the form of grant-in-aid from the Secretary of State (HC 1994, paragraphs 467 and 490). The commissioners must submit a detailed corporate plan to the Secretary of State every year, setting English Heritage's projected budgetary requirements for the following three years. Whether or not the plan obtains ministerial approval depends on the degree to which previous management and policy targets have been achieved. Summaries of the corporate plan are usually published by the commissioners and annual accounts must be laid before Parliament (NHA 1983, schedule 3, paragraph 13(4)). More specific spending and accounting requirements are given to the commissioners in their 'Accounts Directive and Financial Memorandum', which deals with the actual payment of grant-in-aid to English Heritage and how items of income and expenditure are to be considered within the context of the corporate plan. It is notable in this context that some grant-in-aid is expressly allocated to specific purposes, for example the preservation of cathedrals (HC 1994, paragraph 479). The Secretary of State also retains the ability to reduce the amount of annual grant (currently about £100 million) if, for example, the amount of income generated is thought by him to merit such a step.

1.13 English Heritage was established primarily to remove from the civil service part of the old DOE and to constitute the heritage function at 'arms length' from government. The reasons for this included a desire for both increased operational flexibility and a more versatile approach to funding heritage work: the body responsible for issuing statutory consents would, for example, no longer be the body which determined grant applications for related archaeological work. The NHA 1983 expressly provides that English Heritage is neither a servant nor an agent of the

Crown and enjoys no Crown status, immunity or privilege (schedule 3, paragraph 2(1)). An exception is where English Heritage is acting by direction of the Secretary of State under 34(2) of the NHA 1983 (though in such instances the privileges etc. subsist only as long as the Crown functions are delegated and would be lost where, for example, the functions related to Crown land which was subsequently disposed of by the Crown to English Heritage).

Independent management and executive action is a characteristic of these non-departmental arrangements, although it should be remembered that the Secretary of State both retains responsibility for issuing of statutory consents and sometimes intervenes forcefully to require a particular course to be followed. An interesting example is referred to in the National Heritage Committee report (HC 1994, paragraph 362), where the chairman of commissioners says that he was directed by the Secretary of State not to save 'the black and white Tudor house called Pitchford' – a reference to the controversy over Pitchford Hall).

As an independent public body responsible for its own capital and revenue expenditure and without recourse to any tax fund or levy, it is possible in theory for English Heritage to become insolvent. The Secretary of State has a power to fund English Heritage (section 38, NHA 1983) not a duty to do so. In practice English Heritage's independent income generating activities account for only about 10% of its income and the bulk of its liabilities are incurred only after the necessary funds have been allocated by the Treasury. There have been no signs yet that English Heritage aspires to any growth which could alter this position, for example including the extensive use of guarantees under section 35 of the NHA 1983. Such guarantees will usually require Treasury clearance, though in contrast to the provisions of section 33(8) of that Act (English Heritage's power to maintain an overdraft) the Secretary of State's consent is not a statutory requirement. All such matters will usually be dealt with in the Accounts Directive and Financial Memorandum.

1.14 With the consent of the Secretary of State, English Heritage has express power to hold any operational land, i.e. land used for the performance of its functions (section 35 (5)(c), NHA 1983)). It also has extensive powers to acquire ancient monuments and land for ancient monuments purposes (see the AMAA 1979, as amended: section 11 (acquisition by agreement); section 12 (guardianship of ancient monuments) and section 16 (acquisition of easements). Except in the case of easements, acquisition is subject to the Secretary of State's consent. English Heritage cannot acquire land compulsorily under section 10 or section 16 of the AMAA 1979. The NHA 1983 contains no general power for English Heritage to hold land for ancient monuments purposes (with the Secretary of State's consent or otherwise). This is significant because the NHA 1983 has a wider definition of 'ancient monument' than the AMAA 1979 (see paragraph 2.02 below). In some circumstances, for example where English Heritage is party to a joint venture arrangement (or subscribes to a company under section 35 of the NHA 1983) for the purpose of providing catering or car parking or other services or facilities for the public visiting ancient monuments or historic buildings, a power to hold land can be implied. But such a power would probably not be implied, for example, under section 33 (2)(a) of the NHA 1983 (English Heritage's duty to provide

15

educational facilities and services etc. in relation to 'ancient monuments' and 'historic buildings' as defined in that Act). English Heritage's express powers to acquire land of archaeological value are restricted to land which is – or is in the vicinity of – a scheduled monument (see paragraphs 1.21 and 2.3 below) or a monument which, in English Heritage's opinion, is of 'public interest' (the definition of ancient monument contained in section 61(12) of the AMAA 1979).

With the consent of the Secretary of State, English Heritage can acquire historic buildings and land associated with such buildings where, in English Heritage's opinion, the building is either of 'outstanding interest' or, in a conservation area, of 'special interest' (section 5 (1)(a) and (b), HBAMA 1953 as amended). English Heritage may also acquire any land which is 'adjacent or contiguous to or comprises' a building which can be acquired under section 5A(1)(a) and (b) (section 5A(1)(c), HBAMA 1953). Potentially this will permit the acquisition of land of archaeological value which is not of public interest, or scheduled, as section 5A(1)(c) does not require that any 'land acquired' must be necessary to support the building acquired under section 5A(1)(a) or (b). (For objects in historic buildings, and for gardens and endowments, see paragraphs 1.24 and 2.175.)

1.15 English Heritage is not a charity, though many of its activities are charitable in nature; it is also able to participate in charitable corporations under section 35 of the NHA 1983.

Stamp duty is not payable on deeds or other instruments which effect transfers of real property to English Heritage (section 46(3)(c), Finance Act 1983).

For tax purposes English Heritage is treated as a charity

(sections 505 and 507, Income and Corporation Taxes Act 1988, as amended). Significant benefits of this status include income tax refunds on covenanted subscriptions, exemption from tax on capital gains (see also section 271(7), Taxation of Chargeable Gains Act 1992), and the charitable exemption from corporation tax. Property transferred to English Heritage is also exempt from inheritance tax to the extent of the positive value transferred (Capital Transfer Tax Act 1984, schedule 3, as amended).

General Powers and Duties of English Heritage

1.16 Section 33 of the NHA 1983 places on English Heritage duties in respect of the archaeological heritage more general and extensive than those of any other body. Under the AMAA and P(LBCA)A the Secretary of State must maintain the schedule of monuments and lists of buildings of special architectural or historic interest, but in terms of actual conservation his duties are negligible. English Heritage, in contrast, is obliged '*so far as practicable*' to '*provide educational facilities and services, instruction and information to the public in relation to ancient monuments and historic buildings, with particular reference to those in England, and in relation to conservation areas situated in England*' (section 33(2)(a), NHA 1983). Section 33(1) makes this provision a primary responsibility of English Heritage by providing that if the functions in section 33(2) conflict with the duties in section 33(1) the functions in section 33(2) 'shall prevail'. All other functions contained in sections 33(2)-(4) and section 34 of the 1983 Act also prevail against the duties contained in section 33(1). The section 33(1) duties prevailed against are, surprisingly, those duties which are usually regarded by the public as English Heritage's paramount responsibility, namely:

'(a)   *to secure the preservation of ancient monuments and historic buildings situated in England,*

(b)   *to promote the preservation and enhancement of the character and appearance of conservation areas situated in England, and*

(c)   *to promote the public's enjoyment of, and advance their knowledge of, ancient monuments and historic buildings situated in England and their preservation.'*

In archaeological and conservation terms these duties are fairly extensive. The legislature has chosen to limit the scope of the obligations in both sections 33(1) and 33(2) to that which is 'practicable'; a limitation which will be of assistance to English Heritage if there should ever be a failure to carry out a particular function due to lack of resources.

The remainder of section 33(2) provides that English Heritage:

'(b)   *may give advice to any person in relation to ancient monuments, historic buildings and conservation areas situated in England, whether or not they have been consulted;*

(c)   *may, for the purpose of exercising their functions, carry out, or defray or contribute towards the cost of, research relating to ancient monuments, historic buildings and conservation areas situated in England;*

(d)   *may, for the purpose of exercising their functions, make and maintain records in relation to ancient monuments and historic buildings situated in England.'*

The definitions of 'ancient monument' and 'historic building' applicable throughout sections 33(1) and 33(2) are those contained in section 33(8) of the NHA 1983 (essentially any monument or building which English Heritage believes to be of the requisite interest: see paragraphs 1.17 and 2.3 below).

English Heritage may charge for advice or facilities provided under sections 33(2)(a) and (b) (section 33(6), NHA 1983) unless the advice or facilities in question are provided to a minister. This express power to charge is potentially a comprehensive aid to income generation.

Section 33(5)(d) of the NHA 1983 contains a 'sweeping-up' power, whereby English Heritage may do such other things as the commissioners think necessary or expedient in the exercise of their functions. However, this power is unlikely to extend to charging for the matters referred to in sections 33(2)(c) (research) and 33(3)(a) (management or investigation of sites).

1.17 English Heritage is made the statutory adviser to the Secretary of State by section 33(3)(b) of the NHA 1983. Indeed, amendments made to the AMAA by section 33(3) and schedule 4 of the 1983 Act mean that the Secretary of State is usually unable to act without first consulting English Heritage. For example, he is precluded from scheduling a monument or granting a scheduled monument consent (see paragraphs 2.3-2.14 and 2.23 below) without prior consultation. Schedule 4 also amends the HBAMA, as discussed below. English Heritage may give advice to the Secretary of State whether he requests it or not, on any ministerial function under the HBAMA or AMAA.

Section 33(3) and schedule 4 of the NHA 1983 together give English Heritage the power to provide information and other services to the public in affording access to ancient monuments, and also to carry out archaeological investigations. The power to 'undertake, assist in, defray or contribute towards the cost of archaeological investigation of any land in England', which is effected by inserting a new section 45(1A) into the AMAA, does not relate only to monuments which are scheduled, or of public interest (the definition of 'ancient monument' for purposes of the AMAA) but to any land which in the opinion of English Heritage contains anything of archaeological or historic interest. These are extensive powers, especially when one considers the all-embracing definition of 'investigation' contained in section 61 of the AMAA. That Act, however, does not contain express charging powers for English Heritage (or for local authorities); unless from the context in which the powers to investigate are exercised a power to charge can be said to arise by 'necessary implication', the levying of a charge may be unlawful (see generally comments at paragraph 1.35 below). From this perspective it would have been better if the ambit of section 33(6) of the NHA 1983 had not been restricted to the functions prescribed by sections 33(2)(a) and (b), as the sweeping-up power in section 33(5)(d) is unlikely to be sufficient to authorise charging.

English Heritage may, but is not obliged to, publish the results of any archaeological investigation conducted under section 45 of the AMAA.

Section 35 of the NHA 1983 authorises English Heritage to form or participate in the formation of other corporate bodies (including corporations constituted with limited liability). The objects, or main objects, for which such a corporation must be established are one or more of those provided by section 35(2)(a)-(d) of that Act:

'(a)   *the production and publication in England of books, films or other informative material relating to ancient monuments or historic buildings;*

(b)   *the production in England of souvenirs relating to ancient monuments or historic buildings;*

(c)   *the sale in England of informative material relating to ancient monuments or historic buildings, or of souvenirs, and*

(d)   *the provision in England of catering or car parking or other services or facilities for members of the public visiting ancient monuments or historic buildings.'*

'Ancient monument' and 'historic building' in this context have the wider definitions contained in section 33(8) of the NHA 1983. Section 35(3) permits English Heritage to exercise any rights which it holds in such a company and it may provide financial assistance (including the giving of guarantees) to such a company. Section 35 in effect permits English Heritage to be involved in activities which would not be authorised under section 33 of the Act.

Section 37 provides for the Secretary of State to make regulations which empower English Heritage to carry out the Secretary of State's functions in relation to monuments, buildings and gardens situated partly in England. For this purpose the Secretary of State can by Order (passed on affirmative resolution of Parliament) amend sections 33 and 34 or anything amended by schedule 4 of that Act. No Order has so far been made under this section.

Sections 32-37 of the NHA 1983 are reproduced at appendix 1B of this work.

1.18 English Heritage is split into two divisions, 'Historic Properties' and 'Conservation'. Historic Properties is responsible for the ownership and management of those sites which belong to English Heritage or are subject to guardianship arrangements (for guardianship see paragraphs 2.167-2.170 below). In manpower terms Historic Properties takes by far the largest proportion of available resources. Conservation is responsible for the inspection of ancient monuments and historic buildings, conservation in London, general heritage advice (including enhancement of the schedule of ancient monuments under the MPP), and the making of grants for listed building, conservation area, ancient monument and archaeological purposes.

From its grant-in-aid English Heritage also maintains the Central Archaeology Service (formerly the Central Excavation Unit) – its own archaeological investigation arm.

English Heritage's Conservation Function

1.19 As a statutory corporation English Heritage is restricted to the express and implied powers conferred upon it. Moreover, as a relatively recent parliamentary creation, most of English Heritage's powers are to be found in the HBAMA 1953 (as amended), the AMAA 1979 (as amended), the NHA 1983 and the P(LBCA)A 1990 (as amended by the

Planning and Compensation Act 1991).

1.20 English Heritage does not schedule monuments but it must be consulted by the Secretary of State before a monument is scheduled (by him) and must inform owners and other persons that a monument has been scheduled (sections 1 and 1A, AMAA 1979). Likewise, in contrast to the position of Cadw, which grants consents on behalf of the Secretary of State for Wales, English Heritage does not grant scheduled monument consents, although it must be consulted by the Secretary of State before scheduled monument consent is granted (section 2 and schedule I, part 1, AMAA 1979). English Heritage must also be consulted before a class consent is made and before a scheduled monument consent is revoked or modified. English Heritage cannot designate Areas of Archaeological Importance under Part II of the AMAA but it must be consulted before the Secretary of State either designates such an area (section 33, AMAA 1979) or appoints an Investigating Authority (section 34, AMAA 1979). English Heritage is itself the Investigating Authority in default of appointment by the Secretary of State (section 34(4)).

1.21 Under section 1 of the P(LBCA)A the Secretary of State must consult with English Heritage before compiling or amending a statutory list of buildings of special architectural or historic interest. English Heritage will also be an important consultee of local planning authorities when applications for listed building consent are considered. Outside London, English Heritage's powers to protect historic buildings is second to that of local planning authorities, although in Greater London English Heritage can serve both building preservation notices and repairs notices (sections 3(8) and 48, P(LBCA)A) and, with the Secretary of State's involvement, can direct a London Borough Council to refuse an application for listed building consent (section 14(2), P(LBCA)A). Under section 45 of the P(LBCA)A English Heritage can also enforce in Greater London against breaches of listed building control.

A special power enables English Heritage to compile a register of gardens of special historic interest. Any registers so compiled must be notified to the Secretary of State and to the relevant local planning authority. Gardens do not receive any statutory protection by virtue of being entered to such a list, although English Heritage must be consulted by local planning authorities when applications affecting grade I listed gardens are received. Entry on the lists, at any grade, means that the local planning authority should have regard to the garden's historic interest when determining applications for planning permission (see chapter five of this work).

The Secretary of State must consult English Heritage before acquiring an historic building under section 5 of the HBAMA, or an ancient monument under sections 10 or 11 of the AMAA.

English Heritage has powers of entry on and inspection of ancient monuments and land believed to contain ancient monuments (section 6A, AMAA and section 36, NHA 1983; see paragraphs 2.15-2.22 below). English Heritage may 'superintend' and advise on any works on an ancient monument and may charge for such assistance (section 25(3A), AMAA; see also section 33(6), NHA 1983). It also has the power to require information as to interests in land (section 57, AMAA).

Under its general powers of research and record (section 33(c) and (d), NHA 1983), together with its power to offer advice to the Secretary of State, English Heritage is currently re-assessing the schedule of all ancient monuments, with a view to procuring a more representative sample of nationally important archaeological remains (the 'Monuments Protection Programme' – MPP).

1.22 English Heritage undertakes archaeological work under express powers (section 45(1A), AMAA). The power to conduct archaeological investigation is augmented by powers under section 25 of the AMAA and sections 33(c) and 33(d) of the NHA 1983. The Secretary of State is no longer authorised under section 45 to undertake archaeological work in England (section 45(1) of the AMAA as amended by the NHA 1983). Although English Heritage has no express power itself to carry out emergency works on ancient monuments, it may do so if authorised by the Secretary of State.

English Heritage has power under section 17 of the AMAA to enter management agreements which, amongst other things, may restrict the use of ancient monuments. English Heritage may also provide facilities for the public on ancient monuments, or make charges for access (section 20(3) of the 1979 Act and section 33(2)(a) of the NHA 1983). English Heritage can also issue 'licences' under section 42, AMAA, authorising the use of metal detectors in 'protected places' (see paragraph 2.158 below).

1.23 Development by English Heritage on guardianship or

managed sites, for certain ancient monuments purposes, is excepted from the requirements to obtain a specific grant of planning permission by virtue of article 26 of the GPDO. English Heritage, like Cadw, must also be consulted on all planning applications liklely to affect any scheduled monument (article 10(1)(n) of the GD(P)O). A class consent issued under section 3 of the AMAA also excepts from the requirement to obtain a prior grant of scheduled monument consent works carried out by English Heritage (see paragraph 2.30 below), although land held by the commissioners is not Crown land as defined by section 50 of that Act. English Heritage, therefore, enjoys a more favourable position than do government departments which, if they propose works which ordinarily would require a grant of scheduled monument consent, must apply to the Secretary of State for 'scheduled monument clearance'.

1.24 Most of the grants made by English Heritage are a distribution of grant-in-aid received from the Secretary of State. There is a variety of purposes for which English Heritage may award grants in England (usually to the exclusion of the Secretary of State's powers to make equivalent awards). These include:

- research in relation to ancient monuments, historic buildings and conservation areas (section 33(c), NHA 1983);
- archaeological investigation, analysis and publication (section 45, AMAA);
- the preservation, maintenance, management acquisition or removal (for preservation) by any person

of an ancient monument (section 24(3A), AMAA);
- the preservation of historic buildings and their gardens or other land of 'outstanding' historic or architectural interest (including the granting for such purposes of endowments to the National Trust) (section 3A, HBAMA);
- the acquisition by a local authority of listed buildings acquired under their powers of compulsory acquisition, or by the National Trust of historic buildings and land which is of outstanding interest (section 5B, HBAMA).

It is emphasised that English Heritage generally cannot act outside England or, it seems, in territorial waters contiguous to England (see paragraph 2.9 below). Specific restrictions on English Heritage's grant-making powers include the inability to finance the acquisition of chattels or artefacts which are not acquired in relation to a particular heritage site. Nor can English Heritage assist in the funding of archaeological research or education where this is unconnected with the conservation or preservation of 'the heritage'.

The Royal Commission on the Historical Monuments of England (RCHM(e))
[At the time of writing the SSCMS is implementing a merger of RCHM(e) with English Heritage, to form a single lead body for the historic environment. Legal merger will not be possible until English Heritage's functions have been modified by amendments to the NHA 1983. This may be many months ahead. RCHM(e)'s Royal Warrant can be revoked more quickly, by Orders in Council. Delay in full legal merger is not expected, however, to prevent administrative and management functions of the two organizations coming together as planned. The text below should be read

with the new arrangements in mind.]

1.25 Like the Royal Commission on the Ancient and Historical Monuments of Scotland (RCAHM(s)) and the Royal Commission on the Ancient and Historical Monuments of Wales (RCAHM(w)), RCHM(e) was established by Royal Warrant in 1908. The Warrant has been renewed periodically, most recently in 1992. The first Warrant charged RCHM(e):

> '*to make an inventory of ancient and historical monuments and constructions connected with or illustrative of the contemporary culture, civilisation and conditions of life of the people from earliest times, and to specify those which seem most worthy of preservation.*'

The Warrant of 15th April 1992 continues in the same vein, charging RCHM(e):

> '*to provide for the survey and recording of ancient and historical monuments and constructions connected with or illustrative of, the contemporary culture, civilisation and conditions of life of the people of England from the earliest times ... by compiling, maintaining and curating the National Monuments Record of England as the basic national record of the archaeological and historical environment ... by identifying, surveying, interpreting and recording all buildings, sites and ancient monuments of archaeological, architectural, archaeological and historical interest in England ... in order both to enhance and update the National Monuments Record of England and also to respond to statutory needs.*'

RCHM(e) has power under the Warrant to call on persons to provide access to bodies of documents and 'registers'.

RCHM(e) is also charged with: providing advice and information relevant to the preservation and conservation of historic buildings, archaeological sites and 'ancient monuments'; collecting and exchanging data with other record holders; providing an index to data from other sources (increasingly, information held by County Sites and Monuments Records (SMRs)); promoting public use of the National Monuments Record by all available means; and establishing national standards in both archaeological and architectural surveying and recording and in the curation of records.

1.26 RCHM(e) has two main functions, recording and maintenance of records. The fundamental difference between RCHM(e) and English Heritage is that of a research as opposed to a conservation organisation. To the layman this distinction is not always apparent, as the organisations work very closely, with English Heritage placing great reliability on RCHM(e)'s research expertise and data. Until 1994 the organisations occupied adjacent buildings in Savile Row. RCHM(e) has moved its base of operations to Swindon (for the first time the National Monuments Record and the National Archaeological Record are at one location). It has also taken over the supervising function which English Heritage had over SMRs and has developed a new, publicly accessible computer record (MONARCH) which facilitates integration of RCHM(e)'s records.

1.27 The commissioners of RCHM(e) are appointed by the

Crown on the advice of the Prime Minister (effectively the SSCMS). Commissioners are unpaid although they can call upon an extensive and expert staff, formerly divided into archaeological and architectural divisions but reorganised, in 1995, into five divisions (NMR, archaeological survey, architectural survey, Information Services and Development, and Corporate Services). In 1993-1994 the work of the two old divisions together cost £4.7m (RCHM(e) *Annual Report* 1994). These divisions cut across RCHM(e)'s several regional offices, located at Cambridge, Exeter, Keele, Newcastle-upon-Tyne, Salisbury Southampton, Swindon and York. A residual record and field capacity is maintained in London, relating to Greater London. In 1995-1996 expenditure on archaeological and architectural surveys was £3.9m of a total of £12.2m (RCHM(e) *Annual Report*, 1995). This decreased in 1996-97, following the adoption of a new five-year strategic plan which gives urgent priority to the consolidation of and improvement of access to existing inventories.

There are signs that RCHM(e) may soon be losing its distinct identity, by merger with English Heritage. But it is likely that the particular nature of RCHM(e)'s function will remain intact within the new organization, even if subject to a unified body of Commissioners and a single executive. RCHM(e) has a reputation for expertise in field recording and survey, both of the emergency and everyday variety (some of which is now contracted out). It has also been instrumental in securing records of many historic buildings demolished in the country's Urban Development Areas and has carried out extensive surveys of hospitals, textile mills, farm buildings and archaeological landscapes.

This expertise invariably means that RCHM(e) is a useful ally before public inquiries as, although wary of giving evidence itself, RCHM(e) has close ties with several universities, conservation trusts, national archaeological organisations, as well as with the DCMS and, of course, English Heritage. Its expertise, even if not directly available at public inquiries, often informs debate on technical matters.

1.28 Under section 8(2) of the P(LBCA)A works for demolition of a listed building are not 'authorised' unless RCHM(e) has been notified of the proposal and, if it wishes to do so, for the period of one month after the grant of consent, is permitted reasonable access to the building for the purpose of architectural/archaeological recording. It is, in effect, an offence for an applicant not to afford such access or to demolish without notifying RCHM(e) in accordance with the section. However, in contrast with the national amenity societies, RCHM(e) is not involved formally in the listed building consultation process. RCHM(e) has no statutory role at all in relation to scheduled monuments (see chapter 2, especially paragraphs 2.40-2.45.). If a building is both a scheduled monument and a listed building the former procedures will take precedence and, if desired, it will be necessary to secure rights of access and recording for RCHM(e) by a condition in the scheduled monument consent. (This will be less of a problem when RCHM(e) merges with English Heritage.)

RCHM(e) has specific statutory authority to inspect sites or buildings for matters of historical or archaeological interest when an operations notice is served in relation to an Area of Archaeological Importance (section 40(b), AMAA).

Under a scheduled monument class consent (see paragraph 2.32) RCHM(e) and RCAHM(w) may also carry out limited survey work on scheduled monuments without a specific grant of scheduled monument consent.

RCHM(e) has no specific power under the Warrant to engage in contract work for profit. Such contract work as it does carry out is incidental to its express functions.

Grants are available from RCHM(e) for the curation or making of records. SMRs and aerial reconnaissance projects have been notable recipients in recent years. RCHM(e) has no power to grant-aid the physical conservation of buildings and monuments. Likewise, RCHM(e) does not own or manage any monuments, and has no power under the Warrant to do so. Nor does RCHM(e) have any statutory role in the enforcement of listed building or ancient monument control.

1.29 The Warrant emphasises RCHM(e)'s role in promoting public use of its records, especially the National Monuments Record (NMR). The NMR is now housed at Swindon. The original Warrant of 1908 had charged RCHM(e) with the production of inventories but, as it became apparent that publication of all the data amassed was impractical, RCHM(e) has for many years seen the maintenance of the NMR as fulfilling that obligation. RCHM(e) also supplies the Ordnance Survey with archaeological information. The Ordnance Survey itself first compiled what became known as the National Archaeological Record (NAR), but the functions relating to the NAR were transferred to RCHM(e) in the 1950s.

With the increasing importance of data transfer, securing quality control and standards in architectural and archaeological record systems is an additional part of RCHM(e)'s brief. Reference is made above to its supervision of SMRs; the Warrant is also notable for its emphasis of data exchange, the production by RCHM(e) of indexes to archaeological records and the establishing of national standards in architectural and archaeological recording.

The National Heritage Memorial Fund (NHMF)
(References to sections in paragraphs 1.30 and 1.31 are to the NHA 1980 unless otherwise indicated)

1.30 A 'National Land Fund' was established in 1946 with an endowment of £50 million, as a memorial to those who died in World Wars I and II. This fund was rarely used for its intended purpose and was depleted to only £15 million (HC 1987, 406) when in 1980 the National Heritage Act established the NHMF, as a memorial to those who 'have died for the United Kingdom' (section 1(1)), and as successor to the bulk of the National Land Fund's property. The NHMF is administered by trustees who in day to day management are independent of the Government. However, the trustees and the chair of trustees are appointed by the Prime Minister (on the advice of the Secretary of State for Culture, Media and Sport) and the fund receives substantial grant assistance from the Government. The Treasury may give directions for the manner in which government grants can be invested (section 6(2)). Other funds received by the NHMF may be invested in any manner authorised by the Trustee Investment Act 1961, though the trustees must not retain any property other than money except as the

Secretary of State permits (section 5(3)). The Government is entitled to receive an annual financial report from the fund and this must be laid before Parliament (section 7(1)). For taxation purposes the fund is treated as a charity (sections 505 and 507 of the Income and Corporation Taxes Act 1988); this is especially important in relation to any chargeable gains attracting capital gains tax (schedule 29, paragraph 26 of the Income and Corporation Taxes Act 1988; section 271(7) of the Taxation of Chargeable Gains Act 1992).

1.31 The powers of the trustees have been significantly extended by the NHA 1997. Under the old section 3 of the NHA 1980, the trustees could make grants or loans to specified persons or bodies (see below), for the purpose of assisting those persons or bodies to acquire, maintain or preserve:

'(1)   *any land, building or structure which in the trustees' opinion is of outstanding scenic, historic, aesthetic, architectural or scientific interest;*

(2)   *any object which in the trustees' opinion is of outstanding historic, artistic or scientific interest;*

(3)   *any collection or group of objects which, taken as a whole, is in the trustees' opinion of outstanding historic, artistic or scientific interest;*

(4)   *any land or object not within heads (1)-(3) above the acquisition, maintenance or preservation of which is, in the trustees' opinion, desirable by reason of its connection with land or a building or structure falling within head (1); or*

(5)   *any rights in or over land the acquisition of which is in the trustees' opinion desirable for the benefit of land or*

> *a building or structure falling within heads (1) or (4) above.'*

Under the old section 3 the persons or bodies entitled to receive grants or loans ('eligible recipients') were museums, galleries, libraries and similar institutions; bodies involved in the provision, improvement or preservation of amenities for the public; nature conservation bodies; the Secretary of State when acting under section 5 of the HBAMA or sections 11 or 13 of the AMAA 1979; but, significantly, not bodies established for or conducted for profit. The trustees had to be satisfied before making a grant or loan that the item or object to be assisted was both of outstanding interest and important to the national heritage (section 3(2)). Not all scheduled monuments or grade I listed buildings qualified. Conversely, some 'lesser' structures were assisted if considered by the trustees sufficiently important to the national heritage.

Two points are worthy of special note. First, under the old section 3, 'preservation of objects or property' was strictly interpreted by the NHMF; archaeological excavation itself was not sponsored. Secondly, the NHMF looked on itself as a provider of last resort and usually had to be satisfied that other sources of funding were unavailable or inadequate. The NHMF assisted high profile, comprehensive projects (such as the re-endowment of National Trust property at Nostell Priory, West Yorkshire). The fund has also assisted the National Trust on routine repairs, such as the repair of Calke Abbey, Derbyshire, although these were dealt with very much as special cases.

The NHA 1997 and new sections 3 and 4 of the NHA 1980

A proportion of the proceeds from the National Lottery is administered by the NHMF trustees, for heritage purposes, under what is known informally as the 'Heritage Lottery Fund' (HLF). The substantial sums generated by the Lottery and the narrow powers of the NHMF trustees presented an embarrassment of riches as far as heritage awards were concerned. Under the National Lottery etc. Act 1993, a proportion (originally 20% but now 16⅔%) of the proceeds received from the licence arrangements under which national lottery franchises are operated goes to sponsor architectural and artistic projects, very broadly referred to as the heritage. Under section 3 of the NHA 1980 eligible projects had to be capital projects with a public or charitable character: like NHMF but unlike English Heritage grants, HLF grants could not be used to assist purely private projects. The old section 3 was also too narrow to permit funding of archaeological research, education and field investigation. As a result most of the HLF funds disbursed went to the familiar, individually expensive string of architectural and decorative restoration projects involving grade I listed buildings or similar, with less than 1% going to archaeological investigation or research. The size of the fund generated each year is in excess of £100m.

The powers of the NHMF trustees are now transformed by the new section 3, substituted by the NHA 1997. For both NHMF and HLF purposes (in terms of the Act still referred to together as 'the Fund') the trustees may give financial assistance *'in the case of things of any kind which are of scenic, historic, archaeological, aesthetic, architectural, engineering, artistic or scientific interest'* for the purpose of (i) preservation or enhancement of such things, or (ii) encouraging the study or understanding (or disseminating information about) them, or (iii) securing access to them or their display, or encouraging enjoyment of them, or (iv) encouraging the maintenance and development of the skills required for their preservation or enhancement.

The trustees may only assist projects under the new section 3 if the project appears to them to be of public benefit. As the trustees are also required to 'bear in mind' the desirability of public access or public display of the thing in question, and of its enjoyment by the public (section 3(7)), these considerations are, in effect, likely to provide the test of public benefit. The trustees must also be satisfied that the project is of 'importance to the national heritage' (section 3(4)(b); a lower threshold than the test of 'national importance' applicable to the scheduling of monuments (see chapter 2 of this work)). Subject to the above requirements, however, the Fund may now assist a very wide range of projects. There is no longer a stipulation that recipients of assistance must themselves be constituted for some public purpose: the concept of 'eligible recipients' has been scrapped. Archaeological projects, including site investigation carried out by private contractors, will fall within the types of project which the trustees are able to assist. Curation of museum exhibits or historic structures in disrepair clearly falls within the section. In its most recent policy document the Fund mentions five areas where archaeology may be most readily assisted: sites threatened by erosion; recording of locally significant features, e.g. field boundaries; enhancement of SMRs; the publication of old excavation archives where the excavation director is no longer active; and the publication of local fieldwork projects.

Financial assistance may be by way of grant or loan, and conditions may be attached (section 3(5)), including conditions as to access or repayment of grant.

Under a new section 3A public exhibitions and archives may receive financial assistance from the Fund.

The schedule to the NHA 1997 also amends section 4 of the Act so that the old powers of the NHMF to assist conservation other than by way of grant or loan, for example by the purchase of property, are expressly applicable to archaeology (section 4(2)(a); although there is no equivalent express power for archaeological objects, under section 4(2)(b)). Section 4 as amended may be of limited significance as there is still an 'outstanding interest' test linked with importance to the national heritage. However, there is again no longer an eligible recipient test; nor under section 4 is there a public benefit test, although the trustees must bear in mind the desirability of public access (section 4(2)(c)).

Local Authorities, Universities and Museums

1.32 Local authorities have a very different involvement in conservation matters than do universities. Over the past twenty or so years, however, one area of considerable similarity has been the willingness of both to support the establishments of archaeological 'units'. Units may be defined as groups of archaeologists dedicated to the field investigation, especially excavation, of threatened sites; a technical rather than an administrative emphasis on the actual preservation of sites in imminent danger. The term can be extended to certain trusts and similar bodies, but in most cases these have a distinct legal identity, whereas local authority and university units are part of a much larger legal entity.

1.33 Local authority units may consist of several officers on the staff of a local or county museum, in which case they are properly considered an adjunct of the relevant museum service. Units may be grafted onto a local authority's planning staff, for example by the employment of two or three archaeological officers dealing with an authority's conservation function. Some units – in archaeological terms often the more successful – have their own standing with a local authority, either as a division within a local authority department (for example, leisure services, or recreation and tourism), or with their own political identity, such as exist in some of the former metropolitan and other counties reduced to solely district structures, where 'joint committees' for archaeology have emerged. Independent national park authorities constituted under the Environment Act 1995 also have the powers of local authorities to undertake and support archaeological activity in their national park areas (under section 45 of the AMAA 1979, see paragraph 6.34 below). The establishment of a unit is typically between 5-10 staff, though, as with most contractors, many temporary staff may be employed.

The university unit may be part of a department of archaeology, from which some members of staff are seconded to carry out field operations. Perhaps mindful of the potential conflict with the educational needs of students, however, where a university unit is motivated by commercial contracting considerations, the staff involved tend to undertake this work by arrangements 'at arm's length' from the archaeology department itself.

The work of units is often heavily dependent on grant-aid, especially grants from English Heritage under what has in the past been termed the 'rescue archaeology' budget. This funding is not available for establishment costs and is awarded on a project basis, albeit on rolling programmes, with organisations tied to contract work either in the field or on post-excavation analysis. English Heritage funding continues to decline, however, as the units are expected to meet costs through developer funded projects.

1.34 Although usually part of a larger legal entity most units attempt to maintain a high profile with both the conservation public and the funding bodies. Their efforts in influencing funding and legislative policies have been co-ordinated by bodies such as the Standing Conference of Archaeological Unit Managers (SCAUM), part responsible for the British Archaeologists and Developers Liaison Group's Code of Practice (see chapter 6); the Association of County Archaeological Officers (ACAO) and the Association of District Archaeological Officers (ADAO), now merged to form the Association of Local Government Archaeological Officers (ALGAO); the Association of Museum Archaeologists; the Council for British Archaeology (see paragraph 1.44); and the Institute of Field Archaeologists (see paragraph 1.40).

1.35 Amongst the many legal considerations relevant to the work of local authorities, universities and museums as archaeological contractors three are especially worthy of note: (a) powers; (b) profits; and (c) conflict of interests. Local authorities, even when originally constituted under

Royal Charter, are now properly considered statutory bodies; universities are constrained by their charters, though less so by parliamentary statutes; most museums will also usually rely on local authority powers, or powers conferred by a specific Act.

(a) The powers under which a university unit may undertake the work of an archaeological contractor, whether or not the purpose is to trade as contractor, will usually be uncertain, if apparent at all from its charter or other governing instrument. If the work done is incidental to a more general function (for example, the recording of remains as part of a university field project conceived to provide answers to a problem of academic interest) an implied or incidental power will usually exist. However, the very recognition of units as administratively discreet contracting entities usually suggests a role within the parent organisation which is more than incidental. The maintenance of a 'contracting unit' is often more than an adjunct to the development of expertise in particular archaeological techniques. Like any body corporate, if a university or a local authority has neither specific nor implied/incidental power to carry out a function, in this case archaeological contracting, its dealings will be void at the outset, and neither the parent organisation nor a contracting party will be able to enforce any contractual provisions (*Ashbury Railway Carriage and Iron Company v. Riche* (1879) L.R. 7 HL, 653, as applied in *Hazell v. Hammersmith and Fulham London Borough Council* [1991] 1 All E.R. 545 HL). The consequences of such *ultra vires* activity are grave: expenditure incurred may be repayable by those fiduciaries who have spent beyond their authority; third parties may be without remedies for no or poor performance. Where there are doubts, existing corporate powers should be scrutinised and any potentially unlawful activity avoided, curtailed or reduced to the bare minimum which can be justified.

Local authorities have fairly wide, express powers to 'undertake, assist in, or defray or contribute towards the cost of' archaeological investigations of any land in or in the vicinity of their area (section 45(2), AMAA). Investigations are defined in section 61(4) of that Act to include: *'(a) any investigation for the purpose of discovering and revealing and (where appropriate) recovering and removing any objects or other material of archaeological or historical interest situated in on or under the land; and (b) examining, testing, treating, recording and preserving any such objects or material discovered during the course of any excavations or inspections carried out for the purposes of any such investigation'*. The authority must consider that the land in question may contain an ancient monument *'or anything else of archaeological or historical interest.'* Unless special powers are relevant, for example the carrying out of work for other local authorities or for other 'public bodies' under the Local Authorities (Goods and Services) Act 1970, an authority should not participate in archaeological investigations which are neither in nor within the vicinity of its area. Nor can an authority 'trade', in the usual sense of that word, that is, on a commercial basis, for the purpose of accumulating surpluses.

Ancillary powers of local authorities to employ staff are contained in section 112 of the Local Government Act 1972 (as amended). The preceding section of that Act contains the well-known power for authorities to do anything which is calculated to facilitate, or is conducive to or incidental to the discharge of their functions (although it cannot be a function to incur expenditure, including carrying out activities which will require expenditure, except as authorised under the Act). The Public Libraries and Museums Act 1964, the Local Authorities (Historic Buildings) Act 1962, and P(LBCA)A 1990 contain powers which together enable authorities to assist in the support of archaeological survey and curation activity. The AMAA also empowers local authorities to make management agreements and to enter guardianship arrangements in respect of ancient monuments.

The position varies from university to university and between different local authorities, depending on the content of universities' governing instruments and, in the case of local authorities, any local Acts. Specific enquiry is necessary in each case. Individual contracts may now be certified by local authorities under the Local Government (Contracts) Act 1997. In simple terms, this Act can be described as a measure which provides for individual contracting situations where the powers of the relevant authority are uncertain. A local authority is able to certify the contract in question as within its powers and this will then prevent the local authority from relying on the *ultra vires* doctrine and avoiding subsequent liability at *private law*. However, the Act gives no extra powers as such and its provisions should be exercised with caution. Public law remedies against the contractual dealings of an authority and its officers are left intact by the Act.

(b) Neither local authorities nor universities are trading organisations, a fact which is easily obscured by the current pressures upon particular parts of these organisations to operate profitably. The problem is especially acute in the local authority context where once the question of powers to carry out an activity has been settled there are further questions of (i) whether the authority is able to charge for the service provided and (ii) if able to charge, whether the authority can operate the 'chargeable service' as a business.

For (i) either express or implied authority will again be required and it is likely that if an authority is already relying on implied power for carrying out an activity, under section 111 of the Local Government Act 1972 for example, then charging the recipient for that service will be *ultra vires* (*R. v. Richmond-upon-Thames London Borough Council, ex parte McCarthy and Stone (Developments) Ltd.* [1991] 3 W.L.R 941 HL). By this unanimous decision of the House of Lords it was confirmed that a charge cannot be levied by a statutory body for carrying out its functions unless a power to charge is given to the authority either by 'express statutory words or by necessary implication'. In the absence of express words the 'necessary implication' of this test is more demanding than the 'reasonably incidental'. If a local authority does not have power to charge for a service a 'customer' will not be obliged to pay for the service, with obvious and potentially catastrophic results. In *McCarthy and Stone* the lack of power to charge was explained by their Lordships as the impossibility of recognising one incidental power as incidental to another incidental power. This was fatal to the local authority argument in this case because the power to provide the planning advice in question was only incidental (or implied). Under section 45 of the AMAA 1979, however, local authorities do have an express power to carry out archaeological investigations and the court could find in favour of an authority which charged for providing such work. The main difficulty is that the power to carry out the work is accompanied by powers to defray or contribute towards costs, and these are not qualifications which assist in necessarily implying charges. Further, there must be doubt that such an intention could be imputed to Parliament in 1979, when the approach to archaeological contracting was very different from what it is today. *McCarthy and Stone* also confirmed that just because a service is supplied on a 'take it or leave it' basis does not mean that a power to charge will be implied. Because most developers who engage a university or local authority archaeology unit do so in a spirit of co-operation the question is unlikely to come before the courts; however, a developer like McCarthy and Stone, pursuing a point of legal principle, may yet emerge to create significant problems.

(ii) If a local authority or a university is able to charge for the provision of archaeological services, it should still satisfy itself that the purpose of its activity cannot be construed as 'trading for profit'. This will usually be an improper purpose, certainly for local authorities, of which it has been said: *'whereas there is nothing inherently impermissible in anticipating that the provision of [one recreational facility] will be profitable and that such profits may be available for spending on other such facilities, what is impermissible is to provide the facilities in order to create trading revenue' (Crédit Suisse v. Allerdale Borough Council* (1994) QBD, per Colman J., p.74 of the court transcript; now upheld by the Court of Appeal: (1996) *The Times*, May 20). Again, whether a local authority or other statutory corporation is trading in this way depends on the particular facts; attitudes to 'clients' and the treatment of revenues will be as important as the proportion of a particular 'business' which is charged at commercial rates. Advertisement by some university and local authority organisations, of the 'satisfying all your archaeological needs' or 'maximising your investment' variety, suggest legal problems from the outset.

(c) As creatures of charter and statute charged with executing a wide variety of public duties, the need to avoid interests which conflict with those duties, and to act fairly, places further potential restrictions on contracting in an open market. The private company or the individual consultant may adopt a position which is unconscionable or anti-competitive and will suffer the consequences; but for a public authority the risks of acting unlawfully are more pervasive. Commercial activities which in themselves would usually give no rise to a conflict of interest at private law may well do so when carried out by a body delegated to undertake functions in the public interest. For local authorities, significant participation in archaeological contracting may conflict with conservation duties. Within archaeology itself the potential for conflict has already been recognised, with the IFA and others emphasising the need for a 'separation of functions' between 'curators', responsible for conserving archaeological remains, and 'contractors', responsible for undertaking archaeological investigations. This may require more than the establishment of two departments within the same organisation; where a local authority supports the major curatorial role of maintaining the County Sites and Monuments Record for example, the potential for conflict may mean that the authority should avoid archaeological contracting completely.

1.36 Local authorities have general power to provide and

maintain museums and art galleries within their administrative areas, and to do *all such things as may be necessary or expedient for or in connection with the provision or maintenance thereof* (section 12, Public Libraries and Museums Act 1964, as amended by section 272, Local Government Act 1972). Authorities are not expressly empowered to levy a charge for the provision of museums services, though they have express power to charge for admission to museums (section 13 of the 1964 Act). Under *McCarthy and Stone* it is difficult to see how a local authority museum could maintain a contracting field capacity on the back of its museum powers only; maintaining a field unit will, in most cases, be an activity carried on under section 45 of the AMAA (see above).

As an example of the minimum powers which a museum should possess in order to be an archaeological contractor it is instructive to consider the Museum of London. This museum is a distinct corporate body, constituted under the Museum of London Act 1965 (as amended by the Local Government Act 1985 and the Museum of London Act 1986). It is granted specific power to *'provide archaeological services and undertake archaeological investigations and research in connection with land in London ... and to promote the provision of such services and the undertaking of such investigations'* (section 3 of the 1965 Act, as amended). 'London' in this context means Greater London and the surrounding area. The express charging powers in the Acts of 1965 and 1986 do not specify the undertaking of archaeological investigations but, in the case of such a relatively recent statutory provision which speaks of providing archaeological services, charging powers may follow by necessary implication. Even in London, however, the issue is not clear-cut, especially when one considers that the museum is funded by the Corporation of London and the Secretary of State, with English Heritage possessing express grant-making powers for the carrying out of such investigations (section 4 of the 1986 Act).

National Museums and National Societies

1.37 Some influential and respected private institutions play an important role in British archaeology. There are national learned societies such as the Society of Antiquaries of London (founded 1707), the Royal Archaeological Institute, the Prehistoric Society, the Society for the Promotion of Roman Studies, the Society for Medieval Archaeology, and the Association for Industrial Archaeology; campaigning organisations such as RESCUE: The British Archaeological Trust; and, above all, the national museums (for archaeology, essentially the British Museum and the National Museums and Galleries of Wales). The learned societies are primarily representative and academic, sometimes involved in the formulation of long-term conservation policy but concentrating on the publicising of archaeology to a significant but specialised audience. The national museums do likewise but, in addition, tend both to assist the non-specialist public and to provide highly specialised services to archaeology, including laboratory analysis and conservation. None of these institutions carries on archaeological field contracting on a significant scale, and it would be beyond the objects of most to do so. Their influence is perhaps greatest when working with English Heritage and local planning authorities. The national museums are especially well-respected and currently administer finds of treasure on behalf of the Secretaries of State (see chapter 3).

Archaeological Trusts and Societies

1.38 Historically the impetus for field archaeology in the United Kingdom came from a wealth of national, regional and county archaeological societies, mostly formed in the nineteenth century. Today, although various national societies and some of the larger county societies still make a significant contribution to archaeological research, their role as archaeological contractors is negligible. In organisational terms the societies range from relatively small, unincorporated associations to companies limited by guarantee with 1500 or more members. Amongst their membership the latter usually have the technical knowledge, as well as the constitutional power, to undertake fieldwork to a professional standard, and may provide an additional source of archaeological contracting for the future. The Sussex Archaeological Society maintains ancient monuments in its ownership. The Yorkshire Archaeological Society has one of the best archaeological libraries in the country. The Surrey Archaeological Society achieved prominence recently in its efforts to amend the law relating to portable antiquities.

Archaeological Trusts in England, and especially in Wales, tend to be of a different character from that of archaeological societies. Most trusts are of more recent origin, formed to undertake archaeological survey and excavation in circumscribed geographical areas. Although usually charitable, their involvement in contracting requires a commercial approach to management and practice. Some trusts cover relatively large areas, for example the Glamorgan/Gwent Archaeological Trust; others are more limited in their coverage, for example Canterbury Archaeological Trust. In Wales regional trusts have been the norm and have even been responsible for production of regional Sites and Monuments Records. The most well-known trust is probably the York Archaeological Trust for Excavation and Research Ltd (York Archaeological Trust or 'YAT'). Assisted by the special development and marketing opportunities in York, the YAT has grown to be a charitable organisation possessing one of the largest and most skilful archaeological establishments in the country. A separate project management company has also been established by the Trust (Heritage Projects (Management) Ltd).

For archaeological trusts success generally brings its problems. It usually leads to managerial difficulties, as tensions arise between the officers who are daily confronted with a trust's business and the trustees in whom control and responsibility ultimately is vested. The usual result is an organisation which is wary of change and slow to take decisions. Archaeological trusts are also usually limited by geographical area, so that once expansion in its business has occurred maintaining momentum may be difficult.

An archaeological trust carrying out a significant amount of contract work is usually well-advised to incorporate, to limit the potential liability of trustees but also to obtain other benefits such as improved delegation and perpetual succession. 'Directors' of a charitable corporation should be aware, however, that they will remain liable as charity trustees in spite of incorporation. Incorporation may also mean that a person dealing with the trust will no longer have the comfort that the assets of the trustees will be available to meet trust liabilities; this may be an important consideration where, for example, a contractor is also providing consultancy services.

Independent Consultants and Commercial Contractors

1.39 Before the age of 'environmental assessment' and PPG 16 there were some independent archaeological consultants in the United Kingdom, but the growth in this mode of working has been especially significant since the late 1980s. In part the growth can be attributed to the limitations of both trusts and units, but the catalyst has been the Government's fostering of a regime in which private finance is expected to contribute to the archaeological investigation of sites threatened by change in land use. A lot of archaeological work is now required to be funded as part of the development process, much of it unrelated to any wider academic or research strategy. Its organisation, therefore, is increasingly on a private, professional basis.

Independent contractors and consultants have grown in number to exploit this demand. Their legal character is as varied as in any other line of work: sole principal, partnership or companies incorporated under the Companies Acts. The main concern of a client will be the consultant or contractor's ability to properly carry out the job required, a difficult assessment to make given the array of consultants and contractors now available. These range from the sole practitioner offering site evaluation services, to the corporate consultant offering advice on (to quote one recent advertisement) 'development potential and taxation, litigation, historical research, public inquiries, public relations and project specification'. Useful indicators of archaeological ability are membership of appropriate professional bodies, for example the IFA (both individuals and organisations) or, generally, fellowship of the Society of Antiquaries of London (individuals, an honour abbreviated to 'F.S.A.'). Projects satisfactorily completed are, clearly, a useful guide, and business reputation is a helpful indicator, although the overall volume of archaeological consultancy and contracting is insufficient to permit detailed comparisons between providers. There is no national market and few, if any, developed local markets for archaeological services.

A potential client should also consider specifically the legal and financial make-up of the contractor or consultant, to an extent unfamiliar to many who have become accustomed to dealing with local authority units or with English Heritage. In particular, a client will wish to consider: the contractor's legal ability to perform a contract; the assets of the contractor to which it will have recourse if the contractor should default on its obligations (audited accounts, produced under confidentiality arrangements, may suffice); whether a performance bond is desirable; the contractor's quality controls (probably ascertained by an independent inspection of the contractor's premises and sites); and the extent to which the contractor is insured against liabilities which could not easily be met from the contractor's own resources (bearing in mind that professional indemnity insurance cover is desirable where, in addition to undertaking actual investigation, a contractor also offers specialist advice).

The Institute of Field Archaeologists (IFA)

1.40 The IFA is a company limited by guarantee. It was incorporated in 1985 to succeed the unincorporated association of that name which had been growing steadily in membership during the early 1980s. Although possessing an influential voice in the conservation lobby, this is not the IFA's main purpose. Its memorandum of association states that the IFA is established to:

'Advance the practice of field archaeology and allied disciplines; to define and maintain proper professional standards in training and education in field archaeology, in the execution and supervision of work, and in the conservation of the archaeological heritage; to disseminate information about field archaeologists and their areas of interest ...'

Specifically, the IFA is:

'1. to promote the highest standards of competence and practice amongst field archaeologists;
2. to conduct or promote examinations, certificates, or diplomas in the Institute's name;
3. to establish national, regional, local and other groups for the promotion of the objects of the Institute; and
4. to facilitate the interchange of information ideas and practice on all matters pertaining to field archaeology.'

1.41 The memorandum of association gives extensive

coverage of such objects. However, it is more limited in its treatment of the services which the Institute is able to provide for its membership. The bias favours educational, consultative and regulatory, not professional services, inevitably perhaps in a profession which has only recently seen the emergence of significant numbers of independent, full-time practitioners. Only since about 1996 for example, has the IFA offered (through a broker) professional indemnity insurance. The IFA is not a trade union and although providing a jobs service does not operate in any representative manner in employment cases.

1.42 Membership of the IFA stands at more than a thousand, divided amongst the categories, in descending order of status, of honorary member, member, associate and practitioner. Honorary membership is awarded to those who have given special service to field archaeology during their professional lives; members are recognised by the IFA as having the capacity to carry sole responsibility for a substantial archaeological project in one or more areas of field archaeological practice; associates are seen as slightly less experienced than members, where the ability to carry sole responsibility for 'substantial' projects is still to be demonstrated, whilst practitioners (misleadingly) are those who are just beginning their careers in archaeology. The IFA also recognises an affiliate grade of membership which is open to anyone involved in archaeology and who agrees to be bound by the IFA's Code of Conduct (see below). Although for a national organisation its membership is small, in archaeological terms the IFA probably comprises half of all full-time field archaeologists in the country. Moreover, the membership includes archaeological contractors, both public and private, independent consultants, and a significant proportion of the archaeological staff of English Heritage. In 1995 a scheme for the registration of archaeological organisations which meet specified IFA criteria was introduced. This is not a form of corporate membership but recognises that some organisations rely on the professional status for which the IFA stands. The IFA Annual Report for 1997-98 indicates that about 22 organisations are registered, with more applications expected. Registered organisations must *inter alia* designate a named responsible officer and must be open to monitoring.

The essential measure which the IFA's validation committee employs when admitting applicants to either the member, associate or practitioner grade is the 'area of competence'. Formerly there were nine of these 'AOCs', namely: excavation, survey, underwater archaeology, aerial archaeology; environmental archaeology; finds study and collections research, recording and analysis of buildings, cultural resource management, and research and development (of archaeological techniques and applications). These were replaced in 1996 by a reduced list of five AOCs: archaeological field practice; archaeological resource management; finds and environmental study, collections research and conservation; archaeological research and development; and recording and analysis of buildings. An applicant can be registered against any number of AOCs. The degree of responsibility he or she has demonstrated in a specified area is the key to which category of membership is judged appropriate, not the area of competence itself; so, for example, a 'member' may be competent in only one area of practice but an associate may be competent, at that level, in five areas. It should be noted that the principle of validation was introduced only in 1986, after the initial membership of the IFA had been established. These original members, numbering about half of those currently with full membership status, were entitled in 1986 to assess their own competence. Moreover, the peer validation process is the only test for membership; there are, for example, no common exams or assessments.

All members, associates and practitioners agree to be bound by the IFA's by-laws, especially its Code of Conduct (adopted in 1985, with major amendments made in 1988, 1993, 1996 and 1997). The general provisions of the Code are that:

(i)   an archaeologist shall adhere to the highest standards of ethical and responsible behaviour in the conduct of archaeological affairs, so that, for example, he must not undertake work for which he is not adequately qualified;

(ii)   an archaeologist has a responsibility for the conservation of the archaeological heritage, so that, for example, an archaeologist shall ensure that the object of any investigation justifies the destruction which an investigation will entail;

(iii)   an archaeologist shall conduct his or her work in such a way that reliable information about the past may be acquired and shall ensure that the results are properly recorded;

(iv)   an archaeologist has responsibility for making available the results of archaeological work with reasonable dispatch, so that, for example, he or she must not accede to conditions which require permanent suppression of archaeological discoveries;

(v)   an archaeologist shall recognise the aspirations of employees, colleagues and helpers with regard to all matters relating to employment, including career development, health and safety, terms and conditions of employment, and equality of opportunity.

A breach of the Code of Conduct is referable to the IFA's disciplinary committee, under the IFA's Disciplinary Regulations. These regulations provide for a quasi-judicial examination of the complaint, the right of the parties to present evidence, to cross-examine and to appeal against the findings of the panel of inquiry or, when acting in a preliminary matter, a decision of the chairman of the committee. The ultimate sanction is termination of membership, although this would not prevent the person concerned from continuing to work as an archaeological consultant or contractor.

A further code to which all members of the Institute must subscribe is the *Code of Approved Practice for the Regulation of Contractual Arrangements in Field Archaeology* (adopted in 1990, under article 45 of the IFA's articles of association). This Code has far-reaching effects on the information, interests and degree of competence which archaeologists (either as employers or contractors) must disclose, or require to be disclosed, when contracts are made for archaeological services. This code is considered in chapter six, in relation to the provision of archaeological facilities by developers. Breach is again a disciplinary matter referable to the IFA's disciplinary committee, although its day-to-day implementation is in the hands of the Institute's 'Working Practices in Archaeology' committee.

1.43 When looking at its success in forging a general consensus on matters of conduct between field archaeologists, it is easy to forget that the IFA, as an incorporated body, was only formed in 1985. It has taken further steps recently to standardise the quality of work expected of its members (and others) when they carry out particular kinds of archaeological work. 'Standards Guidance' has been adopted relating to desk-based assessments, field evaluation, watching briefs and the recording of standing buildings. A draft standard for excavation has been adopted for a trial period. The Code of Approved Practice for Contractual Arrangements advises compliance with the standards guidance but does not require it.

The IFA is not a recording or investigating body in its own right; neither is it a fund dispensing grants for conservation purposes or primarily a pressure group. It is the main, national body for practising archaeologists. It concentrates on regulation and standardisation of working practices within the profession, the training of archaeologists, and the monitoring of the legislative and administrative framework within which archaeology is carried out.

The Council for British Archaeology (CBA)

1.44 Whereas the IFA is new a body primarily concerned with professional standards and standing, the CBA was formed in 1944 to safeguard Britain's archaeological heritage, by promoting public interest in archaeology and furthering archaeological representation, research, education and publication.

CBA has a strong academic basis. For many years membership was open to institutional members only, including all universities teaching archaeology in the United Kingdom mainland, representatives of which played a significant role on the CBA's governing body (the 'Council') and on its Executive Board. The Executive Board channels the CBA's work into various national committee areas: aerial archaeology, church archaeology, historic buildings, urban archaeology, rural archaeology, nautical archaeology, archaeological science, industrial archaeology and archaeology in schools, universities and adult education. The day-to-day management of the CBA is in the hands of a Director, a salaried officer assisted by a small staff.

The CBA is a charity and a company limited by guarantee. Its patron is HRH The Prince of Wales. Individuals are able to join one of 12 CBA regional groups (or in Scotland the separate sister organisation, the Council for Scottish Archaeology). These groups are autonomous but work closely with the Council and are entitled to send representatives to Council meetings. There is as yet no regional group in Northern Ireland or the Isle of Man. Until recently it was not possible for individuals to join the national CBA, but this has now changed so that individual membership of both the regional groups and the national organisation is permitted.

The annual budget of CBA is about £0.5m of which over 50% is usually grant received from the British Academy. A further 10% is usually received in grant from the Secretary of State, primarily to assist in the CBA's role as one of the national amenity societies formally consulted on listed building applications (see below). The remaining funds arise from the CBA's own investments, publications, subscriptions and the like.

1.45 The CBA is not a research institution. The CBA concentrates instead on assessing research priorities and carrying out archaeological appraisals. Important works include *The Erosion of History* (1972) and *The Archaeology of the Uplands* (1986) (published in conjunction with the RCHM(e)) – respectively, works on the threats to archaeological remains in the historic towns and the uplands of Britain. Both publications have been influential beyond the archaeological profession. The CBA also publishes a reputable newsletter, British Archaeology, ten times per year, and a briefing. But these are a small part of a wide-ranging output which includes an extensive series of archaeological reports.

As one of the national amenity societies, the CBA has a formal consultative role under the listed building consent procedures, though not under the scheduled monument regime (regular, informal consultation between the Welsh Office and the CBA takes place in Wales, however). For its work on listed building applications the CBA receives a small grant from the Secretary of State with which it funds an historic buildings officer. However, the Council is more closely connected with local and national government, and the various agencies, than this specific listed building function suggests. CBA was involved in the formulation of PPG 16 and frequently supports the conservationist cause at local inquires. It is a well-respected consultee on proposed reforms of archaeological and ancient monument legislation, being more independent than are English Heritage, local authorities or even the IFA. The CBA is also in frequent liaison with English Nature, the Ministry for Agriculture, which it advised on the archaeological aspects of environmentally sensitive areas (see chapter four), and the Church of England. The CBA has also been a strong lobbyist in favour of reforming the law relating to portable antiquities and is regularly consulted on such proposals by the British Museum.

As a charity, the CBA is not permitted to pursue profit as an object, nor is it within the CBA's objects to be an archaeological contractor. In the representational sphere it must also take care to ensure that it does not pursue political change as an object, but may instead bring perceived deficiencies in law and administration under greater public scrutiny. Over the years the CBA has proved both active and authoritative: 'the CBA is of established reputation and respected opinion; its policy recommendations have been widely implemented' (Hunter and Ralston, 1993, 40).

The National Trust (for Places of Historic Interest or Natural Beauty)

1.46 The National Trust is probably the best known owner and manager of heritage property in the country. Commensurate with its conservation role it also takes a keen interest in promoting and protecting the archaeological value of its sites.

The Trust was incorporated in 1907 by private Act of Parliament, one of the few private heritage bodies to receive statutory powers. It is empowered to deal with real and other property in a variety of ways, including the power to declare land inalienable if the Trust resolves that a property should be held for the benefit of the nation (section 21, National Trust Act 1907). This protects the land in question from appropriation or acquisition under a number of statutory provisions, including the Acquisition of Land Act 1981 (specific parliamentary authority is then required); the discharge of covenants under section 84 of the Land Property Act 1925; and acquisition by a tenant of a freehold reversion under the Leasehold Reform Act 1967 (as amended). The Trust is now a registered charity.

Amongst its general objects are:

1. Promoting the permanent preservation for the benefit of the nation of land and tenements including buildings of beauty or historic interest (section 4(1), National Trust Act 1907); and
2. Preserving buildings of national interest or architectural, historic or artistic interest (and the augmentation of such buildings, places and their surroundings) (section 3, National Trust Act 1937).

It is mostly these objects which dictate the Trust's involvement in archaeological work. The Trust is custodian of a variety of archaeological sites, ranging from caves and field monuments to castles and Roman villas. Each is managed by the appropriate regional director of the Trust, whose primary concern will be the preservation of such archaeological sites in perpetuity.

CHAPTER TWO

ANCIENT MONUMENTS AND ARCHAEOLOGICAL AREAS

The term 'ancient monument' appears to have entered English law in the Ancient Monuments Protection Act of 1882, an Act intended to protect earthworks, barrows and major national monuments. Later Acts, though extending protection to a greater number of monument types, continued to distinguish archaeological sites from historic buildings and historic areas in towns. Ancient monuments and archaeological sites therefore are a distinct part of the 'heritage'.

Activities which affect ancient monuments and archaeological sites are regulated by several statutory and common law rules, but the most important are the statutory provisions now contained in the AMAA 1979.

The AMAA is usually referred to as an amending and consolidating Act, but it enacted some of the most far-reaching changes in heritage law this century. Some concepts were inherited from earlier legislation; for example, the 'schedule' of monuments, introduced by the 1882 Act, and the payment of compensation, in certain circumstances, to owners who suffer loss attributable to the status of land as a scheduled monument (introduced by the Ancient Monuments Act 1931 and now provided for by compensation for the refusal of 'scheduled monument consent'; see paragraph 2.200). Other concepts were rendered obsolete by the AMAA; for example, the system of 'interim preservation notices' and 'preservation orders' introduced by the HBAMA 1953 (now replaced by scheduled monument consent procedures), and the making of 'acknowledgement payments', under the Field Monuments Act 1972, to owners who practised sympathetic management of scheduled monuments.

The AMAA was amended by the NHA 1983. The amendments were mainly procedural and effected a separation, in heritage matters, of the advisory from the decision making functions of the Secretary of State. English Heritage (see paragraph 1.09) is now statutory adviser to the Secretary of State for Culture, Media and Sport (see paragraph 1.01). The Secretary of State must consult with English Heritage before making just about all important decisions under the AMAA. A similar separation of functions exists in Wales, but there Cadw (Welsh Historic Monuments) is an executive agency of the Welsh Assembly, whereas English Heritage is a distinct statutory corporation.

The legal framework established in 1979 extends to Scotland. Neither the AMAA nor the NHA 1983 extends to Northern Ireland, where archaeology is provided for under the Historic Monuments (Northern Ireland) Act 1971.

Scheduled Monuments
(sections 1 and 61, AMAA are reproduced at appendix 2A of this work)

2.01 The AMAA recognises four categories of monument: monuments; ancient monuments; protected monuments; and scheduled monuments. (The NHA 1983, confusingly, provides another definition of ancient monument, in relation to English Heritage's general obligations and management functions.)

'Monument' is a comprehensive, physical descriptive category which, subject to limited exceptions (see paragraphs 2.05 and 2.08), embraces all types of sites and structures, whatever their importance, including caves and excavations (section 61(7), AMAA). Section 61(7) refers to:

'(a) *any building, structure or work, whether above or below the surface of the land, and any cave or excavation;*

(b) *any site comprising the remains of any such building, structure or work or of any cave or excavation; and*

(c) *any site comprising, or comprising the remains of, any vehicle, vessel, aircraft or other movable structure or part thereof which neither constitutes nor forms part of any work which is a monument within paragraph (a) above.'*

Section 61(9) of the AMAA makes it clear that the site of a monument includes not only the land in or on which the monument is situated but also any land comprising or adjoining it which appears to the Secretary of State, English Heritage or, in appropriate cases, a local authority, to be essential for the monument's support and preservation. This provision anticipates the powers of acquisition and management conferred on those bodies under the Act, whilst also indicating the extent of land which a competent authority may take into account when, for example, deciding to formally enter a monument to the schedule of monuments. But the provision does not mean that parts of a monument which may lie outside of the area which is actually afforded statutory protection are deemed to be scheduled.

2.02 'Ancient monuments' are monuments within the meaning of section 61(7) which are either entered to the statutory schedule compiled by the Secretary of State or, in the Secretary of State's opinion, are *'of public interest by reason of the historic, architectural, traditional, artistic or archaeological interest'* attaching to them (section 61(12), AMAA). In some circumstances, where English Heritage exercises functions under the AMAA, 'ancient monument' can also mean a monument which English Heritage believes to be of public interest etc. Such circumstances are considered more fully below. To add to this complexity, the NHA 1983 introduced yet another definition of ancient monument for English Heritage's management functions under sections 33(1), 33(2) and 35 of that Act. The latter definition does not refer to public interest (see paragraphs 1.16 and 1.17).

'Protected monuments' is a class defined by section 28 of the AMAA, in relation to the offence under that Act of damaging monuments which are owned by or under the 'guardianship' (see paragraph 2.167 for guardianship) of either the Secretary of State, English Heritage or a local authority, *or* monuments which are scheduled monuments.

2.03 'Scheduled monuments' are defined by the AMAA as any monument which for the time being is included in the schedule of monuments maintained by the Secretary of State (section 1(11)). Procedurally this is by far the most important category of monument. The Secretary of State must compile and maintain a schedule of monuments (section 1(1)). On the commencement of the AMAA, he had to include in the schedule all monuments scheduled (or notified as to be scheduled) under previous legislation and was given a discretion to add any other monuments which to him appear to be of 'national importance' (section 1(3)). He must consult with English Heritage before scheduling (or de-scheduling) a monument (section 1(3), AMAA as amended by section 33, NHA 1983). In practice, most proposals to add or delete an entry are received via English Heritage.

2.04 The concept of national importance is considered below, but it should be noted that the AMAA places no duty on the Secretary of State to schedule previously unscheduled monuments and few, if any, legal obligations to do so will be implied. Although the Secretary of State may believe a monument to be of national importance, he is not compelled to schedule it. His discretion here is a broad one and will not be challenged by the court unless irrelevant matters have been taken into account, or relevant matters ignored (*R. v. Secretary of State for the Environment, ex parte Rose Theatre Trust Company* (1990) 59 P. & C. R. 257 at 266 QBD). In this case Schiemann J. accepted that when deciding whether or not to schedule a monument the Secretary of State was entitled to consider a wide range of factors, including:

- the risk of compensation payments;
- the competing pressures of re-development and the preservation of monuments (in London, but probably in any other context where development pressures are great);
- the difficulty in delimiting, accurately, the important parts of a monument;
- that a scheme for protecting the monument in question was, in the opinion of English Heritage, as

    likely as was scheduling to secure the future of the monument;

- that the scheduling of a monument does not mean that a monument will be preserved in perpetuity, only that works affecting the monument will first require the consent of the Secretary of State;
- that developers who had co-operated in providing facilities and resources for archaeological investigation of the monument in question (and other monuments) might be discouraged from doing so in future; and
- that the co-operation of the developer had been instrumental in revealing the full significance of the monument.

Even in emergency situations, however, it must be doubted whether such a range of criteria should generally be taken into account by the scheduling authority. One of the arguments advanced by the Rose Theatre Trust was that such matters could be properly considered at the time an application for scheduled monument consent came to be determined. There is merit in this argument, although *Rose Theatre* represents the law at present.

If the power to schedule monuments is ever granted to English Heritage, the provisions of section 33(1) of the NHA 1983 (see paragraph 1.16 above) could, conceivably, narrow English Heritage's discretion to refuse to schedule if specific statutory wording in any new enabling powers does not provide otherwise.

Statutory and Non-Statutory Criteria

2.05 Section 61(7) of the AMAA defines what may constitute a monument for statutory purposes. This is a much wider definition than the term 'building' which gives rise to the uncertainties familiar in listed building law (see chapter five of this work). Remains accessible only by means of remote sensing techniques, for example geophysical applications or aerial photography, can be monuments and may be scheduled if the evidence is of sufficient quality; so too may roads, relict field boundaries or boulders carved with prehistoric markings. Doubt exists as to whether environmental deposits containing evidence of human activity - stone tools and the use of fire, for example - are within the definition of 'monument'. In practice such sites are scheduled if it is possible to argue that they fall within 'any site comprising the remains of ... a work' (section 61(7)(b), AMAA). To come within section 61(7)(b), however, there must have been a *thing* in question before the existence of remains can be entertained.

As a very rough rule of thumb, most prehistoric, roman and pre-conquest monuments will be considered for scheduling, even if only part-preserved or significantly degraded. Most medieval buildings and settlement sites which survive in something like their complete form will also be considered. Monuments of more recent date, however, will have to be both well-preserved and illustrative of the principal changes in architecture, military engineering, industrial or agricultural technology or public works.

2.06 It is also generally understood, though only a permissive statutory provision, that to be scheduled a monument should be of 'national importance'. This view derives from section 1(3) of the AMAA, which provides that the Secretary of State may on first compiling the schedule, or at any time thereafter, include a monument which appears to him to be of national importance. This is clearly a discretionary power, and there is no rule of law that he must schedule a monument which is of national importance (see paragraph 2.04). The question arises whether he is able to schedule monuments which are of less than national importance, monuments which archaeologists might refer to as 'regionally important'. Current ministerial practice, together with a strict interpretation of section 1(3), suggests not. In any event, it is difficult to conceive of a situation where a monument which the Secretary of State wished to schedule could be said to be of less than national importance.

2.07 There is no statutory definition of national importance. It is a time-honoured phrase whose substance is determined by the Secretary of State in consultation with English Heritage. A representative sample is sought by reference to eight, as yet non-statutory, criteria, first given public prominence by the Secretary of State in 1983. Annex 4 of PPG 16 repeats these criteria, though the headnote to the annex is a reminder that they are not definitive, but 'indicators'. The criteria, not, it is emphasised, in order of importance, are as follows.

(1)   Period: all types of monuments that characterise a category or period should be considered for preservation.

(2)   Rarity: there are some monument categories which in certain periods are so scarce that all surviving examples which still retain some archaeological potential should be preserved. In general, however, a selection must be made which portrays the particular and commonplace as well as the rare. This process should take account of all aspects of the distribution of a particular class of monument, both in a national and a regional context.

(3)   Documentation: the significance of a monument may be enhanced by the existence of records of previous investigation or, in the case of more recent monuments, by the supporting evidence of contemporary written records.

(4)   Group Value: the value of a single monument (such as a field system) may be greatly enhanced by its association with related contemporary monuments (such as a settlement and cemetery) or with monuments of different periods. In some cases, it is preferable to protect the complete group of monuments, including associated and adjacent land, rather than to protect isolated monuments within the group.

(5)   Survival/Condition: the survival of a monument's archaeological potential both above and below ground is a particularly important consideration and should be assessed in relation to its present condition and surviving features.

(6)   Fragility/Vulnerability: highly important archaeological evidence from some field monuments can be destroyed by a single ploughing or unsympathetic treatment; vulnerable monuments of this nature would particularly benefit from the statutory protection which scheduling confers. There are also existing standing structures of particular form or

71

complexity whose value can be severely reduced by neglect or careless treatment and which are similarly well suited by scheduled monument protection, even if these structures are already listed historic buildings.

(7) Diversity: some monuments may be selected for scheduling because they possess a combination of high quality features, others because of a single important attribute.

(8) Potential: on occasion, the nature of the evidence cannot be specified precisely but it may still be possible to document reasons anticipating its existence and importance and so to demonstrate the justification for scheduling. This is usually confined to sites rather than upstanding monuments.

Obviously, these criteria are extremely wide and designed to ensure that a very broad selection can be justified on archaeological grounds: a monument would not need to score highly against each, and criteria 4, 6 and 8 may produce results which the non-archaeologist will find difficult to appreciate. Since about 1985 English Heritage has been reviewing the application of the criteria as part of its 'Monuments Protection Programme' (MPP). The assessment of monuments has been developed to a level of sophistication previously unknown in public archaeology in England (see, for example, Darvill *et al.* (1987)).

2.08 The Secretary of State may schedule any kind of monument except 'buildings occupied as dwelling houses by any person other than a caretaker or his family' (section 1(4), AMAA). Ecclesiastical buildings 'in use for ecclesiastical purposes', any machinery, craft or moveable structure not of public interest, and any wreck or site of a wreck protected under section 1 of the Protection of Wrecks

Act 1973 cannot be scheduled, as these are not monuments within the meaning of section 61(7) of the AMAA (section 61(8) of that Act). A redundant church is not necessarily out of ecclesiastical use, therefore care must be taken in this respect (see chapter five).

Monuments in United Kingdom territorial waters may be scheduled (section 53, AMAA), though for the reason stated in the preceding paragraph this protection cannot be extended to a wreck protected under the 1973 Act. The two codes were intended to be distinct. Marine monuments scheduled under the AMAA are usually denuded architectural and similar structures close to the shore. Restricted areas under the 1973 Act must relate to the site of (or a site which may prove to be) 'a vessel lying wrecked' (section 1(1)(a)), 1973 Act); distinct offences of tampering with, damaging or removing wrecks or depositing material on top of wreck sites, are created by section 1(3) of that Act. Consents for works in such restricted areas are, however, now given by the Secretary of State for Culture, Media and Sport (see appendix 1A of this work).

Monuments on Crown land may also be scheduled (section 50(1)(a)), though the requirement to obtain 'scheduled monument consent' is not applicable to anything done by or on behalf of the Crown on Crown land (section 51(1)(b) (where 'scheduled monument clearance', a non-statutory authorisation, is required).

2.09 English Heritage is not empowered to act outside England, either under the provisions of the NHA 1983 or under the AMAA as amended. This means that it cannot administer ancient monument policy in United Kingdom territorial waters on behalf of the Secretary of State (who may schedule such monuments). The AMAA presents a confused picture with, for example, section 45 limiting English Heritage's powers in the making of grants to England yet section 53 anticipating ownership of monuments in territorial waters by English Heritage. It may not have been appreciated by the draftsman of the 1983 Act that the term 'England', unlike the term 'Great Britain' does not extend to the seabed within territorial waters. In Wales there is, as yet, no such confusion as Cadw, an executive agency and not a separate statutory corporation, has the power to administer ancient monuments policy in territorial waters. There is no universally accepted definition of territorial waters, though as a bare minimum they are acknowledged to extend to at least three miles from low-water mark (section 7, Territorial Waters Jurisdiction Act 1878).

2.10 The Secretary of State formerly published a list of all monuments included in the schedule. Now he only has to supply English Heritage with details of the schedule and English Heritage must then publish the schedule on the Secretary of State's behalf. Section 1(7) of the AMAA permits the publication of the schedule in parts, and in practice the schedule is under continuous review. Lists are currently published on a county basis, even in those areas, for example the Metropolitan areas, where administrative counties no longer exist. Although these published lists can be of legal as well as of archaeological significance, they do not define the extent, but provide only the name or description, and location (by parish and national grid reference) of monument types. The schedule is more than the published lists; at the very least the schedule will usually include a copy of the identification map originally sent to the owner when the monument was scheduled. The Court of Appeal has held that a map produced by the Secretary of State, and supplied to a developer, was definitive of the extent of a scheduled monument, and that the matter did not need to go to the jury for determination as a matter of fact (*R. v. Bovis Construction Ltd* [1994] Crim.L.R. 938). English Heritage will usually produce several pieces of evidence during court or other proceedings. The criminal courts will generally expect that the maps and documents adduced would enable a lay person to determine the extent of the scheduled area, without obtaining specialist advice.

2.11 Entry of a monument to the schedule should be registered by the registering authority (i.e. the appropriate local authority) as a local land charge (section 1(9), AMAA). Failure to register has occasionally been of assistance to defendants in scheduled monument prosecutions. Failure to register may also give rise to compensation claims against the registering authority (section 10, Local Land Charges Act 1975).

2.12 In exercising any of their functions under the AMAA the Secretary of State, English Heritage or local authorities may require a statement in writing of interests in land from occupiers of any land, and any person receiving rent from any land (section 57, AMAA). Such persons can also be required to provide written details of any other estate or interest, including that of a mortgagee, known to them to subsist in the land. Failure to give the required information without reasonable excuse is a summary offence, punishable by a fine of up to level 3 on the standard scale. Knowingly making a misstatement in respect of any information provided is an offence punishable on summary conviction by a fine up to the statutory maximum or, on indictment, by an unlimited fine.

2.13 Although there is no formal appeal against scheduling, advance notice of the intention to schedule is usually given to owners, so that objections and comments may be heard. Argument on the archaeological merits alone is an uphill struggle, and an expert opinion of considerable weight will be the minimum which is required. The more usual results of such notification are discussions on a site's planning history, including the effects of scheduling in the case in question and how these might be mitigated.

2.14 After entering a monument to the schedule the Secretary of State must inform English Heritage of the fact 'as soon as may be' (section 1(6A), AMAA); English Heritage must then notify the relevant owners, occupiers and local authority. Section 56 of the Act provides for acceptable methods of service for this and other purposes; for example, when an owner's address cannot be found the fixing of a notice to the monument is deemed to be good service.

In brief, the main consequences of scheduling are that many otherwise lawful activities, including the use of metal detectors, become illegal unless prior consent is received from the appropriate authority. Compensation may be payable where consent for 'works' is refused, and, generally, sites become potential subjects for a range of management measures. Scheduling also confers rights of access to authorised inspectors, though not to the public. But it does not place an obligation on an owner or occupier to enhance or preserve the monument in question. This is a contrast with listed buildings, as most listed buildings will still have an economic use and failure to maintain such a building may result in the service of a repairs notice (see chapter five); under section 10 of the AMAA an ancient monument may be compulsorily acquired in order to 'secure its preservation', but there is no express statutory provision which requires works to be carried out as a preliminary to the process of compulsory acquisition.

Powers of Entry to Land

2.15 Any person authorised in writing by the Secretary of State or, in England, English Heritage, may enter land at any reasonable time for the purpose of inspecting a scheduled monument (a) to ascertain whether the monument is being damaged, or (b) generally in respect of matters relating to the processing and implementation of a scheduled monument consent (sections 6 and 6A, AMAA). Section 44 of the AMAA provides that not less than twenty-four hours notice of entry must be given to the occupier of the land. If 'works' are to be carried out, under other provisions of the Act, by English Heritage, or the Secretary of State or his representative (otherwise than by consent under part II of the AMAA), 14 days notice must be given. Longer periods of notice are desirable in practice, though it should be noted that 'days' in this context is not restricted to 'working days'.

2.16 Unlike the Secretary of State, English Heritage is not empowered under section 6A to authorise the examination and recording of matters of archaeological interest encountered during the inspection of works carried out under a scheduled monument consent. English Heritage does have wide powers of inspection and recording under section 36 of the NHA 1983 (see paragraph 1.22 above and appendix 2 of this work), but these are expressed to be for maintaining records of sites which English Heritage believes are of archaeological interest. In practice this limitation is of minor importance, as the Secretary of State may authorise English Heritage to inspect works; moreover, conditions attached to a scheduled monument consent will often provide for English Heritage, or other nominated archaeologists, to inspect and record on the Secretary of State's behalf.

2.17 Provided that not less than seven clear days notice is given to the owner and, if not the same person, the occupier of a monument, either the Secretary of State or, on his authorisation in England, English Heritage, may also enter land, at any time, to carry out works which are 'urgently necessary' to preserve a scheduled monument (section 5, AMAA 1979, as amended). The general notice provisions of section 44 do not apply. There is no power under section 5 for the Secretary of State to delegate his functions under that section to a person or body other than English Heritage.

2.18 A monument need not be scheduled for a power of entry to exist under the AMAA. Section 26(1) of that Act empowers persons duly authorised by the Secretary of State (but not English Heritage) to enter and inspect (for the purpose of making records) any land which the Secretary of State knows or has reason to believe contains an ancient monument (as defined by section 61(12) of the Act, see paragraph 2.02 above). The NHA 1983 did not amend section 26, because section 36 of the 1983 Act gives persons duly authorised by English Heritage equivalent powers to inspect any land containing a monument which, in relation to English Heritage's functions under section 33(2)(d) of the NHA 1983, is an ancient monument. An ancient monument in this latter context means any 'structure, work, site, garden or area' which in English Heritage's opinion is of 'historic, architectural, artistic or archaeological interest' (section 33(8), NHA 1983). Not less than twenty-four hours notice must be given to all occupiers when any person enters land under either the powers contained in section 26 or section 36 of the above statutes.

2.19 Certain additional powers of entry are granted by section 13 (relating to guardianship monuments) and section 43 (valuations and surveys) of the AMAA. These powers can be exercised by local authorities when determining the amount of compensation payable under the Act or if they are the guardians of a guardianship monument, as well as by the Secretary of State, English Heritage and their authorised representatives.

2.20 Under both the 1979 and 1983 Acts, supplemental provisions usually require: that entry into a dwelling can take place only with the consent of the occupier; that identification must be produced if requested; and that such equipment (and assistance) may be taken as is reasonably required for the purpose in hand. Intentional obstruction of a person authorised to enter land under the Acts is usually an offence (see paragraph 2.154). Excavation is not authorised under section 6 or section 6A of the AMAA, and under section 26 excavation can only be undertaken with the consent of owners and occupiers (strictly 'every person whose consent to the making of the excavation would be required apart from this section').

2.21 The AMAA anticipates that 'investigations', which includes term excavation (section 61(4)), will usually be undertaken pursuant to conditions attached to scheduled monument consents or under the provisions of part II of the Act (relating to Areas of Archaeological Importance). Where a person entering land is also authorised under the AMAA to carry out investigation of the land that person may also take temporary custody of objects of archaeological or historic interest discovered during the course of 'excavation, examination or operations'. Such objects may be retained for any reasonable length of time which permits them to be examined, tested, treated, recorded or preserved (section 54, AMAA). The Secretary of State or a local authority which has financed an agreed excavation or analysis of the objects may publish the results in such manner and form as they think fit (section 45(3), AMAA). The Crown's right to treasure (see chapter three) is not affected by these provisions (section 54(3)).

2.22 Scheduling, as distinct from guardianship or public ownership, does not confer any rights of public access to monuments where no such rights previously existed.

Scheduled Monument Consent

2.23 The AMAA introduced a new procedure for controlling works affecting scheduled monuments (section 2). A person who intends to carry out works which do not fall within certain exceptions (these are considered below at paragraphs 2.28-2.36) must first obtain a specific grant of 'scheduled monument consent' from the Secretary of State (section 2(3)(a), AMAA). This requirement replaces the old system of Interim Preservation Notices and Preservation Orders, and acknowledges the overriding importance in this context of preservation over normal economic use.

Before the commencement of the AMAA an owner was required to give three months notice to the Secretary of State of an intention to carry out works which could affect a scheduled monument. The Secretary of State would then agree to the works proceeding or would issue an Interim Preservation Notice, either forbidding the works or restricting their scope. Subsequently, the Secretary of State could confirm the notice by serving a 'permanent' Preservation Order. For many reasons this system proved to difficult to operate. The AMAA bringing scheduled monument law more in line with listed building law, begins instead from the premise that '*if any person executes or causes or permits to be executed any works to which this section applies he shall be guilty of an offence unless the works are authorised*' (section 2(1)). Section 2(1) applies to all monuments entered to the statutory schedule from the time the monument is entered to the schedule, not from the time that a local land charge is registered against the property, or the owner notified by English Heritage or Cadw. 'Works', as defined in section 2(2) (see below), will only be authorised if carried out in accordance with a prior grant of scheduled monument consent. An applicant must now wait for the consent to be granted, not for three months to elapse without ministerial response.

2.24 Scheduled monument consent is required for many activities for which a general planning consent may exist by development order, or which would not be classed as development under the planning Acts. This distinction is particularly relevant where compensation for refusal of scheduled monument consent is at issue (see paragraphs 2.201-2.203).

2.25 Scheduled monument consent is also usually required in addition to other forms of statutory control, for example planning controls and controls over disused burial grounds (see chapters six and three respectively). Specific provisions in the P(LBCA)A ensure that, in respect of works to a building which is both scheduled and listed, scheduled monument control takes precedence; dual applications are unnecessary and listed building control, including liability for the main listed buildings offences, is removed (section 61, P(LBCA)A). Section 75 of the P(LBCA)A also removes scheduled monuments from the class of buildings for which conservation area consent must be obtained before demolition of a building in a conservation area.

2.26 Applications for scheduled monument consent must be submitted before any works covered by section 2(2) are begun, namely:

   '(a)   any works resulting in the demolition or destruction of

> *or any damage to a scheduled monument;*
> (b) *any works for the purpose of removing or repairing a scheduled monument or any part of it or of making any alterations or additions thereto; and*
> (c) *any flooding or tipping operations on land in, or under which there is a scheduled monument.'*

Section 2(2) is intended to provide a reasonably definitive list of works, but it does not extend to the more general word 'disturbance'encountered in relation to operations in Areas of Archaeological Importance (see below). The word 'works', although including 'operations' (section 61(1), AMAA) is itself limiting, as can be illustrated by the example of damage caused by shrub roots. Damage to a monument occasioned by roots of shrubs growing at the time of scheduling will not fall within section 2(2); nor will damage caused by shrubs which take hold naturally after scheduling. These cannot be categorised as 'works'. The planting of shrubs after scheduling is considered by English Heritage to require consent, and this is supported by the exclusion from Class 1 of the Class Consents Order 1994 (see below) of 'the planting or uprooting of trees, hedges or shrubs'. However, where the object planted is too small to involve 'operations', something less than commercial operations for example, there may be no 'works' and so, even though damage is caused as a result of growth, no requirement to obtain scheduled monument consent.

2.27 The form and certificates for scheduled monument applications are prescribed by the Ancient Monuments (Applications for Scheduled Monument Consent) Regulations 1981 (S.I. 1981, No.1301; see appendix 2B of this work). As with planning and listed buildings, applications can differ enormously in scale and effect. Where excavation or site evaluation may be required the applicant should obtain archaeological advice at an early stage, as it will be necessary at the application stage to detail the archaeological impacts of proposed works and the programmes which are intended to mitigate these impacts. Where anything more than trial trenching is envisaged, preliminary but extensive discussion of why an excavation is needed should be undertaken with English Heritage (see the additional guidance note published by English Heritage, appendix 2C of this work).

See paragraphs 2.40-2.45 below for scheduled monument consent applications. See also class 7 of the Ancient Monuments (Class Consents) Order.

Class Consents

2.28 Where a monument is scheduled there will be no need to obtain a specific grant of scheduled monument consent if the works commenced before June 14, 1994, and are of a class falling within The Ancient Monuments (Class Consents) Order 1981 (S.I. 1981, No.1302) (as amended by The Ancient Monuments (Class Consents) Order 1984 (S.I. 1984, No.222). After June 14, 1994 the works must be of a class falling within The Ancient Monuments (Class Consents) Order 1994 (S.I. 1994, No.1381).

2.29 Class consents are granted by the Secretary of State under section 3 of the AMAA, and create classes of 'permitted works' for which an application for scheduled monument consent need not be made. By article 2 of the 1981 Order, works for which scheduled monument consent was granted included: agricultural, horticultural or forestry works of the same kind as were executed during the five year period immediately preceding the effective date of the Order (October 9, 1981), but excluding drainage works, hedge planting or removal, or works below the depth of 'normal' ploughing (Class I); works executed at a depth of more than ten metres by the former National Coal Board or its licensees (Class II); works executed by the British Waterways Board on their land for the repair or maintenance (not involving a material alteration) of a monument, which were also works essential for the functioning of a canal (Class III); works for the repair or maintenance of any machinery where no material alteration to a monument was effected (Class IV); and works which were essential for health and safety (Class V). The 1984 Order introduced Class VI into the 1981 Order, namely all works executed by English Heritage.

2.30 The 1994 Order completely revises the existing classes and provides some new ones. Except for the savings for works commenced before June 14, 1994, the old Orders are revoked (article 3(1), 1994 Order). The new classes are:

Class 1. Agricultural, Horticultural and Forestry Works

Permitted works: Agricultural, horticultural and forestry works of the same kind as those previously carried out lawfully in the same location and on the same spot within that location within the period of six years immediately preceding the date on which the works commence; but excluding works falling into one or more of the following categories:

(a)   in the case of ploughed land, any works likely to disturb the soil of any part of that land below the depth at which ploughing of that part has previously been carried out lawfully;

(b)   in the case of land other than ploughed land, any works likely to disturb the soil below the depth of 300 millimetres;

(c)   sub-soiling, drainage works, the planting or uprooting of trees, hedges or shrubs, the stripping of top soil, tipping operations, or the commercial cutting and removal of turf;

(d)   the demolition, removal, extension, alteration or disturbance of any building, structure or work or of the remains thereof;

(e)   the erection of any building or structure;

(f)   in the case works other than domestic gardening works, the laying of paths, hard-standings or foundations for buildings or the erection of fences or other barriers.

Class 2. Works by the British Coal Corporation or their Licensees

Permitted works: Works executed more than 10 metres below ground level by the British Coal Corporation, or any person acting pursuant to a licence granted by the Corporation under section 36(2) of the Coal Industry Nationalisation Act 1946 [now any licensed operator within section 65(1) of the Coal Industry Act 1994]

Class 3. Works by British Waterways Board

Permitted works: Works executed by the British Waterways Board, in relation to land owned or occupied by them, being works of repair or maintenance, not involving a material alteration to a scheduled monument, which are essential for ensuring the functioning of a canal.

Class 4. Works for the Repair or Maintenance of Machinery

Permitted works: Works for the repair or maintenance of machinery, being works which do not involve a material alteration to a scheduled monument.

Class 5. Works Urgently Necessary for Safety or Health

Permitted works: Works which are urgently necessary in the interests of safety or health provided that:

(a)   the works are limited to the minimum measures immediately necessary; and

(b)   notice in writing justifying in detail the need for the works is given to the Secretary of State as soon as reasonably practicable.

Class 6. Works by the Commission (English Heritage)

Permitted works: Works executed by the Commission.

Class 7. *Works of Archaeological Evaluation*

Permitted works: Works of archaeological evaluation carried out by or on behalf of a person who has applied for consent under section 2 of the AMAA being works carried out:

(a)   in order to supply the Secretary of State with information required by him for determination of that application;

(b)   under the supervision of a person approved for that purpose in writing by the Secretary of State or the Commission (*English Heritage*); and

(c)   in accordance with a written specification approved for that purpose by the Secretary of State or the Commission.

Class 8. *Works carried out under certain Agreements concerning Ancient Monuments*

Permitted works: Works for the maintenance or preservation of a scheduled monument or its amenities being works executed in accordance with the terms of a written agreement between the occupier of the monument and the Secretary of State or the Commission (*English Heritage*) under section 17 of the AMAA.

Class 9. *Works grant aided under section 24 of the AMAA*

Permitted works: Works for the preservation, maintenance or management of a scheduled monument being works executed in accordance with the terms of a written agreement under which the Secretary of State or the Commission (*English Heritage*) defray, or contribute towards the cost of those works pursuant to their powers under section 24 of the AMAA.

Class 10. Works undertaken by the Royal Commission on the Historical Monuments of England or the Royal Commission on the Ancient and Historical Monuments of Wales

Permitted works: Works consisting of the placing of survey markers to a depth not exceeding 300 millimetres for the purpose of measured surveying of visible remains undertaken by the Royal Commission on the Historical Monuments of England or by the Royal Commission on the Ancient and Historical Monuments of Wales.

2.31 The 1994 Order introduces four entirely new class consents and significantly amends classes 1 and 5 ('farming operations' and 'health and safety'). The new classes are classes 7, 8, 9 and 10. Classes 2, 3, 4 and 6 are largely unchanged, except for the more accurate reference to 'scheduled monuments' in classes 3 and 4 (in substitution for the word 'monument' in the 1981 Order). What constitutes a material alteration (classes 3 and 4) is a matter of fact in each case, but it will be a relatively low threshold where any works affecting the permanent structure of a monument are concerned.

Class 7 permits archaeological evaluations by persons other than English Heritage or archaeologists nominated by the Secretary of State. Such work is intended to be tightly controlled, but the class opens the way for independent consultants and contractors to evaluate sites when an application has been made for scheduled monument consent and further information is required by the Secretary of State. The class does not confer any general permission to evaluate, and it should be noted that an application must already have been made. The provisions of the Order require the person carrying out the evaluation to work closely with both the Secretary of State, possibly English Heritage, and a nominated supervisor. In effect, the class obviates the need for a separate scheduled monument consent in those cases where works of the kinds referred to in section 2(2)(a) of the AMAA will form part of an evaluation.

New classes 8 and 9 relate to works to which the Secretary of State or English Heritage have already consented by virtue, respectively, of their entering a management agreement under section 17 or a funding agreement under section 24, of the AMAA. The wording of both classes will require that management and funding agreements have to accurately detail the works which are to be carried out, otherwise the classes will be difficult to operate. Class 8 is not applicable to agreements made by local authorities.

2.32 The RCHM(e) and the RCAHM(w) will usually consult English Heritage or Cadw, as appropriate, before surveying a scheduled monument, as scheduled monument consent or a licence to use equipment capable of detecting metal may be required (see paragraph 2.157 below). In most instances, however, works include no more than the positioning of survey pegs in the top-soil of a monument. This limited amount of disturbance is now expressly authorised. Note that organisations other than the two mentioned will *prima facie* require a specific grant of consent to carry out the same kind of work. Surveys by English Heritage fall within class 6.

2.33 For the purposes of section 2 of the AMAA, class 6 authorises all works carried out by English Heritage. However, it does not authorise for all purposes works carried out by English Heritage on scheduled monuments; for example, a specific grant of planning permission will still be required if the operations or use do not fall within English Heritage's permitted development rights under the GPDO (see paragraph 1.23 and chapter six). If a scheduled monument also lies within an Area of Archaeological Importance English Heritage will have to comply with AAI procedures. By virtue of class 6, English Heritage is able to carry out works to structures which are both listed and scheduled without any specific authorisation under those codes, as the scheduled monument code overrides the listed buildings code.

2.34 Class 5 of the 1981 Order referred to works which were essential for health and safety. 'Essential' was sometimes interpreted by landowners to convey a greater element of subjectivity than was originally intended. The new wording 'urgently necessary' is more in keeping with the provisions relating to urgent works to listed building; the phrase is probably to be read disjunctively, i.e. that the works are necessary and urgent, but even if the urgency is due to neglect. The phrase 'necessarily urgent'could have provided a different emphasis, as works would, additionally, still need to be 'immediately necessary' (class 5(a)). Notice of works must be served on the Secretary of State (class 5(b));

a notice served on English Heritage will, technically, be defective.

2.35 Before 1994 agricultural, horticultural and forestry works did not require a specific grant of scheduled monument consent provided that the works in question had been carried out at the location in question during the period of five years before 9 October 1981 and provided that the works were not of a kind referred to at paragraph 2.29 above. The Department of National Heritage's consultation paper on the proposed changes to the 1981 Order, dated November 2, 1993, considered that a rolling cut-off date was desirable: it was becoming difficult to prove whether particular works had been carried out during the period 1976-1981 and, even if they had, it was felt that an occasional use in that period should not justify the resumption of that use at a much later date. The new class 1 therefore introduced a six year rolling period, which applies from June 14, 1994. As under the old Order, works must both fulfil the time criterion and must not be works excepted from the class. Tipping operations, removal of turf on a commercial basis, and removal of top soil are now specifically excluded from the class. Tipping on scheduled monuments, on agricultural land in particular, has been a significant problem, as it was difficult to argue that such works were not authorised under class 1 of the 1981 Order. The new class 1 also now provides two instances where soil disturbance itself will be unauthorised (class 1(a) and class 1(b)). If ploughing has already taken place lawfully during the six year period (usually under the old class 1), any more intensive ploughing *likely* to disturb soil below the original depth of ploughing will not be authorised. The Secretary of

State did not introduce a maximum depth for ploughing, but has, in effect, retained the lawfulness of 'normal ploughing' referred to in the old class 1. Works *likely* to disturb soil which is not ploughed land, at a depth of more than 300 millimetres, will not be authorised. Specific exclusions are now made for both the erection and demolition of buildings, although there is a saving for domestic gardening works.

2.36 Article 2(3) of the 1994 Order provides that any condition or limitation in a specific grant of scheduled monument consent shall not be negated by consent under any class consent. A class consent may be withdrawn by direction of the Secretary of State, in relation to a particular scheduled monument (section 3(3), AMAA). He must consult English Heritage before making such a direction. The Act provides no appeal against a direction and no compensation is payable. An affected person must simply make an application for a specific grant of scheduled monument consent, on refusal of which the normal rules relating to compensation and appeal will come into play (see below).

The Crown and Public Utilities

2.37 Although monuments on Crown land may be scheduled, sections 50(1)(b) and 50(2) of the AMAA do not expressly bind the Crown interest in such land. Under the usual constitutional presumption, therefore, the Crown is not bound, and scheduled monument consent is not required by any ministry or Government department, or for anything done for or on behalf of the Crown. A non-statutory system is in place, whereby Government departments obtain 'scheduled monument clearance'. The provisions of this system are said to mirror scheduled monument consent procedures, though some Government departments, for example the Ministry of Defence, appear in the past to have been comparatively unrestrained.

2.38 There is no saving in the 1979 Act for the operational activities of 'public utilities', and no class consent has ever been issued in respect of works by gas, water, electricity and telecommunications undertakers and the like. Such works will require scheduled monument consent, including works carried out on Crown land which are not carried out 'for or on behalf of the Crown'.

2.39 If any doubts exist as to whether scheduled monument consent is required it is advisable to take independent legal advice and then seek the views of English Heritage's regional inspector. There are no statutory arrangements for determining whether consent is required, such as exist under the TCPA 1990 (as amended). As with so many aspects of scheduled monument law, the procedures are less sophisticated than those encountered in the planning and listed building system, and the applicant will have few precedents on which to base his own assessment. Failure to obtain consent when consent is required will, at least, involve the applicant in negotiations to which no statutory timetable applies and which may, from the developer's perspective, have disastrous land-use consequences. Unauthorised works may also constitute an offence under section 2 of the AMAA.

Applications for Scheduled Monument Consent (SMC)

2.40 The procedure for determining applications is set out in schedule 1, part I of the AMAA. The Secretary of State may refuse to entertain an application which does not include certificates as to the ownership of or interests in the relevant land (schedule 1, part I, paragraph 2(1)), and it is an offence to knowingly or recklessly supply false certificates (*ibid.*, paragraph 2(4)). See appendix 2B of this work for the form of certificate.

2.41 Applications should not be made to English Heritage. The Secretary of State must, however, send a copy of each application to English Heritage as soon as practicable after receipt (schedule 1, part I, paragraph 2A) and must consult English Heritage on the application (*ibid.*, paragraph 3(3)(c)).

2.42 There are no express provisions in the AMAA 1979 relating to the manner in which the Secretary of State must exercise his statutory discretion to grant SMC. The Secretary of State has not issued any formal policy statement on how applications for consent are determined. The clearest indication of ministerial policy is contained in PPG 16 which, although a planning document, reproduces policies which the Secretary of State is known to apply when considering applications for SMC. The leading policy is that remains of national or similar importance should be preserved *in situ* or, in exceptional cases, by record. Scheduled monuments will be of national importance.

2.43 The matters which the Secretary of State will take into account vary very greatly, depending on the nature of the monument and the works proposed (scheduled monuments comprise an even greater variety of structures than listed buildings). There are no general statutory guidelines to compare with those of sections 54A and 70 of the TCPA 1990. However, at the very least, consideration will be given to the following matters:

(a) Whether there is any need for the development which overrides the archaeological value of the monument in question. This is very rare, especially as far as proposals within the mainstream planning system are concerned. PPG 16 contains a *presumption* in favour of the physical preservation of scheduled monuments and other monuments of national importance.

(b) Whether the proposed works are necessary, in the sense of whether there is a reasonably viable alternative. Substantially increased costs of an alternative will not mean that a proposal to disturb a scheduled monument is considered favourably; so, for example, the Secretary of State may require that the route of a new pipeline avoids a scheduled monument, at the cost of building a new pumping station, even where the applicant includes a programme of archaeological investigation in his application. Such an approach conforms with the principle that archaeological remains are finite and fragile. Mitigation works which themselves require SMC will only be permitted if they reduce the archaeological impact to *de minimis* levels.

(c) The importance of that part of a monument which will be affected by the works and whether any preservation by record can be accommodated within archaeological research priorities.

(d)   Whether the integrity or the setting of a monument is affected. The impact of an operation on the monument will not be considered sympathetically if it will have the effect of making access from one part of a monument to another more difficult, or if the appearance of the monument suffers. Direct disturbance of archaeological remains is not always the main criterion, even in applications for SMC.

(e)   Whether the proposed works have already been authorised under other statutory provisions (especially under the planning regime). If they have not, compensation for refusal of SMC will be limited (see paragraph 2.211).

(f)   Although section 2(5) of the AMAA permits the Secretary of State to impose conditions requiring prior excavation of an area to be affected by proposed works, preservation *in situ* of remains is the preferred option in the case of remains which are of national importance. All scheduled monuments will be of national importance (see paragraph 2.6 above) and it does not follow that just because significant funding for archaeological investigation is available there is a reasonable prospect of obtaining SMC.

(g)   Whether a particular programme of mitigation or archaeological work can be secured by binding agreement with the applicant (for example by way of section 106 planning obligation - see chapter six) or by way of grant or management agreement under sections 24 and 17 of the AMAA. English Heritage will be particularly sensitive to the adequacy and enforceability of any such programme.

2.44 Schedule 1, part I, paragraph 3(2) of the AMAA provides that

'Before determining whether or not to grant scheduled monument consent on any application therefor, the Secretary of State shall either:

(a) *cause a public inquiry to be held; or*

(b) *afford to the applicant, and to any other person to whom it appears to the Secretary of State expedient to afford it, an opportunity of appearing before and being heard by a person appointed by the Secretary of State for the purpose.'*

Usually a hearing is offered, though in complex or sensitive cases an inquiry will be held. It appears to be the Secretary of State's policy to call a local inquiry if the applicant prefers this to a hearing. The contents of the proposed decision letter will be discussed thoroughly with the applicant but, in contrast to the planning regime, a final letter will not be issued before the hearing or inquiry (unless the applicant has declined an offer of either). If the applicant does not want a hearing or inquiry the decision letter will usually record the fact that a hearing has been declined.

2.45 There is no statutory period within which decisions

have to be made and there is no obligation on the Secretary of State or English Heritage to advertise applications publicly, or to make applications known to local planning authorities or RCHM(e)/RCAHM(w). English Heritage will have notified the applicant that English Heritage's views have been sent to the Secretary of State, but without disclosing the substance of those views. Current practice is for the Secretary of State to consult on an *ad-hoc* basis, though if a representation is received he must consider it (schedule 1, part I, paragraph 3(3)(a), AMAA), and he must send notice of his decision to all persons making representations (*ibid.*, paragraph 3(4)).

2.46 Whether a hearing or an inquiry is held, the person appointed by the Secretary of State will usually be an inspector of the Planning Inspectorate who is well-versed in conservation policy. An archaeological assessor may sometimes be required. A 'joint' inquiry may be held if the question of scheduled monument consent is to be determined together with a planning appeal relating to the same proposal, though the inquiries remain legally distinct entities, with the inspector fulfilling a slightly different role in each. The importance of the distinction was emphasised by *Woodspring District Council v. Unit Construction South West and Accado* (1989) 4 P.A.D., 20, where the court ordered the Secretary of State to re-open a linked planning inquiry when he accepted revised plans of the developer (which satisfied the scheduled monument requirements) without a further hearing or inquiry under the AMAA. Arrangements for an inquiry will be made by the Planning Inspectorate; arrangements for a hearing, including appointment of the person conducting proceedings, tend to be made directly by the Department for Culture, Media and Sport.

2.47 The role of the inspector at a scheduled monument inquiry tends to be more inquisitorial than at a planning or listed building inquiry because the Secretary of State is not hearing an appeal against another's decision and may already be minded as to a particular view. Nonetheless, the inspector will conduct the proceedings within the spirit of the Town and Country Planning (Inquiries Procedure) Rules 1992, although the rules cannot be said to be binding on the parties except to the extent that they agree to be bound (as the rules relate to the TCPA and its different statutory processes). At both hearings and inquiries the archaeological or historical merits of the case will be examined, something which the court will not attempt should an appeal against the decision be made subsequently under section 55 of the AMAA. Evidence is not taken on oath and the strict rules of evidence do not apply (especially relevant in relation to statements of opinion and the purport of documents). Of course, the weight of expert evidence, in particular, is diminished if the person making a statement is not available for cross-examination of the statement. At least one expert from English Heritage will normally attend on behalf of the Secretary of State. Other witnesses appearing for the Secretary of State might be the local county archaeologist or professor of archaeology. As in most public inquiries the quality of expert evidence tends to be decisive. The evidence of English Heritage is especially weighty on archaeological matters, though independent consultants also possess the degree of knowledge and expertise already familiar to practitioners in other areas of environmental and conservation law.

2.48 The timetable will reflect that of a planning inquiry. Once the intention to hold an inquiry is announced each party must copy its statement of case to the inspectorate and to the other parties. The applicant must file his statement (and its supporting documents) within nine weeks of being notified that an inquiry will take place. The statement of case is vital, providing as it should the factual background to the proposal, the proposal's impact and the policy context. Mitigation measures, possible alternative schemes or the need for the proposal may be relevant at this stage but are usually fleshed out in proofs of evidence. Before finalising proofs it may be desirable to obtain further, specialist advice on any weaknesses in the case. Proofs of evidence and appendices must be copied to the inspector and all other parties at least three weeks before the beginning of the inquiry (or the date when it is known that the evidence in question will be heard). Local inquiries are considered in more detail at paragraphs 6.84-6.98 below.

2.49 The Secretary of State must consider the report of the person holding the inquiry before making his determination (schedule 1, part I, paragraph 3(3)(b), AMAA), and the determination will usually mirror the inspector's findings and reasoning. If it does not, clear and intelligible reasons for the departure and for any new facts or matters introduced must be communicated to the applicant for his additional comments (see the planning law case of *Seddon Properties Ltd v. Secretary of State for the Environment* (1978) 42 P. & C.R. 26). This is an extension of the rules of natural justice (paragraph 2.110 below), and applies also to reports received after a hearing (see, for example, *Welwyn-Hatfield District Council v. Secretary of State for the Environment and*

Morgan Electronics Ltd [1991] J.P.L. 1019, a case concerned with natural justice under the town and county planning written representations procedure).

The parties will be responsible for their own costs at a scheduled monument inquiry/hearing. Costs are not awarded against any party.

2.50 Where large developments are proposed an application for SMC will usually be discussed in detail with English Heritage before ever reaching the Secretary of State. This consultation should result in a scheme whose main elements are acceptable, although the Secretary of State may still call an inquiry, of his own volition, if he thinks the application merits it. (The planning system and listed building or conservation area issues may also still need to be taken into account, at inquiries which run in tandem with the scheduled monument inquiry.) A good example of such an inquiry was that held in 1992 into the proposal by Gloucestershire County Council to build a new magistrate's Court over part of the Roman town of Gloucester (DNH/HSD 9/2/1949). Consultation with English Heritage by the applicant had produced a revised proposal interpreted in the light of a specially commissioned geophysical survey. Prior excavation and a system of piling for building works was proposed within the area of the monument, to be located according to the results of the survey. The inspector's conclusion that there was nothing to suggest that the monument would suffer any significant archaeological effect as result of the excavation or works was accepted by the Secretary of State. Only five conditions are attached to the consent: one relates to prior notification of the commencement of works to English Heritage, another to the avoidance of damage by the use of machinery; the remainder require the works and archaeological investigation to be executed to the satisfaction of the Secretary of State, the excavation report to be made available within three years of the completion of the excavation, and structural piles within the scheduled area to be provided with protective sleeves.

A more complex conundrum faced the inspector at an inquiry into an application to construct five dwellings and access road, for church use, within the scheduled area of St. Albans Abbey, Hertfordshire (DOE HSD 9/2/106; part of the decision letter is also published at [1991] J.P.L. 1096). The applicants did not argue that the need for the development overrode the importance of the site – which it clearly did not – and the main issues were (a) the importance of the site as part of the scheduled monument and (b) the extent to which the proposed scheme might damage archaeological deposits.

On issue (a) an evaluation had proved inconclusive and the evidence before the inspector suggested that the site was probably only a peripheral part of the abbey precinct. However, the inspector still considered that *'whatever information the site could yield would be valuable in continuing to build up an even more accurate picture of the monument's history ...'*. He concluded that the remains should be preserved in situ or be further investigated. On issue (b) the inspector found that a structural raft, designed to limit destruction to archaeological deposits, would fulfil its purpose but that service trenches, which were an impact which could not be mitigated, would still cause significant damage. Because of this it was considered inappropriate to grant scheduled monument consent subject to a condition requiring details of foundations and service trenches to be approved before development commenced. This being the case, there were representations from English Heritage that scheduled monument consent be refused. The inspector accepted that the site was not a priority site in terms of research into the whole monument and that all excavation involves some destruction of deposits. However, he found the argument that the deposits should be left intact until archaeological techniques had improved and the argument that resources would be better used elsewhere to be partly contradictory. The inspector concluded, against English Heritage, that *'no serious harm would arise, and perhaps some benefit from greater knowledge would be gained, if scheduled monument consent were granted subject to full excavation of the whole site being carried out before development commenced.'*

This conclusion was supported by the archaeological assessor at the inquiry and by the Secretary of State subsequently. The excavation condition ultimately attached to the consent following the inquiry was that:

'(a)   a full archaeological excavation of the whole of the application site shall be carried out prior to the commencement of development, in accordance with a research design approved by the Secretary of State and

(b)   the excavation shall be undertaken under the direction of a person approved by English Heritage subject to the final approval of the Secretary of State.'

Conditions Generally

2.51 An applicant will only request a hearing or an inquiry if the Secretary of State's provisional decision indicates that SMC will be refused or will be granted subject to conditions which the applicant finds unacceptable. Section 2(4) of the AMAA provides that *'scheduled monument consent may be granted either unconditionally or subject to conditions (whether with respect to the manner in which or the persons by whom the works or any of the works are to be executed or otherwise).'* As befits the sensitive character of most scheduled sites, this enables very specific and demanding conditions to be imposed. Section 2(5) of the Act expressly authorises conditions requiring prior access to a monument by English Heritage or a person authorised by them, or, outside England, the Secretary of State or his nominated representative, for the purpose of archaeological examination and excavation of the site. Section 2 does not provide for staged authorisation of details, to compare with 'reserved matters' in planning law, but provision is made for SMC to be granted for part only (or several parts) of the area for which consent is requested (schedule 1, part I, paragraph 3(1), AMAA).

2.52 The applicant must be satisfied that he is able to comply with all terms and conditions as failure to comply will render offending works 'unauthorised' (section 2(3)(b), AMAA) and the appropriate person(s) criminally liable (*ibid.*, sections 2(1) and 2(6)). The position on breach of condition is similar to that on breach of condition attached to a listed building consent, but should be contrasted with breach of condition attached to a planning consent, where enforcement measures of some form must be taken before criminal liability arises.

2.53 Conditions should be distinguished from the related but not identical concept of 'terms' or 'limitations' of a consent. Limitations often appear in planning permissions when the development permitted by the consent is expressed to be, for example, for the erection of 'six industrial units and associated car parking' or for 'a hostel for the homeless'. The construction of ten industrial units or a private dwellinghouse would be in breach, respectively, of the limitations in each of these permissions, and consequently would, in each case, be a breach of planning control (section 171A, TCPA 1990). The equivalent in scheduled monument law is the 'term', referred to in section 2(3)(b) of the AMAA. If SMC is granted for the felling of 0.5 hectares of forest and 0.75 hectares are actually felled unauthorised works will have taken place, though there will have been no breach of condition. Section 2(6) will not be applicable in such circumstances unless the extent of the works was also covered by a condition.

2.54 In planning law some conditions are obligatory. In particular, when a local planning authority grants permission for building or other operations, the authority must impose a condition which usually requires the permission to be implemented within the period of five years from the date of grant, or within two years after the final approval of reserve matters (section 92(2), TCPA 1990). There are no such obligatory conditions in scheduled monument law, although section 4(1) of the AMAA achieves a result similar to section 91(2) of the TCPA when it provides that *'if no works to which a scheduled monument consent relates are executed or started within the period of five years beginning with the date on which the consent was granted'* ... or such longer or shorter period specified in the consent ... *'the consent shall cease to have effect at the end of that period'*. Late implementation of the SMC will give rise to criminal liability. SMC, like planning permission, enures for the benefit of the land (schedule 1, part I, paragraph 1(2), AMAA) and is unlikely to be personal to the applicant. This means that if a person acquires (or owns land but is not the applicant) he must be satisfied that the consent meets with his requirements as owner.

The Validity of Conditions

2.55 All discussion of conditions attached to statutory consents must take place against the background of the law relating to the exercise of statutory discretion as encapsulated in the case of *Associated Provincial Picture Houses Ltd v. Wednesbury Corporation* [1948] 1 K.B. 223 CA. The 'Wednesbury test' is nowadays usually distilled to the requirement that a person entrusted with a statutory discretion must, when making his decision:

1. consider all relevant matters;
2. ignore or not take into consideration any matters which are irrelevant; and
3. not arrive at a decision which is so unreasonable that no reasonable person or body entrusted with that discretion could have made it. (Strictly speaking, this third principle is the one to which the case gives its

107

name, the other principles being well-established principles of public law before *Wednesbury*.)

The test has extensive application in planning law and is relevant to statutory discretions exercised by ministers of the Crown (see, for example, *Padfield v. Minister of Agriculture Fisheries and Food* [1969] A.C. 997 or *Congreve v. Home Office* [1976] Q.B. 629 CA). More specific rules, relating to planning conditions and, by implication, other statutory discretions of a land-use nature, arise from planning law cases. The current position is as expressed by the House of Lords decision in *Newbury District Council v. Secretary of State for the Environment* [1981] A.C. 578; [1980] 1 All E.R. 731 at p.761 *per* Lord Lane; that conditions must be (a) applied for a planning purpose, (b) must fairly relate to the development proposed and (c) must not be *Wednesbury* unreasonable. The Secretary of State, as a servant of the Crown, usually has a wider discretion than an authority created by or governed by statute, but *'where a minister is given a discretion and exercises it for reasons inconsistent with the policy of that Act, the courts can intervene'* (per Denning M.R., in *Congreve*). In practice, the tests which the court applies to a ministerial decision will be derived from *Wednesbury*.

2.56 For a condition to be *prima facie* unreasonable in the sense of the third limb of *Wednesbury*, the 'unreasonableness' will have to be 'overwhelming' (*Buckinghamshire County Council v. Hall Aggregates (Thames Valley) Ltd* [1985] J.P.L. 634 CA). This means overwhelming from the legal standpoint, not on the merits or as a matter of literary expression. For example, a condition attached to a scheduled monument consent which required the applicant to fund archaeological work to be carried out by English Heritage would, in the absence of parliamentary authority, run counter to the constitutional settlement contained in the Bill of Rights, that the Crown is not able to impose a levy or tax without the consent of Parliament. Requiring the payment of a sum of money in exchange for a permission may not, at first sight, appear to be a method of raising revenue, but that may well be the essence of what would be happening (see *Att.-Gen v. Wilts. United Dairies* (1921) T.L.R. 884, where the Secretary of State was held to be acting *ultra vires* when charging for the issue of licences to sell milk). If a scheduled monument consent required the payment of a sum of money to a party unconnected with the Secretary of State that would be less likely to offend against this constitutional rule, although the minister may still be acting improperly for want of sufficient legal authority to levy a charge. The AMAA contains no express power for the Secretary of State to charge for the provision of archaeological investigation and he could be caught by a rule similar to that applied by the court to local authorities in *McCarthy & Stone*.

2.57 If a condition has no ascertainable meaning, for example because necessary words have been omitted or because the concepts referred to in the condition have not been adequately formulated, the condition will be void and of no effect. In such circumstances, the court will deem that no reasonable authority could have imposed the condition. However, ambiguity does not necessarily imply that a condition has no ascertainable meaning (see, for example, the planning law case of *Fawcett Properties v. Buckinghamshire County Council* [1981] A.C. 578, where the court tried to find the meaning most closely approximating the meaning which the planning authority had intended). If one meaning cannot be said, however, to be the most probable the condition will fall. The giving of reasons for a decision may assist the court in making an interpretation. However, in contrast to private law, the *contra proferentum* rule – that the meaning of a term or condition which imposes a burden is construed against the party seeking to impose the burden – is not applicable, and will not assist the court in finding some limited, valid meaning in an otherwise meaningless condition (*Crisp from the Fens Ltd v. Rutland County Council* (1950) 1 P. & C. R. 48).

2.58 Where a condition is imposed for a purpose which is beyond the purposes of the statute(s) under which the discretion is exercised, the condition may have been imposed for an ulterior or irrelevant purpose, and so offend, respectively, against both the third and second limbs of *Wednesbury*. A condition attached to a scheduled monument consent must be for an 'ancient monuments' purpose, i.e. for the performance of the Secretary of State's functions under the AMAA or the HBAMA. Planning law provides many examples of conditions which have been declared invalid for seeking to impose obligations beyond the scope of the enabling statute (the most well-known are probably *Hall & Co. Ltd v. Shoreham-by-Sea Urban District Council* [1964] 1 All E.R. 1 CA, where a planning condition required the applicant to dedicate parts of a road to the use of adjacent landowners, instead of approaching the matter under the highway authority's powers; and *Bradford Metropolitan Borough Council v. Secretary of State for the Environment* (1986) 278 E.G. 1473 CA, where a planning condition required the applicant to carry out road widening works at its own expense).

2.59 A condition will also be invalid if it derogates so much from what the SMC purports to grant that the consent is in effect inoperable. A consent which permitted opencast mining but required the *in situ* preservation of many upstanding elements of a scheduled monument would probably fall into this category. If the archaeological constraints are so severe the correct course is for the application for SMC to be refused. All conditions derogate from grant to a greater or lesser extent, and a fine degree of derogation is central to the effectiveness of many valid conditions (see below). The question is really whether a condition derogates from the proposal put by the applicant or whether it derogates from that which a reasonable authority imposing conditions of a similar nature would have authorised. It is the latter which will be most readily subject to challenge.

2.60 A condition must be able to be fulfilled. If the steps required of the applicant are beyond the applicant's control, or incapable of fulfilment for some other reason, the condition will be invalid. In the planning law case of *Hayns v. Secretary of State for the Environment* (1977) 36 P. & C. R. 317, a condition was held to be unreasonable which required the applicant, as part of his development, to construct a road on land not within his ownership. A condition in similar, though not identical form has, however, been upheld by the House of Lords. This required an applicant to secure the closure of a road not within his control before development commenced (*Grampian Regional Council v. City of Aberdeen District Council* [1984] J.P.L. 590). The distinction is that in *Hayns* the condition required the road works to be carried out, as a part of the development; but *Grampian*, by a condition precedent to the carrying out of works, requires that the permission is not implemented before the works have occurred. *Grampian* style conditions have an important role to play in archaeological planning (see chapter six), though it should be remembered that the important issue in the *Grampian* case was whether a condition which, in effect, required works for which there might not be any reasonable prospect of fulfilment could be valid. It is incorrect to refer to all conditions precedent to development as Grampian conditions. In archaeology, such a condition attached to a planning permission may require the applicant to secure a programme of archaeological work, whether or not the applicant is able to obtain and fund the required level of investigation. Similar conditions will, in appropriate circumstances, also be valid when attached to a SMC, though in scheduled monument cases it seems to be the Secretary of State's policy to be satisfied that even the proviso to a negative condition does have a reasonable prospect of fulfilment.

2.61 A condition will not be invalid just because it is difficult to enforce (see the planning law case of *Bizony v. Secretary of State for the Environment* [1976] J.P.L. 306). It is, of course, in the Secretary of State's interest to ensure that enforcement is always a practical possibility.

2.62 Just as it is important that a condition is imposed for a scheduled monument purpose, by analogy with planning law, a condition should 'fairly and reasonably relate to the works authorised' by the consent (*Newbury, ibid.*; see also *Pyx Granite Co. Ltd. v. Minister of Housing and Local Government* [1958] 1 Q.B. 554 at 572 CA). If works or activities are required which cannot be said to fairly and reasonably relate to the application for SMC, it will be necessary to secure them by agreement, for example under an agreement for grant, or a management agreement. The AMAA does not provide powers as wide as those contained in section 106 of the TCPA 1990. Although it may be fair and reasonable to attach a condition to a SMC which requires prior excavation, to a defined standard, by persons approved by the Secretary of State (section 2(4) and 2(5), AMAA), a condition which required the applicant to carry out a research excavation of part of the monument unaffected by the works, or to provide land for a site museum after the works have been completed, would be invalid on this ground. A condition requiring the applicant to publish the results of archaeological investigation carried out under section 2(4) powers may also be invalid unless the publication can be said to assist in the 'preservation of the site by record'. Such conditions, like all invalid conditions, will not become valid because the applicant has suggested or consented to them. In SMC cases, however, the likelihood of challenge in such circumstances is slight, as there is no public consultation on applications.

2.63 If a condition is such an integral or fundamental part of a consent that it is not severable from the consent as a whole, the consent will be a nullity if the condition is invalid. For example, where the Secretary of State imposes conditions on a SMC requiring the prior excavation of a scheduled monument together with the siting of development in accordance with the information provided by that investigation, if either of those conditions was held on appeal to be invalid for a reason unconnected with the archaeological merits, the whole consent would probably fall, with the case remitted to the Secretary of State for re-consideration. The proper decision might then be refusal of consent. The applicant should be wary of making an appeal in circumstances where he would be more willing to accept a consent with onerous conditions than face the prospect of having no consent at all: unlike the general predisposition in favour of granting planning applications which are in accordance with the development plan, the Secretary of State has, for obvious reasons, no policy which favours the granting of scheduled monument consent.

2.64 Following *Newbury*, ministerial guidance on planning conditions is that they should be:

'1. *necessary;*
2. *relevant to planning;*
3. *relevant to the development being permitted;*
4. *enforceable;*
5. *precise; and*
6. *reasonable in all other respects.'*

These guidelines were contained in DOE Circular 1/85 (Welsh Office 1/85), now updated as DOE Circular 11/95 (Welsh Office 35/95), as discussed at paragraph 6.74 below.

The guidelines are followed by the Secretary of State when formulating conditions on scheduled monument consents and the appropriate staff at English Heritage are circulated with a practice note on the application of the guidelines in archaeological cases. These guidelines fall squarely within the requirements already discussed. The exception is the first guideline, that of 'necessity'. This is ambiguous and, in the sense of a condition triggered by the characteristics of a proposal, is much stricter than the requirement that conditions must be relevant to both the purposes of the statute and the particular works to be authorised. When formulating conditions on scheduled monument consents the Secretary of State tends to interpret this guideline as meaning that conditions should not mirror provisions already appearing in the enabling statute or other statutes and regulations.

Specific Conditions

2.65 The kinds of condition most commonly encountered in scheduled monument cases can, for the sake of convenience, be divided into three categories: those which are prescriptive or restrictive of the method of carrying out authorised works; those which limit the extent or the nature of the authorised works; and those which require the applicant to carry out or procure some particular act or thing which, from a scheduled monuments perspective, better facilitates the proper authorisation of the works. As with planning conditions, it is good practice for reasons to be given for the imposition of conditions.

Method or Manner of Working

2.66 The Secretary of State has express statutory authority to regulate the 'manner in which or the persons by whom' works are carried out (section 2(4), AMAA). His preferred model conditions which, in only slightly amended form, appear in many scheduled monument consents are:

A (method of working):   *In order to ensure that the works to which this consent relates are carried out satisfactorily , at least [   ] weeks notice in writing of the commencement of the works shall be given to [the Historic Buildings and Monuments Commission] and you are advised to [discuss the method of working for [   ] with the Commission's representative] [prepare a trial sample of [   ] for inspection by the Commission's representative before works commence].*

B (method of working):   *The works to which this consent relates shall be carried out to the satisfaction of the Secretary of State, who will be advised by the Historic Buildings and Monuments Commission. Not less than [   ] weeks notice in writing of the commencement of work shall be given to [   ] in order that a representative of the Commission is able to inspect and advise.*

Conditions relating to working practices should not become imprecise by, for example, referring to alternatives. Nor should they be detailed beyond the scope of what is ascertainable from the application.

C (person undertaking
works):   *Before any works to which this*
consent relates are begun on site
[   ] shall be permitted to enter
the site for a continuous period of
not less than [   ] weeks for the
purposes of [carrying out an
archaeological   excavation]
[examining all archaeological
remains on the site and carrying
out an archaeological excavation]
[examining and surveying all
archaeological remains on the site].

Examples of standard conditions relating to the conduct of
archaeological excavations are reproduced at appendix 2C.

2.67 The Secretary of State is cautious of delegating his
decisions on any matter relating to SMC applications, for
example by requiring construction works or archaeological
work to be carried out to the satisfaction of 'x' (rather than
the minister himself). This concern is clearly manifested in
model condition B.

2.68 Consents with conditions requiring excavation, or even
survey, are a small proportion of all grants of scheduled
monument consents. This is because most applications do
not relate to large-scale or damaging proposals. One of the
most common archaeological conditions provides for a
'watching brief'.

D (watching brief): *Not less than [   ] weeks before any of the operations to which this consent relates are begun on site [   ] shall be informed in writing of the timetable for the proposed works and either he or his nominated representative shall be given the opportunity to enter the site at any reasonable time for the purposes of inspecting the site and recording any matters of archaeological or historic interest observed in the course of that inspection.*

Note that a watching brief does not permit the representative to undertake excavations or survey work.

2.69 If the archaeological value of the part of the monument to be affected by the works is unknown it might be appropriate to impose a condition which requires an archaeological evaluation followed, if necessary, by an archaeological survey or excavation of sensitive areas. Evaluations carried out in accordance with a specification agreed with the Secretary of State will now fall within class consent 7 (see paragraph 2.30 above), but in some less important cases it may be desirable to grant SMC subject to provisions for evaluation and small-scale investigation. Care should be taken to ensure that the requirement for post-evaluation archaeological work does not derogate unacceptably from the grant. The model condition at C should be phrased to provide for evaluation instead of survey or excavation and then continue in the following form:

E (evaluation):

> *When the results of the evaluation are available the Secretary of State, in consultation with the Commission will determine whether a prior archaeological excavation or other archaeological work is necessary. Should prior excavation or other archaeological work be necessary, [   ] shall be given access to the site for a further period of not more than [   ] weeks before works to which this consent relates are begun for the purpose of carrying out such excavations or other archaeological work.*

2.70 An evaluation as a condition of the grant should, of course, be distinguished from the kind of evaluation envisaged by class consent 7 and PPG 16. In the latter cases a more comprehensive evaluation will be appropriate and will provide information upon which the decision whether or not to grant consent can be based. A proposal for major works, affecting a significant part of a scheduled monument whose particular characteristics are imperfectly understood, will, almost without exception, be preceded by this latter kind of evaluation, with regard to which the question of conditions does not arise.

Limitation of Proposed Works

2.71 When in receipt of an application for SMC it might be readily apparent to the minister that works or operations should not be permitted on the scale proposed, but that they would be acceptable if limited in nature or extent. An application for consent to plough land (which does not fall within class consent 1) might be approved subject to the condition that *'ploughing of the site to which this consent relates shall be restricted to a depth of [300] millimetres'*. Care should be taken to avoid ambiguity or imprecision if reference is made to minimal cultivation techniques; techniques and methods of working should be specified. Equally, if the applicant is a commercial operator care should be taken to avoid conditions which make the proposed works impossible to carry out on any commercial basis. For example, if an application for afforestation is limited by condition which requires that *'the area known as [   ] cross-hatched on the plan attached and measuring approximately [   ] hectares shall not be planted but shall be retained as open moorland'*, this may restrict the scope of the commercial operation to the point where it becomes unviable. If no suitable compromise can be reached SMC should be refused and the applicant invited to submit a new proposal.

2.72 Sometimes, usually following initial discussions with English Heritage, an application will contain detailed proposals for the archaeological treatment of a site. These proposals may relate to 'aftercare' works as well as a programme of archaeological investigation. The Secretary of State's powers to control works extends to aftercare works too, so that he may, for example, limit a proposal to create a visitor centre, access road and car park in the following form:

> '*Access to the visitor centre [to be constructed on the site] shall from the point where the [access road] enters the area of the scheduled monument to [the visitor centre] be on foot only.*'

Quite separately from any planning permission which the applicant may need, the Secretary of State may require the car park to be off-site, involving the applicant in acquiring rights over adjacent land (see below). It would be *ultra vires* the Secretary of State's powers under the AMAA to impose conditions which deal with matters which should properly be dealt with under the TCPA 1990, for example the nuisance to neighbours caused by the erection of a visitor centre, or highway congestion resulting from the development, although on-site elements such as building design and traffic circulation can obviously be dealt with to the extent that they affect the scheduled monument. Conditions which attempt to regulate matters which take place outside the scheduled area of the monument (including the 'setting') run the risk of being *ultra vires* and are better dealt with by way of agreement under the AMAA or some other statutory provision.

Procurement by the Applicant

2.73 Conditions relating to the method or manner of working may require prior investigation of a monument, that is investigation prior to the commencement of the works authorised by the consent. Like planning conditions, SMC conditions are conditions subsequent to the grant, but conditions may be valid if expressed to be conditions precedent to the commencement of the authorised works (see model condition C above). However, the Secretary of State may wish to go further than this and, in keeping with the principle of 'developer funding' supported by PPG 16 (see chapter six), he may wish to impose a condition which obliges the applicant to procure something which at the time of the grant of consent is not under the applicant's control, or requires agreement by the applicant with a third party (the agreement may be for the provision of archaeological services for example). As indicated in the discussion of *Grampian*, above, where the thing to be procured by the applicant is not within the applicant's control, care must be taken to impose a condition precedent to the works rather than a condition which effectively directs the applicant to carry out the procurement.

Conditions requiring the procurement of some species of prior archaeological investigation may be in the following form:

No works to which this consent relates shall be commenced on site until the applicant has secured the implementation [of a programme of archaeological work] [of full archaeological excavation of the area cross-hatched on the plan attached to this consent] in accordance with a written specification submitted by the applicant and approved by the Secretary of State.

This form is similar to that advocated by the Secretary of State at paragraph 30 of PPG 16, save that the prohibition on the commencement of works relates to the whole of the scheduled monument (and not just the archaeologically sensitive part of the area covered by a planning application). Conditions should not require the applicant to make financial contributions to archaeological work (see paragraph 2.56 above), nor should they require the provision of 'facilities' or 'resources'. The latter terms will at best be imprecise.

2.74 Most large-scale works affecting monuments will require a specific grant of planning permission. The local planning authority is required by the GD(P)O to consult English Heritage on proposals which affect a scheduled monument or its setting, and appropriate planning conditions or a planning obligation can be discussed with the applicant. In many cases the planning system provides the desired control and resources and English Heritage can then advise the Secretary of State on the SMC application in the knowledge that a major element in securing preservation (by record or *in situ*) is to be dealt with by other means. For consideration of planning conditions relating to procurement by the applicant for planning permission see chapter six.

2.75 Conditions should usually be resisted which require an applicant to secure rights over land not under his control, or to enter into a legal agreement for management of land within his control. Almost invariably such conditions will be inherently uncertain, relying as they do on the legal compliance of third parties. Where such extra legal arrangements are desirable, under section 17 of the AMAA or section 106 of the TCPA for example, it is advisable to treat the existence of the arrangements as a condition precedent to the issuing of the scheduled monument consent, i.e. they should be negotiated before SMC is granted.

Revocation or Modification of Scheduled Monument Consent

2.76 Scheduled monument consent may be revoked or modified under section 4(3) of the AMAA, by direction of the Secretary of State, following consultation, in England, with English Heritage. The revocation or modification may be to any extent which the Secretary of State considers expedient. The Secretary of State is expressly empowered to modify the period within which works to which a consent relates must be implemented or, indeed, to impose a time-limited consent (section 4(4), AMAA). He may, of course, also exclude works from consent or require authorised works to be carried out in a manner different from that originally authorised.

2.77 Part II of schedule 1 to the AMAA deals with the procedure. A notice must first be served by the Secretary of State on the owner (and, if a different person, the occupier) of the monument, specifying the particular modification or revocation. The notice must contain a 'draft' of the proposed action, together with the reasons for it, and must stipulate the period for objections. At the Secretary of State's discretion other persons may be served with the notice; in relation to any monument in England, English Heritage must be served with a copy. The person served has a minimum 28 days to object to the proposed revocation or modification. If there is no objection or all objections are withdrawn the Secretary of State may make the direction under section 4. English Heritage should already have been consulted and should therefore be in favour of the proposed action.

Where objections are not withdrawn the Secretary of State must either hold a public inquiry or give the applicant a hearing. The latter course is more likely in cases of modification. A direction may still be made after the inquiry/hearing provided that the Secretary of State considers all objections and the report of the person who chaired the inquiry/hearing. Costs of the hearing are to be borne by the Secretary of State unless he believes these should be borne by another party.

2.78 Under a notice of proposed revocation or modification the works specified in the notice will cease to be authorised under part I of the AMAA (e.g. under an existing scheduled monument consent) on the date of service of that notice on the owner/occupier. Criminal liability will arise at this time. Compensation payments may, in relevant circumstances, also be calculated from this date (see paragraph 2.208 below). The works referred to continue to be unauthorised until: 21 months after service of the notice; the date on which a direction is made by the Secretary of State (when the scheduled monument consent will no longer exist in its original form); or the date when the Secretary of State serves a second notice saying that he no longer intends to make a direction (AMAA, schedule 1, part II, paragraph 8(4)).

Areas of Archaeological Importance (AAIs)

2.79 One of the most promising but as yet most disappointing provisions of the AMAA 1979 is the concept of AAIs. Introduced by part II of the Act, AAIs were designed to give archaeologists prior access to land which was to be disturbed, for the purposes of archaeological investigation and recording – facilities which had not always been forthcoming. Whilst planning permission could be refused on archaeological grounds, or conditions requiring access and prior archaeological investigation imposed on a planning consent, it had been difficult for local planning authorities to follow such courses of action when all that was really required was an opportunity to investigate a site to ascertain whether the site was of archaeological value.

2.80 The need for new powers was raised in Parliament as early as 1974. Subsequently, during the passage of the Ancient Monuments and Archaeological Areas Bill through the Lords, Baroness Steadman, outlining the scope of the new provisions, stated that 'it is necessary to reinforce voluntary arrangements by providing a statutory right for the rescue archaeologist to have access for a limited period to selected areas of special importance' (P.P.(HL) 398, col.453). It was intended that the new statutory controls would be flexible enough to allow developers and archaeologists to work side by side. Unfortunately, it seems that the procedures introduced by the creation of AAIs have served only to irritate developers and to fall short of archaeological expectations in those cases where archaeologically valuable sites are discovered as a result of prior investigation under the statutory powers. From the outset there was an acceptance by the Department of the Environment that the majority of sites falling within a particular AAI were expendable, that designation only provided a short respite from imminent destruction during which archaeological salvage could take place. This is a far cry from the increasingly widespread contemporary practice of evaluation as part of the planning process.

Designation of AAIs

2.81 The main characteristics of the system introduced by part II of the AMAA are (1) a geographical area defined by order (the AAI); (2) an archaeological body, the 'investigating authority', appointed by the Secretary of State to respond, in the field, to the service of notices by 'developers'; and (3) the district council or London Borough for the area within which the AAI is situated (effectively, the local planning authority), the recipient of notices from developers that prescribed 'operations' are proposed.

2.82 In contrast to the Secretary of State's duty to maintain a schedule of monuments, there is no duty for any body, public or private, to designate AAIs. Section 33(1) of the AMAA states that *'the Secretary of State [after consultation with the Historic Buildings and Monuments Commission] may from time to time by order designate as an area of archaeological importance any area which appears to him to merit treatment as such for the purposes of this Act'*. A discretion to designate is also given to local authorities (section 33(2); although no regulations have ever been made to prescribe the scale of plans or the content of notices required by schedule 2 to the Act), subject, in England, to prior consultation with English Heritage, and subject generally to confirmation by the Secretary of State (schedule 2, paragraph 13, AMAA). A similar provision applies to the Broads Authority under the Norfolk and Suffolk Broads Act 1988 and to national parks newly constituted under the Environment Act 1995 (though no AAIs are designated in these areas, nor are any likely to be designated). English Heritage has powers to designate AAIs in Greater London (section 33(2A), AMAA), though has not yet made any designations. This contrast with the duty to maintain a schedule of monuments is fundamental and goes some way to explaining why the designation of AAIs has been neither as extensive nor as rapid as was originally anticipated.

2.83 Both ministerial and other designations are effected by 'designation orders', which are registrable as local land charges (section 33(5), AMAA). Before making an order the Secretary of State must consult with the appropriate local authority and, in England, with English Heritage. If he proceeds with the designation he must publish his proposals in the London Gazette and in one or more newspapers circulating in the locality concerned. Copies of the draft order and maps must be submitted for public inspection to the local authority (schedule 2, paragraph 4). The order can then be made after a period of six weeks has elapsed, running from the day when the draft order was first advertised (schedule 2, paragraph 6). The making of an order must again be advertised (as above).

Six months must elapse from the making of the order (or, in the case of a local authority order, from the date of its confirmation) until the order comes into force. Appeals against the making of an order is to the High Court under section 55(2) (see paragraphs 2.106-2.115, below), although non-statutory representations can be made to the minister, English Heritage or the local authority during the public notice stage. An order can be revoked or varied at any time (section 33(4), AMAA). The procedure for revocation is similar to that for designation (schedule 2, paragraph 18).

Variation of an order is confined to a reduction in the size of the area designated.

2.84 The main effect of designation is to place a statutory obligation on anybody proposing to 'disturb the ground', or carry out works which will flood or cause material to be tipped on a site within the AAI ('operations'). Flooding includes covering the land with any liquid or partially liquid substance; tipping includes the tipping of soil or refuse and building materials (section 61(1), AMAA). The statutory obligation is for the person carrying out or intending to carry out the operations (defined by section 35(3) as the 'developer' for the purposes of part II of the Act) to give at least six weeks notice of the beginning of operations to the local planning authority for the area in which the AAI is situated (section 35(1), AMAA). This 'operations notice' must specify the operations to be carried out, the site affected, the date on which it is intended to commence work and, where operations will not take place until the site has been cleared, the date on which the preparatory site clearance will be completed (section 35(4)(a)). Site clearance means *'the demolition and removal of any existing building or other structure on the site and the removal of any other materials thereon so as to clear the surface of the land (but does not include the levelling of the surface or the removal of materials from below the surface)'* (section 41(1)(d), AMAA). The form of operations notice (and the accompanying certificate) are prescribed by *The Operations in Areas of Archaeological Importance (Forms of Notice etc.) Regulations 1984* (S.I. 1984, No. 1285) (see appendix 2E of this work). The notice must be served on the district council(s) or London Borough(s) in whose area the AAI is situated (in

Wales, the appropriate county council or county borough). Where 'operations' is proposed by such a council the notice must be served on the Secretary of State. Where a notice is required to be served it is an offence to undertake works without serving one, to commence operations within the period of six weeks after the service of the operations notice or, where site clearance operations are required, to commence operations without notifying the investigating authority (see below) that site clearance has been completed (sections 35(1)(a), 35(1)(b) and 35(8), AMAA).

2.85 Service of an operations notice confers rights of entry to the site on the investigating authority, the Secretary of State and the Royal Commission on Historical Monuments (see below). The investigating authority may, within a prescribed period, elect to excavate the site.

2.86 An operations notice must also be accompanied by a certificate as to the developer's interest in the land affected (section 36, AMAA). This will ensure amongst other things that the archaeologists who enter the site under the powers contained in section 38 are not trespassing or themselves party to an offence. As operations notices will often be served in a development context the person issuing the certificate may have a limited interest in the site, for example a licence contained in an agreement for lease or in a conditional sale contract. Authorities possessing compulsory purchase powers may serve a certificate which relates to land in which they intend to acquire an interest (section 36(1), AMAA), as may statutory undertakers in relation to any work which they are empowered by statute to carry out (section 36(2)). It is a summary offence to knowingly or recklessly issue a false certificate, punishable by a fine at level 3 on the standard scale (section 36(4)).

2.87 In addition to the exemption which Crown operations enjoy (section 50(3), AMAA), an operations notice will not be required if the investigating authority for the AAI has given consent to the intended operations (section 37(1), AMAA). Under section 37(2) of the Act the Secretary of State has also removed certain operations from the requirements of section 35. By virtue of *The Areas of Archaeological Importance (Notification of Operations) (Exemption) Order 1984* (S.I. 1984, No. 1286; see appendix 2F of this work) an operations notice need not be served in respect of the following works:

–   agricultural, horticultural and forestry operations and landscaping and gardening provided that such operations do not disturb the ground below a depth of 600 mm;

–   mining operations provided that such operations are executed in accordance with the C.B.I. Code of Practice for Mineral Operators dated April 1982 (referring to the C.B.I. Code, now superseded by the Code dated 1991, see chapter six);

–   works of repair and other *de minimis* works by drainage bodies or navigation authorities;

–   certain operations for the repair, maintenance or re-laying of highways, footpaths or railways and routine operations relating to public utilities;

- operations more than ten metres below ground level;

- operations for which scheduled monument consent is granted (either by express grant or by class consent);

- operations started within five years after the service of notice of other operations on the same site.

These exemptions reflect the requirements of public undertakings and the trivial effects of many private operations. Such a lengthy list of exemptions, however, means that it is often difficult for a 'developer' to establish when he will be relieved of his duty under section 35.

Investigating Authorities

2.88 The central role in the AAI system is that of the investigating authority, an authority appointed by the Secretary of State, whom the Secretary of State believes is competent to undertake archaeological investigations in the designated AAI (section 34(1), AMAA). In default of such an appointment, the investigating authority, in England, will be English Heritage or, in Wales, Cadw. The investigating authority is, therefore, additional to the local planning authority (though the same district council may carry out both functions). Usually the functions are split, as in York where the York Archaeological Trust is the investigating authority and the local planning authority is York City Council. The appointment of an investigating authority may be cancelled at any time, in England subject to prior consultation with English Heritage (no such requirement exists in Wales as Cadw remains part of the Welsh Office function).

2.89 In an AAI the investigating authority has the powers conferred by part II of the AMAA, including wide powers of entry to sites and to undertake short-term archaeological excavations of sites in respect of which operations notices have been served. Part II does not, however, permit the investigating authority to require financial contributions from 'developers', and the AMAA does not require the Secretary of State to provide funding to investigating authorities. An investigating authority may authorise any other person to carry out its functions under part II (section 34(5)).

2.90 When an operations notice is served on the local authority (see above), the local authority must notify the investigating authority. The investigating authority is then entitled to enter the site and any land giving access to the site, at any reasonable time, for the purpose of: *'inspecting the site (including any buildings or structures ...) with a view to recording any matters of archaeological interest and determining whether it would be desirable to carry out any excavations on the site'*; and for *'observing any operations carried out on the site with a view to examining and recording any objects or material ...'* (section 38(1), AMAA). These are rights which accrue directly to the investigating authority on the service of an operations notice. The latter power, to observe during operations, subsists after the six weeks period referred to below has expired and continues for as long as the notified operations are being undertaken.

2.91 The investigating authority may excavate the site but only if it notifies the developer, the local authority, the Secretary of State and (in England) English Heritage within four weeks of the service of the operations notice that it wishes to take advantage of its powers to excavate (section 38(3)). The time for excavation is limited to four months and two weeks from a period ending 6 weeks after service of the operations notice (section 38(4)(a), AMAA). The investigating authority must, therefore, very soon after the service of an operations notice, decide on the archaeological significance of the site. Its powers to enter and record the site may continue for many months but it must decide whether to excavate or not within the first four weeks.

2.92 An operations notice may be served many months before development occurs, in respect of a site where buildings are still standing. In such circumstances the AMAA requires the developer to notify the investigating authority of the completion of site clearance (section 35(7); (see section 41(1) for definitions of clearance and site clearance)). It is an offence for the developer to carry out operations without doing so. The period of six weeks, from which the excavation period of four months and two weeks is calculated, is extended to the date when notification of final site clearance is made (section 38(4)(b), AMAA). However, there is no suspension of other time requirements where site clearance is to take place. The investigating authority's powers of entry and inspection still arise arise on service of the operations notice and, problematically, the investigating authority's decision to excavate or not must still be taken within four weeks of service of the operations notice, usually before the site is cleared.

2.93 In most cases the developer and the relevant authorities will wish to reach an understanding outside the statutory requirements. The AMAA recognises this when by agreement it allows the excavation period to run from a date earlier than that prescribed by section 38 (section 38(4)(c)). It is also fairly common for developers to agree an extension to the excavation period when significant remains are discovered. In default of agreement the ability of an investigating authority to excavate is enforced by sections 38(5)-(7). Section 38(6) empowers the authority to enter the site at any reasonable time during the excavation period for the purpose of exercising its rights to excavate; section 38(7), in effect, makes it an offence for the developer to carry out proscribed operations during the excavation period; and, where site clearance operations are being undertaken and the 'excavation period' is therefore postponed, section 38(5) authorises the investigating authority to carry out excavations before site clearance is completed provided that excavation does not interfere with site clearance or operations not covered by the Act.

2.94 There are no statutory regulations or circulars prescribing methods of working in AAIs. If site investigations are grant assisted by English Heritage the usual controls will apply (see paragraphs 2.191-2.194), otherwise the investigating authority may work as it sees fit, though the Secretary of State has reserve powers under sections 38(8) of the AMAA to issue directions to an investigating authority as to the exercise of its powers in respect of any particular archaeological site.

2.95 The AMAA empowers the Secretary of State to authorise any person (now including English Heritage) to enter a site where operations are taking place, for the purpose of inspecting and recording matters of archaeological or historical interest (section 40(a)). A similar power is granted to the RCHM(e) (section 40(b)). In both cases the Secretary of State or English Heritage may indemnify persons against loss when carrying out functions authorised under section 40 (section 46(3)).

2.96 Neither the Secretary of State nor English Heritage have any distinct powers under part II of the AMAA to fund archaeological investigation in AAIs, either by funding the establishment of investigating authorities or funding investigations themselves. However, section 45 powers extend to the funding of investigations of land which either the Secretary of State, English Heritage or the relevant local authority (as appropriate) believes may contain *'anything else'* (other than an ancient monument) *'of archaeological or historical importance'*.

2.97 For subsidiary powers of entry under the AMAA and powers, under section 54, of the investigating authority to take temporary custody of objects discovered during site investigations, see paragraph 2.21 above.

For compensation provisions see paragraphs 2.212 and 2.213, below.

Offences under Part II AMAA 1979

2.98 Unless proscribed operations are exempt (see paragraph 2.87 above), the developer must serve an operations notice in respect of the operations, wait for a minimum of six weeks before commencing operations (where site clearance is not required), notify the investigating authority of the completion of site clearance, and refrain from carrying out the operations at any time when the investigating authority has the right to excavate the site. Failure on the part of any person (or under section 35(8) the developer only) to abide by these requirements will render that person criminally liable (sections 35(1), 35(8) and 38(7), AMAA, respectively), subject in all cases to the defences available under section 37. Except under section 35(8) a person will also be liable if he causes or permits a breach of any of these requirements.

2.99 The offences are triable either way. On summary conviction an offender is liable to a fine to the statutory maximum (currently £5,000), or on indictment to an unlimited fine (section 35(9)). There is no custodial power. Local authorities are expressly empowered to institute proceedings under the section; they are also expressly authorised to apply for injunctions to restrain a 'developer' who is carrying out or is about to carry out proscribed operations on a site which in the relevant authority's opinion is likely to contain anything of archaeological or historical interest which will be disturbed, damaged, destroyed or removed without proper archaeological investigation (section 35(10)).

2.100 Section 37 provides three specific defences to charges under section 35. The accused must prove that either:

(a)   he took all reasonable precautions and exercised all due diligence to avoid or prevent a disturbance of the ground (section 37(5));

(b)   he did not know and had no reason to believe that the site of the operations was within an AAI (section 37(6)(a)); or

(c)   the operations were urgently necessary in the interests of health and safety and that notice in writing of the need for the operations was given to the Secretary of State as soon as was reasonably practicable (section 37(6)(b)).

The accused is likely to have to prove these defences on the balance of probabilities, not beyond reasonable doubt. When considered together with the breadth of the numerous exempting provisions referred to at paragraph 2.87 these defences form a significant obstacle to anybody hoping to construct criminal liability. As recently as 1997 English Heritage had no record of a prosecution under section 35 (*pers. comm.*).

2.101 Prohibitions on the use of metal detectors, under part III of the AMAA, apply in AAIs (see paragraph 2.156 below).

AAIs in Practice

2.102 The administration of an AAI is complex. Designation usually creates a burden of casework for the local authority and English Heritage; this is undoubtedly one of the reasons for the less than enthusiastic adoption of the concept at local level. Only a handful of AAIs have so far been designated, and all of these are in the historic town centres of Chester, Exeter, Canterbury, Hereford and York. These designated on 30 September 1984. Proposals for a further five possible AAIs have been shelved. Whereas the listing of buildings and the scheduling of monuments may proceed from one decade to the next with very variable amounts of funding, the essentially active, non-preservation ethos behind part II of the AMAA demands quick, comprehensive and frequently expensive action to be taken by the investigating authority. English Heritage reported to the House of Commons Environment Committee as long ago as 1986 that *'The Commission has no power to pay for the 'core' costs of the investigating authorities, even if this were considered desirable in principle and the D.O.E. have not been prepared to do so* [fund administrative costs] ... *The process of obtaining funds from other sources is difficult and basically precludes the quick response for which the legislation was intended'* (HC 1987, 204).

English Heritage has since suggested the repeal of part II of the AMAA stating that *'this Part of the Act is no longer a necessary protection, since PPG 16 more than covers the situation and is working well in practice. In contrast, part II of the 1979 Act can be seen as positive incentive to excavate rather than to preserve in situ. It is therefore considered that part II should be repealed in its entirety'* (English Heritage Consultation Paper, April 1994). This proposal met with some resistance (see, for example, Jagger and Scarse (1997) J.P.L. 195). AAIs do provide some protection, against metal detecting for example, and provide exactly those rights of inspection and evaluation which under the planning system are subject to negotiation. In areas like AAIs, which are known to be of archaeological importance, there must be some scope for both linking the service of operations notices with applications for planning permission, and the exercise by the investigating authority of its right to excavate before the implementation of planning permission. This could be effected by amendment of sections 35 and 38 of the AMAA and public financial provision for site inspection and evaluation (but not excavation or large-scale investigation) by investigating authorities.

Ancient Monuments Procedures: Supervision by the Court

2.103 A hearing or public inquiry will usually take place before a final decision on an application for scheduled monument consent is made. This is a contrast to the planning system, where a decision will usually have been made before a public inquiry is held. However, in both systems, whereas an inquiry will address both substantive and legal issues the court, generally, will only be prepared to consider the legal circumstances of the decision; in particular, the courts will not carry out the 'balancing functions' of the Secretary of State, the person entrusted with the statutory discretion by Parliament.

2.104 Both systems of supervision also provide a specific statutory means of challenging the decisions of the public authority. In planning cases the challenge is made under section 288 of the TCPA 1990; in scheduled monument cases the challenge is under section 55 of the AMAA 1979 (see appendix 2A of this work). Section 55 states that *'except as provided by this section the validity of any order or action to which this section applies shall not be questioned in any legal proceedings whatsoever; but nothing in this section shall affect the exercise of any jurisdiction of any court in respect of any failure or refusal on the part of the Secretary of State to take a decision on an application for scheduled monument consent'.*

2.105 Simple non-determination of an application is justiciable outside of the section (there is no deemed refusal in scheduled monument law), as are actions or inactions of the Secretary of State which are not within the AMAA, such as refusal to schedule a monument. For matters outside section 55, application should be made to the court under RSC Order 53 (judicial review; see paragraph 2.116 below). If the matter falls within section 55 judicial review will be precluded, Parliament already having provided a particular method of application. Application under section 55(1) is governed by RSC Order 94. The applicant who fails to follow the correct procedure risks, in the case of a matter which should have been brought under Order 53, having his section 55 application struck out.

Proceedings under section 55 of the AMAA 1979

2.105 To have *locus standi* under this section the litigant must be a 'person aggrieved' by an order or action to which the section applies (section 55(1)). Historically, a person aggrieved was someone whose own legal rights had been denied or threatened but this is no longer the case, and it is now settled law that a third party whose legal rights are not under threat may still fall within this definition (*Bizony v. Secretary of State for the Environment* [1976] J.P.L. 306). Indeed, the requirement of 'sufficient interest', for judicial review, seems in some judges' eyes to be a stricter test.

2.107 Section 55 has two limbs. The first deals with want of power under the Act and procedural irregularities in the making, variation or revocation of orders designating Areas of Archaeological Importance under Part II of the Act (sections 55(1)(a) and 55(2)). The second limb deals with want of power under the Act, or procedural irregularities, in any action of the Secretary of State when deciding an application for scheduled monument consent or modifying or revoking an existing consent. Under both limbs there will be an overlap between want of power and procedural irregularity. The latter, however, must be substantially prejudicial, not merely incidental, whereas a single, technical omission which results in a want of power may be fatal. Section 55(6) is explicit about the procedural requirements in question:

(a)   *in relation to designation orders, the requirements of the AMAA (mainly schedule 2 of the Act) and regulations made under the Act;*

(b)   *in relation to decisions on scheduled monument consents, the requirements of the AMAA (mainly schedule 1, parts 1 and 2), regulations made under the Act and the requirements of the Tribunals and Inquiries Act 1992 (including the regulations made under that Act) as they relate to a scheduled monument consent inquiry.*

2.108 Application under section 55 must be made to High Court within six weeks of the relevant date (section 55(1), AMAA and RSC Order 94, rule 2). Where issue is taken with a designation order the relevant date is the date on which notice of the order was (first) published under schedule 2 to the AMAA. Where issue is taken with a decision on a scheduled monument consent the relevant date is the date of the decision letter (if later than the date of the actual decision), or the date when notice was given to the applicant that he was to be denied a public inquiry (a 'hearing' cannot be refused). These time limits are strict and failure to comply will result in rejection of the application (though see the planning case of *Low v. Secretary of State for Wales and Glyndwyr District Council* [1994] J.P.L. 41 CA, where an application received out of time at the Crown Office but in time at the Central Office was heard by the court).

2.109 Leave of the court is not required when proceeding under section 55. Application is by way of originating motion (RSC Order 94, rule 2) which states the grounds of the challenge. A copy of the grounds and affidavit(s) should be served on the Secretary of State (or, in applications relating to designation order, on English Heritage or the local planning authority, as appropriate).

2.110 The court has wide powers to quash the relevant order or action on the grounds of *Wednesbury* unreasonableness and the decision-maker's interpretation of legal terms, as well as on the grounds specified in section 55 (see above). But the court is unable to re-open the Secretary of State's decision and substitute its own (see, for example, the planning case of *Clarke v. Secretary of State for the Environment* [1992] E.G.C.S.42, CA). A useful overview of the matters which will be uppermost in the judge's mind is provided by *Seddon Properties Ltd. v. Secretary of State for the Environment* (1978) 42 P.& C.R.26. These include:

(a)   'perversity': whether an action or decision is so unreasonable that no reasonable authority could have taken it (reasons should be given for decisions and these reasons should be 'proper, clear, intelligible and adequate');

(b)   relevance: whether all relevant matters were considered and no irrelevant matters (by which the decision or action were influenced) were taken into account (see also the planning case of *North Wiltshire District Council v. Secretary of State for the Environment* [1992] J.P.L. 955 CA);

(c)   that procedures have been complied with, especially the requirements of the Tribunals and Inquiries Act 1992 and the Town and Country Planning (Inquiries Procedure) Rules 1992;

(d)   natural justice: in particular, whether the public body in question has acted in good faith, without bias and with a judicial temper; whether each party has had disclosed to it all documents available to the examining body; whether each party has been given an opportunity to be heard in the presence of the other, to state his case and to contradict the statements of the other; and whether each party has had adequate notice of the facts at issue; and

(e)   want of power; whether the Secretary of State acted within his powers under the Act.

2.111 The Secretary of State should not bring matters into his decision which were not considered at the inquiry unless all parties are given an opportunity for further comment (see, for example, the listed building case of *SAVE Britain's Heritage v. Secretary of State for the Environment*, considered in chapter five below). However, a matter may not constitute a 'new issue' if the Secretary of State attaches a different weight from that attached by the inspector to a matter of which the applicant was already aware by the nature of his proposal (see the planning law case of *Homebase Ltd v. Secretary of State for the Environment* [1994] E.G.C.S. 17, CA).

2.112 Law should always be distinguished from policy. Whereas he cannot depart from the law, the Secretary of State may depart from his own policy as long as he gives 'cogent, clear, intelligible and relevant reasons for doing so': *Westminster City Council v. Portland Estates plc* [1985] A.C. 661; *Bolton Metropolitan Borough Council and Others v. Secretary of State for the Environment* [1995] *The Times*, May 25, HL. If the Secretary of State or the inspector follows policy slavishly, discretion may have been improperly fettered. Moreover policy can be, and sometimes is, wrong in law.

Bolton has also affirmed that the Secretary of State has considerable latitude when formulating a decision letter. He need not refer expressly to *'every argument, however peripheral'*, but need only give reasons in sufficient detail *'to enable the parties to know what conclusion he has reached on the principal, important controversial issues'*.

2.113 Section 55 of the AMAA provides that a designation order or a scheduled monument consent decision may be suspended until the court determines the application before it. On final hearing the order or decision may be quashed entirely or in part only. Section 55 is silent as to whether parts only of an applicant's property may be removed from the scope of the order or act in question. Although judgment under section 55 cannot be said to be discretionary, neither is judgment an applicant's automatic right on making his case: an applicant must demonstrate that the action or designation order, as well as having been improperly made, is also prejudicial.

2.114 Quashing of a decision or order will mean that it is inoperative and the appropriate statutory procedure must be repeated *de novo*. In contrast to judicial review proceedings, section 55, in effect, neither provides for the private law remedies of injunction, declaration or damages (against which see the Crown's special position, below) nor for the prerogative writs of prohibition and *mandamus*. These remedies are precluded for matters within section 55(2) by the operation of section 55(7).

2.115 For matters outside of section 55(2) recourse to the court is under RSC Order 53 (judicial review). Note that some matters which appear to be wholly within section 55(2) and therefore not justiciable under Order 53 may, on closer scrutiny, be open to judicial review because an error of law, for example a misunderstanding of statutory procedures by the Secretary of State, means that the issue in question did not arise from one of the matters which 'fell to be determined under the Act'.

Judicial Review

2.116 Judicial review offers the broadest supervision of public decision making. It comprises a range of private and public law remedies, both of which are generally available to the court, whether on the application of a private or a public body. In ancient monuments cases, however, all remedies sought will usually be public law remedies. Indeed, injunctions will not be granted against the Secretary of State in his public capacity (section 2, Crown Proceedings Act 1947).

2.117 Judicial review is only appropriate if what is being challenged is a matter of public law. Matters of public law include the decisions and actions of the Secretary of State, local authorities and a host of other bodies which make decisions in the public interest, probably including English Heritage in the exercise of its 'public' functions under the NHA 1983. 'Mixed' cases may occur. If there is no private law element to his claim a litigant will have to proceed by way of public law remedies; conversely, where there is a private law element the litigant cannot be forced to seek a public law remedy (*Roy v. Kensington and Chelsea and Westminster Family Practitioner Committee* [1992] 1 AC 624). If a matter is found to give rise to a private law claim the court may convert the action to one in private law (under RSC Order 53, rule 9(5)). Choosing the wrong public law proceedings, however, may also be fatal if the time limits for an alternative application have expired. If the wrong proceedings are taken it will usually be too late to make an alternative application under section 55. For example, where proceedings should have been taken under section 288 of the TCPA the court will refuse to hear a judicial review application and will not convert that application even if still within the six weeks time limit (*R. v. Secretary of State for the Environment, ex parte Johnson and Benn* [1998] J.P.L. B7). For matters falling within section 55 of the AMAA, the only means of challenge will be as described above. Provisions which seek to oust the jurisdiction of the court on a particular matter should be brought to the attention of the judge (in the bundle of statutory materials lodged with the application).

2.118 If a specific appeals procedure is available, either statutory or otherwise, this should usually be followed before judicial review is sought. In fact the judge may want to know that other forms of redress, if any, have been exhausted or are inappropriate before granting leave to apply. The main exception to this rule is where the application alleges an error in law when, as the appeals procedure may be incapable of dealing with the issue, the matter may be justiciable under Order 53 immediately (*R. v. Hillingdon London Borough Council, ex parte Royco Homes Ltd* [1974] Q.B. 720; (1974) 28 P.& C.R.251; see also *R. v. Leeds City Council, ex parte Hendry* (1994), *The Times*, January 20, CA). In some instances leave may be sought and then application for an adjournment made (if leave is granted), pending the outcome of the procedural appeal. This will prevent the application being made out of time, something which may be especially appropriate in ancient monument cases, where, outside of the codes relating to inquiries and tribunals, there are very few statutory time limits. However, the general rule remains that existing appeals machinery should be utilised before resorting to judicial review.

The Grounds of Review

2.119 Generally, the weight given by the Secretary of State to a particular fact or matter is not reviewable by the court. The 'balancing exercise' on substantive, ancient monuments issues is delegated by Parliament to the Secretary of State, not the court. Review of the Secretary of State's actions, decisions or orders purported to be made under the AMAA will be reviewable on grounds very similar to those referred to when considering section 55, namely want of power, procedural error or unfairness, and irrelevance or unreasonableness. A specific ground, that the Secretary of State has failed or refused to act in the determination of an application for scheduled monument consent is also reserved by section 55(7) of the AMAA. Within the scope of these general headings, two alleged grounds will tend to arise most frequently.

(a)   The Secretary of State has not given any reasons, or has given insufficient reasons, for his decision or other action, so that on its face the decision appears gratuitous or not to have been taken in good faith.

(b)   The decision or action taken indicates an error of law, or an error concerning the decision making process itself. Such an error, whether on the face of the record or not, will give rise to review: *Anisminic Ltd v. Foreign And Commonwealth Compensation Commission* [1969] 1 All E.R. 208 HL; *Re Racal Communications Ltd* [1981] A.C. 374.

Procedure

2.120 In contrast to an application under section 55, an applicant for judicial review must first obtain leave of the court. The application for leave should be made promptly and in any event no later than three months after the date when the grounds of review arose (RSC, Order 53, rule 4).

The application is usually heard *ex parte* without appearances before the judge. The judge will consider from the papers filed at court whether the applicant has *locus standi* (see below), has conducted himself properly in the matter (especially relating to time limits and delays) and whether he has a *prima facie* case (see, for example, *Re Friends of the Earth* [1988] J.P.L. 93 CA). In deciding whether there is such a case the judge will usually err on the side of the applicant, but it is vitally important, even at this stage, to ensure that all relevant information within the applicant's knowledge is disclosed, as failure to reveal procedural impropriety by the applicant, or selective quotation of statutory provisions, may have severe cost consequences at the substantive hearing.

Time Limits

In *R. v. North Somerset District Council and Pioneer Aggregates (U.K.) Ltd, ex parte Garnet and Piersenne* [1997] J.P.L. 1015, Popplewell J. refused leave to local residents who sought to review the Council's decision to grant planning permission for the extension of a quarry into part of a park listed grade II on the English Heritage register of parks and gardens. Although made within three months of the decision the application was not brought 'promptly'. Moreover, an applicant's difficulty in learning of the decision will not in some judges' eyes guarantee a sympathetic approach: Keane J. has suggested that when challenging the grant of planning permission by judicial review a six week time limit is appropriate (*R. v. Cotswold District Council, ex parte Barrington Parish Council* [1997] E.G.C.S. 66). It is possible that a similar approach would be taken in an ancient monuments application: the challenge is most likely to be by a third party, section 55 provides a six week period for challenge under the Act, and delay in the implementation of a land-use consent would be in issue.

2.121 The notice of application should be in form 86A (SCP, vol.2) and should be supported by an affidavit by the applicant which verifies the factual statements in the form 86A and exhibits any written record, e.g. minutes of meetings and reports. The application need not be made by counsel as, unlike the substantive hearing, it will not be heard in open court. Indeed, the application is usually made by post, without an oral hearing. Having said that, it is certainly the case that most applications for leave are based on forms 86A and affidavits settled by counsel. If interlocutory relief is desired (a stay of proceedings or an injunction, for example, pending the substantive hearing) an oral hearing, as well as application on notice to the proposed respondent, is usually desirable.

2.122 The *locus standi* requirement for judicial review is a 'sufficient interest' (Order 53, rule 3(7)). This is thought to be a less demanding test than the 'person aggrieved', but there is considerable disparity between the attitudes of individual judges. The recognition of *locus* is not discretionary, however, but is a matter of law and fact: *I.R.C. v. National Federation of Self-Employed and Small Businesses Ltd* [1981] 2 All E.R. 93 HL. The kind of relief sought will be an important consideration. If the applicant is seeking an injunction against a public body he may be required to demonstrate a personal legal interest, just as he would if seeking an injunction against a private person. If, however, the issue of a writ of *mandamus* is sought (to force the minister to act in a specified way) the applicant will not be required to show any infringement of personal legal rights, although the rights of the applicant affected may still need to be greater than if an order to quash a decision is sought. (The different remedies available are considered below at paragraph 2.123.)

In the *Rose Theatre* case (see paragraph 2.04 above) Schiemann J. took the very strict view, that as the applicant trust company had been recently formed by a number of people who individually would not have had sufficient *locus*, the company did not have sufficient standing to bring judicial review proceedings against the Secretary of State for his refusal to schedule the remains of the theatre. This was based on the questionable assumption that an 'ordinary citizen' lacked a sufficient interest to institute judicial review proceedings against the Secretary of State in ancient monuments matters (contrast, for example, *R. v. Stroud District Council, ex parte Goodenough* [1982] J.P.L. 246 DC, where local residents were assumed to have *locus* to challenge the decision of the local planning authority's approach to preservation of listed buildings). Otton J. formed a different view in the *Greenpeace* (THORP) application to review the decision of the Secretary of State not to hold a public inquiry into the desirability of a new nuclear fuel re-processing plant (*R. v. H.M.I.P., ex parte Greenpeace Ltd* (1993), *The Independent,* September 30; [1994] 4 All E.R. 329). He judged that Greenpeace's status as an adviser of U.N.E.S.C.O., together with its 400,000 plus world-wide membership, of whom 2,500 were in Cumbria, gave the applicants *locus standi*. It was also significant that Greenpeace was seeking a writ of *certiorari* and not *mandamus,* and that the matter might not be brought before the court by any other group. The ministerial decision challenged in *Greenpeace* was arguably more amenable to review, as it concerned refusal of a public inquiry rather than the more technical question of whether or not to schedule.

Both Otton J. and Schiemann J. thought the question of *locus* to be one which could be profitably re-examined in detail at the full hearing, where 'the strength of the applicant's interest' would continue to be one of the matters considered. In *Rose Theatre* Schiemann J., by reference to eight propositions, summarised the matters which the court should take into account.

1. Once leave has been given to move for judicial review the court which hears the application ought still to examine whether the applicant has a sufficient interest.
2. Whether an applicant has a sufficient interest is not purely a matter of discretion of the court.
3. Not every member of the public can complain of every breach of statutory duty by a person empowered to come to a decision by that statute. To rule otherwise would be to deprive the phrase 'a sufficient interest' of all meaning.
4. However, a direct financial or legal interest is not required.
5. Where one is examining an alleged failure to perform a duty imposed by statute it is useful to look at the statute and see whether it gives an applicant a right enabling him to have that duty performed.
6. Merely to assert that one has an interest does not give one an interest.
7. The fact that some thousands of people join together and

assert that they have an interest does not create an interest if the individuals did not have an interest.

8. The fact that those without an interest incorporate themselves and give the company in its memorandum power to pursue a particular object does not give the company an interest.

(*R. v. Secretary of State for the Environment, ex parte Rose Theatre Trust Company* (1990) 59 P.& C.R. 257 at 271 QB).

Some of these propositions may be doubted, especially numbers 5 and 7, but as a whole they are a useful indication of the hurdles which may have to be cleared by a conservation group which applies for judicial review. *Rose Theatre* should not deter applicants. Other judges may adopt a different approach. Indeed, in a more recent case, Sedley J. stated that judicial review is not about rights but about misuse of public power and, consequently, a person with no particular stake in a matter may bring an apparent abuse of such power to the attention of the court. The court should assist such a person, not be a hindrance. *Rose Theatre* was specifically not followed (*R. v. Somerset County Council, ex parte Dixon* [1997] C.O.D. 325). As Riley has emphasised ((1997) J.P.L. 25) there is otherwise a risk that unlawful decisions may go unchallenged, as one of the main repositories of know-how – English Heritage – may already be tied into the decision making process.

The Hearing and the Remedies

2.123 Only matters referred to in the application for leave are normally included in the substantive application. The substantive application must be made within 14 days of the grant of leave, by originating motion (RSC Order 53, rule 5(5)). Unlike the application for leave, the substantive application must be on notice to the other parties in the proceedings and an affidavit of service should be filed. The respondent must file his reply by affidavit within 56 days of being served with the applicant's notice of motion and affidavit of application. The reply will be by affidavit, which explains the reasons for the decision or action and how this was taken and seeks to rebut the allegations in the form 86A. The applicant should consider whether a further affidavit, rebutting matters raised in reply, is needed.

2.124 Exceptionally, the respondent might apply to have the application set aside on the grounds that the proceedings are misconceived or defective for want of full disclosure. There is, however, rarely any direction for disclosure of documents, and the judge will not wish to be submerged in a mass of detail; he will be interested only in the vital facts of the case. The parties are expected to reach some consensus on what actually happened, a consensus which should translate itself into the 'skeleton arguments'.

2.125 Applications in respect of the Secretary of State's behaviour in relation to a matter falling within the AMAA will inevitably be concerned with the public law remedies: the prerogative writs (now, strictly, 'orders') of *mandamus*, prohibition and *certiorari*. *Mandamus* will require a public authority to carry out its functions in a specified manner; prohibition will prevent an anticipated decision or course of action being taken; and *certiorari* will quash a decision and, in effect, remit the matter to the decision maker for reconsideration. *Mandamus* and prohibition will be harder to obtain than *certiorari*, although in ancient monuments cases *certiorari* may be the remedy most frequently sought. This should not obscure the fact, however, that the outcome of judicial review proceedings is more difficult to assess than most private causes of action; the overturning of a decision or action, especially that of a minister, is not easily achieved.

Injunctions

2.126 In important cases it may be possible to restrain breaches of the AMAA by injunction. As there is no statutory power under the AMAA to compel offenders to repair damage done to monuments, either speedy action to prevent damage or an injunction which requires reinstatement may be the only effective protection of a site.

Except for breaches of the AAI notification procedures (section 35(10), AMAA) the AMAA does not give express power to local authorities to seek injunctions for ancient monuments purposes. Local authorities still rely on their general powers under section 222 of the Local Government Act 1972 to bring such proceedings 'for the promotion or protection of the interests of the inhabitants of their area'. These are far weaker powers than are conferred in relation to planning breaches by section 187B of the TCPA (see chapter six of this work) and are probably restricted to preventing expected breaches of the ancient monuments code (a prohibitory injunction) rather than obtaining mandatory relief. Unless there is a breach of planning control as well as a breach of the AMAA it is unlikely, therefore, that a local authority would pursue an injunction.

In contrast, English Heritage is given express power by section 33(2A) of the NHA 1983 to 'institute in their own name proceedings for an injunction to restrain any contravention of any provision of that Part ...' i.e. part I of the AMAA. This is a wide power and by analogy with planning law cases under section 187B TCPA would include steps which force an offender to remedy damage caused by unauthorised activity.

It is possible for the Secretary of State to apply for an injunction to restrain an expected breach of the criminal law (*Gouriet v. Union of Post Office Workers* [1978] A.C. 435). In England the possibility of such an action for ancient monuments purposes must be remote given the powers now vested in English Heritage. However, Cadw does not have legal powers separate from those of the appropriate Secretary for Wales, therefore an action by the appropriate government department may still be contemplated.

Private citizens cannot bring proceedings for an injunction unless their own legal rights are infringed. For example, if a neighbour carries out works on his own land which are unauthorised under the AMAA, but which also involve a trespass onto neighbouring land, the owner of that neighbouring land could bring proceedings for an injunction to restrain the trespass but would not be able to do so to force reinstatement of the archaeological site not on his land. The 'archaeological element' would be a public law matter to be taken by the appropriate public authority.

Offences and Enforcement

2.127 The AMAA contains several offences aimed at

securing the preservation of archaeological remains and the effective implementation of scheduled monument and AAI procedures. In addition, liability under the enforcement provisions in the TCPA 1990 may be relevant, as may the offences under the Theft Act 1968 and the Burial Act 1857. Offences under the P(LBCA)A 1990 will not be relevant where a monument is both a listed building and a scheduled monument (though may be relevant where a listed building is an unscheduled archaeological site).

The main provisions intended to protect scheduled monuments and other 'protected monuments' (see paragraph 2.145 below) are found in sections 2 and 28, respectively, of the AMAA. Section 42 of the Act restricts the use of and the recovery of material by metal detectors in 'protected places'. Section 35(1) of the AMAA makes it an offence to carry out prescribed operations in an AAI *inter alia* without first serving an 'operations notice' (and section 35(10) expressly authorises district councils to seek injunctions to restrain breaches of this provision). There are also offences under section 36(4) and schedule 1, part I, paragraph 2(4) of the AMAA (issuing false certificates for statutory purposes); section 44(8) (intentionally obstructing a person authorised to exercise a power of entry under the Act); section 57(3) (knowingly supplying false information under the Act); and section 19(7) (contravening any regulations made under the Act for controlling access to monuments in care).

Section 2 (Unauthorised works to a scheduled monument)
(Section 2, AMAA is reproduced at appendix 2A of this work)

2.128 A person executing or causing or permitting to be executed works to a scheduled monument which require consent under section 2 of the AMAA commits an offence if he fails to obtain consent for the works (section 2(1)) or fails to comply with any conditions attached to the consent (section 2(6)), as the works in question will then be unauthorised for the purposes of section 2(3). Criminal liability is incurred immediately the unauthorised works are executed; there is no need for any notice to be served by the Secretary of State, English Heritage or the local authority, nor is it possible to avoid liability by carrying out works of intended mitigation. Section 2 does not specify any particular *mens rea* (contrast the offence under section 28). The act of executing the works, or having sufficient proximity to the works is enough. Although liability is in this sense 'strict' it is not absolute in the old sense of the word, as the section provides four distinct defences (see below). However, in *R. v. Sims (J.O.) Ltd.* (1993) 96 Cr. App. R. 125 at 128, in accordance with increasingly common usage, the Court of Appeal referred to the offence as 'absolute' whilst at the same time acknowledging the statutory defences.

2.129 Works which require authorisation under section 2 are those already referred to above, namely:

    (a)   *any works resulting in the demolition or destruction of or any damage to a scheduled monument;*

    (b)   *any works for the purpose of removing or repairing a*

> *scheduled monument or any part of it or of making any*
> *alterations or additions thereto; and*
>
> (c)   *any flooding or tipping operations on land in, or under*
> *which there is a scheduled monument*

(section 2(2); for the definition of 'flooding and tipping operations' see section 61, AMAA).

It is probable that subsection 2(2)(a) contemplates something more than *de minimis* works, for example disturbance caused by the lowering of the water table in a relict landscape. The appearance of the word 'damage' after the word 'destruction' suggests that mere disturbance is not enough. English Heritage have indicated that they would prefer the section to be amended to include 'disturbance' expressly within the list of offending operations (EH 1994).

2.130 Works may be authorised by a specific grant of scheduled monument consent or by a class consent. Until relatively recently it was also possible under the transitional provisions in the AMAA, where an operations notice served on the Secretary of State remained unanswered, for a deemed scheduled monument consent to arise. The notice had to be served before the commencement of the Act in 1981, but the works could have been begun as late as 1986 and could be completed even later.

2.131 Offences under section 2(1) and 2(6) are triable either way. In the magistrates court the fine may be up to the statutory maximum (currently £5,000; there is no enhanced fine to compare with that under section 9 of the P(LBCA)A 1990, as amended). In the Crown Court the fine is unlimited.

There is no custodial power under section 2. Whether a defendant or the prosecution prefers one venue or the other depends on the particulars of the alleged offence. As a general rule, a defendant will opt for the magistrates if he believes his offence to be relatively minor; he may also hope to raise evidential (but not legal) questions more easily there. If the prosecution wishes to make an example of an offender, or believes there is a point of general legal interest at issue, the Crown Court is the appropriate venue.

2.132 Prosecutions may be undertaken by the local authority for the area in which the scheduled monument is situated, English Heritage, or indeed a private individual, as well as the Crown. However, Crown Court action will have significant costs implications when compared with the laying of an information before the magistrates, and will be beyond the means, and the inclination, of most private individuals. In the Crown Court a private prosecution will usually be a 'relator' action brought by the Attorney General on behalf of the individual, but the individual still has to meet the costs (and in fact will have to satisfy the Attorney General that costs can be met before proceedings are commenced). English Heritage will usually work closely with the Crown Prosecution Service or any other prosecutor. Indeed, where English Heritage wants to prosecute it is unlikely to do so itself and will usually ask the Crown Prosecution Service to take the case, due to the latter's national coverage and ability to readily involve the police in obtaining evidence. For a private prosecution the co-operation of English Heritage may be of vital importance, not least in establishing that scheduled monument consent was never granted for the works in question and that the monument is scheduled.

A joint circular letter, issued on 22 June 1988 by the county and district local authority associations and English Heritage (as reproduced at BAN (1988) 3(6), 53) clarified the latter's role in archaeological prosecutions, especially where local authorities may be involved. Paragraph 4 of the letter states that '*In most circumstances, English Heritage is not the most effective body to take a case forward to legal proceedings. As a centralised organisation with relatively few staff in the field and very limited in-house resources, English Heritage is in considerable difficulty in investigating the full local circumstances of offences rapidly and thoroughly to provide a secure basis for prosecution'*. Whether this will change with the increasing regionalisation of English Heritage remains to be seen. Annex 3, paragraph 12 of PPG 16 emphasises that speed in the assembling of evidence is often crucial to successful prosecutions ('*before memories fade or vital evidence is concealed'*) and that local authorities are often the first source of information. The letter of 1988 states that '*it is therefore normal English Heritage policy, once preliminary investigation has established a potential case for prosecution, to pass the information to the police for them to take such further action as they consider appropriate. If the police consider that there are adequate grounds for a prosecution, they will in turn pass the information to the Crown Prosecution Service. English Heritage will provide evidence for the police or Crown Prosecutor on the scheduled status of the monument, such damage as appears to have been caused to it and other material matters. If the police are unwilling to prosecute in a case where there does appear to have been significant damage, English Heritage will consider whether to proceed itself'* (paragraph 5). The main thrust of the letter is to encourage local authorities to pursue archaeological prosecutions more vigorously, and to this end, where a local authority is to prosecute and the *'costs of prosecution could be much more substantial'* (than in the magistrates court) *'English Heritage will be prepared to consider making a contribution towards the cost of the proceedings provided that it has supported the case for prosecution and agreed financial assistance in principle before proceedings are instituted. ... In determining the appropriate contribution in any particular case it would be right to take into account, for instance, whether the authority had incurred actual marginal expenditure in instructing private practice solicitors, and whether a significant and unusual division of professional or technical staff time had been involved'* (paragraph 7).

2.133 In addition to obvious evidential lifelines, such as the prosecution's inability to adduce evidence that the monument in question was scheduled at the time the alleged offence took place, there are three statutory defences under section 2.

In the case of a section 2(2)(a) or 2(2)(c) offence it is a defence for the accused to prove that he did not know and had no reason to believe that the monument in question was within the area affected by the works or that the monument was scheduled (section 2(8)).

In the case of a section 2(2)(a) offence, or the offence of breaching a condition attached to a scheduled monument consent, it is a defence for the accused to prove that he took all reasonable precautions and exercised all due diligence to avoid or prevent damage to the monument (section 2(7)) (or, under section 2(6), to avoid contravening the condition).

There is no particular defence to charges brought under section 2(2)(b) – works for the removal or repair of a scheduled monument – but the accused may have recourse to the general defence to all offences under section 2, namely that the works were urgently necessary in the interests of safety or health and that notice in writing of the need for the works was given to the Secretary of State as soon as reasonably practicable (section 2(9)). These are less onerous than the requirements of class consent 5 (see paragraph 2.30 above), which requires urgent works to be the minimum necessary and requires a detailed notice to be served on the Secretary of State.

2.134 Each of these defences requires the accused to prove that he took the necessary action or had the requisite ignorance. Such proof will be on a balance of probabilities, and not 'beyond reasonable doubt'.

These defences present considerable hurdles for the prosecution. The 'ignorance defence' under section 2(8) has no counterpart in listed building law, where the equivalent offence has, with justification, been described as one of absolute liability (see chapter five below). This difference between the two systems of regulation is sometimes referred to the greater difficulty in recognising scheduled monuments than listed buildings, though this argument tends to assume that listed buildings are easily distinguishable from those buildings which are not listed. English Heritage supports the abolition of the ignorance defence in favour of an approach which takes understandable ignorance into account as mitigation when sentencing (EH 1994).

2.135 Sometimes works are necessary in the interests of health and safety, and there will be no opportunity to obtain scheduled monument consent from the Secretary of State.

This defence is paralleled in listed building law, but the section 2(9) defence is more widely drawn. Proposals to amend section 2(9) have been under consideration by the Secretary of State since 1992 but there has been no formal indication that proposals are to be brought before Parliament. The new class consent for works on health and safety grounds (see above) may render such amendment unnecessary.

2.136 The defences under section 2(7) are restricted to the offences of damaging, destroying or demolishing a scheduled monument under section 2(2)(a). The meaning of 'damage' has already been considered (see paragraph 2.129 above) but the extent of the monument in this context, and the meaning of 'reasonable' within this section, are problematical. On the first point, the Secretary of State and English Heritage take the view that all of the area indicated on the scheduling maps as scheduled is covered by the designation 'scheduled monument', although it is still possible for a defendant to take the point that within this area he did not damage a monument if, such is the case, remains could not be affected by his works. On the second point, the 'reasonable precautions' referred to are probably those to be expected of a person with the defendant's training, and not those expected of a person with archaeological training. If it can be proved, however, that the defendant knew the monument was scheduled it is arguable that the use of archaeological assistance would have been a reasonable precaution.

2.137 With section 2 offences the prosecution will often have to deal with multiple defendants. The person executing the works may not be the person who has control of the site, and may not be the person who could have been expected to be responsible for obtaining scheduled monument consent. Section 2(1) expressly provides that liability may attach to any person who causes or permits the offending works. 'Permitted' in this sense will, if the person in question had authority to prevent the works taking place, include 'wilful inadvertence' to a potential breach of section 2. 'Causes' is potentially wider, but requires as a minimum that a person had a degree of control over the works, though not necessarily over the person who executed them. Causation does not imply knowledge or negligence, and a person may cause a particular effect even though he could not have prevented the particular offence from occurring (*National Rivers Authority v. Yorkshire Water Services Ltd* [1995] 1 All E.R. 225 HL, a case brought under section 107(a) of the Water Act 1989; see also *R. v. CPC(UK) Ltd* (1994) *The Times*, August 4, CA, causation not requiring proof that the defendant's acts were the sole cause of the damage sustained).

2.138 A body corporate may be liable under section 2. The penalties available are consistent with corporate liability: there is no custodial provision and no *mens rea* requirement (contrast the offence under section 28, AMAA). The question will be whether the 'controlling mind' of a body corporate was directed to the works undertaken by the directors or managers having day-to-day responsibility for such matters. Over the last five years the courts have found involvement of the controlling mind more readily than hitherto. In *National Rivers Authority v. Alfred McAlpine Homes East Ltd* (1994) *The Times*, February 3, DC, the court held that it was sufficient that those employees who had immediate responsibility on site for the offending works (in this case the illegal escape of pollutants into controlled waters) were acting within the course and scope of their employment. However, as section 2 of the AMAA does not create absolute offences, it may be possible for a corporation to avoid liability by demonstrating that at the relevant time it had a scheme of delegation in place which, if properly followed, would have brought the corporation within one of the statutory defences.

2.139 Directors and managers will not be able to hide behind the person of the body corporate if it is proved that offences were committed with their consent or 'connivance', or as a result of their neglect (section 58, AMAA).

Defendants will frequently face multiple charges, as damage, destruction and demolition are concepts with significant areas of overlap, though care should be taken not to duplicate charges.

The section 2(7) defence is not available to a charge under section 2(2)(b). However, section 2(2)(b) requires proof that the purpose of the works was renewal or repair.

Sentencing

2.140 Prosecutors will normally wish to bring proceedings in the Crown Court, not the magistrates. In addition to greater sentencing powers, the defendant will usually face greater adverse publicity and the court should be more at ease with unfamiliar areas of the law. The defendant will frequently seek a summary trial. The venue is very important for sentencing as the AMAA does not (yet) provide for enhanced fines in the magistrates court.

2.141 Fines in the Crown Court will usually range between £5-20,000, depending, amongst other things, on the degree of damage to the monument and whether or not the defendant's actions are perceived as deliberate or negligent. In *R. v. Seymour* [1989] C.L.R. 360 CA a defendant convicted of damaging the scheduled Roman remains at Alcester, Oxfordshire, successfully appealed against the size of his fine. The fine was reduced from £10,000 to £3,000. The Court of Appeal held that the original fine was 'excessive for an offence which was not an intentional flouting of the law', being an act of negligence which had not brought any personal gain to the defendant. Similar sentiments were expressed by the Court of Appeal in *R. v. Sims (J.O.) Ltd* [1993] 96 Cr.App.R. 125; (1992) *The Independent*, August 3; (1992) CB, July 20, where the degree of negligence of the defendant was seen to be especially relevant to the level of the fine to be imposed. In this case a fine of £75,000 was reduced to £15,000 when account was taken of: the guilty plea; the defendant's good reputation and commercial losses flowing from the prosecution; and that works had ceased when the significance of the damage had been recognised by the defendants. The works in question destroyed substantial medieval remains and a Roman tessellated pavement. The court observed that if the damage had been deliberate, or carried out with express knowledge, the fine would have been 'very large indeed'.

In *Seymour* it could be argued that the plough damage was less severe and more inadvertent. Where an offender has committed more than one offence, or where he has been more destructive, however, fines will be higher. In one case involving three separate charges under section 2, for which fines totalling £30,000 and costs of £10,000 were ordered, the

Court of Appeal saw fit to reduce the fine only to £15,000 and left the costs order intact (*R. v. Simpson* (1993) 14 Cr.App.R.(S.) 602; see also *The Daily Telegraph*, October 22, 1991, for a report on the initial hearing). In *Bovis*, the Court of Appeal accepted that the contractor had a previously good record of work on protected sites and that it had incurred significant costs as a result of its error. The fine was left at £2,000, with £20,000 costs raised to £26,000 (*R. v. Bovis Construction Ltd* [1994] Crim L.R. 938 CA).

2.142 Although protection of the setting will be a planning consideration (see chapter six of this work) and may also be of importance when considering the impact of works on the monument itself, scheduled monument consent is not required either for works on monuments which are not scheduled, or for works on land which merely constitutes the setting of or is contiguous to a scheduled monument. It is legally possible for a monument to be in the care of the Secretary of State or English Heritage and remain unscheduled, in which case an offence under section 2 could not be committed though charges under sections 19 and 28 of the AMAA could be available. On a monument which is scheduled, however, the Secretary of State's identification map will normally be taken as definitive evidence of extent, and where damaging works have taken place within that area there is no issue to be put to the jury on whether a scheduled monument was actually damaged (*Bovis*, above).

2.143 Neither section 2 nor section 5 of the AMAA makes provision for the Secretary of State or the court to require reinstatement of a scheduled monument once unauthorised works have been carried out (contrast the position in listed building law, where an enforcement notice may require remedial works and where the costs of urgent repairs can be recovered from owners). The most that can be obtained under section 5 of the AMAA (urgent works) is the diverting of any criminal compensation to the Secretary of State. If more is required an injunction must be sought under the general jurisdiction of the court (there is no express statutory power for the Secretary of State to do so, though English Heritage has express power see paragraph 2.126 above).

Section 28 (Intentional or reckless damage to a Protected Monument)

2.144 Intentional or reckless damage or destruction of a 'protected monument' without lawful excuse, and knowing that the monument in question is a protected monument, constitutes a separate, more serious offence than the offence under 2. Section 28 deals more with the vandal than does section 2; section 28 offences, therefore, carry potentially greater penalties.

2.145 A protected monument is defined as any scheduled monument or any monument under the ownership or guardianship of the Secretary of State, English Heritage or a local authority (section 28(3)). The offender must:

- know that the monument is a protected monument;
- himself cause destruction or damage to the monument;
- intend to do damage or destruction to the monument

> or be reckless as to whether the monument would be
> damaged or destroyed.

2.146 If not actual knowledge, the prosecution must prove that the accused took active steps to remain ignorant of the facts, or, *per* Parker J. in *Westminster City Council v. Croyalgrange Ltd* [1985] 1 All E.R. 740, that the accused shut his eyes to things which should have been obvious.

2.147 If the accused does not execute the offence himself he will probably have to be acting through an 'innocent agent', for example a minor. It will not avail the accused to plead that he had the owner's consent as section 28(2) expressly provides that the section applies notwithstanding such consent (where a charge of criminal damage could not be brought in the alternative). Problems can arise with causation but determination of cause is 'a matter of common sense for the tribunal of fact' considering that:

> *'the accused need not be the sole cause; the accused need not*
> *foresee the consequences of his act, omission or role; if there is*
> *any intervening cause whether that cause was so powerful as*
> *to reduce the accused's conduct to no cause at all.'*
> *(Empress Car Company (Abertillery) Ltd v. National Rivers*
> *Authority* [1997] J.P.L. 908 DC, causing pollution of
> controlled waters under section 85, Water Resources Act
> 1991).

2.148 The prosecution will usually encounter most difficulty with the *mens rea* requirement of section 28. Although 'intention' does not mean desiring the particular result to occur, the result must have been a virtual certainty of the act of the accused (*R. v. Nedrick* [1986] 3 All E.R. 1 CA; see the very involved debate on what constitutes legal intention in *R. v. Hancock* and *R. v. Strickland* [1986] A.C. 455). Recklessness, in such close proximity to the word 'intending', is very probably 'specific or subjective recklessness', in the sense that the accused was aware of the risks of his actions but nonetheless went on to act as he did (*R. v. Cunningham* [1958] 3 All E.R. 711 CA; not the lower threshold, 'objective' recklessness of the *Lawrence* variety (*R. v. Lawrence* [1982] A.C. 510). In addition, section 28 provides that the accused may escape liability altogether if he had 'lawful excuse' (section 28(1)). This expression does not necessarily mean lawful authority; it may be something less than this, for example a genuine mistake which strips the accused of the required *mens rea*. If the accused brings evidence of such an excuse it is the prosecution's task to rebut it rather than defence's task to prove it.

2.149 The act of destruction or damage cannot constitute an offence if authorised by a specific grant of scheduled monument consent or by class consent (section 28(2)).

2.150 Maximum sentences under section 28 are a £5,000 fine and/or six months imprisonment on summary conviction and an unlimited fine and/or two years imprisonment on indictment. In *R. v. Hope* (1996) *The Times*, July 31, a defendant was fined £8,000 by the Crown Court for carrying out unauthorised excavations at Wymondsley Priory, Hertfordshire. The court considered that the damage had been incurred recklessly, as maintained by English Heritage who instigated proceedings through the Crown Prosecution Service.

Other offences under the AMAA

2.151 Section 19 of the Act authorises the Secretary of State to make regulations 'prohibiting or regulating any act or thing which would tend to injure or disfigure' any monument in the care of either the Secretary of State or English Heritage. He may also make regulations restricting access to such monuments (see, for example, The Stonehenge Regulations, S.I. 1997, No. 2038). Contravention of such regulations is an absolute offence which renders the offender liable to a maximum fine of £1,000 on summary conviction. An omission as well as an act of commission may render a person liable under regulations made under this section.

2.152 For the offence of disturbing the ground in an Area of Archaeological Importance, either without serving an operations notice or within six weeks after effecting such service, see paragraph 2.84 above.

2.153 Under section 57 of the AMAA the Secretary of State, English Heritage or a local authority may require an owner (as defined by section 61 of the Act) or occupier to give written particulars of their interest in a monument, and the name and address of any person known to them to have an interest. Section 57(2) makes it an offence to refuse to give such information, subject to a maximum fine of £1,000 on summary conviction. If a misstatement is knowingly made in the answer to such a request the person making the statement is liable to an unlimited fine on indictment or to a maximum fine of £5,000. There is defence under section 57 of 'reasonable excuse' (section 57(2)). This is a less stringent requirement than 'lawful excuse' but will require something more than simple failure to understand the request; for example, absence from the jurisdiction at the time the request was made.

2.154 It is an offence to intentionally obstruct a person exercising a power of entry under the Act (section 44(8), see paragraph 2.20 above)).

2.155 Criminal liability may also be incurred by the issuing of false certificates when applying for scheduled monument consent (schedule 1, part I, paragraph 2(4)) or when serving an operations notice under part II of the Act (section 36(4)). In either case, if a person issues a certificate which he knows is 'false or misleading in a material particular', or which he issues recklessly and which turns out to be so false or misleading, he will be liable to a fine of up to £1,000 on summary conviction.

Metal Detectors

2.156 The AMAA introduced restrictions on the use of metal detectors (section 42, reproduced at appendix 2A of this work). The restriction applies only in 'protected places' (distinguish 'protected monuments' under section 28), namely scheduled monuments, monuments in the ownership or under the guardianship of the Secretary of State, English Heritage or a local authority, and sites in Areas of Archaeological Importance (section 42(2)). Most archaeological sites, therefore, do not fall within section 42, and it must be conceded that it would be unfair to impose such criminal liability in all cases. Nor do all ancient monuments fall within section 42, as not all ancient monuments are subject to specific legal designation (an ancient monument may simply be a monument which the Secretary of State believes to be of public interest (section 61(12), AMAA).

2.157 A 'metal detector' is defined by section 42(2) as 'any device designed or adapted for detecting or locating any metal or mineral in the ground'. In addition to the usual proprietary metal detecting equipment, all survey tools capable of detecting metal or minerals as discreet entities, such as a magnetometer (though not a resistivity meter) will fall within this definition. English Heritage interprets section 42(2) as including any machine capable of detecting metal, whether or not this is the machine's main purpose.

2.158 Section 42 creates three separate offences:

(a) the use of metal detectors in a protected place without the written consent of the Secretary of State or English Heritage (section 42(1);

(b) the removal of archaeological or historical material so discovered without the written consent of the Secretary of State or English Heritage; (section 42(3)); and

(c) failure to comply with the conditions pursuant to which any such written consent was granted (section 42(5)).

2.159 The person who has consent to use a metal detector will commit an offence if he removes material from a protected place (unless he also has consent to remove the material in question); indeed, his liability will be greater if removing material than simply using a metal detector without consent. For using a metal detector the maximum fine, on summary conviction, is level 3 on the standard scale (currently £1,000; the offence is not indictable). Like other ancient monument offences, however, the offence cannot be described as an absolute offence, because it is a defence to prove that the metal detector in question was being used for a purpose other than detecting objects of archaeological or historical interest (section 42(6)). The defence has been successfully pleaded on a number of occasions, mostly unreported by the legal press. It is also a defence for the accused to prove that he had *'taken all reasonable precautions to find out whether the place where he used the metal detector was a protected place'* and that he also *'did not believe'* that it was a protected place (section 42(7)). For either defence to succeed the accused has more than an initial evidential burden to displace; he would not be claiming that an element of the offence is missing but that he falls within a statutory exception. He will normally be required to prove his defence on a balance of probabilities.

2.160 The removal of material found by metal detector (but not otherwise) from a protected place is a more serious offence. An offender is liable on summary conviction to a fine at the statutory maximum (currently £5,000), or on indictment to an unlimited fine. There is no sanction of imprisonment. It is not a defence when charged under section 42(3) to claim that the metal detector was in use for an 'innocent' purpose (section 42(6)), although the 'reasonable precautions' defence is still available. If the protected place in question is a scheduled monument an offender also risks the further charges under section 28 of the AMAA, and in extreme cases charges may lie under section 2.

2.161 Where a person fails to comply with a condition in a licence to use a metal detector, he will be liable, as appropriate, for unauthorised use and/or unauthorised removal (section 42(5)). Neither the 'innocent purpose' nor the 'reasonable precautions' defence applies to a section 42(5) offence. However, breach of the conditions of a licence should be a rare occurrence as licences are issued both infrequently and in very special circumstances: they have been issued, for example, to an archery club which sought to recover lost arrows, to archaeologists retrieving artefacts from spoil heaps, and to locate unexploded mortar bombs.

The archaeologist's main concern is that the removal of finds discovered by metal detector destroys stratigraphy and provenance. Important finds are also usually hidden from the public. For finds from sites which are not within section 42 of the AMAA there is now a non-statutory code of practice, to encourage the reporting of finds discovered by detectorists (see chapter three, on portable antiquities).

2.162 Although the AMAA does not prevent metal detectors from being used on monuments which are not 'protected places', a person will need permission from the landowner before entering, searching for and removing objects from land. The detectorist is otherwise likely to commit trespass, both to land and other property, and, if he removes objects, he may commit theft. Where items may be treasure (see chapter three), they must be disclosed to the local SMR, public museum or the local coroner.

Ancient Monuments: Acquisition, Guardianship and Management

The AMAA provides for the acquisition, guardianship, protection by agreement and enhancement by grant aid of ancient monuments.

Acquisition

2.163 The Secretary of State may acquire ancient monuments (as defined by section 61(12) of the AMAA) by agreement (section 11(1)) or, for the purpose of securing their preservation, compulsorily (section 10(1)). Compulsory acquisition was a new power created by the AMAA and assurances were given during the passage of the bill through Parliament that compulsory powers would only be used as a last resort. Before any acquisition under sections 10 or 11 of any land in England the Secretary of State must consult with English Heritage.

2.164 By stipulating 'ancient monument', the AMAA makes it clear that to be acquired a monument need not be already scheduled, but if not scheduled it must be of 'public interest' (section 61(12)(b)). The broad definition of ancient monument contained in section 33(8) of the NHA 1983 is not applicable. Current ministerial policy is said to be that acquisition will be considered only where no other party is able to secure the future of the monument and where the monument is of 'primary national importance' (a phrase which reserves to the minister the maximum discretion as to whether to acquire).

2.165 Acquisition by agreement may be for a consideration or by gift (section 11(3)). In the former case, part I of the Compulsory Purchase Act 1965 applies (this implies certain protective provisions for the benefit of the land acquired). On compulsory acquisition the Acquisition of Land Act 1981 applies. The compulsory purchase order must be made by the Secretary of State. Negotiations thereafter will be either under the notice to treat procedure of the Compulsory Purchase Act 1965, or the general vesting declaration procedure of the Compulsory Purchase (Vesting Declarations) Act 1981. In either case compensation will be assessed according to the provisions of the Land Compensation Act 1961, but subject to the section 11(4) of the AMAA, which requires that where a monument is a scheduled monument compensation shall be assessed on the basis that scheduled monument consent would not have been granted for *'any works which would or might result in the demolition, destruction or removal of the monument or any part of it'* (section 10(4)).

Crown land cannot be compulsorily acquired under section 10 (section 50(2)(b)), AMAA).

2.166 An alternative to acquisition by the Secretary of State is acquisition by English Heritage or by the appropriate local authority (sections 11(1A) and 11(2), AMAA). Powers and conditions similar to those relevant to acquisition by the Secretary of State apply, except that if acquiring for a consideration a local authority may only acquire a monument within its area and, where English Heritage is acquiring, the Secretary of State's consent must first be obtained. Neither English Heritage nor local authorities have powers of compulsory acquisition under the AMAA, though a local authority may in the performance of its functions, outside the AMAA, acquire an ancient monument if the Secretary of State is minded to grant scheduled monument consent for any development proposal and is otherwise minded to confirm the CPO. In *Michael Kemis v. Salisbury District Council (Re The Moot, Downton, Wiltshire)* (1994) 34 R.V.R., 172, 5.2 hectares of land, containing the ruins of a scheduled medieval castle and parkland, were compulsorily acquired by the Council for the sum of £42,250. There was a viable proposal to develop a small part of the site as a two storey house, in conformity with conservation area policies. Valuers had been unable to agree a comparable basis of valuation and the claimant had his claim of £150,000 rejected. As the claimant had also been late in making his claim he also lost his costs of the (CPO) inquiry.

A local planning authority can transfer land acquired by CPO to another owner, for example a preservation trust or English Heritage. However, acquisitions by English Heritage are extremely rare, even though the Secretary of State has now almost no role in the acquisition and management of property, in most cases having directed English Heritage to manage those monuments already in ministerial ownership.

Guardianship

2.167 Under section 12 of the AMAA the Secretary of State, a local authority (including a national park) or English Heritage may accept by deed the 'guardianship' of an ancient monument (as defined by section 61(12) of that Act).

This is where *inter alia* a freeholder or leaseholder for an unexpired term of not less than 45 years, a tenant for life under the Settled Land Act 1925, charity trustees, or the trustees of a qualifying trust for sale constitutes one of the aforementioned bodies guardian of a monument. If the person entering the deed is not in occupation the occupant must also be a party. The owner(s) retains his property interest in the monument subject to the provisions of the guardianship deed, for example fresh restrictive covenants. Sections 12(1) and 12(1A) of the AMAA provide that the Secretary of State must consult with English Heritage, and English Heritage must have the consent of the Secretary of State, before accepting monuments in guardianship.

2.168 A guardianship deed is registrable as a local land charge (section 12(7)), as were arrangements under the old system of compulsory guardianship.

An agreement made under section 12 will impliedly oblige the guardian to maintain a monument (section 13(1)). Consequently, a guardianship deed deems the guardian to have full control and management of the monument in question (section 13(2)). Some pre-1979 agreements may not grant full control). The guardian is empowered to do *'all such things as may be necessary for the maintenance of the monument and for the exercise by* [it] *of proper control and management with respect to the monument'* (section 13(3)). Maintenance includes *'fencing, repairing, and covering in ... and the doing of any other act or thing which may be required for the purpose of repairing ... or protecting the monument from decay or injury'* (section 13(7)).

2.169 The guardian of a monument (or a person authorised

on its behalf) may also enter the monument at any reasonable time for exercising its powers under section 13. Section 13(4) expressly authorises a guardian to examine, open up or excavate for the purpose of archaeological or historical examination any monument under its guardianship, or to remove the monument or any part of it to another place for the purpose of preserving it. The statutory powers of a guardian may be extended by agreement between the parties to the deed, and in most cases this will be desirable.

2.170 Guardianship may be renounced or terminated in respect of part of a monument by the guardian, but only with the agreement of the person(s) *'for the time being immediately affected by the operation of the guardianship deed'* (section 14(1), AMAA) and only if the guardian is satisfied that *'(a) satisfactory arrangements have been made for ensuring its preservation after termination of guardianship and (b) that it is no longer practicable to preserve ...'* the monument (whether because of cost or otherwise) (section 14(3)).

An occupier of the monument who is both (a) not bound by the guardianship deed and (b) whose property interest in the monument would have entitled him to put the monument in to guardianship, is able to terminate the guardianship at any time by serving notice on the guardian (section 14(1)).

Guardianship must continue until one of the above events occurs, or the guardian exercises its powers to acquire the monument.

Adjacent Land

2.171 Land not within the boundary of, but which is adjoining or in the vicinity of, an ancient monument may also be placed under guardianship or be acquired (either by agreement or compulsorily), provided that such additional land is *'reasonably required for the maintenance of or access to the monument, proper control or management of the monument, storage of equipment or the provision of facilities to the visiting public'* (section 15(1), AMAA). Adjacent land need not be acquired at the same time as the monument to which it relates (section 15(2)). The powers and obligations affecting adjacent land etc. are similar to those affecting the ancient monument itself. In particular, section 15(5) of the Act implies the duties and powers under section 14(1) and 14(2) (termination of guardianship) in respect of adjacent land.

Easements

2.172 Where a monument is in the ownership of the Secretary of State, English Heritage or a local authority, that owner may acquire any easement (including a newly created easement) necessary for the purpose of maintenance etc. as stipulated in section 15 of the AMAA (see above). Any easement necessary for the like use of adjacent land may also be acquired (sections 16(1), 16(1A) and 16(2) of the Act). This means that easements may be acquired for the use of adjacent land, for example as an interpretation centre, even though the easement does not lead or relate directly to the monument itself. Again, only the Secretary of State is empowered by the AMAA to acquire rights compulsorily.

In England, the Secretary of State must consult English Heritage before acquiring easements, but there is no similar requirement under section 16 for English Heritage to consult the Secretary of State.

2.173 Sections 16(4) to 16(8) of the Act provide broadly equivalent powers for the same bodies to acquire easements in relation to guardianship sites. The requirements and the purposes for which 'guardianship easements' may be acquired are as defined in 16(1), where the acquiring authority is the owner of the monument. Sections 16(5) and 16(6) contain protective provisions which ensure that any relevant easements are still legal easements, even though the guardian may not have any dominant tenement to which the easement could attach. The creation of a 'guardianship easement' should be protected by registration as a local land charge (section 16(8), AMAA).

Public Access

2.174 The public have a general right of access to monuments in public ownership or in guardianship unless, in the case of guardianship monuments, the deed of guardianship restricts the public's right of access (sections 19(1) and 19(9), AMAA). In fact, the right extends to monuments which were acquired under the previous legislative provision of 'compulsory guardianship', and may be a source of conflict between the disgruntled owner of a monument, the public and the guardian.

2.175 However, section 19(2) permits the owner or guardian

to severely restrict this right to particular times of the day, to particular days and to specified parts of the monument in question. The public may also be excluded from part or the whole of the monument for a specified period if the owner or guardian considers it *'necessary or expedient to do so in the interest of health and safety or for the maintenance or preservation of the monument'* (section 19(2)). Any restriction by a local authority must be achieved by way of regulations under section 19, and such regulations must be first approved by the Secretary of State (section 19(8)). If for the purpose of preserving a monument a local authority is to exclude the public completely, the prior consent of the Secretary of State must be obtained (section 19(2)(b)). English Heritage and the Secretary of State have residual power under section 19(2) to exclude etc. without making regulations.

2.176 Section 19 contains general powers to make regulations, in favour of the Secretary of State or a local authority but not English Heritage, although regulations made by the Secretary of State may extend to monuments in the ownership or guardianship of English Heritage (section 19(4A)). In England, when making regulations under this section which relate either to monuments in the ownership or guardianship of the Secretary of State or English Heritage, English Heritage must be consulted by the Secretary of State. Regulations may, amongst other things, regulate public access to monuments in public ownership or guardianship and may prohibit any act or thing which *'would tend to injure or disfigure the monument or its amenities or disturb the public in their enjoyment of it'* (section 19(4)(b)). Breach of regulations made under section 19 will constitute a distinct offence punishable on summary conviction by a fine of up to level 3 on the standard scale (section 19(7)).

2.177 Charges may be made for entry to monuments, both generally (section 19(5)) or by way of regulations (section 19 (4)).

There is a general power to refuse admission to '*any person* [whom the owner or guardian] *has reasonable cause to believe is likely to do anything which would tend to injure or disfigure the monument or its amenities or to disturb the public in their enjoyment of it*' (section 19(6)).

2.178 No right of public access is conferred by scheduling or designation of an AAI. The rights under section 19 arise by virtue of public ownership or guardianship, and not by virtue of statutory protection. Of course a monument may be statutorily protected as well as being in public ownership or guardianship.

Facilities for the Public

2.179 Owners or guardians have no general duty under the AMAA to provide facilities for the public at monuments to which section 19 applies. However, section 20 permits both the provision of such facilities and charging for their use. The facilities permitted by the section must be in connection with affording public access and it is doubtful that this could be construed to include the provision of gift shops and restaurants unless carried out on a restricted basis. Section 33 of the NHA 1983 does not authorise English Heritage to provide much more than this, though under section 35 of that Act English Heritage may participate in companies with far wider objects and powers (see appendix 1B of this work).

2.180 An owner or guardian will, of course, have duties at common law, under the Occupiers' Liability Acts 1957 and 1984 and under the health and safety legislation, to persons visiting its monuments. These duties may require the provision of facilities ensuring safety, for example covered walkways and non-slip surfaces, or resting places and sanitary facilities.

Grant Aid and Management Agreements

2.181 Acquisition and guardianship of ancient monuments, though usually effective in securing their preservation, is expensive and rarely resorted to by the bodies concerned. Indeed, English Heritage frequently states that no new guardianship sites will be created, and acknowledges that acquisition is a step of very last resort. English Heritage, which manages such sites on behalf of the Secretary of State, increasingly views the preservation of monuments outside the top category of visitor attractions as more efficiently secured by a flexible package of management measures. The measures available are of three main types: grants; management agreements and payments; and advice and assistance.

Grants

2.182 Grants can be made by English Heritage (in Wales by

the appropriate committee of the Welsh Assembly, acting through Cadw) under section 24(2) of the AMAA to foster the *'preservation, maintenance or management'* of an ancient monument or to salvage any part of an ancient monument by removal. Alternatively, English Heritage or the Committee, as appropriate, may undertake the work themselves. In either case, grant can only be paid or works undertaken at the request of the 'owner' (defined at section 61(1) of the Act). In England, it is English Heritage which decides whether the monument, if not scheduled, is of public interest (section 24(3B)). Where a local authority provides facilities under section 20 of the AMAA (access arrangements) at ancient monuments, section 24(3) permits grant to be made for the provision of such facilities.

Local authorities (including national parks) are also empowered to grant aid or undertake the preservation, maintenance or management of ancient monuments in, or in the vicinity of, their area (section 24(4)).

Section 24(1) provides for English Heritage and, outside England, the Committee to defray or contribute towards the costs of any person in acquiring an ancient monument, but for the reasons mentioned above this power is rarely used.

2.183 Grant is usually only available where an owner is experiencing or will experience difficulty in preserving an ancient monument, to ensure that preservation takes place. Retrospective applications for works already carried out are not viewed favourably. Scheduled monument consent procedures are the main encouragement to the preservation of ancient monuments when works of repair (or alteration) are authorised for development purposes, but where buildings or structures are of little economic value grant assistance is seen by English Heritage as a very useful stimulus. Grants may be given for works which do not require scheduled monument consent. The Area Inspector of Ancient Monuments is usually the person who will decide whether or not the works in question merit grant aid. If the application is approved, a private owner can expect to receive a reimbursement of about 50% of eligible costs, sometimes a little more if costs are especially high. A local authority may expect only about 25% of its eligible costs to be reimbursed. Value added tax will not be covered by the grant if this is recoverable by the applicant. However, if the works fall within the category of approved alterations (not repairs) to a schedule monument or a listed building, in charitable, ecclesiastical or domestic use no value added tax will be payable (Value Added Tax Act 1994, schedule 8, group 6).

2.184 An offer of grant must normally be accepted within three months and the works to which the grant relates commenced within the period of 12 months after the making of the offer. Any work funded from repair grant will be closely reviewed by English Heritage/Cadw and it is usually a condition of payment that the works are completed to an acceptable standard. Other, non-routine, conditions may be attached to a grant, for example conditions as to the future maintenance, though if the conditions are onerous it is preferable to have the owner enter a separate management agreement under section 17 of the AMAA (see below).

2.185 Works executed in accordance with a written agreement for grant received from the Secretary of State or

English Heritage (but not from a local authority) under section 24 of the AMAA are now exempt from the requirement to obtain a specific scheduled monument consent (Class 9, The Ancient Monuments (Class Consents) Order 1994; see paragraph 2.30 above). Note that this general consent does not extend to works executed in accordance with an agreement for grant paid under section 45 (which may have a very different purpose).

2.186 It is always open to English Heritage/Cadw to carry out the works itself (if the owner consents) or to *advise and superintend* any works on an ancient monument (section 25(2), AMAA). (If recording or survey is required because of grant assisted works, or works carried out pursuant to a scheduled monument consent, the cost will usually be met, if at all, by English Heritage/Cadw under their section 45 powers (see paragraphs 2.196-2.198 below). Sections 33 and 34 of the NHA give English Heritage more general authority in this respect (see chapter one).)

Management Agreements and Payments
(Section 17, AMAA is reproduced at appendix 2A of this work)

2.187 Where repair grant is inappropriate, for example when it is unlikely to provide a solution to a seasonal or recurrent problem, agreements under section 17 of the AMAA are increasingly employed, either in tandem with grant assistance or subject to the additional financial provisions of that section. Such agreements are facilitated by the comprehensive powers to enter into 'management agreements' given to the authorised bodies (English

Heritage, the Secretary of State (including Cadw), and local authorities) under section 17(4). National park authorities can also now enter section 17 agreements in their national park areas, under schedule 9 of the Environment Act 1995.

2.188 Just about all activities which foster the preservation of monuments can be encouraged in this way, while those which are detrimental to preservation or detract from a monument's character can be limited or curtailed. Section 17(4) provides that a management agreement may provide for all or any of the following matters in respect of *ancient monuments*:

(a)   *the maintenance and preservation of the monument and its amenities;*

(b)   *the carrying out of any such work, or doing of any such other thing, in relation to the monument or land as may be specified in the agreement;*

(c)   *public access to the monument or land and the provision of facilities and information or other services for the use of the public in that connection;*

(d)   *restricting the use of the monument or land;*

(e)   *prohibiting in relation to the monument or land the doing of any such thing as may be specified in the agreement; and*

(f)   *the making by the Secretary of State or [English Heritage] or the local authority (as the case may be) of payments in such manner, of such amounts and on such terms as may be so specified (and whether for or towards the cost of any work provided for under the agreement or in consideration of any restriction, prohibition or obligation accepted by any other party thereto);*

and may contain such incidental and consequential provisions as appear to the Secretary of State or [English Heritage] or the local authority (as the case may be) to be necessary or expedient.

2.189 It is fairly common for agreements between English Heritage and an owner to result in the cessation of particular land uses in return for an agreed level of payment to the owner (section 17(4)(f)), sometimes taken together with payments under agricultural set-aside, provided that there is no double subsidy. Or an owner might agree to undertake land management which will directly benefit a monument, such as fencing to prevent animal damage or the practising of minimal cultivation techniques. The system supersedes 'acknowledgement payments' made under the Field Monuments Act 1972 and agreements under section 5 of the Ancient Monuments Act 1931.

2.190 Agreements under section 17 may be registered as local land charges if they contain prohibitions, restrictions or positive obligations which 'run with the land' (i.e. expressed to be binding on successors in title to that land). Section 17(5) provides that agreements may contain such provisions. Section 1(1) of the Local Land Charges Act 1975 provides that such restrictions or obligations are registrable. Such provisions may also be registered at H.M. Land Registry (usually in the charges register of the title in question) or, in unregistered land, as land charges. Section 17 agreements need not be of this nature, however; they may be of limited duration, or personal to the occupier who is party to the agreement. Indeed, where periodical payments are made pursuant to an agreement they are usually covenanted to be made for a period of about three years, though longer terms will be encountered where a lump sum is paid, either under section 17 or 24, at the commencement of a management period.

2.191 A restriction etc. entered under section 17 will oust the jurisdiction of the Lands Tribunal, under section 84 of the Law of Property Act 1925, to discharge the restriction (section 17(7)).

2.192 An applicant is not generally relieved of any duty to obtain scheduled monument consent by virtue of his entry into a section 17 agreement (section 17(8)). However, works executed in accordance with such an agreement with the Secretary of State or English Heritage (but not a local authority) are now exempt from the requirement to obtain a specific scheduled monument consent (Class 8, The Ancient Monuments (Class Consents) Order 1994; see paragraph 2.30 above).

2.193 If an owner remains reluctant to act in concert with English Heritage or Cadw, even where repair or management grant is promised, an acquisition grant can be authorised to assist the purchase of the monument by a new, private sector, owner (this was a new power introduced by the AMAA). Compulsory powers of acquisition and disposal, to a third party, may also be useful to the Secretary of State in such a situation. Payments will be based on the value of the monument as an estate with limited beneficial use (see below).

Advice and Assistance

2.194 The Secretary of State has wide powers under section 25 of the AMAA to '*give advice with reference to the treatment of any ancient monument*' or to '*superintend any work in connection with any ancient monument*'. Where the ancient monument in question is also a scheduled monument he (or in England, English Heritage) is obliged to 'superintend' if he (or it) believes this is advisable. Both the Secretary of State and English Heritage are empowered by section 25(3) to charge for advice and superintendence given under section 25, this power not being restricted to instances where the owner of the monument has requested advice.

Uninvited superintendence on site, where works are not subject to conditions in a scheduled monument consent, clearly requires rights of entry, for which see paragraphs 2.15-2.22 above.

2.195 English Heritage also has authority to give advice to any person in relation to historic buildings and ancient monuments (as therein defined) under section 33(2)(b) of the NHA 1983.

2.196 Although much advice and superintendence is provided during the course of routine work, for example the replacement of fencing or the re-grouting of masonry, a significant amount also includes an element of archaeological 'investigation' (defined by section 61(4) of the AMAA to include excavation, obtaining and recording information, and examining, recording and processing finds). For the Secretary of State's or English Heritage's purposes, however, the funding of such work is considered a distinct head of expenditure, usually falling within section 45 of the AMAA. A grant towards the costs of improvement works (including archaeological supervision) will be separate from a grant for prior archaeological investigation. The grants may in any event be paid to different persons, for example the owner and the archaeological contractor.

2.197 Section 45 funding has a high profile in the archaeological community because it is traditionally the main source of finance for site investigation. This is gradually changing following the application of new development plan policies and PPG 16 by local planning authorities (see chapter six), but not completely and not without lamentation (see, for example, Biddle (1994)).

2.198 Grants under section 45 have recently totalled about £7 million per annum in England (but are reducing, certainly as far as excavation funding is concerned). Local authorities, including national parks, are authorised to make payments under section 45 but rarely do so.

It is usual for section 45 expenditure to be incurred when scheduled monument consent has also been granted. The funded works will therefore be controlled by conditions both in the consent and in the notice of award of grant. Substantial funding under section 45 has, however, also gone to sites which are not scheduled (especially in urban areas) – it is not a requirement under section 45 that a site should be an ancient monument as defined by section 61 (12) of the AMAA – and in such instances the conditions attached to payments of grant take on increased importance. Conditions might include: a right for English Heritage/ Cadw to inspect archaeological work at any time; the provision of interim reports and management accounts before successive stages of payment are made; the acceptance by the grant receiving organisation of all liability with regard to employment protection, health and safety, and indemnities in favour of landowners and occupiers; and deposit of the material and written archives in a suitable museum (suitable according to English Heritage/Cadw published criteria) within a specified period. Breach of grant conditions will, at most, give rise to civil liability, for example repayment of grant, and not criminal liability under section 2 of the AMAA. For further discussion of the funding of archaeological investigation see paragraphs 2.73-2.75 and chapter six.

2.199 Grants are made for particular projects. Payments under section 45 are said by English Heritage to be made according to *'criteria ...'* the same as those *'... which define a monument as being of national importance for purposes of scheduling'* (HC 1987, 203). Central government is anxious to avoid the provision of block grants to organisations as these are believed to fund establishment costs at the expense of field and post-excavation work.

Compensation

2.200 A variety of circumstances may give rise to compensation under the AMAA. The main provisions are found in section 7 (refusal of or grant of scheduled monument consent subject to conditions), section 9 (revocation or modification of scheduled monument consent) and sections 10, 15 and 16 (compulsory acquisition of land or easements for ancient monuments purposes). Section 46 of the AMAA also provides for compensation when land or chattels are damaged by the exercise of a right of entry under section 6, 6A, 26, 38, 39, 40 or 43 of the Act.

Refusal or grant of Scheduled Monument Consent subject to Conditions

2.201 Where a person interested in land incurs expenditure or any loss or damage ('loss etc.') in consequence of the refusal of or granting of scheduled monument consent subject to conditions, compensation may be payable under section 7 of the AMAA. Section 7(2) makes express provision for compensation in certain cases, and subsequent subsections of the section qualify the entitlement in such cases. These qualifications need to be read in conjunction with the usual rules under section 5 of the Land Compensation Act 1961 (applied to the assessment of depreciation in land under the AMAA by section 27, AMAA).

2.202 Where a specific grant of planning permission exists before a monument is scheduled, compensation will lie for loss etc. which is a *consequence* of an inability to undertake works which are *reasonably necessary* for carrying out the authorised development provided that the permission is still valid at the time when the application for scheduled monument consent is made (not the date of the decision on the application) (section 7(2)(a), AMAA). The scope of section 7(2)(a) is qualified by section 7(3) which provides that compensation under section 7(2)(a) is limited to loss etc. sustained by the fact that in consequence of the Secretary of State's decision the works in question were not authorised under section 2(1) of the AMAA. Compensation will not be available for matters preparatory to the application, the production of plans for example, nor will compensation be available just because scheduled monument consent is required.

2.203 Where works do not constitute 'development' or are development authorised by the GPDO (see chapter six) compensation may be payable even where the rights arise after scheduling of the monument (section 7(2)(b)). However, section 7(4) contains the important proviso that unless the works in question are solely operations involved in or incidental to agricultural or forestry use (including afforestation) [which would not require a specific grant of planning permission] compensation will not be available arising from the loss etc. flowing from any works which *'would or might result in the total or partial demolition or destruction of the monument'*. If claiming under section 7(2)(b) special attention should also be paid to section 7(6)(b); the latter requires regard to be had to any undertaking given by the Secretary of State to grant scheduled monument consent for works other than works to which the application in question relates.

2.204 Other compensation entitlements under section 7 are limited. Section 7(2)(c) provides for compensation where works *'which are reasonably necessary for the continuation of any use of the monument for any purpose for which it was in use immediately before the date of the application for scheduled monument consent'* fail to receive authorisation. By a proviso to that subsection uses which would 'contravene legal restrictions' for the time being applying to the monument are to be disregarded. This probably means that any breach of the civil as well as of the criminal law is to be disregarded, although the proviso could have been more explicit. The main 'restriction' which will usually constrain compensation claims is the absence of legal authority for the use under planning law (normally, but not always, by a grant of planning permission for that use).

2.205 It seems fairly certain, given the position of this subsection within the section as a whole, that section 7(2)(c) is intended to refer to 'use' as distinct from 'development'. But problems of interpretation arise because these terms are not mutually exclusive in planning law (in fact a material change of use is 'development' under section 55(1) TCPA 1990). Thus, if before the relevant scheduled monument consent is given, a planning permission is obtained for a material change of use which affects a scheduled monument, that use will fall within section 7(2)(c) and necessary works may be the subject of compensation. The local planning authority, working together with English Heritage/Cadw should be alert to the risks of granting such planning permission, and may refuse permission in appropriate cases. Article 10 of the GD(P)O provides for consultation between local planning authorities and English Heritage or the Secretary of State (as appropriate) on planning applications likely to affect the site of a scheduled monument.

2.206 Scheduling itself does not give rise to compensation under the AMAA. The relevant time for assessing compensation is the time when the application for scheduled monument consent was refused or granted subject to conditions (*Currie's Executors v. Secretary of State for Scotland* [1992] S.L.T. 69 (Lands Tribunal) (not the time when the application was made, though this date is relevant in determining whether compensation will be available under sections 7(2)(a) and (c)).

Compensation must relate to loss etc. suffered as a consequence of the Secretary of State's decision. Not all such loss will relate to depreciation of the land upon which the monument is situated; disturbance and severance, for example, may be claimed. As referred to above, section 27 of the AMAA imports the rules found in section 5 of the Land Compensation Act 1961, which amongst other things provides that land should be assessed as if sold in the open market by a willing seller. Section 27 applies section 5 with 'necessary modifications'. This is far from explicit, and an exposition of the subtleties of land compensation is beyond the scope of this work. However, of the six rules in section 5 of the 1961 Act those found in subsections 5(4) and 5(5) are likely to be more important in scheduled monument matters than is usual in conventional land compensation cases. Section 5(4) expressly applies the general valuation assumption that any increase in the value of land attributable to a use which '*could be restrained by any court, or is contrary to law, or is detrimental to health of the occupants ... or to public health*' shall not be taken into account (although restrictions which are no longer enforceable will be ignored: *Hughes and Hughes v. Doncaster Borough Council* (1990) 61 P. & C. R. 355 HL). Under section 5(5), if the land in question is of a type for which there is no 'general demand or market', a claim may be made on the basis that 'reinstatement' of the use (i.e. continuation of the use) in some other place is *bona fide* intended and compensation assessed accordingly.

2.207 Disputes over compensation are to be settled by the Lands Tribunal (section 47, AMAA). Interest on unpaid compensation is to be assessed according to the prescribed rates for the time being in force. Compensation is paid, in England, by English Heritage, not the Secretary of State. Payments should be registered as a local land charge as this is a pre-condition of the recovery by the Secretary of State of compensation under section 8 of the AMAA (as a condition of the grant of a scheduled monument consent which authorises previously unauthorised works).

For the prescribed method of claim see paragraph 2.214, below.

Revocation or Modification of Scheduled Monument Consent

2.208 Where works affecting a scheduled monument cease to be authorised under part I of the AMAA (sections 2 and 3) compensation may be payable under section 9, to a person interested in the land in question, for the loss etc. which is a consequence of the revocation or modification. There are three cases where section 9 will apply:

(a)   on revocation or modification of a consent granted under section 3 (class consents, see paragraph 2.30 above) (section 9(2)(a)), save that compensation is only payable if a specific application for scheduled monument consent is refused or granted subject to conditions other than those which previously applied under the class consent (section 9(3));

(b)   where a specific grant of scheduled monument consent is revoked or modified by direction of the Secretary of State under section 4 of the AMAA (section 9(2)(b)); or

(c)   where a notice is served under paragraph 5, part II, of schedule 1 to the AMAA preventing the continuance of authorised works (see paragraph 2.77; this will be on a date earlier than the making of a direction by the Secretary of State in such a matter).

In the latter two cases compensation specifically extends to loss etc. incurred in the making of plans and other matters preparatory to the application for the scheduled monument consent which is to be revoked or modified (section 9(4)). But compensation in these cases does not extend to any works undertaken before the granting of scheduled monument consent or in respect of any other loss etc. (except loss related to the depreciation of an interest in land) which arises out of anything done or omitted to be done before the grant of the scheduled monument consent in question (section 9(5)).

2.209 Compensation under this section is again payable by English Heritage/Cadw on behalf of the Secretary of State. Procedural matters are as discussed in relation to section 7.

Compulsory Acquisition of Land and Easements

2.210 Compensation on the compulsory acquisition of land or easements under the AMAA is determined in accordance with section 5 of the Land Compensation Act 1961 (see above), subject, in the case of land acquisition, to the important limitation appearing in section 10(4) of the AMAA. This limitation is that if the monument is scheduled at the time of the compulsory purchase order which authorises its acquisition (but not otherwise) compensation will be assessed on the assumption that scheduled monument consent would not be granted for any works which *'would or might result in the demolition, destruction or removal of the monument or any part of it'*. Planning permission, therefore, will usually be of negligible value if the implementation of such permission would offend against section 10(4). There is no provision, however, permitting a direction for minimum compensation as under section 50 of the P(LBCA)A, and, where buildings are both listed and scheduled, section 61 of the P(LBCA)A precludes compulsory purchase under section 47 of that Act.

2.211 Compensation under sections 10, 15 and 16 will be paid by the acquiring authority (the Secretary of State); the applications procedures prescribed under section 47 of the AMAA do not apply. Application should be made according to the method and timetable appropriate to the CPO.

Compensation under section 46

2.212 Section 46 of the AMAA provides for the payment of compensation in respect of damage caused to land or any chattels on land as a result of the exercise of powers to enter or do anything on land under the following sections of the Act:

Sections 6 and 6A: entry on land to inspect a scheduled

monument;

Section 26: entry on land with a view to recording matters of archaeological or historical interest (including excavation);

Section 38: entry on land by an Investigating Authority in an AAI for the purposes of this section (including excavation);

Section 39: as above but in respect of rights arising when served with notice (not an 'operations notice') by an authority possessing powers of compulsory acquisition;

Section 40: where an operations notice is served in an AAI, entry on land to which the notice relates by persons authorised by the Secretary of State or RCHM(e); and

Section 43: entry on land for purposes of survey or valuation.

2.213 Compensation under section 46 must be met by the person exercising the rights, or who authorised the exercising of the rights. This will usually be English Heritage or Cadw. Section 46(2) provides that compensation arising from the exercise by an Investigating Authority of its powers in an AAI will be met, in England, by English Heritage and in other cases by the Secretary of State.

Claims are to be made on the forms prescribed under section 47.

Prescribed Forms (see appendix 2D of this work)

2.214 The Ancient Monuments (Claims for Compensation) (England) Regulations 1991 (S.I. 1991, No.2512) prescribe the form of application for compensation under sections 7, 9 and 46 of the AMAA. Claims under sections 7 and 9 of the AMAA are to be sent by recorded delivery post to English Heritage, in London, within six months after the decision, direction or notice which gave rise to the claim. The Secretary of State may at his discretion extend this period. Claims under section 46 must be sent to the relevant authority in that case.

The Ancient Monuments (Claims for Compensation) (Wales) Regulations 1991 (S.I. 1991, No.2647) contain similar provisions for Wales, except that applications under section 7 and 9, and applications for extension time, should be addressed to Cadw.

CHAPTER THREE

BURIALS AND PORTABLE ANTIQUITIES

Portable antiquities will frequently lie undiscovered within an ancient monument, an area of archaeological importance or a listed building and benefit, indirectly, from statutory protection; but this is a very different proposition from legal protection of objects in their own right. Unlike land and things annexed to land, portable antiquities are subject to very few heritage provisions.

3.01 There is no general, archaeological restriction on what an owner may do with portable antiquities. Except for the three instances mentioned below, objects of historic or archaeological interest which are not annexed to land or buildings will usually enjoy no more legal protection than other species of chattel. Unless falling within the definition of treasure, for example, there is no general obligation to report the discovery of a portable antiquity, or to submit it for analysis or otherwise deal with such a find in a particular way. As with all chattels, the law of trespass and the offences of theft or criminal damage may be relevant, but these cannot provide the degree of protection afforded sites and buildings under the statutory provisions. Even on a scheduled monument it is not a specific offence in heritage law to remove portable antiquities (unless found by metal detector); though an offence will be committed if unauthorised works etc. are carried out on a scheduled monument in contravention of section 2 of the AMAA, or damage is caused to the monument in contravention of section 28 of that Act. This apparent anomaly reflects the position at English law that 'objects' which are within or annexed to land or a building form part of that land or building and so do not require protection in their own right. However, objects are sometimes easily 'severed from the realty' (see *Fletcher*, paragraph 3.59 below) and the potential profits of effecting such severance are sometimes substantial.

3.02 The exceptions to the generalisation in paragraph 3.01 are found in the incidental protection which may sometimes arise under the law of burial, the law of treasure and the law relating to the export of works of art and antiquities. These are now considered in turn, under the headings (1) Human Remains and Burial Grounds, (2) Treasure and (3) Export of Antiquities.

Human Remains and Burial Grounds

3.03 Interments are frequently encountered during excavations, especially in urban areas. Development and conservation schemes may also affect churchyards or other burial grounds. Both of these eventualities are regulated, primarily by statute but with a historic basis in common law.

Interments Generally

3.04 Section 25 of the Burial Act 1857 provides that (*'except in the cases where a body is removed from one consecrated place of burial to another by faculty granted by the ordinary for that purpose, it shall not be lawful to remove any body, or the remains of any body, which may have been interred in any place of burial, without a licence under the hand of one of Her Majesty's Principal Secretaries of State, and with such precautions as such Secretary of State may prescribe as the condition of such licence ...'*. Failure to obtain such a licence where one is needed, or failure to abide by the conditions of such a licence, is an offence for which the person undertaking the removal is personally liable. The offence is a summary one only. However, an offence is committed on each occasion that a body, or its remains, are removed. The offence is also one of strict liability. For example, following old common law rules, it will be no defence to plead that the body was removed for altruistic purposes, whether these purposes be the provision of a finer resting place or the pursuit of archaeological research. (It was an offence at common law to disinter a dead body without lawful authority and common law rules may still be considered in proceedings under statute.)

3.05 Section 25 is very wide. 'Any place of burial' introduces a definition of a body's resting place which is not restricted to churchyards or even to burial grounds in general, but extends to all sites containing human remains, interred by whatever agencies and for whatever purpose.

3.06 Liability under section 25 is avoided not by any sophistry about what constitutes a burial, a body or an interment, but by pursuing the exceptions provided by prescribed statutory or ecclesiastical procedures. Section 25 itself provides two such exceptions.

3.07 The first arises in relation to burial grounds of the Church of England, where a faculty has been obtained from the ordinary (the bishop of the diocese in question). The Home Secretary considers a faculty to be sufficient authority for the removal of remains from one churchyard to another, not just for removal within the same churchyard. However, this exception requires remains to be moved from one area of *consecrated* ground to another area of *consecrated* ground, and for the purposes of the Act *consecrated* means consecrated by the Church of England. Where the proposal is to reinter elsewhere, and the alternative procedures discussed below, in relation to compulsory acquisition or acquisition under the TCPA 1990, do not apply, the Church is bound by the Act like any other person or authority. The same applies if remains are to be kept in store for a considerable period before reinterment: a faculty will not be sufficient authority and a Home Office licence issued under section 25 may also be required. As a matter of ecclesiastical law, in obtaining a faculty for the removal of remains there is *'a burden on the petitioner ... to show that the presumed intention of those who committed the body or ashes to a last resting place is to be disregarded'* (*Re Atkins* [1989] 1 All E.R. 14 Cst Ct). For the method of petition see the Faculty Jurisdiction Rules 1992 (S.I. 1992, No.2882). Application is usually made to the appropriate diocesan registry.

3.08 The second exception arises where the Home Secretary has granted his licence for the removal of remains (see below).

Home Office Licences (Section 25 of the Burial Act 1857)

3.09 A licence under the Act is obtained from the Home

Office. For 'archaeological applications', i.e. applications to remove remains which are not less than 100 years old, the following details should be provided:

1.   the applicant's own name, address and (if applicable) telephone number;
2.   the name, address and telephone number of the person supervising or carrying out the excavations (if different);
3.   site location, including map reference and A4 location map;
4.   estimated number of bodies;
5.   the suspected period range of the burials, e.g. 'prehistoric' or '500 -1,000 AD';
6.   whether or not the remains are in Church of England consecrated ground;
7.   the estimated duration of the exhumation activity;
8.   where it is intended to conduct a temporary examination of the remains before reinterment or cremation, the length of the examination and the name, address and telephone number of the person responsible for the examination;
9.   the intended means of disposal of the remains, together with the full address of the place where the remains are to be reinterred, cremated or kept in storage; and
10.   a statement that all of the remains discovered on the site in question will be removed.

3.10 If the answer to any of these requirements or questions is not known, the Home Office recommends that the applicant says so. The applicant should also inform the

Home Office of the district council in whose area the burial ground is located, and whether redevelopment of the site is intended, as advice may then be available on whether the restrictions in the Disused Burial Grounds Act 1884 apply (see paragraph 3.20, below).

3.11 The fee for a licence was set at £10, by the Human Remains Removal Licence (Prescribed Fees) Order 1982 (S.I. 1982, No.364). At the time of writing, the Home Office is no longer requiring a fee to be paid. However, the brief list of particulars mentioned above should make it clear that removal of human remains is, if carried out properly, both labour intensive and expensive.

3.12 The Home Office recommended application form is reproduced as form 46 in EFP, vol.6 *Burial and Cremation*. See also Garratt-Frost *et. al.*, appendix 2. However, in exclusively archaeological cases, a form of application which covers all of the matters detailed in paragraph 3.9 above will be acceptable.

3.13 Where archaeological remains are to be dealt with at the same time as remains of more recent date additional procedures and safeguards apply. In such cases the Home Office approved forms should always be used, as they deal with matters such as the consent of relatives of the deceased and the comments of the relevant burial authority. A notice should be published which alerts relatives and personal representatives of the deceased that an application for a section 25 licence is intended. This notice should be circulated in local newspapers over a length of time sufficient to satisfy the Home Office that all reasonable enquiries have been made (for a form of notice see Garratt-Frost *et. al.*, 8). There is no need to follow the section 25 procedure, of course, if removal of burials is to take place pursuant to some other statutory procedure which dis-applies the 1857 Act (see paragraph 3.19 below; the majority of schemes with a non-archaeological element will fall into one of these categories).

3.14 Sometimes human remains will be encountered accidentally during the course of excavation. Removal of the remains will constitute an offence under section 25 unless an appropriate authorisation is obtained. The simplest solution is to apply to the Home Office, by telephone, for an 'emergency' licence. Where the remains have not been removed since discovery the Home Office accepts such applications for authority to remove (or continue the disturbance of) human remains which have been disturbed by accident. No charge is made for the issue of the licence. The conditions attached to the licence may, however, be as detailed and rigorous as those attached to a licence granted before works commence. The licence can be issued on the day of application but where several bodies are anticipated work on site must usually be suspended until an assessment of the extent of burial is obtained.

3.15 Licences issued by the Home Office under section 25 will specify the nature and the location of the remains to be removed. These details will be followed by a list of 'precautions', typically that *'the removal shall be effected with due care and attention to decency'*, and that *'the remains shall not be left to public view, shall be placed in suitable containers and shall be conveyed to a named place of burial or cremation'.*

Precautions relating to the analysis of remains may be included, in particular a date when such analysis must cease (in addition to the date by which the remains must be reinterred).

3.16 The licence, as all licences, is merely a permission to do what would otherwise be unlawful. It does not confer any rights where no rights previously existed, for example a right of entry to land, or a right to build on or re-develop burial land without complying with statutory and common law restrictions. These are separate matters to be arranged by the applicant or his agent.

3.17 The wording of the 1857 Act suggests that the precautions imposed on the grant of a licence will be conditions precedent to the permission. Consequently, breach of one or more precautions may render the entire licence void and the licensee liable as if a licence had never been obtained.

3.18 Statutory provisions which are most likely to apply when building on or otherwise developing a disused burial ground include the P(LBCA)A (conservation area consent); TCPA (planning permission), the Disused Burial Grounds Act 1884 (see below), though scheduled monument consent and listed building consent may be relevant.

3.19 Other authority, disapplying the prohibition in section 25, is found in the Disused Burial Grounds (Amendment) Act 1981, various special development powers contained in, for example, the TCPA 1990 (development of land acquired for planning purposes), section 20 of the New Towns Act

1981 and section 77 of the Housing Act 1988. Each of these Acts contains extensive provisions which enable building to take place on burial grounds following the removal of human remains in accordance with statutory procedures. The Church of England may also remove human remains from and build on a churchyard in pursuance of a Pastoral Scheme; a faculty will not then be required (sections 30 and 65(8) of the Pastoral Measure 1983).

Building on Disused Burial Grounds: the General Position

3.20 Under section 3 of the Disused Burial Grounds Act 1884 it is unlawful for any person to erect a building on a disused burial ground except for the purpose of enlarging a church, chapel, meeting house or other place of worship. The definition of a 'disused burial ground' for the purposes of the Act is provided by the Open Spaces Act 1887 and section 20 of the Open Spaces Act 1906. This includes *'any ground whether consecrated or not which has been set apart for and which is no longer used for interment'* (whether or not the ground has been wholly or partly closed for burial purposes under statute or Orders in Council). Consequently, unless the provisions of the 1884 Act have been dis-applied (under a local statute for example), statutory authority will be needed if a disused burial ground is to be built upon other than for purposes of worship.

3.21 Authority is found in the procedures contained in the statutes referred to at paragraph 3.19 above, of which the Disused Burial Grounds (Amendment) Act 1981 and the TCPA 1990 are discussed in more detail below. As well as circumventing the restrictions contained in the Disused Burial Grounds Act 1884, removal of remains carried out either in accordance with the provisions of the schedule to the 1981 Act (section 2(7), 1981 Act), or in accordance with the procedures laid down in regulations made by the Secretary of State and applicable to removal under the TCPA (see below, paragraphs 3.37-3.38), will mean that a licence under section 25 of the Burial Act 1857 is not required. As Garratt-Frost notes, however, burials in or between the walls of a church, for example in a crypt, will not be burials 'within a burial ground', and so any statutory provision which authorises the removal of remains from a 'disused burial ground' will not, unless there is an express saving, obviate the need for a section 25 licence (or faculty) for the removal of such burials (Garratt-Frost *et. al.*, 2).

3.22 Provisions contained in the New Towns Act 1981 and the Housing Act 1988 are similar to those applicable under the TCPA.

3.23 A pastoral scheme pursuant to the Pastoral Measure 1983 may authorise the building on (or closure of) churchyards and burial grounds of the Church of England. The Pastoral Measure provides a self-contained code for Church of England purposes, as long as the remains in question are to be removed to another Church of England burial ground. Procedures under the Pastoral Measure are, again, similar to those under the Disused Burial Grounds (Amendment) Act 1981 (which does not apply to Church of England land, though the TCPA provisions may apply to Church of England consecrated ground).

3.24 In contrast to the 1981 Act, however, the Pastoral Measure is silent as to section 25 of the Burial Act 1857.

Although a pastoral scheme which applies section 30 of the Pastoral Measure may authorise the removal of human remains (section 65 and schedule 6, Pastoral Measure 1983), a pastoral scheme cannot authorise removal other than to Church of England consecrated ground. When removal is to other ground a section 25 licence is required (indeed, on a strict reading of the Pastoral Measure a section 25 licence will be required whenever a faculty is not obtained, but this cannot have been the intention, as Church of England authority other than a faculty may on occasion authorise the removal of burials).

The Disused Burial Grounds (Amendment) Act 1981
The Pastoral Measure 1983

3.25 These are the instruments of most general application when dealing with the removal of human remains from burial grounds; the Pastoral Measure in relation to Church of England land and the 1981 Act in relation to other land. The enactments contain similar provisions and, for both, the definition of 'burial ground' is important. The 1981 Act, as outlined above, imports the definition of burial ground from the Open Spaces Act 1906. Section 30(6) of the Pastoral Measure defines a burial ground as *'any land set apart and consecrated for the purpose of burial whether or not burials have taken place therein'*. In either case, whether a burial ground is disused is a question of fact: the ground need not have received burials at any time (*Re Ponsford and Newport District School Board* [1894] 1 Ch 454 CA), but there must be an element or period of disuse of the ground (*Till v. Market Weighton Parish Council* [1961] 3 All E.R. 1022).

3.26 Burials in a chapel or church do not fall within either of these definitions. The saving in section 2(7) of the 1981 Act will not apply in such circumstances (a section 25 licence will usually be required); though in Church of England cases a faculty will not be required where such burials are the subject of a redundancy or pastoral scheme.

3.27 The main provisions of the 1981 Act are found in sections 1 and 2 and the schedule to the Act. They are intended to 'enable building to take place on certain disused burial grounds with appropriate safeguards', indeed to extend to other churches and religious bodies, including secular owners of former church property – who, under section 3 of the Act, hold their interest subject to the same obligations, restrictions and duties as the former church – procedures similar to those which, in 1981, already applied under the faculty jurisdiction.

3.28 Section 1 excludes the operation of section 3 of the Disused Burial Grounds Act 1884 in cases where no burial has ever taken place or where, following public notification in accordance with section 1(2), the personal representatives or relatives of any deceased person interred within the last 50 years have not objected to the proposal (or if they have objected, that they have withdrawn the objection). To fall within section 1, removal of remains must also be effected in accordance with section 2 and the schedule to the Act. The section 1(2) procedure therefore is central. Where human remains *may* have been buried in a burial ground, the section requires that the church or its successors to the land must place a notice (a) in a conspicuous place on or near the burial ground, and (b) for two successive weeks in a newspaper circulating in the area in which the burial ground is situated. The notice must invite objections to the proposal within a period which is not less than six weeks after the first publication of the notices. The notice procedure is considered in more detail below.

3.29 At the time of publication it is advisable to contact the Home Office to ascertain whether the Secretary of State is minded to make any 'directions', under powers contained in the schedule to the Act, relating to the removal of the remains (but not tombstones or memorials). The Act does not require such application but gives to the Secretary of State a power to make directions at any time. It is prudent, therefore, to ascertain any concerns of the Secretary of State's at the outset.

3.30 On application by the church or its successors in title the Secretary of State may by Order, under section 2(2), dispense with the requirements of section 2(1) and the schedule, if it appears to him that building on the burial ground in question will not involve the disturbance of human remains (as distinct from no remains ever having been there). Such an Order is registrable as a local land charge but, unlike comparable Orders under the TCPA, may not affect Church of England land. An Order under this section may be subject to conditions and may be amended or revoked (section 2(3)). Application for such an Order should include (1) a location plan of A4 size which shows the development which will not disturb human remains, (2) details of any parts of the development which will involve disturbance of human remains and (3) the name of the district council in whose area the remains are interred. A dispensation order, if granted, is registrable as a local land charge, as successors in title should be bound by its conditions.

Notices under the Disused Burial Grounds (Amendment) Act 1981

3.31 Human remains and tombstones are usually removed in accordance with section 2 and the schedule to the Act, which contain notice requirements additional to those in section 1 (notice of building, see above). Paragraph 1 of the schedule to the 1981 Act provides the notice procedure which must be followed before removing any human remains, undertaking work which will render a grave inaccessible, or before removing tombstones, monuments or 'memorials'. The church or its successors in title ('the applicant') are required to:

1. publish a notice of its intention to carry out the proposed works, in a newspaper circulating in the locality, at least once in two successive weeks;
2. display in a conspicuous place on site a similar notice, again detailing the proposed works;
3. serve a copy of the notice on the Commonwealth War Graves Commission (CWGC); and
4. where remains have been interred within twenty-five years of the date of the notice, serve a copy on the personal representatives or relatives of the deceased (in so far as their names are ascertainable with reasonable enquiry).

By paragraph 2 of the schedule notices must include the following details:

1. an address at which written particulars of the

deceased persons whose graves are affected by the proposal may be inspected;

2. the name of the burial ground or crematorium where reinterment or cremation will take place;
3. the manner in which it is proposed to deal with tombstones, monuments and other memorials;
4. a statement that the applicant will permit the removal of remains and any tombstone, monument or memorial (monument in this context meaning a memorial to the dead) by personal representatives, relatives or the CWGC, provided such removal takes place within two months from the date of notice by them to the applicant of their intention to do so (this notice to be received within the period of six weeks available for objections);
5. a statement about the rights of personal representatives, relatives or (in appropriate cases) the CWGC to make their own arrangements within two months of the date of their notice to the applicant (see below);
6. a statement recording any directions issued by the Home Office under paragraph 7 of the schedule to the Act (manner of removing remains etc.) together with a statement of the intentions of the applicant with respect to the manner of reinterment or cremation and removal or disposal of monuments;
7. a statement that the reasonable expenses of such reinterment, cremation, removal or disposal will be met by the applicant; and
8. a statement that where burial rights are affected compensation may be claimed from the applicant.

3.32 The notices required under sections 1 and 2 of the Act may be consolidated (see the form of notice at appendix 3A) Under such a notice the applicant must allow six weeks for objections to building on the burial ground and will, concurrently, receive proposals from relatives and personal representatives of the deceased to remove remains (at the applicant's expense). There is nothing in the Act which prevents the exercise of these rights to remove remains by relatives and personal representatives if, because of objections, the building scheme cannot proceed. In circumstances where many recent graves are affected it is prudent therefore to have two notices running consecutively, so that the right to request removal of remains does not arise until the applicant is sure that there are no objections which cannot be overcome.

Any relatives or personal representatives wishing to remove remains themselves must do so within 2 months of notifying the applicant of their intention to do so. As soon as possible within this period they should apply for directions in their own right from the Secretary of State.

3.33 In cases where the applicant removes human remains (but not otherwise) it may, if reasonably practicable, re-erect any monument or memorial in the new burial ground or at some other appropriate location (paragraph 5). Alternatively, such monuments or memorials may be left *in situ* (paragraph 6). If a tombstone, monument or memorial is not dealt with in one of these ways, however, paragraph 9 of the schedule to the Act requires that it be broken and defaced before being disposed of. Where a monument or memorial is removed, defaced or made inaccessible, the applicant must within two months deposit with the district council or the London borough council for the area (as appropriate) (a) sufficient particulars of the monument or memorial to permit its identification (including a copy of any inscription), and (b) a statement recording the date and manner of its removal, and its new location, or a statement that it has become inaccessible or has been defaced.

Where remains are removed a certificate of removal which complies with paragraph 8 of the schedule to the Act must be filed with the Registrar General within two months after removal.

3.34 Only after the stringent requirements of section 2 of the Act have been complied with is a burial ground released, under section 4, from the trusts and property restrictions which may have affected it as a burial ground. However, that section 4 does not override charitable trusts affecting the use of the land. It is unlikely that such trusts will be drawn sufficiently wide to enable the land to be sold without the consent of the Charity Commissioners or, if the title documents contain no power of sale, an order of court (see, for example *Oldham Metropolitan Borough Council v. Att-Gen* [1993] 2 All E.R. 432 CA).

Any disputes over compensation, either for loss of burial rights or for costs of removal, may be referred by either party to the County Court (section 8, 1981 Act).

If the requirements of the Act are not properly complied with, and no other authority is obtained, the persons carrying out the removal of remains will be in breach of section 25 of the Burial Act 1857 and, if building takes place, the owner and his agents may be in breach of section 3 of the Disused Burial Grounds Act 1884.

3.35 The 1981 Act has been cited as a statutory application of the maxim that 'the developer must pay' for archaeological excavations in a burial ground (HC 1987, paragraph 141). Although the Act may serve to preserve archaeological information which might otherwise be lost, its ambit is clearly much narrower than that supposed by the Select Committee, being restricted to the removal of remains (and removal and recording of monuments) and not extending to scientific exploration or examination of burial grounds or their contents.

3.36 Procedures under the Pastoral Measure 1983 are similar – in many aspects identical – to those found in the 1981 Act. Section 65 and schedule 6 contain the relevant provisions. The main contrasts are that under the Pastoral Measure:

1. the Bishop can impose conditions as to the removal of remains;

2. notices are to be served on 'the next of kin' of the deceased, not 'relatives' (though these terms today are nearly synonymous); and

3. £50 only is payable to cover the costs of removal of any one burial, plus £15 for any one tombstone (and not 'reasonable expenses' as under the 1981 Act).

For forms applicable in the ecclesiastical jurisdiction see the

Faculty Jurisdiction Rules 1992.

Generally it should be appreciated that in comparison to other churches the Church of England jurisdiction assumes a disproportionate significance in archaeological matters as most early churches and burial grounds are in Church of England ownership. However, if a burial ground is not owned by or connected with a church, either established or non-conformist, neither the 1981 Act nor the Pastoral Measure will be applicable and, unless removal of remains falls within one of the special statutory exemptions (for example section 240 of the TCPA) a section 25 licence is still required.

The Town and Country Planning Act 1990

3.37 Whereas the Disused Burial Grounds (Amendment) Act 1981 applies to church/chapel burial grounds not subject to the Church of England jurisdiction, and the Pastoral Measure applies only to the Church of England, the TCPA 1990 applies to all burial grounds, whether religiously affiliated or not. However, the relevant provisions of the TCPA are restricted to the limited circumstances of development of burial grounds following their acquisition, either by agreement for planning purposes or compulsorily. Under sections 239 and 240 of the TCPA, if removal of human remains and monuments is carried out in accordance with that Act, any burial ground which has been acquired (1) by the Secretary of State, a local authority or a statutory undertaker under Part IX of the Act (or part I of the P(LBCA)A), (2) compulsorily under any enactment, or (3) by a local authority for planning purposes, may be developed without a section 25 licence, and free of the restrictions contained in the Disused Burial Grounds Act 1884, or any provision of ecclesiastical law. Burials within a building also come within the TCPA, so even in these circumstances a section 25 licence will not be required .

3.38 Section 240 requires that regulations be made to provide for: (a) the publication of notices by the owner to inform the public of his intention to remove human remains and monuments (i.e. tombstones and memorials); (b) enabling personal representatives to make their own arrangements for disposing of or removing remains and monuments, subject to the costs being defrayed by the owner; and (c) compliance with directions issued by the Secretary of State and, where consecrated land is affected, conditions imposed by the bishop of the diocese. No regulations have yet been made under this section; the regulations assumed to be still applicable are the Town and Country Planning (Churches , Places of Religious Worship and Burial Grounds) Regulations 1950 (S.I. 1950, No.792), which in most respects reflect the requirements of the procedure under the Disused Burial Grounds (Amendment) Act 1981. The main differences are that under the 1950 regulations the landowner is required to make only a £25 contribution to the costs of removal and the Royal Fine Arts Commission is entitled to request reports on monuments before they are disposed of. A form of notice under the regulations appears at form 47, EFP, vol. 6 *Burial and Cremation.*

Grave Goods and Tombstones

3.39 Under English law, where a person deposits valuables

in or fixes a structure to land owned by another person, the valuables or structure will, assuming no express agreement or provision to the contrary, become the property of the landowner; they will become part of or 'annexed' to the land. Under English law it is also possible for objects to be abandoned, so that title in them vests in a finder. This is a contrast to Scots law, where finds are deemed *bona vacantia* and vest in the Crown (though it is not the case that the doctrine of *bona vacantia* has no application in other branches of English law, for example in the administration of estates). Whenever objects are found, or the original owner of an object cannot be traced, the main claims under English law will, normally, be those of the finder and the owner of the land (or water) where the object was discovered. As is well-known, these claims may frequently be in conflict. Questions of annexation or abandonment are very much dependent on the particular facts. On the sale of land, for example, whether or not furnishings or equipment have become annexed to a property may be crucial. There are, however, some narrow but general exceptions to the usual presumptions in this area of law, and these have a bearing on archaeological finds. The law of grave goods and tombstones is one exception (see below, this chapter, for the exception of treasure).

3.40 As in life, so in death: under English law a body, like a person, cannot be property *(Handyside's case* c.1750; an exception is where a body has acquired different attributes by the application of skill, e.g. disection and preservation, *R. v. Kelly and Another* (1998) *Independent,* June 4, CA). However, grave goods deposited with the deceased may still vest in the personal representatives of the deceased.

Most authority on this point is old and the extent to which it still constitutes good law is uncertain. The doctrine of 'heirloom', whereby specified items of property pass automatically from one generation to the next, is noteworthy in this context, though the doctrine is now probably obsolete and was hardly ever applicable to possessions which had been buried underground.

3.41 A burial shroud was held to be the property of the person who donated it for burial (*Hayne's case*, 1613); the donor need not, of course, be a relative or personal representative of the deceased (though in the context of burial one may well be speaking of the claims made by relatives or personal representatives of the donor!). Cases such as Hayne's are scarcely the most reliable statement of the law, but there is sufficient authority here to justify caution when dealing with grave goods. Any risks should be taken only after having considered the value of the objects concerned and the likelihood of claims.

In the case of grave goods which pre-date the modern era (before 1500-1600, depending on the part of the country concerned) there is virtually no risk, outside the law relating to treasure, of claims arising which are adverse to those of the landowner. In later instances the statutory consultation process conducted before disinterment of remains should assist in alerting the landowner to possible claims.

3.42 The law treats monuments and memorials in the same way as grave goods, namely that a person who erects such a structure has the first claim to the property in it whilst he is still alive (*Corven's case*, 1612). After that person's death the personal representatives or relatives of the person commemorated by the monument or memorial will have the better claim (*Lady de Wyche's case*, 1469). Both of the latter cases were affirmed in the nineteenth century case of *Hitchcock v. Walter* (1838) and may be considered slightly more reliable presumptions than those relating to grave goods. However, the statutory consultation procedures deal directly with the removal etc. of monuments and memorials and, consequently, there should be far less scope for misunderstandings or conflicting claims in this area.

3.43 If rights to grave goods or monuments are infringed a claimant's likely remedy is a civil action for trespass to goods, or for conversion. Conversion will only be applicable if the defendant has dealt with the relevant property as an owner by assuming rights of ownership; trespass is actionable merely on the infringement of the property rights of the owner, no dealing or conversion to the defendant's own use is required. It is sometimes said that liability for criminal damage or theft may also arise. For criminal damage there must be recklessness and recklessness does not necessarily follow from the fact of removal of objects to another place or, in the case of monuments and memorials, their 'defacing' as required by statute. Flouting of statutory procedures or something approaching deliberate destruction of objects will probably be required for such a charge to be upheld. Amongst other things, theft requires both 'dishonesty' and an 'intention permanently to deprive the owner' of the property in question. A person openly disposing of grave goods (whether because of a mistake of civil law or otherwise) may not be acting dishonestly; a person who simply stores grave goods for transfer elsewhere may not intend permanently to deprive the owner. In either instance it would be difficult to establish liability for theft.

The old law of treasure trove had no application to grave goods as such goods were not 'hidden with an intention to recover'. Grave goods may qualify as treasure under the Treasure Act 1996 but the right of the Crown or of a franchisee is subject to any prior interests or rights of a donor or personal representatives of the deceased.

Treasure

After several attempts to reform the law of treasure trove a new Act, the Treasure Act 1996, is now in force. The Treasure Act brings to an end the Crown prerogative of treasure trove and replaces it with a modern system of reporting, assessment and reward for the discovery of treasure. Both the old and the new system need to be considered if the current position is to be understood.

Treasure Trove

3.44 A variant of the law of treasure trove existed in medieval times and probably had its origins in late Saxon law. Possibly conceived in order to restrict the acquisition of gold and silver, according to a right of title vesting in the Crown, treasure trove was said to arise where *'any gold or silver in coin, plate or bullion is found hidden in the earth or any other secret place and belongs to the Crown by prerogative right, unless the person who hid it is known or afterwards discovered, in which case it belongs to him'* (Halsbury, vol.8, paragraph 1513 (as supplemented)). Jurists and commentators have disputed which materials were covered by treasure trove, and how the law operated. But the requirement that the objects concerned were originally 'hidden' was accepted by the Court of Appeal in 1981; the Court also held that to be treasure trove objects had to have a 'substantial' gold or silver content (*Att-Gen of the Duchy of Lancaster v. G.E. Overton (Farms) Limited* [1982] 1 All E.R. 524 CA).

3.45 The notion that base metals or coin generally could be treasure trove was rejected by the Court of Appeal. Indeed, Lord Denning was of the view that substantial in this context might mean at least a 50% gold and/or silver content, and certainly not an insignificant amount (*loc. cit.*). This test, of course, rules out many valuable and exquisite artefacts – most prehistoric implements, for example. Even where objects contained gold or silver the *Overton* test was demanding, possibly requiring higher percentages of precious metal than in some modern jewellery. In many treasure trove inquests, however, juries still appeared to be satisfied with a precious metal content of about 10% or slightly less. Section 1 of the Treasure Act now defines 'treasure' *inter alia* as objects with a gold or silver content of at least 10%.

3.46 The requirement that the objects must have been 'hidden with an intention to recover them', i.e. that they must evidence an *animus revertendi*, was not seriously questioned in *Overton*. In archaeological circles, and elsewhere, this rule was derided, both for its irrelevance to the ownership of almost all objects which are of archaeological interest and also the difficulties of evidence and assumption which this requirement introduced for the treasure trove jury. A jury had to decide, usually on the basis of meagre and suspect evidence, whether from the nature and context of an archaeological find an *animus revertendi* could be imputed. If it could not be imputed, on a balance of probabilities, then the object in question could not be treasure trove. Amongst objects which were excluded were those which were lost accidentally (beneath a bridge for example), objects forfeited to natural disaster, and objects which had been deliberately discarded (votive offerings and grave goods). Palmer observed some years ago that a presumption had arisen that such objects as pass the gold or silver content test were considered to have been originally deposited with an intention to recover ((1981) M.L.R. 178). This presumption was often unjustifiable from a legal standpoint and merely illustrated one of the main inadequacies of the ancient law in dealing with the task which it was expected to perform.

3.47 When an object was substantially of gold and/or silver and was deposited with an intention to recover the two basic treasure trove conditions were met. However, if the original depositor came forward the object was returned to him; in such unlikely circumstances the depositor would have a better title than the Crown. In several parts of the country the Crown has, over the centuries, granted a franchise of treasure trove to non-Crown bodies and persons. Most franchise holders are known, but it was (and still is) conceivable that the Crown's title may be contested by a little known franchise holder. A 'private claim' will only succeed on its own merits, not on any weakness in the claim of the Crown or the franchise holder: *Att-Gen v. Trustees of the British Museum* [1903] 2 Ch 598 at 609. The concept of franchise is still relevant under the Treasure Act.

Section 5 of the Act imports a definition of franchise which derives from the franchise of treasure trove. In a franchise area the franchisee, not the Crown, is the person entitled to treasure under section 4 of the Act.

3.48 Concealment of treasure trove was an offence at common law, but the offence was abolished by the Theft Act 1968, section 32(1)(a). Prosecution for theft – from the Crown or franchise holder – was a possible substitute, as the wide definition of property in the 1968 Act could extend to the appropriation from the Crown of treasure trove. The notion that theft could extend to appropriation of the right of the Crown to have the question of treasure trove determined was considered otiose in *R. v. Hancock* [1990] 3 All E.R. 183 CA, as a charge of theft could be sustained whether or not the finds were in the possession of the Crown. The jury in the criminal trial was thought competent to determine the question of treasure trove on all the evidence before them in the criminal proceedings. Consequently, although it might be difficult to specify the true owner before the question of treasure trove had been determined, in order to sustain a conviction for theft of treasure trove magistrates or jury had to be sure beyond reasonable doubt, not merely as a matter of 'real possibility', that the objects were treasure trove at the time the theft occurred. In the absence of a coroner's inquest, and where objects themselves were not available for examination, the Crown or franchise holder's case in such circumstances became almost impossible to substantiate. The Treasure Act reintroduces specific criminal liability for failure to report a discovery of treasure to the coroner.

3.49 In some circumstances the finder of treasure may also

offend against section 42 of the AMAA, which prohibits the use of metal detectors in 'protected places' (see paragraph 2.165, above). The offences of carrying out unauthorised works on a scheduled monument, or intentionally or recklessly causing damage to a protected monument (see paragraphs 2.137-2.148 and 2.153-2.159) may also be relevant in extreme cases.

Treasure Trove Procedure

3.50 Discovery of a gold or silver object had to be reported to the coroner for the coroner's district in which the objects were found. Reporting could take place either directly or through the local police or museums service. The coroner would decide to hold an inquest to ascertain, by jury, the composition of the find, whether the find was deposited with an intention to recover, and the identity of the finder. Title was not conclusively decided, as property issues between private citizens were (and remain) outside the jurisdiction of coroners (see 3.56 below).

Sometimes a decision could be reached without an inquest, for example where objects were found before the inquest to have no trace of gold or silver. A coroner would normally seek specialist advice on the composition of finds which seemed to be of gold or silver – in England from the British Museum and in Wales from the National Museum of Wales.

3.51 The treasure trove jury came to its verdict on a balance of probabilities. The main question was usually that of *animus revertendi*, although the identity of the finder (where there were conflicting claims), and gold and silver content, were additional questions.

3.52 As a tribunal of fact, the coroner's inquest was not influenced by the findings of other juries on similar but not identical facts. Each new find or collection of finds reported should have been considered on its own merits, together with expert archaeological advice from at least two sources which were independent of one another. If a second discovery of objects was made soon after an earlier discovery then, unless there were strong reasons for believing that the second find came from a physical context identical to that of the first, it was prudent to summon a jury of different constitution from that which considered the earlier question. The location, manner of discovery and lapse of time between different finds were all matters to be taken into account when considering whether a jury was likely to have an unacceptable predisposition to determine the issues in a particular way. Finding alternative juries was a simple enough matter. For example, a jury summoned for purposes unconnected with treasure trove could be asked to consider a treasure trove case at the end of their other deliberations.

A form of treasure trove declaration is reproduced at appendix 3C of this work. Coroner's inquests into treasure under the Treasure Act will be held without a jury unless the coroner directs otherwise. Where a jury is summoned the procedure will be the same as that of the treasure trove inquest, in particular evidence will still be given on oath and those giving false testimony may be prosecuted for perjury (see *R. v. Peach* [1990] 2 All E.R. 966 CA for consideration of perjury during a treasure trove inquest).

3.53 If declared treasure trove, objects became Crown property or, where the franchise of treasure trove has been granted by the Crown to another person, to that person. Notable franchise holders are the Duchy of Lancaster, the Duchy of Cornwall and the cities of London and Bristol (though there are other franchisees). All rights of ownership other than those of the Crown or franchise holder were forfeit. The British Museum or the National Museum of Wales, as appropriate, administered treasure trove on behalf of the Secretary of State for National Heritage and was deputed to consider one of three courses of action: (1) return of the object(s) to the finder; (2) sale of the treasure to a buyer of its choice and transmission of the sale proceeds to the finder; or (3) retention of the object(s) but with the payment to the finder of an *ex gratia* sum equivalent to the object's full market value. The second option was rarely exercised, although another museum could acquire the object(s) from the national museum and defray any award out of its own funds. The third option was the usual method of dealing with finds of any significant value and, of course, is the procedure which both attracts most public interest and is likely to be the option taken most frequently with such finds under the Treasure Act.

3.54 Whichever option was followed it was the finder personally and not his employer, principal or licensor who benefited from any treasure trove reward. If an employer was to retain an interest in the proceeds of treasure trove he had to secure such interest in advance, either by specific assignment or some other form of contractual arrangement. The Treasure Act provides, at section 10, that the Secretary of State may pay rewards to the finder or the occupier or any person with an interest in the relevant land. Employers are therefore likely to be in no better position under the Act. A form of assignment of rights in treasure and finds for general excavation purposes, is reproduced at appendix 3D of this work.

3.55 The finder had no right to a reward for finding treasure trove, nor did he have any redress if the market value determined by the Treasure Trove Reviewing Committee (formerly a Treasury body, but latterly under the auspices of the Department of National Heritage) fixed a market value which he believed to be too low. A finder will be in a comparable position under the Treasure Act. The committee assessed the price as between a willing vendor and purchaser but, of course, was not able to take into account any special 'desire value' which some antique objects attracted. Accordingly, the level of reward was sometimes the subject of criticism, though still appearing sufficient to encourage the reporting of finds. The annual list of rewards paid by the committee usually numbered between 10-30, most of which were less than £5,000 and only two or three of which exceeded £20,000. Awards of £100,000 or more usually appeared only once per year or even more infrequently.

3.56 The treasure trove inquest did not necessarily determine ownership of finds, or any other related civil or criminal issue. On a declaration of treasure trove title vested in the Crown or franchise holder, but not all potential claims to ownership, for example those unrelated to the question of treasure trove, were examined during proceedings before the coroner. The coroner is not empowered to investigate ownership in general; an inquest into treasure trove had to consider ownership only to the extent necessary to determine entitlement under the prerogative. Where objects were not treasure trove the coroner would return the find to the finder. Any other claimant – a landowner, for example – had to contest matters in a civil action. Where objects were declared treasure trove neither the owner of the land where the objects were found nor the finder had a legal claim against the Crown, either to the objects themselves or to the whole or any share of a reward.

3.57 If a jury found as a matter of fact that the objects in question were not deposited with an intention to recover, the Crown had no claim in treasure trove. Such objects were normally returned to the finder, who would then hold the objects subject to third party claims. The original owner or his relatives or descendants (see the case of grave goods above) may still have had a claim which did not come before the coroner. However, in the case of archaeological finds, the strongest claim will usually be that of the owner of the land where the objects were found, as in *Overton*. Such competing claims are contested in the civil courts. Where the finder has taken objects from land dishonestly, whilst treasure hunting for example, he may be liable in theft.

3.58 At civil law it is usual for a finder of objects to have a claim which is weaker than that of the landowner, and a person holding a subsequent interest in land will have a weaker claim than a person with a prior interest, for example a lessee as against his lessor: see *Elwes v. Brigg Gas Co.* [1886-90] All E.R. Rep. 562 and *South Staffordshire Water*

Co. v. Sharman [1895-99] All E.R. Rep. 259. In *Waverley Borough Council v. Fletcher*, Auld L.J. stated the main principles as follows.

> '*In my view, the two main principles established by the authorities, and for good practical reasons, are as stated by Donaldson L.J. in Parker. I venture to restate them with particular reference to objects found on or in land, for he was concerned primarily with objects found in a building. (1) Where an article is found in or attached to land, as between the owner or lawful possessor of the land and the finder of the article, the owner or lawful possessor of the land has better title. (2) Where an article is found unattached on land , as between the two, the owner or lawful possessor of the land has the better title only if he exercised such manifest control over the land as to indicate an intention to control the land and anything that might be found on it*' ([1995] 4 All E.R. 756 at p.764, CA).

The second of these principles may be drawn a little too widely in favour of the finder, as it does not appear to recognise a distinction between land to which a finder has lawful access and land to which he is afforded no such access. Both *Fletcher* and *Parker* (*Parker v. British Airways Board* [1982] 1 All E.R. 834, CA; jewellery found in a public lounge at an airport held to be the property of the finder) dealt, respectively, with land and buildings the subject of public rights. Whether the finder has obtained lawful access or, conversely, has committed acts of trespass, will be an important consideration in practice, usually taken into account before the degree of control exercised by the landowner. There will be borderline cases where a finder commits what amounts to a technical trespass and nonetheless obtains a better title than the landowner to unattached objects, but the second principle tends, by the use of the word 'control', to suggest a standard of treatment of land above that standard which the law would normally expect of a landowner or occupier maintaining property for his own use. Control is probably to be construed as control of land or buildings as against the finder and the degree of actual control necessary to defeat the finder's claim is likely to diminish in proportion with the finder's rights to be present at the place where the find was made.

3.59 It is submitted that the finder's title may be better than the landowner's, therefore, only where the following tests are passed: (1) the item was already separated from the 'realty' (i.e. the land or building in question) (see *Armory v. Delamirie* [1558-1774] All E.R. Rep. 121, where a chimney sweep successfully claimed title to a jewel said to have been found in a chimney); (2) the finder was not a trespasser (either initially or as a result of unauthorised activities on the land) at the time when he made the find, even if his access was only impliedly authorised, for example by an informal licence or public right; and (3) the owner or other lawful occupier of the land did not at the time the object was found manifest an intention to exercise control over the land as against the finder, for example because of control of the public in a public place or because of limitation in a licence given to the finder. Where a finder 'severs objects from the realty' and removes them he will usually have a title better than the landowner only where a licence or other right authorises such severance and removal. In the majority of cases severance will constitute trespass, as an act inconsistent with the purposes for which the finder may have been authorised to enter. *Fletcher* is a case in point: where a person using a metal detector in a public park located and dug down 9 inches to remove medieval jewellery, he was considered by the court to have been a trespasser at the time the jewellery was removed. Title in the finds was held to be in the local council. Use of a metal detector in a public place itself will probably not render a finder a trespasser, unless by-laws or notices expressly prohibit such activities.

Reform: The Treasure Act 1996

3.60 In *Overton* Lord Denning thought it 'very desirable that the law ... relating to small antiquities ... should be amended'. Ninety years ago, in the *British Museum* case (*loc. cit.*, 610), Farwell J., when considering the law of treasure trove, spoke of the 'fanciful suggestions more suitable to the poems of a Celtic bard'. The case for reform was a strong one and it is surprising that the reforms now contained in the Treasure Act were so long in gestation.

3.61 There have been a number of attempts at legislative reform. A Bill introduced in 1982 by Lord Abinger was, in effect, defeated by the Government. The Bill proposed some minor amendments to the law of treasure trove, including the extension of the prerogative to materials other than those of gold and silver. In 1988, the Department of the Environment issued a consultation paper which, amongst other things, considered the compulsory reporting of finds to designated public institutions and whether a system of fines or rewards would most easily secure compliance with such a statutory requirement. But the consultation did not result in any amendment to the law.

3.62 The Surrey Archaeological Society produced another Bill, introduced into the House of Lords by Lord Perth in 1994. Again the intended reforms were modest: ending the *animus revertendi* rule; allowing objects not of gold or silver but found in association with gold or silver objects to become treasure (thus preserving the integrity of hoards); and, most importantly given the uncertainty created by *Overton*, defining 'gold' and 'silver' objects according to specific percentages of metal content (5%, or 0.5% if in coin). The Bill would also have permitted the Secretary of State to extend, by statutory instrument, the categories of objects covered. The Bill did not obtain Government support and fell on its second reading. At the time it was suggested that a more comprehensive review of the law in this area was required.

3.63 The Government did eventually warm to the idea of reform. *Hansard* (Lords) June 7, 1995, recorded the Government's spokeswoman on heritage matters, Baroness Trumpington, giving an assurance that the Government was looking to introduce a Bill similar to the Perth Bill within the year. In December 1995, with Government backing, Sir Anthony Grant, MP introduced the 'Treasure Bill' into the House of Commons. The Treasure Act received the royal assent on July 4, 1996 and came fully into force on September 24, 1997 (S.I. 1997, No.1977; section 11 (the statutory code of practice) has been in force since March 13, 1997). It is similar to the Perth Bill in that it seeks to substitute the law of treasure trove by statutory provisions which redefine 'treasure' and do away with the *animus revertendi* rule (except for the limited purposes of section 1(c)). The Act has 15 sections (reproduced at appendix 3E of this work, as part of the statutory Code of Practice). The first three sections define what constitutes treasure. Section 1 provides that treasure is:

'(a)   any object at least 300 years old when found which
  – is not a coin but has a metallic content of which at least 10 per cent by weight is precious metal
  – when found, is one of at least two coins in the same find which are at least 300 years old at that time and have that percentage of precious metal, or
  – when found, is one of at least ten coins in the same find which are at least 300 years old at that time;
(b)   any object at least 200 years old when found which belongs to a class designated under section 2(1); [designation by order of the Secretary of State of classes of objects which in his opinion are of outstanding historical, archaeological or cultural importance]

(c)   any object which would have been treasure trove if found before the commencement of section 4; [section 4 transfers Crown rights in treasure trove to the exchequer pursuant to sections 4 and 6 of the Act] *or*

(d)   any object which, when found, is part of the same find as
  – an object within paragraph (a), (b) or (c) found at the same time or earlier, or
  – an object found earlier which would be within paragraph (a) or (b) if it had been found at the same time.'

Section 3 defines precious metal as gold or silver (the proportion of each to the other therefore is irrelevant); 'coin' includes any metal token which was or can reasonably be assumed to have been used or intended for use as money. There are also statutory presumptions introduced in favour of age and proximity. Section 3(6), for example, provides that *'an object which can reasonably be taken to be at least a particular age is presumed to be at least that age, unless shown not to be'*. Section 3(5) provides that *'if the circumstances in which objects are found can reasonably be taken to indicate that they were together at some time before being found, the objects are presumed to have been left together, unless shown not to have been'*. In determining whether or not objects are part of the same find (ultimately a matter for the coroner) section 3(4) provides that an object is part of the same find as another if *'(a) they are found together, (b) the other object was found earlier in the same place where they had been left together, or (c) the other object was found earlier in a different place, but they had been left together and had become separated before being found'*.

The Secretary of State has not yet made any orders under section 2(1) of the Act. As things stand single finds of coin will not be treasure under the Act (unless such a find would have fallen within the definition of treasure trove). Many single coins dispersed across a site are unlikely to be treasure, whereas coins in close proximity, for example from a well, are likely to be. Two gold or silver coins found together may be treasure if they are both of at least 10% precious metal. Other objects, which are not themselves treasure, will not become treasure by their association with a single coin. If coins are not of at least 10% precious metal there must be ten or more if they are to qualify as treasure (early drafts of the Treasure Bill put this figure at two but this was amended before the Bill's second reading). Objects other than coin, if not part of the same find as treasure, will always be required either to pass the precious metal test or fall within a class prescribed by the Secretary of State. However, in the Code of Practice published by the Secretary of State under section 11 of the Act (the 'statutory code', reproduced at appendix 3E of this work) the Secretary of State makes it clear that where material which could be treasure forms part of a larger object which itself would not be treasure it may be reasonable to consider the two elements as separate objects (note to paragraph 6 of the statutory code). Such an approach promises to be a fertile ground for argument before the coroner or the court.

Neither unworked, natural objects nor minerals extracted from a natural deposit can be treasure, even if part of the same find as treasure; nor can any object which falls within a class designated by order of the Secretary of State under section 2(2) (e.g. objects found within Church of England consecrated ground, for which exemption has been agreed unless the objects in question would have fallen within the definition of treasure trove: paragraph 16 of the Statutory Code). 'Wreck', within the Merchant Shipping Act 1995, is excluded from the definition of treasure.

3.64 The Treasure Act makes it a criminal offence not to report a find of treasure to the coroner within 14 days of the day after the day of discovery (or 14 days after the day on which the finder 'first believes or has reason to believe' the object is treasure). The offence is punishable summarily by a fine of up to level 5 on the standard scale and/or three months imprisonment (section 8(3)). It is a defence for the defendant to show that he had and continued to have a reasonable excuse for failing to notify the coroner.

The coroner's jurisdiction continues under the Act save that he now has a discretion whether or not to summon a jury (under treasure trove a jury was mandatory). A coroner proposing to hold an inquest must notify the British Museum or, in Wales, the National Museum of Wales (now known as the National Museums and Galleries of Wales); he must also take reasonable steps to notify the finder, the *occupier* of land where the treasure was found and other 'interested persons' whose details have come to his attention (section 9). If an object is found to be treasure it will vest in the Crown or the appropriate franchisee of treasure trove subject to any prior rights of any person in the treasure (section 4). The rights referred to are rights subsisting at the time when the treasure was left where it was found (as with treasure trove): *'if the original owner or his heirs can show that the object belongs to them then their claim will be superior to that of the Crown'* (paragraph 10 of the statutory code).

Section 10 of the Act provides that where treasure vests in the Crown and is to be transferred to a museum, the Secretary of State must before the transfer determine (as he thinks fit): whether a reward is to be paid by the museum; the treasure's market value; the amount of any reward; to whom the reward, if any, should be paid; and, where more than one person is to receive the reward, how much each is to receive. Payment of a reward is made expressly unenforceable against the Secretary of State or a museum. A reward may not exceed market value (section 10(4)). In contrast to treasure trove rewards will not be paid only to 'finders' – section 10(5) provides that rewards may be paid to finders (or other persons 'involved in the find'), occupiers of land at the time of the find or any other person interested in the land, either at the time of the find or subsequently. In many cases one can expect that the reward will be paid to the finder without 'abatement' (see below). It will be prudent in some cases therefore for landowners and employers to take an assignment of any treasure reward from excavators or metal detectorists (although paragraph 76 of the statutory code indicates, without prejudice to the interests of landowners, that rewards will not normally be paid to archaeologists). A form of assignment is reproduced at appendix 3D of this work.

Procedure and Rewards under the Treasure Act 1996 (the statutory code of practice)

The statutory code sets out, amongst other things, the principles and practice to be followed when (a) treasure is found and (b) payments are made under section 10 of the Act (rewards to finders).

3.65 Finders of treasure should report the find to the coroner for the district in which the find was made (paragraph 36). The precise six-figure grid reference of the find-spot should be reported, although this will not be publicised or referred to at the inquest (paragraph 43). The coroner should acknowledge the notification (providing evidence of the finder having complied with his statutory duty) and send instructions to the finder about where to deliver the find for inspection and safe-keeping. An important element of the new procedure is that coroners are expected to have formal agreements with bodies who are able to take delivery of finds, such as local museums or archaeological services. The finder is unlikely to have to deliver the find to the coroner. Whether the coroner, museum or other body takes delivery that person must issue the finder with a receipt which contains the details listed at paragraph 37 of the code.

The coroner should copy all relevant documentation to the person who takes delivery of the find. That person is expected to copy the documentation to the appropriate national museum. If, after inspection, it is decided that an object 'is clearly not treasure', the object may be returned to the finder, who will then await the decision of the coroner (on the documentary records only, without an inquest). If the finds are believed to be treasure the national museum must be notified and the coroner must hold an inquest (though not necessarily before a jury). The exception is where no museum or similar body wishes to acquire the find. In such circumstances, even if such a find may be treasure, the Secretary of State is likely to disclaim the find under section 6 of the Act. The coroner would then be entitled to order the return of the find to the finder without holding an inquest.

If a find appears to be treasure and a museum wishes to acquire it, the coroner must notify the finder, and the occupier and the owner of the land where the find was made, of the date and place of the inquest. These persons will be able to examine witnesses. In some cases the Crown, museums and/or local archaeological officers may be represented at the inquest. Where a find is not treasure it should be returned to the finder together with both an acknowledgement by the coroner that the find is not treasure and a copy of the documentation. Where the find is treasure and the coroner is advised that a museum wishes to acquire it, the coroner must arrange for delivery of the find to the appropriate national museum, which in turn will arrange for valuation by the Treasure Valuation Committee (a Government and not a museum appointed body, successor to the Treasure Trove Reviewing Committee).

3.66 In an attempt to have a more transparent valuation procedure the statutory code proposed that reports from the national museums to the Treasure Valuation Committee will no longer contain valuations and the committee itself will commission reports from independent experts. The committee is not responsible for paying any reward; this is the job of the Secretary of State. Before payment is made, however, all interested parties will be informed of the committee's expert valuations and will be given an opportunity to comment on these, including, in the case of finders and landowners, the right to submit their own expert valuations. Once the committee has recommended a figure to the Secretary of State, interested parties will still be able to make representations to the Secretary of State before he makes his decision. Paragraph 65 of the code envisages a minimum period of 28 days between the committee's recommendation and the ministerial decision. The reader is invited to contemplate judicial review of the decision of the Secretary of State; there can be no doubt that such action could be taken in appropriate cases.

As with treasure trove, a finder has no right to a reward. Government policy is to make *ex gratia* payments to encourage the reporting of finds. The Secretary of State will only make payments once he has received payment from the museum or other institution which wants the treasure. Rewards may be paid to finders, landowners or occupiers of land (see paragraph 3.64 above). In section J of the statutory code we are told that where there is more than one finder a reward may be apportioned. Where a finder establishes that he had permission to be on the land where the find was made (and the code introduces an evidential burden for the finder to this effect) the burden is then placed on the landowner/occupier to establish that there was an agreement to share any reward. The statutory code emphasises that rewards may be abated or withheld where there has been improper conduct. Nine examples of such conduct are given at paragraph 74, ranging from breach of section 8 of the Treasure Act (reporting of finds) and section 42 of the AMAA (use of metal detectors in protected places) to the possibility that the finder was trespassing. The ninth circumstance is *'where there are other factors that the Secretary of State thinks it appropriate to take into account in individual cases'* – a convenient catch-all given the potential legal dangers of such a prescriptive list. We are told that the Secretary of State's decision on any abatement may be judicially reviewed (paragraph 80). As section 10(7) of the Treasure Act obliges the Secretary of State to take into account anything relevant in the statutory code when determining a reward no doubt it will only be a matter of time before the application of section J of the code (rewards) is litigated.

3.67 Under treasure trove, only objects substantially of gold or silver could be treasure and even gold and silver items could not be treasure if lost or discarded with no intention to recover. The Treasure Act (subject to the limited exceptions in section 1(c)) applies to objects irrespective of whether they were discarded, lost or hidden for later recovery. However, unless the Secretary of State provides numerous new categories of treasure by order, the constitution of treasure will still be limited when taken in the context of the great variety of artefacts which are afforded a high value by archaeologists.

Antiquities at Sea

3.68 Local authority planning control does not usually apply to the seabed below low water mark. Operations such as mining or drilling at sea, or the laying of cables, may require ministerial licence and, in some instances, environmental impact assessment may be required (see chapter 4 of this work). Good archaeological practice for seabed developers is encapsulated in a code published in 1995 by the 'Joint Nautical Archaeology Policy Committee'.

Monuments in United Kingdom territorial waters may be scheduled under the AMAA (section 53(1), AMAA) and the usual restrictions under that Act apply (e.g. restrictions on the use of metal detectors); the only exception is that of wreck sites designated as restricted areas under the Protection of Wrecks Act 1973, which are not 'monuments' within section 61(7) of the AMAA (see paragraph 2.08 of this work).

Under section 1(1) of the Protection of Wrecks Act 1973 the Secretary of State may designate historic wreck sites as restricted areas. The site must be in United Kingdom territorial waters and the Secretary of State must be satisfied that the site is or may be the site of a wrecked vessel which because of its historical, archaeological or artistic importance ought to be protected from unauthorised interference. There are approximately 35 wreck sites off England and 5 off Wales. It is an offence under section 1(3) of the 1973 Act to damage such a vessel or to remove any object from it. Only those licensed by the Secretary of State may carry out works otherwise proscribed by section 1. Licences may be given for works of survey, surface recovery, or excavation. They are usually granted on an annual basis by the appropriate minister for Wales or in England by the SSCMS, who is advised by the Advisory Committee on Historic Wreck Sites. Contravention renders the offender liable, on summary conviction, to a fine of up to level 5 on the standard scale; on indictment the fine is potentially unlimited.

Specific but similar protection is extended to military vessels and aircraft in the United Kingdom (including territorial waters) by the Protection of Military Remains Act 1986. The remains in question must date from after the start of the First World War. Sanctions available are similar to those under the Protection of Wrecks Act.

3.69 Property in a wrecked vessel and its contents does not automatically belong to the Crown. Under the Merchant Shipping Act 1995 all 'wreck" ('flotsam, jetsam, lagan and derelict') found in United Kingdom territorial waters must be first notified to the Receiver of Wreck appointed from time to time by the Secretary of State. The Receiver is entitled to take possession of the wreck unless it is claimed by its lawful owner before notification (section 236 of the Act). Even if the Receiver of Wreck has no notice of ownership he must wait one year before the wreck and its contents become vested in the Crown. Section 246(2)(c) of the Act makes it a summary offence to remove any part or parts of a wreck without due authority, punishable by a fine of up to level 4 on the standard scale.

Museum Collections and Title

3.70 Archaeological excavation will usually result in an

archive of finds and an archive of drawn records. Copyright in records normally rests with the archaeologist or archaeological organisation responsible for the investigation. This is considered in more detail in chapter 6. Finds and artefacts will usually be the property of the landowner or lawful occupier of the site, and it is this person who will be the appropriate transferor if the artefacts are to be accessioned by a museum or other curatorial body. The exceptions to this general rule are artefacts which are treasure, objects declared 'wreck' (at sea) and finds to which the finder or depositor has a better title according to the principles governing grave goods and memorials or the discovery of objects unattached to land. Human remains *per se* cannot be property.

3.71 Title in portable objects will usually pass by delivery. There is no legal requirement for writing, either under hand or as a deed. Writing is preferable, however, both as evidence of transfer and so that warranties and/or covenants are given or implied by the transferor (for example, by the giving of a title 'guarantee' under the Law of Property (Miscellaneous Provisions) Act 1994). Simple delivery of an object may give rise to conflicting views and undesirable legal consequences. The depositor may argue that objects were deposited conditionally or on trust, or he may argue that the museum holds deposited objects merely on a bailment. The assertion of such conflicting interests will often only occur on the death of a depositor, when personal representatives are winding up a deceased's estate.

3.72 Protection may be afforded by the limitation period (six years in the case of conversion), so that a museum may argue that a depositor's claim to any finds deposited for six years or more is statute-barred. Some museums, in fact, make a point of notifying depositors of the museum's sole interest in particular finds so that the limitation period begins to run. Such practices are clearly a second best when compared with explicit, signed writing.

The Export of Antiquities

3.73 Although within the jurisdiction of England and Wales there are no general controls on the discovery and retention of antiquities, the Import, Export and Customs Powers (Defence) Act 1939 (as amended) permits the Board of Trade to make Orders which control overseas trade in restricted goods. The Act was originally an emergency measure whose purpose was to prevent 'trading with the enemy' (until 1990 it was capable of repeal by Orders in Council, but The Import and Export Control Act of 1990 has now removed this possibility). Section 3 of the 1939 Act, together with section 68 of the Customs and Excise Management Act 1979, provides that import or export of goods in contravention of an Order will make the goods liable to forfeiture. The importer/exporter of the goods is also liable, on summary conviction, to a fine of up to level 5 on the standard scale or three times the value of the goods (whichever the greater) or, on indictment, an unlimited fine and/or seven years imprisonment.

3.74 Under the 1939 Act, article 2 of The Export of Goods (Control) Order 1992 (S.I. 1992, No.3092), as amended by The Export of Goods (Control) Order 1994 (S.I. 1994, No.1191) prescribes an extensive schedule of restricted goods. The schedule includes 'antiques' found in the United Kingdom or within United Kingdom territorial waters. The definition of 'antiques' is contained in group 2 to the schedule, meaning: *'any goods manufactured or produced more than 50 years before the date of exportation except –*

(1)   *postage stamps and other articles of philatelic interest;*
(2)   *birth, marriage or death certificates or other documents relating to the personal affairs of the exporter or the spouse of the exporter;*
(3)   *letters or other writings written by the exporter or the spouse of the exporter; or*
(4)   *any goods exported by, and being the personal property of, the manufacturer or producer thereof, or the spouse, widow or widower of that person.'*

Article 3 provides for the authorisation of the export or import of prescribed goods under licence of the Secretary of State. Licences are required for exports to other member states within the European Union, although a licence granted under the relevant EU provisions obviates the need for a licence under the Order. A licence can be granted with or without conditions. Article 5 of the Order makes it an offence to knowingly or recklessly make false statements or to furnish false documents to obtain a licence. The offence is punishable on indictment by imprisonment of up to two years and/or a fine, and summarily by imprisonment and/or a fine of up to level 5 on the standard scale. A licence issued in such circumstances will be void *ab initio*.

The Secretary of State granted the Open General Export Licence for antiques in 1993. This authorises the export from the United Kingdom of archaeological material originating outside the jurisdiction provided that such material is between 50-100 years old and has a value of not more than £39,600. If the material is more than a 100 years old it will not be authorised by the Open General Licence. Artefacts of United Kingdom origin do not fall within the Open General Licence. Questions as to whether particular goods need to be licensed should be addressed to the Export Licensing Unit of the DCMS.

3.75 Where archaeological antiquities are to be exported application for a licence is made to the Secretary of State for Culture Media and Sport, who is advised by the British Museum or the National Museums and Galleries of Wales. The museum experts consider whether one or more of the following 'Waverley' criteria apply (not be confused with the recent treasure hunting case of that name). The criteria are whether:

(1)   the object is so closely connected with British history and the national life that its departure would be a misfortune;
(2)   the object is of outstanding aesthetic importance; or
(3)   the object is of outstanding significance for the study of some branch of art and learning or history.

These criteria are designed to ascertain whether an object is *'an essential part of the heritage and whether at least the opportunity should be afforded to keep it in the country'* (HC 1994, paragraph 473).

3.76 If, according to the Waverley criteria, the object is

thought by the Secretary of State's advisers to be an essential part of the national heritage, these advisers and the applicant's advisers may argue their respective cases – usually in writing – before the Reviewing Committee on the Export of Works of Art. This committee then reports to the Secretary of State for Culture, Media and Sport. Where retention in the United Kingdom is recommended, the Secretary of State will defer granting a licence for a period, usually of between three to six months, during which domestic institutions will be allowed to match the market valuation identified by the committee. The valuation is usually influenced by the price offered for the antiquities by the overseas importer. There is no automatic right to a licence once the initial period of deferment has elapsed. This procedure is sometimes applied very flexibly by the Government and is amenable to judicial review if the applicant suffers prejudice (by a further deferment of a licence, for example; see *R. v. Secretary of State for National Heritage ex parte J. Paul Getty Trust* (1994) *The Independent*, November 7 (delay in granting a licence for the export of Canova's *The Three Graces*)).

3.77 If a domestic institution or consortium of institutions raises the necessary funds the applicant may choose to accept an offer made by such a body or simply refuse to sell the object. If he refuses the licence application lapses. The object may not then be exported.

3.78 European controls on the export of antiquities are considered at paragraphs 4.40-4.41 of this work, in particular regulations relating to the recovery of objects unlawfully imported to the United Kingdom.

CHAPTER FOUR

INTERNATIONAL AND EUROPEAN INITIATIVES

INTERNATIONAL

Outside Europe the main international obligations which affect heritage law in the United Kingdom are the various UNESCO conventions on 'cultural property'. These conventions, however, do not have direct effect in the national jurisdictions concerned and, if ratified by governments, only require signatory nations to take such steps as they deem appropriate at the national level.

4.01 The Hague Convention of 1954 provides for the protection of cultural property in the event of armed conflict. It has rarely been properly policed and has had little impact on those nations which were not already predisposed to respect cultural property in the event of war. The Convention on the *'Means of Prohibiting and Preventing the Illicit Import, Export and Transfer of Ownership of Cultural Property'* (1970) has not yet been ratified by the United Kingdom; this international protocol intended to control the smuggling of ancient artefacts and art between nations is also poorly policed, so that co-operation between, for example, American and United Kingdom customs is hindered.

4.02 Perhaps the World Heritage Convention (1972) is now the best known of the conventions, providing for the assessment by committees of experts, from signatory nations, of heritage sites which are 'of outstanding universal value'. The sites themselves are nominated to the committee by the governments of those nations. About 300 such sites have been designated in over 100 countries. A list of designated sites in England appears at paragraph 6.35 of PPG 15, to which should be added the naval and ancillary facilities known for Convention purposes as 'Maritime Greenwich'. Welsh sites consist of the Castles and Town Walls of King Edward in Gwynedd. In the United Kingdom all World Heritage Sites are already protected by restrictive heritage provisions, including (in most cases) scheduling, and the convention adds little additional, legal protection. However, the convention does increase the importance of sites in the planning system. In a number of planning cases attention has focused on the effect of World Heritage Site designation and it is clear that the Secretary of State considers the 'setting' of World Heritage Sites to be extensive and of the utmost sensitivity: see, for example, *Coal Contractors Limited v. Secretary of State for the Environment and Northumberland County Council* (1994) 68 P. & C.R. 285 QBD. A development which does not cause 'demonstrable harm' to a protected landscape may be unacceptable on the separate ground of its adverse impact on the setting of a World Heritage Site. An environmental assessment (see paragraph 4.10 below) will usually be required where such a site is the subject of a proposal to carry out significant development.

Paragraph 2.23 of PPG 15 advises that:

> *'Each Local Authority concerned, taking account of World Heritage Site designation and other relevant statutory designations, should formulate specific planning policies for protecting these sites and include these policies in their development plans. Policies should reflect the fact that all these sites have been designated for their outstanding universal value, and they should place great weight on the need to protect them for the benefit of future generations as well as our own. Development proposals affecting these sites or their setting may be compatible with this objective, but should always be carefully scrutinised for their likely effect on a site or its setting in the longer term. Significant development proposals affecting World Heritage Sites will generally require formal environmental assessment, to ensure that their immediate impact and their implications for the longer term are fully evaluated.'*

Paragraph 2.22 of the PPG refers to World Heritage Sites being a key material consideration when planning and listed building consent applications are determined.

4.03 Although not part of the convention, criteria for the inclusion in the list of World Heritage Sites have been formally agreed by the inter-governmental World Heritage Committee. These criteria require that the site in question should:

- represent a unique artistic achievement, or
- have exerted a great influence, or
- bear a unique or at least exceptional testimony to a

civilisation which has disappeared, or
- be an outstanding example of a type of building which illustrates a significant stage in human history, or
- be an outstanding example of a traditional human settlement, or
- be directly or tangibly associated with events or with ideas or beliefs of outstanding universal significance.

In addition sites must be authentic, must not be the result of reconstruction, must have adequate legal protection and must be the subject of management plans.

For a more detailed discussion of the effectiveness of World Heritage Sites see Evans *et al.* (1994).

EUROPE

4.04 Europe exerts a greater and increasing influence on the United Kingdom than do international conventions, though usually obliquely by virtue of measures directed at broad environmental issues. Influence is greater primarily because the European Communities Act 1972 provides for the transposing of community measures into domestic law; influence is increasing because the force of the Treaty of Rome is now enhanced by European convergence as anticipated by the Maastricht Treaty. Article 128 of the treaty includes a specific provision relating to cultural matters, including heritage conservation issues.

4.05 As environmental and cultural matters are already controlled to varying degrees at the national level the community provisions in this area are usually promulgated by way of directive, not regulation, i.e. by measures having effect between the Council of The European Communities and the governments of member states (articles 249-252, Treaty of Rome), and not effect between the Council and individuals or private organisations of member states. A directive must be transposed into domestic law by appropriate statutory measures, and only then will private individuals and organisations be able to take action between themselves in the domestic courts. A directive will specify a period within which it must be transposed into domestic law.

4.06 If a directive which requires member states to adopt certain rules is not transposed, the citizens of that member state will be unable to rely on the directive between themselves (see, for example, *Paola Faccini Dori v. Recreb Srl* (1994) *The Times*, August 4, ECJ, or *Marshall v. Southampton and South West Hampshire Health Authority* [1986] 2 All E.R. 584 HL). An exception to this rule is where obligations of 'horizontal direct effect' arise, when the terms of a directive are both unconditional and sufficiently precise. But such provisos are unlikely to apply in the conservation context where directives are usually drawn in general terms, to take account of the very different systems and landscapes within the community. Moreover, a legal entity such as a local planning authority, which is not an individual for the purposes of community law, may not rely on a community directive against an individual or private legal person (so that a local planning authority could not, without statutory enactment of the directive, seek to enforce Council Directive 85/337 – requiring environmental assessment of certain projects – against applicants for planning permission: *Wychavon District Council v. Secretary of State for the Environment and Another* ((1994) *The Times*, January 10, QBD). Transposition of a directive by the appropriate United Kingdom measure is, therefore, usually vital if the directive is to be relied upon in the conservation context. The main exception is where a member state (or an 'emanation' of the state, such as a local authority) conducts itself in a manner inconsistent with a directive which should have been implemented, in the sense that implementation is no longer conditional and the subject-matter of the directive is sufficiently precise: Marshall, *loc. cit.*; *Fratelli Costanzo v. Commune di Milano* [1989] ECR 1839. In such cases private citizens and other legal persons within the jurisdiction will often have a cause of action against the relevant government department or body (see *Wychavon; Twyford Parish Council v. Secretaries of State for the Environment and Transport* [1992] Env. L.R. 37 QBD; *R. v. North Yorkshire County Council, ex parte Brown and Cartwright*, a challenge now upheld by the House of Lords, *The Times*, February 12, 1999).

4.07 The community directive on environmental impact assessment (85/337/EEC) has been transposed into national law and has been significant in archaeological conservation. The existing domestic regulations have recently been re-cast in accordance with extensive amendments to the directive made by Council Directive 97/11 (see below). The Return of Cultural Objects Regulations 1994 (S.I. 1994, No.501) (as amended by S.I. 1997, No.1719) are made in response to Council Directive 93/7/EEC. The Environmental Information Regulations 1992 (S.I. 1992, No.3240) are also introduced in response to a European Council Directive

(90/313/EEC). 'Environmentally sensitive areas', are a product of an EC regulation, as are restrictions on the export of antiquities outside of the EU. These provisions are considered below in the following order: (1) Environmentally sensitive areas (2) Environmental assessment (3) EU export restrictions and the return of cultural objects and (4) the Environmental information regulations.

Environmentally Sensitive Areas

4.08 Regulation 19 of Council Regulation 85/797 on farm structures (as amended by Council Regulation 92/2078 and Commission Regulation 95/2772) provides for EU funding for the protection of 'environmentally sensitive areas' (ESAs). In England and Wales these are areas designated under section 18 of the Agriculture Act 1986, as parts of the farming landscape which are required to be managed in an environmentally friendly manner: normal commercial farming is constrained and integrated conservation practices are encouraged. Section 18 specifically mentions *'buildings and other objects of archaeological, architectural or historical interest"* (section 18(1)(b)), and one of the earliest ESAs, at West Penwith, Cornwall, required management guidelines to take account of the need to protect the *prehistoric archaeological interest* from the improvement of dairy pasture.

4.09 Regulation 19 permits member states to declare ESAs *'in order to contribute towards the introduction or continued use of agricultural production practice compatible with the requirements of conserving the natural habitat and ensuring an adequate income for farmers'*. The first ESAs were declared in 1987 and there are now 22 throughout England, including:

- Norfolk Broads;
- Breckland;
- North Peak;
- Clun;
- Pennine Dales;
- Somerset Levels and Moors;
- South Downs;
- Suffolk River Valleys;
- West Penwith;
- Test Valley;
- Avon Valley (Dorset/Hampshire);
- Exmoor;
- Lake District;
- North Kent Marshes;
- South Wessex Downs;
- South West Peak;
- Blackdown Hills;
- Cotswold Hills;
- Essex Coast;
- Dartmoor;
- Shropshire Hills; and
- Upper Thames Tributaries.

The largest is the Lake District ESA, which covers virtually the whole of that region. The South Wessex Downs ESA is one of the smaller examples, though even this contains many hundreds of hectares. ESAs in Wales include the following areas: Cambrian Mountains; Clwydian Range; Lleyn Peninsula; Preseli; Radnor; and Ynys Mon.

Grants, by way of capital payments, are available to support the adoption of ESA policies in all ESAs, although policies differ between ESAs and will be enforced by contrasting legal agreements with landowners. Individual designation orders (many of which were amended in 1996 and 1997 to comply with Council Regulation 92/2078 and Commission Regulation 95/2772) and the appropriate Ministry of Agriculture management plan for the ESA should be consulted in particular cases. Grants may provide for restoring or enhancing historic features, such as walls, stiles, dikes and bridges, and will usually be assessed at a set scale per metre/hectare/feature of the structure in question. Unlike set-aside schemes ESAs provide for positive, integrated management on a continuing basis. They are innovative in conservation terms in recognising a historic basis for designation, rather than seeing historic interest as a peripheral matter. The main drawback from the archaeologist's perspective is that the ministry, which administers ESAs, will not usually reveal details of exactly which landowners are participating in ESA policies, and archaeological work in response to or preparatory to such policies is therefore difficult to co-ordinate. This means that the ministry tends to issue fairly bland guidance about the individual archaeological or historical merits of ESAs, sometimes merely directing the landowner to consult the local SMR. Sites which are already legally protected or well-known usually benefit greatly but there is little effort made to actively preserve or to further investigate sites about which information is sparse. ESA status does not confer any additional importance in terms of national planning policy (PPG 7 *The Countryside – Environmental Quality and Economic and Social Development* (revised), paragraph 4.15).

Environmental Impact Assessment

4.10 The greatest influence of community law in archaeology is probably Council Directive 85/337 on 'the assessment of the effects of certain public and private projects on the environment'. This established the concept of environmental impact assessment by requiring member states to introduce legally binding procedures for securing that such assessment occurred in advance of certain development projects. By article 12(1) of the directive procedures were to be adopted by member states within three years of July 3rd 1985. It is symbolic of the United Kingdom Government's reserve in this area that the statutory instrument which first transposed the directive into national law was made only in 1988, shortly after the due date.

Directive 85/337 has been amended by Directive 97/11 and in the more environmentally aware climate of the 1990s the Government has already introduced new regulations to comply with the amendments.

4.11 In its preamble Directive 85/337 recites that (1) *'the best environmental policy consists in preventing the creation of pollution or nuisances at source, rather than subsequently trying to counteract their effects'* (the 'precautionary principle'); there is a need (2) *'to take effects on the environment into account at the earliest possible stage in all the technical planning and decision-making processes'* and to (3) *'provide for the implementation of procedures to evaluate such effects'*. In particular, the preamble continues, to recite (4) that consent for *'public and private projects which are likely to have significant effects on the environment should be granted only after prior assessment of the likely significant environmental effects of these projects have been carried out'*. The Directive as amended by 97/11 now also requires member states to adopt all measures necessary to ensure that 'development consent' is obtained before approval is given for projects which are likely to have significant effects on the environment. This means that some relevant projects which do not constitute development under domestic law may need to incorporate procedures for development consent, e.g. afforestation schemes. The Directive also envisages that EAs should be conducted on the basis of (5) appropriate information supplied by the developer and other authorities involved in a project.

4.12 Annex I of the Directive stipulates schemes to which environmental assessment must apply (projects likely to have a 'major effect on the environment'). Annex II introduces wide-ranging categories to which environmental assessment may be applicable (see below, paragraphs 4.19 and 4.20). Annex III (as inserted by 97/11) elaborates on the matters to be considered when preparing an *environmental statement*. One of the factors against which environmental impacts have to be assessed is their effects on 'landscapes of historical, cultural or archaeological significance' and areas classified or protected under legislation of member states (annex III, paragraph 2 cases 2(h) and 2(e) respectively). Article 4 of the directive now makes it clear that the full interrelationship of the specified cases – including archaeological landscapes – must be taken into account, one against the other, on a similar basis.

4.13 The Directive is implemented in the United Kingdom by a number of statutory instruments made under section 2(2) of the European Communities Act 1972 (and other enabling legislation where relevant). Domestic regulations now cover a wide range of activities including salmon farming in marine waters, afforestation, land drainage and harbour works. The regulations most frequently of relevance to the work of archaeologists are the Town and Country Planning (Environmental Impact Assessment) (England and Wales) Regulations 1999 (S.I. 1999, No.293); the Highways (Assessment of Environmental Effects) Regulations 1999 (S.I. 1999, No.369); and the Electricity and Pipeline Works (Assessment of Environmental Effects) Regulations 1990 (S.I.1990, No.442) as amended. Appendix 4C below lists the main regulations relating to environmental assessment in England and Wales.

As most development projects in the United Kingdom fall to be authorised under the Town and Country Planning Acts the Government implemented the Directive primarily by regulations which require the provisions of the Directive to be taken into account at the time that applications for planning permission are made. They are referred to only obliquely in the TCPA 1990 (see section 71A, TCPA, for example). Regulations, however, have served to: (a) withdraw most permitted development rights from development which because of its nature requires environmental assessment (article 10, GPDO; originally under the Town and Country Planning (Environmental Assessment and Permitted Development) Regulations 1995 (S.I. 1995, No.417), but now under the main regulations);

and (b) introduce a requirement on a planning enforcement appeal for the applicant to submit an environmental assessment where required by the Secretary of State, so that in appropriate cases planning permission will be given only if the environmental information has been considered (originally under the Town and Country Planning (Environmental Assessment and Unauthorised Development) Regulations 1995 (S.I. 1995, No. 2258), but now pursuant to regulation 25 of the main regulations).

Planning permission can be granted by the Secretary of State in a number of other ways. This means that regulations are also made to require environmental assessment in such cases so that the Directive is not ignored. Reference is made below to the Transport and Works Act regulations. Deemed planning permission may be granted under the Pipelines Act 1962 or the Electricity Act 1989 only after applications have, in appropriate cases, been the subject of environmental assessment under the Electricity and Pipeline Works (Assessment of Environmental Effects) Regulations 1990 (S.I. 1990, No. 442) as amended. The regulations do not apply to particular developments authorised by Act of Parliament, as developments under 'specific acts of national legislation' are expressly exempted by article 1(5) of the Directive.

There are also several instances where projects involving development can proceed without planning permission. The most well-known instance is probably development by the Crown (so, for example, regulations are made in relation to development by the Ministry of Transport, see paragraph 4.15 below). Afforestation is not development requiring planning permission under the TCPA (section 55(2)(e), TCPA). Former regulations required the Forestry

Commission to take environmental statements into account, in appropriate cases, before awarding grants for afforestation projects. In order to comply fully with Council Directive 97/11 new regulations have now been made which also cover non grant-aided afforestation. Less well-known are salmon fishing in marine waters (usually consisting of development outside the geographical jurisdiction of the local planning authority but within territorial waters where the Crown has jurisdiction) and harbour works (authorised by ministerial 'harbour revision orders' under the Harbours Act 1964). In the former case, consents by the Crown, as 'landlord', must be preceded in appropriate cases by environmental assessment; in the latter case ministers must, in appropriate cases, consider an environmental statement before making the Order.

Only environmental assessment in the context of highways projects and conventional planning permission is now considered in detail, although the procedures and methods of assessment are similar whichever regulations are contemplated.

4.14 As will be seen from appendix 4C existing regulations anticipate most eventualities, although section 71A in the TCPA 1990 (inserted by section 15 of the Planning and Compensation Act 1991) allows the Secretary of State to extend environmental assessment to include new processes, even if these processes are not referred to in the Directive. The extension of environmental assessment to wind generators, motorway service areas and coastal protection works, under the Town and Country Planning (Assessment of Environmental Effects) (Amendment) Regulations 1994 (S.I. 1994, No. 677) was a case in point.

Specific, substantive regulations have not been made in relation to projects authorised under the Transport and Works Act 1992 but regulation 5 of the Transport and Works (Applications and Objections) Procedures Rules 1992 (S.I. 992, No. 2902) requires environmental statements to accompany applications for an order (unless the Secretary of State has directed that no statement is needed). The Transport and Works (Assessment of Environmental Effects) Regulations 1995 (S.I. 1995, No. 1541) amend section 14 of the Transport and Works Act 1992 so that the Secretary of State is required to confirm in the order made that the 'environmental information' was taken into account. New regulations, the Transport and Works (Assessment of Environmental Effects) Regulations 1998 (S.I. 1998, No. 2226), have recently amended the TWA so that new rules can be made to bring the transport and works procedure in line with the requirements of 97/11.

The Secretary of State retains power in exceptional cases, and subject to consultation with the European Commission, to exempt projects from the scope of regulations (article 2(3)) of the Directive; see, for example, regulation 4(4) of the main regulations.

The Directive does not require local planning authorities or the Secretary of State to submit 'plans and programmes', e.g. development plans or strategic transport plans, to EIA. A directive along such lines is under consideration by the EC and may soon find its way into domestic law.

Highways

4.15 The Highways (Assessment of Environmental Effects)

Regulations 1999 are important in relation to archaeology. These regulations inserted a new part VA into the Highways Act 1980 and this requires the Secretary of State to address the question of environmental impact assessment when he is considering the construction of a highway or the improvement of an existing highway. The Secretary of State has a duty to decide whether environmental assessment is required and the steps necessary to identify, describe and assess the factors referred to in annex III of the Directive. The New Roads and Street Works Act 1991 imports similar requirements for privately funded roads and the Transport and Works Act (Applications and Objections Procedure) Rules 1992 introduce similar requirements for applications to the Secretary of State for orders relating to transport systems and inland waterways. Under the highways regulations the Secretary of State will usually publish an environmental statement at the time the relevant draft Orders are made. Ministerial advice on the quality of environmental assessment, and the problems encountered by archaeologists, are not dissimilar to those discussed below in relation to environmental impact assessments under the EIA regulations (see paragraph 4.34).

The Town & Country Planning (Environmental Impact Assessment) (England and Wales) Regulations 1999 (the 'planning EIA regulations')

4.16 Regulation 3(2) of the planning EIA regulations prohibits the granting of planning permission for development which requires environmental assessment unless the planning authority (or the Secretary of State or an inspector) has taken the 'environmental information' into consideration. The test for when an environmental impact assessment is required under these regulations originates from the Council Directive (see paragraph 4.12 above) and is applicable to all the regulations made with reference to that directive. Projects likely to have a *major effect* on the environment are automatically required to have a prior environmental assessment (unless exempt). A list of such mandatory (annex I) cases appears at schedule 1 to the planning EIA regulations. Developments which would be likely to have a *significant effect* on the environment due to the development's size, nature or location (annex II cases) may be required to be the subject of prior environmental assessment (a list of the types of development to be considered appears at schedule 2 to the planning regulations, and see paragraph 4.19 below). The Secretary of State may by Development Order direct that development of a specified type which would fall within either schedule 1 or schedule 2 is exempted from the regulations as development for which consideration of environmental information is not required before planning permission may be granted (regulation 4.4; see paragraph 4.14 above). At the time of writing no such Order has been made by the Secretary of State.

EIA Development

The planning EIA regulations refer to schedule 1, schedule 2 or amendment to schedule 1 or 2 development as 'environmental impact assessment development' (EIA development).

4.17 If (a) an applicant for planning permission submits an environmental statement which he expresses to be for the purposes of the planning EIA regulations, or (b) an applicant does not challenge the local authority's view that an application is an application to which the regulations apply, or (c) the Secretary of State directs that the development is EIA development, the regulations will be deemed to apply (regulation 4). It is also possible for the applicant to agree or concede in writing with the local planning authority that an environmental statement is required and an environmental statement will then be necessary. Whether development falls within schedule 1 or schedule 2 is otherwise a matter for the local planning authority and/or the Secretary of State. The question is one of fact and not law, although the decision taken may be challenged on *Wednesbury* grounds (see paragraph 2.55 above for discussion of the *Wednesbury* test). In *R. v. Swale Borough Council and Medway Ports Authority, ex parte Royal Society for the Protection of Birds* [1991] J.P.L. 39 the court, at first instance, held that when determining whether an environmental assessment is required under the planning EIA regulations the relevant body should consider the development for which permission is sought (or development which will inevitably follow from that development) and no less or further. In the wider context only *effects* of specific development could be taken into account, not other development itself. The Directive as amended still does not provide for aggregation of developments which individually would not require EIA into one composite environmental impact which would require EIA.

4.18 Under the planning EIA regulations it is the local planning authority which will first determine whether an environmental assessment is required. This is referred to in the regulations as 'screening'. However, the Secretary of State may make this determination himself in cases where the applicant challenges the local planning authority's view. A local planning authority may also request the opinion of the Secretary of State in relation to its own proposed development. In other cases, whether an environmental assessment is required may depend on the opinion of the relevant ministry or grant-making body (for example, the Forestry Commission in the case of afforestation programmes, the minister for transport in the case of new roads, the Secretary of State for the Environment, Transport and the Regions in the case of applications under the Transport and Works Act 1992, or the Secretary of State for Trade and Industry in relation to applications for licences to generate electricity).

4.19 Schedule 1 projects (major development) include such things as power stations, aerodromes and oil refineries. This schedule has been amended by the Government to include new projects and thresholds contained in Directive 97/11. Overall, 97/11 inserts 12 new and widens six of the existing cases in annex I of 85/337. If not within schedule 1 a project will either be within schedule 2 or outside the regulations. Schedule 2 projects constitute a very extensive list but of particular interest to archaeology are water management for agriculture (case 1), extracting peat and extraction of minerals by opencast mining (case 2), and infra-structure projects (case 10). To require environmental assessment schedule 2 projects must be likely to have significant environmental effects. This is still the appropriate test; the list of projects merely prescribes the types of project to be considered. Directive 97/11 has inserted eight new cases into annex II and these have also found their way into domestic regulations.

4.20 Establishing what are 'significant effects' inevitably involves a degree of subjectivity. Schedule 2 to the regulations provides applicable thresholds and criteria, intended to guide authorities in assessing when they should adopt a 'screening opinion' that EIA is necessary. In contrast to the old regulations, it is now of definite assistance to archaeology that under the new regulations the concept of a 'sensitive area' includes scheduled monuments (regulation 2(1)). If a sensitive area is affected, there is no need to consider the thresholds and criteria. DETR Circular 02/99 (*Environmental Impact Assessment*) contains guidance on when an environmental assessment will be required. In particular, paragraphs 32-34 of the Circular suggest that there are three main categories: (1) major projects of 'more than local importance', for example development which because of its sheer scale is likely to have wide-ranging environmental effects, or development which substantially departs from approved development plans; (2) projects which affect a particularly sensitive or vulnerable location, for example areas of outstanding natural beauty, sites of special scientific interest, national parks or scheduled monuments (although the latter are not expressly referred to in the guidance); and (3) unusually complex cases where expert and detailed analysis of environmental effects is desirable, for example development involving radioactive emissions. Archaeology is not especially well-served by this advice, as the advice gives the impression that only scheduled monuments may be appropriate for environmental assessment. However, it should be remembered that this guidance is indicative of when assessments should be required, not when they may be required. Clearly, monuments of lesser status may be affected by development which is likely to have an impact sufficient to justify an assessment. In both cases the test is still whether the proposed development will have significant environmental effects. It is just that in the case of scheduled monuments ('sensitive areas') the planning authority does not have to consider the thresholds and criteria applicable to the development. In listing the matters which authorities should take into account when screening applications schedule 3 to the regulations includes 'landscapes of historical, cultural or archaeological significance' (i.e. whether scheduled or not).

4.21 Annex A to the Circular contains more specific *indicative* criteria for assessing the likelihood of significant environmental effects. The appendix considers a range of developments, though mainly from the standpoint of size or nature and not any estimate or prediction of their environmental effects on particular parts of the environment. In relation to the archaeological heritage, agriculture, extractive industry, urban development projects and infra-structure projects will be especially relevant. The guidance indicates that sand and gravel working in excess of 15 hectares, or 'urban development projects' exceeding 5 hectares may require environmental assessment.

A vexed question is the extent to which the normal listed building and AMAA controls will render environmental assessment unnecessary. However, the existence of additional controls should, presumably, only influence the decision as to whether an environmental assessment is required to the extent that those controls provide for preliminary work of a kind and extent similar to that which would be provided under formal assessment. Although the Directive as amended permits member states to have one, integrated procedure for considering EA and other pollution controls (e.g. under Council Directive 96/61) there is no possibility, at present, of integrating listed building and scheduled monument consent procedures with EIA.

4.22 A local planning authority which requires planning permission under the TCPA 1990 for the development of its own land must comply with the planning EIA regulations and provide an environmental statement in cases falling within schedule 1 or schedule 2 (regulation 22 of the regulations).

Operation of the Environmental Impact Assessment Regime under the Planning EIA Regulations

4.23 An application for planning permission which falls into either schedule 1 or schedule 2 of these regulations must not be determined by the local planning authority (or the Secretary of State or a planning inspector) unless the relevant decision-maker has 'first taken the environmental information into consideration' (regulation 3(2)). An application will automatically be a schedule 1 or a schedule 2 application (subject to any directions of the Secretary of State) if: (1) the applicant has submitted an environmental statement expressed to be for the purposes of the regulations; (2) the local planning authority has requested an environmental statement and the applicant does not apply to the Secretary of State for a direction; or (3) the applicant has made a written statement to the local planning authority in which he has agreed to submit an environmental statement (regulation 4). In cases 1 and 3, if the applicant has taken the steps indicated, an application for planning permission will then be governed by the planning EIA regulations. In case 2 the regulations will be applicable unless the Secretary of State of his own volition directs otherwise. However, in nearly all cases the preliminary view of the local planning authority should be requested (see paragraph 4.24 below), as envisaged by the regulations.

4.24 'Environmental information' means the environmental statement prepared by the applicant together with all representations made by any body required to be consulted under the regulations or, indeed, any other representations duly made, in either case, being representations about the likely environmental effects of the proposed development (regulation 2(1)). Failure to take such information into account by the Secretary of State may be challenged by application to the High Court under section 288 TCPA 1990 (see regulation 30 of the planning EIA regulations). Failure to request a formal environmental statement by the local planning authority where one could have been requested, as well as encouraging inconsistencies in the interpretation of the environmental information, may be subject to challenge by judicial review (*R. v. Poole Borough Council, ex parte Beebee* [1991] 2 P.L.R. 27). In *Beebee* the local planning authority made a planning decision without the benefit of a formal environmental statement. On review of the authority's decision Schiemann J. held that information placed before the council by the Nature Conservancy Council and others suggested that the relevant environmental matters were sufficiently considered. The authority's decision could not therefore be impugned, although it is clearly preferable to avoid such challenges.

4.25 A procedure exists for the applicant to request the ('screening') opinion of the local planning authority as to whether the regulations apply (regulation 5(1)). This is distinct from requests about the content of environmental statements. The applicant may appeal to the Secretary of State if it disagrees with the local planning authority's view or if the authority does not express its opinion within the prescribed time limits (regulation 5(6)). There is no obligation on an applicant to obtain a preliminary view from the local planning authority but, if the development appears to the applicant to be a borderline case, prior notice of the local planning authority's view is very useful, as environmental assessments will invariably be expensive and, if required after submission of the planning application, difficult to timetable. Regulation 5 prescribes the method of application for the local planning authority's opinion.

Local planning authorities must give their opinion with clear and precise reasons within three weeks of the request (or such longer period as agreed with the applicant) (regulation 5(4)). Further information may be requested by the local planning authority but ministerial advice is that, at this stage, only information which is of a general nature should be requested and not information which will be necessary to process the planning application (see Circular 02/99, paragraph 56; see paragraph 4.29 below). Under regulation 20(2) the request for an opinion, together with the local planning authority's reasons for requiring an environmental impact assessment, must be kept with the planning register, for public inspection. When an application for planning permission is eventually made this information is transferred to the relevant part of the planning register.

If the applicant requires the directions of the Secretary of State an application should be made to the regional office of the Department of the Environment, Transport and the Regions or to the Welsh Office (or to DETR, London in the case of mining or quarrying applications in England). There is no time limit prescribed within which to make this application. Regulation 6 prescribes the written requirements. A copy of the application must be served on the local planning authority.

The Secretary of State must issue his direction within three weeks of the application for directions, or such longer period as the Secretary of State reasonably requires. There is no provision for an inquiry into the merits or otherwise of his decision (challenge is by way of judicial review; the Secretary of State has a very wide discretion: see, for example, *R. v. Secretary of State for the Environment, ex parte Marson* (1998), *The Times,* May 18, CA). Any direction made must be placed on public record (the planning register). The Secretary of State also publicises some decisions in journals and reports.

4.26 If an environmental statement is sent with the planning application the development will automatically be governed by the regulations, though the local planning authority may still require further information under regulation 19. Publicity and notification requirements apply similar to those where an environmental statement is required pursuant to a direction of the Secretary of State or on the advice of the local planning authority (see paragraph 4.31): the local planning authority must post a site notice for not less than 21 days and must put an advertisement in a newspaper circulating in the locality of the development (article 8, GD(P)O). This publicity must alert the public to both the planning application and the environmental statement.

4.27 Several copies of the environmental statement must be provided by the applicant so that the statement can be made available to the public (regulation 17; reasonable charges may be made for supplying copies, see regulation 18). Note that the statutory minimum number of copies has now been amended to four. Together with the planning application and environmental statement the applicant should notify the local planning authority of any statutory consultees or other bodies already served with a copy of the environmental statement. The recipient body must also be informed by the applicant of its right to make representations to the local planning authority (regulation 13). One of the main features of the environmental impact assessment procedure is that statutory consultees must, with certain exceptions contained in regulation 12(5), provide all relevant information in their possession to the applicant (regulation 22).

The applicant must serve a certificate under article 7 of the GD(P)O (certificate as to notices).

4.28 When the local planning authority receives the planning application and environmental statement it must take the steps prescribed by regulation 13(2) of the planning EIA regulations, namely:

(1)   place a copy of the statement on part 1 of the planning register;

(2)   send three copies of the statement to the Secretary of State, together with the application and supporting documentation;

(3)   ask all of the bodies whom the applicant has not served with a copy of the statement but which should be served whether they wish to receive a copy of the statement or any part of it, and inform such bodies that they may make representations;

(4)   inform the applicant of the names and addresses of those bodies who require copies of the statement and ask the applicant whether he wishes to serve those bodies direct or wishes to send the copies to the authority for service; and

(5)   serve on those bodies a copy of any statement sent to them by the applicant for service.

4.29 The local planning authority may at this time request further information from the applicant on any of the matters referred to in paragraph 3 of schedule 3 to the regulations (see appendix 4A below). Such a request must be in writing and the authority must have regard to current knowledge and methods of assessment and the extent to which such further information is reasonably required to give proper consideration to the likely environmental effects of the proposed development. Evidence in support of statements already supplied may also be requested (regulation 19). Regulation 19 extends to planning applications which are dealt with by the Secretary of State or an inspector.

4.30 The bodies to be notified by the applicant are those referred to in article10 of the GD(P)O (old GDO article 18). If not consulted under the applicable provisions of the GD(P)O, the bodies specified by regulation 13(2) of the planning EIA regulations should be consulted, including the Countryside Agency, the Nature Conservancy Council for England (or, in Wales, the Countryside Council for Wales), the Environment Agency (in certain cases) and any principal council for the area in which the development is situated unless that council is the local planning authority. In archaeologically sensitive cases English Heritage or Cadw should be consulted, though article 10 of the GD(P)O only requires consultation where development is likely to affect the site of a scheduled monument (case 'n').

There is no requirement under article 10 to consult the County SMR for the area, nor does ministerial advice recommend this. Such consultation is clearly desirable, however, especially where sites of archaeological importance are already known to exist (see paragraphs 12 and 17 of PPG 16). It can only be concluded that consultation with the local SMR is an integral part of environmental impact assessment where there is any – even a remote – possibility of archaeological remains. Where such consultation has not been carried out it may be reasonable and within regulation 19 for the local planning authority to request additional information. There is no statutory appeal against any request for such further information, although in extreme cases an applicant could choose to contest such a request by judicial review.

4.31 Where an application is made for planning permission without an environmental statement but the local planning authority or Secretary of State determine that an environmental statement should be supplied, there are slightly different publicity requirements. Regulation 14 provides that the applicant, not the local planning authority, must post notices on site and in a newspaper circulating in the locality (regulation 14(2)). When delivering the environmental statement as part of the planning application, the applicant must then certify to the local planning authority that the relevant site notice has been posted or that he could not do so because he had insufficient rights of access to the land in question (regulation 14(5)).

The Decision under the Planning EIA Regulations

4.32 The local planning authority is not permitted to determine an application for planning permission where an environmental impact assessment is required until 21 days after the appropriate site notice has been displayed and 14 days after the appropriate newspaper advert has appeared. In practice the local planning authority will take much longer than this to determine what, invariably, will be a complex proposal; in fact, regulation 32 of the planning EIA regulations extends the period within which an applicant can appeal against non-determination by the local planning authority from 8 to 16 weeks (qualifying article 20 of the GD(P)O; old GDO article 23).

4.33 The local planning authority (or the Secretary of State on call-in, or the Inspector on appeal) should reach its decision in the normal way, that is in 'accordance with the development plan unless material considerations indicate otherwise' (section 54A TCPA 1990, as amended). Once the necessary environmental information is available the regulations do not have any bearing, from a legal perspective, on how the planning application is to be determined, although environmental assessment will have placed more information before the decision-maker, so that the material considerations will be that much more detailed. The preservation of known archaeological remains has been acknowledged as a material consideration in the planning process for more than 20 years (see paragraphs 6.39-6.42 below). The holistic and precautionary emphasis on environmental assessment, supported by the Council Directive 85/337 and the regulations, should be uppermost in the decision-maker's mind when considering the environmental statement and other environmental information. Environmental impact assessment fits in neatly with the philosophy underpinning PPG 16. It will usually be reasonable for the decision-maker to refuse an application where the adverse environmental effects cannot be mitigated, or to impose appropriate conditions where they can.

Whether the application is refused or approved, however, the planning authority must publicise its decision, allow further inspection of all relevant documentation, and give the main reasons and considerations for its decision, including, where permission is granted, a description of the main mitigation measures (regulation 21). In non-EIA cases the requirement to give reasons only applies to instances where planning permission is refused.

Specific concerns

4.34 It should be remembered that environmental impact assessment is only required for major projects or projects likely to have significant environmental effects. The size and nature of the proposed development is a vital consideration, but, it is the significance of the environmental effects themselves not the significance of the scheme in its own right which determines whether formal environmental impact assessment is required. The impact on the cultural heritage should also be taken to include effects arising from the relationship of that heritage with other parts of the environment, for example landscape, soil and even population pressures (see annex III of Directive 85/337). When preparing an environmental statement it is usually apparent that a limited number of environmental effects are of predominant concern; it is rare, however, for these to be entirely archaeological because, to a developer, except perhaps in the case of upstanding field monuments, the mitigation of archaeological threats will seem to be relatively easily achieved. This will often be a misconception by the developer, probably because the desk-based assessment which he has carried out as a preliminary to compiling his environmental statement falls short of what might reasonably be required, or because the archaeological information which is available in inventories, archives, SMRs or aerial photographic records does not permit a reliable assessment to be made.

The developer may encounter problems of access to a site at the early stage when an environmental statement is to be prepared, though this problem can be exaggerated, especially where non-destructive testing is concerned. More significantly, moving to physical examination in the field will both require the appointment of an archaeologist (if one has not already been appointed) and may strengthen the case for further mitigation methods. This, of course, is in the spirit of the whole procedure and developers should be encouraged to instruct an archaeologist where this seems desirable on environmental grounds. Article 5(3) of the Directive as amended now requires environmental statements to include an outline of the main alternatives studied by the developer, together with an indication of the main reasons for the developer's choice, taking into account the environmental effects. If an archaeologist has already been appointed to carry out a desk-based assessment only, it is good professional practice to consider whether further work is required. Failure to do so may lead to problems later, for example with the local planning authority or statutory or other consultees. The planning EIA regulations now provide for a formal opinion, on the preferred scope of the environmental statement, to be obtained from the planning authority (regulation 10). Previously, this procedure had been an informal one, but now that it has statutory recognition environmental statements may be able to cover technical matters in a way which is more amenable to those taking the planning decision.

4.35 It is often said that preliminary archaeological field investigation or 'evaluation' is relatively inexpensive (see, for example, paragraph 21 of PPG 16). In environmental assessment, as in most assessment, the benefit of an evaluation will be directly proportional to the knowledge, experience and money invested in it. If the evaluation consists of field-walking and observation together with mapping costs, expenses will be low. But such assessment will usually be insufficient alone and intensive evaluation, including extensive geophysical survey and selective trial trenching, may be required. These latter costs may not be 'high' but they may be equal to the costs of geological, hydrological or economic studies. It is not possible to specify any hard and fast rules about when such intensive evaluation should be undertaken. The local planning authority's opinion may be vital, as will that of English Heritage, though the developer may prefer to rely on his own, independent archaeological advice. The following are some of the factors which should be taken into account when considering a site intensive evaluation:

(1)   whether there are questions of site demarcation or extent to be answered (as distinct from site inter-relationships);

(2)   whether there are questions of function or chronology that may be answered by artefact finds or other discreet information;

(3)   whether the only evidence currently available was obtained by remote sensing techniques;

(4)   the location of the 'development area' with respect to sites of known archaeological importance outside that area;

(5)   the fragility of the remains to be investigated;

(6)   whether useful comparative data will be produced by intensive evaluation, bearing in mind, for example, the current state of knowledge of the project site type;

(7)   the location and likely effects of the proposed development on the terrain, bearing in mind that

the effects of the development may extend beyond the immediate site boundary; and

(8) whether the main or an important question is the nature and quality of the deposits, in which case geophysical survey alone is unlikely to provide sufficient environmental information.

Of these factors perhaps the least obvious is factor (6). Quantification of archaeological value will rarely be possible, though value may be expressed numerically to enable comparison of complex subjective judgments (see Darvill *et al*, paragraph 2.7 above). However, if it is the belief of a properly informed consultant that evaluation will not assist in the comparison of site value, both between sites within the area of proposed development or between those sites and sites outside that area, evaluation is difficult to justify.

4.36 The results of evaluation should be a more informed environmental statement. Whether the statement is the result of a desk-based assessment or intensive evaluation, the statement should be approached critically. It is not unknown for an environmental statement to repeat very casual and preliminary opinions of a local authority archaeologist, suggesting that the development site is free of archaeological remains. In some instances environmental statements have repeated such comments (probably omitting qualifying wording) whereupon the local authority archaeologist has made representations to the effect that archaeological conditions should be imposed on the planning consent. Even following a relatively sophisticated evaluation it should also be remembered that evaluation is extremely selective of archaeological evidence and that consideration should always be given to the manner in which the implementation of the development, if it is to proceed, should be controlled. Mitigation of adverse effects, and 'preservation by record' of remains which may be disturbed or destroyed, will be the main concern of the decision-maker, but it may be desirable for further and more detailed evaluative work to be undertaken after the planning application is made. Further information to assist in the determination of an application for outline planning permission may be required by the local planning authority under article 3(2) of the GD(P)O, provided that this is information which properly relates to elements of the development which would otherwise be dealt with as reserved matters. This is in addition to the local planning authority's power to request further environmental information under regulation 19 of the planning EIA regulations.

4.37 A good environmental statement should deal thoroughly and in detail with the quality of information upon which the statement is based together with the implications of that knowledge, usually by drawing the decision-maker's attention to several options for dealing with environmental effects and stating the likely effectiveness of each option. In particular, the environmental statement may suggest a programme of mitigation to be undertaken after planning permission has been granted in outline but before both development is commenced and, importantly, before detailed plans are approved. DOE Circular 11/95 (WO 35/95) *The use of Conditions in Planning Permissions* advises that *'for projects subject to environmental assessment, conditions attached to a grant of planning permission may incorporate mitigation measures proposed in an environmental statement'* where such conditions meet the Secretary of State's own tests of necessity, relevance to planning, relevance to the development, enforceability, precision and reasonableness, and do not place unjustifiable burdens on applicants (paragraphs 77 and 14). The Circular acknowledges that planning conditions may require a scheme of mitigation covering matters of planning concern to be submitted and approved in writing before any development is undertaken. Model condition 25 (for landscaping) is suggested as a suitable basis (see appendix 4B of this work).

In special cases, though not mentioned in paragraph 77 of the Circular, the decision-maker may wish to address such mitigation or further, phased evaluation by way of section 106 planning obligation. A planning obligation may, in particular, seek to control the timing of both evaluation and subsequent implementation of planning permission. Such a course of action presumes that the development is to proceed in some form or other and will be of no assistance where the local planning authority is uncertain whether an application should be approved. A programme of further evaluation and/or mitigation is likely to be acceptable only in the case of archaeological sites of known importance (though not necessarily scheduled monuments) when, because of the general desirability of the development, further evidence is required to indicate where mitigation measures should be adopted on site in preference to a programme of archaeological investigation. Although paragraph 77 of the Circular rightly cautions against the use of planning conditions which duplicate other legislative controls, in archaeological matters the AMAA 1979 and the TCPA 1990 are rarely capable, from a technical viewpoint, of dealing with identical issues and so attempts to duplicate or substitute controls are less likely than, say, with listed building controls. A comprehensive approach to archaeological site evaluation is often more easily justified under the TCPA than under the AMAA.

4.38 Reasonably full knowledge of archaeological sites is achieved only by irreversible disturbance (even destruction) of archaeological remains and considerable financial outlay. It is these factors which usually impose the greatest constraints on what can or should be the extent of evaluation. When compared with the techniques of other disciplines there is very little which is technically backward or inadequate in archaeology; and like other disciplines which play a part in environmental assessment, archaeological evaluation should go only so far as is required to assist in the planning decision.

Where archaeological remains are a significant element in an environmental statement, the decision-making body, as well as the developer, will also need access to specialist archaeological opinion. Critical assessment of the statement is vital. The decision-making body should expect an environmental statement to acknowledge any areas of uncertainty and to attempt to quantify benefits and adverse effects independently of one another. Paragraph 1 of *'Environmental Assessment: a guide to the procedures'* (DOE, 1992) states that the environmental statement should also be the result of *'systematic analysis using the best practicable techniques and best available sources of information'*.

For a valuable discussion of the relevant techniques and

assessment of results in an archaeological context see Lambrick (1993). Appendix 10 of the DOE publication *Preparation of Environmental Statements for Planning projects that require Environmental Assessment: A Good Practice Guide* (DOE 1995) contains essential advice on the assessment of the cultural heritage. Archaeology (marine and terrestrial, legally protected or not) is identified by DOE 1995 as an important aspect of the heritage, together with historic buildings, conservation areas, historic landscapes, historic battlefields and parks and gardens. Impacts identified include threats to cultural resources by vibration, air pollution, 'recreation pressure' and ecological damage (paragraph 22). Paragraphs 23-30 deal with scoping, baseline surveys, the prediction of impacts and their mitigation. On scoping the three main components of assessment are identified as archaeology, historic buildings and historic landscapes. Lack of documented information does not mean that a site is devoid of cultural interest and investigation – especially of archaeology and historic landscape features – may still be required. *'The scoping phase should end with identification of any requirements for further information to be collected during the baseline studies'*. Baseline surveys and prediction of impacts should be undertaken by 'an expert in cultural heritage'. Baseline surveys may consist of archival research, field study (including geophysical survey) and trial excavation. In the case of nationally important sites and landscapes the most appropriate form of mitigation of impacts is considered to be complete avoidance, leaving a suitable buffer zone around the site (paragraph 27). Where destruction of sites is unavoidable 'appropriate provisions' may be necessary to excavate and record remains before development commences. If a site is 'unpredictable' in its archaeological potential, it may be necessary to arrange for the construction stage to be overseen by an archaeologist (paragraph 29).

4.39 A prescribed outline for the content of environmental statements is set out in schedule 4 to the planning EIA regulations (reproduced at appendix 4A of this work). The archaeological heritage is now specifically referred to at paragraph 3 of the schedule.

The Return of Cultural Objects Regulations
(see paragraph 4.07)

4.40 Directive 93/7/EEC seeks to impose a duty on each member state to protect the cultural objects of other member states when such objects are removed from the territory of a member state unlawfully. The cultural objects in question must be either national treasures and above specified financial values, or fall into those categories of objects listed in the Directive (ecclesiastical treasures or objects from public collections, for example). The objects must also have been removed from the relevant national territory on or after January 1, 1993. When requested to do so by the first member state the duty placed on the other member state(s) is to seek and preserve the relevant object with a view to returning it to the state from which it was taken. In the United Kingdom, regulations 4 and 5 of the regulations empower the Secretary of State to apply to court for orders facilitating the search for and preservation of objects.

It is the responsibility of the requesting state to pursue the return (rather than the protection) of the object in question. The regulations recognise a specific cause of action for the purpose. An action must be commenced within 30 years from the date of unlawful removal from the requesting member state (75 years in the case of removal from public collections); nor can an action be brought more than one year after the requesting state first became aware of the location of the object and of the identity of the person holding it.

4.41 The domestic regulations on the return of cultural objects must be read together with EU Regulation 3911/92, a measure of direct effect in member states, whose objective is to control the unlawful export of 'cultural goods' from the EU. 'Unlawful' in this sense means in contravention of domestic law of the member state from which an object is to be exported out of the EU. As it is the member state which in each instance is able to grant a licence which satisfies the provisions of the Regulation. Article 2(4) of the Regulation exempts objects which are of (i) 'limited archaeological or scientific interest', are (ii) not the direct product of excavations or finds within a member state and (iii) are on the market lawfully. However, export licences cannot be granted if the issuing authority has notice that the goods have been unlawfully removed from the jurisdiction of another member state. For the purpose of the Regulation cultural goods include:

- archaeological objects which are more than 100 years old and are the product of excavations or finds on land or underwater (annex A1 of the Regulation); and
- any dismembered parts of an artistic, historical or religious monument where such monument is over

100 years old (annex A2 of the Regulation).

The domestic Regulations and EU Regulations have had limited impact on preserving the archaeological heritage as that term is understood by archaeologists, but with the new Treasure Act (see chapter 3) and with progress on various European conventions (see below) improvements in the protection of portable antiquities may be expected in the long term.

The Environmental Information Regulations
(see paragraph 4.07)

4.42 These are aimed more at the accessibility of information relating to pollution than the presence of archaeological sites but the definition of environment in regulation 2(2) includes 'the state of any soil or the state of any natural site or other land'. It is conceivable that information retained by English Heritage, Cadw, the appropriate Royal Commission on Historical Monuments, or local authorities may fall within the regulations, although annex D to the Department of the Environment guidance issued in December 1992 does not refer to these specific heritage organisations. English Heritage, for example, should be considered 'an emanation of the state' for the purposes of the Council Directive, notwithstanding its constitution under a distinct Act.

If a body bound by the regulations refuses to supply information in its possession which the applicant is entitled to see, that decision may be reviewable by the court. In *R. v. British Coal Corporation, ex parte Ibstock Building Products Limited* [1995] J.P.L. 836 QBD the mere granting of leave to apply for an order of *mandamus* against the British Coal

Corporation resulted in the Corporation disclosing the requested information. Harrison J. took a broad view of the information falling within the regulations so that as well as information about the presence of naval munitions in a disused mineshaft, the Corporation had, in addition, to disclose the identity of the person who originally supplied statements to the Corporation. In the circumstances, the identity of the person making the statements was held to be of importance in evaluating the reliability of the basic information supplied by the Corporation (so much so that British Coal was unsuccessful in arguing that it should not have to stand the applicant's costs of the action).

Other European and International Initiatives

4.43 European initiatives which do not yet have legal effect include the conventions promulgated by the Council of Europe, a body consisting of appointees of member states (acting through the Council of Ministers). A Cultural Heritage Committee of the Council carries out the detailed work of preparing such official documentation. The Council of Europe has no legislative capacity and is outside the formal structures of the EU. In heritage matters it has produced the revised *'European Convention on the Protection of the Archaeological Heritage'* (endorsed at Valetta, 1992). This convention is extensive and makes relatively detailed provision for the safeguarding and management of the archaeological heritage.

For the purposes of the convention the archaeological heritage: (1) shows humanity's past; (2) retraces the history of mankind and its relationship with the natural environment; (3) is studied in the main by excavations or discoveries and other methods of research into mankind and the related environment; and (4) is within the jurisdiction of one or more signatories. Article 1 provides a non-exclusive list of the elements of the archaeological heritage to which the convention applies, including *'structures, constructions, groups of buildings, developed sites, moveable objects, monuments of other kinds as well as their context, whether situated on land or under water'* (article 1(3)). Difficulties in reliably defining the extent of national jurisdiction at sea are avoided by accepting whatever jurisdiction signatories assume, be this the territorial sea, the 12 mile zone contiguous to the territorial sea, or some other zone, for example the continental shelf or zone recognised by international economic treaty. The main provisions of the convention are that (a) in the investigation of sites there is an overriding principle of least destruction and maximum information capture, with states preventing illicit excavation of material (article 3); (b) measures should be taken to ensure physical preservation of the heritage, either by preservation *in situ* or in repositories (article 4); (c) planning consultation and environmental impact assessment should have a central role in management of the heritage (article 5); (d) the material resources available for archaeological site rescue should be increased (article 6); and (e) states should make improved arrangements to prevent the illicit trade in antiquities (article 10).

Although the text of the convention has been accepted by 20 signatory nations, to be binding on a national government it must be ratified by the relevant national government. The United Kingdom has yet to ratify. Even when ratified the convention gives signatory states some latitude in implementing its provisions; for example, if a state believes existing controls are already adequate no new measures will be required. One area in which the convention may be a potent moral force, however, is in the United Kingdom attitude to the protection of 'portable antiquities' (see chapter 3, above). For a general discussion of the convention see O'Keefe (1993).

4.44 A step further removed from direct, legal application in the United Kingdom is the *International Charter on Archaeological Heritage Management* (ICAHM), a document drafted during the 1980s and passed by the General Assembly of the International Council on Monuments and Sites (ICOMOS) in 1990, at Lusanne. ICOMOS is an organisation with no particular government links, either in the United Kingdom or in Europe. It is an independent body with national branches, composed mainly of academics and other professionals, active in the development of management standards and conservation frameworks (recently having produced a draft charter for management of the underwater cultural heritage). ICOMOS recommendations in the ICAHM are typically comprehensive and ambitious, probably the stuff of long-term policy change rather than immediate legal impact.

The ICAHM defines the archaeological heritage as '*that part of the material heritage in respect of which archaeological methods provide primary information*' ... comprising '*all vestiges of human existence*' and consisting of '*places relating to all manifestations of human activity, abandoned structures, and remains of all kinds (including subterranean and underwater sites), together with all the portable cultural material associated with them*'. The charter's main principles are that (a) land use must be controlled in order to minimise the destruction of the archaeological heritage (article 2), (b) the protection of the archaeological heritage is a collective public responsibility which must be acknowledged through relevant legislation and the provision of adequate funds (article 3), (c) the compilation of databases recording the heritage should be seen as a continuous process (article 4), (d) archaeological investigation should cause the minimum possible destruction to the archaeological heritage (article 5), (e) preservation of archaeological sites and monuments *in situ* is preferred but any investigations which are undertaken should be according to a justifiable list of priorities (article 6), (f) presentation and reconstruction of sites should not destroy archaeological information and should be seen as a continuing activity (article7) and (g) professional standards amongst archaeologists should be established and maintained and international co-operation encouraged (articles 8 and 9). This list is a greatly distilled summary of the ICAHM, which is a detailed and sophisticated document. For example, article 3 ('legislation and the economy') includes requirements that legislation should *'in principle require full archaeological investigation and documentation in cases where destruction of the archaeological heritage is authorised'* and should make provision for *'the temporary protection of unprotected or newly discovered sites and monuments until an archaeological evaluation can be carried out'*. Article 3 also requires that environmental impact assessment at the developer's own cost should be *'embodied in appropriate legislation'*. The full text of the ICAHM is reproduced in *Antiquity* 67 (1993), 400-402.

CHAPTER FIVE

LISTED BUILDINGS AND HISTORIC LANDSCAPES

A significant amount of archaeology is practised on or in relation to historic buildings, most of which are buildings listed as of special architectural or historic interest. Archaeological remains in the traditional sense, of below ground strata, are accepted as a probable incident of many higher grade listed buildings; there is also an increasing tendency to extend the disciplines of archaeology into the interpretation of above ground remains, for example the phasing or historic development of buildings. Inevitably, those dealing with listed buildings on a regular basis will sooner or later have to consider archaeological matters, whilst archaeologists will find themselves considering listed building law and procedures. In either case it is necessary to have a knowledge of both how listed building law affects historic structures and associated archaeological remains, and how listed building law relates to other parts of the law which are more readily recognised as of relevance to archaeology.

The Statutory and Policy Context

5.01 Listed buildings are the subject of a distinct and

detailed statutory code, now removed from the Town and Country Planning Act and contained in the Planning (Listed Buildings and Conservation Areas) Act 1990 (the 'P(LBCA)A'). The provisions of the P(LBCA)A were just about identical to the listed building provisions of the Town and Country Planning Act 1971 from which they were taken, but subsequently they have been amended in limited but important ways, especially in relation to enforcement, by the PCA 1991.

The main statutory regulations are contained in the Planning (Listed Buildings and Conservation Areas) Regulations 1990 (the 'P(LBCA)R'), which superseded the 1987 regulations; the Town and Country Planning (Enforcement) (Inquiries Procedure) Rules 1992; and the rules relating to public inquiries (see chapter six of this work).

5.02 Listed buildings law, like much of heritage law, is heavily influenced by central government policy. Current advice for England is contained primarily in PPG 15: *Planning and the Historic Environment* (issued jointly by the Secretary of State for National Heritage and the Secretary of State for the Environment in September 1994). PPG 15 summarises Government policy on listed buildings, conservation areas and related matters, and supersedes the advice contained in DOE Circular 8/87 . The directions in 8/87 continued in force until Environment Circular 14/97: *Planning and the Historic Environment: Notification and Directions* (issued jointly by the SSETR and the SSCMS on August 24, 1997). In Wales policy is contained in *Planning Guidance (Wales) Planning Policy* and WO Circular 61/96: *Planning and the Historic Environment: Historic Buildings and*

Conservation Areas (issued on December 5, 1996). New directions in Wales are given in WO Circular 1/98: *Planning and the Historic Environment: Directions by the Secretary of State for Wales* (issued on February 2, 1998).

Until 1992 the listed building functions of the Government were administered by the Secretary of State for the Environment (and, in Wales, by the Secretary of State for Wales). In England, the creation of the Department of National Heritage resulted in a division in listed building and conservation area functions between the two departments, with the Secretary of State for the Environment retaining listed building appeal functions and the Secretary of State for National Heritage assuming responsibility for policy and conservation (see chapter one of this work). The functions of the Secretary of State for the Environment now fall to the SSETR, whilst those of the Secretary of State for National Heritage fall to the SSCMS. In Wales the appropriate committee of the Welsh Assembly is responsible, in consultation with Cadw, for both the policy and appeal functions.

5.03 According to PPG 15, paragraph 6.6, there are over 440,000 listed buildings in England and Wales (20 times the number of scheduled monuments). There can be no doubt that 'listing' is a constraint more readily applied by the Secretary of State. Of course, the true position is more complex than a simple comparison of numbers suggests. There are three grades (non-statutory) of listed building: grade I, grade II* and grade II (unstarred), whereas there is only one category of scheduled monument. If we speak of grade I and grade II* listed buildings only a fairer numerical comparison is achieved (about 27,000 listed buildings, of which about 9,000 are listed grade I). There may be fewer archaeological sites than there are historic buildings, although reliable estimates place the number of archaeological sites in England and Wales at over 600,000.

5.04 To be listed a building must be a *'building of special architectural or historic interest'* (section 1(1), P(LBCA)A). Historic in this sense is taken to mean historic fabric and not association with historic events or people (PPG 15, paragraph 6.15 emphasises that listing due to historical association alone will be exceptional). There must usually be some physical, historic or archaeological structure. This accords with the practice when scheduling monuments. When considering a listing, however, the scope of the Secretary of State's discretion is expressly enhanced by the statutory power contained in section 1(3) of the P(LBCA)A namely that *'in considering whether to include a building in a list compiled or approved under this section, the Secretary of State may take into account not only the building itself but also –*

(a) *any respect in which its exterior contributes to the architectural or historic interest of any group of buildings of which it forms part;*
(b) *the desirability of preserving, on the ground of its architectural or historic interest, any feature of the building consisting of a man-made object or structure fixed to the building or forming part of the land and comprised within the curtilage of the building.'*

There is no comparable express power contained in the AMAA 1979, although a relatively wide definition of 'monument' is applied by section 61(7) of that Act.

5.05 The detailed criteria applied by the Secretary of State when assessing a monument for scheduling are reproduced at paragraph 2.07 of this work. These criteria contrast with those outlined at paragraphs 6.10-6.12 of PPG 15 (and annex C, paragraph 1 of WO 61/96), where, in relation to listed buildings, it is stated that:

'*The following are the main criteria which the Secretary of State applies as appropriate in deciding which building to include in the statutory lists:*

— *architectural interest: the lists are meant to include all buildings which are of importance to the nation for the interest of their architectural design, decoration and craftsmanship; also important examples of particular building types and techniques (e.g. buildings displaying technological innovation or virtuosity) and significant plan forms;*

— *historic interest: this includes buildings which illustrate important aspects of the nation's social, economic, cultural or military history;*

— *close historical association: with nationally important people or events;*

— *group value: especially where buildings comprise an important architectural or historic unity or a fine example of planning (e.g. squares, terraces, or model villages).*

Not all these criteria will be relevant to every case, but a particular building may qualify for listing under more than one of them.'

6.11 *'Age and rarity are relevant considerations, particularly where buildings are proposed for listing on the strength of their historic interest. The older a building is, and the fewer the surviving examples of its kind, the more likely it is to have historic importance. Thus, all buildings built before 1700 which survive in anything like their original condition are listed; and most buildings of about 1700-1840 are listed, though some selection is necessary. After about 1840, because of the greatly increased number of buildings erected and the much larger numbers that have survived, greater selection is necessary to identify the best examples of particular building types, and only buildings of definite quality and character are listed. For the same reasons, only selected buildings from the period after 1914 are listed. Buildings which are less than 30 years old are normally listed only if they are of outstanding quality and under threat. Buildings which are less than 10 years old are not listed.'*

(WO 61/96, annex C talks of 'key examples' rather than 'selected buildings' for the post-1914 period).

These criteria appear to be a summary of the detailed guidance issued in the form of a manual to the historic buildings investigators employed by the Secretary of State. The differences between the manual and the PPG are due to the need for far more rigorous architectural and historic guidelines when assessing individual and borderline cases. It is, nonetheless, obvious from the above criteria that pre-conquest or medieval buildings, and buildings with medieval timber, should usually be listed. The incorporation of remains of such stonework or timber work in buildings of much later date will in itself be some justification for listing, and there are many examples of this. Seventeenth or eighteenth century buildings surviving intact are invariably listed, and the survival of seventeenth or eighteenth century features in a later building will be significant. In later periods, urban planning, the use of iron construction, or association with a specific industrial or architectural technique, are some of the factors which may be persuasive. For a full discussion reference should be made to one of the historic buildings investigators' manuals.

5.06 The best preliminary advice is to make an objective assessment of the building in question, as far as this can be ascertained by detailed, visual inspection and by research in local archives (maps are especially useful but must be used critically). In the nineteenth and twentieth centuries especially a building may be listed (or listed at a higher grade than one might expect) because of its architect or because of its innovative technical features. Earlier buildings may have important features in the roof space, including evidence of firehoods or prefabrication of timbers, or may have changed uses several times over the centuries. There is no substitute for detailed investigation, as discovered in 1988 by the person who recommended the listing of Moss Fen Lodge (see *Medieval gem proves fake*, (1988) *The Guardian*, April 11; a recently built replica, re-assembled from an assortment of medieval timbers, listed and then de-listed when its owner alerted the Secretary of State to the building's origins).

5.07 PPG 15, WO 61/96 and the selection criteria contained in them are, like their predecessors, only advisory. The criteria are not legal requirements; the only statutory test is whether or not a building is of special architectural or historic interest. As with scheduled monuments, the Secretary of State has a statutory duty to compile lists but he has a discretion whether or not to include any individual building in those lists.

There is no statutory definition of what constitutes 'special interest' under section 1(1) of the P(LBCA)A. What is special is within the Secretary of State's discretion having taken the appropriate professional advice and having come to an objective judgment.

'Buildings'

5.08 The term 'building' is part defined by section 91(2) of the P(LBCA)A, which imports the definition contained in section 336(1) of the TCPA 1990, a definition which extends to *any structure or erection and any part of a building, structure or erection* but not any plant or machinery comprised within it. In practice 'building' has come to mean any permanent structure which cannot be easily moved without being dismantled (*Barvis Limited v. Secretary of State for the Environment* (1971) P. & C.R. 710 CA). Section 61(7) of the AMAA includes this wording in relation to the definition of machinery which may be part of a scheduled monument. However, the P(LBCA)A creates an ambiguity in that section 91(2) excludes machinery whilst section 1(5) includes machinery; the *Barvis* definition must still be imported into the listed buildings context from case law. Kerr (C.B. November 1993) cites a listed building appeal inquiry concerning Stotford Water Mill, Bedfordshire, where the inspector decided that section 1(5) overrode section 91(2) and therefore considered all machinery within the mill as included in the listing. But this may not always be the case.

5.09 A greater range of structures may be listed than is usually supposed. Mileposts, guide-stoops, standing stones and crosses, telephone kiosks, gravestones and even stone cobbles have been listed. Ornamental urns set in a garden were the subject of an unsuccessful complaint to the Parliamentary Commissioner for Administration (Fourth report of the P.C.A. (1974-1975, 68-70) where, by listing the urns, the Secretary of State was found not to have listed personal property). The usual property law tests of degree and purpose of annexation are the determining factors. In *Corthorn Land and Timber Co. v. Minister of Housing and Local Government* (1966) 17 P. & C.R. 210, it was held that a building preservation order could attach to chattels which had become so affixed to the land as to become part of the freehold. The property law case of *Berkeley v. Poulett* (1976) 241 E.G. 911; 242 E.G., 32 CA, contains the most authoritative statement on the tests for ascertaining whether an object has become part of the land or building to which it relates. Applying a test originating in the case of *Leigh v. Taylor* [1902] A.C. 157, the Court of Appeal held that (i) if a chattel is fixed to the realty it will become part of the realty unless (ii) the object was fixed in order to improve the enjoyment of the object itself and not the realty. The notion of 'fixing', however, is probably not to be interpreted as meaning that annexation can only take place by means of physical connection. In particular, Scarman L.J. (as he then was) thought that an object simply resting on land under its own weight could be a fixture, although there was a presumption to be displaced that such an object remained a chattel. Degree and purpose of annexation were also accepted as the relevant test by the House of Lords in the landlord and tenant case of *Elitestone Ltd. v. Morris and*

Another [1997] 2 All E.R. 513 (wooden bungalows fixed on concrete pillars deemed to be part of the land).

The *Berkley v. Poulett* test is tacitly acknowledged by PPG 15 at paragraphs 3.31-3.32. The case of *R. v. Secretary of State for Wales, ex parte Kennedy* [1996] J.P.L. 645 confirmed that the property law test applies to listed buildings cases (in this instance the decision of an inspector to uphold a listed building enforcement notice against the removal of a carillon clock from Leighton Hall, Welshpool). The appellant's argument that the clock was machinery and, by virtue of section 91(2) of the P(LBCA)A, outside the ambit of listing, was considered by Ognall J. to be untenable on the facts of the case. The respondent local planning authority had argued that an item of plant or machinery, if a fixture, is to be treated as part of the listed building for the purposes of the listed buildings legislation.

5.10 Structures other than machinery need separate consideration. In *Watson-Smyth v. Secretary of State for the Environment and Cherwell District Council* (1992) 64 P. & C.R. 156 QBD, the court held that a ha-ha could be protected as a structure within the curtilage of a listed building. If a ha-ha can be a structure for the purposes of section 1(5) of the P(LBCA)A such a structure might also be a structure for the purposes of section 1(1) of that Act and be listable in its own right. This argument could apply also to moats and other boundary features whether or not the building which they enclose is listed, and so enable some monuments, which are of less than national importance (and therefore outside scheduling) to receive statutory protection. However, in *Watson-Smyth* the element of construction necessary for constituting the structure in question was an important consideration. Moreover, the original, functional link between such structures and the listed building which they enclose is an important consideration. In *R. v. North Devon District Council, ex parte Tarn* (February 20, 1998; unreported) *Watson-Smyth* was distinguished, when the court at first instance found that a 'hedgebank of traditional construction faced with dry stonework' was originally an old field boundary and not erected for the purpose of enhancing the listed building. Consequently, the court held that the hedgebank was not a curtilage structure.

Exceptions

5.11 Dual listing and scheduling is said to be a historic phenomenon: current policy is to avoid such overlaps where possible (PPG 15, paragraph 6.34). Dual protection usually occurs because scheduling of monuments was introduced into national law before listing, but also because some structures which are first listed are subsequently considered better protected by the 'closer' controls afforded by scheduling. Where a building is both listed and scheduled, the scheduled monument controls take precedence. This precedence has now received statutory acknowledgement in the form of section 61 of the P(LBCA)A, by which the requirement to obtain listed building consent, the ability to serve building preservation notices, the power to compulsorily acquire or carry out section 54 (urgent repairs) works and the ability to prosecute for listed building offences are all dis-applied in relation to buildings which are also scheduled. The anomaly of dual listing and scheduling is to be addressed, in England, by the Monuments Protection Programme (MPP) currently being undertaken by English Heritage. However, where some higher grade listed buildings are de-scheduled, ancillary earthwork structures and the like could benefit from additional protection under listed building controls, particularly where the scheduling was defined on an area rather than a buildings basis.

5.12 A distinction should be drawn between the problems associated with the law of buildings and the law of 'curtilage'. The question of whether a curtilage structure is covered by a listing may present problems similar to the question of whether an object is a building at all, but the curtilage question should be asked only after the buildings test is seen to have been satisfied. If a structure or object is neither a building nor a fixture to a building (or land) it cannot be protected by listing, as a curtilage structure or otherwise.

5.13 At paragraph 2.08 it was explained that a building which is occupied as a dwelling (otherwise than by a caretaker or his family) cannot be a scheduled monument. A building in ecclesiastical use cannot be a monument and so cannot be scheduled as such (section 61(8), AMAA). Neither of these limitations exists in listed building law. Ecclesiastical buildings, including churches and other buildings in use for ecclesiastical purposes, can be listed – though special controls apply when the question of listed building consent falls to be determined (see paragraphs 5.62-5.66, below) – and according to convention are graded A, B or C, in contrast to the secular grades of I, II* and II. Of course, many dwellinghouses are listed. This fact alone emphasises a great difference between the scheduling and listing regimes.

5.14 Crown land may be scheduled and Crown buildings may be listed (section 83(1), P(LBCA)A). To the extent that a listed building is held in the right of the Crown most provisions of the Act (including the requirement to obtain listed building consent) do not apply to that interest. Paragraph 3.40 of PPG 15 cites DOE Circular 18/84: *Crown land and Crown development*, namely the Government's commitment to manage Crown land as if conservation and heritage restrictions apply. Similar commitments are given in WO 61/96, paragraph 129, where WO Circular 37/84 is cited. As with scheduled monuments, the controls are again informal. Section 84 of the P(LBCA)A provides for the grant of listed building consent in anticipation of a Crown disposal of Crown land. There is no such provision in scheduled monument law, but under the AMAA the Crown remains the sole body responsible for issuing scheduled monument consents.

Objects or Structures fixed to Buildings

5.15 Section 1(5) of the P(LBCA)A provides that ... '*listed building means a building which is for the time being included in a list compiled or approved by the Secretary of State under this section; and for the purposes of this Act –*

    (a) any object or structure fixed to the building;
    (b) any object or structure within the curtilage of the building which, although not fixed to the building, forms part of the land and has done so since before 1 July 1948,

shall be treated as part of the building.'

In most instances section 1(5) widens the scope of an individual listing. It is important to note that the description of a building in the certified list of buildings is for information and identification purposes only, and is not an inventory of all the features of architectural or historic interest which a building possesses. The tests relating to fixtures – degree of annexation, for example – apply to the items which may come within the listing. Common examples of fixtures and fittings which will probably be covered include friezes, wood panelling, datestones, plaster, stucco, frescos and mosaic, chimney pieces, fireplaces, window frames and shutters, statuary in relief, shelving or fitted furniture, architraves, balustrades and balconies. Often it will be the removal of the best fixtures of a building which most significantly affects its special character. This is all the more reason to form an accurate view of what is covered by the listing before alterations are carried out. What might appear to be minor works may be fundamental to the building's historic interest, especially if the removal damages historical and archaeological relationships so that a site or structure is more difficult or impossible to interpret.

The expression *'an object or structure fixed to a building'* is unlikely to include a distinct but physically connected building (*Debenhams Plc v. Westminster City Council* [1987] 1 A.C. 396). Such a structure will usually have to be considered under the curtilage rule, if at all.

The Curtilage

5.16 A building is probably only capable of having one

curtilage at any one time, and this must be contiguous to the building in question. This is because any curtilage will usually serve *'the enjoyment of the building (or buildings) and, in this sense, will be ancillary to it'* (see *Watson-Smyth, loc. cit.*, 160, where an important ingredient in determining whether an object was within the curtilage was the ha-ha's ancillary nature in relation to the principal building). The larger the piece of land in question, or the more distant from the main building are particular parts of the land, the more likely it is that the building facilitates the enjoyment of the land (or parts of the land), and not vice-versa. This tends to exclude such land from the curtilage. A curtilage is usually *'in the nature of a garden, courtyard, croft or yard, or a service building'* (*Pilbrow v. St. Leonard, Shoreditch Vestry* [1895] 1 Q.B. 433). However, there is no limit in principle to the size or functional nature of a curtilage as things will depend very much on the building which the curtilage serves. In *Dyer v. Dorset County Council* [1988] 3 W.L.R. 213 CA, the Court of Appeal held that a house at the perimeter of the grounds of an agricultural college, and fenced off from the college grounds, was not within the curtilage of the college in spite of forming part of the same hereditament. The tenant of the house was therefore able to exercise a right-to-buy under the Housing Acts. However, in that case Nourse L.J. and Donaldson M.R. were unable to satisfy themselves that there was a clear or settled definition in English law of the concept of curtilage (*loc. cit.*, 355-358). PPG 15 and WO 61/96 (at paragraphs 3.36 and 90, respectively) both wisely state that *'great caution must therefore be exercised in attempting to extrapolate any general principles from recent decisions, and this guidance does not purport to be definitive'*. Because of the difficulties encountered, the Secretaries of State attempt to list individually all buildings on a site which qualify for listing.

5.17 A question of particular importance has been the effect which change of ownership or change of function may have on the determination of a curtilage or the definition of discreet structures as curtilage buildings. The deceptively obvious considerations taken into account in *Att.-Gen., ex rel. Sutcliffe, Rouse and Hughes v. Calderdale Metropolitan Borough Council* (1983) 46 P. & C.R. 399 were: (i) the physical layout of buildings; (ii) the past and present ownership of the buildings; and (iii) the past and present function and use of the buildings. Clearly, there can be considerable changes in any or all these elements after the date on which a building is first listed. However, in *Sutcliffe*, the court held that where terraced houses were so closely related physically and geographically to a mill, even though the mill and houses were in different ownerships at the applicable time, the houses were still within the curtilage of the mill.

5.18 It is good practice to compare the physical layout of a site at the time of listing and subsequently, especially in relation to boundary structures. The functional relationship of building and lands to the main building at the time of listing and subsequently should be considered especially in relation to subsidiary or complimentary uses. There is no rule that changes in ownership have to take place for a curtilage to be reduced or extinguished; this can occur by the erection of new structures which imply functional changes, or by virtue of functional changes themselves. However, changes in ownership remain significant events in the management of a building and it is at such times that curtilage relationships are most affected. In *Watts v. Secretary of State for the Environment* [1991] J.P.L. 718 QBD, the owner of a barn and manor house sold the manor house in 1981 but retained the barn and connecting wall in its own grounds. The manor house was listed in 1985. The wall was demolished, in part, after the listing and without listed building consent but, at first instance, the court held that as the section of wall formed part of a property separate from the listed building at the date of the listing, the wall was ancillary to a building other than the manor house. The Secretary of State advises that when a self-contained building is fenced or walled-off from the rest of a site at the time of listing, regardless of the reason for the erection or occupation of the new building, it is likely to be regarded as having a separate curtilage (PPG 15, paragraph 3.34).

5.19 *R. v. London Borough of Camden, ex parte Bellamy* [1991] J.P.L. 255 CA concerned very different facts, namely the inclusion (or otherwise) of a coach house within the curtilage of a house in Hampstead Village Conservation Area. As both houses were within the same ownership at the date of listing (1950) and the coach house was at that time probably used as a garage ancillary to the house, the court took the coach house to have been included in the listing.

The problem of curtilage is still a difficult and intractable one. '*In the meanwhile, it is difficult to offer general guidance other than the characteristically safe but unhelpful formula: each case must be considered on its own facts*' (Mynors (1993) J.P.L., 99).

5.20 Whether or not an object or structure falls within the curtilage of a listed building is of obvious importance for listed building control. In theory, controls apply to curtilage objects and structures to the same extent as to principal buildings. There may also be tax savings, especially on business rates and, where alterations are carried out, on value added tax.

5.21 There is no equivalent to the curtilage rule in scheduled monument law. Scheduled monuments are either within the boundary of the scheduled site or they are not. The 'setting' of a monument is a material consideration when *planning permission* is sought (see chapter six), although the setting of a monument, like the setting of a listed building, is difficult to define.

The Setting of a Listed Building

5.22 'Setting' plays an important role in listed building control, perhaps more so than in scheduled monument law. The planning authority must have special regard to the desirability of preserving *inter alia* the setting of a listed building (a) when considering whether to grant listed building consent (section 16(2), P(LBCA)A) and (b) when considering whether to grant planning permission (section 66(1), P(LBCA)A). Specific notice and advertisement requirements apply to a planning application which falls within section 66 (section 67, P(LBCA)A).

PPG 15, paragraph 2.17 advises that the 'setting' of a building should not be interpreted too narrowly; setting may be limited to land which is obviously ancillary but may include land which is some distance away from the building. An authority may be *Wednesbury* unreasonable in concluding that the construction of a large warehouse 80 metres from a listed building does not affect the setting of the listed building (*R. v. South Hertfordshire District Council, ex parte Felton* [1990] E.G.C.S. 34 CA, where the Court of Appeal also held that whether or not a proposal affects the setting is not to be read as 'substantially affects'). In *Worsted Investments Limited v. Secretary of State for the Environment and Uttlesford District Council* [1994] E.G.C.S., 66 QBD; [1994] J.P.L., B111-112, a developer proposed a B1 use building of c. 9,500 square metres with ancillary car parking and an access road, all adjacent to, but beyond the grounds of, Thremhall Priory, Essex. The Priory, a semi-derelict, grade II (unstarred) listed building, was not part of the application site, but the setting of the building was affected. The proposal, which included an element of 'planning gain' to facilitate restoration of the derelict building, was only acceptable to the local authority with a section 106 planning obligation which provided for the protection of the setting of the priory, including a former moat. On appeal against the planning authority's refusal of outline planning permission, the inspector appointed by the Secretary of State found that the alternative scheme would so harm the setting of the building that the harm was not outweighed by the proposed restoration. On appeal to the High Court against the inspector's findings, David Keene Q.C., sitting as a deputy judge of the High Court, held that although policy dictates that every effort has to be made to save listed buildings this does not mean that restoration had to be carried out at all costs, for example by works which would detract from a building's setting.

5.23 The AMAA does not place any duty on local planning authorities in relation to scheduled monuments comparable to the duty under section 66 of the P(LBCA)A. Nor is there a duty comparable to that contained in section 16(2), P(LBCA)A, as local planning authorities do not determine any scheduled monument consent applications (though in POH the Government has consulted on the desirability of delegating this function). There is, therefore, no express statutory duty to take the setting of scheduled monuments into account when determining applications for planning permission; although it may be unreasonable on policy and *Wednesbury* grounds for a planning authority not to do so, and consultation with English Heritage is required under the GD(P)O when a planning proposal is *inter alia* likely to affect the site of a scheduled monument.

In cases of dual listing and scheduling, section 66, P(LBCA)A is still relevant when planning applications fall to be determined, as section 66 is not one of the provisions disapplied by section 61 of the Act.

Group Value

5.24 The possibility of structures being considered together as a group, though individually not meriting listing, is recognised by section 1(3), P(LBCA)A and in scheduled monument law by section 61(10)(b) of the AMAA. In listed building manuals the notation 'GV' denotes group value. Each building in the group should contribute to the whole, otherwise protection for individual buildings as unlisted buildings in a conservation area (or entry on a non-statutory list) might be more appropriate. The wide definition of 'building' in section 336 of the TCPA may apply to a group of structures in close proximity to each other, for example a mounting block, a stile and a gatepost, so that the group is accorded group value.

Parks and Gardens

5.25 English Heritage is empowered to maintain records and make information available to the public under section 33(2) of the NHA 1983, and one of its functions since 1984 has been to compile a Register of Parks and Gardens. Section 8C of the HBAMA 1953, as inserted by the NHA 1983, schedule 4, tacitly acknowledges the existence of a 'register of gardens and other land' in England which appears to English Heritage to be of special interest.

Section 8C provides that where such a list is compiled English Heritage must notify the owner and occupier, the district and county planning authorities and the Secretary of State as soon as reasonably practicable after entering a particular site to the list. A copy of the list description should be served together with the notice.

In Wales Cadw produces a similar list of parks and gardens although this forms part of a more comprehensive register of 'Landscapes, Parks and Gardens of Special Historic Interest'.

5.26 Maintaining the registers of parks and gardens of special historic interest is not a statutory requirement. The inclusion of a garden or park in the registers does not of itself import any statutory restriction or control of the land in question. However, the registers are extensively researched and are authoritative. Initially, the English Heritage list was produced without maps but since about 1992 maps have been available. The format of entries is similar to entries in the list of buildings; the register is also produced in many volumes (like the buildings list but in contrast to the Register of Historic Battlefields). Sites are graded I, II* and II, signifying a similar hierarchy to the listed building grades.

5.27 There is no reason why a garden of sufficient antiquity and importance cannot be protected as a scheduled monument. A relict garden – the remains, for example, of the grounds of a robbed-out medieval fortified house – may be protected in this way, whether or not there are significant architectural remains surviving. The chances of scheduling are enhanced by the existence of other architectural features such as gateways, bridge piers, and outbuildings. The usual criteria for assessing a monument's importance will be applied (see chapter two of this work).

Individual historic features, especially architectural features, may be listed and serve to enhance the protection afforded the garden as a whole, both through the curtilage rules and the duty placed on planning authorities by section 66 of the P(LBCA)A. Many parks and gardens are also formally designated as conservation areas and so require the planning authority to pay special attention to the desirability of preserving or enhancing the character or appearance of the area when exercising their powers under the TCPA or the HBAMA 1953.

5.28 The registers of parks and gardens are an additional, planning constraint, of particular relevance where the landscape or architectural value of gardens and parks merits protection in their own right, without necessary reference to any other historic features which they might serve or with which they might be associated. The grading of a park or garden is independent of the grade given to any listed building which falls within it. The main focus of the registers is the thousands of gardens and parks which are under threat from piecemeal encroachment, unsympathetic development or neglect. '... *Local planning authorities should protect registered parks and gardens in preparing development plans and in determining planning applications. The effect of proposed development on a registered park or garden or its setting is a material consideration in the determination of a planning application*' (PPG 15, paragraph 2.24). Paragraph 131 of *Planning Guidance (Wales) Planning Policy* contains similar advice, though emphasising the interim nature of the register in Wales. The preservation or investigation of archaeological remains in this context is secondary to the well-being of the historic garden or park in question; indeed gardens can benefit at the expense of listed buildings and archaeological remains, although conflicting priorities should be rare.

In England, the status of historic parks and gardens has increased greatly since 1984. Since June 1995 article 10(1)(o) of the GD(P)O has required planning authorities in England to consult English Heritage on all applications affecting grade I and II* gardens or parks; the Town and Country Planning (Consultation with the Garden History Society) Direction 1995 (see DOE Circular 9/95, appendix C) also requires consultation with the Garden History Society on planning applications affecting gardens or parks of any grade. In Wales, Cadw should be consulted instead of

English Heritage. The arrangements are not yet statutory, but will become so when the register is formally adopted. Support at national level for the preservation and enhancement of gardens and parks is strong. Consequently, restrictive interpretation of policy by local planning authorities is usually supported by the Secretary of State or inspectors at appeal.

Battlefields

5.29 In June 1995 English Heritage published a non-statutory Register of Historic Battlefields. There are 43 sites listed, from the earliest (Battle of Maldon) to the most recent (Battle of Sedgemoor), each depicted by a map showing the military positions of the protagonists and the surviving landscape features of note. Paragraph 6.39 of PPG 15 states that there is no intention to grade such sites but emphasises that the current list records only those battlefields which are both important and sufficiently documented to be located on the ground. The Register was maintained by English Heritage for some years before publication and is to be kept under review. Like the parks and gardens register, the Register of Historic Battlefields does not entail any additional statutory controls but is a planning document which will assist planning authorities in considering the effects of development proposals on particular registered sites (PPG 15, paragraph 2.25)

As there are far more planning authorities than registered sites, it follows that many authorities will have no recourse to the Register. Where a registered site is taken into account when making the planning decision, planning authorities should be clear that (i) each entry in the register, inevitably, tends to err on the side of inclusion rather than exclusion, and not every impact will be of major significance; but (ii) the register is compiled with few entries, at national level, and is more likely than are the registers of parks and gardens (or even the statutory list of buildings) to identify sites which, in their entirety are of national importance, by reason of their authenticity, visual amenity, integrity and accessibility. Battlefield sites are in their very nature a testament to transient activity which often leaves little in the way of physical remains; sometimes natural features will be the most important features. Structural remains may include small ditches, palisades or siege works but these rarely define the battlefield, which is just as likely to be identified by its concentration of 'portable antiquities' and human remains (see chapter three of this work).

There is no equivalent, published list of battlefield sites in Wales.

Hedgerows

5.30 Under section 97 of the Environment Act 1995 the appropriate Committee for Wales or, in England, the Secretary of State for Environment, Transport and the Regions and the Minister of Agriculture, Fisheries and Food, are empowered to make regulations for or in connection with the protection of hedgerows. The regulations may contain provisions prohibiting the removal of hedgerows and other prescribed acts, in the interests of environmental conservation. The phrase 'environmental conservation' includes conservation *'of features of archaeological or historic interest'* (section 97(8)). The section makes unauthorised removal of a protected hedgerow punishable on indictment by an unlimited fine or, on summary conviction, by a fine up to the statutory maximum.

The section is a watered down version of the wording originally proposed. The concept of an 'important hedgerow' is likely to be construed narrowly; assessment will require national criteria to be established, in consultation with a limited range of environmental consultees (in the historic sphere, almost exclusively English Heritage and Cadw). The level of fines specified for the removal of hedgerows suggests a serious offence, akin to unauthorised works to listed buildings or scheduled monuments. Permitted development rights will, in effect, be restricted where hedgerows become protected, notably in the agricultural sphere.

Section 97 may be especially useful in protecting linear archaeological features traditionally associated with hedgerows, for example prehistoric and medieval roads and tracks. Ditches and other structural features of field monuments may also benefit, although many of these features will already be scheduled and hedgerows on such sites tend to be limited in extent. Hedgerow protection promises to be most useful in preventing the deterioration of wider landscape areas.

5.31 Regulations been made (The Hedgerows Regulations 1997; S.I. 1997, No.1160) but have been placed under review by the incoming Government. Reconsultation with statutory consultees has taken place: i.e. bodies representative of affected businesses; landowners and local authorities; 'such bodies whose statutory functions include the provision to

Ministers of the Crown of advice concerning matters relating to environmental conservation'; and 'other bodies'. Regulations must be laid before Parliament, for approval on affirmative resolution of both houses.

The minimum extent of hedgerow to which the regulations apply is *'any hedgerow growing in or adjacent to, any common land, protected land, land used for agriculture, forestry or breeding or keeping of horses, ponies or donkeys, if (a) it has a continuous length of, or exceeding, 20 metres; or (b) it has a continuous length of less than 20 metres and, at each end, meets (whether by intersection or junction) another hedgerow'* (regulation 3(1)). Hedgerows within the curtilage or marking the curtilage of a dwellinghouse are excluded (regulation 3(3)). A person wishing to remove such a hedge must serve a 'hedgerow removal notice' (in the form prescribed by schedule 4 of the regulations) on the local planning authority. Removing a hedgerow to which the regulations apply will constitute an offence, punishable as stated above, unless (a) the period of 42 days has elapsed since service of the notice and the planning authority has not responded, or (b) the planning authority has consented to the removal in writing.

If the local planning authority objects to the removal and the hedgerow is an 'important hedgerow' (but not otherwise) the authority must serve a 'hedgerow retention notice' on the applicant, unless the authority is *'satisfied, having regard in particular to the reasons given for its proposed removal in the hedgerow removal notice, that there are circumstances which justify the hedgerow's removal'* (regulation 5(5)(b)). A hedgerow cannot be 'important' unless it, or the hedgerow of which it is a part *'(a) has existed for 30 years or more, and; (b) satisfies at least one of the criteria listed in part II of schedule 1'* to the regulations (regulation 4). Part II of that schedule provides archaeological, historical, wildlife, and landscape criteria. The archaeological and historical criteria are as follows:

'1. *The hedgerow marks the boundary, or part of the boundary, of at least one historic parish or township; and for this purpose 'historic' means existing before 1850.*

2. *The hedgerow incorporates an archaeological feature which is –*

   (a) *included in the schedule of monuments compiled by the Secretary of State under section 1 (schedule of monuments) of the Ancient Monuments and Archaeological Areas Act 1979; or*
   (b) *recorded at the relevant date in a Sites and Monuments Record.*

3. *The hedgerow –*

   (a) *is situated wholly or partly within an archaeological site included or recorded as mentioned in paragraph 2 or on land adjacent to and associated with such a site; and*
   (b) *is associated with any monument or feature on that site.*

4. *The hedgerow –*

   (a) *marks the boundary of a pre-1600 AD estate or manor recorded at the relevant date in a Sites and Monuments Record or in a document held at that date at a Record Office; or*

      (b) is visibly related to any building or other feature of
           such an estate or manor.

5. *The hedgerow –*

      (a) is recorded in a document held at the relevant date at a
           Record Office as an integral part of a field system
           pre-dating the Inclosure Acts; or
      (b) is part of, or visibly related to, any building or other
           feature associated with such a system, and that system–

           (i) is substantially complete; or
           (ii) is of a pattern which is recorded in a document
               prepared before the relevant date by a local planning
               authority, within the meaning of the 1990 Act, for
               the purposes of development control within the
               authority's area, as a key landscape characteristic.'

(The 1990 Act referred to is the TCPA. The 'relevant date' is the date of the regulations, i.e. March 24, 1997, so that later additions to Sites and Monuments Records etc. cannot be taken into account. 'Sites and Monuments Record' is not restricted to County Sites and Monuments Record but extends to any 'record of archaeological features and sites adopted by resolution of a local authority or, in Greater London, by English Heritage'. 'Record Office' includes any place at which documents are made available for inspection under section 1 of the Local Government (Records) Act 1962, places where documents are held subject to tithe redemption arrangements and public record depositories.)

A hedgerow retention notice must specify the applicable schedule 1 criteria(on). Removal of a hedgerow the subject of such a notice is a separate offence, punishable as stated above (regulation 7(1)). A person served with a retention notice may appeal to the Secretary of State who, after hearing the appellant and the local planning authority (by written representations or local inquiry) may quash, modify or uphold the notice.

World Heritage Sites

For sites designated as World Heritage Sites see paragraph 4.02 of this work.

Historic Landscapes Generally

5.32 There is no specific statutory protection in English law for areas of historic landscape, that is extended areas containing a number of monuments and associated features, not necessarily of one historic or prehistoric period. Some argue that the existing controls are already sufficient, although the balance of informed opinion seems to be that the availability of a historic landscape designation would be useful. The most important 'area designation' which does exist is that of national park. Here development is strictly controlled and the new authorities constituted under the Environment Act 1995 are now under a duty to conserve and enhance the cultural heritage as well as the natural landscape. Positive initiatives to preserve historic areas in the national parks should increase. However, other designations – for example, Areas of Outstanding Natural Beauty or Environmentally Sensitive Areas (see chapter 4 of this work) – may often encourage preservation of historic remains, but the historic elements of the landscape may lack the kind of protection which would follow from specifically historic, protective measures. The same can also be said of many conservation areas, designated on particular architectural grounds, where the duty to preserve or enhance the area may run counter to protection of historic remains *per se*.

5.33 Gardens, battlefields and World Heritage Sites succeed mainly in raising the profile of a landscape when a decision is taken on an application for planning permission. This is useful but a far cry from statutory protection, especially in cases where development may take place without a specific grant of planning permission. Under section 66 of the P(LBCA)A, the planning authority must have special regard to the desirability of preserving the setting of a listed building; there is no like statutory duty under the AMAA for scheduled monuments, although preservation of a monument's setting is an important planning consideration. The combined effect of one or more higher grade listed buildings or scheduled monuments in a landscape is to enhance the preservation of the features in that area that are associated with the buildings or monuments in question; the preservation of historic features which are not related and not protected under statute is another matter. Policies in development plans provide for the identification of archaeological sites which are not scheduled monuments (see chapter six); policies may identify areas – usually part of a 'special landscape area' designation, or similar – as well as discreet sites, although a considerable amount of preparatory work is required to justify such an approach at local inquiry. But such identification is only effective as far as a grant of planning permission is required; even then, the designation will influence rather than determine the planning decision. Deliberate or negligent damage to sites is not readily punishable in such circumstances. In rural areas especially, designation of Areas of Archaeological Importance (see chapter 2 of this work) could be a restraint on damage or works undertaken without the need for planning permission, but there is no intention by government, central or local, to make such designations. In Wales there are no AAIs at all.

5.34 English Heritage has not published any list or register of historic landscape areas for England. Paragraph 6.40 of PPG 15 states that *'much of its* [the wider historic landscape] *value lies in its complexity, regional diversity and local distinctiveness, qualities which a national register cannot adequately reflect'*. In Wales, Cadw includes historic landscapes in its register of landscapes, parks and gardens of special historic interest. 'Landscapes' include larger areas than could be covered by the English Heritage register of parks and gardens. However, the prospect of statutory protection for historic landscapes in either England or Wales still seems remote.

Listing Building Procedures

5.35 The Secretary of State has a duty to compile a list of buildings of special architectural or historic interest, and may approve, with or without modification, such lists compiled by English Heritage, Cadw or other heritage bodies or persons (section 1(1), P(LBCA)A). A similar duty has existed since the Town and Country Planning Act of 1947. There is no statutory or formal right of appeal against listing (PPG 15, paragraph 6.26 (and WO Circular 61/96, paragraph 58), advises on informal requests to have a building 'de-listed' on the historical or architectural merits).

Before compiling, approving or amending a list of buildings in England, the Secretary of State must consult English Heritage and such other bodies or persons having special knowledge or interest in buildings of special architectural/historic interest as he thinks appropriate (section 1(4), P(LBCA)A). There is no statutory duty to consult the relevant local authority, local heritage bodies or the national amenity societies, though consultation does take place between local planning authorities and English Heritage/Cadw before systematic re-surveys are submitted to the Secretary of State. It should be added that English Heritage relies on extensive consultation with the RCHM(e) as, in Wales, does Cadw with the RCAHM(w).

5.36 Listing which is not the product of systematic re-surveys is usually referred to as 'spot-listing' and often occurs when local heritage bodies or local planning authorities make individual recommendations to the Secretary of State. Systematic re-survey and spot-listing are legally indistinguishable. More unusual paths to listing, however, include 'deemed listing' of a building. This occurred on January 1, 1968 when all unlisted buildings subject to a Building Preservation Order were deemed to be listed. Listing can also occur when an application for a 'certificate of immunity from listing' fails to be granted by the Secretary of State. The latter procedure was introduced in the wake of *Amalgamated Investment and Property Company v. John Walker and Sons* [1976] 3 All E.R. 509 CA, where between exchange of contracts and completion of the sale of a bonded warehouse, the warehouse was listed and, as far as the purchaser was concerned, greatly depreciated in value. The Court of Appeal held that the purchaser had no remedy, listing being a risk which the purchaser had to accept. Schedule 15 of the Local Government, Planning and Land Act 1980 accordingly inserted section 54A into the Town and Country Planning Act 1971, the successor provisions to which are now contained in section 6 of the P(LBCA)A. Under section 6, if a planning application has been made for development which involves the alteration, extension or demolition of a building, or if planning permission for such development has been granted, any person can apply to the Secretary of State for a certificate that the building will not be listed. If a certificate is given the building cannot be listed – and a Building Preservation Notice cannot be served – for five years after the date of the certificate. The procedure may be useful to developers but it carries a risk that the Secretary of State will refuse a certificate and so list the building. Paragraph 6.29 of PPG 15 and paragraph 61 of WO 61/96 advise that a building is usually completely re-assessed; this will be the case even if already assessed as part of systematic survey. It is not only the occupier, owner or applicant for planning permission who may apply for a certificate; any person may apply (section 6(1)(b), P(LBCA)A). If a certificate is issued local planning authorities are notified and the certificate should be disclosed in response to planning enquiries of the relevant local authority as part of a conveyancing search.

5.37 In addition to listing by the Secretary of State, local planning authorities (including national park authorities but excluding county councils) may serve Building Preservation Notices (BPNs) on owners in respect of any unlisted building which, in the opinion of the authority, is (a) of special architectural or historic interest, and (b) in danger of demolition or alteration in such a way as to effect its character (section 3, P(LBCA)A). These notices must be distinguished from the now defunct building preservation *orders*. English Heritage is also empowered to serve BPNs in London. Once issued such a notice comes into immediate effect. After issue the authority is under an obligation to request the Secretary of State to list the building (section 3(2), P(LBCA)A). A BPN remains in force for six months or the earlier date on which the Secretary of State includes the building in the statutory list or advises the authority concerned that he will not include the building in the list. Whilst in force the notice has the effect of making the building subject to the provisions of the P(LBCA)A as if it were listed. If the building in question does not become listed as a result of this process the authority will be liable to pay compensation to the persons affected, including compensation arising from breaches of contract which the notice may have induced (section 29, P(LBCA)A). There is no provision which enables the Department for Culture, Media and Sport or the Welsh Office to indemnify an authority or otherwise assist in the process. Paragraphs 46-48 of DOE Circular 8/87 formerly urged local authorities to make full use of their section 3 powers; the sober advice at paragraphs 6.23-6.25 of PPG 15 is more realistic.

5.38 There is no 'immunity certificate' procedure under

scheduled monument law. Nor are there provisions comparable to the service of a Building Preservation Notice. Local authorities have no power to issue such a notice in respect of monuments which are not buildings, although when a breach of planning control threatens such a monument enforcement under the TCPA 1990 may be a possibility (see paragraph 6.37-6.39 below).

The Statutory List

5.39 The statutory list takes the form of booklets, each covering the several constituent parts of each local authority area. Booklets should be certified on behalf of the Secretary of State; uncertified booklets may be provisional lists or copy lists which could not be adduced as evidence of listing. It is the signing of the list or, in the case of spot-listing, the individual list entry, which effects the listing (the *John Walker* case, above). Each building is recorded by reference to a map sheet number, a postal address, listing grade (I, II* or II), indication of group value (GV), if appropriate, and a textual description. The list should be read with the relevant map sheets. In contrast to scheduled monument law, neither the textual description nor the map sheets define the extent of listing. They are in effect for information purposes, with the extent of listing only ascertainable from an inspection of the building in question.

The Local Authority Role

5.40 The list of buildings must be open to public inspection (section 2(4), P(LBCA)A). The most accessible are those circulated to local planning authorities and SMRs. It is the task of local authorities to notify owners and occupiers of a new listing (schedule 4 to the P(LBCA)R prescribes a form for the purpose), unlike scheduled monuments, where English Heritage or Cadw makes the notifications. The local authority should also register the listing as a local land charge (section 2(2) of the P(LBCA)A deems the registering local authority to be the originator of the charge).

Immediately a building is listed or is subject to a Building Preservation Notice consent, known as 'listed building consent', will usually be required to demolish it or to alter or extend it in any way which would affect the building's character as a building of special architectural or historic interest. The application for consent is made to the relevant local planning authority. Without listed building consent, and compliance with the attendant statutory requirements, works may be in breach of section 7, P(LBCA)A, and thereby constitute a criminal offence.

5.41 Listing also places the planning authority under a specific duty when determining an application for planning permission under the TCPA. The duty is to have *'special regard to the desirability of preserving the building or its setting or any features of special architectural or historic interest which it possesses'* (section 66, P(LBCA)A). Where listed buildings are part of an integrated archaeological site or landscape this section is an important reminder of the potential materiality of historic remains to planning decisions (see paragraph 6.54 of this work).

Constraints

5.42 Under listed building control, consent may be required for many works which would be permitted development by virtue of the GPDO, or which would not be development at all under the TCPA. Examples include replacement of doors and windows, replacement of low boundary walls or painting the exterior of a building (painting the exterior of a building in 'deep pink with black detailing' was held to be capable of requiring listed building consent in *Royal Borough of Windsor and Maidenhead v. Secretary of State for the Environment and Others* (1988) 56(3) P.C.R. 427 QBD). Works to the interior of a listed building will also require consent if the proposed works affect the character of the building as a building of special architectural or historic interest (section 7, P(LBCA)A). It is not necessary for the parts of the interior (or exterior) affected to be mentioned in the list description. According to the rules already considered at paragraphs 5.15-5.19, works which affect objects or structures fixed to or within the curtilage of a listed building may also require consent.

5.43 Works for the alteration or extension of a listed building will be authorised if:

'(a)   *written consent for their execution has been granted by the local planning authority or the Secretary of State; and*
(b)   *they are executed in accordance with the terms of the consent and of any conditions attached to it'* (section 8(1), P(LBCA)A).

Alterations and extensions which are unsympathetic may be

as damaging as demolition. Case law and appeals indicate the scope of matters which must be considered: the addition of doors to a storm porch has been held on appeal to be capable of requiring listed building consent ((1985) J.P.L. 416), as has the reduction in the roof space of a barn ((1989) J.P.L. 308). Partial demolition in order to make way for an extension has been held to be demolition nonetheless (*R. v. Hertfordshire District Council, ex parte Sullivan* (1981) J.P.L., 752). However, in *Shimizu (U.K.) Ltd v. Westminster City Council* [1997] 1 All E.R. 481 the House of Lords decided that a proposal to remove chimney breasts from a building, whilst retaining chimney stacks and the main facade, could be properly considered as a proposal to alter and not to demolish part of a listed building. The Lords did not accept that the term 'listed building' could be limited to part of a listed building and so concluded that demolition meant *'pulling down a building so that it was destroyed completely and broken up'*. Appendix E of Environment Circular 14/97 (*Planning and the Historic Environment – Notification and Directions by the Secretary of State* (issued jointly by the SSETR and SSCMS on 24 August 1997)) gives timely and appropriate advice:

> *'Whether works are for demolition or alteration is still a matter of fact and degree in each case, to be decided in the light of guidance given by the House of Lords. Major works which comprise or include acts of demolition falling short of complete destruction of a listed building e.g. facade retention schemes may still constitute works of demolition, therefore, depending on their extent. However, many works which were previously regarded as demolition, because they involved destruction of part of the fabric of the building, will now fall into the category*

of alterations and will require consent only if they affect the building's character as a building of special architectural or historic interest.'

One result of this new interpretation of demolition is that applications for consent for alterations will have to be more closely scrutinised by decision makers to ensure that adequate conditions are attached to any consents granted (for example, rights for the appropriate Royal Commission may need to be secured by condition if there is no demolition at law and the statutory provisions below are, therefore, inapplicable).

5.44 Works for the demolition of the whole or part of a listed building will be authorised if (i) consent is received; (ii) demolition takes place in accordance with the consent and any conditions attached to it; (iii) *'notice of the proposal to execute the works has been given to the Royal Commission'* [RCHM(e) or RCAHM(w), as appropriate], *'and either –*

for a period of at least one month following the grant of such consent, and before the commencement of the works, reasonable access to the building has been made available to members or officers of the Royal Commission for the purpose of recording it, or

the Secretary of the Royal Commission, or another officer of theirs with authority to act on their behalf for the purposes of this section, has stated in writing that they have completed their recording of the building or that they do not wish to record it' (section 8(2), P(LBCA)A).

5.45 '*In considering whether to grant listed building consent for any works the local planning authority or the Secretary of State shall have special regard to the desirability of preserving the building or its setting or any features of special architectural or historic interest which it possesses*' (section 16(2), P(LBCA)A). The listed building code, therefore, imposes a specific duty on the decision maker, as well as on the applicant, when works are proposed which affect a building's special character. Such a specific heritage duty is not found in scheduled monument law, where the Secretary of State's discretion is free of such express obligation.

5.46 When an application for listed building consent falls to be determined, advertisement and notification will usually have ensured that the decision maker has received a number of representations from statutory bodies, amenity societies and the public. Such representations must be considered by the decision maker (regulation 5, P(LBCA)R 1990) together with any other matter which the decision maker sees as material, in line with the duty imposed by section 16(2). Section 16 does not refer to 'material considerations' (contrast section 70, TCPA). Section 70 will only be relevant if an application for planning permission is required. Development plan policies may be instructive but, again, will only be directly relevant to applications which entail an element of development.

5.47 Decision makers should comply with the advice given in PPG 15 or its Welsh equivalents unless there are good reasons for not doing so. Paragraph 3.3 of the PPG advises that '*there should be a general presumption in favour of the preservation of listed buildings, except where a convincing case can be made out, against the criteria set out in this section, for alteration or demolition'*. In paragraph 3.5 the general criteria which may be relevant are said to be:

'i. *the importance of the building, its intrinsic architectural and historic interest and rarity, in both national and local terms ...;*

ii. *the particular physical features of the building (which may include its design, plan, materials or location) which justify its inclusion in the list: list descriptions may draw attention to features of particular interest or value, but they are not exhaustive and other features of importance (e.g. interiors) may come to light after a building's inclusion in the list;*

iii. *the building's setting and its contribution to the local scene, which may be very important, e.g. where it forms an element in a group, park, garden or other townscape or landscape, or where it shares particular architectural forms or details with other buildings nearby; and*

iv. *the extent to which the proposed works would bring substantial benefits for the community, in particular by contributing to the economic regeneration of the area or the enhancement of its environment (including other listed buildings).'*

These criteria are repeated in paragraph 70 of WO 61/96 and a similar presumption in favour of preservation is stated at paragraph 119 of PG(W)PP.

5.48 Paragraphs 3.6 of PPG 15 and paragraph 71 of WO 61/96 remind authorities that in principle there is no distinction to be drawn in applying the statutory controls to different grades of listed building. Grade is a material consideration, especially in the context of proposed alteration or extension, but it is not a reliable guide to the sensitivity of a building to alteration. Paragraphs 3.12-3.15, together with annex C, of the PPG contain relevant guidance on alterations (now amended in accordance with appendix E of Environment Circular 14/97 as a result of *Shimizu*). Authorities are reminded that listed buildings *'may comprise not only obvious visual features such as decorative facades or, internally, staircases or decorated plaster ceilings, but the spaces and layout of the building and the archaeological or technological interest of the surviving structure or surfaces'*.

Consent for Demolition

5.49 Not surprisingly the Secretary of State is reluctant to sanction the demolition of listed buildings. Even where a listed building has been completely demolished – and, in the case in question, was awaiting shipment overseas – a listed building enforcement notice may validly require its return to site and re-construction, if a sufficient part of the building still remains and re-construction is feasible (*R. v. Leominster District Council, ex parte Antique Country Buildings Ltd. and Others* (1988) 56 P. & C.R. 240, QBD.; timbers from a dismantled, grade II(unstarred), timber-framed barn, comprising 70-80% of a recoverable whole required to be returned and re-constructed *in situ*). The owner in such circumstances is the owner of the constituent parts of the building notwithstanding the translation of the building from realty into chattels.

5.50 Paragraph 3.19 of PPG 15 (as amended) develops the thinking behind paragraph 89 of old DOE Circular 8/87, in particular that the relevant authority should take into account specified matters when considering an application for total or substantial demolition of a listed building. The specified matters are as follows:

'i.   *the condition of the building, the cost of repairing and maintaining it in relation to its importance and to the value derived from its continued use. Any such assessment should be based on consistent and long-term assumptions. Less favourable levels of rents and yields cannot automatically be assumed for historic buildings. Also, they may offer proven technical performance, physical attractiveness and functional spaces that, in an age of rapid change, may outlast the short-lived and inflexible technical specifications that have sometimes shaped new developments. Any assessment should also take account of the possibility of tax allowances and exemptions and of grants from public and charitable sources. In the rare cases where it is clear that a building has been deliberately neglected in the hope of obtaining consent for demolition, less weight should be given to the costs of repair;*

ii.   *the adequacy of efforts made to retain the building in use. The Secretaries of State would not expect listed building consent to be granted for demolition unless the authority (or where appropriate the Secretary of State himself) is satisfied that real efforts have been made without success to continue the present use or to find compatible alternative uses for the building. This should include the offer of the unrestricted freehold of the building on the open market at*

> *a realistic price reflecting the building's condition (the offer of a lease only, or the imposition of restrictive covenants, would normally reduce the chances of finding a new use for the building);*
>
> iii. *the merits of alternative proposals for the site. Whilst these are a material consideration, the Secretaries of State take the view that subjective claims for the architectural merits of proposed replacement buildings should not in themselves be held to justify the demolition of any listed building. There may very exceptionally be cases where the proposed works would bring substantial benefits for the community which have to be weighed against the arguments in favour of preservation. Even here, it will often be feasible to incorporate listed buildings within new development, and this option should be carefully considered: the challenge presented by retaining listed buildings can be a stimulus to imaginative new design to accommodate them.'*

These considerations illustrate the differences underpinning the listed building and scheduled monument codes. In determining an application for scheduled monument consent, the first two considerations would be of little, if any, relevance. Gradual collapse and ruination of a scheduled historic structure, although persuasive in the support of consent for repairs, could never merit the grant of consent for demolition of a scheduled monument.

5.51 Paragraph 3.16 of the PPG concedes that occasionally there will be cases when demolition of a listed building is unavoidable. This may be on grounds of health or safety or some other exceptional circumstance. Economic considerations are also frequently of central importance, to an extent unknown in scheduled monument cases.

Listed building consent has been granted for the demolition of a warehouse where there was held to be no reasonable prospect of saving it or otherwise developing the surrounding area ((1981) J.P.L. 72 and 306). Indeed, although Government guidance advocates a stern treatment of economic arguments, it has been held that where a decision maker fails to give proper consideration to the costs of restoration, even where these might not be prohibitive, the decision may be unlawful and quashed as a consequence (*Kent Messenger Ltd. v. Secretary of State for the Environment* (1976) J.P.L. 372). That said it is debatable whether any positive conclusions can be drawn from the various listed building consent appeals which have considered economic arguments. Each application is best dealt with openly, on its own merits, with a reasonable approach by all parties. The basic legal background is that:

(a) economic factors are relevant, especially in relation to implementation within a reasonable timescale;

(b) funding by way of 'enabling development' (i.e. a proposal linked with the works for which listed building consent is sought), or from the development itself, may be lawfully considered; and

(c) consent for demolition or alteration will not be granted simply because a proposal is demonstrably viable from the economic standpoint and no viable, but less damaging, proposal has been identified.

Each case will bring with it particular, often unique, economic and historic considerations. The determination which the decision maker (national or local) arrives at in these difficult circumstances is rarely one so perverse that the court will overturn it. One recent case serves to demonstrate the latitude which the decision maker enjoys. In *R. v. West Dorset District Council, ex parte Searle* (1998), unreported, the Court of Appeal considered an application to quash the decision of the local planning authority to grant planning permission and listed building consent for the conversion of Downe Hall, Bridport (grade II listed, conversion to five residential units together with eight new houses in the grounds). English Heritage had written to the planning authority requesting that the developer's financial appraisal be tested against other financial scenarios. Apparently this was not done, but the court declined to hold that the planning authority had acted outside its jurisdiction. No doubt English Heritage would, in such circumstances, expect to refer confidently to its own guidance, i.e. that contained in paragraphs 3.3 (economic appraisal) and 3.4 (enabling development) of its advice note on the historic environment, EH 1995. Paragraph 3.3 states *inter alia 'if a proposal would involve material detriment to the special interest of a listed building or the character or appearance of a conservation area, a decision on its acceptability needs to be informed, among other considerations, by an economic appraisal of the scheme and also of alternative scenarios, including a realistic assessment of what would happen if the development were not to go ahead'.* Paragraph 3.4 then states *inter alia* that *'permission should not be granted for otherwise undesirable enabling development just to secure the repair of an important listed building, even one which is seriously at risk. Developers should understand that they cannot expect to receive permission for such proposals in order to cover an anticipated deficit, when the speculative purchase price for a listed building and the cost of repairing and converting it to the most beneficial use consistent with its historic form and character will be significantly in excess of the subsequent value of the repaired building'*. But in *Searle* the court, like the planning authority, was not persuaded that such an approach had to be taken for the decision to remain within the authority's statutory discretion. No doubt a challenge by the applicant, of a refusal of consent, would have met with a similar judgment from the court as long as the planning authority had taken the financial appraisal into account, albeit without detailed consideration of other financial scenarios.

5.52 Very occasionally, economic factors may be considered entirely in the context of development benefit, and so outweigh the question of restoration or even survival of the building itself. In *R. v. Westminster City Council, ex parte Monahan* [1989] 2 All E.R. 74 CA the Court of Appeal, upholding the first instance decision, would not quash a decision of the Secretary of State to grant consent for the demolition of a grade II(unstarred) building (a nineteenth century pavilion-cum-hall), where demolition was thought to be necessary for the continued prosperity and functioning of the adjacent opera house (the Royal Opera, Covent Garden). In *SAVE Britain's Heritage v. Secretary of State for the Environment* [1991] 2 All E.R. 10 the House of Lords upheld the minister's decision to permit the demolition of a row of eight grade II (unstarred), nineteenth century houses so that a development proposal which promised local environmental and design improvements could proceed. This must be considered one of those proposals which principle iii, paragraph 3.19 of the PPG refers to as providing 'substantial benefits for the community'. Certainly, in general policy terms, such treatment of listed buildings finds little support; this was the background to SAVE's application to court. The court provided a useful, if unfortunate, reminder that circulars and PPGs are guidance and no more – persuasive but not binding.

5.53 In Wales, *Planning Guidance (Wales): Planning Policy*, paragraph 120, repeats paragraph 3.17 of PPG 15 almost verbatim when addressing the specific circumstances in which demolition may be authorised. Paragraph 120 states that '... *the Secretary of State would not expect consent to be given for total or substantial demolition of any listed building without convincing evidence that all reasonable efforts have been made to sustain existing uses or find viable new uses, and these efforts have failed; that preservation in some form of charitable or community ownership is not possible or suitable; or that redevelopment would produce substantial benefits for the community which would decisively outweigh the loss resulting from demolition'*.
Like paragraph 3.17 of the PPG this adds little to the more comprehensive ministerial statements on the matter (paragraph 3.19 of the PPG 15, for example).

5.54 The demolition of an unlisted building in a conservation area will require conservation area consent if the demolition is to be lawful (section 74, P(LBCA)A 1990; an ecclesiastical building may be exempt). If the building is listed or scheduled, however, no conservation area consent is required; listed building consent or scheduled monument consent will suffice. Following *Shimizu* 'partial demolition' is to be construed as a contradiction in terms and so what was formerly referred to as partial demolition of an unlisted building in a conservation area no longer requires conservation consent. However, demolition remains an operation which may in itself constitute development, albeit that an express grant of planning permission is rarely required (see paragraphs 6.18-6.20 of this work).

5.55 Works not involving demolition will not need conservation area consent but if constituting development for which an express grant of planning permission is required must be considered by the decision making authority in the light of section 72(1) of the P(LBCA)A, i.e. that *'special attention shall be paid to the desirability of preserving or enhancing the character or appearance'* of the conservation area. In *South Lakeland District Council v. Secretary of State for the Environment* [1992] 2 W.L.R. 204 HL, the House of Lords held that, in this context, to 'preserve or enhance' does not mean that development must make a positive contribution to the conservation area; development may either make such a contribution or, alternatively, may be such as will not harm the conservation area.

The Grant of Listed Building Consent

5.56 In most cases where listed building consent is required the local planning authority is the body which receives applications in the first instance (the Crown does not need listed building consent and ecclesiastical bodies may benefit from limited exemptions but otherwise must comply; county councils must apply to the appropriate district council). The main exception is for local planning authorities' own applications (which must be made to the SSETR or the relevant Committee for Wales, as appropriate). In the case of works to be carried out by English Heritage on its own property or property in its care or prospective ownership application is to the SSETR (paragraph 32, Environment Circular 14/97). By virtue of section 61, P(LBCA)A the latter procedure does not apply to works to buildings which are also scheduled monuments.

5.57 If the intended works also constitute development for which planning permission is required under the TCPA, an application to the local planning authority for planning permission will be necessary. It is usual for the listed building and planning applications to be considered together. Delays may occur whilst consultation takes place on the listed building proposals.

5.58 The local planning authority is usually the district or the London Borough Council for the area in which the building is situated, although an urban development corporation, the Broads Authority or a national park authority may be the appropriate body. Section 10(2) of the P(LBCA)A outlines the information to be provided to the local planning authority when applying for listed building consent, although in practice most authorities have their own application forms which, in accordance with regulation 3, P(LBCA)R) require detailed descriptions and plans of the works. As with applications for scheduled monument consent no fee is payable.

5.59 Unless relating only to the interior of a grade II (unstarred) building applications received by the local planning authority must be advertised (regulation 5,

P(LBCA)R). The advert must be placed in a local newspaper and on the site, after which there must be a minimum period of twenty one days during which representations from any person may be made to the authority. Regulation 5(2)(b) requires the planning authority to take all representations received into account when determining the application.

5.60 Usually, when a local authority is minded to grant listed building consent it must notify the Secretary of State (section 13, P(LBCA)A), at the appropriate regional office. (Special and complex provisions apply in Greater London, which are not considered further in this work.) The planning authority must wait twenty eight days from the date on which it first notifies the Secretary of State and cannot grant listed building consent during this period. The Secretary of State may direct that the application be referred to him for his own decision (section 12, P(LBCA)A). If he does call-in the application for his own decision a public inquiry or hearing will be held if the applicant or the local planning authority so requests. However, this general position is subject to specific notification requirements which are both involved and subject to periodic revision. In practice not all applications need to be referred; the principal applications which must be referred are those:

(a) affecting grade I and grade II* buildings;
(b) grade II (unstarred) buildings which involve demolition of the principal building, a principal external wall of the principal building or demolition of all or a substantial part of the interior of the principal building

[where a proposal to retain less than 50% of the surface area of any elevation is deemed to be a proposal for demolition of a principal external wall and a proposal for demolition of *'any principal internal element of the structure including any staircase, load-bearing wall, floor structure or roof structure'* it is to be treated as a proposal for demolition of a substantial part].

(Environment Circular 14/97).

Notification in relation to curtilage buildings or by reference to cubic capacity of buildings (DOE Circular 8/87) is no longer required.

Most minor works to grade II (unstarred) listed buildings, for example the construction of a new porch or the replacement of windows, are not required to be notified to the Secretary of State or English Heritage. This means that some applications of archaeological significance will be determined by the local authority without referral; examples would be the construction of a boundary wall which cuts through archaeological deposits, the filling-in of part of a moat which encloses a grade II(unstarred) manor house or the replacement of the roof timbers (without demolishing the roof structure) in such a building.

In Wales Cadw is required to be notified of any application which involves demolition, or affects either the interior or exterior of a grade I or grade II* building, the exterior (but not the interior only) of any grade II (unstarred) building, or any listed building grant aided under Section 4, HBAMA 1953 (WO Circular 61/96, paragraph 72A, as amended).

In addition to notifying the Secretary of State when minded to grant listed building consent, as soon as they receive a valid application for certain proposals local planning authorities are directed to notify and copy the relevant papers to English Heritage as soon as a possible. The applications which are notifiable are the same as those which should be notified to the Secretary of State under section 13 of the P(LBCA)A, albeit at an earlier stage than notifications to the minister (Environment Circular 14/97, direction 15(2)). By the time an authority is minded to grant consent for an application which is subject to the direction to notify the Secretary of State, therefore, it will usually have consulted English Heritage.

Where a local planning authority receives an application for the demolition of a listed building, or for alterations which include demolition of any part of a listed building, the national amenity societies must also be notified, together with the appropriate Royal Commission (Environment Circular 14/97, direction 15(1); WO 61/96, paragraph 72(B)). The national amenity societies in question are the Ancient Monuments Society, the Council for British Archaeology, the Society for the Protection of Ancient Buildings, the Georgian Group and the Victorian Society. Failure to notify the national amenity societies, the Royal Commission or English Heritage may result in one of those bodies asking the Secretary of State to consider the application himself.

Both the English and the Welsh circulars also require local planning authorities to consult English Heritage/Cadw in relation to planning applications for proposals which in the opinion of the authority (acting reasonably) affect the setting of a grade I or grade II* listed building, and for some applications within conservation areas.

5.61 Local authorities remain central to the listed building system. For this and other reasons, in England, it is the SSETR and not the SSCMS who retains control of listed building consent procedures. This is a contrast with scheduled monument consent procedures where the SSCMS both schedules monuments and determines applications for consent.

The Ecclesiastical Exemption

5.62 Some of the most archaeologically significant works on listed buildings are those which affect historic churches and cathedrals. However, subject to any directions made by the Secretary of State under section 60(5) of the P(LBCA)A *ecclesiastical buildings for the time being in use for ecclesiastical purposes* are exempt from listed building control (section 60(1), P(LBCA)A). All places intended for and currently used for worship, even if only partly so used, are capable of falling within the ecclesiastical exemption, although the Secretary of State has issued a general direction under section 60(5) of the Act which removes the exemption from all ecclesiastical buildings which are not subject to acceptable, independent controls (see below).

5.63 This general, statutory exemption is long-standing, having originated with the notion that the internal procedures of the Church of England (the faculty jurisdiction) offered a suitable alternative – although cathedrals, and some structures within their precincts, are outside the faculty system and other Church of England controls apply. As currently drafted the exemption is not only from listed building control, but also the provisions relating to urgent repairs, repairs notices and CPO procedures, temporary listing, and criminal liability under section 59 of the Act. Listed building enforcement notices and the section 9 offence have no application to buildings falling within the exemption. Conservation area consent is not required for demolition of unlisted ecclesiastical buildings in conservation areas (section 75(1)(b), P(LBCA)A; again subject to compliance with independent controls).

5.64 The definition of 'ecclesiastical building' for the purposes of the P(LBCA)A is now acknowledged to include all Christian denominations and some non-Christian places of worship (*Att.-Gen., ex rel. Bedfordshire County Council v. Trustees of Howard United Reformed Church, Bedford* [1976] A.C. 363). Section 60(3) also stipulates that a building used or available for use by a minister of religion wholly or mainly as a residence from which to perform the duties of his office is not an ecclesiastical building within the meaning of section 60(1). Buildings or land not intended for worship but which are used as such do not fall within the exemption.

There was always some difficulty in interpreting the breadth of the exemption in practice, especially in relation to curtilage buildings or buildings adjoining a church but used for purposes ancillary to worship. The Ecclesiastical Exemption (Listed Building and Conservation Areas) Order 1994 (S.I. 1994, No.1771), interpreted according to the guidance contained in part 8 of PPG 15 (part 5 of WO 61/96), now provides greater control and clarity.

5.65 The Order restricts the exemption to the Church of England and those denominations or faiths which, when considering the effects of proposed works on listed buildings, have their own internal procedures which accord with a code of practice approved by the Secretary of State (see paragraphs 8.4 and 8.5 of the PPG and paragraph 142 of the Welsh Circular). In addition to the Church of England, the Church in Wales, the United Reformed Church, the Roman Catholic Church, the Methodist Church, the Baptist Union of Great Britain and the Baptist Union of Wales have procedures which comply with the code. The main elements of the code are that:

1. A body independent of the church council or committee which proposes the changes should consider the application (this body does not need to be independent of the particular religious organisation itself, of course);
2. The independent body should have some expertise in – or have arrangements for obtaining advice on – archaeological as well as architectural matters;
3. All proposals should be publicly advertised and consultation should take place with the appropriate local planning authority, the national amenity societies and English Heritage/Cadw;
4. The desirability of preserving historic remains must be taken into account at the time any works are authorised; and
5. Records of decisions taken by the independent body must be kept and the results of the decisions must be notified to relevant amenity societies.

The Order also clarifies the building types to which the exemption is intended to apply, i.e. only buildings whose primary use is as a place of worship, including any object or structure within the building and any object or structure fixed to the building or within the curtilage of the building (unless, in the case of fixtures or curtilages, the objects or structures in question are separately listed). From the procedural point of view the code makes it clear that proposals which affect archaeological deposits should be treated in similar fashion to proposals which affect architecture.

5.66 In applying the new system of exemption the Secretary of State has particular regard to the extent to which the relevant ecclesiastical authorities are able, through their internal procedures, to subject those proposing works to informed decision making and legally binding obligations. The faculty jurisdiction of the Church of England is a case in point. Under section 12 of the Faculty Jurisdiction Measure 1964 archdeacons may authorise minor repairs and decorations to churches, but where more than minor alterations or works are to be undertaken authorisation is required by the chancellor of the appropriate consistory court for the diocese (parishioners will 'petition the court for a faculty'). The chancellor must seek the advice of the relevant Diocesan Advisory Committee ('DAC', a body for the diocese which as well as church representatives includes representatives of some of the national amenity societies and the local planning authority) before determining the petition. However, the extent to which archaeological advice is taken by the chancellor varies between different dioceses. For many years the Council for British Archaeology exhorted the Church to have at least one archaeological expert in attendance at committee meetings. These exhortations found formal recognition in the Care of Churches and Ecclesiastical Jurisdiction Measure 1991 (amending the 1964 Measure), under which each DAC is required to have at least one member who possesses a knowledge of archaeology. The chancellor is not bound by the advice of the DAC. Contested cases will be heard before a formal session of the court (which tends to operate on a peripatetic basis).

5.67 Although cathedral churches are outside the faculty system, they are governed by the Care of Cathedrals Measure 1990 and the Care of Cathedrals Rules 1990 (S.I. 1990, No. 2335) (as amended). Under section 2 of the Measure the cathedral church body must obtain prior approval of any proposed works which will materially affect (a) the architectural, archaeological, artistic or historic character of the cathedral church or any building within the precinct of the cathedral church which is for the time being used for ecclesiastical purposes, (b) the immediate setting of the cathedral church, or (c) any archaeological remains within the precinct of the cathedral church. Archaeological remains are defined by section 20(1) of the Care of Cathedrals Measure as *'the remains of any building, work or artefact, including any trace or sign of the previous existence of the building, work or artefact in question'* – a definition of remains which borrows from section 61(13) of the AMAA.

In the case of work which includes the *disturbance or destruction of any archaeological remains within the precincts of the cathedral* approvals are from the Cathedrals Fabric Commission for England. The Cathedrals Fabric

Commission may direct that other, 'special' applications be referred to it (section 6, Care of Cathedrals Measure). Application for routine matters, for example matters not of special archaeological or historic interest, will be determined by the Fabric Advisory Committee of the cathedral pursuant to section 15 of the Measure; rule 11 of the Care of Cathedrals Rules makes special provision for the documentation to be provided in proposals for works affecting listed buildings and scheduled monuments. Rule 10 provides for notification of decisions of a committee of review to English Heritage, the national amenity societies and the RCHM(e). The Fabric Commission is required to have at least one archaeologist amongst its membership (schedule 1, paragraph 3(g) of the Measure), as must the relevant cathedral Fabric Advisory Committee, unless the cathedral is not of archaeological significance (section 12(2) of the Measure). In deciding applications the cathedral authorities are required to carry out a balancing exercise similar to that required of the consistory courts in the faculty jurisdiction.

5.68 The general position regarding listed buildings in the faculty jurisdiction is as expressed in *Re St. Mary's, Banbury* [1987] 1 All E.R. 247 and *Re St. Luke the Evangelist, Maidstone* [1995] 1 All E.R. 321 (both decisions of the Arches Court, Canterbury). In brief, these cases provide that (a) there is a strong presumption against change which adversely affects a church's character as a building of special architectural or historic interest; (b) works which would permanently affect a listed church in this way must be necessary and not just desirable from a liturgical point of view. '*Although the exemption is necessary so that in such cases the dead hand of the past shall not prevent the proper use of a building consecrated to the worship of God, a listing does indicate that a faculty which might affect the special nature of the architectural or historic interest ... should only be allowed in cases of clearly proved necessity'* (Re St. Mary's, Banbury, per Dean Sir John Owen, *loc. cit.,* 250). The balancing exercise which the consistory court hearing the petition (for the faculty) is required to carry out will include an assessment of: *'the pastoral needs of the parish ... the importance of the listed building ... the contribution which the building makes to the area in which it stands ... the costs of preserving the building and where a church has been almost totally destroyed [as in the case in question] what possibility there is of rebuilding the church in anything like its original condition'* (Re St. Barnabas' Church, Dulwich (1994) *The Times,* January 20, Southwark Cst. Ct.). With specific reference to below ground archaeology, conditions requiring archaeological work to be carried out in advance of or as part of alterations to a church may be attached to a faculty (Re St. Mary, Thame); ecclesiastical authorities are expected to consider and make proper provision for the recording of archaeological remains even where the exemption applies. Paragraph 8.5 of PPG 15 advises that: *'In considering proposals for such works* [to ecclesiastical buildings in use], *any effects on the archaeological importance of the church or archaeological remains existing within its curtilage should be taken into account along with other relevant factors. Where works of repair or alteration are to be carried out which would affect the fabric of listed churches or churches in conservation areas, denominations should attach any necessary conditions for proper recording in accordance with the principles set out in paragraphs 3.22-3.24 and, in respect of archaeological remains, in paragraph 2.15.'* Paragraph 8.12 of that PPG reminds authorities of the importance of below ground archaeology as well as the above ground, historical remains.

5.69 Even where buildings fall within the ecclesiastical exemption for listed building purposes, planning permission will be required for 'development' (see chapter 6 of this work). It follows that the planning authority must have regard to its duties under sections 66 and 72 of the P(LBCA)A where appropriate. However, an ecclesiastical building in use for ecclesiastical purposes cannot be a monument within the AMAA (section 61(8) of that Act) and so cannot be scheduled; although until proposed legislative changes are made the ground beneath a church may be affected by scheduling.

5.70 Burial grounds, whether consecrated or not, may fall within the faculty jurisdiction of the Church of England, but they do not fall within the ecclesiastical exemption. Moreover, special rules apply to building on disused burial grounds and the removal of human remains (see chapter 3 of this work). In some cases the internal procedures of the Church of England may provide sufficient authority for dealing with burial grounds, but in non-Church of England cases other statutory provisions come into play. Where gravestones and other memorials are listed and are to be affected by work or development, authority to remove or make inaccessible (in accordance with the Disused Burial Grounds (Amendment) Act 1981 or other, similar provisions) will not obviate the need for listed building consent.

5.71 An ecclesiastical building which falls within the

exemption will cease to do so in relation to a proposal for total demolition of the building, as the building in question cannot then be treated as in use for ecclesiastical purposes (see the *Howard Church Trustees* case, *loc. cit.*). A Church of England church which has become formally redundant under the Pastoral Measure 1983 would, therefore, no longer attract the exemption if not for section 60(7), P(LBCA)A which provides that demolition of a redundant church, undertaken in pursuance of a redundancy or pastoral scheme, benefits from a specific statutory exemption. Other denominations and faiths are outside section 60(7) and so will require listed building consent in such circumstances.

Conditions to the Grant of Listed Building Consent

5.72 The power to grant listed building consent subject to conditions is found in section 16(1) of the P(LBCA)A. Section 17(1) of the Act then expressly authorises matters which may be the subject of conditions, namely:

'(a)   *the preservation of particular features of a building, either as part of it or after severance from it;*

(b)   *the making good, after the works are completed, of any damage caused to the building by the works; and*

(c)   *the reconstruction of the building or any part of it following the execution of any works, with the use of the original materials so far as practicable and with such alterations of the interior of the building as may be specified in the conditions.'*

These are extensive powers and are permissive, not

exclusive.

5.73 Section 17(2) expressly authorises conditions which require later approval of specified details once works have been begun. Such conditions are already permissible in the planning context as 'reserved matters' but in listed building law they may relate to matters not set out in the application for consent; in this way they may provide for works necessary to deal with a contingency, e.g. the discovery of suspected but unknown architectural or archaeological features which are part of a building's structure. There is a danger, of course, that section 17(2) conditions may be treated by authorities as authorising the use of 'outline' applications for listed building consent. This is warned against in paragraph B.10 to annex B of PPG 15, where authorities are reminded of the importance of an adequate understanding of the impact of a proposal before granting consent.

5.74 When demolition of a listed building is proposed, section 17(3) of the P(LBCA)A authorises conditions which require a contract for carrying out relevant development works (and/or the grant of planning permission for the development) to be in place before demolition commences. The purpose of such a condition would be to safeguard the appearance of the locality in which the building is situated. The provision gives no additional powers to the decision making authority to stipulate what should appear in the contract for redevelopment or to secure archaeological resources by contract (though resources may, in limited circumstances, be secured by condition: see below).
    The effectiveness of a condition imposed under section

17(3) will also depend on the continued solvency of the applicant and the desire of the relevant third party to enforce performance of the contract.

5.75 A listed building consent must normally be implemented within five years of grant, but a longer or shorter period may be specified (section 18, P(LBCA)A). Consent will usually enure for the benefit of the building although a personal consent is possible (section 16(3) of the Act). A purchaser or funding institution should be wary of a personal consent.

5.76 Breach of a condition may be as serious as executing works without consent. In either case the offending works will be unauthorised for the purposes of section 7 and, unlike a planning breach, may constitute an offence without any further action by the planning authority. The offender may also be subject to a listed building enforcement notice or an injunction.

5.77 Matters which may be the subject of conditions include the following.

  (a)   Removal of building fabric by hand; see the case of 74-82 Lombard Street, Birmingham, where the inspector granted consent for the demolition of part of grade II(unstarred) listed terrace by 'pick, jemmy crowbar or other approved hand tools only' ([1992] J.P.L., 492).

  (b)   Retention of existing features or features which may be revealed by the authorised works (paragraph 3.24, PPG 15; paragraph 83, WO 61/96). This may include features revealed by attendant architectural or archaeological investigation.

(c)   Severance of and preservation of particular features of a building, for example a sundial or a datestone (the purpose behind the demolition by hand, referred to at (a) above, was to preserve items for the local museum).

(d)   Carrying out works under architectural/ archaeological supervision, usually in the nature of a watching brief, to facilitate recording. Below ground works will usually entail development and the powers available under the planning Acts can then be relied on. A condition requiring access for the relevant Royal Commission will be unnecessary in demolition cases due to the statutory provisions of section 8(2), P(LBCA)A. It is customary for the consent simply to notify the applicant of the statutory rights of the appropriate Royal Commission.

(e)   'Exploratory opening up' as contemplated by paragraph 3.24 of PPG 15; i.e. an obligation is placed on the applicant to investigate the impact of the main works on suspected features of value. (Exploratory works, if destructive, may be the subject of an independent listed building consent, as there is a danger of derogating unacceptably from grant in attaching a condition where exploratory investigation suggests a drastic variation of the main work. Such an approach is preferable where early on in a proposal an applicant is attempting to satisfy the authority as to the archaeological value of a building and its curtilage.)

Draft conditions and some specific issues of *vires* and reasonableness are considered in relation to planning conditions and conditions attached to scheduled monument consents (chapters 2 and 6 of this work). Conditions attached to listed building consents should, like planning conditions, be necessary, relevant (to the listed buildings code), enforceable, precise and reasonable in all respects.

5.78 In archaeology, the most vexing question is the extent to which the applicant can be required to carry out archaeological/architectural recording as a condition of a listed building consent, as distinct from a planning permission (for which ministerial guidance is now comparatively unequivocal) or a scheduled monument consent. Paragraph 3.23 of PPG 15 and paragraph 82 of WO 61/96 state that *'local planning authorities should also consider, in all cases of alteration or demolition, whether it would be appropriate to make it a condition of consent that applicants arrange suitable programmes of recording of features that would be destroyed in the course of the works for which consent is being sought'*. Even PPG 16 falls short of requiring applicants (for planning permission) to finance or provide resources for archaeological work and, not surprisingly, PPG 15 and WO 61/96 remind authorities not to require applicants to finance such programmes of recording in return for the granting of listed building consent. Indeed, PPG 15 may be considered more restrictive than PPG 16 on two counts: (a) it talks of 'arranging for' rather than 'providing' a programme of archaeological recording; while (b) 'recording of features that would be destroyed' suggests a narrow purpose to recording and something less intensive than the 'preservation by record' alluded to in the planning context.

5.79 In some instances archaeological remains will be a physical part of the listed building affected (a redundant wall or floor levels, for example); but in other instances they will not (a foundation trench of an earlier building). However, even in the latter case, remains may be deemed part of the listed building, as an object or structure within the curtilage of the building which *'although not fixed to the building, forms part of the land and has done so since before 1st July 1948'* (section 1(5)(b), P(LBCA)A). A limited but intensive archaeological investigation, sometimes involving excavation, may be the only way of adequately recording the remains. There is no legal reason why a listed building consent cannot have a condition attached which requires such works to be carried out before the alteration or demolition authorised by the consent is begun. A requirement for this might arise, for example, where a listed building consent does not authorise any demolition but the RCHM(e) or RCAHM(w) wishes to record archaeological features before alterations are carried out. In cases involving demolition the relevant Royal Commission will have a statutory right of access but a condition may still be required to secure the appropriate level of access and facilities.

The Position of the Applicant for Listed Building Consent

5.80 Carrying out works without listed building consent when consent was required will usually render the offender criminally liable. As with scheduled monument cases, the criminal liability is immediate and does not depend on non-compliance with some notice or order specifying a breach.

5.81 In contrast to scheduled monument law, however, the listed building code also provides for the service of enforcement notices (section 38 of the P(LBCA)A). The listed building enforcement notice is a useful measure for securing remediation of any damage caused to a building by a breach of listed building control, provided that remedial action is still possible (note the *Antique Country Buildings* case, above). A distinct appeals procedure applies to listed building enforcement notices; appeal is pursuant to section 39 of the P(LBCA)A (see below). The absence of equivalent procedures under the AMAA may originate in the perceived difficulty of remedying damage to archaeological deposits, but this is not a persuasive argument. In some cases the substance of a monument is little different from that of a listed building; moreover, although a monument is not assumed to have reasonably beneficial use, it is beyond dispute that the archaeological value of a site can frequently be salvaged. (A listed building enforcement notice cannot be served in relation to a building which is both listed and a scheduled monument; section 61 of the P(LBCA)A disapplies section 9 of the Act in such instances and so there can be no breach against which to enforce.)

5.82 Section 8(3) of the P(LBCA)A recognises that the local planning authority may be granted for works already executed; hence the notion of 'retrospective consent' in listed building cases. An application for such consent is determined in the usual way, as if the works to which it relates had not been carried out. Paragraph 3.42 of PPG 15 warns local authorities against accepting a *fait accompli*. As consent is only effective from the date of the decision and not from the date when the works were executed, a residual liability remains and a prosecution could be brought in respect of the period when the works were not authorised. Enforcement action is, of course, no longer possible in respect of works for which retrospective consent has been granted. Where a listed building enforcement notice has been served and an owner makes a retrospective application for listed building consent for the works as well as appealing the notice, the application will be determined as part of the enforcement notice inquiry.

Appeals against refusal of listed building consent

5.83 Appeal lies to the Secretary of State under section 20 of the P(LBCA)A where the local planning authority:

(a) refuses an application for listed building consent or grants it subject to conditions (which the applicant finds unacceptable), or

(b) refuses an application for the discharge of a condition (or grants such an application but imposes new, unacceptable conditions), or

(c) refuses an application for later approval of details, for example under a condition imposed by virtue of section 17(2).

5.84 Appeal also lies where the local planning authority does not notify the applicant – within the prescribed period of eight weeks (regulation 3(4), P(LBCA)R) – of their decision or of their referral of the application to the Secretary of State. If the matter is 'called-in' by the Secretary of State and there are substantive objections to the grant of consent a public inquiry will usually be held.

5.85 Appeals must be lodged with the Secretary of State for the Environment, Transport and the Regions/appropriate Committee of the Welsh Assembly within six months of the date of the decision etc. which gives rise to the appeal (either the actual date of the decision notice or the date from which the planning authority is in default: regulation 8 of the P(LBCA)R). Section 21(3) of the Act provides that the notice of appeal may include as a ground that the building in question does not merit inclusion in and should be removed from the statutory list.

5.86 On appeal, the legal and technical issues under consideration mean that the appellant is usually well-advised to enlist specialist assistance, both legal and architectural. There are no rules specific to the conduct of listed building consent appeals. The planning inquiries rules apply (see chapter 6 below). Appeals may be heard either by way of written representations or by inquiry or hearing, and the costs rules apply. If the decision on a parallel application for planning permission is also to be appealed both may be taken together. It is possible to succeed in one appeal and fail in the other (for an example see the appeal decisions on 7 Winckley Square, Preston, [1993] J.P.L. 600).

5.87 Section 22(3) of the P(LBCA)A states that the decision of the Secretary of State on an appeal shall be final. This refers to the listed building merits – and so to any archaeological merits of the Secretary of State's decision. An appellant may appeal to the High Court on a point of law (section 63, P(LBCA)A) within six weeks of the decision letter. Section 62(1) of the Act precludes any legal challenge except in accordance with the provisions of section 63. This means that the High Court will take a restrictive view of the availability of judicial review.

For High Court actions, both under statute and under the inherent jurisdiction of the Court, see chapter two of this work.

Listed Building Enforcement Notices

5.88 The enforcement notice is primarily a measure to secure remediation of works carried out without the appropriate consent, or in breach of condition. Section 38(2) of the P(LBCA)A specifies restoration of a building, or mitigation of the damage done to a building, as within the scope of a listed building enforcement notice:

> '(2) A listed building enforcement notice shall specify the alleged contravention and require such steps as may be specified in the notice to be taken ...
>
> (a) for restoring the building to its former state;

(b) *if the authority consider that such restoration would not be reasonably practicable or would be undesirable, for executing such further works specified in the notice as they consider necessary to alleviate the effect of the works which were carried out without listed building consent; or*

(c) *for bringing the building to the state in which it would have been if the terms and conditions of any listed building consent which has been granted for the works had been complied with'* (section 38(2), P(LBCA)A).

5.89 In contrast to the situation where a 'repairs notice' is issued a listed building enforcement notice cannot require works to be undertaken which would result in an improvement on the condition of the building immediately before the unauthorised works took place (*Bath City Council v. Secretary of State for the Environment* [1983] J.P.L. 737). Restoration works specified should also be reasonably practicable, although an inspector, on appeal, may be able to exercise his discretion to amend a notice which goes beyond this test (*Bath City Council, loc. cit.*). An enforcement notice should not be issued in relation to damage occasioned by accident or malicious damage by a third party (fire damage or terrorist activity, for example: see (1981) J.P.L., 443). As long as the works are properly specified it seems that a notice will not be rendered invalid merely because the issuing authority is on record as desiring (but not requiring) more extensive work (*R. v. Elmbridge Borough Council, ex parte Active Office* (1997), *The Times*, December 29 QBD).

5.90 The Town and Country Planning (Enforcement Notices and Appeals) Regulations 1991 (S.I. 1991, No.2804) prescribe the form of notice. Unlike a planning enforcement notice there are no time limits within which a listed building enforcement notice must be issued. Unauthorised works to a listed building are a source of potential continuing criminal liability, as well as constituting an offence from the time of their inception. The local planning authority must specify in the notice a date when the notice becomes effective and the date by which each step covered by the notice must be carried out. The notice cannot become effective until at least 28 days after service on the recipient, and must be served not later than 28 days after issue. Notices are usually issued by the local planning authority but the Secretary of State may issue (section 46, P(LBCA)A) provided that he consults beforehand with the appropriate local planning authority and English Heritage.

5.91 Failure to comply with the steps specified in a notice is a distinct criminal offence, punishable on summary conviction with a fine of up to £20,000 and on indictment with an unlimited fine (section 43, P(LBCA)A). The PCA 1991 inserted a new section 43 into the P(LBCA)A which provides *inter alia* that in criminal proceedings under the section it is a defence for the accused to show that '*he did everything he could be expected to do to secure that all the steps required by the notice were taken*' (section 43(4)(a)). This defence requires more than all reasonable steps and probably approaches 'best endeavours'. Formerly it was not open to recipients to argue that they had done all that they could to comply: they had to comply and could be prosecuted if they did not (*Mid-Devon District Council v. Avery* [1994] J.P.L. 40 DC, a case actually heard in 1992). In *Avery* the defendant argued before the magistrates that he was unable to obtain replacements for UPVC windows within the 28 days specified in the notice due to the general demand for carpentry services following widespread storm damage. The magistrates accepted this as defence under the old section 43 but on appeal by way of case stated the Divisional Court remitted the matter to the justices with a direction that the case be found proved. The 'defence' of insufficient time to comply should be taken as a ground of appeal to the Secretary of State, not necessarily on prosecution.

5.92 As well as prosecuting for non-compliance an authority which issues a notice may carry out works in default. The power arises under section 42(1) of the P(LBCA)A. Expenses incurred in carrying out the work may be recovered from the 'owner' (as defined at section 336, TCPA 1990) of the land. It is an offence punishable by a fine up to level 3 on the standard scale for any person to wilfully obstruct a person exercising rights arising under section 42(1).

5.93 Where a listed building enforcement notice is considered too onerous, or unacceptable for some other historic building reason, the proper course is an appeal to the Secretary of State under section 39, before the date on which the notice becomes operational. Indeed, section 64 of the Act provides that the validity of a listed building enforcement notice shall not be questioned in any proceedings except by way of appeal under section 39 (for a failed attempt to judicially review the issuing of two listed building enforcement notices, where the Divisional Court took a strict view of section 64, see *R. v. Dacorum Borough Council and another, ex parte Cannon* [1996] E.G.C.S. 97 DC).

Until the appeal is determined or withdrawn the enforcement notice is of no effect: no criminal liability arises under section 43, nor are works in default possible under section 42. The Secretary of State has full powers to correct or vary a notice – as well as uphold or quash a notice – provided he is satisfied that the variation or correction will not cause injustice to the appellant or the local planning authority (section 41(1), P(LBCA)A). Appeals are conducted under the rules applicable to planning enforcement inquiries. These are broadly similar to the general inquiries procedure rules which are discussed briefly in chapter six. Costs may be awarded in listed building enforcement notice appeals (see DOE Circular 8/93, annex 7).

5.94 Section 39(1) provides eleven separate grounds of appeal, all of which are listed on the forms of appeal printed by the DETR and provided to the recipient with the notice. The grounds are:

(a)   *that the building is not of special architectural or historic interest;*

(b)   *that the matters alleged to constitute a contravention of section 9(1) or (2) have not occurred [unauthorised works];*

(c)   *that those matters (if they occurred) do not constitute such a contravention;*

(d)   *that works to the building were urgently necessary in the interests of safety or health or for the preservation of the building, that it was not practicable to secure safety or health or, as the case may be, the preservation of the building by works of repair or works for affording temporary shelter, and that the works carried out were limited to the minimum measures immediately necessary;*

(e)   that listed building consent ought to be granted for the works, or that any relevant condition of such consent which has been granted ought to be discharged, or different conditions substituted;

(f)   that copies of the notice were not served as required by section 38(4);

(g)   except in relation to such a requirement as is mentioned in section 38(2)(b) or (c) that the requirements of the notice exceed what is necessary for restoring the building to its condition before the works were carried out;

(h)   that the period specified in the notice as the period within which any step required by the notice is to be taken falls short of what should reasonably be allowed;

(i)   that the steps required by the notice for the purpose of restoring the character of the building to its former state would not serve that purpose;

(j)   that steps required to be taken by virtue of section 38(2)(b) exceed what is necessary to alleviate the effect of the works executed to the building; and

(k)   that steps required to be taken by virtue of section 38(2)(c) exceed what is necessary to bring the building to the state in which it would have been if the terms and conditions of the listed building consent had been complied with.

5.95 Examples of relatively minor unauthorised works which have been the subject of a listed building enforcement notice upheld on appeal include:

(i)   painting of the front elevation of a grade II (unstarred) listed building ((1979) J.P.L. 782; (1981) J.P.L. 607);

(ii)   replacement of artificial roof slates with slates in natural stone ((1991) J.P.L. 287);

(iii)   replacement of park gates, within the curtilage of a stately home, in breach of condition requiring prior approval of local planning authority (1993) J.P.L. 987);

(iv)   the fixing of a blue painted alarm box on the front elevation of a grade II* listed building, when white would have matched the colour scheme of the building ((1993) J.P.L., 606); and

(v)   the insertion of a lift shaft in the arched entrance to a grade II(unstarred) building (lift to be removed although the inspector holding that the compliance period be extended to eight years; decision upheld in *Hounslow London Borough Council v Secretary of State and Lawson* [1997] J.P.L. 141 QBD).

Of course, enforcement notices remain an effective measure against more serious breaches such as demolition of facades, removal of architectural fittings or demolition of whole buildings.

Injunctions
(see also paragraph 6.41 of this work)

5.96 Local authorities and English Heritage are now expressly authorised to seek injunctions for actual or anticipated breaches of sections 7 and 9 of the P(LBCA)A (section 44A, P(LBCA)A and section 33, NHA 1983). These may be sought in either the County Court or the High Court. There is no requirement that a listed building enforcement notice or other enforcement action must first have been taken but, by its very nature and potential expense, an injunction should be sought only in circumstances where other remedies are thought to be insufficient due to the urgency or public profile of the case.   An injunction is a discretionary remedy of the court, not a remedy which a plaintiff is entitled to once the case is proved. It must be equitable for the injunction to be granted; an injunction will not be granted therefore if, for example, there has been either undue delay in bringing the proceedings or inequitable behaviour on the part of the plaintiff. In *Kirklees Metropolitan Borough Council v. Batchacre Ltd* ((1987), Unreported) the Council failed to obtain an injunction at the substantive hearing when it emerged that, unknown to the Council's planning department, the Council's building control section had consented to the demolition of the grade II (unstarred) listed mill in question. Rose J. found that the need for an injunction was nothing more than 'self-induced'. The *Antique Country Buildings* case (*loc. cit.*) is an example of a successful application for injunctive relief (see *Leominster District Council v. British Historic Buildings and SPS Shipping* [1987] J.P.L. 350 for the injunction proceedings in this matter, which restrained the defendants from shipping the historic timbers of a dismantled historic building overseas).

Criminal Liability for Unauthorised Works or Damage

The Section 9 Offence

5.97 The offence of carrying out works which are unauthorised is contained in section 9 of the P(LBCA)A. The offence consists of a contravention of section 7 of the Act which states that *'no person shall execute or cause to be executed any works for the demolition of a listed building or for its alteration or extension in any manner which would affect its character as a building of special architectural or historic interest, unless the works are authorised'*. Authorisation usually takes place pursuant to section 8 of the Act (see above). Works carried out in contravention of a condition contained in a consent are also unauthorised and so may attract the same penalty.

5.98 Section 9(1) says simply that *'if a person contravenes section 7 he shall be guilty of an offence'*. The offence has been held to be one of strict liability (*R. v. Wells Street Metropolitan Stipendiary Magistrates, ex parte Westminster City Council* [1986] 3 All E.R. 4; (1987) 53 P. & C.R. 421). This follows the test in *Gammon (Hong Kong) Ltd v. Att.-Gen. of Hong Kong* [1985] A.C. 1 PC, that in cases which give rise to issues of social concern the creation of strict liability is effective to promote the objects of the statute, whether or not imprisonment was a possibility. If the main ingredients of the offence are present, the defendant will be liable unless he can avail himself of the statutory defence; he will be unable to argue, for example, that he was unaware either that the building was listed or that the works were detrimental to its status as a listed building.

The *Wells Street* decision has been influential (see the reasoning of the Divisional Court in *Mid-Devon District Council v. Avery (loc. cit.)*). Indeed, the fact of strict liability has been sufficient to result in the quashing of a conviction where the prosecution adduced evidence of the defendant's state of mind (*R. v. Sandhu (Major)* [1997] J.P.L. 853). In *Sandhu*, unnecessary evidence was adduced that the defendant had been unconcerned about flouting listed buildings law and had ignored his surveyor's advice. Given that considerable weight was placed on this by the judge in his summing up, the introduction of such evidence could have prejudiced the jury against him and the conviction was held to be unsafe. The Court of Appeal considered that the defendant's state of mind in such circumstances may be relevant in sentencing but not in establishing guilt.

5.99 The statutory defence – to be proven on a balance of probabilities and not simply raised in rebuttal – is contained in section 9(3):

'(a)   *that works to the building were urgently necessary in the interests of safety or health or for the preservation of the building;* [and]

(b)   *that it was not practicable to secure safety or health or, as the case may be, the preservation of the building by works of repair or works for affording temporary support or shelter;* [and]

(c)   *that the works carried out were limited to the minimum measures immediately necessary;* and

(d)   *that notice in writing justifying in detail the carrying out of the works was given to the local planning authority as soon as reasonably practicable.'*

5.100 Where a building is damaged by accident or act of God the damage will not be caught by section 9, which refers specifically to works. Accidental fire, a fallen tree or a colliding motor vehicle will not constitute works, although in extreme instances they may be instrumental in deliberate damage to a building and so the subject of prosecution under section 59 of the Act.

The word 'causes' is to be construed as requiring neither proof of fault or knowledge, nor proof that the one act was the sole cause of the harm. In all cases it is a question of fact (*R. v. CPC(UK) Ltd* (1994) *The Times*, August 4, CA). A mistake as to the identity of a building, as in the demolition of Monkspath Hall, Solihull, should be no defence. Here a listed building was demolished by mistake when a contractor employed by the local authority misdirected his bulldozer. Both the defendant driver and the company which employed him were fined – the company for causing the demolition for want of proper supervision and the driver for executing the works ((1981) *The Times*, May 19). The defence of mistake was not accepted; clearly such a set of facts does not fall within the kinds of accidents referred to above.

5.101 Private individuals as well as public bodies may initiate proceedings under section 9. In the magistrates court it is a matter of laying an information and obtaining a summons signed by the Clerk to the Justices. In the Crown Court, whereas public bodies may bring proceedings (though not in their own name) private individuals will usually require the consent of the Attorney General, primarily to satisfy the Court that sufficient funds are available to meet any costs which may be awarded. Perhaps the most famous, private success was that achieved by the Society for the Protection of Ancient Buildings in 1981, in their prosecution of the unauthorised demolition of the Welby Almshouses, Lincolnshire (proceedings brought under section 55, Town and Country Planning Act 1971, the precursor to section 9, P(LBCA)A).

5.102 Sentences in the magistrates court can be a £20,000 fine and/or imprisonment for up to six months; in the Crown Court an unlimited fine can be imposed and/or up to two years imprisonment (section 9(4), P(LBCA)A). These high levels of fine, inserted by the PCA, reflect the seriousness which Parliament now attaches to listed building offences. A fine of £10,000 was imposed as long ago as 1975 (*R. v. Endersley Properties Ltd* (1975) P. & C.R., 399, a case concerning an unauthorised demolition), but it is only since 1992 that such levels of fine have been available in the magistrates court.

5.103 Section 9(5) of the P(LBCA)A requires the court (now the magistrates court as well as the Crown Court) to have particular regard to any financial benefit which has accrued or is likely to accrue to the defendant in consequence of the offence. An exceptional example of the application of this provision (in its old form) is found in *R. v. Chambers* [1989] J.P.L. 229, Cambridge Cr. Ct. Two company directors were convicted of causing the demolition of two grade II (unstarred) cottages, on the very day before an inspector's decision letter was issued, dismissing an appeal against the planning authority's refusal of listed building consent. The directors had bought the property with full knowledge of the listing and, in pursuit of financial gain, had allowed the buildings to deteriorate. There were no mitigating circumstances. The directors were each fined on each of two separate counts a sum of £17,000, plus £1100 costs. The company of which they were directors was fined £1,000 on two counts, plus £1,000 costs. The judge leant in favour of heavy fines rather than imprisonment because of the financial benefits which had accrued.

A heavier fine still was imposed in the more recent case of *R. v. McCarthy & Stone (Developments) Ltd* [1998] C.L.R. 424, Newport Cr.Ct. Here, property developers were given oral notice of listing of a building on a site earmarked for housing development. The following day the developer demolished the building. Not until five days later was formal notice of listing given by fax. On prosecution under section 9, the developer was fined £200,000 and ordered to pay £12,000 costs for a 'deliberate and cynical act intended to frustrate the listing of the building'.

Note that in applying section 9(5), however, the court must still have regard to the financial means of the offender, as required by section 19(2) and (3) of the Criminal Justice Act 1991 (*R v. Browning* [1996] 1 P.L.R., 61 CA, a planning enforcement case but the concurrent duty is applicable also to listed building cases).

The Section 59 Offence

5.104 '*If, with the intention of causing damage to a listed building, any relevant person does or permits the doing of any act which causes or is likely to result in damage to the building, he shall be guilty of an offence ...*' (section 59(1), P(LBCA)A).

The offence of doing or causing an act which does or is likely to do damage to a listed building must be done with the intention of causing damage – not necessarily of the kind occasioned – and must be done by a 'relevant person' as defined in section 59(2), P(LBCA)A). A relevant person is a person who would be entitled to do the act in question if not for the prohibition contained in section 59(1). Any person who would not be entitled as a matter of private law would instead probably be committing criminal damage under the Criminal Damage Act 1971.

5.105 The relevant person requirement prescribes a class which is narrower than the class under section 28 of the AMAA 1979 (intentional damage to protected monuments). Section 59(3) also excludes from the ambit of section 59(1) works which are authorised by a grant of planning permission under the TCPA, as well as works authorised under section 8, P(LBCA)A. In contrast to section 9 offences there is no statutory defence, although the requisite intention may be an onerous element for the prosecution to prove. 'Damage' is more than physical disturbance and probably connotes some destruction of the building's architectural or historic character.

5.106 A section 59 prosecution can only be brought in the magistrates court. A fine of up to level 3 on the standard scale may be imposed. There is no power to imprison. Following conviction, if the defendant fails to take such reasonable steps as may be necessary to *'prevent any damage or further damage resulting from the offence'* he is liable to further prosecution and on conviction to a fine of up to one tenth of the level 3 fine for each day on which he is in breach of this provision (section 59(4), P(LBCA)A).

Scheduled Monuments and Listed Buildings

5.107 Where a building is a scheduled monument and also listed, the scheduled monument regime takes precedence. Under section 61, P(LBCA)A, listed building consent is not required for works affecting a scheduled monument. Section 9 and listed building enforcement notices (which relate to breaches of section 9) have no application. Repairs notices and urgent works notices under the P(LBCA)A cannot be served (though the more restricted urgent works provisions and CPO proceedings under the AMAA will apply).

The ancient monuments offences under sections 2 and 28 of the AMAA must be charged in appropriate cases, and not the offences under sections 9 and 59 of the P(LBCA)A. Whereas offences against section 59 are punishable only before the magistrates, the section 28 offence may be tried in the Crown Court, with the considerably greater sentencing options of an unlimited fine and two years imprisonment. The marked difference in potential punishment requires some explanation. Scheduled monuments are of higher status than the majority of listed buildings, and scheduled monuments, because they frequently have little economic value, may be more prone to destruction. These factors could account for the discrepancy between the penalties for carrying out unauthorised works. Under section 2 of the AMAA imprisonment is not possible, whereas imprisonment is possible under section 9 of the P(LBCA)A. Section 9 has more onerous financial penalties, particularly before the magistrates and, unlike section 2, does not recognise a defence based on ignorance.

These contrasting penalties seem to imply that intentional damage or destruction is a more serious issue where ancient monuments are concerned, whereas unauthorised works are a more serious issue in the context of listed buildings. Such an interpretation is supported by the absence of an enforcement notice procedure in ancient monument law and the absence of a repairs notice procedure in advance of compulsory purchase. These are fundamental differences, though not necessarily justifiable. They do mean, however, that any amalgamation of the two codes into a 'unified heritage code' (see Scarse (1991) and Jewkes (1993)) will require careful assessment of some very basic principles. Proposals under consideration by the Government may bring ancient monument law more in line with listed building law (POH, see the introduction to this work).

Repairs Notices, Urgent Works and Dangerous Buildings

In addition to remedies designed to counter acts of commission the P(LBCA)A also provides remedies to redress instances of neglect, notably the provisions of sections 47 and 54 of the Act.

Section 54 (Urgent Works)

5.108 Section 54 provides that when it appears to a local authority, or the Secretary of State or English Heritage, that works are urgently necessary to preserve an unoccupied listed building, they may execute the works, including works to provide temporary shelter or support. In England, English Heritage acts on behalf of the Secretary of State, whereas in Wales the Welsh Assembly, through Cadw, acts in its own right. In London, English Heritage may exercise the power concurrently with the relevant London borough council. No action can be taken in respect of exempt buildings, that is scheduled monuments, ecclesiastical buildings in use (section 54(4), P(LBCA)A), buildings in which the relevant interest is a Crown interest (section 83, P(LBCA)A) or buildings which are occupied, unless only partly occupied (section 101(3), P(LBCA)A).

5.109 Action must be preceded by a notice, served on the owner, which (a) describes the works required to be carried out and (b) gives at least seven days notice of the authority's intention to act (section 54(5), P(LBCA)A). The authority is empowered to recover the cost of the works from the owner (section 55(2), P(LBCA)A), although the authority should be careful not to do more works than are strictly urgent (see below). Costs may include the 'continuing expense' of making available apparatus and materials (section 55(3)(a), P(LBCA)A).

5.110 Within 28 days of receiving a notice from the authority which sets out the costs incurred in carrying out the works an owner may make representations to the Secretary of State that (i) some or all of the works were unnecessary, (ii) that works of temporary support or shelter continued for an unreasonable length of time, (iii) that the amount specified in the notice is unreasonable, or (iv) recovery would cause hardship (section 55(4), P(LBCA)A). The Secretary of State will then determine what, if anything, should be recovered by the relevant authority together with reasons for his findings.

5.111 DOE Circular 8/87, paragraph 129 advised that a local planning authority should consider the means of the owner before carrying out the works under section 55, particularly where large buildings in the ownership of charities or voluntary organisations were concerned. PPG 15, paragraph 7.8 continues in this vein and advises that *'if an authority intends to attempt to recover the cost of the works, the financial circumstances of the owner should be taken into account at the outset and any sums the authority wishes to recover should not be unreasonable in relation to his or her means'*. The economic viability of the building should also be taken into account so that if, for example, consent for demolition may be granted in the relatively short term the extent of works specified in the notice should reflect this (see the appeal decision relating to 29/31 Bell Street, Romsey, Hampshire (1978) J.P.L. 637). This decision is also authority for saying that the notice served should also stipulate a fixed amount for the works so that the owner knows his potential liability; additional works should be the subject of a new notice. An owner must be able to assess whether or not to make representations to the Secretary of State (*Bolton Metropolitan Borough Council v. Jolley* [1989] 1 P.L.R., 97). A notice which required an owner to 'take all such steps as may be necessary' was quashed by the court (*R. v. Camden London Borough Council, ex parte Comyn Ching* (1984) 47 P. & C.R., 417).

5.112 'Urgent works' should be construed narrowly, for example works to keep a building wind and weather proof and safe from collapse or vandalism. Authorities going beyond this may find themselves with initial problems similar to those experienced by Swansea City Council ((1997) J.P.L. 162), where an inspector appointed by the Secretary of State for Wales did not recognise most of the works carried out by the Council as urgently necessary. The inspector accepted that the replacement of roof-ridge cover pieces, timber treatment to lower parts of the roof, the propping of floor joists and temporary covering of the roof were within section 54. However, a completely new roof, dwarf wall to alleviate ingress of flood water, new doors and windows and recladding of a porch in new slate were considered excessive. Indeed, in the case of the dwarf wall and the blocking of a rear door the inspector found that listed building consent (on a presumed application by the Council) should be refused. Of costs of over £4,000, £56 only was found to be recoverable. The inspector's decision has now been successfully challenged by the Council (*R. v. Secretary of State for Wales, ex parte Swansea City Council*, December 14, 1998), the court finding that the Council had acted reasonably in the circumstances and should not be 'hamstrung' in deciding what is urgently necessary. But the guidance and the approach taken by inspectors still favours a narrow interpretation of section 54, albeit not quite so narrow as favoured by the inspector in this case.

Section 47 (Repairs Notices and Compulsory Purchase)

5.113 When it appears to the Secretary of State that reasonable steps are not being taken to properly preserve a listed building he may make an order, or may confirm an order by the appropriate local planning authority, for the compulsory acquisition of the building (section 47, P(LBCA)A). The order may extend to any land comprising or contiguous or adjacent to the building which appears to the Secretary of State to be required for the preservation of the building, or securing amenities, access or proper control and management. The section would authorise the compulsory acquisition of land containing archaeological remains in appropriate cases. Where the building in question is situated in England, the Secretary of State must consult English Heritage before making or confirming an order and he must be satisfied that acquisition is expedient. The Acquisition of Land Act procedure applies (see chapter two of this work).

5.114 The powers in section 47 cannot be exercised unless a repairs notice is first served by the acquiring authority under section 48 of the P(LBCA)A. Service must take place at least two months before the compulsory purchase process is started. The 'repairs notice' must specify the works which the acquiring authority *'consider reasonably necessary for the proper preservation of the building'*, and it must be accompanied by a note which explains the compulsory purchase and repairs notice procedure (section 48(1), P(LBCA)A).

5.115 There is no sense in which the section 48 notice can be used as an alternative to an urgent works notice or a listed building enforcement notice. All are concerned with the preservation of listed buildings but a repairs notice should only be served if there is a genuine intention to acquire the building. This necessarily renders the repairs notice a suitable vehicle for dealing with major repairs and restoration work. If the authority does not believe that compulsory acquisition is needed to secure the preservation of the building it may well be compromised during discussions with the owner to the extent that the CPO will not be confirmed (see the planning law case of *R. v. Secretary of State for the Environment, ex parte Leicester City Council* (1988) P. & C.R. 364, where land was not genuinely required for development purposes, the CPO being used as a bargaining ploy and therefore found by the court to be compromised). The service of a repairs notice is undoubtedly a major stimulus to most owners. Indeed, the majority of repairs notices do not lead to compulsory acquisition.

5.116 A repairs notice can be an onerous document as far as an owner is concerned. There is House of Lords authority for the proper interpretation of such notices and this interpretation is strict and unambiguous (*Robbins v. Secretary of State for the Environment* [1989] 1 All E.R. 878 HL; notices served under the precursor of section 48, section 115 of the Town and Country Planning Act 1971). In *Robbins* the court held that a repairs notice is not bad for stipulating 'works of restoration' as long as the notice both requires sufficient 'works of preservation' to be done and states that failure to execute these works will result in a CPO being made. Lords Bridge and Ackner both emphasised the owner's recourse to the magistrates court to question the instigation of the CPO procedure (now contained in section 47(4)) and that an owner should not do nothing on receipt of an onerous notice in the expectation that the onerous requirements would invalidate the notice. Moreover, their lordships held that although preservation does imply an objective limitation on the extent of works required to be undertaken, preservation is to be considered in the context of the condition of the building at the time the building was first listed (*loc. cit.*, 884-885). 'Restoration', interpreted to mean works to put a building in a condition better than when first listed, is beyond the scope of a repairs notice; but comprehensive and large scale preservation is within section 48 even if to the owner, who may have acquired a property some years after the listing, the required works seem to be works of restoration. *'The interest of the owner, if he is unwilling to undertake the necessary works in retaining his property, has to yield to the public interest in the same way and on the same terms as the interest of any other property owner whose property is acquired for some necessary public purpose'* (per Lord Bridge, *loc. cit.*, 885b).

5.117 The broad sweep of section 47 is attributable to the nature of compulsory purchase, whose purpose is to provide for more than the immediate future of a building and to compensate the owner fairly for the loss of his property. Compensation will be assessed under the Land Compensation Act 1961 but subject to the assumptions contained in section 49, P(LBCA)A. PPG 15 and its Welsh equivalents remind authorities that a CPO must be considered expedient and that the resources for repair must be available. If there are objections to the CPO the Secretary of State will usually hold a local inquiry. Compensation will sometimes be very limited in listed buildings CPOs – the costs of repair will be high and development values low. The acquiring authority may also include a direction in the CPO that a minimum amount of compensation is due to the owner (section 50, P(LBCA)A). Under section 50 the acquiring authority must be satisfied that *'the building has been deliberately allowed to fall into disrepair for the purpose of justifying its demolition and the development or redevelopment of the site or any adjoining land'*. There should be clear evidence of an intention to allow a building to fall into disrepair to justify its demolition (PPG 15, paragraph 7.15; WO 61/96, paragraph 139). If the CPO is confirmed by the Secretary of State with the direction intact minimum compensation – usually one pound – will be payable.

5.118 The resources of the owner and his ability to meet any expenses necessitated by complying with a repairs notice are not a ground of appeal to the magistrates under section 47(4), nor does the acquiring authority need to take such matters into account when serving a repairs notice (*Rolf v. North Shropshire District Council* (1988) P. & C.R. 242 CA). An acquiring authority may serve a repairs notice and make a CPO under section 47 even though it has no intention of carrying out the works itself and when acquired will transfer the building to a third party (*Rolf, loc. cit.*). 'Back-to-back' transfer is indeed the Secretary of State's preferred course of action. PPG 15, paragraph 7.13 and paragraph 137 of WO 61/96 advise that '*privately owned historic buildings should, whenever possible, remain in the private sector*'. PPG 15 continues: '*local planning authorities are encouraged to identify a private individual or body, such as a building preservation trust, which has access to the funds to carry out the necessary repairs and to which the building will be sold as quickly as possible. Suitable covenants should be negotiated to ensure that repairs will be carried out by a purchaser*'. The in-and-out rules under the Local Authorities (Capital Finance) Regulations 1990 (as amended) applied where the building was transferred within two years after acquisition by the local authority and so no set-aside of capital money was required. Where onward transfer is intended the acquiring authority is well-advised to have a development agreement in place with the private sector partner in order to secure repairs and timescale.

5.119 A good example of compulsory purchase under section 47 is documented at [1995] J.P.L. 641. The CPO concerned properties at 26-30 Normanby Street, Alton, Hampshire, a grade II (unstarred) house originally consisting of three, eighteenth century, two-storey houses. The building had been listed following the service of a Building Preservation Notice by East Hampshire District Council. The Council had twice served urgent repairs notices but the building remained in a state of disrepair. The Council served a repairs notice, with which the owner did not comply (at all). The inspector found that *'despite the Council's willingness to discuss the building with the owner, and its offer of 40 per cent of the costs of repair, the owner twice applied to have the building de-listed. He had belatedly put forward an inappropriate scheme for converting and extending the building. The Council considers that the lack of action by the owner amounts to deliberate neglect designed to allow the property to fall into such a condition as to lead to its demolition. In its view, the only means to ensure proper preservation of the building would be a change of ownership with a legal agreement to ensure proper repair; the Council has had discussions with the Hampshire Buildings Preservation Trust and the Alton Building Preservation Trust (which gave evidence at the inquiry to support repair and conversion of the building). Alternatively, the Council could sell the land to a private owner, or undertake repairs itself before marketing'*. The Secretary of State found that the owner had done nothing which aided the repair of the building; that the building was correctly listed; that the owner had failed to understand the 'basic approach to the preservation of the character and fabric of the building'; that adjacent backland was properly included in the Order, as it was required for amenity and possibly for access. As there was also evidence to suggest that the owner's neglect did contemplate demolition the Secretary of State confirmed the CPO with a direction for minimum compensation.

Dangerous Buildings

5.120 Under section 56 of the P(LBCA)A a local planning authority must consider whether it should first exercise its powers under sections 47 and 54 before taking any steps to obtain a dangerous structure order in respect of a listed building (under section 77 of the Building Act 1984). This follows the decision of the Divisional Court in *R. v. Stroud District Council, ex parte Goodenough and Others* (1982) J.P.L., 246 where it was held that the local authority should have explored all of its powers under the listed buildings code before consenting to the making of such an order. Emergency measures under section 78 of the 1984 Act are still not covered by this provision but would, in any case, probably not fall foul of section 9, P(LBCA)A if immediately necessary on the grounds of safety or health.

Section 56, P(LBCA)A applies to the similar but separate provisions in sections 62, 65 and 69 of the London Buildings (Amendment) Act 1939. Special provisions apply to demolition orders in respect of listed buildings under the Housing Act 1985 (see the 'closing order' provisions under sections 303-306 of that Act).

Listed Building Purchase Notices

5.121 In accordance with the principle that a listed building should retain an economic use, section 32 of the P(LBCA)A provides that owners of listed buildings may in certain circumstances serve a notice on the local planning authority which requires the authority to buy the building. There must have been a refusal of listed building consent, a grant of consent subject to conditions, or a consent must have been revoked or modified, as a result of which, in any of these instances, an owner is able to demonstrate that:

1. The building (and any adjacent or contiguous land) has become incapable of reasonably beneficial use;
2. Where consent has been granted subject to conditions compliance with the conditions will render the building incapable of reasonably beneficial use; and
3. The building cannot be rendered capable of reasonably beneficial use by carrying out works for which consent has been granted.

(Section 32(2), P(LBCA)A).

5.122 In determining what is 'reasonably beneficial use' section 32(4) provides that no account is to be taken of '*any prospective use which would involve the carrying out of development* [other than development following war damage, building reconstruction etc ...] *or any works requiring listed building consent ... other than works for which the local planning authority or the Secretary of State have undertaken to grant such consent*'.

CHAPTER SIX

ARCHAEOLOGY AND PLANNING LAW

C hapter two and chapter five considered controls specific to conservation of the archaeological and historic heritage. Provisions which have a wider environmental purpose may, however, also assume an important role in archaeological conservation; in chapter four environmental impact assessment was discussed, and for many years the archaeological heritage has also been taken into account in the mainstream planning system.

6.01 The treatment of archaeological sites as isolated, environmental features governed only by a narrow, regulatory framework may encourage a destructive approach where special circumstances cannot be pleaded at the national level. The background to *Hoveringham Gravels* (paragraphs 6.47-6.48 below) was a case in point, with the developer arguing in effect, that protection of monuments and archaeological sites was not a material consideration in the determination of planning applications. In recent years, and especially since the publication of PPG 16: *Archaeology and Planning*, in November 1990, government, planning authorities and developers have come to accept that an effective method of archaeological conservation may lie in a more rigorous application of the procedures available under the Town and Country Planning Acts, the Highways

Act and, to a lesser extent, the enabling statutes of the public utilities. Indeed, the scale, the frequency, the usually lengthy lead-in times, and the developed consultation processes associated with these procedures have made them a sophisticated channel of archaeological procurement. The situation in Wales is comparable except that PPG 16 (Wales): *Archaeology and Planning* did not appear until November 1991 and is now superseded by WO Circular 60/96, *Planning and the Historic Environment: Archaeology* and paragraphs 134-140 of *Planning Guidance (Wales) Planning Policy.*

This chapter is divided into three parts. The first part deals with the authorisation of development in general, both under the TCPA 1990 and otherwise. The second part discusses archaeology as a consideration in the grant of planning permission and the drafting of development plans under the TCPA 1990. The third part considers the securing of 'archaeological facilities', particularly in relation to site investigations.

(I) The Authorisation of Development

The Town and Country Planning Act 1990

6.02 The basis of the system is that a prospective developer of land must first obtain permission for that development (section 57(1), TCPA 1990). In most instances this means permission from the appropriate district council, London borough council or, since the commencement of the Environment Act 1995, the appropriate national park authority. County councils retain planning powers in respect of 'county matters', i.e. mineral development or matters designated county matters by the Secretary of State. Formerly only the Lake District and the Peak District national parks were planning authorities in their own right. The district or borough council is usually the local planning authority for metropolitan and other unitary authorities. In those shire counties which remain, county councils and district councils are both planning authorities. In Urban Development Areas (UDAs), where planning control for a designated area is removed from the hands of the relevant local authority by order of the Secretary of State, the Urban Development Corporation (UDC) for the UDA is the local planning authority.

This composite structure is regulated by the Secretary of State for the Environment, Transport and the Regions. He may intervene in the process at almost any level and, amongst his many powers, he may constitute and dissolve UDCs; call-in, from a local planning authority, applications for planning permission made to that authority so that he himself may decide whether or not to grant planning permission; and he may make statutory instruments and directions which have a fundamental effect on how the TCPA is applied. The Secretary of State or an inspector appointed by him will hear appeals under section 78 TCPA 1990 (appeals against decisions or non- determinations of the local planning authority) and appeals against enforcement notices.

The meaning of 'Development' under the TCPA 1990

6.03 *Development* is defined by section 55(1) TCPA 1990 as

'the carrying out of building, engineering, mining or other
operations in, on over or under land or the making of any material
change of use of any buildings or other land'. Many activities are
expressly excluded from this definition by section 55(2),
including (but not limited to): works of maintenance,
improvement or alteration of a building which only affect its
interior or do not affect its external appearance; the use (i.e.
excluding operations) of land for agricultural or forestry
purposes together with the use for either of these purposes
of any building occupied together with such land; or works
by local authorities and statutory undertakers for the
inspection, repair or renewal of roads, sewers, cables etc.
'Building operations' now include demolition of a building
(section 55(1A)(a), TCPA 1990), although the GPDO grants
permission for demolition on specified grounds and
provided prescribed procedures are followed (see
paragraph 6.18 below). These consents under the GPDO are,
of course, without prejudice to other statutory controls,
namely the Building Regulations, the P(LBCA)A and the
AMAA.

6.04 Whether or not operations involve development
requiring planning permission is sometimes a difficult
question. For example, the cultivation of bushes as a means
of enclosure may not be development whereas the
construction of a wall or fence will be. However, the
construction of a wall or fence of one metre or less in height
(all cases) or two metres or less in height (except if adjacent
to a highway used by vehicular traffic) is permitted
development under part 2 of the GPDO (though not if the
wall or fence is within the curtilage of a listed building).

6.05 Where development or material change of use is proposed and the proposal (a) is not exempted from the requirement to obtain planning permission (see paragraph 6.21); (b) is not development permitted under the GPDO (see paragraph 6.8); and (c) is not authorised by 'some other Act or authority', the developer must first apply to the local planning authority for the area to which the proposal relates for a specific grant of planning permission.

6.06 The method of application is prescribed by the Town and Country Planning (Applications) Regulations 1988 (S.I. 1988, No.1812). There is no standard form, each local planning authority produces its own. Planning authorities have specific authority to charge fees for processing applications, calculated according to the Town and Country Planning Fees Order from time to time in force (fees vary greatly, depending on the size and nature of the proposed development, though not on any specific environmental impacts). Planning authorities do not, however, have authority to charge for pre-application advice (*R. v. Richmond-upon-Thames London Borough Council, ex parte McCarthy and Stone (Developments) Ltd* [1991] 3 W.L.R. 941 HL).

Development Plans

6.07 Applications for planning permission are determined within a complex policy framework. Policy reflects ministerial advice and circulars, and 'development plans' for the county and local area. The 'development plan' for a shire county is the structure plan and local plans taken together. In most areas now governed at local level by unitary authorities the development plan is the unitary development plan (UDP) or, if the UDP is not yet at an advanced stage, the old structure plan and local plans as they relate to the unitary area. Some new unitary authorities will simply produce district wide local plans within the framework of existing structure plans. Structure plans are produced by the county and contain strategic policies, such as how much new housing is needed over the plan period (usually about 10-20 years); how much retail shopping provision is desirable; or policies defining the extent of the county's commitment to the preservation of the built heritage. The structure plan does not usually identify individual sites. Local plans are produced by the districts and contain site specific policies, such as the allocation of land to housing or industry, the location of ancient monuments and conservation areas, or the extent of recreational land. Formerly there could be several local plans for one district area, but the requirement is now for a local plan covering each local planning authority area. UDPs contain in part I what would normally be structure plan policies, with 'local plan policies' in part II (though UDPs are formulated in part according to Secretary of State's guidance which is currently more prescriptive than that for local and structure plans). The general form and content of development plans is prescribed by the Town and Country Planning (Development Plans) Regulations 1991 (as amended).

The relevant development plans must be taken into account when an application for planning permission is determined by the local planning authority (section 70(2), TCPA 1990). In fact the Planning and Compensation Act

1991 inserted a new section (54A) into the TCPA which requires applications to be determined in accordance with the development plan 'unless material considerations indicate otherwise' (see paragraph 6.44 for material planning considerations). If the local planning authority is minded to grant planning permission on an application which conflicts materially with the development plan the application, in certain circumstances, will be referred to the Secretary of State, who may 'call-in' the application. The publicity requirements are also more onerous for development which conflicts with the development plan (article 8, GD(P)O).

Permission granted by Order, Statute or some other Act or Authority

By Order (the GPDO)

6.08 Article 3 of the GPDO grants planning permission for the classes of development listed in schedule 2 to the Order ('permitted development'). The classes are extensive (the schedule has 33 *parts* and runs to over 50 pages) and deal with matters ranging from operations within the curtilage of a dwelling house to aviation development. Most classes consist of a short statement of the development for which the Secretary of State is granting permission by the Order, followed by a number of limitations and conditions on such permission. Limitations frequently appear in the case of listed buildings and development within the curtilage of listed buildings. Limitations are also made in respect of 'article 1(5)' land (article 1(5) of the GPDO), that is land within a national park, an AONB, a conservation area, the

Norfolk Broads, or land falling within section 41(3) of the Wildlife and Countryside Act 1981.

6.09 Part 4 of the schedule grants permission for temporary operations and uses. The period permitted is no more than 28 days per year in the case of a temporary use, and some uses, for example the holding of markets or motor sports rallies, are excluded. Where operations are 'permitted development' or authorised in some other way part 4 also grants permission for the temporary provision of buildings, works and plant (for example a site cabin, a compound and spoil heaps) in connection with those operations. Mining operations are excluded as are operations for which planning permission is required but has not been granted. Part 4 may be important when archaeological work is ancillary to a development authorised by a specific grant of consent (though planning permission may be required, for a cabin and canteen for example, if archaeological investigations are to take place in advance of planning permission being granted). Any lengthy or extensive archaeological excavation may, however, require planning permission in its own right, though field survey or other investigations which do not involve significant disturbance of the ground obviously will not, no matter what form they take. A short excavation of, say, three weeks duration, may be an irritant to the local planning authority. Such an excavation would not fall either within part 4 (as a temporary *use*) or, except in remarkable circumstances, within any other part of schedule 2 (even part 26, see below). It may then be unauthorised development but would be difficult to enforce against.

6.10 The most significant parts of schedule 2 as far as archaeology is concerned are part 6 (agricultural buildings and operations), part 7 (forestry buildings and operations), part 11 (development under local or private Acts or orders), part 14 (development by drainage bodies), part 16 (development by or on behalf of sewerage undertakers), part 17 (development by statutory undertakers), part 22 (mineral exploration), part 26 (development by English Heritage) and part 31 (demolition of buildings).

6.11 Part 6 – Grants permission for agricultural development, including the construction of buildings and the carrying out of excavations, within certain limits. There are no conditions or limitations within this class for the benefit of archaeological sites or historic buildings, though the local planning authority may be able to give directions as to the siting and appearance of structures. Works authorised by this part can easily destroy archaeological remains; an article 4 direction should be considered in appropriate cases (see paragraph 6.26, below).

6.12 Part 7 – Grants permission for forestry development, including the construction of buildings, 'private ways' and other operations. The comments on part 6 are applicable.

6.13 Part 11 – Grants permission for development which is already authorised by parliamentary authority provided that the empowering statute or order 'designates specifically' the nature of the development and the land on which the development may be carried out. Article 3(7) of the GPDO requires that where the empowering statute or order post-dates July 1, 1948 and requires the consent or approval of any person development will not be authorised by part 11 until that consent or approval is obtained. Large and sensitive developments are often authorised by such parliamentary authority. It is important, therefore, to obtain appropriate protection for archaeological sites in the relevant statute or order, e.g. requiring the promoters to obtain the prior consent of the local planning authority and English Heritage to specified works.

6.14 Part 14 – Grants permission for drainage development by drainage bodies. This may sometimes affect the survival of waterlogged archaeological deposits. Although not presenting the scale of threat posed by peat extraction, attendant works and reductions in water table can have adverse effects on waterlogged archaeological deposits.

6.15 Parts 16 and 17 – Grant permission for most routine works and construction by sewerage, railway, gas, electricity and water undertakers. Major works, for example new lines or pipelines, usually require either ministerial consent or a specific grant of planning permission and archaeological matters may be considered when such consent or permission is sought. Undertakers may also be required to 'have due regard to' archaeological sites when formulating their development proposals; they should be reminded of these provisions, especially if proceeding only under the GPDO.

6.16 Part 22 (read in conjunction with article 7 of the GPDO) - Grants permission for mineral exploration, i.e. the drilling of boreholes, the carrying out of seismic surveys or other excavations in pursuit of minerals other than petroleum.

Class A of part 22 relates to exploration for a period not exceeding 28 consecutive days; class B relates to exploration of any duration. Permission under class A does not extend to exploration involving operations in a national park, an AONB, or on a Site of Specific Scientific Interest or a *'site of archaeological interest'*. To fall within class B the developer must first notify the planning authority of its intention to explore, and then wait either for a period of 28 days to elapse from the date of service of the notice, or for earlier confirmation from the planning authority that the exploration may proceed. Within the period of 21 days from receipt of the notice the planning authority may, on prescribed grounds, issue a direction under article 7 withdrawing the permitted development rights granted under article 3, i.e. requiring the developer to make an application for a specific grant of planning permission. The prescribed grounds include development within those areas and sites referred to when considering class A of part 22, the Broads (article 7(2)(a)) and development which would adversely affect the setting of a grade I listed building. Development consisting only of operations which in an Area of Archaeological Importance (AAI) would be exempt from AAI controls (under the Areas of Archaeological Importance (Notification of Operations)(Exemptions) Order 1984) cannot be the subject of such a direction.

A direction under article 7 may be overruled by the Secretary of State at any time within the period of 28 days after which it was made.

The expression *site of archaeological interest* means for the purposes of the GPDO land which is a scheduled monument (but excluding its setting), is within an AAI or which is within a site *'registered in any record adopted by resolution by a county council and known as the County Sites and Monuments Record'* (article 1(2)). When first introduced into the General Development Order 1977 the reference to registered sites had a cut-off date in 1986. This has since been removed, both under the GDO 1988 and the GPDO. The requirement for adoption of the County SMR by resolution of a 'county council' alludes to the fact that permission for mineral development would normally be determined by the county planning authority. This may cause some problems of interpretation for SMRs maintained by joint authorities or district councils.

6.17 Part 26 – Grants permission for development by or on behalf of English Heritage consisting of (a) the maintenance, repair or restoration of any building or monument; (b) the erection of screens, fences or covers designed or intended to protect or safeguard any building or monument; or (c) the carrying out of works to stabilise ground conditions by any cliff, watercourse or the coastline. The expression 'building or monument' is limited in this context to any building or monument owned, managed or controlled by, or in the guardianship of, English Heritage. The class does not authorise the extension of any building or monument nor, apparently, does it authorise archaeological investigations, where these would require planning permission. When works are executed to stabilise cliffs etc. temporary structures must be removed after six months unless the planning authority agrees otherwise.

6.18 Part 31 – Grants permission for *any building operation consisting of the demolition of a building* (class A), subject to specified limitations and conditions. Class B of this part grants permission for any building operation consisting of the demolition of the whole or any part of a gate, fence, wall or other means of enclosure. These general permissions are necessary given the amendment of section 55(1) of the TCPA 1990, in line with case law, which provides that demolition of buildings is now included within the definition of 'building operations' (section 55(1)(1A); see paragraph 6.3 above). DOE Circular 10/95 (WO 31/95): *Planning Controls over Demolition* explains the complexities of the new regime.

If consent for demolition is required under any statutory provision other than the TCPA such consent must still be obtained, as part 31 only authorises demolition in so far as demolition is development requiring planning permission. Note also that in the case of class A development permission is not granted where the building in question has either been rendered unsafe or uninhabitable due to the action or inaction of any person having an interest in the land on which the building stands, or if it is practicable to secure safety or health by temporary support works. Even where class A works do not fall within these limitations, unless the works are urgently necessary in the interests of health or safety, notice of the intended demolition must still be served on the planning authority for approval of the *method of demolition and any proposed restoration of the site*. A 28 day period is prescribed for such approval and demolition must be in accordance with the approved details. The developer must also display a site notice.

Demolition of parts of buildings may be authorised impliedly or expressly by schedule 2 to the GPDO but article 3(9) of the Order limits the permission granted for the demolition of whole buildings to that granted by part 31 of the Order.

6.19 Article 4(2) of the GPDO permits any planning authority which follows the procedure laid down by article 6 of that Order to direct that specified classes of development in the whole or a part of a particular conservation area will require a specific grant of planning permission. No confirmation by the Secretary of State is required for such article 4 directions for such conservation purposes. The development to which an article 4(2) direction can relate are given in article 4(5) and include the enlargement, alteration, improvement, painting, and re-roofing of houses at locations fronting highways, waterways or open space. Note that conservation consent is required in any event for demolition of buildings within a conservation area and so, in relation to demolition, article 4(5) refers only to demolition authorised by class B of part 31 (gates, fences etc.).

6.20 Directions of the planning authority under article 4 remove the general planning consent granted by the Secretary of State and his approval for such directions is normally required (article 5(1), GPDO). In addition to the exception to this rule relating to conservation areas however, the need for the consent of the Secretary of State is not required to a direction ('article 4(1) direction') which relates solely to a listed building, being a *building which is notified to the authority by the Secretary of State as a building of architectural or historic interest*, or development within the curtilage of a listed building (article 5(3), GPDO). The exception to this is where the development in question is that of a statutory undertaker, in which case the Secretary of State's approval must still be obtained. Section 5(3) does not apply to development affecting a scheduled monument or its setting, only to listed buildings and similar. Its main focus is on curtilage development, and minor operations and change of use which might affect the appearance or setting of a listed building.

By Statute or some other Act or authority (Development authorised other than under the TCPA and GPDO)

6.21 Not all development is authorised under the TCPA or the GPDO. An Act of Parliament or an order made under statute may authorise development and, in addition, provide for the suspension of normal listed building and scheduled monument procedures. Such development is often part of a proposal which also involves compulsory purchase of the necessary interests in land.

6.22 Private local Acts, i.e. statutes not promoted by the Government and relating to only part of the jurisdiction, were the main means by which new undertakings of all kinds were authorised in the nineteenth century, especially where proposals were for linear features, such as railways and canals, which required the acquisition of a succession of land holdings. Some of the more recent private local Acts have again related to linear features, for example urban tramways and bridges.

Such Acts contain within them the 'planning permission' which the promoter requires. There is a lengthy parliamentary procedure (which can begin in a committee of either house) during which detailed plans and proposals for development are argued by parliamentary counsel and objections or requests for conditions are settled. If the objection is one of principle this should usually be taken in the 'first house', i.e. the house where the Bill was introduced; if one of detail it may be acceptable to wait until the Bill is discussed later, perhaps with the comfort of a 'second house undertaking' from the promoter, that it will not object to a particular matter being raised at the later stage.

6.23 Section 42 of the Local Government (Miscellaneous Provisions) Act 1976 provides that any local Act passed after or during 1976 will, unless the relevant Act expressly provides otherwise, take effect subject to normal planning controls. It is usual therefore for promoters of such Acts to secure the necessary express powers, although an Act may contain limitations and conditions which require the promoters to notify or consult with specialist bodies and gain the approval of details, of any development authorised, from the local planning authority. Part 11 of the GPDO grants permission for all development authorised by private or local Acts subject to the conditions and limitations in that part (see paragraph 6. 13 above).

6.24 As a means of securing authority for infrastructure works, private Acts may be superseded by Orders under the Transport and Works Act 1992 (the 'TWA'). In keeping with the trend to skeleton Acts and increased delegation of legislative powers, the TWA enables the Secretary of State to authorise major infrastructure projects, including private roads, railways and waterways, by ministerial Order (sections 1 and 3, TWA). The Act provides for public local inquiries rather than opposed Parliamentary committees as the forum for resolving objections and disputes. The applicant for an Order under the TWA must supply details of the scheme to the relevant local planning authority at the time when the application is made. The planning authority, affected landowners and statutory undertakers may make representations to the Secretary of State (who may require an environmental assessment to be provided). If the Secretary of State makes an Order he may deem that planning permission is granted for the development, pursuant to section 16 of the TWA and section 90(2A) of the TCPA 1990. Regulations provide for the consolidation with the main application of any listed building and scheduled monument consent applications required (The Transport and Works Applications (Listed Buildings, Conservation Areas and Ancient Monuments Procedure) Regulations 1992 (S.I. 1992, No.3138): it is the applicant's duty to refer to all such consents required in his draft order and supporting documents (section 17, TWA).

6.25 Development may also be authorised by a host of other ministerial Orders and licences. Perhaps the most significant in archaeological terms are Orders made by the Secretary of State under the Highways Act 1980 (providing for new trunk roads and motorways). A draft Order is usually published by the Secretary of State within a period of 13 weeks from first publishing notice of the proposed scheme. Objections can be made to the draft and presented at a public local inquiry convened for the purpose. The local planning authority and highway authority will make representations and appear but there may be a less sympathetic approach to lay objectors than is found at local planning authority committees.

A good example of development by 'licence' is provided by section 36 of the Electricity Act 1989, which reserves to the Secretary of State for Trade and Industry the right to license the generation of electricity, if above prescribed minimum thresholds. Licences may authorise the building of power stations; planning permission from the local planning authority will not be required (see sections 90(2) and 268 TCPA 1990). The Secretary of State for Trade and Industry may also grant licences under the Telecommunications Act 1984. These authorise installation of predominantly underground cables for television and other communications purposes. There are many other kinds of ministerial licence or consent, ranging from those relating to petroleum exploration at sea to the construction of land drainage works. The need for environmental assessment in such circumstances will usually be dealt with under regulations already referred to in chapter 4 of this work.

Section 90(1) of the TCPA 1990 (as amended) provides that *'where the authorisation of a government department is required by virtue of an enactment in respect of development to be carried out by a local authority or by statutory undertakers who are not a local authority, that department may, on granting that authorisation, direct that planning permission for that development shall be deemed to be granted subject to such conditions (if any) as may be specified in the direction'*. The TCPA applies to such decisions as if the matter had been called-in by the Secretary of State under section 77, except that part XII of the Act (the right to challenge orders and notices in the High Court) does not apply.

6.26 Development by the Crown on Crown land does not fall within the TCPA: the general rule is that the Crown is not bound by an enactment unless the Act in question so provides, either by express words or by necessary implication. This exception does not extend to non-Crown development on Crown land, for example where the Crown has a commercial tenant, nor does it extend to bodies which may be 'emanations of the state' but which do not act on behalf of the Crown (English Heritage, for example, in contrast to the RCHM(e) which – at the time of writing – is a Crown agent). Probably the most obvious examples of Crown exemption are those enjoyed by the Secretaries of State for Defence and Health. Government departments or agencies which are legally still part of a department will usually be outside the normal planning controls and will be subject only to the non-statutory procedures summarised in DOE Circular 18/84. However, the Crown is able to take the benefit of the TCPA, for example by obtaining a grant of planning permission which takes effect once the disposal to a non-Crown body has been made (section 299, TCPA 1990), or by entering planning obligations (sections 106 and 299A, TCPA 1990). The Government is currently considering curtailing the exemption for Crown development.

The Duties of Statutory Undertakers and Persons Licensed under Statute

6.27 When carrying out development for which a grant of planning permission from the local planning authority is not required statutory undertakers and public utilities have long had to comply with provisions relating to archaeology and the built heritage, usually contained in the statutes by which the undertakers or utilities in question were established. The number of such organisations has increased substantially with the privatisation of gas, electricity, water and telecommunications. As the appropriate statutory machinery has been re-worked or newly devised, archaeological provisions have been updated.

6.28 These provisions tend to be 'strategic', imposing a general duty on an undertaker to consider the archaeological interest within the undertaker's entire range of activities. A typical provision is 'to have regard to the desirability of protecting' sites of archaeological interest when formulating proposals.

6.29 The provisions relating to listed buildings and scheduled monuments apply to statutory undertakers and licensees, unless enjoying Crown exemption or exercising rights specifically conferred by Parliamentary authority. Statutes and licences often emphasise that the powers granted do not obviate the need for listed building and scheduled monument consent where this would normally be necessary. Where the TCPA or the P(LBCA)A would require planning decisions to take the setting of a building or monument into account similar, though simplified, requirements may be present in a statutory licence. For example, licences granted by the Secretary of State for Trade and Industry to telecommunications code system operators under the Telecommunications Act 1984 usually contain wording along the following lines:

Condition [ ]

In respect of the Statutory List of Buildings, except in the case of emergency works, the Licensee shall give written notice to the

*Planning Authority before installing Lines or other tele-
communications apparatus (a) on any listed building; or (b) on or
above the ground in proximity to any grade I listed building.*

*Where the Planning Authority notifies the Licensee in writing
within 28 working days of the giving of the notice that the
installation would detrimentally affect the character or appearance
of the building, or its setting, and that the installation should not
take place, the Licensee may install the apparatus only if the
Planning Authority subsequently agrees in writing or if the
Secretary of State, after having consulted the Planning Authority,
so directs in writing.*

*For the avoidance of doubt it is hereby declared that nothing in
this Licence affects: (a) the statutory requirement that the consent
of the Secretary of State shall be obtained before any work is carried
out which will affect the site of an ancient monument scheduled
under sections 1 and 2 of the Ancient Monuments and
Archaeological Areas Act 1979; or (b) the obligation imposed on
the Licensee by virtue of section 7 of the Planning (Listed
Buildings and Conservation Areas) Act 1990 to obtain listed
building consent for any works which affect the character of a
listed building, or involve the demolition of any part of such
building.*

Some old statutes contain very basic savings for sites
protected under the AMAA. Section 47(d) of the Coast
Protection Act 1949 provides that *'nothing in this Act or in any
order made thereunder shall ... authorise or require any person to
carry out any work or do anything in contravention of the
[Ancient Monuments and Archaeological Areas Act 1979]'.*
Section 67(3) of the Land Drainage Act 1991 and section
183(2) of the Water Resources Act 1991 contain similar
formulae. Section 40(2)(a) of the Forestry Act 1967 excludes

from the powers of compulsory purchase conferred by that Act *'land which is the site of an ancient monument or other object of archaeological interest'*.

But such provisions do not subject development to the rigours of public participation, PPG 16 or even development plan policies, such as would be the case if the works in question had to be authorised by a specific grant of planning permission. As will be apparent from discussion of the GPDO and the general duties of statutory undertakers (see below) robust archaeological provisions are the exception rather than the rule.

6.30 In most parts of the country SMRs enjoy good relationships with the planning arms of statutory undertakers, especially water and gas. Prior consultation on proposals is the norm, assistance for archaeological survey is frequent and the funding of archaeological investigation is not unusual. The assistance and consultation of statutory undertakers often goes beyond what is required under statute, as will be clear when the rather circumscribed requirements of those statutes are considered.

6.31 The Electricity Act 1989 requires licensee companies to *'have regard to the desirability ... of protecting sites, buildings and objects of architectural, historic or archaeological interest'* when formulating any relevant proposals (section 38; schedule 9, paragraph 1(1)(a)). The requirement is an internal one for the licence holder and will be effective in conservation terms only to the extent that archaeological opinion is taken into account. Consultation on individual proposals is not required by the Act but within 12 months of being granted a licence holders must produce 'statements' (i.e. policy documents) on how they intend to comply with their statutory duties. In producing such a statement the licensee is obliged to set out its procedures, including consultation procedures. Consultation must also take place with English Heritage (or in Wales with the Historic Buildings Council for Wales) when compiling the statement. The statement must be modified from time to time as new circumstances dictate (schedule 9, paragraphs 2(1) and 2(2)).

6.32 The Water Resources Act 1991 placed a duty on water companies (and on the former National Rivers Authority ('NRA')), in relation to their functions under that Act, to *'have regard to the desirability of protecting and conserving buildings, sites and objects of archaeological, architectural or historic interest'* (section 16(1)(b)). Codes of practice published by the companies under section 18(4)(c) of the Act require the prior approval of English Heritage/Cadw. Again, consultation on individual proposals is not required by statute, though the water companies have adopted informal procedures with many heritage bodies, including SMRs.

6.33 Under the Environment Act 1995 the NRA is abolished and its functions assumed by the Environment Agency. The Agency and the appropriate minister have a duty *'when formulating or considering ... any proposal relating to any functions of the Agency ... to have regard to the desirability of protecting and conserving buildings, sites and objects of archaeological, architectural, engineering or historic interest'* ... and to *'take into account any effect which the proposals would have on the beauty or amenity of ... any rural or urban area or any such ... buildings, sites or objects'* (sections 7(1)(c)(i) and (ii) of the Act). These duties mirror those placed on the Ministry of Agriculture, Fisheries and Food and relevant undertakers under section 3(2)(b) and (c) of the Water Industry Act 1991. The need to 'have regard to' may imply a slightly higher duty than to 'take into account'; the former suggests some constraining influence of the matters under consideration whereas the latter does not.

6.34 Part 3 of the Environment Act 1995 redefines the functions of national parks. They become independent planning authorities for their areas. In particular they now have a duty to conserve and enhance the natural beauty, wildlife and *cultural heritage* of their areas. For this purpose schedule 9 to the 1995 Act recognises national parks as local authorities for the purposes of parts I and II of the AMAA (giving national parks power *inter alia* to expend money on archaeological investigations, to enter into management agreements under the AMAA or to become guardians of ancient monuments).

Planning Enforcement

6.35 The English Heritage consultation paper of 1994 and the Department of National Heritage consultation *Protecting our Heritage* (1996) both advocate the end of Areas of Archaeological Importance. They do so, in part at least, because PPG 16 and the planning system are thought to provide a more effective way of controlling development which threatens archaeological remains in urban areas. The main elements of this control within the planning system are (a) the conditions which the local planning authority is able to attach to grants of planning permission and (b) the sanctions which can be applied when unauthorised development is undertaken.

Development may be authorised in a variety of ways (see above, this chapter). If development appears to be taking place without authorisation the local planning authority, and in most cases the Secretary of State, may take steps to secure compliance with the planning legislation. These steps include the service of an enforcement notice (together, in urgent cases, with a stop notice) or, in serious or difficult cases, obtaining an injunction. Where the breach of planning control is non-compliance with a planning condition, failure to properly fence a site for example, the local planning authority may issue a breach of condition notice.

6.36 In preparing for enforcement action the local planning authority should take advantage of the statutory provisions which require disclosure of or otherwise assist in the gathering of information. These are:

- section 330 TCPA 1990, a general planning Act power to require information as to interests in land from owners, occupiers and persons receiving rents; in contrast to a planning contravention notice (see below) a notice under this section may require the recipient to specify the use of land;
- section 171C TCPA 1990 (planning contravention notice), the notice introduced by the PCA 1991 which enables the planning authority to require details about development of a kind specified in the notice, especially the time when the development in question commenced, and the names and addresses of

anybody known to the recipient to have been involved with carrying out the development;
- section 16 Local Government (Miscellaneous Provisions) Act 1976, a general power enabling local authorities to require information on holdings and interests in land.

A notice served under any of these sections renders the person served liable to criminal sanctions if he or she does not comply. Providing incorrect information usually results in heavier penalties than simple non-compliance.

Additional sources of information are the planning registers, site visits (possibly under section 196A TCPA 1990), the local SMR and English Heritage's Field Monument Warden reports.

6.37 Development which threatens archaeological remains will usually be operational development and operational development which, in the majority of cases, must be curtailed or controlled quickly if the damage to remains is to be prevented or abated. Current Government guidance on the use of the various enforcement measures is contained in Environment Circular 10/97, *Enforcing Planning Control: Legislative Provisions and Procedural Requirements.*

Enforcement notices are issued by the planning authority under section 172 TCPA. The notice should specify either that unauthorised development has taken place (a 'breach of planning control' within section 171A(1)(a), TCPA) or that there has been a failure to comply with a specified condition or limitation subject to which planning permission was granted (a breach within section 171(A)(1)(b), TCPA).

An enforcement notice may require remedy of the breach of planning control *inter alia* 'by discontinuing any use of the land or by restoring the land to its condition before the breach took place' (section 173(4)(a), TCPA). A notice may, therefore, be mandatory as well as prohibitive. In archaeological cases prohibitive action will be the norm as reinstatement of deposits and site relationships, although desirable, is not usually an option. However, there may be scope for mandatory action where historic structures are concerned, particularly masonry or ditches and banks which form part of a monument. If there is a breach of planning control in relation to a building which is also listed as of special architectural or historic interest a listed building enforcement notice may be served at the same time as a planning enforcement notice. Where sub-surface remains and deposits are concerned the only notice is likely to be served under the planning legislation, as there are no enforcement notice provisions under the AMAA.

An enforcement notice must only be issued by the planning authority once the appropriate committee or officer authorisation has been given. Where relevant, the personal circumstances of the person to be served should be considered by the enforcing authority (*R. v. Kerrier District Council, ex parte Uzell* [1996] 71 P & C.R. 566). The issuing authority must be satisfied that it is expedient to issue, having regard to the development plan and other material considerations. The notice should specify the breach of planning control, the land to which it relates, the steps required to remedy the breach and the period for compliance (from a date – the 'effective date' – stipulated in the notice). The period for compliance cannot be less than 28 days. A plan should be attached to the notice. Service should be personal or by recorded delivery post. All persons with an interest in the land affected should be served, including mortgagees. Service must take place no later than 28 days after the notice is 'issued' (i.e. dated) by the local planning authority. Failure to comply with a valid enforcement notice against which there has been no appeal lodged (or against which an appeal has been dismissed) will render the owner and/or controller of an interest in the land affected liable on summary conviction to a fine of up to £20,000, or an unlimited fine in the Crown Court (section 179, TCPA). Where there is such non-compliance the local planning authority is also empowered to enter land and remedy the breach, charging the owner its reasonable costs (section 178, TCPA).

6.38 Enforcement is not possible against operational development (as distinct from a change of use) which occurred or was substantially completed more than four years before enforcement action is taken (section 171B(1), TCPA). Most archaeological enforcement cases will not be affected by this provision as they tend to relate to the imminent destruction of fragile, buried remains or the partial destruction of remains by operations which if reversed might cause further loss of archaeological material. Enforcement action could be taken against an unauthorised archaeological excavation, as an archaeological excavation will usually constitute operational development for which it is difficult to argue that planning permission is granted by the GPDO. But the temporary nature of such excavations makes the service of an enforcement notice alone an ineffective step, as even if the operations cease within the period for compliance the damage to archaeological remains may be extensive and impossible to remedy. Steps which are impossible to comply with may render the notice invalid on *Wednesbury* grounds. Failure to specify steps and talk instead of 'a scheme to be approved' may be void for uncertainty (*Kaur v. Secretary of State for the Environment and Greenwich London Borough Council* [1990] J.P.L. 814). Where compliance requires works which would go beyond what is necessary to remedy the breach an appeal will lie under section 174, TCPA. Where an appeal is lodged before the effective date and the local planning authority does not seek a court order under section 289(4A), TCPA (notice to have effect pending determination of appeal) compliance is not required until the Secretary of State has upheld the notice or the appeal is withdrawn (section 175(4), TCPA).

6.39 *Stop notices* may be issued by the local planning authority in any case where the authority has resolved to issue an enforcement notice and before the enforcement notice takes effect. A stop notice proscribes some or all of the activities the subject of the enforcement notice by a much earlier date. The period for compliance is often about two or three days after service. Under section 186, TCPA compensation is payable if the enforcement notice to which the stop notice relates is not upheld on appeal; it is prudent therefore to fully investigate the potential compensation liability and possible defences of the developer before seeking authority to issue. Environment Circular 10/97 also advises that stop notices should be drawn as narrowly as practicable. Archaeological cases which are of sufficient importance to merit the service of an enforcement notice will often require a stop notice to prevent destruction of remains. A stop notice is effective notwithstanding an appeal against the enforcement notice to which it relates, hence the availability of compensation on determination of the enforcement notice appeal.

The mechanics of drafting and serving a stop notice are similar to enforcement notices. Both are frequently served and entered in the planning register together.

Failure to comply with a stop notice is an offence for which the offender will be liable to a fine before the magistrates of up to £20,000 or an unlimited fine on indictment (section 187, TCPA). The court must have regard to any financial benefit which has accrued or is likely to have accrued to the offender in consequence of the breach, although this duty does not override the court's duty, under section 18 of the Criminal Justice Act 1991, to have regard to the financial circumstances of the offender (*R. v. Browning* [1996] 1 P.L.R. 61); the two duties must be exercised together.

A stop notice will cease to have effect once the compliance period in the enforcement notice expires or, if there has been an appeal, when the notice is upheld. The enforcement notice itself is then operative and if compliance does not take place an offence is committed under the enforcement notice. The penalties are the same as for non-compliance with a stop notice.

6.40 *Appeal* against an enforcement notice must be made before the effective date, on the form of appeal which the local planning authority should have enclosed with the notice. An appeal must be on one or more of the grounds in section 174(2), TCPA. The appeal may be considered on written representations, by hearing or by inquiry, depending on the complexity of the issues involved and the preferences of the parties. The procedure for making an appeal is contained within the Town and Country Planning (Enforcement Notices and Appeals) Regulations 1991 (S.I. 1991, No.2804).

6.41 *Injunctions* may be sought by the planning authority to restrain breaches of planning control. There is now express authority in the form of section 187B, TCPA. It is likely that an injunction will be sought only where the breach is serious and susceptible to restraint, although the section refers to an injunction being 'necessary or expedient' for restraining any actual or apprehended breach of planning control. In contrast to an enforcement or stop notice there is no need for the breach to have already occurred. Moreover, the word 'restrained' in section 187B is not to be construed narrowly and includes mandatory remedies (*Croydon London Borough Council v. Gladden* [1994] 1 P.L.R. 30 CA; *South Hams District Council v. Halsey* [1996] J.P.L. 761).

English Heritage has no express powers to obtain injunctions to restrain breaches of planning control but is empowered under section 33(2A) of the NHA 1983 to seek injunctions for listed buildings purposes (local planning authorities also have a similar but narrower power under section 44A, P(LBCA)A) or to restrain breaches of part I of the AMAA.

Application may be made under section 187B to either the High Court or the County Court, though the limited experience of some judges in the latter may dictate a High Court action. The grant of an injunction is always in the discretion of the court. A breach of planning control can be restrained by interlocutory injunction (*Runnymede Borough Council v. Harwood* [1994] 1 P.L.R. 22 CA). The court should consider the interlocutory application on the 'balance of convenience' at the time of that application (*American Cyanamid v. Ethicon Limited* [1975] A.C. 396). To obtain a prohibitive injunction, restraining the defendant from excavating foundations, for example, the plaintiff should not need to show that he will be successful at trial; although for a mandatory injunction there should be a high degree of probability that such an injunction will be granted at trial. Costs undertakings from the applicant are not a prerequisite of the granting of an injunction but remain in the discretion of the judge (*Kirklees Metropolitan Borough Council v. Wickes Building Supplies Limited* [1993] A.C., 220). An injunction may be sought even though the defendant has been acquitted on a criminal charge for the same act (*Halsey, loc. cit.*).

6.42 Under section 171A of the TCPA an enforcement notice can be served in respect of a breach of a condition or limitation in a planning permission. However, the PCA 1991 introduced a new notice, the 'breach of condition notice' (section 187A, TCPA), issued by the local planning authority but specifically in relation to breach of condition once the planning permission has been implemented. There is no statutory appeal against a breach of condition notice and failure to comply with the notice is an offence punishable by a fine of up to level 3 on the standard scale. A notice will not be effective if the condition to which it relates is invalid. In the case of major breaches of condition – not implementing a programme of archaeological work before commencing development, for example – an injunction or stop notice will be required. But for relatively minor breaches, especially those of long standing, the section 187A procedure is a useful, additional method of enforcement.

(II) Archaeology as a Planning Consideration

Planning Considerations Generally

6.43 The extent to which a planning authority takes account of a particular representation or matter when determining a planning application depends on all the circumstances of the case, but the authority must (a) have regard to the provisions of the development plan so far as these are material to the application and (b) to any other material considerations (section 70(2), TCPA 1990). The planning authority must determine the application in accordance with the development plan unless material considerations indicate otherwise (section 54A, TCPA 1990, as inserted by section 26, Planning and Compensation Act 1991). PPG 1, *General Policy and Principles* (revised February 1997) advises that *'where the development plan contains relevant policies, applications for development in accordance with the plan shall be allowed unless material considerations indicate otherwise'* (paragraph 2). Paragraph 40 of the guidance states that *'applications which are not in accordance with relevant policies in the plan should not be allowed unless material considerations justify granting a planning permission'*. Those deciding such applications or appeals are advised to *'take into account whether the proposed development would cause demonstrable harm to interests of acknowledged importance'*.

The content of adopted (and emerging) development plans is, therefore, vital. Before the amendment of 1991 development plans were very important but now they are expressly prescriptive. It has been said that 'the introduction of section 54A to the Act of 1990 requires a local planning authority or the Secretary of State when deciding whether to grant planning permission for a development to give priority to the provisions of the development plan' (*Loup and Others v. Secretary of State for the Environment and Salisbury District Council* [1996] J.P.L. 22, CA, per Glidewell L.J.). This 'priority' in section 54A sets up a presumption in favour of the development plan; the presumption may be rebutted by other, sufficiently persuasive, considerations (see, for example, *St. Albans District Council v. Secretary of State for the Environment and Allied Breweries Ltd* [1992] E.G.C.S. 147), but these considerations should, by implication, be of more than equivalent weight to the development plan policy which they seek to supplant. The additional considerations need not necessarily derive from considerations outside of the development plan in question, as section 54A does not itself refer to *other* material considerations. There cannot be a 'legitimate expectation' that any particular planning application will be determined solely by reference to the applicable development plan (*Loup and Others, loc. cit.*). It is insufficient, however, for the planning authority to consider a matter generally if it should be given consideration specifically as a matter covered by the local plan (*R. v. Redditch Borough Council, ex parte Albutt, Clews and Scott* [1996] J.P.L. B85 QBD).

Development plans and archaeological policies are considered in more detail at paragraph 6.47 *et. seq.* Whatever the policies in a development plan, however, there will invariably be a number of other considerations which are material.

6.44 What constitutes a 'material consideration' is impossible to define accurately (see, for example Purdue, (1989) J.P.L 156). Development plans in the course of preparation, ministerial policies, existing development rights, retention of existing use, fear of setting a precedent, availability of alternative sites, and the existence of alternative statutory controls are all factors which may be relevant in appropriate circumstances; as will be the views of landowners adjoining the application site or persons who are otherwise specially affected, and persons with specialist knowledge. To be material a consideration does not have to be a matter of public law. In fact the interests of individual occupiers of land and the concerns of local interest groups are to be considered a part of the public interest as a whole (*Barratt Development (Eastern) Ltd v. Secretary of State for the Environment and Oadby & Wigston Borough Council* [1982] J.P.L. 648). '*Any consideration which relates to the use and development of land is capable of being a planning consideration*' (*Stringer v. Minister of Housing and Local Government* [1971] 1 All E.R. 65).

6.45 The financial implications, in bald terms, of refusing planning permission are not a material consideration, so that undesirable development can be rejected whatever the economic cost to the applicant (*J. Murphy & Sons Ltd v. Secretary of State for the Environment* [1973] 2 All E.R. 26). However, the financial implications of refusal can almost never be taken in isolation. Conversely, development which would not normally be acceptable but which provides economic benefits outweighing the initial difficulties may be treated favourably (*Brighton Borough Council v. Secretary of State for the Environment* (1978) 39 P.& C.R. 46). Pertinent heritage cases include: *R. v. Westminster City Council, ex parte Monaghan* [1989] 2 All E.R. 74 CA, where development involving demolition of grade II listed buildings was permitted in order to sustain Covent Garden as an international opera house; planning appeal decision T/APP/Q3115/A/93/221244/P7, reported at (1994) J.P.L. 479, where permission was granted for the construction of a golf course in an area of special landscape value subject to the establishment of an endowment fund to be applied over a 20 year period for the repair of nearby listed buildings; and planning appeal decision T/APP/U1240/A/ 88/112039/P7, reported at (1996) J.P.L. 158, where, against green belt policy, permission was granted for the construction of 26 terraced cottages within the curtilage of Henbury Hall, Dorset, a grade II* listed building, so that a £450,000 residual profit from the scheme could be applied to stabilising the hall. For a discussion of 'planning gain' as it relates to archaeology see the discussion of section 106 planning obligations at paragraphs 6.123-6.135.

6.46 Archaeological considerations must be balanced by the local planning authority against all other material considerations, even if archaeological considerations arise from compliance with archaeological policies in the development plan. 'Other considerations' may themselves be reflected in development plan policies. Examples would be a need within a particular plan period to provide a specified number of new dwellings or a pre-determined landfill capacity, or a recreational land use allocation in a plan. Other considerations may also arise from ministerial policy; for example, the general principle of *permitting owners of land to use or develop their land as they judge best unless the consequences for the environment or the community would be unacceptable* (PPG 1, paragraph 36). Such a 'presumption' must now of course be read in conjunction with section 54A of the TCPA, which will restrict its operation to the extent that development is not in accordance with the development plan. Of course, in some instances, conservation considerations may justify the approval of a development proposal which on policy grounds would otherwise be unacceptable.

Archaeology Itself

6.47 The leading case on the materiality of archaeology as a planning consideration is *Hoveringham Gravels Ltd v. Secretary of State for the Environment* [1975] 1 Q.B. 754 CA; a case decided under the TCPA 1971 and the Ancient Monuments Act 1931. The ratio of this case was that a local planning authority could lawfully refuse planning permission for a development which would have destroyed a scheduled monument (and the Secretary of State was not, as the plaintiff company argued, bound to pay full compensation by treating the ancient monuments legislation as an entirely separate code). There were also obiter statements that the protection of unscheduled monuments could be a material consideration in the planning process; see, for example, the statement of Lord Scarman that '*a local planning authority might well consider an ancient monument [sic] to be of sufficient local importance to justify its protection by the refusal of planning permission to a development which would destroy it, and the Secretary of State could reasonably uphold the decision of the local planning authority, even though the monument did not qualify for protection as a monument of national importance' (loc. cit.,* at 771C).

6.48 The decision lent support to the practice of taking as a material consideration evidence of the presence of archaeological remains on an application site. This follows from the notion of 'locally important monuments', as it is the local planning authority in this context which, on advice, must decide what to accept as locally important. If an archaeological site or monument of local importance is in evidence the local planning authority may take steps, including refusal of planning permission, to protect it. To quote Lord Scarman: *'the mere fact that the monument can be protected under the Ancient Monuments Acts cannot mean that in the absence of such protection permission to develop must be given. The factor remains a material consideration to which the planning authority will give such weight as it thinks fit in the context of the planning of land use in the area for which it is responsible' (loc. cit.,* at 771A).

6.49 *Hoveringham Gravels* is also authority for the continued relevance of planning controls to sites which are protected as scheduled monuments. The Ancient Monuments Act 1931 was held to be no exclusive code which restricts or ousts the planning powers of the local authority (see the comments of Lord Justice Orr, *loc. cit.,* 765). This ruling can be extrapolated to the position under the AMAA and the TCPA 1990 and is, in fact, only a recognition of the principle that a statute is binding on all matters within its purview, including matters addressed by other statutes unless those statutes expressly provide otherwise.

6.50 The protection of unscheduled monuments from developments which would destroy or would adversely affect them was consistent with ministerial policy before PPG 16 (see, for example, DOE Circular 22/84 and DOE Circular 8/87). It is incorrect to say, therefore, that it was PPG 16 which first made the protection of unscheduled archaeological sites a material consideration, either as a matter of case law or ministerial guidance. However, PPG 16 and its Welsh equivalents are without doubt the most significant pieces of ministerial guidance ever on the treatment of archaeological sites in the planning system. The guidance contains one of the increasingly rare presumptions against allowing development. In national policy guidance the only current presumptions of this kind are (a) against inappropriate development in the green belt (PPG 2) and (b) against proposals which would involve significant alteration or cause damage to nationally important archaeological remains or their settings (PPG 16 and PG(W)PP). Perhaps even more significant was the major policy shift represented by PPG 16 in its general endorsement of what are popularly known as 'preservation by record' and 'developer funding'. The two now tend to go hand in hand. Of developer funding, PPG 16 says *'where planning authorities decide that physical preservation in situ of archaeological remains is not justified in the circumstances of the case and that development resulting in the destruction of archaeological remains should proceed, it would be entirely reasonable for the planning authority to satisfy itself before granting planning permission that the developer has made appropriate and satisfactory provision for the excavation and recording of the remains'* (paragraph 25). This advice is repeated in PG(W)PP at paragraph 138.

6.51 PPG 16 is also important for its formalisation, in policy terms, of what by the late 1980s had become accepted practice in the more forward-looking planning authorities. Paragraph 18 states that *'the desirability of preserving an ancient monument [sic] and its setting is a material consideration in determining planning applications whether that monument is scheduled or unscheduled'*. (It does not appear to have been the intention when drafting PPG 16 to limit 'materiality' to ancient monuments as defined by the AMAA, but to talk of monuments generally.) The support which the Secretary of State is likely to give to this policy is emphasised by the invitation in that paragraph to use article 4 directions (removal of permitted development rights) in appropriate cases. This advice has been repeated more recently at WO Circular 60/96, paragraph 10.

6.52 Significantly, both PPG 16 and its Welsh equivalents also provide guidance on how such material considerations should be approached. In addition to developer funding and the practicalities of enforcing policy either by means of planning conditions or planning obligations, the guidance is emphatic both in its support for archaeology in development plans (PPG 16, paragraphs 14 and 15) and about the necessity of archaeological advice and evaluation at an early stage in the planning process. All planning authorities are advised to make use of county archaeological officers, SMRs and, in Wales, the relevant archaeological trusts (a full appendix of addresses is attached to the guidance). Persons requiring archaeological advice are also referred (by PPG 16, but not the newer Welsh guidance) to the directory of members of the IFA. Local planning authorities are invited to consider giving directions to applicants to provide more archaeological information as part of their applications (under regulation 4 of the Town and Country Planning (Applications) Regulations 1988).

6.53 It is the breadth and boldness of PPG 16, especially in comparison to what went before, which accounts for its impact. However, the note remains guidance; although it indicates how the Secretary of State or an inspector may decide an appeal against the refusal of planning permission on archaeological grounds, PPG 16 does not have mandatory force. It is itself a material consideration, albeit a persuasive one, to be taken into account together with all other material considerations by local planning authorities. Paragraph 27 of PPG 16 and paragraph 16 of WO 60/96 wisely emphasise the need to treat each application for planning permission on its individual merits *'taking into account the archaeological policies in detailed development plans* [i.e. local plans and part II of unitary development plans] *together with all other relevant policies and material considerations, including the intrinsic importance of the remains and weighing these against the need for the proposed development'.*

Moreover, there are dangers both for the local planning authority or the Secretary of State in 'slavishly adhering' to any set policy, or otherwise fettering a discretion vested in them by Parliament (see, for example, *Stringer, loc. cit.,* where the planning authority was held to have unfairly fettered its discretion by agreeing previously with a third party to restrict development in the vicinity of a radio telescope network). Policy may be rejected for sound and express reasons whenever this seems fair and reasonable to the decision-maker (see, for example, *SAVE Britain's Heritage v. Secretary of State for the Environment and Others* [1991] 2 All E.R. 10 HL, where their lordships held that the Secretary of State was entitled to reject his own policy against the demolition of listed buildings which were still capable of reasonably beneficial use, in favour of a scheme believed by him to be of superior architectural value).

6.54 In England planning applications with archaeological implications will also require consideration of ministerial guidance contained in PPG 15: *Planning and the Historic Environment* (DOE/DNH 1994). In Wales the relevant sections of PG(W)PP and WO Circular 61/96, *Planning and the Historic Environment: Historic Buildings and Conservation Areas* together contain advice almost identical to that in PPG 15 (see chapter five of this work). Although some listed building applications do not involve development and, strictly speaking, are outside of the TCPA 1990 and development plans and ministerial guidance adopted under that statute, most applications for listed building consent will involve development. The protection of historic buildings and historic areas is certainly a material planning consideration. Indeed, where development proposals may affect a listed building, local planning authorities are required to have special regard to the desirability of preserving the listed building, its setting or any features of special architectural or historic interest which the building possesses (section 66(1), P(LBCA)A; note also the comparable requirement for the planning authority to pay special attention to the desirability of preserving or enhancing the character or appearance of any conservation areas affected, as required by section 72(1) of the P(LBCA)A). Paragraph 2.11 of PPG 15 emphasises that the impact of development on historic features and areas should be a matter for concern: *'The Secretary of State attaches particular importance to early consultation with the local planning authority on development proposals which would affect historic sites and structures, whether listed buildings, conservation areas, parks and gardens, battlefields or the wider historic landscape. There is likely to be much more scope for refinement and revision of proposals if consultation takes place before intentions become firm and timescales inflexible'*. The clear implication is that the protection of historic features may be a material planning consideration even where the features in question are neither listed buildings or listed in the English Heritage register of garden sites nor within a conservation area. As might be expected, World Heritage Sites are accorded high status by PPG 15, as a 'key' material consideration (paragraph 2.22 of the PPG).

Paragraph 2.11 of PPG 15 goes on to say that local planning authorities *'expect developers to assess the likely impact of their proposals on the special interest of the site or structure in question, and to provide such written information or drawings as may be required to understand the significance of a site or structure before an application is determined'*. Paragraph 2.16 of the PPG also advises that where permission is to be granted consideration should also be given to whether or not adequate arrangements have been made for the recording of the archaeological interest of historic buildings (or of archaeological sites in their vicinity). This advice is applicable to all historic structures associated with archaeological remains, not just those buildings which enjoy some form of statutory protection.

Paragraph 131 of PG(W)PP states that ... *'local planning authorities should...take full account of the historic landscape in preparing their development plans and in determining planning applications'*. ... *'The inclusion of a site in the World Heritage List highlights the outstanding international importance to be taken*

into account by local planning authorities in determining
planning applications and listed building consent applications,
and by the Secretary of State in determining cases on appeal and
following call-in' (paragraph 132).

Development Plans

6.55 Local planning authorities have a statutory duty to
assess their areas, to produce and publicise draft plans
(notably consultation and deposit drafts), and to consider
representations (including representations from the public)
during the appropriate consultation periods. A public local
inquiry will be held before a local plan, or a unitary
development plan is formally adopted. Adoption of a
structure plan is preceded by an 'examination in public'.
District-wide local plans, like UDPs and structure plans are
now mandatory. It is this thorough programme of
consultation and investigation, together with the
requirements of section 54A of the TCPA 1990, which gives
adopted plans their prescriptive force. Although
development not in accordance with one or more
development plan policies may be authorised, either by the
local planning authority or, in prescribed circumstances, on
call-in to the Secretary of State, this is the exception rather
than the rule; an application which conflicts with plan
policies will usually encounter resistance from the outset
and may be referable to the Secretary of State as a departure
from the plan. The adoption of many development plans is
taking a very long time, in part at least because prospective
developers are anxious to secure sympathetic policies.

6.56 In 1987 a survey of archaeological policies in English

and Welsh structure and local plans illustrated the variety of policies adopted by planning authorities (Manley (1987)). Many structure plan policies were demonstrably weak in their treatment of heritage matters, and this weakness was transmitted to local plans. The protection offered by some structure plans was only of the kind that *'sites of archaeological and historical interest will be protected from adverse developments as far as practicable'*. Rarely did such policies expressly refer to other, relevant policies in the same plan, e.g. to recreation and leisure or general policies, for example policy on 'planning gain'. Archaeological policies in local plans only addressed the question of different categories of site in the vaguest terms, for example distinguishing scheduled monuments from other sites, but little more. Reasoned justification and explanatory material were too limited. There was little and sometimes no emphasis on the importance of early evaluation of archaeological remains when applying for planning permission, and this was not helped by the identification of very few sites either on the proposals map or in other planning documents.

6.57 Many counties could have benefited from policies similar to those in the Essex structure plan (although even these look restrained by today's standards):

Policy C4: Development which would substantially and adversely affect an area or site of outstanding archaeological interest will not normally be permitted; and

Policy C6: Applications for planning permission for development affecting ancient monuments or archaeological sites will normally be refused if there is an overriding case for

*preservation. Where there is no overriding case for
preservation, development of such sites will not normally be
permitted until adequate opportunities have been provided for
the recording and where desirable the excavation of such sites.*

6.58 However, even the Essex policies suffered from an
unfortunate terminology, elements of which continue to
appear in more recent development plans, for example
newly drafted unitary plans. The most common ambiguity
is reference to 'ancient monuments' (a term which has an
express statutory definition under the AMAA), when what
seems to be intended is 'monuments'. PPG 16 is not entirely
free of such confusion. Many plans used words such as
'outstanding' or 'archaeological interest' with no attempt to
define these terms; variants frequently encountered include
'exceptional', 'archaeological concern', 'archaeological value'
and 'archaeological importance'. Sometimes there is
reference to 'areas of archaeological importance' when there
are no such (statutorily designated) areas within the locality
covered by the plan. The position has improved greatly in
the 1990s. Some recent development plan drafts employ
terms which avoid confusion of such statutory and
non-statutory terminology. These plans also apply terms
more in keeping with those adopted in ministerial guidance
and have the advantage of a more detailed consideration of
archaeological policies at the consultation stage.

In the 1980s it was often considered an achievement by
archaeologists if they were able to obtain a policy which
raised a presumption against development which would
damage or destroy sites of archaeological importance; it was
a significantly greater achievement to obtain a policy which
required prior investigation of sites, even important sites,

before they were destroyed by adverse development. The draft Replacement Berkshire Structure Plan (1988), in policy (EN26 (a)), provided that 'scheduled ancient monuments' and the 'most important non-scheduled archaeological sites' were to be preserved intact; policy (EN26 (c)) would then have required developers to provide for archaeological work before and during development affecting archaeological sites. The first policy was accepted by the Secretary of State; but EN26 (c) was modified to read:

> *In the case of archaeological sites and monuments of unknown importance and areas of high potential, consideration will be given to the need for, and provision will be made, as appropriate, for investigations before and during development.*

This did not go so far as the planning authority had intended but, in some respects, it foreshadowed the guidance on such matters contained in PPG 16 and its Welsh equivalents.

6.59 The status of archaeological policies in development plans has increased considerably since the late 1980s. There are three main reasons:

(a)   the Government's desire to tackle the question of archaeological conservation, including the provision of funds for archaeological investigation, primarily through the planning system;

(b)   following the enactment of section 54A TCPA 1990, the need, more than ever before, for local planning authorities to secure comprehensive plan policies;

(c)   the Government's determination to update many obsolete development plans and, in some areas, the introduction of the new system of unitary development plans (UDPs) and district-wide local plans, which have encouraged a fundamental reassessment of policy.

6.60 PPG 16, at paragraph 8, states that *'Where nationally important archaeological remains, whether scheduled or not, and their settings, are affected by proposed development there should be a presumption in favour of their physical preservation. Cases involving archaeological remains of lesser importance will not always be so clear cut and planning authorities will need to weigh the relative importance of archaeology against other factors including the need for the proposed development'*. This advice is repeated in PG(W)PP, paragraph 134 and WO 60/96, paragraphs 17 and 18.

    Paragraph 14 of PPG 16 then goes on to emphasise the key role of local authorities, as planning, education and recreation authorities, where *'appropriate planning policies in development plans ... will be especially important'*. PPG 16 does not venture any model policies but it does go on to advise, at paragraph 15, that detailed development plans (i.e. local plans and part II unitary development plans) should include policies for the *protection, enhancement and preservation* of sites of *archaeological interest* and of their settings. *'The proposals map should define the areas and sites to which the policies and proposals apply'*. Paragraph 8 of WO 60/96 contains identical wording. Such statements are at variance with advice from English Heritage which says that the proposals map should only *'show monuments which are scheduled at the time the plan is adopted and could indicate easily definable areas of particular importance or vulnerability'* (EH 1992). Whether all sites covered by restrictive plan policies should be identified on the proposals map is an important question, but not one which English Heritage is prepared to answer in the affirmative.

Paragraph 16 of PPG 16, following on from the statement in favour of preservation in paragraph 8, provides some general guidance on the treatment of nationally important remains, and other remains, in development plans: *'Archaeological remains identified and scheduled as being of national importance should normally be earmarked in development plans for preservation. Authorities should bear in mind that not all nationally important archaeological remains meriting preservation will necessarily be scheduled; such remains and, in appropriate circumstances, other unscheduled archaeological remains of more local importance, may also be identified in development plans as particularly worthy of preservation'*. Paragraph 135 of PG(W)PP repeats this advice. National policy therefore recognises at least two categories of remains, the nationally and the locally important. In terms of importance the guidance does not recognise three categories of site. However, local planning authorities familiar with the identification of scheduled monuments in their development plans frequently retain this category and then recognise a second category of un-scheduled monuments of probable national importance, followed by a third category of local importance. Ministerial advice is merely permissive in relation to locally important remains and unscheduled monuments but is almost directory in relation to scheduled monuments. EH 1992 is of no further assistance when considering the bulk of remains not of national importance. It emphasises instead the changing nature of archaeological knowledge and the need to approach each planning application individually in the light of all available information. In this sense the archaeological issues are no different from any other expert issues. The predictive capacity of a plan, like the fund of archaeological knowledge, is accepted as limited.

In contrast to paragraph 15 (paragraph 8 of the WO 60/96), paragraph 16 of PPG 16 (paragraph 135, PG(W)PP) refers to 'important' archaeological remains, rather than sites of archaeological 'interest'. 'Interest' suggests a weaker requirement though is perhaps merely an example of ambiguous drafting. Perhaps paragraphs 15 and 8 refer to remains (there called 'sites') which can be accurately delineated and paragraph 16 and 135 refer to all remains including those of unknown extent. The better view is that paragraphs 15 and 8 are intended to deal with the general treatment of archaeological considerations, with paragraphs 16 and 135 addressing the particular question of how the presumption in favour of preservation is to be applied.

6.61. English Heritage, English Nature and the Countryside Agency have produced their own joint guidance on *Conservation Issues in Strategic Plans* (1993) and *Conservation Issues in Local Plans* (1996) ('CLP'). The narrative and specimen wording in CLP has proved useful to local planning authorities when preparing local plan policies for archaeology and the historic environment. For example, at box 4.8 CLP recommends policies to cover *inter alia*:

- *'preserving and enhancing internationally and nationally important archaeological sites or areas, with a strong emphasis on preservation in situ;*

- *preserving and enhancing sites of regional, county or local archaeological importance, with a preference in favour of preservation in situ;*
- *ensuring that areas of archaeological potential are properly evaluated and that where preservation in situ is not warranted there is proper recording prior to any damage or destruction of deposits; and*
- *conserving and enhancing important historic landscapes including historic parks and gardens and battlefields.'*

CLP emphasises the increasingly high value which archaeologists place on whole landscapes and the historic character of areas: *'Many local plans currently confine their attention to known archaeological sites, historic buildings or historic parks and gardens......Planning authorities should now take a more comprehensive view of the historic landscape'* (page 14). An approach the agencies particularly recommend consists of (i) characterising and assessing the historic 'dimension' of the whole local plan area; (ii) drafting policies which seek to protect the historic fabric and character of the landscape; and (iii) identifying any aspects of the landscape which are of special interest and which merit more detailed attention in considering proposals for development. In this context a Cotswold District Council policy (Deposit Draft 1994) is quoted with approval:

'1. *Development will not be permitted which would destroy, damage or adversely affect the character, appearance or setting of an historic landscape, or of any of its features, including parks and gardens of special historic interest.*
2. *Schemes to improve, restore, and manage the historic landscape will be sought in connection with, and*

> *commensurate with the scale of, any new development affecting an historic landscape.'*

Individual sites and features obviously remain an important consideration in policy terms and paragraphs 4.36 and 4.37 of CLP talk of scheduled monuments, nationally important sites which are, nonetheless, un-scheduled and world heritage sites. Paragraph 4.40 provides helpful advice on the policy treatment of nationally important sites (scheduled or not). *'Known sites of this type should be shown on the proposals map, but since knowledge is incomplete plans should indicate that in assessing the archaeological effects of proposed development account will be taken of up to date SMR information, linked with application of the Secretary of State's non-statutory criteria for identifying monuments of national importance and the results of evaluations carried out by developers. The written statement will therefore need to make clear that not all archaeological constraints are shown on the map, and assessments of importance are likely to change with greater knowledge in the future. It may be helpful to show areas of archaeological potential rather than specific known sites, so that map information is less incomplete. In urban areas, plans should make reference to urban archaeological assessment and strategies.'*

Paragraph 4.42 of CLP acknowledges that some local planning authorities may wish to recognise at least two categories of site which are of less than national importance, e.g. sites of local or county importance. CLP doesn't recommend such an approach, neither does it reject it. Instead all sites of less than national importance are considered together. *'As well as monuments which are already scheduled, or which are known to be of national importance, there are many other sites or areas which are of more local importance.*

They may be significant within a region, a county, a district or even more locally, perhaps at parish levels, but cannot, at least on the basis of present knowledge and current understanding, be regarded as of national importance. These sites also require protection and in deciding on appropriate policies attention must be given to local values and perceptions ... however, there will need to be an appropriate differential in the degree of protection afforded to these sites in policies, compared with those that are of national importance' (paragraph 41). *'Policies for these archaeological sites of more local importance should indicate that development may be refused unless it can be shown that it has no adverse effect on the special interest of area. If development is permitted, on the basis of adequate understanding, then depending on the importance of the archaeological remains and the effect of the proposed development provision must be made for appropriate archaeological investigation and recording and compensatory enhancement elsewhere on the site. All such sites may be included in one policy, although we recognise that some authorities may wish to distinguish between those of significance at a regional and county level and those that are more locally important'* (paragraph 4.42).

Paragraph 4.43 suggests that the proposals map should record 'broad zones' rather than individual sites for locally important remains. Planning authorities are also advised that the written statement should indicate that such map information is not definitive and that other sources will be taken into account when assessing development proposals.

6.62 It is questionable to what extent local planning authorities are comfortable in ascribing national importance to sites which are not scheduled monuments. The idea that authorities might be at ease with two categories of site – the nationally important and the less than nationally important

– is unconvincing. Indeed, the Macclesfield Borough Council policies (Deposit Draft 1994) reproduced by CLP identifies three categories, the most important of which lumps scheduled monuments together with sites of county importance. Its provisions are as follows:

> '*BE23 Scheduled ancient monuments and sites of county importance will normally be preserved. Development which would adversely affect such remains will normally be refused.*
>
> *BE24 Developments which would affect sites of district importance and areas of archaeological potential may be refused. Any proposal may require the submission by the applicant of an archaeological evaluation to assess the importance of the site. Development proposals must be designed to accommodate the archaeological remains where planning permission is granted.*
>
> *BE26 Development which would affect other sites of archaeological interest not meriting preservation may be permitted provided that the applicant makes adequate provision for an agreed programme of archaeological investigation to take place.'*

[The use of the word 'normally' in policies is no longer recommended by the Secretary of State but these policies pre-date the change].

Policies such as these clearly require reliable information if the subtle differences between archaeological site values are to be ascertainable. In many localities this is manifestly not the case and the application of policy is little more than a terminological confidence trick. However, policy itself can assist in the provision of information in order to facilitate such crucial assessments. Specific policies relating to archaeological evaluation are the obvious answer and CLP reproduces the Cherwell District Council policy (Deposit Draft 1992) for guidance:

> *'C27 Before the determination of an application for development which may affect a known or potential site of archaeological interest, prospective developers will be required, where necessary, to make provision for an archaeological field evaluation. This evaluation should seek to define:*
>
> – *the character and condition of any archaeological monuments or remains within the application site;*
> – *the likely impact of the proposed development upon such features;*
> – *the means of mitigating the effect of the proposed development by redesign of the proposal to achieve physical preservation or, where this is not practicable or desirable, provision for archaeological recording prior to the destruction of the monument or remains.'*

In some instances a mix of preservation *in situ* and appropriate investigation and recording may be required.

Other Planning Policy Guidance and Development Plans

6.63 PPG 1 places all planning decisions in an environmental context when in states at paragraph 4 that *'sustainable development seeks to deliver the objective of achieving, now and in the future, economic development to secure higher living standards while protecting and enhancing the environment'*. Environmental effects frequently may be negligible, but potential impact on the environment is a question at the heart of what constitutes the sustainable development to which the Government is committed. *'The planning system, and the preparation of development plans in particular, is the most effective way of striking the right balance between the demand for development and the protection of the environment'* (paragraph 39, PPG 1).

Statutorily approved and adopted plans provide all concerned – residents and amenity bodies, developers and other business interests, and those responsible for providing infrastructure – with a measure of certainty about what types of development will and will not be permitted. However, in achieving this certainty, detailed development plans should not contain so much detail that they become obsolete before the date of review (usually on a 10-15 year cycle). *'The precise level of detail'* [in local plans and part II of UDPs] *'is a matter for local decision, but authorities should bear in mind that the more detailed the plan, the longer it is likely to take to adopt, and the greater the chance that it will not be up-to-date when it is adopted'* (PPG 12, *Development Plans and Regional Planning Guidance*, paragraph 5.15; repeated in proposed revised PPG 12, paragraph 3.11). Plan policies should also be kept under review (PPG 1, paragraphs 2 and 46).

6.64 Section 36(3) of the TCPA does not list conservation of the built or archaeological heritage as matters which must be included in local plans, but ministerial advice is that detailed development plans may include policies which seek to control *'development in particular parts of the plan area, by reference to locally or nationally designated areas (whether to protect the built or natural heritage) or to the physical or geological characteristics that may influence development'* (PPG 12, paragraph 5.54(c)). In addition:

> *'the proposals map should illustrate each of the detailed policies and proposals in the written statement, defining sites for particular developments or land uses and the areas to which specified development control policies will be applied. Boundaries of locally or nationally designated areas such as heritage coasts, conservation areas and Areas of Outstanding Natural Beauty should be shown if necessary to illustrate that a range of particular development control policies apply there'* (PPG 12, paragraph 7.14; repeated in proposed revised PPG 12, annex A, paragraph 26).

EH 1992 alerts authorities to the importance of qualifying the explanations which accompany allocations for specific uses, for example housing or industry, if there may also be archaeological interest in the areas identified. English Heritage's advice is not, of course, ministerial advice but it should be borne in mind by policy makers.

It has been the practice of most local planning authorities, for many years, to include specific policies for scheduled monuments in their local plans and to identify the extent of such sites on the proposals map. But the advent of English Heritage's reassessment of scheduled monuments, the Monuments Protection Programme, has encouraged some authorities, and some English Heritage inspectors, to argue that identification of even scheduled monuments on the proposals map may be misleading and reduce certainty. Where specific policies have been applied however, non-identification on the proposals map is not within the guidance of either PPG 12, PPG 16, EH 1992 or CLP. The word 'necessary' in paragraph 7.14 of PPG 12 refers to the necessity which follows from the inclusion of specific policies within the plan, and not any more general necessity. Most plans contain fairly restrictive policies as far as scheduled monuments and un-scheduled monuments of national importance are concerned, and it is helpful to have the affected areas identified on the proposals map. If both scheduled and un-scheduled monuments of national importance are identified this greatly limits the possibility of uncertainty: there is a reasonably accurate consensus within the archaeological profession about which monuments in a given area are nationally important. The disadvantage of new sites emerging, or of existing sites being re-classified – both of which eventualities can be catered for within the plan – is small when compared with the absence of any identification on the proposals map.

6.65 PPG 12 refers to locally as well as nationally designated sites while PPG 16 and PG(W)PP refer to remains scheduled as of national importance, un-scheduled remains of national importance, and remains of more local importance. In most cases it will be impractical to identify all locally important sites on the proposals map, especially if, as is often the case, locally important sites within a plan area number several hundred.

Plan Policies in Statutory Context

6.66 If the development plan is material to an application the application must be determined in accordance with the plan unless material considerations indicate otherwise (section 54A, TCPA 1990). The material considerations in question need not be 'other' material considerations (contrast the wording of section 70(2) TCPA 1990). The 'materiality of the plan' refers to the whole plan, and so the general purpose of the plan as gleaned from policies other than those dealing directly with the issues in question may be relevant. It should be noted that 'material considerations', are not required by section 54A to be of a weight sufficient to contradict the specific policies in question, but only need to 'indicate' that this is the case. However, paragraph 40 of PPG 1 states that *'applications which are not in accordance with the relevant policies in the plan should not be allowed unless material considerations justify granting a planning permission.'*

6.67 Considerations which do not arise from the development plan are the ones which most applicants will anticipate could prevail against a particular plan policy. Plan policies should aim to respect the statutory provisions of the AMAA and P(LBCA)A but the necessary detail will not always be present in the plan, and the planning authority may decide to override a plan policy if, for example, the statutory requirements to have special regard to the preservation of a listed building or its setting, or to preserve or enhance a conservation area, outweigh a policy which conflicts with these requirements. The conflict may be either way, that is the statutory (heritage) requirements may suggest that a restrictive housing policy should not be applied (*Heatherington (U.K.) Limited v. Secretary of State for the Environment and Westminster City Council* 69 P.& C.R. (1995), 374 QBD), or that a permissive policy should be overridden (*Chorley and James et al v. Secretary of State for the Environment and Basingstoke and Deane Borough Council* [1993] J.P.L. 927 CA).

6.68 There is no specific statutory provision requiring that the preservation of a scheduled monument is taken into account when a planning decision is being made, although under the GD(P)O English Heritage/Cadw must be consulted on such an application.

Planning Permission and Planning Conditions

6.69 Planning permission may be refused, granted unconditionally or granted subject to such conditions as the local planning authority thinks fit (section 70(1), TCPA 1990). A local planning authority may decline to determine an application if within the preceding two years an application which (in the planning authority's opinion) is similar to the current application has been refused on appeal.

An unconditional grant of permission is unusual, and at the very least there will be a condition regulating the period within which the permission must be implemented. This period is usually five years, in accordance with the provisions of section 91(3) of the TCPA, although the period may be extended by express condition. Sections 91 and 92 of the TCPA contain the general timing provisions against which all permissions granted under the Act are interpreted.

6.70 The bulk of applications are either granted subject to conditions or are refused. Where conditions are imposed or an application is refused reasons should be given. In archaeologically sensitive cases refusal should, as a minimum requirement, include statements on the site's archaeological value, the impact which the proposed development would have on such value and why this impact is considered unacceptable by the planning authority.

6.71 Section 70(1)(a) authorises such conditions as the local planning authority 'thinks fit'. Section 72(1)(a) of the TCPA contains a provision expressly authorising conditions which regulate *'the development or use of any land under the control of the applicant (whether or not it is land in respect of which the application was made) or requiring the carrying out of works on any such land'*, if the local planning authority believes such conditions to be expedient in connection with the development authorised by the permission. But neither of these provisions, of course, means that the authority has an unlimited discretion to impose conditions. There are public law constraints similar to those covered in the discussion of scheduled monument consents (see paragraphs 2.55-2.64 and 2.128), and every local planning authority must take account of the particular purposes of the TCPA. Under section 70(2) of the TCPA the authority must also have regard to all material considerations, giving that weight to development plans required by section 54A of the Act (see paragraph 6.35).

6.72 Over the years the court has intervened many times in the examination of planning conditions and there now exists a substantial case law on what is acceptable. Judgments and dicta of the court are not the same, either in content or at law, as ministerial guidance. Ministerial guidance contains principles supplementary to those promulgated by the court; unless guidance conforms with the law it carries no legal force.

6.73 As planning cases typically concern very particular facts from which the courts are invited to draw quite general principles about the operation of a statutory discretion, it is not surprising that there is no integrated code of legal principles in this area. A starting point is the case of *Fawcett Properties Ltd v. Buckingham County Council* [1960] 3 All E.R. 503 HL (in which the court affirmed its earlier but less transparent findings in *Pyx Granite Co. Ltd v. Minister of Housing and Local Government* [1959] 3 All E.R. 1 HL). In deciding whether or not planning conditions which tied cottages to occupation by farm workers were lawful (they were) the House of Lords stated that all conditions must: (a) fairly and reasonably relate to the development for which planning permission is sought; (b) not be wholly unreasonable; and (c) not be uncertain. The first of these principles received judicial scrutiny in *Newbury District Council v. Secretary of State for the Environment* [1980] 1 All E.R. 731 HL. In essence, all conditions must serve a useful planning purpose, and so a condition which required the demolition of buildings on grounds not expressed to be planning grounds was void. *Newbury* also confirmed that conditions must fairly and reasonably relate to the development for which permission is given and that conditions must not be unreasonable in the *Wednesbury* sense (speech of Lord Lane in *Newbury, loc. cit.*, at 761). Unreasonableness and uncertainty have been considered in relation to the Secretary of State's discretion when determining applications for scheduled monument consent, as has the effect of striking out conditions (paragraph 2.56, 2.57 and 2.63 above).

6.74 Ministerial policy on conditions is contained in DOE

Circular 11/95 (WO 35/95): *The Use of Conditions in Planning Permissions*. The Secretary of State recognises six tests for conditions, that they should be: (a) necessary; (b) relevant to planning; (c) relevant to the development to be permitted; (d) enforceable; (e) precise; and (f) reasonable in all other respects (paragraph 14 of the Circular). The preamble to these tests, influenced by *Newbury*, also suggests that conditions should not place unjustifiable burdens on applicants. The tests are the same as those appearing in earlier DOE guidance (Circular 1/85).

Necessity
Unless it is clear that an application would have to be refused if a particular condition is not attached a condition needs *special and precise* justification. Conditions should only be attached because there is a definite need for them and they should be commensurate with that need. A condition will be void to the extent that it is wider in scope than the objective it is intended to secure.

Relevant to Planning
If irrelevant to planning a condition will be void as outside the powers of the local planning authority to impose it under the TCPA. The Circular refers to conditions requiring the dedication of open space to the public (usually secured by legal agreement) or the control of dealings with land. Relevance is an especially high hurdle for many archaeologically desirable conditions to clear (the requirement, as a planning condition, for the results of investigation to be published would probably be void on this ground). A planning condition should not duplicate other statutory controls, for example listed building or

scheduled monument controls, though the Circular recognises that judicious use of planning conditions may avoid the need for later, urgent action under other statutes. (The example given is of action under the Public Health Acts but one can envisage archaeological conditions relating, for example, to the carrying out of works in the vicinity of a scheduled monument which would reduce the need for subsequent management agreements.)

Relevant to the Development to be Permitted
This test, derived from case law, qualifies the general need for relevance required by the preceding test. A condition can be *ultra vires* even if imposed for a planning purpose if that purpose does not fairly and reasonably relate to the development in question. The Circular gives the example of a condition requiring additional car parking where the need for such car parking does not arise from the development permitted but from an existing business carried on by the applicant near to the application site. The Circular also seeks to distinguish between the effects of a development and a development's own features. Alluding to *Newbury*, the circular observes that a condition requiring the demolition of a building may be justified if allowing two buildings on the application site would result in over-development (so that existing infrastructure could not cope with the increased burdens placed upon it). In archaeologically sensitive applications, and as part of an overall scheme of re-development, it may be that redundant buildings, of no particular historical interest, are required to be demolished so that an area of archaeological concern can be properly investigated. Alternatively, it may be that archaeological remains adjacent to the application site should be

investigated by remote sensing techniques, to ascertain and make provision for any associated effects of the development once it is brought into operation.

Enforceable

Enforcement in this context means enforcement by breach of condition notice or planning enforcement notice under the TCPA 1990. If it is physically impossible to detect any breach of a condition the condition will be of no effect. Most conditions affecting archaeological remains will clearly relate to physical matters and so non-compliance should be detectable. The Circular provides examples of when enforcing compliance may be unreasonable. Two different situations are envisaged: (a) the action required of the developer is not within the developer's control at the time when the condition should be fulfilled; (b) a condition cannot be enforced because, although in other respects it is valid, it relates to a development which was never carried out (citing *Handoll and Others v. Warner Goodman and Streat (A Firm) and Others* (1995) 25 E.G. 157; (1995) 70 P. & C.R. 627 CA, where a development built in a manner which diverged materially from the approved scheme should have been treated as development without planning permission, in relation to which a condition attached to the 'permission' requiring occupation only by persons engaged in agriculture became unenforceable). The latter case can only be prevented by effective monitoring of development by the local planning authority. Avoiding the former case requires a comprehensive and detailed understanding of the circumstances surrounding each application, especially the timing of each action required of the developer, and conditions which are drafted accordingly.

Precise

Here the Circular refers to matters which are clear in the mind but are not properly expressed on paper. The example given is of a condition which states that 'a landscaping scheme shall be submitted for the approval of the local planning authority', without specifying that the scheme must be implemented. Sometimes the thinking behind a condition may also be muddled, resulting in ambiguity or vagueness. The Circular stresses that if an applicant cannot ascertain (in this context meaning ascertain after having taken legal advice if necessary) what is required of him by a condition, the condition will be *ultra vires.* Where a condition requires any matter to be undertaken to the satisfaction of the local planning authority it is important that the matter itself is accurately defined and the satisfaction of the local planning authority is referable to details or subsidiary elements of that action. In an archaeologically sensitive application, for example, it would be acceptable to attach a condition requiring compliance, to the satisfaction of the local planning authority, with a particular scheme of investigation already familiar to the applicant; but it would be unacceptable to impose a condition which required an investigation to the satisfaction of the local planning authority. The usual wording of course is for the condition to provide for agreement between the applicant and the authority on the content of the investigation. Clarity may be improved by annexing plans to a permission. This is especially pertinent to permissions which refer to an 'area of archaeological interest' or 'area of archaeological concern'.

Reasonable in all other respects

Even if it passes all other tests a condition may still be void for unreasonableness. This is essentially a *Wednesbury* requirement. The Circular imports ministerial policy into what is reasonable, but the test is whether a condition is so unreasonable that no local planning authority could have properly imposed it, not whether the condition reasonably conforms with ministerial policy. The Circular cautions against conditions which derogate so much from what purports to be granted by the permission as to nullify the permission. Such conditions should be avoided and the application refused. As a matter of policy – though not law – the Circular warns against conditions which place onerous burdens on developers, for example conditions which would deter the involvement of funding institutions (paragraph 36). Operations on land which is not under the applicant's control and the way in which these are addressed by condition is identified as a further source of potential unreasonableness. Care must be taken to word such conditions negatively (see the *Grampian* case, paragraph 2.60 above). Although neither *Grampian* nor the more recent case of *British Railways Board v. Secretary of State for the Environment and Hounslow London Borough Council* [1994] J.P.L. 32 HL held the timescale within which a negative condition had to be fulfilled to be a fundamental element of such a condition, the Secretary of State's policy is that *'such a condition should only be imposed on a planning permission if there are at least reasonable prospects of the action in question being performed within the time-limit imposed by the permission'*. Conditions affecting land not within the application site but which is within the applicant's control are expressly permitted under section 72 of the TCPA, but care must be taken to ensure that such conditions still relate to the development of the non-application land.

6.75 The need for and the scope of conditions will be dictated by the circumstances of each application. PPG 16 emphasises that even in difficult, archaeologically sensitive, cases there is no justification for the taking of uninformed planning decisions. In an appeal against the refusal of planning permission for a workshop, offices and other accommodation at Hazel Farm, Ledbury (T/APP/G1820/A/94/233991/P5) the inspector found that a scatter of flints and Roman pottery was consistent with historical manuring of the site, not the existence of buildings. He rejected the planning authority's request for an archaeological condition and because no evidence of the archaeological interest was presented in advance of the inquiry awarded costs against the authority. The local planning authority, if it believes that insufficient detail has been submitted, can request further information under regulation 4 of The Town and Country Planning (Applications) Regulations 1988; an environmental statement may be appropriate in important cases (see chapter four of this work). English Heritage or Cadw should have been consulted, as required by the GD(P)O, if an application affects a scheduled monument or its setting, but these agencies may also be of assistance in other cases. Early consultation with the appropriate SMR should take place (PPG 16, paragraph 23); in fact most SMRs maintain a reliable list of scheduled and other sites, and are an invaluable first port of call.

6.76 PPG 16, paragraph 21 and WO 60/96, paragraph 13 both advise applicants to commission 'evaluations' if preliminary discussions or research *'indicate that important archaeological remains may exist'*. The difference between an 'assessment' and an evaluation needs to be appreciated. There is no universally accepted definition of either, but the IFA has adopted formal standards for 'desk-based assessments' and 'field evaluations'. The IFA definition of an assessment is *'an assessment of the known or potential archaeological resource within a specified area or site (land-based, inter-tidal or marine), consisting of a collation of existing written and graphic information, in order to identify the likely character, extent and relative quality of the actual or potential resource'*. The IFA definition of an evaluation is *'a limited programme of non-intrusive and/or intrusive fieldwork which determines the presence or absence of archaeological features, structures, deposits, artefacts or ecofacts within a specified area or site (land-based, inter-tidal or underwater). If such archaeological remains are present Field Evaluation defines their character and extent, and relative quality; and it enables an assessment of their worth in a local, regional, national or international context as appropriate'*. 'Assessment' is sometimes used to connote an element of field-walking, so that previously unrecorded sites might be identified. This necessarily falls outside the IFA definition. Some would also require an evaluation to *accurately* define the extent of archaeological remains, within certain tolerances and in reliance on specified investigative techniques. The details will invariably depend on the specification to which the person carrying out the evaluation is working. From the legal perspective an activity will probably constitute an evaluation if any work has been done on-site to establish the character and extent of archaeological remains. Whether the evaluation was of sufficient quality or comprehensive is a matter for the planning authority.

6.77 It follows that an applicant should have carried out an assessment at the earliest stages of formulating his proposal. The evaluation should assist in defining the weight to be given to archaeological matters by the planning authority. Some recent development plans (see above) require evaluations to be undertaken, in appropriate circumstances, as a matter of plan policy. Where such policies are to retain public confidence they must be applied to remains which at least are likely to be important (as evidenced by the desk-based assessment). The policies must also be applied uniformly, so that evaluations are usually required if the planning circumstances suggest this is appropriate. Developers are usually eager to obtain planning permission notwithstanding extra costs, and it will be counter-productive for them to resist the planning authority's request for better information. Developers may appeal to the Secretary of State against non-determination or, in exceptional cases, seek judicial review. But such cases will be rare. Ministerial guidance and appeal decisions weigh heavily against the argument that requiring an evaluation is excessive or onerous. It would probably have to be demonstrated that there were really no archaeological grounds for requiring an evaluation, adducing evidence of a dearth of remains together with an absence of records indicating archaeological sites or features. Such a course would have to be taken on principle because the appellant would need to carry out what amounted to an assessment in order to have a reasonable chance of success in the appeal.

Archaeological Conditions

6.78 What may appear the final chapter of an archaeological

saga to a developer will only be the beginning for the archaeologist. A glance at the English Heritage publication *Management of Archaeological Projects* (1991) reveals the basic characteristics of each stage of archaeological projects, namely post evaluation work, project planning, fieldwork (including recording), 'assessment of potential for analysis', analysis and report, and dissemination. English Heritage has successfully addressed – if not solved – the problem of standardising these terms, although archaeological circumstances still result in fieldwork and analysis of greatly differing scale and character.

6.79 When fully informed of the archaeological implications of a development proposal the planning authority should be able to decide which of the following courses of action to take: (a) grant permission without archaeological conditions; (b) grant permission which contains conditions requiring a watching brief and/or other archaeological work which is incidental to the development timetable; (c) grant a permission which contains conditions relating to the mitigation of the archaeological impact, for example, conditions intended to secure the implementation of an agreed programme of archaeological investigation before and/or during the implementation of the permission, or conditions regulating the timing and method of construction of the development; or (d) refuse permission because of an archaeological impact which cannot be satisfactorily mitigated by conditions.

6.80 Option (a) (grant of permission without any archaeological conditions) tends to speak for itself, though the circumstances in which this response is appropriate vary. Conditions may be not required because an applicant has agreed to amend his application to avoid archaeological remains (although it will usually be prudent in such cases to grant permission subject to model condition 53 of DoE Circular 11/95: fencing of archaeological remains). Conditions may not be required because a parallel scheduled monument consent application will be dealing with all archaeological matters. The bulk of planning permissions contain no archaeological conditions because archaeological remains are not material to most applications.

Option (d) (refusal of planning permission on archaeological grounds) is referred to at PPG 16, paragraph 28 and WO 60/96, paragraph 18 as the option of 'last resort'. In fact it will rarely be necessary to refuse on archaeological grounds alone as a plethora of environmental and related considerations usually impinge on the development of such important remains. Refusal solely on archaeological grounds will be appropriate, however, where a site is known to be of archaeological importance (after evaluation or otherwise) and one or more material considerations indicates that demonstrable harm to the site, or some other element of the archaeological interest, of an unacceptable nature, would result if the development was allowed to proceed even with the benefit of a programme of archaeological investigation. The 'interests of acknowledged importance' (paragraph 40 of PPG 1) which would be harmed if physical destruction is permitted include a site's recreational and educational value. But there is also the archaeological integrity of the site to consider, both between different parts of the same monument and the whole monument's landscape setting. For refusal of permission due to adverse impact on the setting of a monument see the extensive discussion surrounding the refusal of four applications for planning permission to install a microwave radio station on The Trundle, an iron age hill fort in West Sussex (T/APP/L3815/A/90/ 148258-60 & 151738/P5). The scenario would usually require that a substantial part of the archaeological remains are within the site or monument believed to be of archaeological importance, or that spatially discreet remains are so valuable that they should not be disturbed; otherwise conditions providing for mitigation strategies – either by avoiding or recording remains – might be more appropriate than outright refusal (see option (c) below). Indeed, the scheduled monument consent case of St. Alban's Abbey illustrates the possibility that even the loss of scheduled remains may be acceptable, without any overriding need for the development in question, if '*no serious harm would arise, and perhaps some benefit from greater knowledge would be gained, if ... consent were granted subject to full excavation of the whole site ... before development commenced*' ((1991) J.P.L. 1096). Only if a development cannot proceed and at the same time preserve by record or *in situ* what is important about an archaeological site, ranging from the value of its setting to its intrinsic archaeological worth, should permission be refused outright.

6.81 As with any refusal, refusal of an application on archaeological grounds will be more easily defended by the planning authority if the relevant development plan contains a suitably worded policy. Paragraph 16 of PPG 16 advises that all scheduled monuments should – and other important monuments may – be 'earmarked for preservation' in development plans. Such policies will be a considerable hurdle for the applicant on appeal. The local planning authority will in any event be constrained by section 54A of the TCPA 1990 to determine applications in accordance with the development plan unless material considerations indicate otherwise. An officer's recommendation for refusal, communicated to the applicant, may be accompanied by a recommendation of withdrawal of the application if there is a reasonable prospect that further discussions will permit a more acceptable application to be made.

6.82 Option (c) - detailed investigation or amendment of plans to mitigate impact - is the most difficult to apply in practice and is discussed more fully at paragraphs 6.85-6.91 below. Option (b) - incidental archaeological work - is more straightforward, at least from the planning perspective, and was the favoured strategy of most local planning authorities until about the mid-1980s, even where the archaeological impact of a development proposal was significant. At its most basic there would be an archaeological condition that:

> *'The developer shall give a minimum of [21] days notice in writing of the commencement on site of [works] [development][other-specify] to [name and address of nominated archaeologist] an archaeologist nominated by the local planning authority and no [works][development][other] shall commence until the [21] day period has expired; thereafter the developer shall afford access to the site to such nominated archaeologist at all reasonable times during the [works] [development][other] for the purpose of observing the progress of excavations and recording any objects and features of archaeological interest.'*

This condition permits the recording of information only and is usually referred to as a 'watching brief'. Paragraph 81 of Circular 11/95 recognises the continued importance of the watching brief. The model condition suggested by the Secretary of State is as follows:

> '*The developer shall afford access at all reasonable times to any archaeologist nominated by the local planning authority, and shall allow him to observe the excavations and record items of interest and finds (model condition 54).*'

Such a condition does not provide for the investigation of archaeological remains and was in this sense inadequate where remains were to be destroyed. Unfortunately, there are still some instances where such a condition is considered sufficient by the local planning authority when controlled investigation is clearly required.

6.83 A further condition is sometimes attached which requires that after the 21 day period has expired, and in addition to maintaining a watching brief, either '*reasonable access to the site be afforded to the nominated archaeologist for the period of [   ] weeks for the purpose of archaeological investigation*' or '*the developer shall afford the nominated archaeologist reasonable facilities for the purpose of archaeological investigation in the period of [   ] weeks thereafter*'. Paragraph 29, of PPG 16 supports the use of such provision for archaeological investigation. WO 60/96 appears to be less enthusiastic about providing for what would be unprogrammed excavation, although erroneously suggests that a watching brief may assist in the excavation and recording of features. Reserved matters relating to the development of land at

King's Road, Brentwood, Essex were approved on appeal subject to a condition that: *'the Essex County Planners Environmental Services Branch shall be given one month's notice of commencement of development of the site. Thereafter, reasonable facilities for archaeological excavation should be afforded to the County Council including a right of regular access by a person or persons authorised by the County Council before and during the construction works in order to prepare archaeological records. A timetable and a scheme of archaeological works shall be agreed in writing between the owners or the developers of the site and the County Planner before the commencement of any construction works'* (T/APP/H1515/A/94/234183/P4). However, such conditions are likely to result in conflicts on site between the developer's timetable and that of the archaeologists. Where there is a very good working relationship between developer and archaeologist such conditions may be workable, but this is usually more through luck than judgment. The wording of the conditions themselves is certainly of little assistance in determining the nature of investigation or what constitutes 'reasonable facilities'. The latter condition offends against ministerial advice on precision in conditions (see above) and both may lead to unanticipated delays in carrying out the development. Once development has commenced on site *'conditions should not require work to be held up while archaeological investigation takes place'* (note to model condition 54, Circular 11/95) unless the developer has either expressly or impliedly agreed to such delays. Agreement would normally be by the developer's prior approval of a particular programme of archaeological work, in which case conditions formulated under option (c) would probably be more appropriate. In some cases it has to be accepted that the decision maker will not be in possession of information sufficient to justify the imposition of a negative condition. This was the position in the Brentwood appeal. 'Old-style' conditions still have a part to play in such cases if a watching brief is thought to be inadequate and further evaluation is impractical.

6.84 A watching brief will be an appropriate level of response where a site is of suspected archaeological 'interest' but an assessment has not suggested anything of archaeological importance or where an evaluation, if undertaken, has revealed nothing of importance. It may sometimes be appropriate if no archaeological remains are recorded in the appropriate SMR (see the case of Henbury Hall above, paragraph 6.45), though this is rarely an adequate test. If important remains are known or suspected, however, a condition along the lines of those in the preceding paragraph are likely to be inadequate. At best such conditions result in a scramble to record remains and fail to provide for unsuspected discoveries. A fairly casual approach along these lines was adopted by many local planning authorities before PPG 16 and before environmental assessment emphasised the feasibility of timetabling development to respect environmentally sensitive features. In the cities of London and York, and to a lesser extent in other areas, lamentable situations were only salvaged by the goodwill of developers; though some archaeological planning disasters did occur due either to surprise discoveries (see, for example, the case of Huggin Hill: N.L.J. (1989), 676) or a failure to secure an appropriate programme of archaeological work.

6.85 Option (c) (mitigation) can be viewed in two essentially different ways: 'preservation by record' or 'preservation by avoidance'. Most programmes of work will comprise some elements of each. Both kinds of preservation can be costly and require detailed planning and project designs.

6.86 Avoidance measures might include piling, so that a newly constructed building sits above archaeologically sensitive deposits (though there may be problems encountered with air penetration of waterlogged deposits as a result of piling). Piling also involves some loss of archaeological deposits and many archaeologists would argue that there is never an 'acceptable level of loss' such as the 5% maximum loss assumed by the *York Development and Archaeological Study* (Ove Arup and Partners: 1992) ('YDAS'). The developer's counter blast to this is that the costs of full excavation, especially in an urban context, will jeopardise his scheme unless external funding is available (see page 5 of the YDAS).

Removal of basements or underground car parks from a development proposal may be possible if alternative arrangements can be made or parking policies relaxed, though it would be an unreasonable derogation from grant to impose such a condition if the development would, as result, fall foul of statutory highways requirements.

Occasionally it may be acceptable to simply seal a deposit and develop over it, without causing disturbance to archaeological remains beneath the surface, though most urban land uses will result in increased compression of strata and, of course, the remains will become inaccessible. Sealing is usually acceptable only in the case of robust features such as floor levels, courtyards, paving or other, clearly definable, horizontal strata. For fragile remains, e.g.

multi-occupation urban sites with existing voids and intrusions, the costs of sealing are themselves often considerable, and may be resisted by a developer's consultants if the remains cannot be shown to be important. Even where remains are accepted as nationally important (but unscheduled) there may be pressure, usually from the planning authority or the appropriate county archaeologist, to 'preserve by record' on the ground that the study of archaeology is better served by investigation. In an appeal against refusal of planning permission for redevelopment of offices at 82-90 Park Lane, Croydon (T/APP/L5240/A /245769/P2) the inspector found against the local planning authority and in favour of the appellant's proposal to seal the remains of an Anglo-Saxon burial ground *in situ*. The appellants' proposal for preservation *in situ* had the support of English Heritage while the Council, supported by an evaluation conducted by the Museum of London Archaeological Service, believed that the remains should have been excavated. In this instance the inspector applied the presumption in PPG 16 (and the development plan) that archaeological remains of national importance should be preserved *in situ*. There was no evidence before him that the remains would deteriorate more quickly if sealed.

Alteration of the layout or surface extent of a development is a more effective mitigation measure. If it is possible to build partly on land outside the initial application site or, for example, to re-route a pipeline so that it avoids the area of archaeological importance, this would be preferable to a scheme which attempts to mix new development with archaeological conservation. However, discussions must take place at an early stage, preferably before a scheme has been designed in detail by the developer's consultants. Avoidance strategies will rely on the content of approved drawings; planning conditions will require full compliance with these drawings by the developer and further, restrictive conditions may be desirable.

6.87 If at the time when the planning decision is to be taken the planning authority is still unsure about the extent or exact location of archaeological remains it may, in cases where it suspects important remains await discovery, give a permission which reserves approval in respect of the siting and character of buildings (article 1(2) of the GD(P)O lists siting, design, external appearance, means of access and landscaping of a site as 'reserved matters'). The development must, obviously, be able to cope with any amendments anticipated by the planning authority, and for this reason making such aspects the subject of reserved matters is only likely to be acceptable where archaeological remains will cover a small part of the application site. Conditions can only be placed on subsequent approval for reserved matters to the extent that these were indicated in the permission to which such matters relate. This requires the planning authority to have a thorough knowledge of the whole scheme at the outset and its likely impact on the archaeological remains. A typical scenario would be for approval of the siting of buildings to be reserved pending the results of further archaeological evaluation. The 'outline' permission as well as requiring further evaluation would, when stipulating the matters for which approval is reserved, state all conditions which may be imposed on the grant of approval, for example a condition requiring piling or even the securing by the applicant of a full programme of archaeological work. However, if there is a strong suspicion that a programme of archaeological work is required, except in cases where outline permission must be granted as a matter of urgency, it is better practice to call for further evaluation from the developer before the permission is granted and then, by condition, postpone all development on the application site until after such a programme of archaeological work has been carried out (in accordance with the model condition at paragraph 6.90, below).

Newly discovered archaeological remains may be scheduled under section 1 of the AMAA and the local planning authority may revoke an existing planning permission under section 97 of the TCPA (if the developer objects, as he usually will, the Secretary of State's consent is required to the revocation). Either course of action is extremely unlikely because of the potential compensation payments. Local authority members will be concerned to ensure that they are acting reasonably, while *Rose Theatre* has established that the fear of compensation payments is a legitimate ground for the Secretary of State to rely upon when refusing to schedule a monument.

6.88 'Preservation by record' is a term which acquired general currency in the late 1980s. It implies an approximation to preservation of archaeological remains *in situ* and an availability of resources limited only by archaeological constraints. Archaeologists continue to debate the principle extensively, particularly as it tends to limit the scope for research excavation i.e. archaeological work which is carried out to answer questions which are of particular importance to archaeology as an academic discipline (see the *Croydon* appeal, above at paragraph 6.86).

Academic archaeologists tend to be unhappy with the concept; consulting archaeologists tend to support it as a concept which places archaeological work in a commercial context. From the planning perspective it should be said that the concept places greater demands on the planning system if, as is frequently the case, a developer cannot or will not voluntarily arrange for a programme of archaeological work.

6.89 Paragraph 25 of PPG 16 states that *'such excavation and recording should be carried out before development commences, working to a project brief prepared by the planning authority and taking advice from archaeological consultants'*. The paragraph contemplates a voluntary conclusion of arrangements for archaeological work in advance of the grant of planning permission, though the reality of most modern development schemes is that contractual liabilities will not be incurred by the developer until planning permission is obtained. Smaller developers may also be reluctant to incur the expense of appointing archaeological consultants (whose job it will be to assess and advise on the project brief prepared by the planning authority) at a stage when planning permission is not secured.

6.90 Paragraph 28 of PPG 16 advises in these terms: *'There will no doubt be occasions, particularly where remains of lesser importance are involved, when planning authorities may decide that the significance of the archaeological remains is not sufficient when weighed against all other material considerations, including the need for the development, to justify their physical preservation in situ, and that the proposed development should proceed ... planning authorities will, in such cases, need to satisfy themselves that the developer has made appropriate and satisfactory arrangements for the excavation and recording of the archaeological remains and the publication of the results. If this has not already been secured through some form of voluntary agreement, planning authorities can consider granting planning permission subject to conditions which provide for the excavation and recording of the remains before development takes place.'* WO 60/96, paragraph 18 contains similar advice.

A good example of remains of 'less than national importance' preserved by record was provided by the appeal of Eton College, against refusal of planning permission for a rowing lake at Dorney, Buckinghamshire (T/APP/A0400/A/92/206972 and 206973). Bronze Age remains of regional importance were in evidence due to a prior evaluation, but the inspector concluded that as the condition of the archaeological remains was not good and the benefits of the rowing lake were substantial, it was desirable that preservation of remains *in situ* should not stand in the way of the project. As sealing of the remains was neither desirable nor practical the appellant had to provide for their full investigation.

Whether archaeological arrangements are secured by the threat of withholding planning permission or the imposition of planning conditions, the planning authority will need to be in detailed discussion with the developer. Even where the developer has arranged voluntarily for a programme of archaeological work acceptable to the planning authority the planning authority should still seek its implementation by attaching a suitable planning condition. This will be applicable in all cases where the archaeological work has not been completed, or where there are no satisfactory contractual arrangements existing, before planning permission is granted. In cases where the planning authority decides that a condition is necessary to secure the excavation and recording of remains before development takes place the suggested model condition is:

'*No development shall take place within the area indicated [this would be the area of archaeological interest] until the applicant has secured the implementation of a programme of archaeological work in accordance with a written scheme of investigation which has been submitted by the applicant and approved by the planning authority*' (PPG 16, paragraph 30; WO 60/96, paragraph 23, which refers also to 'approval in writing').

This is to be interpreted in accordance with model condition 55 of Circular 11/95 which, rightly, refers to persons other than the applicant (the applicant's agents, or successors in title) and refers to the *local* planning authority. Both model conditions are accompanied by a reminder to developers that the archaeological investigation must be accounted for in the timing of the whole scheme; delay of the developer's initial scheme is implied, but as a negative condition (sometimes inaccurately referred to as a *Grampian* condition) and not as a condition which would interfere with development once it is lawfully commenced.

6.91 A condition of the type considered at paragraph 6.90 should only be imposed if sufficient information is available to justify refusal should the condition not be imposed. The local planning authority should obtain further information by assessment or evaluation if there is any doubt that the condition can be justified on appeal. Such an appeal would, of course, raise different issues from an appeal against non-determination (at which the local planning authority may argue that the developer has not supplied sufficient archaeological information). In practice, assessments should also be provided to the local planning authority by the local authority archaeological officer who, in most cases, will have requested the condition. The decision may need to be deferred to allow time for further negotiation, for identification of suitable archaeological contractors, an accurate assessment of the developer's liability and consideration of public sources of finance (the latter are especially pertinent if the developer is not developing on a profit-making basis).

When taking the planning decision, if the local planning authority still wishes to reserve its position with regard to 'avoidance' or 'recording' mitigation, it could consider imposing a variant of model condition 55, to provide for the approval of one of two different programmes of archaeological work furnished by the developer. However, such a condition must be approached with caution (for want of precision) and is not advisable where the area of archaeological interest comprises a large portion of the application site. In many cases such a condition would also place an onerous burden on an applicant. If the planning decision must be taken and the planning authority really has little idea of the scope of the archaeological work which may be required a 'two-stage condition' is preferable. When granting permission on appeal for a motel and petrol filling station, on a site off the A1 near Peterborough, the inspector decided to deal with the unquantified but obvious archaeological value of a site by imposing the following condition:

'The area of archaeological interest to be the subject of further investigation shall be agreed with the local planning authority before work on site is commenced; and no development shall take place within the agreed area until there has been secured the implementation of a programme of archaeological work in accordance with a written scheme of investigation which has been submitted to and approved by the local planning authority' (condition 18, appeal decision reference T/APP/H0520/A/93/226056/P5).

The first part of this condition could be criticised for lack of certainty in that it requires the applicant and the planning authority to agree yet does not provide a mechanism for agreement. In practice, however, the effect of the condition would be to encourage the applicant to carry out (further) archaeological evaluation of the site, in order to persuade the planning authority of the sufficiency of the programme of archaeological work which he will propose. The scale of the programme would be entirely dependent on the results of evaluation (see paragraph 6.111).

6.92 The local planning authority's views on the archaeological requirements should be supplied to all the parties either informally or as part of a formal project brief. The developer needs to appreciate that a project brief is not a specification for archaeological work; the local planning authority will not, usually, be seeking to undertake the work itself. It is for the developer to satisfy the 'archaeological curator' (often the sites and monuments record officer for the relevant county) that contractual arrangements will be adequate.

Increasingly, therefore, developers must employ their own archaeological consultants to work closely with the developer's professional team. The consultant may be engaged under a contract for services, much like any other consultant, or will be retained in-house on a contract of service. The consultant will formulate the programme of archaeological work for the developer. He will not necessarily carry out the archaeological investigation as contractor to the developer any more than would an architect be expected to construct the development. Sometimes the developer will have to employ a consultant simply to identify a suitable contractor, as archaeologists, unlike other consulting disciplines, are not exclusively regulated by a professional body enforcing a comprehensive set of training requirements. The IFA (see chapter 1) publishes a directory of archaeologists possessing specified 'areas of competence'; this is a useful, though not exhaustive, summary of the field expertise of a large proportion of the archaeologists practising in Britain. Members of the IFA are obliged by its main code of practice not to undertake archaeological work for which they are not qualified. In addition, the IFA 'Code of Approved Practice for the Regulation of Contractual Arrangements in Field Archaeology' (1990) provides that: *'An archaeologist shall not offer, recommend the offer of, or accept a contract of work unless he or she is satisfied that the work can be satisfactorily discharged. The archaeologist undertaking the work shall have the requisite qualifications, expertise and experience and be able to meet the project timescale'* (paragraph 11 of that Code). Paragraph 12 of the Code states that: *'An archaeologist involved in the commissioning of or undertaking works will satisfy himself that the scope of any agreed brief or specification is adequate for the declared purpose, conforms with academic standards and does not needlessly put the resource at risk'.*

Developers will also wish to be satisfied that the preferred archaeological contractor can call directly on the professional resources necessary to quickly implement an investigation of the scale required and whether sub-contracting of the work will be acceptable.

Developers may decide to put archaeological work out to tender. In this case, the developer's archaeological consultant will usually produce a detailed specification which meets the requirements of the planning authority. The consultant will also need to advise on the relative merits of any bids to do the work. It may be simpler in most cases for the developer to adopt the project brief which has found favour with the planning authority and obtain estimates from a variety of contractors for the work which the brief appears to require. A contract drawn around mutually acceptable heads of terms, including a specification, can then be prepared. The latter option has the advantage for the developer of placing consultants' costs later in the funding cycle. It has the disadvantage of producing very little on paper, in the early stages, with which to persuade the local planning authority.

Planning Appeals

6.93 When a local planning authority refuses planning permission or refuses an application for any consent or other approval required either by a condition of an existing permission or development order, the applicant may appeal to the Secretary of State under section 78 of the TCPA.

Under section 78(2) an applicant may also appeal against the failure of the local planning authority to determine his or her application within the period prescribed by the GD(P)O, currently eight weeks. This period of eight weeks can be extended by agreement in writing between the planning authority and the applicant.

The prescribed time limit for making an appeal under section 78 is six months (article 23, GD(P)O). The Secretary of State may accept appeals outside this period in exceptional circumstances. Article 23 also prescribes the documents which the applicant needs to send to the Secretary of State (and the local planning authority) in order to make a valid appeal. It should be emphasised that even where archaeological issues arise on appeal they will do so alongside other issues. Inquiries or hearings in which archaeological issues are the main issue are unusual and inquiries where archaeological issues are the only issue are exceptional outside hearings and inquiries under the AMAA.

6.94 When the papers are received by the Planning Inspectorate officers will decide on whether the appeal is best heard by written representations, an informal hearing or a local inquiry. The appeal may only be heard by way of written representations if neither of the parties requests to be heard. The inspectorate will otherwise decide between a hearing or a local inquiry and, if the latter, depending on the complexity and importance of the issues involved, the Secretary of State may reserve the decision to himself and not 'transfer' his jurisdiction to a planning inspector (although a planning inspector would in either case conduct the inquiry).

6.95 The essentials of the written representations procedure are summarised in annex 1 of DOE Circular 15/96 *Planning Appeal Procedures*. A decision will be based on the written submissions of the local planning authority and the applicant. Paragraph 16 of the Circular states that *'this is by far the most common procedure and normally offers the quickest, simplest and cheapest way of deciding appeals'*. A decision may be issued within three months of appeal. However, given the technical, environmental and aesthetic arguments which frequently arise the procedure is likely to be unsuitable in most archaeological cases.

6.96 *'A hearing is suitable where the development is small-scale; there is little or no third party interest; complex legal, technical or policy issues are unlikely to arise; and there is no likelihood that formal cross-examination will be needed to test the opposing cases'* (paragraph 3, annex 2, Circular 15/96). The atmosphere is intended to be more relaxed and informal than a local inquiry. The parties will sit around a table in a discussion in which the inspector will probe the opposing cases in a fair and impartial manner. The code of practice for hearings (see annex 2 of the Circular) is not statutory and the inspector cannot compel the attendance of witnesses on summons. Unlike the written representations procedure, however, costs may be available against a party who has behaved unreasonably (see below). Third parties may be heard. The target timetable for hearings is twelve weeks from the start date notified by the inspectorate to the parties.

6.97 An inquiry will usually be held under the 'inspectors rules', that is unless the appeal is referred to the Secretary of State under section 77 of the TCPA, or the Secretary of State decides himself to determine the appeal under section 78 or the provisions of the P(LBCA)A, in which case the 'Secretary of State rules' will apply. Annex 3 of Circular 15/96 provides ministerial advice on the interpretation of both sets of rules. Decisions under the Secretary of State rules usually take a little longer, as the inspector who takes the inquiry has to report to the minister's representative for the decision. Archaeologically significant appeals taken together with a hearing under the SMC procedures contained in the AMAA will usually be under the Secretary of State rules. The inspectors rules are found in the Town and Country Planning Appeals (Determination by Inspectors) (Inquiries Procedure) Rules 1992 (S.I. 1992, No. 2039). The Secretary of State rules are found in the Town and Country Planning Appeals (Inquiries Procedure) Rules 1992 (S.I.1992, No. 2038).

6.98 Although the Planning Inspectorate endeavours to fix a date for the inquiry within six months of the appeal (indeed, rule 10 of the inspectors rules prescribes a period of no more than 22 weeks from the 'relevant date' unless this is impracticable), due to the burden of continuing development plan inquiries appellants are currently waiting up to a year for an inquiry date. Decision letters, however, may now be issued only four to six weeks after the close of the inquiry. Many inquiries last only one or two days; a five day inquiry into an appeal under section 78 is a big inquiry. Local plan and UDP inquiries, or structure plan examinations in public, may take several months. The target timetable for the main stages in a local inquiry into a section 78 appeal is as follows:

- the inspectorate receives the appeal and notifies the local planning authority and the appellant, by letter, of the 'relevant date' i.e. the date from which the procedural clock starts to run (usually the date of the letter);
- the inquiry date is settled by inspectorate after discussion with the parties;
- the local planning authority sends its statement of case ('rule 6 statement') to the appellant and the inspectorate within six weeks after the relevant date; the appellant has nine weeks from the relevant date to serve his statement of case;
- third parties receive notification of the appeal and are invited to appear at the inquiry;
- proofs and summaries of evidence are exchanged no later than three weeks before the inquiry date (with plans, maps, documents and statements to be agreed where possible).

6.99 The main documents specifically produced for an inquiry are the proofs of evidence of each witness and the statements of case. Statements of case are drafted and served at an early stage. They outline the case to be put by a party. Proofs are the detailed, justified arguments and opinions of each witness of a party: where the evidence of these witnesses survives cross-examination intact the inquiry will usually be decided entirely on the merits or otherwise of this written evidence.

Statements of Case

6.100 '*The statement of case should contain the full particulars of the case which a party proposes to put forward at the inquiry, together with a list of relevant documents. If the parties know as much as possible about each other's case at an early stage, this will ensure that, where there is scope for negotiation, it takes place well before the inquiry is due to commence, thereby avoiding late cancellations or requests for postponement of inquiries. It will also help the parties to concentrate on the matters which are in dispute; it will help the inquiry to run efficiently; and avoid unnecessary adjournments, which can lead to awards of costs. Parties should normally provide with their statements the data, methodology and assumptions used to support their submissions'* ... (paragraph 18, annex 3, DOE Circular 15/96). A statement of case on archaeological issues will usually rely heavily on national and local policy documents. Accurate archaeological site descriptions and plans will be fundamental. Planning history may be important, especially in cases where the cumulative impact of development is challenged. Details will be needed even at this stage to clarify why certain proposals should be accepted and why others should not, and why some mitigation strategies would be workable and others would not. Paragraph 18 of 15/96 suggests that tables, graphs, diagrams, maps etc. should be produced as part of the statement of case. There are limits to this, however, and information and opinion justifying the case – which should appear in the proofs of evidence – should not appear here. Convenient divisions in a statement of case are: description of the application; description of the site; description of the envisaged effects of the application on the site; planning history; local policy context; national policy context; effects of own proposals; effects of other's proposals; conclusion. Reference, by name, should be made to all policy and other documents to be relied upon but there is no need to enclose any documents or, indeed, to quote from the relevant provisions. This will come later, with the proof.

Proofs of Evidence

6.101 *'Proofs should be concise and ideally contain facts and expert opinions deriving from witnesses' own professional or local knowledge as applied to individual cases. It would also be helpful if they were to address the question of conditions to the extent appropriate to the witnesses' evidence.*

Where it is necessary to set out facts in detail, proofs should focus on what is really necessary for the matter in hand and avoid including unnecessary material. Details such as site description and planning history if not in an agreed statement, can usually be dealt with in appendices with only a succinct statement of the crucial facts in the proof itself. Suitable plans can be used to illustrate and enhance the understanding of such material. The text of national or regional guidance need not be repeated in the text of the proof or any appendices since the parties and the inspector are assumed to have access to such documents as Planning Policy Guidance Notes. Relevant local policies are best presented in the form of extracts which should be included in appendices and normally quoted only as necessary in the proof. [Original copies of all local policy documents which are relevant should be referenced and handed to the inspector, however.] *Where in the text of a proof a point is made in reliance upon a document, the page and paragraph number in that document should always be identified. Proofs should have their pages and paragraphs numbered. Any appendices should also be paginated throughout and there should be a list of the appendices with page references at the beginning of the bundle'* (paragraphs 9 and 10, annex 5, DOE Circular 15/96).

6.102 If a proof is more than 1,500 words a summary should also be provided. Increasingly, the summary will be the written statement to which the witness will speak at inquiry, although cross-examination may still cover the full proof and all other matters on which the witness may be reasonably expected to have knowledge. It is normal to have one expert witness per topic. Where an archaeological issue arises, as one of the main issues, it is helpful for at least two witnesses to appear, one who has experience sufficient to speak on the technical aspects of mitigation, the other to speak on the value of the site and the archaeological resource context. It is rare for one archaeologist or conservationist to have a mastery of both areas, especially in light of the frequent split, in practice, of archaeological curation and contracting.

6.103 A proof should: identify on its frontsheet the inquiry, the party and the name of the witness; provide a brief statement of the qualifications and experience of the witness; provide an introduction to what the evidence will address; describe the site concisely; give details of any archaeologically relevant planning history; discuss site specific matters extensively; address the strengths and weaknesses of opposing views, justifying the witness's own case by technical information; list the main points of evidence in a brief conclusion. Reference may be made to comparable archaeological sites, in order to emphasise site value, for example, or to illustrate the perceived effects of development or of mitigation strategies. Previous development on the site may be relevant to both the planning history (policy arguments, e.g. precedents for permitting development) and the assessment of impact of new development. It is unusual but not unknown for photographic slides to be used to support expert evidence. Like photographs such slides should be marked with orientation and date and have the position from which they were taken marked on an agreed location plan.

6.104 An archaeologist, like any other expert, will be open to cross-examination which questions his general archaeological knowledge of the intellectual and geographical areas relevant to his proof – this will extend to his methodologies and working theories (to the extent that these produce assumptions which have been applied in the selection and interpretation of data). Many archaeologists are familiar with lecturing and public speaking but not all will be comfortable presenting expert evidence the cross-examination of which will often, in part, be an inquisition into intellectual and technical competence. A lot can be gained at the outset if the expert is made fully aware of the need to avoid making bald statements or using emotive language in the proof. Cross-examination is often gruelling, even if the inspector exercises his discretion to protect a witness from intimidation or ridicule or to avoid repetition. The advocate for the other party is responsible for showing why his witness should prevail and the other party's witness should not. Cross-examination is an integral part of an inquiry to the extent that it: (i) tests the validity of the facts and assumptions on which a case is based, in order to expose defects; (ii) identifies and narrows the issues in dispute; and (iii) explores how the application of policies and proposals would meet the objectives intended. If the technical details are complex the inspector, who would, ordinarily, already be a person with some special knowledge of archaeological matters, may be assisted by an assessor, i.e. somebody with expert knowledge.

Archaeological policy is still very much national policy. Where development plans include comprehensive archaeological policies they usually do so according to criteria which appear in PPG 16. In inquiries where the decision is to be taken by the Secretary of State this often has the advantage, from the local planning authority's perspective, of bringing the appellant into conflict with ministerial policy.

6.105 In an inquiry hearsay evidence is admissible and so the evidential problems which can be a cause for concern in, for example, court proceedings for the determination of an open market rent, do not arise. Hearsay which is not first hand hearsay is, however, likely to carry less weight. Evidence is not taken on oath.

6.106 Conditions should be considered by both the appellant and the planning authority, if only to ensure that the inspector knows what the unsuccessful party believes is reasonable in this respect. Proofs may refer to conditions in an appendix but it is of benefit to all parties if a list of those conditions which can be agreed is produced for the inquiry. A planning obligation may also be produced to the inquiry, executed by all relevant parties or unilaterally by the appellant. If an obligation is not completed by the time of the inquiry – the obligation will be expressed to come into effect only on release of the decision letter or later – the inspector may permit an agreed draft to be submitted during the inquiry and the executed engrossment to be forwarded shortly after the close (paragraph 38 of annex 5 to DOE Circular 15/96 indicates that no more than four weeks will be allowed after the close for the completed document to be forwarded).

Costs

6.107 The Secretary of State is empowered to make an award as to the costs of the parties at a hearing or an inquiry but not on an appeal by way of written representations (unless the written representations relate to an appeal against enforcement action). The power arises under section 250(5) of the Local Government Act 1972 (as amended) in conjunction with section 320, schedule 6 and section 322A of the TCPA 1990. Costs do not 'follow the event' as in litigation but are awarded according to a jurisdiction separate from the jurisdiction to determine the appeal. Costs may be awarded against a successful party without any costs being awarded against the unsuccessful party, as the latter may have presented a poor case but without behaving in a way which justifies an award of costs. An application for costs should be made at the end but before the close of the inquiry once the substantial business of the appeal has been completed.

Costs are available for unreasonable behaviour of the other party (and sometimes a third party appearing at the inquiry), provided that such behaviour has caused the applicant for costs to have wasted expenses unnecessarily. This waste can arise from either procedural or substantive unreasonableness. The principles are expounded in annexes 1, 2 and 3 to DOE Circular 8/93, *Award of Costs Incurred in Planning and Other (Including Compulsory Purchase Order) Proceedings.* Examples of unreasonable behaviour are given in the appendix to the Circular and include: pursuit of an appeal which has no reasonable prospect of success, including one which flies in the face of national planning policies; or any failure, by the local planning authority, to provide evidence, on planning grounds, to substantiate each reason for refusing planning permission, or any general failure by the authority to take into account both relevant policy statements in ministerial advice and decisions of the court.

(III) Securing Archaeological Facilities

6.108 The contents of a typical archaeological project brief and specification are outlined at appendix 6A. The application of section 106 planning obligations is considered later in this section and a precedent form of planning obligation by agreement is reproduced at appendix 6B.

Developers are occasionally panicked into hasty arrangements at the prospect of a protracted archaeological investigation. A number of obvious precautions should be taken throughout the negotiations with the local planning authority and the archaeological curator.

6.109 (a) The developer should form his own, professional opinion on whether the curator's views are reliable and that the suggested project is reasonable in its requirements. For example, the curator's idea of what is necessary may not be determined entirely in accordance with the impact of the proposed development. Conversely, the curator may undervalue the archaeological remains, as a result of which there may be unsuspected discoveries during the course of construction.

(b) The developer should be wary of disclosing the costs of 'avoidance' mitigation. Initially such costs may be disclosed to the local planning authority in an attempt to emphasise the difficulty of safeguarding the archaeological interest, but these figures may then influence the local planning authority or curator when considering the scope of the project brief.

(c) The developer should always clarify whether the curator is likely to obtain any direct or indirect economic benefit from the programme of archaeological work. Although the roles of curator and contractor should be independent of one another, some organisations are active in both areas (especially local authorities). There is a risk in such circumstances that the nature and cost of the recommended programme of archaeological work will meet the requirements of the contractor more than those of the developer. When most archaeological contracting was carried out by an archaeological unit or trust, restricted to operations in a relatively small geographical area (a county council area, for example), this was a considerable problem, especially as the archaeologist upon whom the planning authority would invariably rely for advice was an archaeologist employed by the local authority. Paragraph 29 of PPG 16 refers to a 'nominated archaeologist' (i.e. nominated by the local planning authority) as the person who will be carrying out archaeological investigations, and it was within this context that such bias was easily accommodated. As archaeological contracting has become more widespread the risk of such economic proximity of curator and contractor has decreased, but the position in each case still bears reasonable scrutiny. WO 60/96 poignantly omits reference to 'nominated archaeologists'.

6.110 The local planning authority should be careful to make its determinations in good faith and according to the *Wednesbury* requirements. There may also be *vires* issues where a local authority maintains an archaeological contracting capacity (see paragraph 1.35). In extreme cases there may also be a suggestion of 'selling planning permission' and, in effect, levying an unauthorised 'tax'. Such risks can easily be exaggerated, but the dangers may be greater in the consideration of proposals such as archaeological programmes where the desirability and worthiness of the ultimate objective tends to obscure the legal position.

If the planning authority, in accordance with a condition in the form of model condition 55 (or PPG 16 paragraph 30), does not approve the programme of archaeological work which the developer is prepared to fund, the developer may appeal to the Secretary of State against such non-approval; in fact, the CBI *Code of Practice for Mineral Operators* (1991) alerts developers to this course of action, at paragraph 2.10. The time (six months) for appeal in such circumstances does not start to run until permission is refused or deemed to be refused on the expiry of the eight week period stipulated in article 20 of the GD(P)O. However, if the developer knows, and is dissatisfied with, the requirements of the local planning authority before the planning permission is granted he should make his dissatisfaction clear, with a view to further negotiations.

6.111 The developer must not underestimate the

archaeological requirements but should take an active and critical role in the assessment of the archaeological threat of the development proposal. Planning appeal decisions surveyed by Pugh-Smith and Samuels (1993) illustrate the willingness of planning inspectors to reject appeals against conditions requiring archaeological evaluation and/or investigation (or appeals against non-determination where the local planning authority has requested, but not received, further archaeological data).

6.112 In an appeal in 1995 the inspector considered that the appellant's reluctance to undertake 'an exploratory investigation' contributed to the weight of the argument against the case for planning permission (appeal reference T/APP/L5810/A/94/238757/P5). This appeal was against the refusal of permission by the London Borough of Richmond-upon-Thames for six flats and removal of houseboats at Ducks Walk, Twickenham. The appeal was ultimately dismissed on conservation area grounds but in reaching this conclusion the inspector had to take account of a UDP designation, of the area in which the application site was situated, as an 'Area of Archaeological Priority', the area being subject to UDP policies which reflected the advice of PPG 16. A Roman settlement had been discovered in the locality and there was a suggestion that further remains, possibly including waterlogged Roman timber, could lie near to the Thames foreshore. The inspector found that *'Remains of well-preserved rural Roman timber buildings are rare in south-east England and would be of national significance if found ... The proposal to construct piled foundations could, but would not necessarily, permit remains to be preserved in situ. If nationally important remains are present, changes in the burial environment caused by piling could be detrimental to their condition. It would be inappropriate to grant planning consent before the receipt of detailed archaeological information'.*

The planning authority had suggested a preliminary evaluation, before the grant of planning permission, at an estimated cost of £5,000. The applicant did not oblige. The inspector heard from the applicant that (a) previous investigations in the locality (in 1990) had uncovered nothing of archaeological interest, (b) the possibility of identifying remains of a rare Roman timber building should not be a justifiable reason for the refusal of planning consent and (c) that unless planning permission was given, subject to appropriate conditions, archaeological investigation of the area would be unlikely to occur. The inspector dismissed these arguments, finding that: *'the archaeological evidence indicates that there is an array of features indicating previous occupation of the Thames banks over some distance both upstream and downstream of the site. In the circumstances I am not convinced that the fact that previous works have not revealed anything of archaeological interest conclusively demonstrates the absence of them. In view of the potential importance of the locality it therefore seems to me appropriate to require an exploratory investigation. As your client is unwilling to undertake it before the grant of planning permission I consider that contributes to the weight of argument against his case'.*

6.113 The rationale behind the Twickenham decision also appears in the determination of an appeal against the refusal of Stroud District Council to grant planning permission for a small residential development at Painswick, Gloucestershire (appeal reference T/APP/C1625/A /94/237629/P7). Although the applicants in this case expressed themselves willing to accept a condition which required archaeological evaluation of the application site, the inspector found *'that it would be wrong to grant planning permission subject to such a condition because, if the evaluation revealed the existence of important archaeological remains, it may not be possible to implement the permission. The Archaeology Officer* [the county archaeological officer] *stated that the projected line of a known medieval road (County SMR 9665) runs through the eastern part of the appeal site. He felt that the development may disturb that or any settlement remains associated with it. He went on to point out that there is the further possibility of Roman or prehistoric remains associated with the precursor of the medieval road. In the light of this advice, it seems to me that the balance of probability is that remains may be present under that part of the site on which it is proposed to concentrate the development, which could result in demonstrable harm to important archaeological remains. In these circumstances, paragraph 21 of PPG 16 requires that an archaeological evaluation be carried out before the application, or in this case, the appeal is determined. Therefore, notwithstanding my conclusions on the planning merits of the case, I am not able to allow this appeal'.*

6.114 Paragraph 21 of PPG 16 advises that it is reasonable for the planning authority to request the applicant to arrange for an evaluation where important archaeological remains may exist. WO 60/96, paragraph 13 advises that the local planning authority should require an evaluation in such circumstances. The developer may believe that the suspected remains are not important. If so, he should obtain his own specialist advice which will be reliable on appeal. Paragraph 22 of PPG 16 and its Welsh equivalent, however, talk of 'good reason to believe that there are remains of archaeological importance' and so suggest some degree of certainty before the planning authority can require an application to contain the results of evaluation. Here, as in many places, in an attempt to achieve flexibility the guidance becomes ambiguous. Nonetheless, prior evaluation is obviously a matter to be properly addressed in circumstances where evidence indicates the possible presence of important (or 'significant') archaeological remains. A good example is where the planning authority relies on cropmark evidence to support the existence of important remains. The applicant may be inclined to take little or no advice to ascertain whether the evidence is persuasive, in spite of the established value of this technique in the discovery of sites. Pugh-Smith and Samuels (1993) cite in particular the dismissal of an appeal at Flecknoe, Warwickshire (T/APP/E715/A/92/201430/P7). Where the applicant decides to commission an evaluation, if this is expected to cost several thousand pounds it will be prudent for the developer to obtain prior advice on the suggested importance of the remains, by independent desk-top assessment, if he has not already done so.

A survey commissioned by English Heritage concludes that between the years 1988-1991 about 40% of evaluations of suspected archaeological sites revealed archaeological remains, while 17% turned up archaeological remains unexpectedly (*Planning for the Past*, Volume I (English Heritage, 1995)). The same survey also states that the costs of evaluation over this period were usually below £10,000, with only about one evaluation in ten costing more than this.

Major Costs

6.115 The major costs of archaeological work are only incurred with 'detailed' or 'full' investigation of a site. Whether or not the investigation involves intensive excavation, publication or dissemination costs are likely to be a significant element of the archaeological requirement (though see the comments at paragraph 6.128 on the lawfulness of such requirements). Where excavation is involved it is by nature expensive, especially underwater or in multi-context urban deposits; excavation also necessitates interpretation and long-term storage of finds. In the past costings were often produced on an assumption of about a 50:30:20 breakdown, that is 50% for investigation, 30% for post-excavation interpretation and 20% for publication and storage. But recent trends in interpretation and storage have changed these general proportions (which are very sensitive to site-type and conditions) to something more in line with a 25:50:25 breakdown.

6.116 The publication *Towards an Accessible Archaeological Archive* (Society of Museum Archaeologists, 1995) highlights the problem of museum storage. At page 34 guidelines state that archive repositories are now forced to charge for entry of finds and records into storage and for their long-term curation. This situation, it is said, arises from the increase in projects funded privately. '*The project archaeologist should make it clear to the project funder at the tender stage that the storage charge will be an expense which the project funder will have to cover*' (though, clearly, it is difficult to make this a cost within the contract for archaeological services as the extent of the finds and record archives will be unknown at the time the contract is made). The publication envisages a one-off payment to meet the costs of storage, to be agreed with the museum when the size of the archive has been ascertained.

Trends to greater selectivity in excavation have also ensured that post-excavation analysis is expected to produce more information than ever. As publicly funded schemes decrease and the number of privately funded schemes increases there are also more managerial and administrative costs to be allocated on a project (rather than establishment) basis; where a programme of works is to take place outside of its own control there may also sometimes be a reluctance by the planning authority to accept tightly costed investigations.

6.117 Although circumstances differ considerably between different sites and different archaeological organisations, very general figures for the costs of intensive investigation, including all post-investigation work, range from between £50,000 and £5m. A 'small' excavation is one which should be fully funded at about £100,000; a 'medium-sized' excavation may cost between £100,000 and £500,000; a few excavations will cost over £500,000 in their lifetime and will probably be of national significance. Few, if any, intensive excavations will be undertaken for less than £50,000. A £20,000 excavation in advance of pipe-laying or road construction, for example, will be partial and more in the nature of a salvage excavation (and probably no answer at all to the problem of 'preservation by record'). Specified programmes of archaeological work in excess of about £5m are, as yet, extremely rare though some centrally funded projects, which have taken 10 or 20 years to complete, have expended several million pounds.

6.118 Such sums clearly need to be 'secured' to the satisfaction of the person most interested in the proper completion of the programme of works. This is usually the local planning authority and, more particularly, their archaeological officers and the regional inspectorate of English Heritage. The developer will also have to obtain the funds required by the scheme, either through savings (typically on acquisition prices), from its funding institution or partners (thereby decreasing margins), or from increased profits.

6.119 The contract for archaeological work – comprising, for example, specification, tender, form of agreement and conditions of contract – will be the primary documentation setting out the developer's archaeological obligations. Letting such a contract is obviously a major step towards fulfilling the requirements of the project brief which the planning authority seeks to implement. The local authority may be satisfied that the existence of such a contract is sufficient to ensure the completion of the programme, especially if it has access to the developer's recent accounts and business documents (as it may well do if the developer is working closely with a public sector organisation). The existence of a contract, however, does not mean, of course, that there are funds available to ensure that the contract is fully performed.

6.120 Grant aid is discussed in the context of scheduled monuments in chapter 2, where it will be seen that grant is paid under arrangements which ensure that the necessary works are carried out. Full grant assistance for excavation, however, is now exceptional, and the most that will usually be obtained is a top-up award to ensure that a project is viable.

6.121 Contractual obligations may be secured by a bond. A bond is a promise to pay, in this context by a third party on the default of a contracting party under one or more of its obligations. The complication as far as archaeological works are concerned is that the developer's contract for archaeological services may not be with the local authority, and so where the local planning authority wishes to be in a position to enforce the contract or bond the authority will require a separate contractual relationship between itself (the bondsman, if relevant) and the developer, providing for the developer to comply with the requirement to secure the programme of archaeological work. Such an additional contract often takes the form of a section 106 obligation, but it may be a relatively straightforward deed of covenant. It is not necessary to incorporate the terms of the developer's contract for archaeological services; reference to the contract and its provisions is sufficient.

6.122 The promise to pay is conditional on the default of the developer; nothing will be payable if the developer fully performs its obligations. The bondsman is usually a bank, insurance house or other institution of sound financial reputation. The developer will pay a fee to the institution for assuming the risk of default. The bondsman will first satisfy itself that the risk is acceptable, bearing in mind the nature and record of the developer's business. Where the bond covers only a proportion of the liability under the contract the amounts payable should be payable on demand; a simple surety or guarantor in such circumstances will be able to raise a set-off for work actually carried out, which may still leave a shortfall. If the bond is for all liability under the contract a surety/guarantor covenant will usually be acceptable.

If the developer expects to have sufficiently large cash reserves it may, instead of a bond, prefer to pay a cash deposit to the local authority to be held in a stakeholder account or on some other form of trust until the programme of works is completed. This may be cheaper for the developer in the long-run as no premium will be payable to a financial institution. Monies will be released from the account as successive stages of the works are completed.

Section 106 Planning Obligations

6.123 Obligations under section 106 of the TCPA 1990 (as amended by section 12 of the PCA 1991) are a specific kind of legally binding arrangement which, amongst other things, may ensure that sufficient resources are available to meet the requirements of a particular programme of archaeological work, especially where planning conditions are incapable of delivering the financial or transactional certainty required by the planning authority. Until recently it was a moot point whether planning obligations had to deal only with matters which could be properly considered by the planning authority when deciding a planning application. *Good v. Epping Forest District Council* [1994] J.P.L. 372 CA held that the scope of planning *agreements* under section 52 of the TCPA 1971 (the precursor of section 106) could be wider than planning conditions, and this case was cited by Lord Keith when observing that the parallel between material considerations when making a planning decision and the test for planning obligations is not exact (*Tesco Stores Ltd v. Secretary of State for the Environment and Others* [1995] 2 All E.R. 636 at 646 HL). The *Newbury* test for the validity of planning conditions (see paragraph 6.73 above), thought by some commentators to be the appropriate test, was said by Lord Keith to be *'not particularly helpful for the purpose of deciding whether a particular planning obligation is a consideration material to the determination of a planning application with which the obligation is associated'*. The legal position after *Tesco* is that (a) if a planning obligation is relevant to a planning application it is a material consideration (if it is not relevant it will be unlawful); and (b) if a planning obligation has some connection with the planning application which is not *de minimis* regard has to be had to that obligation. This is far more permissive and, at the same time, of less practical assistance than ministerial policy as advocated by circulars and planning policy guidance notes (see paragraph 6.126 below). The regard which is to be paid to a relevant consideration is a matter for the decision maker within the context of ministerial and development plan policy.

6.124 The practice of most planning authorities is to resort to planning obligations when benefits need to be secured which for either political, practical or legal reasons may be difficult to deal with by planning conditions alone. Examples of such matters are the payment of financial contributions (expressly authorised by section 106(1)(d)), the imposition of positive covenants to carry out specific operations or activities on land (section 106(1)(b)) or restrictions or directions affecting land (section 106(1)(a) and (c)), in relation to phasing for example. In all cases such restrictions and obligations will be binding on the land. The developer and the planning authority may also prefer to deal confidentially with such matters (this may be an improper motive for entering a section 106 obligation but will probably not render the obligation unlawful if it can be construed as an incidental benefit: *Daniel Davies & Co. v. London Borough of Southwark* [1994] J.P.L. 1116 CA). Ministerial guidance advises against the secretive use of planning obligations as a way of side-stepping open and accountable local government (DOE Circular 1/97: *Planning Obligations*, paragraph B19).

The degree of control which the planning authority can achieve by requiring a planning *agreement* was demonstrated in *R. v. West Oxford District Council, ex parte Pearce Homes* [1986] J.P.L. 523 QBD. Here the local planning authority had resolved to grant planning permission conditional on the developer entering a planning agreement. Even though the application had been approved by committee (subject to an agreement being completed) the court held that the planning authority did not behave unlawfully when, because further archaeological remains were discovered in the interim, it refused to release the permission.

There is no express power in section 106 authorising the transfer of land, but if a bilateral obligation implies powers other than section 106 powers, as they often do, the potential want of authority may be avoided. In the case of a unilateral planning obligation, where the developer offers a binding deed to the planning authority in support of a planning application, such additional powers will, obviously, not apply (see *Wimpey Homes Holdings Limited v. Secretary of State for the Environment and Winchester City Council* [1993] 2 P.L.R 54 QBD). Under a unilateral undertaking the planning authority could not in any event be compelled to transfer land. Circular 1/97, at paragraph B25, advises against the use of planning obligations for the transfer of land.

6.125 Current ministerial guidance is contained in paragraph 36 of PPG 1 and PPG 16, as well as Circular 1/97. The tenor of all ministerial guidance is that even in difficult cases planning obligations should be the exception rather than the rule. Paragraph B20 of 1/97 also advises that *'if there is a choice between imposing conditions and entering into a planning obligation, the imposition of a condition which satisfies the policy tests of DoE Circular 11/95 is preferable because it enables the developer to appeal to the Secretary of State'*. The CBI *Code of Practice for Mineral Operators* (1991) states at paragraph 2.10 that *'the use of the model* [planning] *condition* [see paragraph 6.90] *should mean that legal agreements are unnecessary in normal circumstances'* and suggests that 'special' archaeological circumstances would usually be necessary to justify a planning obligation. The special circumstances contemplated by the CBI may be the making of financial contributions by the mineral operator to the costs of archaeological works (addressed in the subsequent paragraph of the Code). The question of planning conditions as an alternative to planning obligations has been considered *inter alia* by Colcutt (1997). Colcutt's general conclusion is that negative conditions (and programmes agreed pursuant to such conditions) are capable in routine cases of lawfully securing all proper financial provision which a reasonable planning authority might require.

PPG 16 pre-dates the appearance of 'planning obligations'. However, it approves the use of planning agreements (now falling within section 106) between developers, archaeologists and planning authorities. Paragraph 25 of the PPG speaks of agreements to secure *'appropriate and satisfactory provision for the excavation and recording of remains'* and states that such agreements should also *'provide for the subsequent publication of the results of the excavation'*. It is clear from what follows in paragraph 26 that paragraph 25 contemplates agreements of all kinds, with the emphasis on what the guidance note tellingly refers to as 'voluntary agreements'. This expression refers to a truly consensual approach, unlike that which usually results when a planning obligation is a *de facto* condition precedent to the granting of planning permission; indeed, paragraph 27 of PPG 16 suggests that planning conditions may secure 'excavation and recording' where agreement cannot be reached. Although paragraph 26 suggests that developers and the local planning authority may wish to enter planning agreements therefore, this advice refers particularly to 'voluntary planning agreements' and is not very helpful in illustrating what resources may generally be *required* of the developer by the planning authority. The planning authority may take some comfort from references to excavation, recording and publication in paragraph 25 but ministerial guidance which expressly relates to planning obligations indicates that benefits sought can easily become too remote and therefore unreasonable.

Paragraph 36 of PPG 1 advises that planning agreements must not be used to *'require benefits from property owners which do not have land-use planning justification, or are unrelated to the development under consideration'*. This conforms with

Tesco as such benefits would not be relevant to planning; the principle has a long judicial pedigree. Paragraph 26 of PPG 1 then indicates criteria with regard to which the reasonableness of planning obligations might be assessed, including: the need for the works; the scale of the works in relation to the problem(s) posed by the development; and other methods of financing the works, for example taxation or charges to the public. The availability of grants under section 45 of the AMAA would be a relevant consideration in the latter context as grant conditions may secure works, without recourse to a planning obligation.

6.126 PPG 1 contains no more than the basic principles of ministerial policy. Detailed guidance on the scope and reasonableness of planning obligations is found in DoE Circular 1/97. The new guidance is addressed both to developers and planning authorities (Circular 16/91 was addressed to planning authorities only). Circular 1/97 is premised by the assertion that existing ministerial policy on planning obligations is lawful. That said, the guidance goes much further than does the law in restricting the potential use of planning obligations. *Tesco* confirmed the potentially wide discretion of planning authorities and the Secretary of State but at the same time did not find this discretion inconsistent with policy which could be more restrictive than the law.

The general policy contained in paragraph B2 of 1/97 is that if they are to influence the decision on a planning application planning obligations must be *relevant* to planning and *directly related* to the development to be permitted. Relevance is required by law but a 'direct' relationship is not; law requires only that the relevance must be more than *de minimis (Tesco)*. The guidance also states that when a planning obligation is sought by the planning authority the obligation should be *necessary* in order to make the proposal acceptable in land-use planning terms. However, an obligation need not be necessary if offered by the applicant, so relieving the decision maker from the accusation in such circumstances of taking into account matters which are irrelevant on policy grounds. If an obligation relates to works which are not on the application site, ministerial advice is that there should be a direct relationship between the off-site works and the development to be permitted. Paragraph B3 of the guidance repeats the advice of 16/91, that *'Acceptable development should never be refused because an applicant is unwilling or unable to offer benefits. Unacceptable development should never be permitted because of unnecessary or unrelated benefits offered by the applicant. Those benefits or the parts of those benefits which go beyond what is necessary should not affect the outcome of a planning decision. Local planning authorities should not seek such benefits and should not allow themselves to be improperly influenced by them ...'.*

This easy statement of principle is difficult to apply in practice. It is clear that an archaeological site should not be destroyed without record because, for example, a developer agrees to provide a museum near to the application site to house finds from a another site which are already in storage; equally, a substantial or wealthy developer should not be refused planning permission because he refuses to offer extensive benefits in relation to a site which, even after evaluation, is of uncertain archaeological value. But in many cases, where remains should be preserved and funds for detailed preservation by record are offered by the developer, the decision is not clear-cut. The benefit must relate to the development, but whether these are *de minimis* or directly related is a matter within the reasonable discretion of the local planning authority. Acceptance of preservation by record as a suitable alternative to preservation *in situ* is a decision almost impossible for a third party to challenge. It seems that only in blatant cases of impropriety or unreasonableness will the court take the planning authority to have acted unlawfully in this respect; for example, cases where the planning authority has acted in bad faith (to establish a precedent which ought not to be established, for example), for an improper motive (to avoid capital receipt controls, for example) or where the authority is simply mercenary (obtaining funding mainly to secure jobs in its own archaeological contracting arm). The position at inquiry will, of course, be more strictly construed, in accordance with the Circular, although even at law guidance cannot be ignored or disregarded.

Unlike 16/91, 1/97 does not provide extensive tests for what are reasonable benefits. Nonetheless, paragraph B9 advises that it will be reasonable to seek a planning obligation *'if what is sought or offered (a) is needed from a practical point of view to enable the development to go ahead and (b) in the case of a financial payment, will meet or contribute towards the cost of providing such necessary facilities in the near future ... or, (c) is necessary from the planning point of view and is so directly related to the proposed development and to the use of land after its completion that the development ought not to be permitted without it'*. The guidance mentions benefits in connection with road improvements, car parking and open space, but does not give any archaeological examples. There is a passing reference to reducing harm to 'protected sites and species acknowledged to be of importance' (paragraph B11), though according to footnotes the sites alluded to appear to be nature reserves and the like.

If benefits are *relevant* to planning, *directly related* to the development being permitted and (where an obligation is sought by the planning authority) necessary, the Secretary of State's policy is that the benefits should still be fair and reasonable in scale and kind when compared with the proposed development (paragraph B12). In the sense that benefits should not have a disproportionate influence on the planning decision this advice is consistent with the principles of relevance and directness. Paragraph 12 goes further than this, however, and warns against the use of planning obligations to secure benefits which, even if of direct relevance to a development proposal, should really be secured from other sources. The example given is that of infrastructure schemes. Developers should only be required to improve infrastructure to the extent that it will not be able to cope with additional burdens placed on it by their proposals, not to resolve any pre-existing problems with infrastructure. By analogy it would not be fair or reasonable to require a developer to carry out detailed archaeological investigation of a substantial area outside the application site unless that area would be adversely affected by implementation of the development proposal.

Paragraph 28 of 1/97 reminds local authorities and developers that the Secretary of State is unlikely to support demands (or offers) which go beyond the guidance. Although not law, the guidance emphasises that contravention will result in lost appeals and may result in unfavourable awards of costs. *Tesco* has shown how difficult it is to challenge successfully this ministerial discretion.

6.127 Archaeological benefits which may be part of a section 106 obligation include the funding of archaeological investigations or the provision by a developer of facilities such as footpaths and soft landscaping. It may be important for the planning authority that the archaeological provision is both detailed and binding on the developer (and the land) as a positive covenant, according to an agreed timescale, at the time the planning permission is issued. This may be because the planning authority is concerned about its own ability to enforce a scheme of archaeological investigation either at all (for example, against a body corporate constituted mainly for selling-on the site), or in accordance with a programme which may be largely independent of the developer's preferred timetable. Note that the conditions attached to the planning permission cannot require the applicant to enter a section 106 obligation as the conclusion of the agreement is not within the applicant's control. A planning obligation by agreement will be required as a condition precedent to the issuing of the decision letter.

6.128 It is now common practice for funding for archaeological investigation to include the costs of post-excavation analysis of finds and other material, without which archaeological data are not very meaningful. However, the local planning authority's requirements may extend to the funding of publication of the results of analysis in book form, or long-term curation of finds after analysis. It is questionable whether publication is a direct benefit of the kind mentioned in ministerial guidance, although analysis of finds (and other remains) and the production of an *archive* is so intimately connected with the notion of preservation by record that no practical distinction can be made between investigation and post-investigation analysis and record. By analogy with infrastructure projects, referred to at paragraph B14 of 1/97, 'subsequent costs of maintenance and other recurrent expenditure' should normally be borne by the eventual owner of the relevant asset. This guidance is intended to alert local authorities to the potential unreasonableness of requiring developers to fund the maintenance of assets which they do not own. However, as with publication, this could mean that the planning authority is also on shaky ground when requiring a developer to fund the long-term costs of storing records and finds, title to which should not remain with the developer (see chapter three of this work).

6.129 Planning obligations may restrict the use of land in accordance with an archaeological mitigation strategy. But the life of a planning obligation is potentially quite short as the developer can now appeal against the local planning authority's refusal to discharge or modify an obligation which is five or more years old. In routine cases, as an alternative to a planning obligation, a simple deed of covenant may be sufficient, provided that no positive covenants or default powers are required. Such a covenant could not be the subject of an appeal to the Secretary of State if the planning authority refused to release it five years later. Where ancient monuments are affected consideration should also be given as to whether a management agreement under section 17 of the AMAA could be of assistance. Most local planning authorities will have the power to enter such agreements, which can be effective in restricting the use of archaeological sites, though these agreements are no substitute for planning obligations if control of development or securing facilities for investigation is important. It is a mistake to resort to a deed under section 33 of the Local Government (Miscellaneous Provisions) Act 1982 in a development context; that section is now amended and no longer applies to covenants entered into in pursuance of the development of land (reference to section 33 agreements at page 331 of Suddards and Hargreaves (1996) is in the author's opinion incorrect). In cases where the local authority is itself disposing of the application site a restrictive covenant can be imposed by the deed of transfer.

6.130 Development plan policies may outline the circumstances in which a planning obligation will be required by the planning authority and may also indicate the type of benefits which may be sought. These may be along the following lines: *'where development would not be otherwise acceptable and a condition would not be effective, prior to granting a planning permission a planning obligation may be required to secure the proper preservation in situ or by record of archaeological remains, having regard to the archaeological importance of such remains and other planning considerations'.* Paragraph 16 of 1/97 states that local planning authorities should make it clear in detailed development plans whether they are likely to seek obligations in relation to particular types of development or site. As with conditions, development plan policies should not require the payment of money (or euphemistic equivalents). Such policies will be unreasonable and in any event would probably be the subject of directions by the Secretary of State.

The Formalities

6.131 The formalities required of a planning obligation are prescribed by section 106(9) TCPA 1990 (as amended). The obligation must be a deed; state that it is a planning obligation for the purposes of section 106; identify the land in which the person entering the obligation is interested and identify the person(s) entering the obligation, stating his interest in the land; and identify the local planning authority by whom the obligation is enforceable. There is no requirement to refer to a particular planning application, or to state that the obligation is entered into in furtherance of better planning of an area, though in some circumstances such recitals may be desirable. A planning obligation should also usually be a discrete instrument, although there is no legal requirement to this effect and a covenant in any deed may take effect as a section 106 covenant provided the section 106 formalities are complied with.

A modification or discharge must also be by deed (section 106A(2)). The Town and Country Planning (Modification and Discharge of Planning Obligations) Regulations 1992 (S.I. 1992, No. 2832) provide the procedures; see also DOE Circular 28/92 (Welsh Office 66/92).

It is a prerequisite that the planning authority should be satisfied with the developer's and the landowner's title to the land intended to be bound by the obligation and to remain satisfied in this respect until completion of the obligation (by updating conveyancing searches, for example). As a matter of general law the obligation will only bind the interests of persons (and their successors in title) who execute the deed and who have an interest at the time the deed is completed. Third party interests arising before completion will not be bound unless the holder of that interest agrees to be bound; the planning authority should require all mortgagees interested in the land, together with the landowner if not the developer, to be party to the deed, and should resist the temptation to accept a letter of consent or other document 'under hand'. Practitioners will frequently come under pressure to adopt novel approaches to the completion of planning obligations, but the surest way to avoid errors is to rely on established conveyancing rules and practice. Contracting only with a party who does not have a legal interest in the land in question – the holder of an option or a conditional contract, for example – is asking for trouble, regardless of whether the aims of the planning authority might be assisted by conditions on the planning permission.

6.132 The operative provisions of the obligation, particularly the schedule of works and financial arrangements, are specific to each case. The developer will usually be well-advised to limit his liability to the period during which he has an interest in the site and to ensure that the obligation does not become effective immediately on completion of the deed (the usual provision here is for commencement on implementation of planning permission or some other specified activity which does not require planning permission but would constitute an archaeological threat). The developer will not wish to accept covenants which compel observance of planning conditions as this will inhibit the scope for effective appeal against those conditions. A developer will also resist covenants which require development to be carried out, although in archaeological cases this may be justifiable where remains are deteriorating or would deteriorate if a permission was part implemented. Any phased programme of archaeological mitigation should be completed and the planning authority may reasonably require that the developer is legally obligated in this respect.

A precedent form of planning obligation by agreement is produced at appendix 6B, together with some optional clauses.

6.133 The advantages of a planning obligation as far as a planning authority is concerned include:

(a) the ability to enforce development provisions under contract (there is an express power for planning authorities to seek injunctions under section 106(5), and specific performance of contractual obligations may also be sought);

(b) the ability under section 106(6) and (7) to enter land to carry out works in default, recovering the cost of doing so from anybody against whom the obligation is enforceable (including successors in title to the land in question);

(c) the creation of obligations which will be binding on the land (section 106(3)) and registrable as local land charges (section 106(11)).

The Crown may enter a planning obligation in advance of a Crown disposal of land but the obligation will be enforceable only against successors in title, not against the Crown.

6.134 There are some potential disadvantages for the local planning authority in entering a section 106 obligation which is intended to restrict the use of land. Unlike section 52 and old-style section 106 agreements (which like other covenants could only be released, on narrow grounds, by application to the Lands Tribunal under section 84 of the Law of Property Act 1925) application to discharge a section 106 obligation may be made after only five years (section 106A(4), TCPA). A person bound by a section 52 agreement was always able to apply to the planning authority for release of his covenants but such an application is now a more serious proposition. It is expressly provided that section 84 of the Law of Property Act 1925 (discharge of old restrictive covenants) is of no application to covenants imposed under the new section 106.

The ability to impose positive covenants which run with the land is nearly always seen as one of the principal benefits of a section 106 obligation. But this should not obscure the fact that works may still fail to materialise and the planning authority may not have the resources necessary to carry them out. For example, where a planning authority disposes of land comprising a monument and requires the monument to be conserved as part of an environmental improvement scheme, if the developer defaults and is not worth pursuing the authority may have transferred title to the land and then find itself without any immediate prospect of the conservation of the monument. A bond or other form of security may assist but the charge on the land created by a planning obligation is not a charge which permits realisation of the land to meet the liabilities which the planning authority may incur. Section 106(12) empowers the Secretary of State to make regulations providing for the placing of charges on land in relation to sums 'required to be paid' but no regulations have yet been made. The planning charge in such a situation would simply devalue the land until removed, on payment of the local authority's costs.

6.135 A developer may challenge a planning authority's demands for a planning obligation, as part of a planning appeal to the Secretary of State under section 78 of the TCPA 1990. Costs may be awarded against an authority which requires a planning obligation unreasonably. Application may also be made to the court under section 288, on a point of law, in the usual way. Once an obligation is in force there is no statutory right of appeal against the operation of the obligation except an appeal to the Secretary of State from refusal of the local planning authority to discharge or modify the obligation. Section 288 of the TCPA does not apply to the decision of the Secretary of State in such circumstances. The covenantor's remedy would be judicial review. Disputes between the parties as to the operation of the contract contained within a planning obligation may be referred to the court under common law rules.

HERITAGE ORGANISATIONS AND THEIR FUNCTIONS

RESPONSIBILITIES FOR CONSERVATION POLICY AND CASEWORK

DOE/DNH JOINT CIRCULAR 20/92;1/92   29 JULY 1992

---

1. This circular sets out the new departmental responsibilities following the creation of the Department of National Heritage (DNH).

2. Policy responsibility for archaeology and the conservation of the built heritage now rests with the Secretary of State for National Heritage. The Secretary of State has also assumed sponsorship responsibilities for English Heritage, the National Heritage Memorial Fund, the Royal Commission on the Historical Monuments of England, the Royal Fine Art Commission, and other heritage public bodies.

3. To ensure that the necessary co-ordination of planning and conservation policy is maintained, formal jurisdiction on certain types of heritage casework remains with the Secretary of State for the Environment. There will be close consultation between the two Departments on many issues, including, in particular, cases raising wider policy questions, and cases where the Department of the Environment (DOE) is disposed not to accept advice from English Heritage that an application should be called in, or an application or appeal rejected. Details of the formal responsibilities are set out below.

CASEWORK TRANSFERRED TO DNH

4. In addition to general responsibility for conservation policy, the following casework has transferred to DNH:

(i)   listing of historic buildings (sections 1-6 and 29-30 of the Planning (Listed Buildings and Conservation Areas) Act 1990);

(ii)   scheduling of ancient monuments and scheduled monument consents (sections 1 and 2 of the Ancient Monuments and Archaeological Areas Act 1979);

(iii)   repairs notices, urgent works notices and associated land acquisition (sections 47-48, 50, 52-55 and 76 of the 1990 Act);

(iv)   procedures and reserve powers in respect of the designation of conservation areas (sections 69-70 of the 1990 Act);

(v)   responsibility for the protection of wrecks (section 1 of the Protection of Wrecks Act 1973), and for nautical archaeology generally;

(vi)   grants to heritage bodies under the Special Grants Programme and Environmental Grant Fund;

(vii)   responsibilities in respect of the ecclesiastical exemption (sections 60 and 75 of the 1990 Act).

CASEWORK REMAINING WITH DOE

5. The following casework remains the responsibility of DOE:

(i)   decisions on call-in of listed building and conservation area consent applications (sections 12-15 and 74 of the 1990 Act);

(ii)   decisions on called-in applications, on applications by local planning authorities, and on appeals against refusal of listed building or conservation area consent (sections 16-22 and 74 of the 1990 Act), and determinations under the non-statutory arrangements for development by Government Departments set out in Part IV of DOE Circular 18/84;

(iii)   all related enforcement, modification/revocation, purchase notice and compensation procedures (sections 24-26, 28, 30, 34-35, 39-41, 46 and 74 of the 1990 Act);

(iv)   decisions on requests to confirm Article 4 Directions in conservation areas (Town & Country Planning General Development Order 1988);

(v)   consideration of proposals put forward by the Church Commissioners for the demolition of a church (when listed, or when unlisted in a conservation area) under the Pastoral Measure.

Contacts

6. Existing arrangements, under which planning authorities are required to consult English Heritage when preparing development plan proposals, to notify English Heritage and the national amenity societies of certain

categories of listed building consent application, and to refer certain cases to DOE before issuing a decision, are unaffected by these departmental changes. Notifications of the designation of conservation areas should continue to be sent to English Heritage and DOE regional offices.

7. The former Heritage Division of DOE is now part of DNH; office addresses and telephone numbers remain the same. For the time being, all correspondence and enquiries should be addressed as they would have been prior to these changes. Where necessary, detailed notification of transfers of work and new office addresses will be given later.

8. Any inquiries about this circular should be addressed to Mr A.S. Gordon., Room C9/06, 2 Marsham Street (071 276 3748).

HERITAGE ORGANISATIONS AND THEIR FUNCTIONS

SECTIONS 32-37 OF THE NATIONAL HERITAGE ACT 1983 (AS AMENDED)

---

32 Establishment of Commission

(1) There shall be a body known as the Historic Buildings and Monuments Commission for England.

(2) Schedule 3* shall have effect with respect to the Commission.

(*details the composition and conduct of meetings of the Commission)

33 The Commission's general functions

(1) It shall be the duty of the Commission (so far as practicable) –

(a) to secure the preservation of ancient monuments and historic buildings situated in England,
(b) to promote the preservation and enhancement of the character and appearance of conservation areas situated in England, and
(c) to promote the public's enjoyment of, and advance their knowledge of, ancient monuments and historic buildings situated in England and their preservation,

in exercising the functions conferred on them by virtue of subsections (2) to (4) and section 34; but in the event of a conflict between those functions and that duty those functions shall prevail.

(2) The Commission –

(a) shall (so far as practicable) provide educational facilities and services, instruction and information to the public in relation to ancient monuments and historic buildings, with particular reference to those in England, and in relation to conservation areas situated in England;
(b) may give advice to any person in relation to ancient monuments,

historic buildings and conservation areas situated in England, whether or not they have been consulted;

(c) may, for the purpose of exercising their functions, carry out, or defray or contribute towards the cost of, research in relation to ancient monuments, historic buildings and conservation areas situated in England;

(d) may, for the purpose of exercising their functions, make and maintain records in relation to ancient monuments and historic buildings situated in England.

[(2A)   In relation to England, the Commission may -

(a) prosecute any offence under Part I of the Ancient Monuments and Archaeological Areas Act 1979 or under the Planning (Listed Buildings and Conservation Areas) Act 1990, or

(b) institute in their own name proceedings for an injunction to restrain any contravention of any provision of that Part or of that Act of 1990.]*

(* *words in square brackets were inserted pursuant to section 29(1) of the PCA 1991*)

[(2B) In relation to England, the Commission may make, or join in the making of, applications under section 73(1) of the Leasehold Reform, Housing and Urban Development Act 1993, and may exercise, or participate in the exercise of, any rights or powers conferred by a scheme approved under section 70 of that Act.]*

(* *words in square brackets were inserted pursuant to section 187(1) of the Leasehold Reform, Housing and Urban Development Act 1993*)

(3) Schedule 4 shall have effect to amend the enactments there mentioned –

(a) for the purpose of conferring functions on the Commission in relation to England (including functions of making grants in relation to historic buildings and conservation areas, acquiring historic buildings, acquiring or becoming guardian of ancient monuments, providing information and other services to the public in connection with affording them access to ancient monuments, and undertaking archaeological investigation and publishing the results), and

(b)   for connected purposes (which include allowing the Secretary of State to approve lists of historic buildings compiled by the Commission, and imposing requirements for him to consult with the Commission before he includes a monument in the schedule of monuments or grants scheduled monument consent or designates an area of archaeological importance).

(4) Without prejudice to the generality of subsection (2)(b), the Commission may advise the Secretary of State with regard to the exercise of functions exercisable by him in relation to England under the Historic Buildings and Ancient Monuments Act 1953 and the Ancient Monuments and Archaeological Areas Act 1979, whether or not they have been consulted.

(5)   For the purpose of exercising their functions the Commission may, subject to the provisions of this and any other Act –

(a)   enter into contracts and other agreements;

(b)   acquire and dispose of property other than land;

(c)   with the consent of the Secretary of State, acquire land for providing the Commission with office or other accommodation and dispose of the land when no longer required for such accommodation;

(d)   do such other things as the Commission think necessary or expedient.

(6)   The Commission may make such charges as they may from time to time determine in respect of anything provided under subsection (2)(a) or given under subsection (2)(b) to any person other than a Minister of the Crown.

(7)   With the consent of the Secretary of State, the Commission may borrow temporarily by way of overdraft such sums as they may require for meeting their obligations and discharging their functions.

(8)   In subsections (1) and (2) –

"ancient monument" means any structure, work, site, garden or area
    which in the Commission's opinion is of historic, architectural,
    traditional, artistic or archaeological interest;
"conservation area" means an area designated as a conservation area
    under section 69 of the Planning (Listed Buildings and Conservation
    Areas) Act 1990;
"historic building" means any building which in the Commission's
    opinion is of historic or architectural interest.

34   Commission to exercise certain ministerial functions

(1)   Subject to subsection (4), this section applies to –

(a)   functions of management exercisable by the Secretary of State for
      the Environment (whether by virtue of an enactment or otherwise)
      in relation to any ancient monument or historic building situated
      in England;
(b)   functions of management exercisable by the Secretary of State for
      the Environment (whether by virtue of an enactment or
      otherwise), for purposes connected with such a monument or
      building, in relation to any land which is situated in England and
      which adjoins or is in the vicinity of the monument or building.

(2)   If the Secretary of State for the Environment directs the
Commission to exercise functions to which this section applies and which
are specified in the direction, in relation to any monument, building or
land so specified, the Commission shall exercise them on his behalf in
such manner as he may from time to time direct.

(3)   In subsection (1) "ancient monument" means any structure, work,
site, garden or area which in the opinion of the Secretary of State for the
Environment is of historic, architectural, traditional, artistic or
archaeological interest and "historic building" means any building which
in his opinion is of historic or architectural interest.

(4) This section does not apply to –

(a)   a function of making regulations or other instruments of a legislative character;
(b)   a function exercisable in relation to any royal palace or land adjoining it or in its vicinity.

35   Power of Commission to form companies

(1)   The Commission may form or take part in forming one or more bodies corporate which (or each of which) has as its main object or objects one or more of those mentioned in subsection (2).

(2)   The objects are –

(a)   the production and publication in England of books, films or other informative material relating to ancient monuments or historic buildings,
(b)   the production in England of souvenirs relating to ancient monuments or historic buildings,
(c)   the sale in England of informative material relating to ancient monuments or historic buildings, or of souvenirs, and
(d)   the provision in England of catering or car parking or other services or facilities for members of the public visiting ancient monuments or historic buildings.

(3)   The Commission may hold interests in any such body, exercise rights conferred by the holding of interests in it, and provide financial or other assistance to or in respect of it (including assistance by way of guarantee of its obligations).

(4)   In this section "ancient monument" and "historic building" have the same meanings as in section 33.

(5)   This section is without prejudice to any power of the Commission to undertake anything mentioned in subsection (2) by virtue of section 33.

Appendix 1B

36 Records: powers of entry

(1) Any person duly authorised in writing by the Commission may at any reasonable time enter any land in England for the purpose of inspecting it with a view to obtaining information for inclusion in the Commission's records made under section 33(2)(d); and the following provisions of this section shall apply to any such power of entry.

(2) The power includes power for any person entering any land in exercise of the power to take with him any assistance or equipment reasonably required for the purpose to which the entry relates and to do there anything reasonably necessary for carrying out the purpose.

(3) The Commission may not authorise the power to be exercised in relation to any land unless they know or have reason to believe there is in, on or under the land an ancient monument or historic building; and in this subsection "ancient monument" and "historic building" have the meanings given by section 33(8).

(4) A person may not in the exercise of the power –

(a) enter any building or part of a building occupied as a dwelling house without the consent of the occupier;
(b) demand admission as of right to any land which is occupied unless prior notice of the intended entry has been given to the occupier not less than 24 hours before admission is demanded.

(5) A person seeking to enter any land in exercise of the power shall, if so required by or on behalf of the owner or occupier of the land, produce evidence of his authority before entering.

(6) Where any works are being carried out on any land in relation to which the power is exercisable, a person acting in the exercise of the power shall comply with any reasonable requirements or conditions imposed by the person by whom the works are being carried out for the purpose of preventing interference with or delay to the works; but any requirements or conditions so imposed shall not be regarded as reasonable for the purposes of this subsection if compliance with them would in effect frustrate the exercise of the power or the purpose of the

entry.

(7)   Any person who intentionally obstructs a person acting in the exercise of the power shall be guilty of an offence and liable on summary conviction to a fine not exceeding level 3 on the standard scale*

(* currently £1,000)

(8)   Where in the exercise of the power damage has been caused to land or chattels on land, any person interested in the land or chattels may recover compensation in respect of the damage from the Commission.

(9)   Any claim for compensation under subsection (8) shall be made within the time and in the manner prescribed by regulations made by the Secretary of State for that purpose; and the power to make regulations under this subsection shall be exercisable by statutory instrument subject to annulment in pursuance of a resolution of either House of Parliament.

(10) Any question of disputed compensation under subsection (8) shall be referred to and determined by the Lands Tribunal; and in relation to the determination of any such question sections 2(2) to (5) and 4 of the Land Compensation Act 1961 shall apply (construing the references in section 4 to the acquiring authority as references to the Commission).

37   Monuments etc. partly situated in England

(1)   The Secretary of State may by order provide that the Commission shall have such functions as –

(a)   he thinks appropriate (having regard to their functions in relation to monuments, buildings, gardens, areas or sites situated in England), and
(b)   are specified in the order,

in relation to the parts situated in England of any monuments, buildings, gardens, areas or sites which are only partly so situated and which are specified in the order.

(2)   For the purpose of making such provision, any such order may contain –

(a)   amendments of section 33 or 34, and
(b)   amendments of any section or Schedule amended by Schedule 4 (including consequential amendments relating to the parts of monuments, buildings, gardens, areas or sites not situated in England).

(3)   Any such order shall have effect subject to such supplementary provisions (which may include savings and transitionals) as may be specified in the order.

(4)   Nothing in this section permits the Commission to be given a function of making regulations or other instruments of a legislative character.

(5)   The power to make an order under this section shall be exercisable by statutory instrument, and no such order shall be made unless a draft of the order has been laid before and approved by resolution of each House of Parliament.

ANCIENT MONUMENTS AND ARCHAEOLOGICAL AREAS

THE ANCIENT MONUMENTS AND ARCHAEOLOGICAL AREAS ACT 1979 (Sections 1-4, 7, 17, 42, 45, 55 and 61, and Schedule 1) (AS AMENDED)

1 Schedule of monuments

(1) The Secretary of State shall compile and maintain for the purposes of this Act (in such form as he thinks fit) a schedule of monuments (referred to below in this Act as "the Schedule").

(2) The Secretary of State shall on first compiling the Schedule include therein –

(a) any monument included in the list last published before the commencement of this Act under section 12 of the Ancient Monuments Consolidation and Amendment Act 1913; and

(b) any monument in respect of which the Secretary of State has before the commencement of this Act served notice on any person in accordance with section 6(1) of the Ancient Monuments Act 1931 of his intention to include it in a list to be published under section 12.

(3) Subject to subsection (4) below, the Secretary of State may on first compiling the Schedule or at any time thereafter include therein any monument which appears to him to be of national importance. [The Secretary of State shall consult the Historic Buildings and Monuments Commission for England (in this Act referred to as "the Commission") before he includes in the Schedule a monument situated in England]*.

(4) The power of the Secretary of State under subsection (3) above to include any monument in the Schedule does not apply to any structure which is occupied as a dwelling house by any person other than a person employed as the caretaker thereof or his family.

(5) The Secretary of State may –

(a) exclude any monument from the Schedule; or

(b) amend the entry in the Schedule relating to any monument (whether by excluding anything previously included as part of the monument or adding anything not previously so included, or otherwise).

[In the case of a monument situated in England, the Secretary of State shall consult with the Commission before he makes an exclusion or amendment]*.

(6) As soon as may be after –

(a) including any monument in the Schedule under subsection (3) above;

(b) amending the entry in the Schedule relating to any monument; or

(c) excluding any monument from the Schedule;

the Secretary of State shall [(subject to section (6A) below]* inform the owner and (if the owner is not the occupier) the occupier of the monument, and any local authority in whose area the monument is situated, of the action taken and, in a case falling within paragraph (a) or (b) above, shall also send to him or them a copy of the entry or (as the case may be) of the amended entry in the Schedule relating to that monument.

[(6A) Subsection (6) above shall not apply as regards a monument situated in England, but as soon as may be after acting as mentioned in paragraph (a), (b) or (c) of that subsection as regards such a monument, the Secretary of State shall inform the Commission of the action taken and, in a case falling within paragraph (a) or (b) of that subsection, shall also send to the Commission a copy of the entry or (as the case may be) of the amended entry in the Schedule relating to that monument.]*

(7) [Subject to subsection (7A) below]* the Secretary of State shall from time to time publish a list of all the monuments which are for the time being included in the Schedule, whether as a single list or in sections containing the monuments situated in particular areas; but in the case of a list published in sections, all sections of the list need not be published simultaneously.

[(7A) Subsection (7) above shall not apply as regards monuments situated in England, but the Secretary of State shall from time to time supply the Commission with a list of all the monuments which are so situated and are for the time being included in the Schedule, whether as a single list or in sections containing the monuments situated in particular areas; but in the case of a list supplied in sections, all sections of the list need not be supplied simultaneously.]*

(8) The Secretary of State may from time to time publish amendments of any list published under subsection (7) above, and any such list (as amended) shall be evidence of the inclusion in the Schedule for the time being –

(a)   of the monuments listed; and
(b)   of any matters purporting to be produced in the list from the entries in the Schedule relating to the monuments listed.

[(8A) The Secretary of State shall from time to time supply the Commission with amendments of any list supplied under subsection (7A) above.]*

(9) An entry in the Schedule recording the inclusion therein of a monument situated in England and Wales shall be a local land charge.

(10) (*Scotland only.*)

(11) In this Act "scheduled monument" means any monument which is for the time being included in the Schedule.

[1A Commission's functions as to informing and publishing

(1) As soon as may be after the Commission –

(a)   have been informed as mentioned in section 1(6A) of this Act, and
(b)   in a case falling within section 1(6)(a) or (b) of this Act, have received a copy of the entry or (as the case may be) of the amended entry from the Secretary of State,

the Commission shall inform the owner and (if the owner is not the occupier) the occupier of the monument, and any local authority in whose area the monument is situated, of the inclusion, amendment or exclusion and, in a case falling within section 1(6)(a) or (b), shall also send to him or them a copy of the entry or (as the case may be) of the amended entry in the Schedule relating to that monument.

(2) As soon as may be after the Commission receive a list or a section in pursuance of section 1(7A) of this Act, they shall publish the list or section (as the case may be).

(3) The Commission shall from time to time publish amendments of any list published under subsection (2) above, and any such list (as amended) shall be evidence of the inclusion in the Schedule for the time being –

(a)   of the monuments listed; and
(b)   of any matters purporting to be reproduced in the list from the entries in the Schedule relating to monuments listed.]*

2 Control of works affecting scheduled monuments

(1) If any person executes or causes or permits to be executed any works to which this section applies he shall be guilty of an offence unless the works are authorised under this Part of this Act.

(2) This section applies to any of the following works, that is to say –

(a)   any works resulting in the demolition or destruction of or any damage to a scheduled monument;
(b)   any works for the purpose of removing or repairing a scheduled monument or any part of it or of making any alterations or additions thereto; and
(c)   any flooding or tipping operations on land in, or under which there is a scheduled monument.

(3) Without prejudice to any other authority to execute works conferred under this Part of this Act, works to which this section applies are authorised under this Part of this Act if –

(a)   the Secretary of State has granted written consent (referred to below in this Act as "scheduled monument consent") for the execution of the works; and

(b)   the works are executed in accordance with the terms of the consent and of any conditions attached to the consent.

(4) Scheduled monument consent may be granted either unconditionally or subject to conditions (whether with respect to the manner in which or the persons by whom the works or any of the works are to be executed or otherwise).

(5) Without prejudice to the generality of subsection (4) above, a condition attached to a scheduled monument consent may require that

[(a)   a person authorised by the Commission (in a case where the monument in question is situated in England), or

(b)   the Secretary of State or a person authorised by the Secretary of State (in any other case)]*

be afforded an opportunity, before any works to which the consent relates are begun, to examine the monument and its site and carry out such excavations therein as appear to the Secretary of State to be desirable for the purpose of archaeological investigation.

(6) Without prejudice to subsection (1) above, if a person executing or causing or permitting to be executed any works to which a scheduled monument consent relates fails to comply with any condition attached to the consent he shall be guilty of an offence, unless he proves that he took all reasonable precautions and exercised all due diligence to avoid contravening the condition.

(7) In any proceedings for an offence under this section in relation to works within subsection (2)(a) above it shall be a defence for the accused to prove that he took all reasonable precautions and exercised all due

diligence to avoid or prevent damage to the monument.

(8) In any proceedings for an offence under this section in relation to works within subsection (2)(a) or (c) above it shall be a defence for the accused to prove that he did not know and had no reason to believe that the monument was within the area affected by the works or (as the case may be) that it was a scheduled monument.

(9) In any proceedings for an offence under this section it shall be a defence to prove that the works were urgently necessary in the interests of safety or health and that notice in writing of the need for the works was given to the Secretary of State as soon as reasonably practicable.

(10) A person guilty of an offence under this section shall be liable –

(a) on summary conviction or, in Scotland, on conviction before a court of summary jurisdiction, to a fine not exceeding the statutory maximum; or

(b) on conviction on indictment to a fine.

(11) Part I of Schedule 1 to this Act shall have effect with respect to applications for, and the effect of, scheduled monument consent.

3 Grant of scheduled monument consent by order of the Secretary of State

(1) The Secretary of State may by order grant scheduled monument consent for the execution of works of any class or description specified in the order, and any such consent may apply to scheduled monuments of any class or description so specified. [Before granting consent in relation to monuments of a class or description which includes monuments situated in England, the Secretary of State shall consult with the Commission in relation to the monuments so situated.]*

(2) Any conditions attached by virtue of section 2 of this Act to a scheduled monument consent granted by an order under this section shall apply in such class or description of cases as may be specified in the order.

(3)   The Secretary of State may direct that scheduled monument consent granted by an order under this section shall not apply to any scheduled monument specified in the direction, and may withdraw any direction given under this subsection. [Before making a direction in relation to a monument situated in England, or withdrawing such a direction, the Secretary of State shall consult with the Commission.]*

(4) A direction under subsection (3) above shall not take effect until notice of it has been served on the occupier or (if there is no occupier) on the owner of the monument in question.

(5) References below in this Act to a scheduled monument consent do not include references to a scheduled monument consent granted by an order under this section unless the contrary intention is expressed.

4 Duration, modification and revocation of scheduled monument consent

(1) Subject to subsection (2) below, if no works to which a scheduled monument consent relates are executed or started within the period of five years beginning with the date on which the consent was granted, or such longer or shorter period as may be specified for the purposes of this subsection in the consent, the consent shall cease to have effect at the end of that period (unless previously revoked in accordance with the following provisions of this section).

(2) Subsection (1) above does not apply to a scheduled monument consent which provides that it shall cease to have effect at the end of a period specified therein.

(3) If it appears to the Secretary of State to be expedient to do so, he may by a direction given under this section modify or revoke a scheduled monument consent to any extent he considers expedient. [Where a

direction would (if given) affect a monument situated in England, the Secretary of State shall consult with the Commission before he gives such a direction.]*

(4) Without prejudice to the generality of the power conferred by subsection (3) above to modify a scheduled monument consent, it extends to specifying a period, or altering any period specified, for the purposes of subsection (1) above, and to including a provision to the effect mentioned in subsection (2) above, or altering any period specified for the purposes of any such provision.

(5) Part II of Schedule 1 to this Act shall have effect with respect to directions under this section modifying or revoking a scheduled monument consent.

7 Compensation for refusal of scheduled monument consent

(1) Subject to the following provisions of this section, where a person who has an interest in the whole or any part of a monument incurs expenditure or otherwise sustains any loss or damage in consequence of the refusal, or the granting subject to conditions, of a scheduled monument consent in relation to any works of a description mentioned in subsection (2) below, the Secretary of State [or (where the monument in question is situated in England) the Commission]* shall pay to that person compensation in respect of that expenditure, loss or damage.

References in this section and in section 8 of this Act to compensation being paid in respect of any works are references to compensation being paid in respect of any expenditure incurred or other loss or damage sustained in consequence of the refusal, or the granting subject to conditions, of a scheduled monument consent in relation to those works.

(2) The following are works in respect of which compensation is payable under this section –

(a) works which are reasonably necessary for carrying out any development for which planning permission had been granted (otherwise than by a general development order) before the time when the monument in question became a scheduled monument and was still effective at the date of the application for scheduled monument consent;

(b) works which do not constitute development, or constitute development such that planning permission is granted therefor by a general development order; and

(c) works which are reasonably necessary for the continuation of any use of the monument for any purpose for which it was in use immediately before the date of the application for scheduled monument consent.

For the purpose of paragraph (c) above, any use in contravention of any legal restrictions for the time being applying to the use of the monument shall be disregarded.

(3) The compensation payable under this section in respect of any works within subsection (2) (a) above shall be limited to compensation in respect of any expenditure incurred or other loss or damage sustained by virtue of the fact that, in consequence of the Secretary of State's decision, any development for which the planning permission in question was granted could not be carried out without contravening section 2(1) of this Act.

(4) A person shall not be entitled to compensation under this section by virtue of subsection (2) (b) above if the works in question or any of them would or might result in the total or partial demolition or destruction of the monument, unless those works consist solely of operations involved in or incidental to the use of the site of the monument for the purposes of agriculture or forestry (including afforestation).

(5) In a case where scheduled monument consent is granted subject to conditions, a person shall not be entitled to compensation under this section by virtue of subsection (2) (c) above unless compliance with those conditions would in effect make it impossible to use the monument for the purpose there mentioned.

(6) In calculating, for the purposes of this section, the amount of any loss or damage consisting of depreciation of the value of an interest in

land –

(a) it shall be assumed that any subsequent application for scheduled monument consent in relation to works of a like description would be determined in the same way; but

(b) in the case of a refusal of scheduled monument consent, the Secretary of State, on refusing that consent, undertook to grant such consent for some other works affecting the monument in the event of an application being made in that behalf, regard shall be had to that undertaking.

(7) References in this section to a general development order are references to a development order made as a general order applicable (subject to such exceptions as may be specified therein) to all land.

17 Agreements concerning ancient monuments and land in their vicinity

(1) The Secretary of State may enter into an agreement under this section with the occupier of an ancient monument or of any land adjoining or in the vicinity of an ancient monument.

[(1A) The Commission may enter into an agreement under this section with the occupier of an ancient monument situated in England or of any land so situated which adjoins or is in the vicinity of an ancient monument so situated.]*

(2) A local authority may enter into an agreement under this section with the occupier of any ancient monument situated in or in the vicinity of their area or with the occupier of any land adjoining or in the vicinity of any such ancient monument.

(3) Any person who has an interest in an ancient monument or in any land adjoining or in the vicinity of an ancient monument may be a party to an agreement under this section in addition to the occupier.

(4) An agreement under this section may make provision for all or any

of the following matters with respect to the monument or land in question, that is to say –

(a) the maintenance and preservation of the monument and its amenities;

(b) the carrying out of any such work, or the doing of any such other thing, in relation to the monument or land as may be specified in the agreement;

(c) public access to the monument or land and the provision of facilities and information or other services for the use of the public in that connection;

(d) restricting the use of the monument or land;

(e) prohibiting in relation to the monument or land the doing of any such thing as may be specified in the agreement; and

(f) the making by the Secretary of State or [the Commission or the local authority (as the case may be)]* of payments in such manner, of such amounts and on such terms as may be so specified (and whether for or towards the cost of any work provided for under the agreement or in consideration of any restriction, prohibition or obligation accepted by any other party thereto);

and may contain such incidental and consequential provisions as appear to the Secretary of State or [the Commission or the local authority (as the case may be)]* to be necessary or expedient.

(5) Where an agreement under this section expressly provides that the agreement as a whole or any restriction, prohibition or obligation arising thereunder is to be binding on the successors of any party to the agreement (but not otherwise), then, as respects any monument or land in England and Wales, every person deriving title to the monument or land in question from, through or under that party shall be bound by the agreement, or (as the case may be) by that restriction, prohibition or obligation, unless he derives title by virtue of any disposition made by that party before the date of the agreement.

(6) *(Scotland only.)*

(7) Neither –

(a)   section 84 of the Law of Property Act 1925 (power of Lands Tribunal to discharge or modify restrictive covenants); nor

(b)   (*Scotland only*)

shall apply to an agreement under this section.

(8) Nothing in any agreement under this section to which the Secretary of State is a party shall be construed as operating as a scheduled monument consent.

(9) [References to an ancient monument in subsection (1A) above, and in subsection (3) above so far as it applies for the purposes of subsection (1A), shall be construed as if the reference in section 61(12)(b) of this Act to the Secretary of State were to the Commission.]*

42   Restrictions on use of metal detectors

(1) If a person uses a metal detector in a protected place without the written consent of the [Commission (in the case of a place situated in England) or of the Secretary of State (in any other)]* he shall be guilty of an offence and liable on summary conviction or, in Scotland, on conviction before a court of summary jurisdiction, to a fine not exceeding [level 3 on the standard scale]***.

(*** *words in brackets were inserted pursuant to section 46, Criminal Justice Act 1982*)

(2) In this section –

"metal detector" means any device designed or adapted for detecting or locating any metal or mineral in the ground; and
"protected place" means any place which is either –

(a)   the site of a scheduled monument or of any monument under the ownership or guardianship of the Secretary of State [or the Commission]* or a local authority by virtue of this Act; or

(b)   situated in an area of archaeological importance.

(3) If a person without [written consent]* removes any object of archaeological or historical interest which he has discovered by the use of a metal detector in a protected place he shall be guilty of an offence and liable on summary conviction to a fine not exceeding the statutory maximum or on conviction on indictment to a fine. [The reference in this subsection to written consent is to that of the Commission (where the place in question is situated in England) or of the Secretary of State (in any other case).]*

(4) A consent granted by the Secretary of State [or the Commission]* for the purposes of this section may be granted either unconditionally or subject to conditions.

(5) If any person –

(a)   in using a metal detector in a protected place in accordance with any consent granted by the Secretary of State [or the Commission]* for the purposes of this section; or

(b)   in removing or otherwise dealing with any object which he has discovered by the use of a metal detector in a protected place in accordance with any such consent;

fails to comply with any condition attached to the consent, he shall be guilty of an offence and liable, in a case falling within paragraph (a) above, to the penalty provided by subsection (1) above, and in a case falling within paragraph (b) above, to the penalty provided by subsection (3) above.

(6) In any proceedings for an offence under subsection (1) above, it shall be a defence for the accused to prove that he used the metal detector for a purpose other than detecting or locating objects of archaeological or historical interest.

(7) In any proceedings for an offence under subsection (1) or (3) above, it shall be a defence for the accused to prove that he had taken all reasonable precautions to find out whether the place where he used the metal detector was a protected place and did not believe that it was.

45 Expenditure on archaeological investigation

(1) The Secretary of State may undertake, or assist in, or defray or contribute towards the cost of, an archaeological investigation of any land [(other than land in England)]* which he considers may contain an ancient monument or anything else of archaeological or historical interest.

[(1A) The Commission may undertake, or assist in, or defray or contribute towards the cost of, an archaeological investigation of any land in England which they consider may contain an ancient monument or anything else of archaeological or historical interest; and the reference to an ancient monument in this subsection shall be construed as if the reference in section 61(12)(b) of this Act to the Secretary of State were to the Commission.]*

(2) Any local authority may undertake, or assist in, or defray or contribute towards the cost of, an archaeological investigation of any land in or in the vicinity of their area, being land which they consider may contain an ancient monument or anything else of archaeological or historical interest.

(3) The Secretary of State [or the Commission]* or any local authority may publish the results of any archaeological investigation undertaken, assisted, or wholly or partly financed by them under this section in such manner and form as they think fit.

(4) Without prejudice to the application, by virtue of section 53 of this Act, of any other provision of this Act to land which is not within Great Britain, the powers conferred by this section shall be exercisable in relation to any such land which forms part of the sea bed within the seaward limits of United Kingdom territorial waters adjacent to the coast of Great Britain [(or, as regards the powers mentioned in subsection (1A) above, England)]*.

55 Proceedings for questioning validity of certain order, etc

(1) If any person –

(a) is aggrieved by any order to which this section applies and desires to question the validity of that order, on the grounds that it is not within the powers of this Act, or that any of the relevant requirements have not been complied with in relation to it; or

(b) is aggrieved by any action on the part of the Secretary of State to which this section applies and desires to question the validity of that action, on the grounds that it is not within the powers of this Act, or that any of the relevant requirements have not been complied with in relation to it;

he may, within six weeks from the relevant date, make an application under this section to the High Court or (in Scotland) to the Court of Session.

(2) This section applies to any designation order and to any order under section 33(4) of this Act varying or revoking a designation order.

(3) This section applies to action on the part of the Secretary of State of either of the following descriptions, that is to say –

(a) any decision of the Secretary of State on an application for scheduled monument consent; and

(b) the giving by the Secretary of State of any direction under section 4 of this Act modifying or revoking a scheduled monument consent.

(4) In subsection (1) above "the relevant date" means –

(a) in relation to an order, the date on which notice of the making of the order is published (or, as the case may be, first published) in accordance with Schedule 2 to this Act; and

(b) in relation to any action on the part of the Secretary of State, the date on which that action is taken.

(5) On any application under this section the High Court or (in Scotland) the Court of Session –

(a) may by interim order suspend the operation of the order or action, the validity whereof is questioned by the application, until the final determination of the proceedings;

(b) if satisfied that the order or action in question is not within the powers of this Act, or that the interests of the applicant have been substantially prejudiced by a failure to comply with any of the relevant requirements in relation thereto, may quash that order or action in whole or in part.

(6) In this section "the relevant requirements" means –

(a) in relation to any order to which this section applies, any requirements of this Act or of any regulations made under this Act which are applicable to that order; and

(b) in relation to any action to which this section applies, any requirements of this Act or of the Tribunals and Inquiries Act 1992 or of any regulations or rules made under this Act or under that Act which are applicable to that action.

(7) Except as provided by this section, the validity of any order or action to which this section applies shall not be questioned in any legal proceedings whatsoever; but nothing in this section shall affect the exercise of any jurisdiction of any court in respect of any refusal or failure on the part of the Secretary of State to take a decision on an application for scheduled monument consent.

61   Interpretation

(1) In this Act –

"ancient monument" has the meaning given by subsection (12) below;
"area of archaeological importance" means an area designated as such under section 33 of this Act;
"designation order" means an order under that section;
["the Commission" means the Historic Buildings and Monuments Commission for England;]*
"enactment" includes an enactment in any local or private Act of Parliament, and an order, rule, regulation, byelaw or scheme made

under an Act of Parliament;

"flooding operations" means covering land with water or any other liquid or partially liquid substance;

"functions" includes powers and duties;

"guardianship deed" has the meaning given by section 12(6) of this Act;

"land" means –

(a) in England and Wales, any corporeal hereditament;

(b) (*Scotland only*);

including a building or a monument and, in relation to any acquisition of land, includes any interest in or right over land;

"local authority" means –

(a) in England and Wales, the council of a county or district, ... the council of a London borough, and the Common Council of the City of London; and

(b) (*Scotland only*);

"monument" has the meaning given by subsection (7) below:

"owner", in relation to any land in England and Wales means (except for the purposes of para.2(1) of Schedule 1 to this Act and any regulations made for the purposes of that paragraph) a person, other than a mortgagee not in possession, who, whether in his own right or as trustee for any other person, is entitled to receive the rack rent of the land, or where the land is not let at a rack rent, would be so entitled if it were so let;

"possession" includes receipt of rents and profits or the right to receive rents and profits (if any);

"prescribed" means prescribed by regulations made by the Secretary of State:

"the Schedule" has the meaning given by section 1(1) of this Act;

"scheduled monument" has the meaning given by section 1(11) of this Act and references to "scheduled monument consent" shall be construed in accordance with section 2(3) and 3(5) of this Act;

"tipping operations" means tipping soil or spoil or depositing building or other materials or matter (including waste materials or refuse) on any land; and

"works" includes operations of any description and, in particular (but without prejudice to the generality of the preceding provision) flooding or tipping operations and any operations undertaken for purposes of agriculture (within the meaning of the Town and Country Planning Act [1990] or, as regards Scotland, the Town and Country Planning (Scotland) Act 1972) or forestry (including afforestation).

(2) In this Act "statutory undertakers" means –

(a) persons authorised by any enactment to carry on any railway, light railway, tramway, road transport, water transport, canal, inland navigation dock, harbour, pier or lighthouse undertaking, or any undertaking for the supply of ..., ... hydraulic power;

(b) ... the Civil Aviation Authority, the Post Office and any other authority, body or undertakers which by virtue of any enactment are to be treated as statutory undertakers for any of the purposes of the Town and Country Planning Act [1990] or of the Town and Country Planning (Scotland) Act 1972; and

(c) any other authority, body, or undertakers specified in an order made by the Secretary of State under this paragraph.

(3) For the purposes of sections 14(1) and 21(2) of this Act and paragraph 6(1)(b) and (2)(b) of Schedule 3 to this Act a person shall be taken to be immediately affected by the operation of a guardianship deed relating to any land if he is bound by that deed and is in possession or occupation of the land.

(4) For the purposes of this Act "archaeological investigation" means any investigation of any land, objects or other material for the purpose of obtaining and recording any information of archaeological or historical interest and (without prejudice to the generality of the preceding provision) includes in the case of an archaeological investigation of any land –

(a) any investigation for the purpose of discovering and revealing and (where appropriate) recovering and removing any objects or other material of archaeological or historical interest situated in, on or under the land; and

(b) examining, testing, treating, recording and preserving any such objects or material discovered during the course of any excavations or inspections carried out for the purposes of any such investigation.

(5) For the purposes of this Act, an archaeological examination of any land means any examination or inspection of the land (including any buildings or other structures thereon) for the purpose of obtaining and recording any information of archaeological or historical interest.

(6) In this Act references to land associated with any monument (or to associated land) shall be construed in accordance with section 15(6) of this Act.

(7) "Monument" means (subject to subsection (8) below) –

(a) any building, structure or work, whether above or below the surface of the land, and any cave or excavation;

(b) any site comprising the remains of any such building, structure or work or of any cave or excavation; and

(c) any site comprising, or comprising the remains of, any vehicle, vessel, aircraft or other movable structure or part thereof which neither constitutes nor forms part of any work which is a monument within paragraph (a) above;

and any machinery attached to a monument shall be regarded as part of the monument if it could not be detached without being dismantled.

(8) Subsection (7)(a) above does not apply to any ecclesiastical building for the time being used for ecclesiastical purposes, and subsection (7)(c) above does not apply –

(a) to a site comprising any object or its remains unless the situation of that object or its remains in that particular site is a matter of public interest;

(b)   to a site comprising, or comprising the remains of, any vessel which is protected by an order under section 1 of the Protection of Wrecks Act 1973 designating an area round the site as a restricted area.

(9) For the purposes of this Act, the site of a monument includes not only the land in or on which it is situated but also any land comprising or adjoining it which appears to the Secretary of State [or the Commission]* or a local authority, in the exercise in relation to that monument of any of their functions under this Act, to be essential for the monument's support and preservation.

(10) References in this Act to a monument include references –

(a)   to the site of the monument in question; and
(b)   to a group of monuments or any part of a monument or group of monuments.

(11) Reference in this Act to the site of a monument –

(a)   are references to the monument itself where it consists of a site; and
(b)   in any other case include references to the monument itself.

(12) "Ancient monument" means –

(a)   any scheduled monument, and
(b)   any other monument which in the opinion of the Secretary of State is of public interest by reason of the historic, architectural, traditional, artistic or archaeological interest attaching to it.

(13) In this section "remains" includes any trace or sign of the previous existence of the thing in question.

SCHEDULE 1

CONTROL OF WORKS AFFECTING SCHEDULED MONUMENTS

PART I

APPLICATIONS FOR SCHEDULED MONUMENT CONSENT

1. (1) Provision may be made by regulations under this Act with respect to the form and manner in which applications for scheduled monument consent are to be made, the particulars to be included therein and the information to be provided by applicants or (as the case may be) by the Secretary of State in connection therewith.

(2) Any scheduled monument consent (including scheduled monument consent granted by order under section 3 of this Act) shall (except so far as it otherwise provides) enure for the benefit of the monument and of all persons for the time being interested therein.

2. (1) The Secretary of State may refuse to entertain an application for scheduled monument consent unless it is accompanied by one or other of the following certificates signed by or on behalf of the applicant, that is to say –

(a)   a certificate stating that, at the beginning of the period of twenty-one days ending with the application, no person other than the applicant was the owner of the monument;

[(aa)   a certificate stating that –

(i)   notice of the concurrent application has been given in accordance with rules made under section 6 of the Transport and Works Act 1992 to all persons (other than the applicant) who were, at the beginning of the period of 28 days ending with the date of the application, the owners of the monument; and

(ii)   every such notice contains a statement that an application for scheduled monument consent has been, or is to be, made in respect of the monument]**

(b) a certificate stating that the applicant has given the requisite notice of the application to all the persons other than the applicant who, at the beginning of that period, were owners of the monument;

(c) a certificate stating that the applicant is unable to issue a certificate in accordance with [any]** of the preceding paragraphs, that he has given the requisite notice of the application to such one or more of the persons mentioned in paragraph (b) above as are specified in the certificate, that he has taken such steps as are reasonably open to him to ascertain the names and addresses of the remainder of those persons and that he has been unable to do so;

(d) a certificate stating that the applicant is unable to issue a certificate in accordance with paragraph (a) above, that he has taken such steps as are reasonably open to him to ascertain the names and addresses of the persons mentioned in paragraph (b) above and that he has been unable to do so.

(2) Any certificate issued for the purposes of sub-paragraph (1) above:

(a) shall contain such further particulars of the matters to which the certificate relates as may be prescribed by regulations made for the purposes of this paragraph, and

(b) shall be in such form as may be so prescribed,

and any reference in that sub-paragraph to the requisite notice is a reference to a notice in the form so prescribed.

(3) Regulations made for the purposes of this paragraph may make provision as to who, in the case of any monument, is to be treated as the owner for those purposes.

(4) If any person issues a certificate which purports to comply with the requirements of this paragraph and which contains a statement which he knows to be false or misleading in a material particular, or recklessly

issues a certificate which purports to comply with those requirements and which contains a statement which is false or misleading in a material particular, he shall be guilty of an offence and liable on summary conviction or, in Scotland, on conviction before a court of summary jurisdiction, to a fine not exceeding [level 3 on the standard scale].

[(4A)In this paragraph, "concurrent application" means an application made under section 6 of the Transport and Works Act 1992 relating to proposals for the purposes of which the granting of scheduled monument consent is required in respect of the monument.]**

[2A. As soon as practicable after receiving an application for scheduled monument consent in relation to a monument situated in England, the Secretary of State shall send a copy of the application to the Commission.]*

3. (1) The Secretary of State may grant scheduled monument consent in respect of all or any part of the works to which an application for scheduled monument consent relates.

(2) Before determining whether or not to grant scheduled monument consent on any application therefor, the Secretary of State shall either –

(a)   cause a public local inquiry to be held; or
(b)   afford to the applicant, and to any other person to whom it appears to the Secretary of State expedient to afford it, an opportunity of appearing before and being heard by a person appointed by the Secretary of State for the purpose.

(3) Before determining whether or not to grant scheduled monument consent on any application therefor, the Secretary of State –

(a)   shall in every case consider any representations made by any person with respect to that application before the time when he considers his decision thereon (whether in consequence of any notice given to that person in accordance with any requirements of regulations made by virtue of paragraph 2 above or of any publicity given to the application by the Secretary of State, or otherwise); and

(b)   shall also, if any inquiry or hearing has been held in accordance with sub-paragraph (2) above, consider the report of the person who held it [and

(c)   shall, if the monument in question is situated in England, consult with the Commission]*.

(4) The Secretary of State shall serve notice of his decision with respect to the application on the applicant and on every person who has made representations to him with respect to the application.

4. (1) Sub-sections (2) to (5) of section 250 of the Local Government Act 1972 (evidence and costs at local inquiries) shall apply to a public local inquiry held in pursuance of paragraph 3(2) above in relation to a monument situated in England and Wales as they apply where a Minister or the Secretary of State causes an inquiry to be held under sub-section (1) of that section.

(2) *(Scotland only.)*

(**   *words in brackets inserted pursuant to regulation 4(2) of The Transport and Works Applications (Listed Buildings, Conservation Areas and Ancient Monuments Procedure) Regulations 1992 (S.I. 1992, No. 3138))*

PART II

MODIFICATION AND REVOCATION OF
SCHEDULED MONUMENT CONSENT

5. (1) Before giving a direction under section 4 of this Act modifying or revoking a scheduled monument consent the Secretary of State shall serve a notice of proposed modification or revocation on -

(a)   the owner of the monument and (if the owner is not the occupier) the occupier of the monument, and

(b)   any other person who in the opinion of the Secretary of State would be affected by the proposed modification or revocation.

[(1A) Where the monument in question is situated in England, the Secretary of State shall consult with the Commission before serving a notice under this paragraph, and on serving such a notice he shall send a copy of it to the Commission.]*

(2) A notice under this paragraph shall –

(a) contain a draft of the proposed modification or revocation and a brief statement of the reasons therefor; and

(b) specify the time allowed by sub-paragraph (5) below for making objections to the proposed modification or revocation and the manner in which any such objections can be made.

(3) Where the effect of a proposed modification (or any part of it) would be to exclude any works from the scope of the scheduled monument consent in question or in any manner to affect the execution of any of the works to which the consent relates, the notice under this paragraph relating to that proposed modification shall indicate that the works affected must not be executed after the receipt of the notice or (as the case may require) must not be so executed in a manner specified in the notice.

(4) A notice of proposed revocation under this paragraph shall indicate that the works to which the scheduled monument consent in question relates must not be executed after receipt of the notice.

(5) A person served with a notice under this paragraph may make an objection to the proposed modification or revocation at any time before the end of the period of twenty-eight days beginning with the date on which the notice was served.

6. (1) If no objection to a proposed modification or revocation is duly made by a person served with notice thereof in accordance with paragraph 5 above, or if all objections so made are withdrawn, the Secretary of State may give a direction under section 4 of this Act modifying or revoking the scheduled monument consent in question in

accordance with the notice.

(2) If any objection duly made as mentioned in sub-paragraph (1) above is not withdrawn, then, before giving a direction under section 4 of this Act with respect to the proposed modification or revocation, the Secretary of State shall either –

(a) cause a public local inquiry to be held; or

(b) afford to any such person an opportunity of appearing before and being heard by a person appointed by the Secretary of State for the purpose.

(3) If any person by whom an objection has been made avails himself of the opportunity of being heard, the Secretary of State shall afford to each other person served with notice of the proposed modification or revocation in accordance with paragraph 5 above, and to any other person to whom it appears to the Secretary of State expedient to afford it, an opportunity of being heard on the same occasion.

(4) Before determining in a case within sub-paragraph (2) above whether to give a direction under section 4 of this Act modifying or revoking the scheduled monument consent in accordance with the notice, the Secretary of State –

(a) shall in every case consider any objections duly made as mentioned in sub-paragraph(1) above and not withdrawn; and

(b) shall also, if any inquiry or hearing has been held in accordance with sub-paragraph (2) above, consider the report of the person who held it.

(5) After considering any objections and report he is required to consider in accordance with sub-paragraph (4) above the Secretary of State may give a direction under section 4 of this Act modifying or revoking the scheduled monument consent either in accordance with the notice or with any variation appearing to him to be appropriate.

7. As soon as may be after giving a direction under section 4 of this Act the Secretary of State shall send a copy of the direction to each person

served with notice of its proposed effect in accordance with paragraph 5 above and to any other person afforded an opportunity of being heard in accordance with paragraph 6(3) above.

8. (1) Where in accordance with sub-paragraph (3) of paragraph 5 above a notice under that paragraph indicates that any works specified in the notice must not be executed after receipt of the notice, the works so specified shall not be regarded as authorised under Part I of this Act at any time after the relevant service date.

(2) Where in accordance with that sub-paragraph notice under that paragraph indicates that any works specified in the notice must not be executed after receipt of the notice in a manner so specified, the works so specified shall not be regarded as authorised under Part I of this Act if executed in that manner at any time after the relevant service date.

(3) Where in accordance with sub-paragraph(4) of paragraph 5 above a notice under that paragraph indicates that the works to which the scheduled monument consent relates must not be executed after receipt of the notice, those works shall not be regarded as authorised under Part I of this Act at any time after the relevant service date.

(4) The preceding provisions of this paragraph shall cease to apply in relation to any works affected by a notice under paragraph 5 above –

(a)   if within the period of twenty-one months beginning with the relevant service date the Secretary of State gives a direction with respect to the modification or revocation proposed by that notice in accordance with paragraph 6 above, on the date when he gives that direction;

(b)   if within that period the Secretary of State serves notice on the occupier or (if there is no occupier) on the owner of the monument that he has determined not to give such a direction, on the date when he serves that notice; and

(c)   in any other case, at the end of that period.

(5) In this paragraph "the relevant service date" means, in relation to a notice under paragraph 5 above with respect to works affecting any

monument, the date on which that notice was served on the occupier or (if there is no occupier) on the owner of the monument.

9. (1) Subject to sub-paragraph (2) below, sub-sections (2) to (5) of section 250 the Local Government Act 1972 (evidence and costs at local inquiries) shall apply to a public inquiry held in pursuance of paragraph 6(2) above as they apply where a Minister or the Secretary of State causes an inquiry to be held under sub-section (1) of that section.

(2) Sub-section (4) of that section (costs of the Minister causing the inquiry to be held to be defrayed by such local authority or party to the inquiry as the Minister may direct) shall not apply except in so far as the Secretary of State is of opinion, having regard to the object and result of the inquiry, that his costs should be defrayed by any party thereto.

(3) *(Scotland only.)*

(* words in square brackets were inserted pursuant to section 33 and schedule 4 to the National Heritage Act 1983)

ANCIENT MONUMENTS AND ARCHAEOLOGICAL AREAS

The Ancient Monuments (Applications for Scheduled Monument Consent) Regulations 1981 (S.I. 1981, No.1301)
In force from October 9, 1981

The Secretary of State for the Environment and the Secretary of State for Wales, in exercise of the powers conferred by paragraphs 1(1) and 2(1) (2) and (3) of Schedule 1 to the Ancient Monuments and Archaeological Areas Act 1979(a), hereby make the following regulations:

Citation, commencement, application and interpretation
1. (1) These Regulations may be cited as the Ancient Monuments (Applications for Scheduled Monument Consent) Regulations 1981 and shall come into operation on 9th October 1981.

(2) These regulations apply only to England and Wales.

(3) In these regulations, "the Act" means the Ancient Monuments and Archaeological Areas Act 1979.

Applications for scheduled monument consent
2 (1) An application to the Secretary of State for scheduled monument consent under Part I of the Act shall be in the form set out in Schedule 1 to these Regulations, and shall contain the particulars required by that form.

(2) The application shall be accompanied by a plan identifying** the monument to which it relates and such other plans or drawings as are necessary to describe the works which are the subject of the application.**

(3) The applicant shall supply the Secretary of State with such further information as he may at any time require to enable him to determine the application.**

Certificates and notices
3. (1) A certificate which by virtue of paragraph 2(1) of Schedule 1 to the Act accompanies an application shall be in whichever of the forms set out in Part I of Schedule 2 to these regulations is appropriate, and shall

contain the particulars required by that form.

(2) The requisite notice for the purposes of paragraph 2(1) of Schedule 1 to the Act shall be in the form set out in Part II of Schedule 2 to these regulations, and shall contain the particulars required by that form.

Persons to be treated as the owners of monuments

4. In relation to any monument, a person shall for the purposes of paragraph 2 of Schedule 1 to the Act be treated as the owner of the monument if he is for the time being the estate owner in respect of the fee simple in the monument or is entitled to a tenancy of the monument granted or extended for a term of years certain of which not less than seven years remain unexpired.**

SCHEDULE 1   **Regulation 2(1)**

FORM OF APPLICATION FOR SCHEDULED MONUMENT CONSENT

APPLICATION FOR SCHEDULED MONUMENT CONSENT

ANCIENT MONUMENTS AND ARCHAEOLOGICAL AREAS ACT 1979

(To be completed by or on behalf of the applicant in BLOCK CAPITALS or typescript)

1. Applicant

    Name ....

    Address ....

    .... Post Code .... Tel No ....

2. Occupier of monument – if not the applicant

    Name ....
    Address ....

.... Post Code .... Tel No ....

3. Monument to which application relates

Name (if any) of monument ....

Address or Location ....

....

....

County Monument Number ....

National Grid Reference ....

4. Description of proposed works ....

....

....

5. List of plans and drawings accompanying application

....

....

....

....

6. Any other information relevant to application

....

....

....

....

I/We hereby apply for scheduled monument consent for the works described in this application and shown on the accompanying plans and drawings.

Signature . . . . Date . . . .

on behalf of . . . . *

* Where the application is being dealt with by an agent to whom correspondence should be sent, state the –

Name of agent . . . .

Address of agent . . . .

. . . . Post Code . . . . Tel No . . . .

SCHEDULE 2   **Regulation 3**

PART I

**FORMS OF CERTIFICATE FOR THE PURPOSES OF
Paragraph 2(1) OF SCHEDULE 1 TO THE ACT**

Certificate in accordance with paragraph 2(1)(a)
It is hereby certified that no person other than the applicant was the owner (x) of the monument to which the accompanying application relates at the beginning of the period of twenty-one days which ended on the date of the application.

Signature . . . . Date . . . .

Certificate in accordance with paragraph 2(1)(b)
It is hereby certified that the applicant has given the requisite notice of the accompanying application to all the persons other than the applicant who, at the beginning of the period of twenty-one days which ended on the

567

date of the application, were owners (x) of the monument to which the application relates, namely (y).

Signature . . . . Date . . . .

Certificate in accordance with paragraph 2(1)(c)
It is hereby certified –

(1) that the applicant is unable to issue a certificate in accordance with either paragraph 2(1)(a) or (b) of Schedule 1 to the Ancient Monuments and Archaeological Areas Act 1979;

(2) that the applicant has given the requisite notice of the accompanying application to the following persons who, at the beginning of the period of twenty-one days which ended on the date of the application, were owners (x) of the monument to which the application relates, namely (y); and

(3) that the applicant has taken such steps as are reasonably open to him to ascertain the names and addresses of the remainder of the persons who at the beginning of that period were owners (x) of that monument and has been unable to do so.

Signature . . . . Date . . . .

Certificate in accordance with paragraph 2(1)(d)
It is hereby certified that the applicant is unable to issue a certificate in accordance with paragraph 2(2)(a) of Schedule 1 to the Ancient Monuments and Archaeological Areas Act 1979, but has taken such steps as are reasonably open to him to ascertain the names and addresses of the other persons who, at the beginning of the period of twenty-one days which ended on the date of the accompanying application, were owners (x) of the monument to which the application relates and has been unable to do so.

Signature . . . . Date . . . .

FOOTNOTES

(x) "owner" means a person who is for the time being the estate owner in respect of the fee simple in the monument or is entitled to a tenancy of the monument granted or extended for a term of years certain of which not less than seven years remain unexpired.

(y) Insert names and addresses.

PART II

FORM OF NOTICE FOR THE PURPOSES OF
Paragraph 2(1) OF SCHEDULE 1 TO THE ACT

Notice of application for scheduled monument consent
(Delete the words in square brackets, as appropriate, and omit the brackets.)

This notice relates to the ancient monument at (x).

An application is to be made [by] [on behalf of] (y) to the Secretary of State for [the Environment]* [Wales] for scheduled monument consent under the Ancient Monuments and Archaeological Areas Act 1979 to carry out the following works:
(z).

An opportunity to make representations with respect to the application will be afforded by the Secretary of State before the application is determined.

Signature . . . . Date . . . .

FOOTNOTES

(x) State the address or location of the monument, and the name (if any).
(y) Insert name and address of applicant.
(z) Insert brief description of the proposed works.

* The Secretary of State for Culture, Media and Sport is now the relevant minister.

** The regulations are amended where applicable by The Transport and Works Applications (Listed Buildings, Conservation Areas and Ancient Monuments Procedure) Regulations 1992 (S.I. 1992, No.3138). They are applicable after January 1, 1993 either where an application for SMC is made within 10 weeks after the main application for a Transport and Works order is made to the minister, or if the Secretary of State on receiving a Transport and Works application directs that the concurrent procedure should apply. The amendments are as follows:

(2) In paragraph (2) of regulation 2, there shall be substituted, for the words commencing "a plan identifying" to the end of the paragraph –

"the following –

(a)   a plan identifying the monument to which it relates;
(b)   such other plans and drawings as are necessary to describe the works which are the subject of the application, and which may include –

    (i)   detailed plans, drawings and sections; or
    (ii)   extracts from the plans and sections submitted with the concurrent application; or
    (iii)   (where no such plans, drawings or sections have been prepared) a clear written description of the works which are the subject of the application supported by such other materials as the applicant is reasonably able to provide.".

(3) In regulation 2, after paragraph (2), there shall be inserted –

"(2A) The application shall also be accompanied by a statement that the application is made for the purposes of proposals included in the concurrent application and the statement shall give (where the same are known) the date and reference number of the concurrent application".

(4) In regulation 2, after paragraph (3), there shall be inserted –
"(3A) In this regulation, "concurrent application" has the meaning given by paragraph 2(4A) of Schedule 1 to the Act"*

(** *i.e. an application under the Transport and Works Act 1992; see schedule 1 to the AMAA above)*

(5) For regulation 4 there shall be substituted -

"4. In relation to any monument, a person shall for the purposes of paragraph 2 of schedule 1 to the Act be treated as the owner of the monument if he is a person, other than a mortgagee not in possession, who is for the time being entitled to dispose of the fee simple of the monument (whether in possession or reversion) or is a person holding, or entitled to the rents and profits of the land under, a lease or other agreement the unexpired term whereof exceeds three years.".

(6) In part I of Schedule 2, there shall be inserted after the words "Certificate in accordance with para.2(1)(b)", the following –

"Certificate in accordance with para.2(1)(aa)

It is hereby certified –

(1) that the applicant has served, in accordance with rules**(n)** made under section 6 of the Transport and Works Act 1992, all notices required to be served upon the persons (other than the applicant) who were, at the beginning of a period of 28 days ending with the date of an application under the said section 6, owners of the monument;

(2) every such notice contains a statement that the accompanying application for scheduled monument consent has been made in respect of the monument.

Signature . . . . Date . . . .

(n)   The Transport and Works (Applications and Objections Procedure) Rules 1992 (S.I. 1992, No. 2902)

ANCIENT MONUMENTS AND ARCHAEOLOGICAL AREAS

Guidance note on the matters to be addressed when seeking SMC for excavation of a scheduled monument (issued by English Heritage (the 'Commission') in 1990, whose correspondence address is Fortress House, 23 Savile Row, London W1X 2HE).

The time taken by the Commission to provide advice to the Department of the Environment can be unnecessarily extended by having to request additional information. Applicants are therefore advised to consult with the Inspectorate of Ancient Monuments at the above address before making the formal application and to provide the following information when submitting it.

1. CONDITION OF THE MONUMENT

Describe present condition, including a report of its current land use and the date of this information.

2. PREVIOUS ARCHAEOLOGICAL WORK AT THE MONUMENT

Dates and results of all previous archaeological work on the monument should be summarised (citing references where possible) together with the director(s) and organisation(s) involved. The location of existing site archives and finds should also be noted.

3. PROJECT SITE RECONNAISSANCE AND RESEARCH

Record fieldwork, geophysical survey, documentary or other research undertaken or planned as part of the proposed excavation. (If air photographs are available, please supply, quoting source and reference). If possible, attach a sketch plot at 1:10,000 or 1:2,500 to the background papers submitted with this application. Please state whether an evaluation of the archaeological deposits is planned.

4. RESEARCH DESIGN OF EXCAVATION

In preparing the design include if possible an evaluation of the project in its regional and national context, together with a general statement of aims and in particular an explicit exposition of the problems that the project is designed to solve. Explain why this project cannot take place at another unscheduled site.

5. EXCAVATION METHOD AND STRATEGY

Include an outline of the overall method of and strategy for the excavation, accompanied by plans (preferably at A4 or A3 finished size) at either 1:10,000/1:10,560, 1:2,500 or where appropriate 1:100 scales (or similar suitable equivalents), indicating the precise location of the monument, the position of any previous archaeological investigation(s) and the siting and disposition of the proposed excavation area(s). Describe the methodological approaches to be employed in the project in detail: for example, sampling procedures, recording and recovery techniques.

6. DURATION OF THE PROPOSED EXCAVATIONS

State the proposed start and finish dates for the excavation. If the project proposed involves more than one season's work, a timetable for the whole project should be put forward, together with detailed objectives for each season's work.

7. EXCAVATION DIRECTOR

Provide name and address of proposed director, if not the applicant.

8. PROPOSED DIRECTOR'S EXCAVATION AND RESEARCH EXPERIENCE

Particular reference should be made to experience of excavation on sites relevant to this application. Also list any outstanding commitments on grant-aided excavations and/or post-excavation work. Unless exceptional circumstances apply, permission to excavate is not normally given to directors with a significant backlog of unpublished excavations.

9. SIZE AND STRUCTURE OF EXCAVATION TEAM

If the excavation director is not normally to be present on site, the name of the person(s) responsible for the day-to-day running of the site should be given.

10. SPONSORING ORGANISATION FOR THE PROPOSED EXCAVATION

The status of the organisation concerned should be specified: in addition, applicants should be prepared to supply the names of two referees, to whom the Commission may refer in connection with the project and the project Director's suitability and experience for undertaking it.

11. SPECIALIST HELP AND REPORT

Please indicate which specialists (including environmentalists) have agreed to be involved with the project, whether they will be working on site during the proposed excavation, and the planned level of their commitment particularly during post-excavation processing and the production of the final archive/report.

12. CONSERVATION AND STORAGE PROGRAMME

Arrangements should be made for on-site conservation of excavated material (where necessary), for conservation work (including X-rays) prior to the production of the final excavation archive/publication, and for the satisfactory treatment of all excavated material prior to its final deposition with a suitable museum or other body.

13. POST-EXCAVATION STAFF AND PROGRAMME

The nature, staffing and timetable of the post-excavation processing should be made clear. It is accepted that such a programme may require substantial subsequent revision.

14.   PUBLICATION PROCEDURE AND PROGRAMME

At this stage, an outline of the likely shape of the archive and published report, together with an indication of how and where the Report is to be published, should be provided. Note: it is advisable to make a copy of the site records as work proceeds, to be kept separately in case of loss of or damage to the originals.

15.   DEPOSITION OF ORIGINAL ARCHIVE

Describe arrangements to be made.

16.   PROJECT FUNDING

Indicate the budget allocation for the satisfactory execution of a programme of excavation, post-excavation and publication (including the preparation and deposition of the final archive).

. . . .

Some standard conditions imposed by the Secretary of State on SMCs where archaeological excavation is to take place.

1. that the works to which this consent relates shall be carried out only by (name excavation director) and his/her nominated excavation team.

2. that this consent shall cease to have effect on

(probably no later than 3 months after the date excavation is programmed to end)

3. that not less than one month's written notice of the location and commencement of the excavation is given to

4. that the excavation shall be backfilled within 3 months of completion of the excavation to the satisfaction of the Secretary of State who will be advised by the Commission

or:

5. that any masonry remains exposed in the course of the excavation shall either be backfilled within 3 months of completion of the excavation or, if they are to be the subject of subsequent consolidation and display, shall be protected from the elements until such time as consolidation works commence, all such protection works to be carried out to the satisfaction of the Secretary of State

6. that an interim excavation report shall be sent to the Historic Buildings and Monuments Commission for England at Fortress House, 23 Savile Row, London W1X 2HE within 6 months of completion of the excavation and that a final report of the excavation shall be published within 5 years of completion of the excavation.

ANCIENT MONUMENTS AND ARCHAEOLOGICAL AREAS

ANCIENT MONUMENTS (CLAIMS FOR COMPENSATION) (ENGLAND) REGULATIONS 1991
(S.I. 1991, No.2512)
In force from 5 December 1991

Citation, commencement, interpretation and extent

1. (1) These Regulations may be cited as the Ancient Monuments (Claims for Compensation) (England) Regulations 1991, and shall come into force on 5th December 1991.

(2) In these Regulations, "the Act" means the Ancient Monuments and Archaeological Areas Act 1979.

(3) These Regulations apply only in relation to monuments or land, or to chattels on land, in England.

Claims for compensation under sections 7, 9 or 46 of the Ancient Monuments and Archaeological Areas Act 1979

2. (1) A claim for compensation under sections 7, 9 or 46 of the Act shall be made in the form set out in Part 1 of the Schedule hereto, or in a form substantially to the like effect, and shall be delivered or sent by the recorded delivery service to the person against whom the claim is made.

(2) Subject as mentioned below, a claim for compensation under sections 7, 9 or 46 of the Act shall be made within a period of six months beginning with –

(a) in the case of a claim under section 7 of the Act, the date of the refusal, or grant subject to conditions, of scheduled monument consent;

(b) in the case of a claim under section 9 of the Act –

(i) where subsection (2)(a) applies (scheduled monument consent granted by order under section 3 of the Act ceasing to apply), the date when, on an application for scheduled monument consent for the works in question, consent is refused, or is granted subject to conditions other than those which previously applied under the order;

(ii) where subsection (2)(b) applies (modification or revocation of a scheduled monument consent under section 4 of the Act), the date when the direction is given under section 4(3) of the Act;

(iii) where subsection (2)(c) applies, the date when in accordance with paragraph 8 of Schedule 1 of the Act the works specified or indicated in a notice of proposed modification or revocation of scheduled monument consent under paragraph 5 of that Schedule cease to be authorised; or

(c) in the case of a claim under section 46 of the Act, the date on which the damage occurred,

but in any particular case the Secretary of State may at any time extend the said period or allow further time within which a claim may be made.

Claims for compensation under section 36(8) of the National Heritage Act 1983

3. A claim for compensation under section 36(8) of the National Heritage Act 1983 shall be made in the form set out in Part 2 of the Schedule hereto, or in a form substantially to the like effect, and shall be delivered or sent by the recorded delivery service to the Historic Buildings and Monuments Commission for England, Fortress House, 23 Savile Row, London W1X 2HE within a period of six months beginning with the date on which the damage occurred but in any particular case the Secretary of State may at any time extend the said period or allow further time within which a claim may be made.

SCHEDULE

PART 1

ANCIENT MONUMENTS AND ARCHAEOLOGICAL AREAS ACT 1979
CLAIM FOR COMPENSATION UNDER SECTIONS 7, 9 OR 46 OF THE 1979 ACT

To: Name of the person against whom the claim is made (see footnote 1):
....

1. Person making the claim ("the claimant")
   (in BLOCK LETTERS):

   Full Name

   Address

   If claimant is a limited company or other corporate body give registered or principal office.

   Telephone No.

2. Address or location of the monument or land to which the claim relates:

An accurate plan should be supplied showing any area to which the claim relates

3. (a) State claimant's interest in the land:
   (b) State name and address of any other person known or believed to have an interest in the land and specify that interest:

4. Where the claim is under section 7 (compensation for refusal of scheduled monument consent) –

   (a) give details of the date and the reference number (if known) of the refusal, or grant subject to conditions, of scheduled monument consent in relation to the works mentioned at (b) below:

   (b) (i)   give a brief description of the works for which compensation is claimed (see footnote 2):
        (ii) in the case of works to which section 7(2)(a) applies, give the following details in connection with the planning permission – the name of the authority by which it was granted; the date; the reference number (if known); and a brief description of the development for which planning permission was granted:
        (iii) in the case of works to which section 7(2)(b) applies, give

the reasons why it is considered the works do not constitute development, or constitute development for which planning permission is granted by a general development order:

(iv) in the case of works to which section 7(2)(c) applies, give a brief description of the relevant use of the monument immediately before the date of the application for scheduled monument consent:

(c) give details of the expenditure and any other loss or damage in respect of which the claim is made (see footnote 3):

5. Where the claim is under section 9 (compensation where works affecting a scheduled monument consent cease to be authorised – see footnote 4), give details of –

(a) the works which have ceased to be authorised:

(b) the order, direction or notice by virtue of which the works have ceased to be authorised (in a case to which section 9(2)(a) applies, also gives details of the relevant refusal, or grant subject to conditions, of scheduled monument consent - see footnote 5):

(c) the expenditure (including any expenditure incurred upon the preparation of plans for the purposes of any works, or upon other similar preparatory matters) and any other directly attributable loss or damage in respect of which the claim is made (see footnote 3):

6. Where the claim is under section 46 (compensation for damage to land or chattels caused in the exercise of certain powers under the 1979 Act) (see footnote 6) –

(a) identify on the plan any land (including any building on it) which has been damaged and give particulars of that damage:

(b) specify any chattels on the land which have been damaged and give particulars of that damage:

(c) state the claimant's interest in any damaged chattels:

(d) state the name and address of any other person believed to have

an interest in those chattels and (if known) state that interest:
(e) give brief details of the circumstances in which the damage took place and of the identity of the person (if known) who is believed to have caused the damage:
(f) give particulars of how the amount of the compensation claimed has been calculated:

7. I/We hereby claim the amount of £   (see footnote 7)

Signature of claimant or agent*

Date

* If this claim form is being submitted by an agent state:

Name of agent

Address of agent

Telephone No.

IMPORTANT: SERVICE OF THIS CLAIM FORM. This claim form is to be delivered or sent by the recorded delivery service to the person against whom the claim is made *within six months* of the decision, direction, notification or damage giving rise to the claim for compensation. The Secretary of State may, on request, in any particular case, extend this period. [An application to extend this period should be made to the Secretary of State for the Environment, Room C9/06a, 2 Marsham Street, London SW1P 3EB.]

[Now to be made to the Secretary of State for Culture, Media and Sport.]

Footnotes

1. Claims for compensation under sections 7 and 9 of the Ancient Monuments and Archaeological Areas Act 1979 (as amended by the National Heritage Act 1983, Schedule 4, paragraphs 33 and 35 respectively) concerning a monument situated in England should be made to the Historic Buildings and Monuments Commission for England, Fortress House, 23 Savile Row, London, W1X 2HE.

Claims for compensation under section 46 of the 1979 Act (as amended by the National Heritage Act 1983, Schedule 4, paragraph 62) should be made to the authority by or on whose behalf the power of entry, or other power, was exercised; except that where damage was caused in the exercise of any such power by a person holding appointment as the investigating authority for an area of archaeological importance under section 34 of the 1979 Act the claim shall be made to the Historic Buildings and Monuments Commission for England, Fortress House, 23 Savile Row, London W1X 2HE.

2. Section 7(2) of the 1979 Act provides that the following are works in respect of which compensation is payable –
   (a) works which are reasonably necessary for carrying out any development for which planning permission had been granted (otherwise than by a general development order) before the time when the monument in question became a scheduled monument and was still effective at the date of the application for scheduled monument consent;
   (b) works which do not constitute development, or constitute development such that planning permission is granted therefor by a general development order; and
   (c) works which are reasonably necessary for the continuation of any use of the monument for any purpose for which it was in use immediately before the date of the application for scheduled monument consent.

   However, section 7(4) of the 1979 Act provides that compensation shall not be payable by virtue of section 7(2)(b) if the works in question or any of them would or might result in the total or partial demolition or destruction of the monument, unless those works consist solely of operations involved in or incidental to the use of the site of the monument for the purposes of agriculture or forestry (including afforestation).

3. Compensation payable under sections 7 or 9 of the 1979 Act in respect of any loss or damage consisting of depreciation of the value of an interest in the land is to be assessed on the basis of the rules set out in section 5 of the Land Compensation Act 1961 (section 27 of the 1979 Act).

   Section 7(3), (5) and (6) provide limitations on the entitlement to compensation in certain circumstances.

4. Section 9(2) of the 1979 Act provides that the section only applies where the works cease to be authorised –
   (a) by virtue of the fact that a scheduled monument consent granted by order under section 3 of the 1979 Act ceases to apply to any scheduled monument (whether by virtue of variation or revocation of the order or by virtue of a direction under subsection (3) of that section); or
   (b) by virtue of the modification or revocation of a scheduled monument consent by a direction given under section 4 of the 1979 Act; or
   (c) in accordance with paragraph 8 of Schedule 1 to the 1979 Act, by virtue

of the service of a notice of proposed modification or revocation of a scheduled monument consent under paragraph 5 of that Schedule.

5. Compensation is not payable under section 9(2)(a) of the 1979 Act unless, on an application for scheduled monument consent for the works in question, consent is refused, or is granted subject to conditions other than those which previously applied under the order (section 9(3) of the 1979 Act).

6. These powers relate to rights of entry and connected matters arising under sections 6, 6A, 26, 38, 39, 40 and 43 of the 1979 Act.

7. Under section 47(2) of the 1979 Act any question of disputed compensation shall be referred to and determined by the Lands Tribunal.

The Ancient Monuments (Claims for Compensation) (Wales) Regulations 1991 are in almost identical form. Reference there is to the Secretary of State for Wales and to Cadw

PART 2

NATIONAL HERITAGE ACT 1983
CLAIM FOR COMPENSATION FROM THE HISTORIC BUILDINGS AND MONUMENTS COMMISSION FOR ENGLAND FOR DAMAGE CAUSED TO LAND OR CHATTELS UNDER SECTION 36(8) OF THE 1983 ACT

To: The Historic Buildings and Monuments Commission for England
1. Person making the claim ("the claimant")
(in BLOCK LETTERS)

Full Name

Address

If claimant is a limited company or other corporate body give registered or principal office.

Telephone No.

2. Address or location of land entered by a person authorised by the

Commission (see footnote 1):

An accurate plan should be supplied showing any area to which the claim relates

3. Damage –

(a) identify on the plan any land (including any building on it) which has been damaged and give particulars of that damage:

(b) specify any chattels on the land which have been damaged and give particulars of that damage:

(c) state the claimant's interest in the damaged land or chattels:

(d) state the name and address of any other person believed to have an interest in the damaged land or chattels and (if known) specify that interest:

(e) give brief details of the circumstances in which the damage took place and the identity of the person (if known) who is alleged to have caused the damage:

(f) give particulars of how the amount of the compensation claimed has been calculated:

4. I/We hereby claim the amount of £   (see footnote 2)

Signature of claimant or agent*

Date

* *If this claim form is being submitted by an agent state:*

Name of agent

Address of agent

Telephone No.

IMPORTANT:
SERVICE OF THIS CLAIM FORM. This claim form is to be delivered or sent by the recorded delivery service to the Historic Buildings and Monuments Commission for England, Fortress House, 23 Savile Row,

London, W1X 2HE *within six months* of the damage occurring. The Secretary of State may, on request, in any particular case extend this period. [An application to extend this period should be made to the Secretary of State for the Environment, Room C9/06a, 2 Marsham Street, London SW1P 3EB.]

[Now to be made to the Secretary of State for Culture, Media and Sport.]

Footnotes

1. The claim for compensation must be in respect of damage caused to land or chattels on land in the exercise by a person authorised by the Commission of a power of entry under section 36 of the 1983 Act.
2. Under section 36(10) of the 1983 Act any question of disputed compensation shall be referred to and determined by the Lands Tribunal.

ANCIENT MONUMENTS AND ARCHAEOLOGICAL AREAS

OPERATIONS IN AREAS OF ARCHAEOLOGICAL IMPORTANCE (FORMS OF NOTICE ETC.) REGULATIONS 1984 (S.I. 1984, No. 1285)
In force from August 17, 1984

Citation, commencement, application and interpretation

1. – (1) These Regulations may be cited as the Operations in Areas of Archaeological Importance (Forms of Notice etc.) Regulations 1984 and shall come into operation on August 17, 1984.

(2) The following requirements of these Regulations apply only in relation to operations in areas of archaeological importance in England and Wales.

(3) In these Regulations "the Act" means the Ancient Monuments and Archaeological Areas Act 1979.

Form of an Operations Notice

2. The form set out in Part I of Schedule 1 hereto or a form substantially similar thereto is prescribed as the form required for the purposes of section 35 of the Act (an "operations notice").

Form of a Certificate

3. The form of certificate set out in Part II of Schedule 1 hereto or a form substantially similar thereto is prescribed as the form of certificate required by section 35(4)(b) of the Act to accompany a notice under section 35.

Prescribed steps to be taken by local councils

4. A district or London borough council on whom an operations notice is served in accordance with section 35(5) shall –

    (a)   within seven days of receipt of the notice serve a copy of it (together with the certificate and any other documents accompanying the notice) –

        (i)   on the investigating authority appointed for the relevant area of archaeological importance; or

        (ii)   where no particular authority is so appointed, on the Historic Buildings and Monuments Commission for England as respects a site in England, or on the Secretary of State for Wales as respects a site in Wales; and

(b) if the operations described in the notice are to be carried out after clearance of the site, advise the developer in writing within 14 days of receipt of the notice of the name and address of the relevant investigating authority and of his duty under section 35(7) of the Act to notify the investigating authority of the clearance of the site immediately on completion of the clearance operations.

Notice of Intention to Excavate

5. The form set out in schedule 2 hereto or a form substantially similar thereto is prescribed as the form to be used to give notice pursuant to section 38(3) of the Act (notice of intention to excavate to be given by investigating authorities).

SCHEDULE 1   **Regulation 2**

PART I

FORM OF NOTICE TO BE GIVEN BEFORE CARRYING OUT IN AN AREA OF ARCHAEOLOGICAL IMPORTANCE, OPERATIONS WHICH DISTURB THE GROUND, FLOODING OPERATIONS, OR TIPPING OPERATIONS

OPERATIONS NOTICE

ANCIENT MONUMENTS AND ARCHAEOLOGICAL
AREAS ACT 1979: SECTION 35

(To be completed by or on behalf of the Developer (*footnote 1*) in BLOCK CAPITALS or typescript)

    I/We, Name: ....

    Address: ....

. . . .
Postcode: . . . . *Tel. No.:* . . . .

hereby give notice of my/our intention to carry out the operations described below.

A certificate in accordance with section 35 of the Ancient Monuments and Archaeological Area Act 1979 accompanies this notice.
I/We understand that if within six weeks of serving this notice I/we carry out or cause or permit to be carried out any operations referred to in this notice I/we may be guilty of an offence under section 35 of the 1979 Act.

Particulars of proposed operations

1. *Description of proposed operations (footnote 2):*
2. The Site on which the operations are to be carried out:
    Name (if any): . . . .
    Address or Location: . . . .
    Ordnance Survey National Grid Reference: . . . .

(NOTE: Where the extent of the site cannot be accurately identified from its address or location a clear plan of the site of the operations should be provided.)

3. The date on which it is proposed to begin the operations:
. . . .

*[4. Where the operations are to be carried out after clearance of the site (*footnote 3*), the Developer's estimated date for completion of the clearance operations (*footnotes 4 and 5*) . . . .
. . . .
. . . .].

* Delete if not applicable.

    Signature . . . . Date: . . . .
    on behalf of . . . .

Where the notice is being given by an agent to whom correspondence should be sent, state the –

Name of agent . . . .
Address of agent . . . .
. . . .
Postcode . . . . Tel. No. . . . .

SERVICE OF THIS NOTICE

This notice is to be served on the district council or London borough council or (as the case may be) on each district council or London borough council in whose area the site of the operations is wholly or partially situated except that where the developer is any such council, this notice shall be served on the Secretary of State at 2 Marsham Street (HS Division), London, SW1P 3EB where the site is in England and at Cathays Park, Cardiff CF1 3HQ where the site is in Wales.

FOOTNOTES

1. "Developer" means any person carrying out or proposing to carry out any operations: (section 35(3) of the 1979 Act).
2. "Operations" means operations which disturb the ground; flooding operations; and tipping operations (section 35(2) of the 1979 Act). "Flooding operations" means covering land with water or any other liquid or partially liquid substance (section 61(1) of the 1979 Act). "Tipping operations" means tipping soil or spoil or depositing building or other materials or matter (including waste materials or refuse) on any land (section 61(1) of the 1979 Act). A reference to operations on any land includes a reference to operations in, under or over the land in question (section 41(1)(c) of the 1979 Act).
3. "Clearance of the site" means the demolition and removal of any existing building or other structure on the site and the removal of any other materials thereon so as to clear the surface of the land (but does not include the levelling of the surface or the removal of the materials from below the surface) (section 41(1)(d) of the 1979 Act).
4. "Clearance operations" means operations undertaken for the purpose of or in connection with the clearance of any site (section 41(1)(e) of the 1979 Act).
5. Immediately on completion of clearance of the site the developer must notify the investigating authority for the area of archaeological importance in question. The council will inform the developer of the name and address of

that investigating authority.

6. It is not necessary to serve a notice in this form in a case where the Areas of Archaeological Importance (Notification of Operations) (Exemption) Order 1984 provides exemption for the proposed operations.

SCHEDULE 1

PART II

FORM OF CERTIFICATE FOR THE PURPOSES OF SECTION 35 OF THE ANCIENT MONUMENTS AND ARCHAEOLOGICAL AREAS ACT 1979

Certificate accompanying an operations notice

I/We, Name: ....

Address: ....
....

Postcode: .... *Tel. No.:* ....

hereby certify that with regard to the accompanying operations notice dated ....
.... (*insert date*) given by or on behalf of ....
.... (*insert name of the Developer in the operations notice*):
relating to operations at ....
(give particulars of the site of the proposed operations)

(a)   I/We have an interest in the site of the operations which
□ (apart from any restrictions imposed by law) entitles me/us to carry out the operations in question; or

(b)   I/We have a right to enter on and take possession of the
□ site of the operations under section 11(1) or (2) of the Compulsory Purchase Act 1965 (powers of entry on land subject to compulsory purchase); or

(c) This certificate is issued by statutory undertakers entitled
☐   to carry out the operations in question by or under the following
     enactment
     (footnote) .... *(insert enactment).*

Tick the box which applies.

Signed .... Date ....
on behalf of ....

*Where the certificate is given by an agent to whom the correspondence should be
sent, state the -*

Name of the agent ....
Addres of the agent ....
....
Postcode .... *Tel. No.* ....

2. *(To be completed only where the person issuing this certificate is not the
Developer)*

I .... *(name of person issuing this
certificate)* hereby state that I have authorised the Developer mentioned
in the accompanying operations notice dated ....
(insert date of operations notice) to carry out the operations referred to in that
notice.

Signed .... (Signature of the person issuing this Certificate)
Date ....

NOTE: If any person issues a certificate which purports to comply with
the requirements of this form and which contains a statement which he
knows to be false or misleading in a material particular, or recklessly
issues a certificate which purports to comply with these requirements and
which contains a statement which is false or misleading in a material
particular, he shall be guilty of an offence.

FOOTNOTE

"Enactment" includes an enactment in any local or private Act of Parliament, and order, rule, regulation, byelaw or scheme made under an Act of Parliament (section 61(1) of the 1979 Act).

SCHEDULE 2

FORM OF NOTICE TO BE GIVEN BY ANY INVESTIGATING AUTHORITY OF ITS INTENTION TO EXCAVATE

ANCIENT MONUMENTS AND ARCHAEOLOGICAL AREAS ACT 1979; SECTION 38(3)

NOTICE OF INTENTION TO EXCAVATE

To: ....
....
.... *Name and Address of Developer*

1. TAKE NOTICE that *I/We* ....
....
....
Name and address of investigating authority

being [the investigating authority] [authorised by section 34 [(4)] [(5)] of the Act to exercise the powers of the investigating authority] (*footnote 1*) for the area of archaeological importance in which is situated the site referred to in an operations notice dated .... (*insert date*) and served by you on the ....
council(s) (insert name of council(s)) on ....
(*insert date*) intend, during the period set out in paragraph 2 below, to carry out excavations on that site for the purpose of archaeological investigation (*footnote 2*)

2. The period allowed for excavations is four months and two weeks beginning with –

(a) .... (*insert the date immediately following the end of the period of six weeks beginning with the date of service of the operations notice on the council(s)); or*

(b) if later (and where relevant), the date of receipt by me/us of the notification of clearance of the site pursuant to section 35(7) of the 1979 Act; or

(c) any earlier date agreed between us [such date being ....]. (*If such a date has been agreed before the service of this notice it should be inserted here and (a) and (b) should be deleted; if no such date has been agreed delete words in square brackets).*

NOTE: In a case where (b) is relevant (operations to be carried out after clearance of the site) the investigating authority has the right to carry out excavations before the relevant period begins provided that the authority does not thereby obstruct the execution on the site by the developer of clearance or other operations to which section 35 of the 1979 Act does not apply (*footnote 3*)

3. An investigating authority may at any reasonable time enter the site and any land giving access to it for the purpose of exercising its right to excavate.

4. It may be an offence for any person to carry out operations to which the operations notice relates at a time when the investigating authority has a right to excavate the site.

Signature .... Date ....
on behalf of ....

SERVICE OF THIS NOTICE

This notice must be served on the developer before the end of four weeks beginning with the date of service of the operations notice on the council (section 38(3) of the 1979 Act).

Copies of this notice are to be served upon, (1) the council(s) served with the operations notice; (2) The Secretary of State (unless the functions of the investigating authority are for the time being exercised by him) at 2 Marsham Street (HS Division) London, SW1P 3EB as respects a site in England and at Cathays Park, Cardiff CF1 3HQ as respects a site in Wales;

and (3) the Historic Buildings and Monuments Commission for England (unless the investigating authority is for the time being that Commission), as respects a site in England.

FOOTNOTES

1. Delete whichever is inapplicable. The powers of an investigating authority are exercisable by any authority duly authorised to exercise those powers. Where no authority is appointed, the powers of such an authority are exercisable by the Commission in the case of an area in England and the Secretary of State in the case of an area in Wales.
2. "Archaeological investigation" means any investigation of any land, objects or other material for the purpose of obtaining and recording any information of archaeological or historical interest and (without prejudice to the generality of the preceding provision) includes in the case of an archaeological investigation of any land –
    (a) any investigation for the purpose of discovering and revealing and (where appropriate) recovering and removing any objects or other material of archaeological or historical interest situated in, on or under the land; and
    (b) examining, testing, recording and preserving any such objects or material discovered during the course of any excavations or inspections carried out for the purpose of any such investigation (section 61(4) of the 1979 Act).
3. Section 35 of the 1979 Act applies to operations which disturb the ground; flooding operations; and tipping operations but it does not apply to any of those operations carried out with the consent of the investigating authority or to any operations exempted by an order under section 37* of that Act.

---

*   *See appendix* 2F *of this work for the prescribed exemptions.*

ANCIENT MONUMENTS AND ARCHAEOLOGICAL AREAS

AREAS OF ARCHAEOLOGICAL IMPORTANCE
(NOTIFICATION OF OPERATIONS)
(EXEMPTION) ORDER 1984
(S.I. 1984, No. 1286)
In force from September 30, 1984

1. (1) This Order may be cited as The Areas of Archaeological Importance (Notification of Operations) (Exemption) Order 1984 and shall come into operation on September 30, 1984.

(2) This Order applies only to operations in areas of archaeological importance in England or Wales.

(3) In this Order –

"the Act" means the Ancient Monuments and Archaeological Areas Act 1979;

"drainage body" and "navigation authority" have the same meanings as in the Land Drainage Act [1991]; and

"mining operations" means the winning and working of minerals in, on or under land, whether by surface or underground working.

2. (1) Section 35 of the Act (notice required of operations in areas of archaeological importance) shall not apply to the carrying out of operations of the descriptions specified in the Schedule hereto.

(2) The exemptions afforded by paragraph (1) are subject to any particular conditions mentioned in the said Schedule.

SCHEDULE

EXEMPT OPERATIONS

1. Operations in connection with the use of land for agriculture, horticulture or forestry; provided that such operations do not disturb the ground below a depth of 600 millimetres.

2. Operations in connection with the landscaping (including screening by the erection of fences or walls), layout, planting, or maintenance of public or private gardens, grounds or parks; provided that such operations do not disturb the ground below a depth of 600 millimetres.

3. Tunnelling or other operations affecting the ground in the area only at a depth of 10 metres or more.

4. Mining operations, provided that the operations are carried out in accordance with the Code of Practice for Minerals Operators dated April 1982*.

* The code is now updated, see para.2.87 of this work.

5. Works of repair, renewal or maintenance or emergency works carried out by a drainage body or a navigation authority.

6. Operations for the repair, maintenance, relaying or resurfacing of a highway within the meaning of the Highways Act 1980 or of a footpath as defined in that Act, or of a railway; provided that such operations do not disturb the ground below a depth of 600 millimetres or below the existing foundations, if deeper.

7. Operations for the repair, maintenance or renewal of mains, pipes, cables or other apparatus connected with the supply of electricity, gas, water, drainage services, sewerage services, highway or transport authority services or telecommunication services.

8. Operations for the installation or laying of new mains, pipes, cables or other apparatus connected with the supply of electricity, gas, water, drainage services, sewerage services or telecommunication services where there is a duty by or under any enactment to undertake those operations and to do so within six months of the duty first arising.

9. Operations for the erection or repositioning of street lighting columns not involving excavations to a depth exceeding 1.5 metres.

FORM OF NOTICE OF INTENTION UNDER THE DISUSED BURIAL GROUNDS (AMENDMENT) ACT 1981 (Intention to remove human remains and/or tombstones, monuments or memorials, or to render graves inaccessible). After a form produced by Gillian Harrison, I.F.A. Technical Paper no. 11 (1992). **This form may require amendment to suit particular circumstances.**

Disused Burial Grounds (Amendment) Act 1981
Notice of intention to (Remove Human Remains and/or Tombstones, Monuments or other Memorials) (render Grave inaccessible)(from/at)
. . . . **Church Yard/Burial Grounds/Cemetery***

1. For the purpose of the erection of a building for (state use to which to be applied), it is necessary to remove certain human remains/to remove tombstones, monuments and/or other memorials commemorating deceased persons or render certain graves inaccessible.*

2. In accordance with the provisions of the Disused Burial Grounds (Amendment) Act 1981, notice is hereby given that ** . . . .
. .intend two months after the date of first publication of this notice to remove the remains of the persons whose names, so far as they can be ascertained, are as follows;/to remove tombstones, monuments or other memorials commemorating the persons whose names, so far as they can be ascertained are as follows:*

. . . .

3. A plan of the present place of burial showing the positions of the graves/tombstones, monuments and other memorials*, and a statement containing details thereof, are now deposited at (full address) and may be inspected free of charge between . . . . and . . . .
from Monday to Friday, excluding public holidays, before (insert date).

4. Any personal representatives or relative of any deceased person whose remains were interred less than fifty years ago may give formal notice in writing to the undersigned of objection to the proposal to erect the building and, if such objection be not withdrawn, the proposal to erect the building shall not have effect.

5. Any person who is heir, executor, administrator or relative of any

deceased person whose grave will be rendered inaccessible/remains and/or any monument tombstone or other memorial are/is to be removed,* or in the case of a Commonwealth war burial, the Commonwealth War Graves Commission, may give written notice to the undersigned before (insert date of expiry of not less than six weeks from the date of the first publication of the notice) of intention to undertake the removal of such remains and/or any tombstone, monument or other memorial commemorating the deceased person* and thereupon (s)he will be at liberty, provided that (s)he applies for the Secretary of State's directions for the removal of human remains as soon as possible after giving such notice and that such directions are issued, to cause such remains to be removed and reinterred in any churchyard, burial ground or cemetery in which interments may legally take place or, if desired, cremated. Applications for the Secretary of State's directions should be made to the Under Secretary of State, Home Office, E Division, Room 978, 50 Queen Anne's Gate, London SW1H 9AT. (The Secretary of State's directions are not required to effect the removal of any tombstone, monument or other memorial).** .... will defray the reasonable expense of such removal and, where appropriate, reinterment or cremation.

6. If the notice in paragraph 5 above has been given within the prescribed time, or if after such notice has been given, the persons giving notice have not removed the remains and/or tombstones or monuments or other memorials,** .... will cause all such tombs monuments or other memorials to be disposed of as follows:

and/or all those human remains to be removed and reinterred/cremated in accordance with the following directions given by the Secretary of State:

[insert directions given to the church etc. by the Secretary of State]

7. Any person entitled to burial rights in the burial ground mentioned above at the date of this notice may claim compensation in respect of the loss of such rights by writing to the undersigned.

Dated this .... day of .... 199[]

SIGNED (on behalf of ** ....

Address ....

* strike out the alternative(s) not applicable
** insert name of church etc.

A copy of the notice should be served on the Commonwealth War Graves Commission (at 2 Marlow Road, Maidenhead, Berkshire, SL6 7DX) in accordance with paragraph 1© of the schedule to the 1981 Act.

When applying for the directions of the Secretary of State the following information should be forwarded:

1. The full names and date of death of all those whose remains are to be exhumed (or, where this is impractical, a plan which delineates the area from which the remains are to be removed);
2. Details of the ultimate method of disposal (either burial ground or crematorium) and, where relevant, the museum or laboratory where remains will be stored temporarily for analysis;
3. The name of the district council in whose area the original burial ground is situated.

Where directions are sought by a church etc. which intends to remove remains in preparation for building on a burial ground the directions issued should be recited in the published notice (see form above). Where, on publication of the notice, the Secretary of State receives applications for directions from personal representatives or relatives the church etc. will be notified.

Where it is known that no burials have ever taken place in the part of burial ground to be built upon application can be made to the Secretary of State for an Order dispensing with the requirements of the 1981 Act. An A4 plan which delineates the area of the works should be sent to the Home Office, together with the name of the relevant district council. An Order may contain restrictions on the way in which the land which is built upon is to be treated and as such will be registered as a local land charge.

Statutory Sources for the law relating to the removal of Burials

Primary Legislation:

Burial Act 1857, section 25

Disused Burial Grounds Act 1884
Disused Burial Grounds (Amendment) Act 1981

Open Spaces Act 1887
Open Spaces Act 1906, section 20

Local Government, Planning and Land Act 1980, sections 104,
                                141-144 and schedules 20 and 28

New Towns Act 1981, section 20

Housing Act 1988, section 77 and schedule 10

Town and Country Planning Act 1990, sections 239 and 240

Pastoral Measure 1983, sections 30, 65 and schedule 6

Secondary Legislation:

Town and Country Planning (Churches, Places of Religious Worship and
Burial Grounds) Regulations 1950 (S.I. 1950, No. 792)

Faculty Jurisdiction Rules 1992 (S.I. 1992, No. 2882)

Human Remains Removal Licence (Prescribed Fees) Order 1982 (S.I. 1982,
No. 364)

FORM OF DECLARATION OF TREASURE TROVE

An inquiry of [day and month   ] 199[ ] at [name of town and county
] taken before [   ], Her Majesty's Coroner for the [name of county
or district] upon the oath of [number of jurors] lawful men and true of the
said [county or district] duly sworn and charged and sworn to inquire for
Our Sovereign Lady the Queen as to where, when, how and by whom
certain treasure lately discovered and here produced was found

Having evidence upon oath and *upon their oaths* the Jurors say that the
said treasure, namely [description of treasure
          ] was found on [   ] 199[ ] by [name(s) of finder(s)
               ]

And the said treasure was deposited, hidden and concealed in ancient
times and as the owner thereof cannot now be known is **Treasure Trove**
and the property of our said Lady the Queen

And the said Treasure Trove is to be handed to [Her Majesty's
Treasury][name of franchise holder] on behalf of our said Lady the Queen
for which purpose I, the said Coroner, have taken and seized the said
Treasure Trove into Her Majesty's hands

In witness whereof we have set our hands this   day of [   ] 199[ ]

Jurors

In the presence of :_____ **Coroner**

SHORT FORM ASSIGNMENT BY A FIELDWORKER OF RIGHTS IN FINDS AND TREASURE (not appropriate in Scotland, where all finds usually vest in the Crown)

This Assignment is made the   day of   199[ ]

Between (1)   [name of individual fieldworker] of [address of fieldworker ('the Assignor')

(2)   [name of landowner or sponsoring organisation] of [address of landowner or sponsoring organisation] ('the Assignee')

Whereas:

(A) The Assignee intends to carry out archaeological investigations at and in the locality of the site known as [   ] ('the Investigation')

(B) In consideration of [the invitation extended by the Assignee to the Assignor to participate in the Investigation and the proper preservation of any finds discovered] the Assignor has agreed to assign to the Assignee all of [his][her] interest in all artefacts and other objects discovered during the course of the Investigation

Now this deed witnesses as follows:

1. The Assignor **hereby assigns** to the Assignee all interests claims and entitlements (whether present or future actual or contingent) of the Assignor in any and all finds and other items portable or immovable discovered during or as a result of the Investigation

2. The Assignor **hereby agrees** that [he][she] shall pay to the Assignee on demand all sums received by the Assignor whether in the form of grants bounties rewards ex gratia awards compensation or other receipts from whatever source made to the Assignor in respect of any or all finds discovered during or as a result of the Investigation which are at any time declared treasure trove or treasure within the Treasure Act 1996

SIGNED AS A DEED and

DELIVERED by the said

[   ]

in the presence of: _____
                                                              Signature of Assignor

_____Signature of witness
_____Name of witness
_____Address of witness

Treasure Act 1996: the Statutory Code of Practice

Introduction

Notes: This Code has effect in England and Wales; a separate code has been prepared for Northern Ireland.

A Welsh language version of the Code is available on request from the Department of National Heritage.

When the term 'national museum' is used in this document it is intended to refer to the British Museum in the case of finds from England and the National Museum of Wales (now known as the National Museums & Galleries of Wales) in the case of finds from Wales. References to the 'Secretary of State' are to the Secretary of State for National Heritage.

If finders or others need further advice about any matters relating to the Treasure Act or this Code, then they are recommended to contact the Department of National Heritage, the British Museum or (for Wales) the National Museums & Galleries of Wales. Addresses and telephone numbers are given in Appendix 3.

In many places this Code gives examples of what may or may not constitute treasure and provides advice as to how coroners may approach an inquest. It is intended to provide guidance for all those concerned with treasure. It is emphasised, however, that questions of whether or not any object constitutes treasure and how a coroner should conduct an inquiry into treasure are for the coroner to decide on the facts and circumstances of each case. Nothing in this Code obviates the need for a finder to give independent consideration as to whether something he has found might constitute treasure and where there is any doubt it will usually be appropriate to report the find.

A. Summary

1. The Treasure Act 1996 ('the Act') replaces the common law of treasure trove in England, Wales and Northern Ireland. Treasure trove hitherto provided effectively the only legal protection afforded antiquities found in England, Wales and Northern Ireland. Under the law of treasure trove, there was a requirement that finds of objects made of gold or silver were reported to the coroner. Before an object could be declared treasure trove and be the property of the Crown, it had to pass three test: it had to be made substantially of gold or silver, it had to have been deliberately hidden with the intention of recovery, and its owner or his heirs had to be unknown. In practice, national and local museums had the opportunity to acquire finds of treasure trove. If a museum chose to do so, the lawful finder normally received the full market value (assessed by the Treasure Trove Reviewing Committee); if not, the object was returned, normally to the finder. The Act (see Appendix 1) removes the need to establish that objects were hidden with the intention of being recovered, except in a very few cases (see paragraph 9); it sets out the precious metal content required for a find to qualify as treasure; and it extends the definition of treasure to include other objects found in archaeological association with finds of treasure. The Act confirms that treasure vests in the Crown or the franchise if there is one, subject to prior interests and rights. It simplifies the task of coroners in determining whether or not a find is treasure and it includes a new offence of non-declaration of treasure. Lastly, it states that occupiers and landowners will have the right to be informed of finds of treasure from their land and that they will be eligible for rewards.

The Code of Practice: the provisions of the Act

2. Many of the principles formerly followed in the administration of treasure trove are retained under the Act, although in a modified form. Section 11 of the Act requires the Secretary of State to prepare a Code of Practice relating to treasure, to keep it under review and to revise it when appropriate (see paragraph 84). The Code sets out the guidelines to be followed by the Secretary of State when considering whether or not treasure should be offered to a museum or to the finder or to any other person, when determining a reward and when deciding whether to disclaim the Crown's title to treasure. The Code may also provide guidance for finders, museums, coroners and others who are concerned with treasure. Before preparing the Code, the Secretary of State must consult such interested parties as appear to be appropriate and the Code, or any revision of it, will not come into force until it has been approved by a resolution of each House of Parliament. The Secretary of State is required to publish the Code in such a way as will bring it to the attention of all interested parties and the Secretary of State may publish separate Codes for (a) England and Wales and (b) Northern Ireland and © for different parts of England, Wales and Northern Ireland if appropriate. This Code has effect in England and Wales; a draft of it was issued for consultation in December 1996 and it has been revised in the light of comments received. The Government recognises that this Code needs to be distributed as widely as possible to all interested parties: especially to metal detectorists, landowners, archaeologists, museums, dealers, coroners and the police. The Department of National Heritage will also produce a leaflet (or leaflets) summarising the main requirements of the Act, which will be distributed as widely as possible.

Relationship between this Code and the Government's proposals for the recording of Portable Antiquities

3. The Act is intended to provide a mechanism to allow the public acquisition of finds that come within its scope, but it is not primarily intended to deal with the recording of finds. This issue was the subject of *Portable Antiquities: a discussion document* published by the Department of National Heritage in February 1996. In December 1996 the Government announced that it will fund a two-year project of pilot schemes for the voluntary recording of all archeological finds. The text of the announcement is given in Appendix 2. It should be stressed that the proposals to record archaeological objects that do not fail within the definition of treasure under the Act (paragraphs 5-16) are voluntary, but the Government believes that they are of equal importance in ensuring that vital evidence about our history is preserved. Wherever possible, finders are encouraged to report all archeological finds to the relevant organisations, as identified by the local agreements described in paragraphs 38-41. The Government expects that these pilot schemes will also play a role in providing local reporting arrangements for finds of treasure.

B. Commencement of the Act

4. Under section 15 of the Act the Secretary of State has the power to determine by statutory instrument the date of commencement of the Act (see Appendix 1). The Secretary of State intends to make an Order to the effect that the Act will commence on Wednesday 24 September 1997. The provisions of the Act will only apply to objects found after this time; the burden of proof in seeking to show that an offence has been committed under section 8 of the Act because an object of treasure that has not been reported was found after the commencement of the Act will rest with the prosecution.

C. Definition of Treasure

I. The Definition in the Treasure Act

5. The Treasure Act provides that the following categories of object will be treasure after the commencement of section 4 of the Act (see Appendix 1):

(i) Objects other than coins (section 1(1)(a))
6. any object other than a coin provided that at least 10 per cent by weight of metal is precious metal (that is, gold or silver) and that it is at least 300 years old when found. This means that objects plated in gold or silver will not normally be treasure (unless they are found in association with objects that are treasure).[1]

(ii) Coins (section 1(1)(a) and section 3(2))
7. all coins that contain at least 10 per cent of gold or silver by weight of metal and that come from the same find, provided a find consists of at least two coins with a gold or silver content of at least 10 per cent. The coins must be at least 300 years old at the time of discovery. In the case of finds consisting of coins that contain less than 10 per cent of gold or silver there must be at least ten such coins; they will also need to be at least 300 years old. (A list of coins that are commonly found in England and Wales that contain less than 10 per cent of gold or silver is given in Appendix 4.) It is important to stress that only under certain circumstances are groups

---

1. However, where an object is made up of distinct components, only one of which is precious metal (for example, a gold binding on an amber object), the components will normally be treated as individual, associated objects.

of coins likely to be regarded as coming from the 'same find': see paragraphs 12-14. Single coins will not be treasure, unless they are found in association with objects that are treasure, or unless there is exceptionally strong evidence that they were buried with the intention of recovery (see paragraph 9: for example, a single coin found in plough soil without any sign of a container would not provide such evidence). Section 3 (2) defines the term 'coin' as including any metal token that was, or can reasonably be assumed to have been, used or intended for use as or instead of money. This definition only includes coins and tokens made after the introduction of the first coinage into this country during the Iron Age period and excludes objects made earlier such as iron currency bars. jettons or reckoning counters are also excluded from this definition.

(iii) Objects found in association with objects that are treasure (section 1(1)(d))

8. any object, of whatever composition, that is found in the same place as, or that had previously been together with, another object that is treasure. The object may have been found at the same time as, or later than, the item of treasure (see paragraphs 12-14). However, unworked natural objects will not be treasure (see paragraph 11), even if they are found in association with objects that are treasure.

(iv) Objects that would have been treasure trove (section 1(1)(c))

9. any object that would previously have been treasure trove, but does not fall within the specific categories given above. (Only objects that are less than 300 years old, that are made substantially of gold or silver, that have been deliberately hidden with the intention of recovery and whose owners or heirs are unknown will come into this category. In practice, such finds are rare and the only such discoveries that have been made within recent years have been hoards of gold and silver coins of the eighteenth, nineteenth or twentieth centuries. Single coins found on their own will not qualify under this provision unless there is exceptionally strong evidence to show that they were buried with the intention of recovery: for example, a single coin found in plough soil without any sign of a container would not provide such evidence.) Therefore gold and silver objects that are clearly less than 300 years old will not be treasure unless the finder has reason to believe that they may have been deliberately hidden with the intention of recovery[2].

II. Explanatory notes

(i) Scope of the Act
10. The Act applies to objects found anywhere in England, Wales and Northern Ireland, including in or on land, in buildings (whether current occupied or ruined), in rivers and lakes and on the foreshore (that is the area between mean high water and mean low water), provided that the object does not come from a wreck (on which, see paragraph 15). However, if the original owner or his heirs can show that the object belongs to them, then their claim will be superior to that of the Crown.

(ii) Naturally occurring objects
11. Unworked natural objects (such as fossils, minerals or human or animal remains) will not be treasure (section 1(2) of the Act: see Appendix 1).

(iii) Associated objects
12. The Act states that an object is part of the 'same find' as another object if it is found in the same place as, or had previously been left together with, the other object (section 3(4) and 3(5) of the Act: see Appendix 1). It

---

2. In addition, under the terms of section 2-of the Act the Secretary of State has the power to designate as treasure classes of object which are at least 200 years old and which in the Secretary of State's opinion are of outstanding historical, archaeological or cultural importance. Section 2 of the Act o gives the Secretary of State a corresponding power to remove classes of objects from the definition of treasure. (This power to remove classes of object from the definition of treasure applies both to those objects that are currently defined as treasure by the Act and to any class of object which may have been added to the definition by in order under section 2 of the Act.) An order made under this power will be made by statutory instrument which would need the approval of both Houses of Parliament under the affirmative resolution procedure. These powers cannot be used to apply retrospectively to an object which has already been found. A review will be carried out once the Act has been in operation for three years to consider whether any adjustments need to be made to the definition of treasure (see paragraph 84).

will be for the coroner's inquest to establish these facts and circumstances will vary from case to case. The coroner may seek advice from the finder and also from a local archaeologist or museum curator identified in accordance with the local agreement described in paragraphs 38-41 as to whether objects reported as treasure should be considered as coming from the 'same find'. In general, the definition of the 'same place' should be taken to mean a place of deposition where the contents of a hoard, purse or votive deposit (see paragraph 13) or a group of qualifying finds is either found in physical association or, if dispersed, may reasonably be supposed to have once been in physical association. Dispersal might, for example, occur through agricultural activity or construction work, through the burrowing of animals, or through other agencies. The current and previous use of the land where the find has been made will often be a determining factor. However, if there is any doubt as to whether an object is part of the same find as another object it will be for the coroner to decide.

13. So far as concerns finds consisting exclusively of coins, again any decision will be for the coroner, but only the following three categories will usually be considered treasure: (a) hoards, which have been deliberately hidden; (b) groups such as the contents of purses, which may have been dropped or lost and © votive or ritual deposits. In the case of votive deposits, the 'same place'(see paragraph 12) may include deposition in a well or sacred spring or within a temple precinct, or within a similar location judged to be of ritual purpose. (All groups of fewer than ten base metal coins found on their own are excluded.) Assemblages of coins that may reasonably be interpreted as individual losses accumulated over a period of time and that were in all probability never deposited in physical association (for example those found on settlement sites or on fair sites) should not normally be considered treasure. Most hoards and purses are not associated with settlement or fair sites, although they may be.

14. A number of objects found over a period of time may qualify as treasure, including those that would not have been treasure but for an earlier find of treasure. The find may consist of different classes of objects and it will not need to have been found at the same time or by the same person. However, the Act will not have retrospective effect; for example, if a finder discovers first one coin on a particular site, which will not be treasure, and then subsequently discovers more coins on the same site, which will then qualify as treasure, the original discovery will not be considered as treasure. This applies regardless of whether the earlier find was made before or after the commencement of the Act. The duty to report such finds will rest with the finder who will have a legal duty to report a find if he believes or has reasonable grounds for believing his find to be treasure (see paragraphs 21-24). The Sites and Monuments Record may contain information concerning similar finds made in the same area in the past which may be relevant in determining whether the new find may be treasure (see paragraph 39).

(iv) Objects found on the foreshore (section 3(7))

15. The Act applies to objects found along tidal rivers and on the foreshore (that is the area between mean high water and mean low water) and such finds will be eligible for consideration as treasure unless there is evidence that they have come from a wreck (see also footnote to paragraph 74). If an object was originally deposited on land it may be treasure, provided that it qualifies under the definition of treasure set out in the Act (see paragraphs 5-9); if it has come from a wreck then it will be subject to the salvage régime that applies to wreck under the Merchant Shipping Act 1995. The Receiver of Wreck must legally be notified of all property recovered following the loss of a vessel; and the salvor is entitled to a reward related to the value of the object either from the owner, if he can be identified or, failing that, from the Crown. The existing provisions of salvage law in relation to wreck will not be affected by the Treasure Act.

(v) Objects found on consecrated ground

16. The Government has given a commitment to the Church of England that it will bring forward an order under section 2 of the Act exempting objects found in association with human burials in a consecrated place and objects (except for treasure trove) covered by the Church of England' own legal systems of controls. The Church has indicated that all the objects will be dealt with under the ecclesiastical law in a manner that is analogous to that proposed under the Act. The Government agreed to do this on the basis that the Church of England is in a unique position in having its own legal régime applying to moveable articles that belong to it and the purpose of the order is essentially to provide a clarification of the law in so far as it applies to such objects. Its scope will be limited to the Church of England. (It is not expected that such cases will arise very often.)

D. Ownership of Treasure; Franchisees

(i) Ownership of treasure

17. Section 4 of the Act provides that treasure (as defined in section 1 of the Act) vests in the Crown or in the appropriate franchisee of the Crown, if there is one (see below), but the rights of original owners or their heirs, where known, are fully protected. The Act confirms that the Crown or the franchisee will enjoy the same rights over treasure as they currently do in respect of treasure trove. Objects that qualify as treasure under section 1 of the Act will be treasure irrespective of the circumstances in which they came to be in the place where they were found and, in particular, irrespective of whether they were lost, buried in a grave or abandoned.

(ii) Objects found within treasure franchises

18. It has from time to time been the practice of the monarch to make grants of franchises of treasure trove to various individuals and bodies, although none has been made in recent times. The principal bodies that are believed to hold valid treasure trove franchises are the Duchy of Lancaster the Duchy of Cornwall and the Corporation of London; the City of Bristol may also hold a treasure trove franchise. Section 5 of the Act states that those individuals and bodies who hold treasure trove franchises at the time when the Act commences will continue to enjoy the same rights in respect of treasure and it confirms that Her Majesty and the Duke of Cornwall are to be treated as holders of treasure trove franchises with regard to the Duchy of Lancaster and the Duchy of Cornwall respectively and that they will continue to be so treated after the commencement of the Act.

19. Section 10(8) of the Act makes provision for the holders of treasure franchises to request that the Secretary of State shall follow the guidelines set out below for the payment of rewards in respect of finds from areas for which they hold a franchise. The Duchy of Lancaster has confirmed that, without prejudice to Her Majesty's right to treasure trove in Right of Her Duchy of Lancaster, they expect to follow the provisions of the Act and this Code of Practice in respect of any finds of treasure from their franchise. The Duchy of Cornwall has similarly confirmed that, without prejudice to The Prince of Wales' right to treasure trove in Right of His Duchy of Cornwall, they expect to follow the provisions of the Act and this Code of Practice in respect of any finds of treasure from their franchise. The City of Bristol has confirmed that, without prejudice to any rights enjoyed by Bristol City Council in respect of treasure trove, the City would expect to follow this Code in respect of any finds of treasure from any franchise that the City may enjoy. The Corporation of London has a long-held practice of paying rewards for finds of treasure trove and there is no expectation that the Corporation would wish to change this policy with regard to the additional categories of object that will come within the scope of the Treasure Act.

20. Consequently, objects of treasure that are found within a treasure franchise should be reported by the finder to the coroner in the normal way and shall otherwise be dealt with according to the principles laid down in this Code, with the exception that the Museum of London will have the first right to acquire any finds of treasure made within the franchise enjoyed by the Corporation of London and Bristol Museums and Art Gallery will enjoy a similar right in respect of any finds of treasure made within any franchise that may be enjoyed by the City of Bristol (see paragraph 60(1)). Section 6 of the Act gives the Secretary of State the power to disclaim treasure (see paragraphs 45-48); although this power does not specifically apply to franchise-holders, they may choose to follow this practice if they so wish. Finds from the Corporation of London's franchise and from any franchise that may be enjoyed by the City of Bristol may be disclaimed by the Corporation of London on the advice of the Museum of London, or by the City of Bristol on the advice of Bristol Museums and Art Gallery and these museums may consult the national museum if they wish. Finds from the franchises of the Duchy of Lancaster and from the Duchy of Cornwall may be disclaimed by Her Majesty and The Prince of Wales on the advice of the national museum, following the procedure in paragraph 46.

E. Guidance for Finders and others concerned with Treasure

I. The requirements of the Act: the duty to report finds (section 8)

21. Section 8 of the Act states that a person who finds an object which he believes or has reasonable grounds for believing is treasure must notify the coroner for the district in which the object was found before the end of the notice period, which is 14 days beginning with the day after the find or, if later, the day on which the finder first believes or has reason to believe the object is treasure. Paragraphs 36-41 provide guidance on how finds should be reported and a list of coroners with addresses and telephone numbers is given in Appendix 3. It is important to stress that the Act requires a finder to report his find within 14 days of his making the find or within 14 days of his realising that the find was treasure and not to deliver it within that period. If a finder discovers an object that he does not immediately believe to be treasure but learns subsequently that it may be treasure, for example after cleaning it (see paragraph 44 and Appendix 5 for advice on cleaning) or examining it more closely at a later date, or after showing it to others, or after having it identified by a museum, then he should report it within 14 days of realising that it may be treasure.

22. It is a criminal offence, punishable by a maximum term of imprisonment of three months or a fine not exceeding level 5 (currently £5,000), or both, not to report a find of treasure to the coroner. It will, however, be a valid defence for a prosecution for non-declaration of treasure if the defendant can show that he had a 'reasonable excuse' for failing to notify the coroner. The court will take account of the circumstances of the individual concerned when deciding whether a finder has 'reasonable grounds' for believing an object not to be treasure or a 'reasonable excuse' for not reporting treasure. For example, in considering a case, a court may take into account whether the finder could have been expected to know that his find was treasure.[3] Where it is alleged that a criminal offence has been committed under the provisions of the Act, it win always be for the prosecution to prove their case beyond reasonable doubt.

23. If finders are in any doubt as to whether any of the objects they have found are treasure, they are strongly advised to report them. The duty to report lies with the individual who made the find and this duty to report

---

3. This matter was discussed in the Parliamentary debates on the Treasure Bill: see the statements of the Minister of State, Mr Iain Sproat, reported in Hansard, House of Commons, 8 March 1996, col.579 and 10 May 1996, cols.587-8.

applies to everyone, including archaeologists. However, in the case of an archaeological excavation, it may be convenient for one member of the excavation team to take the responsibility for ensuring that the coroner is informed about all finds of potential treasure made during the course of the excavation.

24. As regards finds of potential treasure made at detecting rallies, if a person were to find an object that qualified as treasure on its own, then that person will have a duty to report the object. If, however, it seemed that, for example, a dispersed hoard of coins had been discovered and that several individuals had discovered coins from the hoard, the individual finders would have a duty to report their finds and the rally organiser or the finds recorder should tell them that this was the case.

II. Guidance

(i) Searching for artefacts

25. The Government recognises that metal detectorists have been responsible for discovering many objects of great importance for the nation's heritage and this Act is not intended in any way to restrict the activities of responsible, law-abiding detectorists.

26. The Government recommends metal detectorists to join a recognised metal detecting club or Organisation in order to take advantage of the wider knowledge of a group and so that they can most effectively be informed about the Treasure Act and Code of Practice and the Government's initiative for pilot schemes for the voluntary recording of all archaeological objects. However, it is recognised that special steps may have to be taken to draw the provisions of the Act and this Code to the attention of those metal detectorists who choose not to join a metal detecting Organisation.

27. The Government urges all metal detectorists to abide by articles 1 and 7 of the National Council for Metal Detecting's Code of Conduct:

1. Do not trespass. Ask permission before venturing on to any private land.

7. Familiarise yourself with the law relating to archaeological sites. Remember it is illegal for anyone to use a metal detector on a scheduled ancient monument unless permission has been obtained[4] ... Also acquaint yourself with the practice of treasure trove.

28. It is important to stress that all those intending to search for objects or to undertake archaeological excavations that may lead to the discovery of such objects must obtain the necessary permissions. In the case of publicly owned land, it cannot be assumed that detectorists will automatically have the right to search there. For example, some local authorities have specific policies restricting the use of metal detectors on their land and finders should always satisfy themselves that they have permission before searching on any council-controlled land. As regards finds made on the foreshore (that is the area between mean high water and mean low water), see footnote to paragraph 74.

29. If there is evidence that the finder has been trespassing or that he has made his find in a 'protected place' without the written consent of English Heritage or, in Wales, of Cadw, he may expect to receive no reward at all or an abated reward, in accordance with the principles laid down in paragraph 74.[5]

30. Anyone who intends to search for artefacts is strongly recommended, when seeking permission to search, to make an agreement with the occupier and the landowner (if different) as to how any reward should be divided between them.

31. If searching on cultivated land, metal detectorists should take care to

---

4. In England permission should be obtained from English Heritage and in Wales from Cadw (see paragraph 29).
5. Under section 42 of the Ancient Monument and Archaeological Areas Act 1978 it is an offence to use a metal detector in a protected place without permission. A 'protected place' is defined by the 1979 Act as (a) the site of a scheduled ancient monument; (b) any monument under the ownership or guardianship of the Secretary of State or a local authority by virtue of the Act and (c) a place situated in an area of archaeological importance (at present the only areas that are so designated are the historic centres of the following five towns: Canterbury, Chester, Exeter, Hereford and York).

recover items only from the plough-soil. If they discover something large (for example, in a container), unusual or below the plough-soil they are strongly recommended to obtain appropriate archaeological help. Finds may be associated with features that are not immediately visible, such as a pit or building. If individual objects are removed from these positions without archaeological supervision the chance to understand and date the feature may be lost. Similarly, archaeological involvement at this stage may help to discover why the object was put there in the first place. It may also be in a finder's interests to obtain appropriate archaeological help in excavating unusual or fragile finds. If, while removing it from the ground, a finder were, deliberately or recklessly, to cause significant damage either to the actual object or to a surrounding monument or to the archaeological deposits making up the contexts which may explain the circumstances in which the object became buried or concealed, then this will be reflected in any *ex gratia* reward that may be payable in respect of the find (see paragraph 74(viii)). If a finder does not remove the whole of a find from the ground but reports it, thus affording the opportunity for the archaeological excavation of the remainder of the find, the original finder will normally be eligible for a reward for the whole find and not just that part which he himself had removed from the ground, although the Secretary of State will need to examine the individual circumstances of each case (see paragraph 73). (The local agreements to be drawn up in accordance with paragraphs 38-41 will provide advice on how to obtain help; alternatively the local Sites and Monuments Record or local authority archaeologist will be able to give advice: see list in Appendix 3.)

32. Finders are also recommended, where possible, to note information such as where the find was made, how deep the find was, whether the find- spot is on cultivated land or under grass and anything else they have found or noticed in the ground (such as metal objects, pottery fragments or building rubble) in the surrounding area at the time of the discovery or previously.

33. The great majority of known archaeological sites are not 'protected places' under the Ancient Monuments and Archaeological Areas Act 1979 (see paragraph 29). Although there are no legal restrictions on metal detecting on such sites, the Government strongly recommends to all metal detectorists that, if they do find significant archaeological objects that are not treasure on a particular site, they should consult the local authority archaeologist in England (or, in Wales, the Regional Trust) responsible for the Sites and Monuments Record or the local museum to ensure that they will not be causing damage or loss of archaeological evidence on a known archaeological site that is registered on the Sites and Monuments Record.[6] The archaeologist or museum will in any case welcome such information. A list of all Sites and Monuments Records is given in Appendix 3.

34. It is recognised that there will be occasions where the reporting of finds by detectorists from unscheduled sites will lead to an archaeological investigation of the site, with the landowner's and/or the occupier's permission, and that very occasionally such investigations may lead to the discovery of significant archaeological remains, so that it may be desirable to suspend further independent or group metal detecting on that site for a fixed period of time. Where this happens, archaeologists should ensure that the detectorist who originally reported the find is kept fully informed, by explaining to the finder what subsequent archaeological action will be taken, by sharing with them the new understanding that results from the find and by giving the original finder due acknowledgement for his

---

6. Concern has been expressed by metal detectorists that if they report finds from a site then it might lead to the site being scheduled with the result that they would no longer be allowed to detect there. However, there is no known example where new detector finds on their own have led to a site being scheduled. Scheduling is carried out systematically under the Monuments Protection Programme, by which English Heritage is reviewing England's archaeology and making recommendations for scheduling to the Secretary of State for National Heritage. To qualify for scheduling, a site must meet very stringent criteria in order to satisfy the Secretary of State that, in accordance with the legislation, it is of national importance and that its management and protection is best achieved by the controls of the scheduled monument system, Isolated detector finds on their own do not provide sufficient justification for scheduling, although such sites may be scheduled if other, more detailed, archaeological information about them exists. In any event, only a small proportion of the total number of known archaeological sites will be scheduled. At present (1997) there are about 17,000 scheduled monuments and the Monuments Protection Programme is likely to increase this to no more than about 32,000 monuments. This will represent less than 10 per cent of the currently known monuments, sites and find-spots, and many scheduled monuments are buildings that are totally unsuited to detecting.

discovery in any subsequent publication of the find. Archaeological bodies are urged to co-operate in this way because the logic of the pilot schemes for the voluntary recording of all archaeological finds (see paragraph 3 and Appendix 2) is that they should be based on co-operation between archaeologists and metal detectorists.

35. Archaeologists should, wherever practicable, give the finder the opportunity to be actively involved in any future archaeological investigation of the site where the find was made. The finder should be given full acknowledgement for his discovery in any publication of the find.

(ii) Reporting finds of treasure; local agreements

36. The Government recognises the need to make it as easy as possible for finders to fulfil their legal obligations under the Act. Finders are required to report their finds to the coroner for the district in which the find was made and this may be done by contacting the appropriate coroner (see Appendix 3). Such a report may be made in person, by letter, by fax or by telephone. The coroner or his officer will give or send the finder an acknowledgement that he has reported the find and will give instructions as to where the finder should deliver his find. This could be to the coroner himself or, in most instances, to a museum or to a local authority archaeological service or other appropriate archaeological Organisation, in accordance with the terms of the local agreement outlined in paragraph 38. The coroner will copy the relevant documentation to that body which will copy it to the relevant national museum.

37. The coroner or the body receiving the object on behalf of the coroner will give the finder a receipt when delivering his find. This receipt will specify the following:

(a) the name and address of the finder(s);

(b) brief description of the object(s) together with a note of its condition (in some cases it may be best if the body receiving the find were to do this by means of a photograph);

(c) a note of exactly where the object(s) was found; a precise location will be needed, to the equivalent of at least a six-figure grid reference wherever possible. (Since this information will be kept confidential, it may be advisable to keep a separate record of it: see paragraph 43.);

(d)   the date when the object(s) was found;

(e)   the name and address of the occupier of the land;

(f)   the name and address of the owner of the land where the find was made (if known) and;

(g)   a contact name and telephone number so that the finder will be able to find out about the progress of his find.

38. The Government proposes that, for each coroner's district in England and Wales, it will be desirable to draw up local agreements between coroners, local government archaeological officers (in Wales, the Regional Archaeological Trusts) and local or national museums, as appropriate, as to how the arrangements for the delivery of finds of treasure will work in each area and that local metal detecting organisations should be informed of those arrangements. It is not possible to lay down a single blueprint as to how this will work across the whole of England and Wales because of the great variety of local archaeological and museum provision that exists across the country, and the form of the agreement will be for each coroner to determine for his district. Where good arrangements for the reporting of finds already exist, the intention will be to build on them. These arrangements will need to be publicised locally, but the Department of National Heritage will maintain a complete record of all such arrangements and may be contacted on 0171 211 6000. Further sources of advice are given in Appendix 3.

39. One of the chief aims of such local agreements will be to ensure, wherever possible, that the location and context of each find of potential treasure is, where appropriate, immediately inspected, accurately pinpointed and recorded and that the recovery process does not cause damage or loss to the preservation or understanding of the national heritage. It will also be necessary to ensure that the appropriate Sites and Monuments Record is informed at the earliest possible opportunity (see list in Appendix 3). The Sites and Monuments Record may contain information concerning similar finds made in the same area in the past which may be relevant in determining whether the new find may be treasure (see paragraph 14).

40. Another aim of such local agreements will be to ensure that the

instructions given by coroners to the finders as to where they should deliver their finds will be, so far as possible, convenient to all parties. It is recognised that some finders may wish to show their finds at metal detecting clubs which may meet monthly and this will still be possible, with the agreement of all concerned, as long as the reporting requirements have been met.

41. According to the agreement that has been reached in each coroner's district, it is expected that the coroner will generally direct a finder who has reported a find to take the same to a local museum curator or a local authority archaeological officer (or an archaeological unit), who will be able to provide a preliminary opinion as to whether an object that a finder believes may be treasure is likely to be treasure. The local museum curator or archaeological officer will be able to return those objects that, in their opinion, are clearly not treasure, either in their own right or by association, to the person who has reported them, pending the decision of the coroner. The museum curator or archaeological officer will then give his opinion on the objects to the coroner and, where his opinion is that the object is not treasure, it will not normally be necessary to hold an inquest. The national museum will be able to provide advice where experienced advice is not available locally and in addition the national museum will need to be informed if the local museum curator or archaeological officer believes that the find may be treasure (see paragraphs 46 and 51 for more details on the procedure to be followed in such cases). The Government accepts that the pilot schemes for the voluntary recording of all archaeological objects will have a valuable role to play here (see Appendix 2).

42. If an object that may be treasure is shown to a person other than the coroner, a museum or a local government archaeological officer, such as a dealer, then that person should remind the finder of his legal duty to report the object to the coroner. However, the obligation to report finds rests with the finder alone. Dealers should abide by the codes of their professional organisations (in particular the Antiquities Dealers Association, the British Association of Antique Dealers, the British Numismatic Trade Association, LAPADA (the Association of Art and Antique Dealers) and the Society of Fine Art Auctioneers) and they should bear in mind that if they acquire, whether knowingly or unknowingly, an object that is treasure or that turns out to be treasure and that has not been disclaimed or returned, they have no title to it. The Government appreciates the need to make information about finds that have been disclaimed or returned easily available in order that dealers may avoid unwittingly purchasing undeclared objects. When they sell objects that have either been reported as potential treasure and disclaimed or which have been declared to be treasure at a coroner's inquest and returned because no museum acquired them, dealers and auction houses are urged to include a note to this effect whenever the object is described in an auction catalogue or sales list. In paragraph 48 it is recommended that the relevant documentation should be kept with the object. In any case, a provenance normally enhances the value of such an object.

43. In order to preserve the integrity of the site of the find for possible further archaeological investigation and to deter trespassers, it will not be necessary to report publicly the precise location of the find, either during an inquest or otherwise. As a general guideline, the civil parish or else a four-figure national grid reference (one square kilometre) will be sufficient in most cases, although in particularly sensitive cases a more general description of the location may be appropriate. The landowner's views will also be taken into account in deciding this matter. However, the finder should report the precise find-spot of his find to the coroner (wherever possible to the equivalent of at least a six-figure national grid reference) and failure to do so may be taken into account when determining any reward for which the finder may be eligible (see paragraph 74(iv)). This information will be treated as confidential by the coroner, by those bodies from whom the coroner has sought advice and by the Sites and Monuments Record.

(iii) Advice on the care of finds
44. Some materials, when removed from the ground, can be identified without cleaning; examples are pure gold or silver-gold alloys. If an object has changed in appearance as a result of having been buried in the ground, it may still be possible to identify the material from a visual examination or from comparison with other similar objects. Further information on how to identify altered materials without cleaning is given in section 2 of appendix 5. Some finders may feel it is necessary to carry out limited cleaning of objects, for example to remove the soil from them, in order to determine whether or not they are likely to qualify as treasure.

In such cases cleaning should be kept to a minimum. In any event, cleaning alone will not necessarily help finders tell what the object they have found is made of and so they are encouraged to seek a professional opinion as soon as possible. More extensive cleaning should only be undertaken by, or with the advice of, a professional archaeological conservator. Inappropriate cleaning can reduce the value (both archaeological and commercial) of finds. Further information on the care of finds and sources of advice are given in Appendix 5. See also paragraph 53.

F. Secretary of State's Power to Disclaim Objects

45. Under Section 6 of the Act the Secretary of State has the power to disclaim objects that have been submitted as potential treasure. Since it is anticipated that museums will not wish to acquire all of the objects that will qualify as treasure, this provision means that it will not normally be necessary to hold treasure inquests in such cases.

46. Although the Secretary of State will be able to use this power at any stage once a find of potential treasure has been reported to the coroner, the normal procedure will be as follows. All finds of treasure must to be reported to the coroner. The coroner will then seek advice either from the local museum or local authority archaeological officer or archaeological unit or from the national museum, in accordance with the arrangements that have been agreed for each coroner's district (see paragraphs 38-41). The local museum or archaeological officer and the national museum should agree whether to advise the Secretary of State that the object should be disclaimed; in some cases it may be necessary for the object to be delivered to the national museum for further study and it is noted in paragraph 51 that the national museum can also provide specialist conservation or metallurgical analysis. The local museum or archaeological officer and the national museum will also consult any other museums registered with the Museums and Galleries Commission that they believe may have a potential interest in acquiring the find. If as a result of this process of consultation, no museum wishes to acquire the object(s), then the national museum will advise the Secretary of State that the Crown's interest in the find should be disclaimed, and will inform the coroner. The coroner will not then need to proceed with an inquest and will take the steps set out in paragraph 47. If information about the find has not already been passed on to the appropriate Sites and Monuments Record (see list in Appendix 3), then it will be done at this stage (see paragraph 39). Only a complete find (for example, a complete coin hoard) may be disclaimed in this way; if a museum wishes to acquire any objects from a find, then the whole find will need to be considered at a treasure inquest.

47. Any objects disclaimed in this way will be treated as though they had never been treasure and will be returned by the coroner. The coroner will give notification to the occupier and the landowner (if different) that he intends to return them to the finder not less than 28 days after the date of his notification unless he receives an objection from either of them. If the coroner receives such an objection, the find will be retained by the coroner, or by the body to whom he has entrusted it, pending the resolution of the dispute between the parties. The coroner does not have the power to make a legal determination as to title as between the occupier, the landowner and the finder, and this question will, if necessary, need to be resolved in the courts.

48. It is recommended that a record of the coroner's findings and documentation relating to the disposal of the object should be kept with it. The person to whom objects have been returned in this way win be free to dispose of them as he wishes. However, all such objects will require an export licence from the Department of National Heritage if they are to be exported abroad. Application forms for export licences may be obtained from the Cultural Property Unit of the Department of National Heritage (0171 211 6000).

49. The procedure outlined in paragraphs 46-48 may also be followed in the case of objects, such as those from archaeological excavations, where no reward is payable because the finder has waived his rights to a reward, provided that this is done in accordance with a pre-existing agreement between the parties concerned and provided that the Secretary of State is satisfied with the arrangements for their disposal. Such finds should also be reported to the coroner in the normal way and the coroner should be informed of the outcome. (See also paragraph 76.)

G. Procedure when a Find has been reported to the Coroner; Treasure Inquests

50. Detailed guidelines on the procedure to be followed by coroners in treasure inquests will be set out in a Home Office Circular. This section of the Code is intended to summarise the main points insofar as they affect those who are likely to have an interest in treasure inquests (finders, occupiers, landowners, museums, etc.).

51. The coroner will hold an inquest on any find that has been reported to him and that he has reasonable grounds for believing to be treasure, except where the find has been disclaimed by the Secretary of State. On the other hand, it is expected that all those finds that no museum wishes to acquire will already have been disclaimed under the procedure laid down in paragraph 46, so it will effectively only be necessary to hold inquests on those finds that a museum wishes to acquire. A report on the find will be prepared for the coroner by national and local archaeologists in conjunction, as appropriate (see paragraph 41).[7] The coroner is required by the Act to inform the national museum if he intends to hold an inquest. In addition, the national museum will be able to provide specialist conservation and analytical facilities. Where necessary the coroner will make arrangements for the object to be delivered to the national museum. (However, the coroner may ask the national museum to make arrangements regarding the delivery of fragile objects.)

52. The body that is providing advice to the coroner in accordance with paragraph 51 will give the coroner a report giving brief details of the objects together with an assessment as to whether they fall within the definition of treasure and, if so, on what grounds. The report will not contain a valuation of the objects.

53. In the case of objects other than coins, it may be necessary to obtain a scientific analysis, wherever possible without sampling, of one or more objects from the find in order to determine whether they fall within the definition of treasure under the Act. It will not normally be necessary to

---

7.   In the case of finds from Wales, the coroner will normally ask for a report from the National Museums & Galleries of Wales.

obtain an analysis of the metal content of coins. In some cases it may also be necessary to clean the objects so that they can be identified (see Appendix 5, section 6).

54. The coroner will have the duty of notifying the finder, the occupier and the owner of the land where the find was made of the place and date when he intends to hold an inquest. These persons will be given an opportunity to examine witnesses at the inquest and may, according to the coroner's discretion, be represented at the inquest. Since it may not always be straightforward for the coroner to discover the identity of the landowner, the Act requires the coroner to ask the finder or the occupier who the landowner is and the coroner will then take reasonable steps to ensure that he is informed.

55. The inquest will be held without a jury unless the coroner, at his discretion, decides otherwise. In some cases the Crown and/or the national museum and/or the local museum or local archaeological officer (as identified in paragraph 51) may wish to be represented at the inquest. The recommendation in paragraph 43 about the desirability of keeping find-spots confidential applies.

56. If an object is found not to be treasure as a result of an inquest, then it will be returned by the coroner according to the principles set out on the return of objects that have been disclaimed in paragraph 47. The recommendation that relevant documentation be kept with the object and the conditions regarding the export of such objects in paragraph 48 also apply. The coroner will be informed by the Department of National Heritage about the decision taken by the Secretary of State in relation to the objects with which he has been concerned.

57. If a find is declared treasure and if the coroner is advised that a museum may wish to acquire either the whole find or an object from it, the coroner shall arrange for the find to be delivered to the national museum so that it can be valued by the Treasure Valuation Committee. (However, the coroner may ask the national museum to make arrangements regarding the delivery of fragile objects.)

58. The decision of the inquest will be subject to the jurisdiction of the courts by way of judicial review. In certain circumstances coroners' inquests may also be reviewed under section 13 of the Coroner's Act 1988.

59. The coroner or the body into whose care a find has been entrusted win take reasonable steps to ensure its safe custody and, in the event of an object being lost or damaged, except by the negligence of the party concerned, the Secretary of State may make an *ex gratia* payment to the person who would have been entitled to the reward under the guidelines contained in paragraphs 66-80 of this code, subject to a lower limit of £100.

H. Acquisition of Treasure

60. The current practice is that objects that are declared treasure trove are offered in the first instance by the Secretary of State to the national museum and that, if the national museum does not wish to acquire the objects, it offers them to other museums. This system will continue (subject to a review after three years: see paragraph 84), but the following procedures and principles will be followed by the national museum in dealing with finds of treasure:

(1) The Museum of London will have the first right to acquire any finds of treasure made within the franchise enjoyed by the Corporation of London. Bristol Museums and Art Gallery will enjoy a similar right in respect of any finds of treasure made within any franchise that may be held by the City of Bristol.

(2) Finds of national importance should be kept intact and will normally be acquired by the national museum. In England, it is expected that only a small proportion of finds of treasure will normally be classed as being of national importance. The national museum will consult the local registered museum[8] over such finds. In the event that a find of regional or local interest cannot be acquired by the local registered museum or by another registered museum, the national museum may then consider acquiring it.

---

8. This museum will already have been identified under the procedure outlined in paragraphs 38-41 and 46.

(3) In the case of other finds not of national importance there may also be good reasons both academically and archaeologically for keeping them intact. If the local registered museum wishes to acquire such a find intact, then it will have the opportunity to do so; if the local museum does not wish to acquire the find, it may be offered to another registered museum in the United Kingdom with a relevant interest in the objects contained in the find. When considering to which local registered museum a find will be offered, account will be taken of the collecting areas and collecting policies of any interested local museums. The documentation relating to the find will be copied to the museum that acquires it.

(4) If no museum wishes to acquire the find intact, then one or more of the museums listed in (2) above may wish to select some of the objects from the find for their collections by mutual agreement. Those objects that are not required by museums will be returned by the coroner according to the principles laid down in paragraph 47. The documentation relating to the whole find will be copied to each museum that acquires some objects from the find.

(5) There is a presumption that objects of treasure found during the course of archaeological excavations will be kept with the rest of the archaeological archive.

(6) A find from consecrated land that would have qualified as treasure trove under the common law of treasure trove, and which will therefore fall outside the scope of the order described in paragraph 16, will be offered to a local church museum (if there is one) if the national museum does not wish to acquire it.

(7) If finders and anyone else with an interest in the find wish to waive their right to a reward on condition that the find is deposited in a particular registered museum, their wishes will be taken into account.

(8) The references to 'registered' museums above are to museums with registration from the Museums and Galleries Commission. (9) The Department of National Heritage's review of museum policy, *Treasures in Trust*, was based on the premise that 'a museum's corrections are to be held on behalf of the public as inalienable cultural

assets' (3.2) and this applies to acquisitions of treasure. Any museum that acquires treasure may only dispose of it in accordance with the registration guidelines of the Museums and Galleries Commission (paragraph 4.2.5) (or its successor), and in accordance with any conditions on disposal imposed by any grant-awarding bodies that may have assisted in the acquisition of the object.

(10) It is expected that museums that acquire finds of treasure will generally wish to place them on exhibition. However, where finds of treasure are not on exhibition, finders and any other interested members of the public will have access to them on request, in accordance with the Museums and Galleries Commission's registration guidelines.

I. Valuation of Treasure

61. The Government strongly reaffirms the principle behind the establishment of the Treasure Trove Reviewing Committee, which was established in 1977 to provide independent scrutiny of valuations of finds of treasure, in the belief that it has worked very well. The Committee will therefore be retained; but it will be renamed the Treasure Valuation Committee in order to reflect more accurately its role. Its terms of reference will be to recommend to the Secretary of State valuations for the items brought before it which correspond as closely as possible, taking account of all relevant factors, to what may be paid for the object(s) in a sale on the open market between a willing seller and a willing buyer; and to provide advice to the Secretary of State in cases where there may be grounds for either no reward to be paid to the finder, or for a reduced reward to be paid, or where there is a dispute as to the apportionment of the reward between the finder and the occupier/owner of the land or between the occupier and a person having a superior interest (see paragraphs 64 and 71).

62. However, the Government recognises that it is important not just that the valuations agreed by the Committee should be fair but that they should be seen to be fair. Therefore, in order to ensure the widest possible confidence in treasure valuations, the Committee will commission reports from independent experts drawn from the trade on all finds that come before it, and the reports submitted by the national museums will cease to contain valuations but will simply contain a description of the objects. In most cases of treasure the valuations will be straightforward and it will be sufficient for the Committee to commission a single valuation, but the Committee will have the discretion to commission more than one valuation where it deems it to be desirable. All interested parties (finders, occupiers and landowners, if eligible for rewards, and any museum that intends to acquire objects from the find) will be given the opportunity to comment on these valuations and on the reports of the national museums before the Committee reaches its decision; in addition, finders and occupiers and landowners, if eligible for rewards, will continue to have the right to submit their own evidence to the Committee. Such evidence may be in the form of valuations commissioned by these parties.

63. It is important to bear in mind that a finder who fails to report a find of treasure in contravention of section 8 of the Act and sells it to a dealer is, besides committing an offence, likely also to obtain a much lower price for it than if he had reported it in the proper way. Reporting a find of treasure in accordance with the requirements of the Act is the best guarantee of receiving a fair reward.

64. In addition, the Secretary of State may request the Treasure Valuation Committee to investigate the circumstances where there may be any grounds for the abatement of the reward under the terms of paragraphs 79 and 80 and to make a recommendation.

65. Should an interested party (as defined in paragraph 62) be dissatisfied with the Committee's recommendation, that party will have the right to make representations to the Secretary of State before a decision is made. The Secretary of State will normally allow one month after the finder (or the occupier or landowner) has been notified of the Committee's recommendation to allow any representation to be made before making the order. The Secretary of State's decision will be subject to the jurisdiction of the courts by way of judicial review. Any claim of maladministration can be investigated by the Parliamentary Commissioner for Administration.

J. Rewards

I. Objectives
66. These guidelines replace the current practice in the payment of rewards for treasure trove, which was most recently re-stated in the *Report of a Review of Ex Gratia Awards to Finders of treasure Trove* (H M Treasury, 1988). The paramount objective in the payment of rewards for finds of treasure is to encourage the reporting of finds and to ensure that there are adequate incentives to finders while at the same time discouraging wrong behaviour. The Department of National Heritage will pay the reward to the person entitled to it according to the provisions in these guidelines. The Department will only make such payment after having received an equivalent sum of money from the museum or museums which wish to acquire the objects.

II. Guidelines for the payment of rewards where the finder is searching for artefacts

67. Where the finder has a valid permission from the occupier to be on the land where he made his find in order to search for and remove artefacts, he will receive the reward in full. The burden of proof as to whether he has permission will rest with the finder.

68. If it is established that the permission to enter the land was subject to the finder and occupier and/or the owner agreeing to share any reward, the Secretary of State will be prepared to apportion the reward with reference to the agreement. If there is a dispute as to the terms of such an agreement, the Secretary of State will determine what is appropriate. Where permission to enter land in order to search for treasure has been established, the burden of proving that it was subject to an agreement to share the proceeds of the reward will be with the occupier or the owner (where different).

69. There may be occasions where an occupier for the time being, because of the extent and nature of his interest in the land, did not have the capacity to give permission and should not have done so; for example, an agricultural tenant may be prohibited from authorising a treasure search under the terms of his tenancy. It is not thought appropriate to abate the finder's reward unless it appears to the Secretary of State that the finder was aware, or could reasonably have established, that the person who granted consent to enter into the land had no authority to do so. Where the Secretary of State does abate the finder's reward, the balance of the abated reward will be paid to the person who would have been entitled to give permission to enter the land to search for treasure (usually the owner).

70. Following from this, there may also be occasions where an occupier for the time being, because of the extent and nature of his interest in the land, would be liable to a person having a superior interest in the land for the proceeds of the sale of any object found on the land and the Secretary of State intends to give effect to this in making the reward. If there is a dispute as to how a reward should be apportioned between the occupier of the land and the person having the superior interest (usually the owner), the Secretary of State will determine what is appropriate.

71. Whenever there is a dispute as to whether a reward should be abated or as to how it should be apportioned, the Secretary of State will have regard to any representations made by the parties and may ask for advice from the Treasure Valuation Committee.

72. If there is more than one finder, that part of the reward to which they are entitled will be divided equally between them except where there is an agreement to the contrary.

73. If a finder does not remove the whole of a find from the ground but reports it, thus affording the opportunity for the archaeological excavation of the remainder of the find, the original finder will normally be eligible for a reward for the whole find and not just that part which he himself had removed from the ground, although the Secretary of State will need to examine the individual circumstances of each case.

74. Finders may expect to receive no rewards at all or abated rewards under the following circumstances:

(i)   where the finder has committed an offence under section 8 of the Act by failing to report treasure within 14 days of making the find or within 14 days of believing or of having reasonable grounds for believing that the find was treasure, without a reasonable excuse;

(ii)   where the finder has committed an offence under section 42 of the 1979 Ancient Monuments and Archaeological Areas Act (unauthorised use of a metal detector on a protected place) (see paragraph 29);

(iii) where there is evidence of illegal activity in relation to a find whether or not a prosecution has been mounted;

(iv)   where all the relevant circumstances surrounding a find, including the find-spot, were not reported;

(v)   where there is evidence that only part of a find has been handed in;

(vi)   where there are reasonable grounds for believing that a find was made elsewhere than on the alleged site;

(vii) where there are reasonable grounds for believing that the finder was trespassing;[9]

(viii) where significant damage has been done deliberately or recklessly either to the actual object, or to a surrounding monument or to the archaeological deposits making up the contexts which may explain the circumstances in which the object became buried or concealed, when the object was removed from the place where it was found;

(ix)   where there are other factors that the Secretary of State thinks it appropriate to take into account in individual cases.

It will be within the discretion of the Secretary of State to decide by how much the reward to the finder is to be abated in such circumstances or whether no reward will be payable at all to the finder.

75. In such circumstances the occupier or the landowner will be eligible for the whole of the balance of the reward in such proportion as the Secretary of State may determine, according to the principles laid down

9.   As regards finds made on the foreshore (that is the land between mean high water and mean low water), the Crown Estate confirms that a finder on Crown Estate foreshore will ordinarily be treated as being on the land with permission, that is, riot trespassing, but this implied permission does not include permission to search. (just over half of the foreshore on the coast of England, Wales and Northern Ireland is Crown land).

in paragraph 69, provided that there is no evidence that they have been a party to wrong behaviour on the part of the finder. The museum that acquires the find will only have to pay that part of the reward that is actually payable.

76. Rewards will not normally be payable when the find is made by an archaeologist. This will not affect any interest that the occupier or the landowner may have in any reward. (See also paragraph 49.)

III. Guidelines for the payment of rewards where the finder was not searching for artefacts

77. Where the finder, who has not been searching for artefacts, makes a chance find and where he clearly has permission to be where he made his find and where he has reported his find according to the law, then the reward will be divided in whatever proportions the Secretary of State thinks fit, taking account of the circumstances of each case. In most cases the finder may expect to receive half of the reward; that part of the reward for which the occupier and the landowner may be eligible will be divided between them according to the principles laid down in paragraph 69.

78. Where the finder has not been searching for artefacts and there are reasonable grounds for believing that the finder did not have permission to be where he made the find, then it may be appropriate for the reward to be divided between the finder, the occupier and the landowner, the Secretary of State being able to use discretion according to the individual circumstances of the case.

IV. Amount of abatement

79. Decisions about the level of rewards in individual cases will be taken in the light of the particular circumstances of each case and in making a decision the Secretary of State shall be guided by the recommendations of the Treasure Valuation Committee. In making its recommendations, the Committee shall seek to find a balance between the objective of those rewards to encourage the prompt and proper reporting of finds and the need for those rewards not themselves to provide an incentive for illegal

or improper behaviour. The Committee shall also take account of the archaeological and historical significance of the effect of illegal or improper behaviour involved in the specific circumstances of a particular case. In such cases the interested parties will have the opportunity to submit evidence to the Committee. The Secretary of State will notify the parties concerned of the decision, giving such reasons as may be necessary.

80. The Secretary of State's decision will be subject to the jurisdiction of the courts by way of judicial review. Any claim of maladministration can be investigated by the Parliamentary Commissioner for Administration.

K. Annual Report

81. The Act requires the Secretary of State to report to Parliament annually on the operation of the Act. This report will take the form of an annual report listing all cases of treasure and also those cases that have been disclaimed by the Secretary of State.

L. Speed of Handling Cases

82. The Government believes that it is very important that cases of treasure and potential treasure should be dealt with by all bodies concerned (museums, archaeologists and the police to whom such objects may be reported, coroners, the national museums, the Treasure Valuation Committee) as expeditiously as possible and urges these bodies to do all that they can to ensure this; as a general rule the target should be that the period between the find being received by the coroner or by the Organisation to whom he has directed that the find be delivered and the payment of an *ex gratia* reward should not be longer than twelve months, although it may be necessary to exceed this period in exceptional cases such as large hoards of coins or finds that present particular difficulties. The Department of National Heritage for its part undertakes to keep finders and other interested parties fully informed of the progress of their cases once a find has been declared to be treasure and a museum wishes to acquire it. The target time between a find having been valued and the payment of the reward should be three months or four months in cases where museums have to seek grants from other bodies, provided that no interested party (as defined in paragraph 62) makes a representation to the Secretary of State concerning the Treasure Valuation Committee's recommendation. In cases where finds are disclaimed before an inquest is held in accordance with the procedure laid down in paragraphs 45-48, the target time should be six months between the receipt of the find by the coroner or by the Organisation to whom he has directed that the find should be delivered and the coroner notifying his intention to return the object or, in the case of finds of single objects, three months.

83. This matter will be examined in the context of the review of the Code which it is proposed (paragraph 84) should be carried out after the Act has been in operation for three years.

M. Codes of Practice

84. The Act requires the Secretary of State to keep this Code under review. A review will be carried out once the Act has been in operation for three years and that review will consider whether any adjustments need to be made to the definition of treasure, according to the powers in section 2, and whether any revisions need to be made to this Code; it will examine, amongst other things, the target times for the handling of cases, the arrangements for the acquisition of finds set down in paragraph 60 and the valuation of treasure. Those bodies who have been consulted on this Code will also have the opportunity to participate in the review.

APPENDIX 1

Treasure Act 1996

CHAPTER 24

Arrangement of Sections

Meaning of "treasure"
Section
1. Meaning of "treasure".
2. Power to alter meaning.
3. Supplementary.

Ownership of treasure
4. Ownership of treasure which is found.
5. Meaning of "franchise".
6. Treasure vesting in the Crown.

Coroners' jurisdiction
7. Jurisdiction of coroners.
8. Duty of finder to notify coroner.
9. Procedure for inquests.

Rewards, codes of practice and report
10. Rewards.
11. Codes of practice.
12. Report on operation of Act.

Miscellaneous
13. Application of Act to Northern Ireland.
14. Consequential amendments.
15. Short title, commencement and extent.

ELIZABETH II c. 24

Treasure Act 1996

1996 CHAPTER 24

An Act to abolish treasure trove and to make fresh provision in relation to treasure. [4th July 1996.]

Be it enacted by the Queen's most Excellent Majesty, by and with the advice and consent of the Lords Spiritual and Temporal, and Commons, in this present Parliament assembled, and by the authority of the same as follows:

Meaning of Treasure
1. – (1) Treasure is –
(a) any object at least 300 years old when found which –
(i) is not a coin but has metallic content of which at least 10 per cent by weight is precious metal/
(ii) when found, is one of ate least two coins in the same find which are at least 300 years old at that time and have that percentage of precious metal; or
(iii) when found, is one of at least ten coins in the same find which are at least 300 years old at that time;
(b) any object at least 200 years old when found which belongs to a class designated under section 2(1);
(c) any object which would have been treasure trove if found before the commencement of section 4;
(d) any object which, when found is part of the same find as –
(i) an object within paragraph (a), (b) or (c) found at the same time or earlier; or
(ii) an object found earlier which would be within paragraph (a) or (b) if it had been found at the same time.
(2) Treasure does not include objects which are –
(a) unworked natural objects, or
(b) minerals as extracted from a natural deposit,
or which belong to a class designated under section 2(2).

2. – (1) The Secretary of State may by order, for the purposes of section 1(1)(b), designate any class of object which he considers to be of outstanding historical, archaeological or cultural importance.
(2) The Secretary of State may by order, for the purposes of section 1(2), designate any class of object which (apart from the order) would be treasure.
(3) An order under this section shall be made by statutory instrument.
(4) No order is to be made under this section unless a draft of the order has been laid before Parliament and approved by a resolution of each House.

3. – (1) This section supplements section 1.
(2) "Coin" includes any metal token which was, or can reasonably be assumed to have been, used or intended for use as or instead of money.
(3) "Precious metal" means gold or silver.
(4) When an object is found, it is part of the same find as another object if –

(a) they are found together,

(b) the other object was found earlier in the same place where they had been left together,

(c) the other object was found earlier in a different place, but they had been left together and had become separated before being found.

(5) If the circumstances in which objects are found can reasonably be taken to indicate that they were together at some time before being found, the objects are to be presumed to have been left together, unless shown not to have been.

(6) An object which can reasonably be taken to be at least a particular age is to be presumed to be at least that age, unless shown not to be.

(7) An object is not treasure if it is wreck within the meaning of Part IX of the Merchant Shipping Act 1995.

Ownership of treasure

4. – (1) When treasure is found, it vests, subject to prior interests and rights -

(a) in the franchisee, if there is one;

(b) otherwise, in the Crown.

(2) Prior interests and rights are any which, or which derive from any which–

(a) were held when the treasure was left where it was found, or

(b) if the treasure had been moved before being found, were held when it was left where it was before being moved.

(3) If the treasure would have been treasure trove if found before the commencement of this section, neither the Crown nor any franchise has any interest in it or right over it except in accordance with this Act.

(4) This section applies

(a) whatever the nature of the place where the treasure was found, and

(b) whatever the circumstances in which it was left (including being lost or being left with no intention of recovery).

5. – (1) The franchisee for any treasure is the person who –

(a) was, immediately before the commencement of section 4, or

(b) apart from this Act, as successor in title, would have been,

the franchisee of the Crown in right of treasure trove for the place where the treasure was found.

(2) It is as franchisees in right of treasure trove that Her Majesty and the Duke of Cornwall are to be treated as having enjoyed the rights to treasure trove which belonged respectively to the Duchy of Lancaster and the Duchy of Cornwall immediately before the commencement of section 4.

6. – (1) Treasure vesting in the Crown under this Act is to be treated as part of the hereditary revenues of the Crown to which section 1 of the Civil List Act 1952 applies (surrender of hereditary revenues to the Exchequer).

(2) Any such treasure may be transferred, or otherwise disposed of, in

accordance with directions given by the Secretary of State.

(3) The Crown's title to any such treasure may be disclaimed at any time by the Secretary of State.

(4) If the Crown's title is disclaimed, the treasure –

(a) is deemed not to have vested in the Crown under this Act, and

(b) without prejudice to the interests or rights of others, may be delivered to any person in accordance with the code published under section 11.

Coroners' jurisdiction

7. – (1) The jurisdiction of coroners which is referred to in section 30 of the Coroners Act 1988 (treasure) is exercisable in relation to anything which is treasure for the purposes of this Act.

(2) That jurisdiction is not exercisable for the purposes of the law relating to treasure trove in relation to anything found after the commencement of section 4.

(3) The Act of 1988 and anything saved by virtue of section 36(5) of that Act (saving for existing law and practice etc.) has effect subject to this section.

(4) An inquest held by virtue of this section is to be held without a jury, unless the coroner orders otherwise.

8. – (1) A person who finds an object which he believes or has reasonable grounds for believing is treasure must notify the coroner for the district in which the object was found before the end of the notice period.

(2) The notice period is fourteen days beginning with –

(a) the day after the find; or

(b) if later, the day on which the finder first believes or has reason to believe the object is treasure.

(3) Any person who fails to comply with subsection (1) is guilty of an offence and liable on summary conviction to -

(a) imprisonment for a term not exceeding three months;

(b) a fine of an amount not exceeding level 5 on the standard scale; or

(c) both.

(4) In proceedings for an offence under this section, it is a defence for the defendant to show that he had, and has continued to have, a reasonable excuse for failing to notify the coroner.

(5) If the office of coroner for a district is vacant, the person acting as coroner for that district is the coroner for the purposes of subsection (1).

9. – (1) In this section "inquest" means an inquest held under section 7.

(2) A coroner proposing to conduct an inquest must notify –

(a) the British Museum, if his district is in England; or

(b) the National Museum of Wales, if it is in Wales.

(3) Before conducting the inquest the coroner must take reasonable steps to

notify –
(a) any persons who it appears to him may have found the treasure; and
(b) any person who, at the time the treasure was found, occupied land which it appears to him may be where it was found;
(4) During the inquest the coroner must take reasonable steps to notify any such person not already notified.
(5) Before or during the inquest, the coroner must take reasonable steps -
(a) to obtain from any person notified under subsection (3) or (4) the names and addresses of interested persons; and
(b) to notify any interested person whose name and address he obtains.
(6) The coroner must take reasonable steps to give any interested person notified under subsection (3), (4) or (5) an opportunity to examine witnesses at the inquest.
(7) In subsections (5) and (6), "interested person" means a person who appears to the coroner to be likely to be concerned with the inquest –
(a) as the finder of the treasure or otherwise involved in the find;
(b) as the occupier, at the time the treasure was found, of the land where it was found, or
(c) as having had an interest in that land at that time or since.

Rewards, codes of practice and report
10. – (1) This section applies if treasure –
(a) has vested in the Crown under section 4; and
(b) is to be transferred to a museum.
(2) The Secretary of State must determine whether a reward is to be paid by the museum before the transfer.
(3) If the Secretary of State determines that a reward is to be paid, he must also determine, in whatever way he thinks fit –
(a) the treasure's market value;
(b) the amount of the reward;
(c) to whom the reward is to be payable; and
(d) if it is to be payable to more than one person, how much each is to receive.
(4) The total reward must not exceed the treasure's market value.
(5) The reward may be payable to –
(a) the finder or any other person involved in the find;
(b) the occupier of the land at the time of the find;
(c) any person who had an interest in the land at that time, or has had such an interest at any time since then.
(6) Payment of the reward is not enforceable against a museum or the Secretary of State.
(7) In a determination under this section, the Secretary of State must take into account anything relevant in the code of practice issued under section 11.
(8) This section also applies in relation to treasure which has vested in a

franchisee under section 4, if the franchisee makes a request to the Secretary of State that it should.

11. – (1) The Secretary of State must –
(a) prepare a code of practice relating to treasure;
(b) keep the code under review; and
(c) revise it when appropriate.
(2) The code must, in particular, set out the principles and practice to be followed by the Secretary of State –
(a) when considering to whom treasure should be offered;
(b) when making a determination under section 10; and
(c) where the Crown's title to treasure is disclaimed.
(3) The code may include guidance for –
(a) those who search for or find treasure; and
(b) museums and others who exercise functions in relation to treasure.
(4) Before preparing the code or revising it, the Secretary of State must consult such persons appearing to him to be interested as he thinks appropriate.
(5) A copy of the code and of any proposed revision of the code shall be laid before Parliament.
(6) Neither the code nor any revision shall come into force until approved by a resolution of each House of Parliament.
(7) The Secretary of State must publish the code in whatever way he considers appropriate for bringing it to the attention of those interested.
(8) If the Secretary of State considers that different provision should be made for –
(a) England and Wales, and
(b) Northern Ireland,
or that different provision should otherwise be made for treasure found in different areas, he may prepare two or more separate codes.

12. – As soon as reasonably practicable after each anniversary of the coming into force of this section, the Secretary of State shall lay before Parliament a report on the operation of this Act in the preceding year.

Miscellaneous
13. – In the application of this Act to Northern Ireland -
(a) in section 7 –
(I) in subsection (1), for "section 30 of the Coroners Act 1988" substitute "section 33 of the Coroners Act (Northern Ireland) 1959";
(ii) in subsection (3), for the words from "1988" to "practice etc.)" substitute "1959";
(b) in section 9(2), for the words from "British Museum" to the end substitute "Department of the Environment for Northern Ireland".

14. – (1) In section 33 of the Coroners Act (Northern Ireland) 1959 (inquest on treasure trove), for "treasure trove" substitute (treasure").

(2) In section 54(3) of the Ancient Monuments and Archaeological Areas Act 1979 (saving for rights in relation to treasure trove) for "in relation to treasure trove" substitute "under the Treasure Act 1996".

(3) In Article 42 of the Historic Monuments and Archaeological Objects (Northern Ireland) Order 1995 (reporting of archaeological objects) –

(a) after paragraph (1) insert –

"(10A) This Article does not apply in relation to an object if the person who found it believes or has reasonable grounds for believing that the object is treasure within the meaning of the Treasure Act 1996.";

(b) in paragraph (11)(a) for "treasure trove" substitute "any treasure within the meaning of the Treasure Act 1996".

(4) Subsections (2) and (3)(b) have effect in relation to any treasure found after the commencement of section 4.

(5) Subsection (3)(a) has effect in relation to any object found after the commencement of section 8.

15. – (1) This Act may be cited as the Treasure Act 1996.

(2) This Act comes into force on such day as the Secretary of State may by order made by statutory instrument appoint; and different days may be appointed for different purposes.

(3) This Act does not extend to Scotland.

APPENDIX 2

Government Announcement on Pilot Schemes for the Voluntary Recording of all Archaeological Finds (see paragraph 3)

Mr Iain Sproat MP, Minister of State, Department of National Heritage, made the following statement on 16 December 1996 in answer to a parliamentary question:

In the discussion document on Portable Antiquities published in February 1996 we sought views on proposals for a scheme for the recording of all archaeological finds, of which perhaps as many as 400,000 a year are currently being discovered, in the belief that there was an urgent need to improve the current arrangements. We received a total of 173 responses and I would like to pay tribute to the care which many of the respondents took with their replies. There is a great deal of invaluable advice in the responses which will guide us as we take the initiative forward. I would like in particular to single out the detailed statements from the Standing Conference on Portable Antiquities and the National Council for Metal Detecting. I have this morning placed copies of the responses in the Library of the

House and also my Department's Library.

Everyone who responded agreed on the importance of recording archaeological finds and on the need to improve the current arrangements, while the balance of opinion was strongly in favour of a voluntary rather than a compulsory system. This means that for the first time we have a broad consensus for the way in which this should be taken forward.

In the light of these responses and following further consultation by my Department, I can now announce that we intend to establish a two-year programme of pilot schemes to commence on 1 September 1997 and that we are making £50,000 available for the eight-month period that falls within the year 1997-98. The scheme will be coordinated directly by this Department and the funding will be channelled through the Museums and Galleries Commission. The aim of the pilot schemes will be to enable an accurate estimate to be made of the resources that would be needed to extend the scheme across the whole of England. The funding will be directed towards employing additional staff in three or four areas to record finds. Our first step will be to invite any suitable body –– museums but also perhaps County Planning Departments or other archaeological bodies – to express an interest in bidding for funding and we intend to do this early in the new year.

(Source: *Hansard*, 16 December 1996, WA 444-5.)

APPENDIX 3

Sources of Further Advice

A. CORONERS

Note: The information in this list is liable to change. The Department of National Heritage (0171 211 6000) will maintain a current list; alternatively addresses and telephone numbers of coroners can be found in the telephone directory (under 'Coroners') or by asking the police. Where an individual coroner has several addresses written communications should generally be sent to the first address.

District	*Address*	*Telephone Number*
1. England		
AVON	**Coroner – P E A Forrest**	
	Coroner's Court, Blackfields, Upper York Street,	Tel: 0117 942 8322
	Bristol BS2 8QP	Fax: 0117 944 5492
BEDFORDSHIRE	**Coroner — D S Morris**	Tel:01234275263/4
	Coroner's Office, Grayfriars, Bedford MK40 1HR	Fax: 01234 275266

Luton Police Station, Buxton Road,	Tel: 01582 394263
Luton LU1 1SD	Fax: 01582 394350

BERKSHIRE

East (Bracknell, Slough, Windsor and Maidenhead and Wokingham)

Coroner — R W Wilson

Thames Valley Police, Langley Police Station,	Tel: 01753 506531
Langley, Slough, Berks SL3 8NF	Fax: 01753 506527
Thames Valley Police, Bracknell Police Station	Tel: 01753 506731
Bracknell, Berks	Fax: 01753 506826
Thames Valley Police, Bridge Road,	Tel: 01753 506931
Maidenhead, Berks SL6 8LP	Fax: 01753 506960

Reading

Coroner — Dr A J Pim

The Mortuary, Royal Berkshire Hospital	Tel: 01189 863116
London Road, Reading RG1 5AN	Fax: 01189 863116

West (Newbury)

Coroner — C Hoile

Police Station, 20 Chapel Street, Thatcham,	Tel: 01235 776085
Berks RE18 4QL	Fax: 01235 776075

BUCKINGHAMSHIRE AND MILTON KEYNES

Buckinghamshire (Aylesbury Vale, Chiltern, South Bucks and Wycombe)

Coroner — R A Hulett

Thames Valley Police, Police Station	Tel: 01296 396531
High Wycombe, Bucks HP11 1BE	Fax: 01296 396512
Thames Valley Police, Police Station	Tel: 01753 506531
Langley, Slough, Berks SL3 8NF	Fax: 01753 506527
Thames Valley Police, Police Station,	Tel: 01296 396116
Wendover Road, Aylesbury, Bucks HP21 7LA	Fax:012965396116

Milton Keynes

Coroner – R H G Corner

Milton Keynes Police Station, 302 North Row,	Tel: 01908 686031
Witan Gate East, Central Milton Keynes	Fax: 01908 686160
MK9 2DS	

CAMBRIDGESHIRE

Cambridge: City and Southern (Cambridge City, East Cambs, South Cambs)

Coroner – J M Smith

Addenbrooke's Hospital, Cambridge	Tel: 01223 217101
Castle Court, Shire Hall, Cambridge, CB3 0AP	Tel: 01223 717587
	Fax: 01223 216980

Huntingdon

Coroner – D S Morris

11-13 Ferrars Road, Huntingdon,	Tel: 01480 456111
Cambs PE18 6DQ	Fax: 01480 455187

Northern (Fenland)

Coroner – W R Morris

1 and 2 York Row, Wisbech, Cambs PE13 1EA	Tel: 01945 461456
	Fax: 01945 63218

Peterborough	**Coroner – G S Ryall** Thorpe Wood Police Station, Peterborough, CambsTel: 01733 63232	
CHESHIRE	**Coroner – J F Hibbert** Griffiths Building, Bank Street, Warrington WA1 2AW	Tel: 01925 444216 Fax: 01925 444219
CORNWALL **East (North** Cornwall, Restormel)	**Coroner – Dr J D Bruce** Bodmin Police Station, Priory Road, Bodmin Cornwall PL31 2AA	Tel: 01208 79980 Fax: 01208 76513
Truro and West (Carrick, Kerrier, Penwith)	**Coroner— E T Carlyon** Police Station, Truro, Cornwall Police Station, Penzance, Cornwall	Tel: 01872 76211 Tel: 01736 331145
Isles of Scilly	**Coroner — D W Pepperell** Police Station, Penzance, Cornwall	Tel: 01736 331145
CUMBRIA **Furness** (Barrow- in-Furness, part of South Lakeland)	**Coroner – I Smith** Central Police Station, Market Street, Barrow-in-Furness, Cumbria LA14 2LE	Tel: 01229 848868 Fax: 01229 848899
North Eastern (Carlisle and parts of Allerdale and Eden)	**Coroner – I H Morton** Carlisle Police Station, Rickergate, Carlisle	Tel: 01228 28191
Southern (part of South Lakeland)	**Coroner — T C Prickett** Kendal Police Station, Kendal, Cumbria LA9 4RJ	Tel: 01539 722611 Fax: 01539 818799
Western (Copeland and parts of Allderdale and Eden)	**Coroner – J C Taylor** 38-42 Lowther Street, Whitehaven, Cumbria CA28 7JU	Tel:01946692461/3 Fax: 01946 692015
DERBYSHIRE **Derby and South** (Derby, Erewash and South Derbyshire and parts of Amber Valley and Derbyshire Dales)	**Coroner – P G Ashworth** 18 St Mary's Gate, Derby DE1 3JR	Tel: 01332 222159 Fax: 01332 294942
High Peak (High Peak and parts of Amber Valley and West Derbyshire)	**Coroner – C Rushton** 10 Buxton Road, Hazel Grove, Stockport SK7 6AD	Tel: 0161 419 9626 Fax: 0161 419 9604

Scarsdale   **Coroner – T Kelly**
(Chesterfield and   71 Saltergate, Chesterfield, Derbyshire S40 1JS   Tel: 01246 201391
North East   Fax: 01246 221081
Derbyshire)

DEVON
Exeter and East   **Coroner – R J Van Oppen**
(East Devon and   Raleigh Hall, Fore Street, Topsham,   Tel: 01392 876575
Exeter and parts of   Exeter EX1 2LR   Fax: 01392 876574
Mid Devon and
Teignbridge

North and West   **Coroner – B D Hall-Tomkin**
(North Devon,   Devon and Cornwall Constabulary, North Walk,   Tel: 01271 335222
Torridge and West   Barnstaple, Devon EX31 1DQ   Fax: 01271 335288
Devon and part of
Mid Devon

Plymouth and   **Coroner – D H B Bishop**
South West   Scott Lodge, Milehouse, Devonport,   Tel: 01752 500111
(Plymouth and   Plymouth PL2 3DD   Fax: 01732 563403
part of South Hams)

Torbay and South   **Coroner – H M Turner**
(Torbay and parts   2 Vaughan Parade, Torquay TQ2 5EF   Tel: 01803 296221
of South Hams and   Fax: 01803 296823
Teignbridge)   Torbay Hospital, Lawesbridge, Torquay TQ2 7AA Tel: 01803 655206

DORSET
Bournemouth,   **Coroner – N E N Neville-Jones**
Poole and Eastern   (Bournemouth) Divisional Police HQ,   Tel: 01292 222190
Dorset   Madeira Road, Bournemouth, Dorset
(Bournemouth,   (Poole) Central Police Station, Civic Centre,   Tel: 01202 223342
Christchurch, Poole Park Road, Poole, Dorset
Purbeck and
Wimborne)

Western (North   **Coroner – M C Johnston**
Dorset, West Dorset, The Coroner's Office, The Plocks, Blandford   Tel: 01305 223033
Weymouth and   Forum, Dorset DT11 7QB   Tel: 01258 453733
Portland)   Fax: 01258 455747

DURHAM
South (Darlington, **Coroner – C E Penne**
Sedgefield, Teesdale Police Office, St Cuthbert's Way, Darlington,   Tel: 01325 467681
and Wear Valley)   Co. Durham DL1 5LW   Fax: 01325 742110
    Police Office, Woodhouse Lane, Bishop   Tel: 01388 603566
    Auckland, Co. Durham DL14 6LB   Fax: 01325 742310

North
(Chester-le-Street, **Coroner – A Tweddle**
Derwentside, Police Station, New Elvet, Durham City   Tel: 0191 386 4222
Durham and Police Station, Stanley, Co. Durham   Tel: 01207 232144
Easington)

ESSEX
No. 1 District   **Coroner – W M Weir**
Basildon, Braintree, (Clacton) Police Station, Clacton on Sea,   Tel: 01235 221312
Brentwood, Essex C015 1ET   Fax: 01255 221312
Chelmsford,   ext: 16210
Colchester, Epping (Colchester) Colchester General Hospital,   Tel: 01206 832300
Forest, Harlow, Turner Road, Colchester, Essex C04 5JL   Fax: 01206 845628
Maldon, Tendring (Chelmsford) Police Station, New Street,   Tel: 01245 491212
Thurrock and Chelmsford, Essex CM1 1NF   Fax: 01245 491212
Uttlesford)   ext: 60826
                     (Basildon Grays) Basildon Hospital,   Tel: 01268 593770
                     Nethermayne, Basildon, Essex SS16 5NL   Fax: 01268 593754
                     (Harlow) 2 Orchard Croft, The Stow, Harlow, Tel: 01279 641212
                     Essex CM20 3BA   ext: 26201
                     (Romford) Oldchurch Hospital, Oldchurch   Tel: 01708 746431
                     Road, Romford, Essex PM7 OBE   Fax: 01708 757032

No. 2 District   **Coroner – P Dean**
(Castle Point, Rochford Police Station, South Street,   Tel:01702530911/
Rochford, Rochford, Essex SS4 1BL   547241
Southend-on-Sea)   Fax: 01702 530188

GLOUCESTERSHIRE
Cheltenham   **Coroner – A L Maddrell**
(Cheltenham and 107 Promenade, Cheltenham, Glos GL50 1NS   Tel: 01242 221064
Cotswold, parts of   Fax: 01242 226575
Stroud and Tewkesbury

Gloucester   **Coroner – D M Gibbons**
(Gloucester and 57 Westgate Street, Gloucester GL1 2NY   Tel: 01452 305661
Forest of Dean and   Fax: 01452 307935
parts of Stroud and
Tewkesbury)

HAMPSHIRE
Central   **Coroner – G A Short**
                     Coroner's Office, 19 St Peter Street, Winchester, Tel: 01962 844440
                     Hants S023 8BU   Fax: 01962 842300

North East   **Coroner – A M Bradley**
                     Police Station, London Road, Basingstoke,   Tel: 01256 473111
                     Hants   Fax: 01256 58199

Portsmouth and South East
Coroner – J R Kenroy
Kingston Crescent Police Station, Portsmouth, Hants P02 8BU
Tel: 01705 891517
Fax: 01705 891574

Southampton
Coroner – K S Wiseman
Coroner's Office, Police Station, Civic Centre, Southampton SO14 7LG
Tel: 01703 581111 ext 3149
Fax: 01703 223631

HEREFORD AND WORCESTER
Central (Worcester and Wychavon and part of Malvern Hills)
Coroner – V F Round
Coroner's Office, Police Station, Deansway, Worcester WR1 2JQ
Tel: 01905 723888 ext: 4943
Fax: 01905 723888 ext: 4943

North Eastern (Bromsgrove, Redditch and Wyre Forest)
Coroner – V F Round
Kidderminster Police Station, Mason Road, Kidderminster DY11 6AN
Police Station, Grove Street, Redditch
Tel: 01562 820888
Fax: 01562 583794
Tel: 01527 584888
Fax: 01527 68399

Western (Hereford, Leominster, South Herefordshire and part of Malvern Hills)
Coroner – D M Halpern
36/37 Bridge Street, Hereford HR4 9DJ
Tel: 01432 355301
Fax: 01432 356619

HERTFORDSHIRE
Hertford (Broxbourne and parts of East Herts, North Herts and Welwyn Hatfield)
Coroner – A Lawson
Eastern Coroner's Officers' Unit, Stevenage Police Station, Lytton Way, Stevenage, Herts SG1 1HF
Tel: 01438 757087
Fax: 01438 757037

Hitchin (Stevenage and parts of East Herts, North Herts and Welwyn Hatfield
Coroner – Dr J A S Vick
Eastern Coroner's Officers' Unit, Stevenage Police Station, Lytton Way, Stevenage, Herts SG1 1HF
Tel: 01438 757021
Fax: 01438 757037

St Albans, Watford and Hemel Hempstead (Hertsmere, St Albans, Watford, Dacorum and Three Rivers and part of Welwyn Hatfield)
Coroner – E G Thomas (St Albans, Watford and Hemel Hempstead)
Western Coroner's Officers' Unit, North Watford Police Station, North Orbital Road, Garston, Watford, Herts WD2 6ER
Tel: 01923 472336
Fax: 01923 472337

(Barnet/Bushey) Bushey Police Station, 43 Clay Hill, Bushey, Herts WD2 1AF
Tel: 0181 733 5387
Fax: 0181 733 5390

ISLE OF WIGHT	**Coroner – J A Matthews**	
	3-9 Quay Street, Newport, Isle of Wight	Tel: 01983 520697
	P030 5BB	Fax: 01983 520697

KENT

Ashford and	**Coroner — B N D Smith**	
Shepway	Teagues, High Street, Flimwell, Wadhurst,	Tel: 1580 879301
	East Sussex, TN5 7PA	Fax: 01580 879269
	(Ashford) Ashford Police Station, Tufton Street,	Tel: 01233 664880
	Ashford, Kent TN23 1BT	Fax: 01233 664880
	(Shepway) Folkestone Police Station,	Tel: 01303 289118
	Shorncliffe Road, Folkestone, Kent CT20 2SG	Fax: 01303 289117

East Kent	**Coroner – R H B Sturt**	
(Canterbury and	Canterbury Police Station, Old Dover Road,	Tel:01227817060/
Dover)	Canterbury, Kent CT1 3JQ	817110
		Fax: 01227 817109
	Dover Police Station, Ladywell, Dover,	Tel: 01304 218121
	Kent CT16 1DQ	Fax: 01304 218152

Mid Kent and	**Coroner – R J Sykes**	
Medway	Police Station, Palace Avenue,	Tel: 01622 608119
(Maidstone,	Maidstone ME15 6NF	Fax: 01622 608118
Gillingham,	Police Station, Painham, Gillingham,	Tel: 01634 385150
Rochester-upon-	Kent ME8 7LP	Fax: 01634 385159
Medway and Swale)		

North West	**Coroner – R L Hatch**	
(Dartford,	Tonbridge Police Station, Tonbridge, Kent	Tel: 01732 745007
Gravesham, Sevenoaks,		Fax: 01732 745009
Tonbridge and	Police Station, Instone Road, Dartford, Kent	Tel: 01322 283121
Malling and		Fax: 01322 283141
Tunbridge Wells)		

Thanet	**Coroner – Miss R M Cobb**	
	5 Lloyd Road, Broadstairs, Kent CT10 1HX	Tel: 01843 863260
		Fax: 01843 603927

LANCASHIRE

Blackburn,	**Coroner – A J A Rebello**	
Hyndburn and	7 Richmond Terrace, Blackburn,	Tel: 01254 263091
Ribble Valley	Lancashire BB7 1BB	Fax: 01254 681442
		e-mail: Fpsols@clara.net
	Coroner's Officer, Mortuary, Royal Infirmary,	Tel: 01254 294116
	Blackburn, Lancs	Fax: 01254 294563

Blackpool and	**Coroner – S G Lee**	
Fylde	Coroner's Office, 283 Church Street,	Tel: 01253 25731
	Blackpool, Lancs FY1 3PG	Fax: 01253 291915

East (Burnley, Pendle and Rossendale)	**Coroner – D A Smith** Mackenzie House, 68 Bank Parade, Burnley, Lancs BB11 1UB	Tel:01282422711/ 427601 Fax: 01282 36357
North (Lancaster and Wyre)	**Coroner – G C Howson** Lancs. Constabulary, Lancaster	Tel: 01524 596675
Preston and South West (Chorley, Preston, South Ribble and West Lancs)	**Coroner – M H McCann** Coroner's Office, Lawson Street, Preston, Lancs Ormskirk Police Station, 1 Derby Street, Ormskirk, Lancs Chorley Police Station, St Thomas's Road, Chorley, Lancs	Tel: 01772 258297 Tel: 01695 566365 Fax: 01695 566365 Tel: 01257 269021 Fax: 01257 269021

LEICESTERSHIRE

Leicester City and South (Blaby, Harborough, Leicester, Oadby and Wigston)	**Coroner – J M Symington** 10 New Street, Leicester LE1 ND Windsor Building, Leicester Royal Infirmary,	Tel: 0116 2516624 Fax: 0116 2514326 Tel: 0116 2586097 Fax: 0116 2586097
North (Charnwood, Hinckley and Bosworth, Melton, North West Leics and Rutland)	**Coroner – P J Tomlinson** 34 Woodgate, Loughborough, Leicestershire LE11 2TY	Tel: 0116 2484040 Fax: 01509 210744

LINCOLNSHIRE

Boston and Spalding (Boston and South Holland)	**Coroner – Miss M Taylor** Boston Police Station, Lincoln Lane, Boston, Lincs	Tel: 01205 366222 ext: 2217 Fax: 01205 356483
Grantham (part of South Kesteven)	**Coroner – T J Pert** Police Station, Stonebridge House, St Catherine's Road, Grantham, Lincs NG31 9DD	Tel: 01476 562501 Fax: 01476 567004
Lincoln (Lincoln and parts of North Kesteven and West Lindsay)	**Coroner – R Atkinson** Divisional Police HQ, West Parade, Lincoln LN1 1YP	Tel: 01522 885217 Fax: 01522 513110
Louth (parts of East and West Lindsay)	**Coroner – N A N Sharpley** Police Station, Eastfield Road, Louth, Lincs LN11 7AN	Tel: 01507 604744 or 01522 558490 Fax: 01522 558490

North and	**Coroner – J S Atkinson**	
Grimsby (North	25 Oswald Road, Scunthorpe, Lincs DN15 7PS	Tel: 01724 864215
East Lincs and		Fax: 01724 280253
North Lincs)	Police Station, Prince's Road, Cleethorpes, Lincs	Tel: 01472 204565
Sleaford (part of	**Coroner – R S R Warnes**	
North Kesteven)	Police Station, Stonebridge House, St Catherine's	Tel: 01476 562501
	Road, Grantham, Lincs NG31 9DD	Fax: 01476 567004
Spilsby (part of	**Coroner – S P G Fisher**	
East Lindsay)	Police Station, Eastfield Road, Louth,	Tel: 01507 604744
	Lincs LN11 7AN	or 01522 558490
		Fax: 01522 558490
Stamford (part of	**Coroner – G S Ryall**	
South Kesteven)	Police Station, Stonebridge House, St Catherine's	Tel: 01476 562501
	Road, Grantham, Lincs NG31 9DD	Fax: 01476 567004

LONDON, GREATER

City (Corporation	**Coroner – Dr D R Chambers**	
of London)	City of London Coroner's Court, Milton Court,	Tel: 0171 332 1598
	Moor Lane, London EC2Y 9BL	Fax: 0171 601 2714
East (Barking and	**Coroner – Dr H Price**	
Dagenham,	Coroner's Court, Queen's Road,	Tel: 0181 520 7245
Havering,	Walthamstow, E17 8QP	Fax: 0181 521 0896
Newham, Redbridge		
and Waltham Forest)		
Inner North	**Coroner – Dr S M T Chan**	
(Camden, Hackney,	St Pancras Coroner's Court, Camley Street,	Tel: 0171 387 4882
Islington and Tower	London NW1 OPP	Fax: 0171 383 2485
Hamlets)	Poplar Coroner's Court, 127 Poplar High Street,	Tel: 0171 987 3614
	London E14	Fax: 0171 538 0565
Inner South	**Coroner – Ms S Lynch**	
(Greenwich,	Southwark Coroner's Court, Tennis Street,	Tel: 0171 407 5611
Lambeth, Lewisham	London SE1 1YD	Fax: 0171 378 8401
and Southwark)	Lewisham Office	Tel: 0181 690 2327
		Fax: 0181 314 1230
	Greenwich Office	Tel: 0181 692 0530
		Fax: 0181 694 8692
Inner West	**Coroner – P A Knapman**	
(Kensington and	Westminster Coroner's Court, 65 Horseferry	Tel: 0171 834 6515
Chelsea, Merton	Road, London SW1P 2ED	Fax: 0171 828 2837
and Wandsworth)	Battersea Office, 48 Falcon Road,	Tel: 0171 228 6044
	London SW11 2LR	Fax: 0171 738 0640

North (Barnet, Brent, Enfield, Haringey and Harrow	**Coroner – Dr W F G Dolman**	
	Hornsey Coroner's Court, Myddelton Road, Hornsey N8 7PY	Tel: 0181 348 4411 Fax: 0181 347 5229
	Barnet General Hospital Mortuary, Wellhouse Lane, Barnet, Herts EN5 3DJ	Tel: 0181 732 4939
	Edgware Police Station, Whitchurch Lane, Edgware, Middlesex HA8 6LA	Tel: 0181 733 3567
	Southgate Police Station, 25 Chase Side, Southgate, London N14 5BW	Tel: 0181 345 4771

South (Bexley) Bromley, Croydon and Sutton	**Coroner – P B Rose**	
	Coroner's Court, The Law Courts, Barclay Road, Croydon CR9 3NE	Tel: 0181 681 5019 Fax: 0181 681 3491
	Bexley Office: Queen Mary's Hospital	Tel: 0181 300 3700 ext: 4004 Fax: 0181 300 3700
	Bromley Office	Tel: 0181 460 6015 Fax: 0181 460 6015
	Farnborough Office: Farnborough Hospital	Tel: 016898 56399 Fax: 016898 56399
	Sutton Office: Sutton Public Mortuary	Tel: 0181 641 3240 Fax: 0181 644 1709

West (Ealing, Hammersmith, Hillingdon, Hounslow, Richmond-upon-Thames and Kingston-upon-Thames)

Coroner – Dr J D K Burton
Hammersmith Coroner's Court, 25 Bagleys Lane, London SW6 2QA — Tel: 0171 371 9935 Fax: 0171 384 2762

MANCHESTER, GREATER

Manchester	**Coroner – L M Gorodkin**	
	Coroner's Court, Fire Station Premises, London Road, Manchester M1 2PH	Tel: 0161 236 4542 Fax: 0161 237 3479

North (Bury, Oldham and Rochdale)	**Coroner – B Williams**	
	Fourth Floor, Telegraph House, Baille Street, Rochdale OL16 1QY	Tel: 01706 49922 Fax: 01706 40720

South (Stockport, Tameside and Trafford)	**Coroner – J S Pollard**	
	(Trafford) Trafford General Hospital Mortuary, Davyhulme, Manchester	Tel: 0161 746 2504
	(Stockport) Stepping Hill Hospital Mortuary, Stockport	Tel: 0161 419 5632
	(Tameside) Tameside General Hospital Mortuary, Ashton under Lyne	Tel: 0161 331 6528

West (Bolton, Salford and Wigan)	**Coroner – M J Coppel** First Floor, Paderborn House, Civic Centre, Bolton BL1 1JW	Tel: 01204 527322 Fax: 01204 387674

MERSEYSIDE

Knowsley, St Helens and Sefton	**Coroner – G H H Glasgow** (Swefton North) Southport Police Station, Law Courts, Southport	Tel: 0151 777 3480
	(Sefton South) Maghull Police Station, Maghull, Liverpool	Tel: 0151 777 3380
	(Whiston and St Helens) Coroner's Office Whiston Hospital, Whiston, Merseyside	Tel: 0151 430 1238 Fax: 0151 426 6694
Liverpool	**Coroner – S R Barter** Coroner's Court, Castle Chambers, 43 Castle Street, Liverpool L2 9SH	Tel: 0151 777 4285 Fax: 0151 777 4289
Wirral	**Coroner – C W Johnson** Midland Bank Building, Grange Road, West Kirby, Wirral L48 4EB	Tel: 0151 624 6538 Fax: 0151 625 7757

NORFOLK

Dereham (parts of Breckland, Broadland, North Norfolk and South Norfolk)	**Coroner – J C M Starling** Coroner's Office, The Priory, Church Street, Dereham, Norfolk NP19 1DW	Tel: 01362 692424 Fax: 01362 698858
Diss and Great Yarmouth (Great Yarmouth and parts of Breckland and South Norfolk)	**Coroner – K M Dowding** 11 Queen Street, Great Yarmouth, Norfolk NR30 2QW Paget Hospital, Lowestoft Road, Gorleston, Great Yarmouth, Norfolk	Tel: 01493 855555 Fax: 01493 330055 Tel: 01493 452477 Fax: 01493 452177
Kings' Lynn (King's Lynn and West Norfolk)	**Coroner – W R Knowles** King's Lynn Police Station, St James Street, King's Lynn, Norfolk PE30 5DE Queen Elizabeth Hospital, Gayton Road, King's Lynn, Norfolk PE30 4ET	Tel: 01553 691211 Fax: 01553 769084 Tel: 01553 613613 Fax: 01553 613700
Norwich (Norwich and parts of Broadland, North Norfolk and South Norfolk)	**Coroner – W J Armstrong** Dencora House, Theatre Street, Norwich NR1 2PG	Tel: 01603 276910 Fax: 01603 633051

NORTHAMPTONSHIRE

	Coroner – Mrs A Pember (Northampton) Campbell Square Police Station,	Tel: 01604 703618

	Northampton NN1 3EB	Fax: 01604 703716
	(Kettering) Kettering Police Station	Tel: 01536 511653
	Road, Kettering, Northants NN15 7PQ	Fax: 01536 510474

NORTHUMBERLAND

North (Alnwick and Berwick-upon-Tweed and parts of Castle Morpeth and Wansbeck)
Coroner – I G McCreath
Northumbria Police, Lintonville Terrace, Ashington, Northumberland NE63 8HD
Tel: 01661 872555 ext: 61654

South (Blyth Valley and Tynedale and parts of Castle Morpeth and Wansbeck)
Coroner – C B Gallon
1 Stanley Street, Blyth, Northumberland NE24 2BS
Tel: 01670 354777
Fax: 01670 355951

NOTTINGHAMSHIRE

Coroner – Dr N D Chapman
The Guildhall, Burton Street, Nottingham NG1 4BN
Tel: 0115 941 2322
Fax: 0115 950 0141

OXFORDSHIRE
Coroner – N G Gardiner
(City) Coroner's Office, New Post Mortem Suite, John Radcliffe Hospital, Headley Way, Oxford OX3 9DU
Tel: 01865 744011
Fax: 01865 742453

(North) Police Station, Thames Valley Police, Warwick Road, Banbury, Oxon OX16 7AE
Tel: 01865 266658
Fax: 01865 266612

(South West) Police Station, Thames Valley Police, Bridge Street, Abingdon, Oxon OX14 3HW
Tel: 01235 776631
Fax: 01235 776612

(South) Police Station, Thames Valley, Market Place, Henley-on-Thames, Oxon OX5 2NX
Tel: 01734 536509
Fax: 01734 536506

THE ROYAL HOUSEHOLD
Coroner – Dr J D K Burton
Hammersmith Coroner's Court, 25 Bagleys Lane, London SW6 2QA
Tel: 0171 371 9935/8
Fax: 0171 384 2762

SHROPSHIRE

East (The Wrekin and parts of Bridgnorth and North Shropshire)
Coroner – M T Gwynne
Police Station, Wellington, Telford, Shropshire
Tel: 01952 256464

Mid and North West (Shrewsbury and Atcham, Oswestry and part of North Shropshire)
Coroner – R D Crawford-Clarke
West Mercia Constabulary, Police HQ, Clive Road, Monkmoor, Shrewsbury SY2 5RW
Tel: 01743 264711
Fax: 01743 264735

South (South   **Coroner – A F T Sibcy**
Shropshire and part 18 Broad Street, Ludlow, Shropshire SY8 1NG   Tel: 01584 873918
of Bridgnorth)   Fax: 01584 876787

SOMERSET
Eastern (Mendip   **Coroner – N L Rheinberg**
and South Somerset) Avon and Somerset Constabulary, Horsey Lane,   Tel: 01935 402128
   Yeovil, Somerset   Fax: 01935 402184

Western   **Coroner – M R Rose**
(Sedgemoor,   Police Station, Shuttern, Taunton,   Tel: 01823 363271
Taunton Deane   Somerset TA1 3QA   Fax: 01823 363215
and West Somerset)

STAFFORDSHIRE
North (Newcastle-   **Coroner – E J Wain**
under-Lyme,   Coroner's Court and Chambers, 547 Hartshill   Tel: 01782 711666
Staffordshire   Road, Hartshill, Stoke-on-Trent,   Fax: 01782 714620
Moorlands and   Staffordshire ST4 6HF
Stoke-on-Trent and
part of Stafford)

South (Cannock   **Coroner – R A Browning**
Chase, East Staffs,   (Stafford) Stafford Borough Police Station,   Tel: 01785 234083
Lichfield, South   Eastgate Street, Stafford
Staffs, Tamworth   (Cannock), Rugeley Police Station, Anson
and part of Stafford) Street, Rugeley, Staffs   Tel: 01785 234319
   (Burton on Trent) Stapenhill Police Station,   Tel: 01785 234783
   Stapenhill, Burton on Trent, Staffs

SUFFOLK   **Coroner – N St J Watkins**
Ipswich (Ipswich   Ipswich Police Station, Civic Drive,   Tel: 01473 383167
and parts of   Ipswich IP1 2AW   Fax: 01473 281300
Babergh, Suffolk
Coastal and Mid Suffolk)

Lowestoft (Waveney **Coroner – A G Leguen de Lacroix**
and parts of Mid   Suffolk Police, Old Nelson Street,   Tel: 01986 835167
Suffolk and Suffolk Lowestoft, Suffolk NR32 1PE   or 01502 562121
Coastal)

West (Forest Heath, **Coroner – H B Walrond**
St Edmundsbury   Police Headquarters, Raingate Street,   Tel: 01284 774167
and parts of   Bury St Edmunds, Suffolk
Babergh and Mid Suffolk)
   The Mortuary, West Suffolk Hospital,
   Bury St Edmunds, Suffolk   Tel: 01284 713686

SURREY	**Coroner – M J C Burgess**	
	Weybourne House, St Peter's Hospital,	Tel: 01932 874136
	Guildford Road, Chertsey, Surrey KT16 OPZ	Fax: 01932 874757
	Police Station, Margaret Road,	
	Guildford, Surrey GU1 4BR	Tel: 01483 31111
	Police Station, 79 Reigate Road, Reigate,	
	Surrey RH2 ORY	Tel: 01737 765040
	Epsom General Hospital, Dorking Road,	
	Epsom, Surrey	Tel: 01372 735264
	Camberley Police Station, Portesbury Road	
	Camberley, Surrey GU15 3SZ	Tel: 01276 677598
	Ashford General Hospital, London Road,	
	Ashford, Surrey	Tel: 01784 255503

SUSSEX, EAST AND BRIGHTON

Hastings, Rother	**Coroner – D Wadman**	
and Eastbourne,	Eastbourne District	
Wealden and	Police Station, Grove Road, Eastbourne,	Tel: 01323 414007
Lewes	East Sussex BN21 4UF	Fax: 01323 414048
	Hastings and Rother District	
	Police Station, Bohemia Road, Hastings,	Tel: 01424 456009
	East Sussex TN34 1BT	Fax: 01424 456009
	Wealden and Lewes District	Tel: 01323 414067
	Police Station, Hailsham, East Sussex	Fax: 01323 414038
Brighton and	**Coroner – Ms V Hamilton-Deeley**	
Hove	Brighton Police Station, John Street,	Tel: 01273 606744
	Brighton, East Sussex BN2 2LA	Fax: 01273 665543
SUSSEX, WEST	**Coroner – R J Stone**	
	Police Station, Kingsham Road, Chichester,	Tel: 01243 520217
	W Sussex	Fax: 01243 520270
	Police Station, Union Place, Worthing,	Tel: 01243 843507
	W Sussex	Fax: 01234 843546
	Police Station, Bolnore Road, Haywards Heath,	Tel: 01444 445808
	West Sussex	Fax: 01444 445857
	Police Station, Hurst Road, Horsham,	Tel: 01243 520286
	West Sussex	Fax: 01243 520315

TEESSIDE

Central and East	**Coroner – M J F Sheffield**	
(Redcar and	Police HQ, Ladgate Lane, Middlesborough	Tel: 01642 326326
Cleveland,	TS8 9EH	Fax: 01642 60521
Middlesborough, Stockton-on-Tees)		
North (Hartlepool)	**Coroner – O J Bjorkeroth**	
	Police HQ, Ladgate Lane, Middlesbrough	Tel: 01642 326032
	TS8 9EH	Fax: 01642 301115

TYNE AND WEAR

South Tyneside
(Gateshead and
South Tyneside)

Coroner – W Duffy
Northumbria Police HQ, Keppel Street,
South Shields
Northumbria Police HQ, High West Street,
Gateshead

Tel: 0191 510 2020
Fax: 0191 563 5139
Tel: 0191 232 3451
Fax: 0191 221 9188

Newcastle upon Tyne

Coroner – L Coyle
Coroner's Court, Bolbec Hall, Westgate Road,
Newcastle upon Tyne NE1 1SE

Tel: 0191 261 2845
Fax: 0191 261 2952

North Tyneside

Coroner – C B Gallon
1 Stanley Street, Blyth, Northumberland
NE24 2BJ

Tel: 01670 354777
Fax: 01670 355951

Sunderland

Coroner – M C Shaw
Police HQ, Gillbridge Avenue, Sunderland

Tel: 0191 454 7555

WARWICKSHIRE

Coroner – M F Coker
(Warwick) Police Station, Priory Road,
Warwick CV34 4NA
(Stratford upon Avon) Police Station,
Rother Street, Stratford upon Avon
CV37 6PD
(Nuneaton) Police Station, Vicarage Street,
Nuneaton CV11 4DW

(Rugby) County Police Office,
Newbold Road, Rugby CV21 2DH

Tel: 01926 415628
Fax: 01926 415724
Tel: 01926 451111
ext: 4156
Fax: 01926 415755
Tel: 01203 641111
ext: 3149
Fax: 01926 415756
Tel: 01926 451111
ext: 3749
Fax: 01926 415752

WEST MIDLANDS

Birmingham
(Birmingham and
Solihull

Coroner – Dr R M Whittington
Coroner's Court, 50 Newton Street,
Birmingham B4 6NE

Tel: 0121 235 3920
Fax: 0121 233 4841

Coventry

Coroner – D R Sarginson
Police HQ, Little Park Street, Coventry

Tel: 01203 539018
Fax: 01203 539804

Dudley

Coroner – V F Round
Dudley Police Station, New Street,
Dudley DY1 2LZ

Tel: 0121 626 8018
Fax: 0121 626 8914

Sandwell North

Coroner – D L Prichard
Smethwick Police Station, Piddock Road,
Smethwick, Warley, West Midlands B66 3BL

Tel: 0121 626 9036
Fax: 0121 626 9060

Sandwell South — Coroner – P J Turner
Smethwick Police Station, Piddock Road, Smethwick, Warley, West Midlands B66 3BL
Tel: 0121 626 9186
Fax: 0121 626 9060

Walsall — Coroner – A K Cotter
Kelvin House, 23 Lichfield Street, Walsall, West Midlands WS1 1UL
Tel: 01922 725515
Fax: 01922 643403
Police Station, Green Lane, Walsall, W Midlands
Tel: 01922 439019
Fax: 01922 439223

Wolverhampton — Coroner – S King
Police Station, Bilston Street, Wolverhampton, W Midlands
Tel: 01902 649018
Fax: 01902 649202

WILTSHIRE — Coroner – D C Masters
Lloyds Bank Chambers, 6 Castle Street, Salisbury, Wilts SP1 1BB
Tel: 01722 326870
Fax: 01722 332223
Divisional Police HQ, Wilton Road, Salisbury, Wiltshire SP2 7HP
Tel: 01722 435293
Fax: 01722 435291
County Police Station, New Park Street, Devizes Wiltshire SN1O 1DZ
Tel: 01380 728885
Fax: 01380 720775
Divisional Police HQ, Prince's Street, Swindon, Wiltshire SN1 2HZ
Tel: 01793 507841
Fax: 01793 507840

YORKSHIRE, EAST
East Riding and Kingston upon Hull — Coroner – Dr R M Butler
Coroner's Court and Office, Essex House, Manor Street, Kingston upon Hull HU1 1YU
Tel:01482 613009/ 613011
Fax: 01482 613020

YORKSHIRE, NORTH
Eastern (Hambleton, Scarborough and Ryedale) — Coroner – M D Oakley
Scarborough Police, Northway, Scarborough, North Yorkshire
Tel: 01723 509332
Fax: 01723 509813
Police Station, 72 High Street, Northallerton, North Yorkshire DL7 SBR
Tel: 01609 789458
Fax: 01609 789413

Western (Craven, Harrogate, Richmondshire and Selby) — Coroner – J D Cave
Divisional Police HQ, North Yorkshire Police, North Park Road, Harrogate, North Yorkshire HG1 5PJ
Tel: 01423 539332
Fax: 01423 539313

York — Coroner – W D F Coverdale
North Yorkshire Police Divisional HQ, Fulford Road, York YO1 4BY
Tel: 01904 669332
Fax: 01904 669313
York District Hospital, Wigginton Road, York YO3 7HE
Tel: 01904 453044
Fax: 01904 454332

YORKSHIRE, SOUTH

East (Doncaster and **Coroner – E S Hooper**
Rotherham)

(Doncaster) Coroner's Court and Office,	Tel: 01302 385031
5 Union Street, Off Sepulchre Gate West,	Fax: 01302 364833
Doncaster DN1 3AE	
(Rotherham) Police Station, Main Street,	Tel: 01709 832031
Rotherham S60 1QU	Fax: 01709 832185

West (Barnsley and **Coroner – C P Dorries**
Sheffield)

(Sheffield) Medico-Legal Centre, Watery Street,	Tel: 0114 273 8721
Sheffield S3 7ET	Fax: 0114 272 6247
(Barnsley) Police Station, Churchfield,	Tel: 01226 736031
Barnsley, South Yorks	Fax: 01226 736295

YORKSHIRE, WEST

Eastern (Leeds and **Coroner – D Hinchliff**
Wakefield)

(Wakefield) 71 Northgate, Wakefield WF1 3BS	Tel: 01924 293237
	Fax: 01924 291603
(Pontefract) Pontefract Police Station, Ream	Tel: 01977 301060
House, Ream Terrace, Pontefract WF8 1DP	Fax: 01977 79231
(Otley) Otley Police Station, Bridge Street,	Tel: 01943 858037
Otley LS21 3BA	Fax: 01943 85802
(Leeds Central) Pearl Chambers,	Tel: 0113 241 4103
22 East Parade, Leeds LS1 5BY	Fax: 0113 244 851
(Morley) Morley Police Station,	Tel: 0113 238 2037
Corporation Street, Morley, Leeds LS27 9NB	Fax: 0113 238 2012

Western (Bradford, **Coroner – R Ll Whittaker**
Calderdale and
Kirklees)

(Bradford) West Yorkshire Police HQ, The Tyrls,	Tel: 01274 373037
Bradford, West Yorks	
(Keighley) West Yorkshire Police, Keighley	Tel: 01535 617057
Division, Keighley, Dewsbury	
(Dewsbury) West Yorkshire Police, Dewsbury	Tel: 01924 431037
Division, Aldams Road, Dewsbury	
(Huddersfield) West Yorkshire Police,	Tel: 01484 436700
Huddersfield Division, Civic Centre,	
Huddersfield	
(Halifax) Coroner's Office, 8 Carlton Street,	Tel: 01422 354606
Halifax HX1 2AL	

2. Wales

BRIDGEND AND **Coroner – P M Walters**
GLAMORGAN
VALLEYS

Police Station, Swan Street, Merthyr Tydfil	Tel: 01658 724228
	Fax: 01658 724262
Police Station, Berw Road, Pontypridd	Tel: 01443 743698
	Fax: 01443 743624

CARDIFF AND THE VALE OF GLAMORGAN	**Coroner – Dr L S Addicott** Coroner's Court, Central Police Station, Cathay's Park, Cardiff CF1 3NN	Tel: 01222 222111 exts: 20 and 390 Fax: 01222 220638

CARMARTHENSHIRE

	Coroner – W J Owen Police HQ, Waunlanyrafon, Llanelli, Dyfed	Tel: 01554 772222 Fax: 01554 741118
	Police Station, Friars Park, Carmarthen, Dyfed	Tel: 01267 232000 Fax: 01267 234262

CEREDIGION	**Coroner – P L Brunton** Aberystwyth Police Station, Boulevard Street, Brieuc, Aberystwyth SY23 1PH	Tel: 01970 612791 Fax: 01970 625174
GWENT	**Coroner – D T Bowen** Victoria Chambers, 11 Clytha Park Road, Newport, Gwent NP9 4PB	Tel: 01633 264194 Fax: 01633 841146
NEATH PORT TALBOT	**Coroner – Dr D J Osborne** South Wales Police, Pontardawe Police Station, High Street, Pontardawe, Swansea SA8 3JL Coroner's Office, Sybil Street, Clydach, Swansea SA6 5EU	Tel: 01792 562784 Fax: 01792 562750 Tel: 01792 845058 Fax: 01792 844902
NORTH EAST WALES (Wrexham County Borough and Flintshire)	**Coroner – J B Hughes** Police Station, Bodhyfryd, Wrexham, Clwyd	Tel: 01978 290222
NORTH WALES CENTRAL (Denbighshire and Conwy)	**Coroner – J B Hughes** Police Station, Prestatyn	Tel: 01978 290222
NORTH WEST WALES (Gwynedd and Anglesey)	**Coroner – D P Pritchard Jones** 19 Bangor Street, Caernarfon, Gwynedd LL55 1AW	Tel: 01286 673387 Fax: 01286 672804
	Bangor Police Station, Garth Road, Bangor, Gwynedd	Tel: 01248 370333

PEMBROKESHIRE

	Coroner – M S Howells 25 Hamilton Terrace, Milford Haven, Pembs SA73 3JJ	Tel: 01646 698129 Fax: 01646 690607

POWYS	Coroner – J Hollis	
	Milwyn, Jenkins and Jenkins, Mid Wales House	Tel: 01686 412166
	Great Oak Street, Llanidloes SY18 6BN	Fax: 01686 413580

SWANSEA	Coroner – J R Morgan	
	Central Police Station, Alexandra Road,	Tel: 1792 456999
	Swansea	
	and	
	Calvert House, Calvert Terrace, Swansea	Tel: 01792 655178
	SA1 6AP	Fax: 01792 467002

B. SITES AND MONUMENTS RECORDS AND LOCAL GOVERNMENT ARCHAEOLOGISTS

Note: The information in this list is liable to change. The Royal Commission on the Historical Monuments of England (National Monuments Record Centre, Kemble Drive, Swindon, Wilts SN2 2GZ, Tel: 01793 414700) maintains a current list of all Sites and Monuments Records.

1. England
BEDFORDSHIRE

Sites and Monuments Record Officer, Heritage Group, Planning	Tel:01234228071/2
Department, County Hall, Cauldwell Street, Bedford MK42 9AP	Fax: 01234 228232

Luton

Curator, Luton Museum Service, Wardown Park, Luton LU2 7HA	Tel: 01582 546719
	Fax: 01582 746763

BERKSHIRE

Sites and Monuments Record Officer, Babtie Group, Shire Hall,	Tel: 01189 234914
Shinfield Park, Reading PG2 9XG	Fax: 01189 310268

BUCKINGHAMSHIRE

County Archaeologist, Buckinghamshire County Museum, Technical	Tel: 01296 696012
Centre, Tring Road, Halton, Aylesbury HP22 5PJ	Fax: 01296 696012

CAMBRIDGESHIRE

Senior Archaeologist (Sites and Monuments Record), Archaeology	Tel:01223317436/
Section, Cambridgeshire County Council, Castle Court, Shire Hall,	717312
Cambridge CB3 OAP	Fax: 01223 362425

CHESHIRE

Sites and Monuments Record Officer, Cheshire County Council,	Tel: 01244 603160
Environmental Planning Service, Commerce House, Hunter Street,	Fax: 01244 603110
Chester CH1 2QP	

Chester
City Archaeologist, Chester City Council, The Forum,
Chester CH1 2HS
Tel: 01872 323603

CORNWALL
County Archaeologist, Cornwall Archaeological Unit,
Kennall Building, Old County Hall, Station Road, Truro TR1 3AY
Tel: 01872 323603
Fax: 01872 323804

CUMBRIA
Sites and Monuments Record Officer, Cumbria County Council,
Economy and Environment, County Offices, Kendal LA9 4PQ
Tel:01539773432/
773428
Fax: 01539 726276

DERBYSHIRE
Sites and Monuments Record Officer, Planning Department,
Derbyshire County Council, County Offices, Matlock DE4 3AG
Tel: 01629 580000
ext: 7125
Fax: 01629 580119

DEVON
Sites and Monuments Register, Environment Department, Devon
County Council, County Hall, Topsham Road, Exeter EX2 4QW
Tel: 01392 382266
Fax: 01392 382135

Exeter
Archaeology and Planning Officer, Planning Services, Exeter City
Council, Civic Centre, Paris Street, Exeter EX1 1NN
Tel: 01392 265223
Fax: 01392 265180

North Devon
North Devon Museums Service, Museum of North Devon,
The Square, Barnstaple EX32 8LN
Tel: 01271 46747
Tel: (01271 346747
from Sept. 1997)

Plymouth
Archaeological Officer, Plymouth City Council, Environmental
Planning and Design, Directorate of Development, Civic Centre
Armada Way, Plymouth PL1 2EW
Tel: 01752 264818
Fax: 01752 264931

DORSET
Sites and Monuments Record Officer, Environmental Services
Directorate, County Hall, Colliton Park, Dorchester DT1 1XJ
Tel:01305224921/
224277
Fax: 01305 224914

DURHAM
Sites and Monuments Record, Arts, Libraries and Museums, Durham
County Council, County Hall, Co Durham DH1 5TY
Tel: 0191 383 4212
Fax: 0191 384 1336

ESSEX
Sites and Monuments Record Officer, Essex Planning Department,
County Hall, Chelmsford CM1 1LF
Tel: 01245 492211
ext: 51637
Fax: 01245 258353

Chelmsford
Keeper of Archaeology, Chelmsford Museums Service, Old Cemetery
Lodge, 1 Writtle Road, Chelmsford CM1 3BL
Tel: 01245 281660
Fax: 01245 280642

Colchester
Curatorial Services Manager, Colchester Borough Council Museums
Service, Museum Resource Centre, 14 Ryegate Road,   Tel:01206282931/2
Colchester CO1 1YG   Fax: 01206 282925

GLOUCESTERSHIRE
Sites and Monuments Record Officer, Environment Department, Tel: 01452 425705
Gloucestershire County Council, Shire Hall, Gloucester GL1 2TH Fax: 01452 425356

Bristol
City Archaeologist, Bristol City Council, Planning and Development Tel: 0117 922 3044
Services, Brunel House, St George's Road, Bristol BS1 5UY

Gloucester
Director, Gloucester Archaeology, City Museum, Brunswick Road, Tel: 01452 526342
Gloucester GL1 1HP   Fax: 01452 503050

South Gloucestershire
Archaeological Officer, South Gloucestershire Council, c/o Civic Tel: 01454 863649
Centre, High Street, Kingswood, Bristol BS15 2TR

HAMPSHIRE
Sites and Monuments Record Officer, Environment Group, Tel: 01962 846735
The Castle, Winchester SO23 8UE Fax: 01962 846776

Southampton
Archaeological Officer, Archaeology Section, Tower House, Tel: 01703 832242
Town Quay, Southampton SO1 1LX

Test Valley
Field Director, Test Valley Archaeological Trust, Orchard House, Tel: 01794 515775
Orchard Lane, Romsey, Hants SO51 8DP

Winchester
City Archaeologist, Winchester Museum Service, Historical Resources Tel: 01962 848269
Centre, 75 Hyde Street, Winchester SO23 7DW Fax: 01962 848299

HEREFORD AND WORCESTER
Sites and Monuments Record Officer, County Archaeological Tel: 01905 611086
Service, Hereford and Worcester County Council, Tolladine Road, Fax: 01905 29054
Worcester WR4 9NB

Worcester
Archaeological Officer, Worcester City Museum, Queen Elizabeth Tel: 01905 722369
House, Trinity Street, Worcester WR1 2PW Fax: 01905 722350

HERTFORDSHIRE
Sites and Monuments Record Officer, Environment Department, Tel: 01992 555244/5
County Hall, Hertford SG13 8DN Fax: 01992 555251

North Hertfordshire
Keeper of Field Archaeology, North Hertfordshire District Council, Tel:01462456305/
North Hertfordshire Museums Service, Museums Resource Centre, 434896
Burymead Road, Hitchin SG5 1RT Fax: 01462 434883

St Albans
District Archaeologist, City and District of St Albans, Planning and Tel: 01727 819252
Heritage Department, Civic Centre, St Peter's Street, Fax: 01727 863282
St Albans AL1 3JE

HUMBERSIDE
Sites and Monuments Record Officer, Humberside Archaeology Tel: 01482 217466
Partnership, The Old School, Northumberland Avenue, Kingston Fax: 01482 531897
upon Hull HU2 OLN

ISLE OF WIGHT
Archaeological Officer, Isle of Wight Archaeological Centre, 61 Tel: 01983 529963
Clatterford Road, Carisbrooke, Newport, Isle of Wight P030 1NZ Fax: 01983 823810

KENT
Sites and Monuments Record Officer, Kent Planning Department, Tel:01622696096/
Springfield, Maidstone ME14 2LX 671411
Fax: 01622 687620

LANCASHIRE
Sites and Monuments Record Officer, Lancashire County Council Tel:01772261550/1
Planning Department, PO Box 160, East Cliff County Offices, Fax: 01772 264201
Preston PR1 3EX

LEICESTERSHIRE AND RUTLAND
Keeper of Archaeology, Leicestershire County Council, County Tel: 0116 265 6791
Hall, Glenfield, Leicester Fax: 0116 265 6788

Leicester
Sites and Monuments Record Officer, Jewry Wall Museum, Tel: 0116 247 3023
St Nicholas Circle, Leicester LE1 7BY Fax: 0116 251 2257

LINCOLNSHIRE
Lincolnshire Sites and Monuments Record Officer, Lincolnshire Tel: 01522 575292
City and County Museum, 12 Friars Lane, Lincoln LN2 5AL Fax: 01522 552811

Boston
Community Archaeologist, Boston Borough Council, c/o Heritage Tel: 01529 461499
Lincolnshire, The Old School, Cameron Street, Heckington, Fax: 01529 461001
Sleaford NG34 9PW

Lincoln
Archaeology Officer, City of Lincoln, Department of Planning, City
Hall, Beaumont Fee, Lincoln LN1 1DF
Tel: 01522 564477
Fax: 01522 567934

North East Lincolnshire
Sites and Monuments Record Officer, North East Lincolnshire
Archaeology Section, Thruscoe Centre, Highgate,
Cleethorpes DE35 8NX
Tel: 01472 323586
Fax: 01472 323555

North Kesteven
Heritage Officer, North Kesteven District Council, c/o Heritage
Lincolnshire, The Old School, Cameron Street, Heckington,
Sleaford NG34 9RW
Tel: 01529 461499
Fax: 01529 461001

South Kesteven
Community Archaeologist, South Kesteven District Council,
c/o Heritage Lincolnshire, The Old School, Cameron Street,
Heckington, Sleaford NG34 9PW
Tel: 01529 461499
Fax: 01529 461001

LONDON, GREATER
Greater London Archaeological Advisory Service, English Heritage,
23 Savile Row, London W1X 1AB
Tel: 0171 973 3735
Fax: 0171 973 3792

Southwark
Archaeologist, Regeneration and Environment Department, Southwark
Council, Chiltern House, Portland Street, London SE17 2ES
Tel: 0171 525 5448
Fax: 0171 525 5432

MANCHESTER, GREATER
Sites and Monuments Record Officer, Greater Manchester
Archaeological Unit, University of Manchester, Oxford Road,
Manchester M13 9PL
Tel: 0161 275 2314
Fax: 0161 275 2315

MERSEYSIDE
Archaeological Officer, Liverpool Museum, William Brown Street,
Liverpool L3 8EN
Tel: 0151 478 4258
Fax: 0151 478 4390

NORFOLK
Sites and Monuments Record Officer, Norfolk Landscape
Archaeology, Union House, Gressenhall, East Dereham NR20 4DR
Tel: 01362 861187
Fax: 01362 860951

NORTHAMPTONSHIRE
Sites and Monuments Record Officer, Northamptonshire Heritage,
PO Box 287, 27 Guildhall Road, Northampton NN1 1BD
Tel: 01604 237242
Fax: 01604 236696

NORTHUMBERLAND
Sites and Monuments Record Assistant, Archaeology Section,
Planning and Environment Division, Northumberland County
Council, County Hall, Morpeth NE61 2EF
Tel: 01670 534 060
Fax: 01670 533086

Newcastle upon Tyne
Sites and Monuments Record Officer, Planning Department,   Tel: 0191 232 8520
Newcastle City Council, Civic Centre, Barras Bridge, Newcastle
upon Tyne NE1 8PH

NOTTINGHAMSHIRE
Sites and Monuments Record Officer, Nottingham County Council,   Tel: 0115 9772116
Department of Planning, Trent Bridge House, Fox Road, West
Bridgford, Nottingham NG2 7QX

OXFORDSHIRE
Sites and Monuments Record Officer, Oxfordshire County Council,   Tel:01865810825/
Leisure and Arts, Centre for Oxfordshire Studies, Central Library, 810115
Westgate, Oxford OX1 1DJ   Fax: 01865 810187

Oxford
Oxford Archaeological Advisory Service, Janus House, Osney Mead, Tel: 01865 263805
Oxford OX2 OES

SHROPSHIRE
Sites and Monuments Record Officer, Environment Department,   Tel:01743252558/
Shropshire County Council, The Shire Hall, Abbey Foregate,   252563
Shrewsbury SY2 6ND   Fax: 01743 252505

SOMERSET
Sites and Monuments Record Officer, Department for the   Tel: 01823 356089
Environment, Somerset County Council, County Hall,   Fax: 01823 355613
Taunton TA1 4DY

Bath
Archaeological Officer, Bath and North East Somerset Council,   Tel: 01225 477651
Development and Environmental Services, Trimbridge House, Trim   Fax: 01225 477641
Street, Bath BA1 2DP

SOMERSET, NORTH
Archaeological Officer, North Somerset Council, PO Box 141,   Tel: 01275 882046
Town Hall, Weston super Marc BS23 1UJ

STAFFORDSHIRE
Sites and Monuments Record Officer, Staffordshire County Council, Tel: 01785 277280
Development Services Department, Riverway, Stafford ST16 3TJ   Fax: 01785 223316

Stafford
Borough Archaeologist, Stafford Borough Council, Development   Tel: 01785 223181
Department, Civic Offices, Riverside, Stafford ST16 3AQ   ext: 351
                                                                  Fax 01785 249371

667

Stoke on Trent
Field Archaeologist, Stoke on Trent City Museum and Art Gallery,   Tel: 01782 232323
Bethesla Street, Hanley, Stoke on Trent ST1 3DW

SUFFOLK
Sites and Monuments Record Officer, Suffolk County Council,   Tel: 01284 352445
Archaeological Section, Shire Hall, Bury St Edmunds IP33 2AR; also at: Fax: 01284 352053

Archaeological Service Manager, Environment and Transport   Tel: 01473 583288
Department, Suffolk County Council, St Edmund House, County   Fax: 01473 288221
Hall, Ipswich IP4 1LZ

SURREY
Sites and Monuments Record Officer, Surrey County Council,   Tel: 0181 541 9402
Planning Department, County Hall, Kingston upon Thames KT1 2DT   Fax: 0181 541 9447

SUSSEX, EAST
County Archaeologist, Planning Department, East Sussex County   Tel: 01273 481608
Council, Southover House, Southover Road, Lewes BN7 1YA   Fax: 01273 479040

SUSSEX, WEST
Assistant Archaeologist, West Sussex Planning Department,   Tel: 01243 756858
County Hall, Tower Street, Chichester P019 1RL   Fax: 01243 756862

TEESSIDE
Tees Archaeology, Sir William Gray House, Clarence Road,   Tel:01429523455/6
Hartlepool TS24 8BT   Fax: 01429 523477

WARWICKSHIRE
Sites and Monuments Record Officer, Museum Field Services,   Tel: 01926 412734
The Butts, Warwick CV34 4SS   Fax: 01926 412974

WEST MIDLANDS
West Midlands Sites and Monuments Record, Joint Data Team,   Tel: 0121 704 6550/
PO Box 1777, Clarendon House, Solihull B91 3RZ   6930
    Fax: 0121 704 6554
Birmingham
Planning Archaeologist, Birmingham City Council, Department of   Tel: 0121 235 3161
Planning and Architecture, PO Box 28, Baskerville House,
Broad Street, Birmingham B1 2NA

Coventry
Archaeology Officer, Coventry Museums, Herbert Art Gallery and   Tel: 01203 833333
Museum, Jordan Well, Coventry CV1 5QP

Dudley
Borough Archaeologist, Planning and Leisure Department, Dudley   Tel: 01384 814190
Metropolitan Borough Council, 3 St James Road, Dudley DY1 1HZ

Sandwell
Borough Archaeologist, Department of Technical Services, Sandwell   Tel: 0121 569 4632
Metropolitan Borough Council, Pennyhill Lane, West Bromwich B71 3PZ

WILTSHITE (excluding Swindon)
County Archaeologist, Wiltshire Library and Museums Service,   Tel: 01225 713733
County Hall, Bythesea Road, Trowbridge, BA14 8BG   Fax: 01225 713993

YORKSHIRE, NORTH
Sites and Monuments Record Officer, Heritage Unit, Environmental   Tel: 01609 780780
Services, North Yorkshire County Council, County Hall,   ext: 2331
Northallerton DL7 8AH   Fax: 01609 779838

York
Principal Archaeologist, City of York Council, Directorate of   Tel: 01904 613161
Development Services, 9 St Leonard's Place, York YO1 2ET

YORKSHIRE, SOUTH
Sites and Monuments Record Officer, South Yorkshire   Tel: 0114 273 1687
Archaeology Service, Sheffield City Museum, Weston Park, Western
Bank, Sheffield S1O 2TP

YORKSHIRE, WEST
Senior Archaeologist, West Yorkshire Archaeology Service,   Tel: 01924 306791
14 St Johns North, Wakefield WF1 3QA   Fax: 01924 296810

Bradford
Archaeological Officer, Bradford Metropolitan Borough Council,   Tel: 01943 600066
Manor House Art Gallery and Museum, Castle Yard, Ikley LS29 9DT

NATIONAL PARKS
Dartmoor National Park
Principal Archaeologist, Dartmoor National Park, Parke, Haytor Road, Tel: 01626 832093
Bovey Tracey, Newton Abbot TQ13 9JQ   Fax: 01626 834684

Exmoor National Park
Archaeologist, Exmoor National Park, Exmoor House, Dulverton,   Tel: 01398 323665
Somerset TA22 9HL   Fax: 01398 323150

Lake District National Park
Archaeologist, Lake District National Park Authority, National Park   Tel: 01539 724555
Office, Murley Moss, Oxenholme Road, Kendal LA9 7RL   ext: 215
  Fax: 01539 740822

North York Moors National Park
Archaeological Conservation Officer, North York Moors National   Tel: 01439 770657
Park, The Old Vicarage, Bondgate, Helmsley York YO6 5BP   Fax: 01439 770691

Northumberland National Park
Archaeologist, Northumberland National Park, Eastburn, South Park, Tel: 01434 6050000
Hexham NE46 1BF   Fax: 01434 605522

Peak District National Park
Archaeologist, Peak District National Park, Archaeology and Heritage Tel: 01629 816200
Group, Aldern House, Baslow Road, Bakewell DE4 1AE   ext: 206
    Fax: 01629 816310

Yorkshire Dales National Park
Archaeological Conservation Officer, Yorkshire Dales National Park, Tel: 01969 650456
Yorebridge House, Bainbridge, Leyburn DL8 3PB   Fax: 01969 650025

2. Wales
NORTH EAST WALES
Clwyd-Powys Archaeological Trust, 7A Church Street, Welshpool, Tel: 01938 553670
Powys SY21 7DL

Denbighshire County Council
County Archaeologist, Denbighshire Countryside Service, Directorate Tel: 01824 708073
of Planning and Economic Development, Trem Clwyd, Canol y Dre,
Ruthin, Denbighshire LL15 1QA

Wrexham
Senior Archaeologist, Wrexham County Borough Council, County Tel: 01978 358916
Buildings, Regent Street, Wrexham LL11 1AY   ext: 27
    Fax: 01978 353882

NORTH WEST WALES
Gwynedd Archaeological Trust Ltd., Craig Beuno, Garth Road, Tel: 01248 352535
Bangor, Gwynedd LL57 2PT   Fax: 01248 370925

SOUTH EAST WALES
Glamorgan-Gwent Archaeological Trust Ltd., Ferryside Warehouse, Tel: 01792 655208
Bath Lane, Swansea, West Glamorgan SA1 1RD

SOUTH WEST WALES
Cambria Archaeology, Shire Hall, Carmarthen Street, Tel:01558823131/
Llandeilo, Dyfed   823121
    Fax: 01558 823133

NATIONAL PARKS
Brecon Beacons National Park
Archaeologist, Brecon Beacons National Park, National Park Offices, Tel: 01874 624437
7 Glamorgan Street, Brecon, Powys LD3 7DP   Fax: 01874 622574

Snowdonia National Park

National Park Archaeologist, Archaeological Section, Snowdonia   Tel: 01766 770274
National Park, Penrhyndeudraeth, Gwynedd LL48 6LS

C. OTHERS

Department of National Heritage

Buildings Monuments and Sites Division, Department of National   Tel: 0171 211 6000
Heritage, 2-4 Cockspur Street, London SWLY 5DH

British Museum

Department of Coins and Medals, British Museum,   Tel: 0171 636 1555
London WC1B 3DG (for enquiries relating to coins)   or 0171 323 8404
    Fax: 0171 323 8171

Department of Prehistoric and Romano-British Antiquities, British   Tel: 0171 636 1555
Museum, London WC1B 3DG (for enquiries relating to prehistoric   or 0171 323 8667
and Roman objects other than coins)   Fax: 0171 323 8588

Department of Medieval and Later Antiquities, British Museum,   Tel: 0171 636 1555
London WC1B 3DG (for enquiries relating to medieval and   or 0171 323 8629
modern objects other than coins)   Fax: 0171 323 8496

National Museums & Galleries of Wales

Department of archaeology and Numismatics, National Museums   Tel: 01222 397951
& Galleries of Wales, Cathays Park, Cardiff CF1 3NP   Fax: 01222 373219

For advice on conservation see section 7 of Appendix 5.

APPENDIX 4

Coins commonly found in England and Wales that contain less than 10 per cent of Gold or Silver

In section 1 of the Act it is stated that if the coins from the same find (for clarification on what is meant by this term see paragraphs 12-14) contain less than 10 per cent of gold or silver, then the find must contain at least ten coins to be treasure (see paragraph 7). This list, which includes those coins that are commonly found in England and Wales that contain less than 10 per cent of gold or silver, is for guidance only and is not intended to be definitive. Many contemporary forgeries may also contain less than 10 per cent of gold and silver, but these cannot be listed here, although they may also be considered as treasure. In case of any doubt finders are advised to check with museums.

A. Celtic

The following issues are listed with reference to P D Van Arsdell, *Celtic Coinage in Britain* (VA). Although this list is quite long, in practice these coins are relatively rare and museums would always be glad to have the chance to record any examples. It does not include Continental Celtic bronze coins that are sometimes found in this country.

Cantii (Kent)
potin coins (VA 102-39); uninscribed (VA 154); Dubnovellaunus (VA 166-7, 173, 180-1); Vosenos (VA 187); Amniinus VA 193, 195)
Atrebates (Berkshire, Sussex and parts of Hants)
Eppillus (VA 450-3)
Durotriges (Dorset and parts of Somerset, Wiltshire and Hants)
uninscribed (VA 1290, 1322-70)
Trinovantes/Catuvellauni (north of the Thames)
'Thurrock type' cast bronzes (VA 1402-42);Addedomarus (VA 1615, 1629, 1646); Dubnovellaunus (VA 1665-9); Tasciovanus (VA 1705-17, 1750, 1808-26); 'Sego' (VA 1855); 'Andoco' (VA 1871-3); 'Dias' (VA 1882); 'Rues' (VA 1890-1903); Cunobelin (VA 1963-89,2081-2137)

B. Roman

(1) All early imperial bronze coins (sestertii, dupondii and asses) made between the reign of Augustus (27 BC – AD 14) and that of Postumus (AD 260-9). These large bronze coins are fairly common finds and are easily recognizable.

(2) All late imperial base silver and bronze coins made after AD 260 (i.e. from the sole reign of Gallienus or, in the Gallic Empire, from the last, debased, issue of Postumus), down to AD 400. This category includes about three-quarters of all Roman coins found in Britain. The main groups are:

(a) all debased radiates made during the sole reign of Gallienus and later (including those of Claudius II and the Gallic emperors Victorinus and Tetricus I and II) and all 'barbarous radiates'.
(b) the reformed radiates of Aurelian and his successors down to Diocletian (AD 270-94).
(c) the radiates of the British emperors Carausius and Allectus (AD 287-96).
(d) all 4th century base silver and bronze coins.

C. Medieval

Northumbrian stycas of the 9th century AD.
All lead and lead-tin alloy tokens.

D. Modern (until 1700)

James I (1603-25)
　Royal copper farthing tokens (for example, 'Harrington' farthings)

Charles I (1625-49
　Royal copper farthing tokens (for example, 'Richmond' and 'Rose' farthings)

Charles II (1660-85)
　Copper halfpennies of 1672, 1673 and 1675
　Copper farthings of 1672-6 and 1679
　Tin farthings of 1684-5

James II (1685-88)
　Tin halfpennies of 1685-7
　Tin farthings of 1684-7

William and Mary (1688-94)
　Tin halfpennies of 1690-2
　Tin farthings of 1689-92
　Copper halfpennies and farthings of 1694

William II (1694-1702)
　Copper halfpennies of 1695-1701
　Copper farthings of 1695-1700

All 17th century traders' tokens
All lead and lead-tin alloy tokens

APPENDIX 5

The Care of Finds

Once any find of potential treasure has been removed from the ground there is always the risk that it may deteriorate. The first priority must be not only to minimise any risk of deterioration but also to preserve evidence. Dirt and corrosion products on the surface of an object may retain important information about how it was used; for example, the corrosion layer on coins may bear traces of a textile wrapping and such evidence can easily be lost through inappropriate cleaning. It will generally be best if finds are packed and stored appropriately as soon as they are removed from the ground. If that is done, the deterioration of the object will be minimised.

The following notes are intended for general guidance only and cover the period between removal of objects from the ground and treatment by or with the advice of an archaeological conservator. More advice is provided in the references in the bibliography. Finders are strongly recommended to seek the advice of a professional archaeological conservator as soon as possible, via one of the sources of conservation advice listed in section 7.

1. NATURE OF FINDS
1.1. Materials
Under the Act a wider range of materials, in addition to silver and gold, could come within the definition of treasure, including metals (iron, copper alloys, zinc, lead, tin and pewter), ceramics, glass, stone, bone, antler, ivory, amber, jet, shale, wood and leather.

1.2. Condition
The condition of an object removed from the ground is likely to be very different from that of an object of the same material that has never been buried. The excavated object may look different, it will be much more fragile and it will be very susceptible to further deterioration. Its actual condition and appearance will be determined by a number of factors including the type of material, the condition when buried and the nature of the burial environment.

1.3. Evidence
Soil and corrosion concretions around objects may contain much important evidence about how the object was made or used and about the environment at the time of burial. Inappropriate cleaning can easily remove this evidence and so corrosion and soil concretions should be left undisturbed and the professional advice of an experienced archaeological conservator should be sought.

Finders should be particularly aware that:

*   The original surface of a metal object, especially iron, copper and silver alloy objects, is usually preserved within the corrosion layers and is not at he level of any surviving bright metal. Cleaning methods (chemical and mechanical) that indiscriminately strip off corrosion layers are therefore also likely to remove the original surface of the subject.
*   The original surface of a flaking and discoloured decayed glass object will not be at the uncorroded glass surface and so the corroded layers should not be cleaned off.
*   What appears to be 'corrosion' on a metal object may also be preserving the only evidence of organic materials that were part of it, or in close proximity to, the object when buried. Traces of textile, leather, wood, bone, horn and

other animal and vegetable products may survive in such a condition that they are not obvious to the untrained eye but can be recognised and identified when examined by a specialist.
* 'Corrosion' layers may also incorporate gilding, inlays, enamel and niello, all of which can easily be removed by inappropriate cleaning.
* Soil deposits in vessels and other containers may include pollen, seeds and other organic evidence of the vessel's contents, as well as providing clues to the environment at the time of burial. Whenever possible, the contents of vessels, including the soil, should be left in place until examined by a specialist. If the contents are removed, the soil deposits should be packed separately and kept with the find.
* Ceramic pots may retain traces of their contents (food or liquids) on the surface and within the fabric of the clay. These will not be visible but may be detectable by scientific analysis. Washing will remove this evidence.
* Traces of paint, gilding and ground (gesso or plaster) may survive on stone, wood and leather objects. These traces are all easily missed and can be lost by indiscriminate removal of soil and burial concretions.

2. IDENTIFYING MATERIALS WITHOUT CLEANING

Some materials, such as pure gold or silver-gold alloys, are easy to recognise even after hundreds of years in the ground. Other materials, particularly other metals and some types of glass which have been buried, will have a very different appearance from their modern equivalents. Also, the condition and appearance of the same material can differ considerably depending upon the burial environment. The following table provides some clues to identifying materials whose appearance may be greatly altered by the burial environment, without cleaning them. For more detailed information on the changes that happen to buried materials, finders are recommended to works in the bibliography, particularly *First Aid for Finds*.

Material	Visual clues to identifying materials which have been altered by burial from their possible appearance on excavation
Gold:	gold colour (pure metal); or, if alloyed with silver and/or copper, may have appearance of the corrosion products of these metals.
Silver:	dull grey/white - turns dull lilac colour when excavated; or green patches or totally green (if alloyed with copper); or black surface.
Copper	green: condition of corrosion can vary from smooth dark patina to powdery

alloys:	or warty and very fragile;
	or black, solid patina with shiny metallic patches.
Iron:	orange brown; white to light grey; black or deep orange/red (burnt); or
	black; may have blue patches when waterlogged;
	corrosion often incorporates soil deposits.
	(N.B. Iron, even when corroded, will be attracted by a magnet.)
Lead, tin,	lead: likely to be heavy relative to size; heavier than silver;
pewter	lead and pewter: white to dull grey under fine light brown soil; may
or zinc:	have lighter patches and darker warts;
	lead: red spots/patches;
	zinc: dull grey with white powdery encrustations, deep pits;
	tin: dull earthy surface;
	tin, pewter: black, often smooth surface.
Enamels	
(usually	may no longer retain original colour;
on copper	may be very fragile and powdery and resemble copper corrosion.
alloys)	
Amber:	translucent yellow, cream, orange brown to red, may have crazed crust.
Glass:	opaque or black iridescence, flaking layers.

3. EFFECT OF REMOVAL FROM THE BURIAL ENVIRONMENT

When a buried object is removed from the soil there is a sudden and drastic change to its environment. This change can so destabilise an object (which may have survived in the ground for hundreds of years) that its condition can deteriorate very rapidly and irreversibly. To prevent this deterioration, objects should be placed in an environment that is appropriate to the type of material and its condition as soon as possible after removal from the ground.

4. PACKAGING AND STORAGE

4.1 Storage Environments

If finds are stored in an appropriate environment from the moment they have been retrieved from the ground, this can help to minimise any risk that they might subsequently deteriorate. The following table is intended as a general guide to storage environments for different materials. The books listed in Section 8 will provide more information. Section 4.3 describes methods for creating different storage environments.

Material	Storage environment
Metals (iron and copper alloys with signs of 'bronze disease')	very dry (e.g. desiccated) with silica gel
Metals (non ferrous): e.g. gold, silver and copper alloys Ceramics Unpainted stone	ambient (dry)
Glass Ceramics if low-fired or with flaking glaze Painted stone and plaster Metals with substantial or important organic remains (non-mineralised) Bone and ivory Amber Jet and shale	damp, cool (refrigerated, but not frozen) and dark
All materials from underwater marine sites Wood, leather and textiles from waterlogged burial environments	wet, cool (refrigerated, but not frozen) and dark

4.2 Packaging Materials

Packaging materials should provide objects with physical protection, they should enable an appropriate storage environment to be created, and they should be chemically inert so that in themselves they do not cause deterioration of the objects. The following are recommended and are in common use by museums and archaeologists. They may be available from high street shops; otherwise finders are recommended to contact their local museum or one of the sources for conservation advice given in section 7 below.

Polyethylene boxes: with self-seal (snap on) lids, such as freezer storage boxes.

Polyethylene bags: self-sealing if possible. Make numerous small holes near the top.

Polystyrene boxes ('crystal' boxes): clear, rigid plastic with hinged or detachable lids.

Polyethylene foam (non absorbent): e.g. 'Jiffy' foam, or 'Plastazot'.

677

Polyether foam (absorbent):	foam with open cell structure.
Acid-free tissue paper	
Polyethylene labels:	e.g. 'Tyvek' (will not deteriorate in the dampest storage environments).
Markers for boxes, bags and labels:	permanent black felt tip pens; black ballpoint pen (do not use these to mark the actual objects).
Silica gel:	used to create a very dry storage environment. Separate sachets can be made by filling perforated polythene bags with loose gel. The sachets are then placed in a sealed polythene box with metal finds. Gel should not be in direct contact with finds as it can cause abrasion. Self-indicating blue gel turns pink as is absorbs moisture. Pink silica gel can be dried out by heating it in an oven at about 100^0 C until dark blue again. Loose silica gel (removed from polythene bags) can be spread out on a baking tray to dry in the oven.
Relative humidity indicator strips:	if placed inside polythene boxes will indicate dryness or dampness of micro-environment.
Aluminium foil/glass jars:	if samples (for example of pot sherds) are retained for analysis of organic residues, they should not be packed in plastics.

4.3 Packing finds and creating storage environments

Robust small finds can be individually packaged in polyethylene bags. Some padding can be provided with 'Jiffy' foam. Delicate small finds should be placed in individual 'crystal' boxes and padded with 'Jiffy' foam or acid free tissue or in a polyethylene foam (e.g. 'Plastozote') cut out to provide firm but gentle support. Tissue paper should only be used where finds are to be kept dry and should not be used with lead alloys. The individually packaged finds can then be packed into the polyethylene boxes in which a micro-environment can be created. Different materials should be placed in different boxes. Any empty space in the outer box can be packed with foam or bubble wrap to prevent objects rattling about when moved.

If the find is a hoard (for example, of coins), it should wherever possible be lifted as one, in its original container if it survives. The original container, with its contents undisturbed, can then be packed into a rigid container, padded with acid-free tissue paper or 'Jiffy' foam and covered, for example in a plastic bucket covered with Polythene sheeting. Where the hoard is not in an original container, the objects should be lifted as a group with surrounding soil. The latter may not only contain important evidence but will also act as a support for fragile objects. The objects plus surrounding soil can then be placed in a rigid container as above.

* A **very dry environment** (e.g. for some metals) can be created by placing bagged silica gel in the polyethylene box with the finds. As a rough guide, one should use an approximately equal weight of silica gel to finds. The silica gel may need to be changed/dried out several times, and at frequent intervals, before a very dry environment is created for newly excavated finds.

* A **damp environment** can be created by placing pads of damp (absorbent, not wet) foam in the polyethylene box with the finds. Glass to be kept damp can be packed between layers of damp foam in the polyethylene box.

* A **wet environment** can be created either by immersing the finds (in their polyethylene bags) completely in water or by placing very wet pads of foam in the box; the latter is more practical for transport purposes. Waterlogged and marine finds do present special problems and professional advice should be sought as soon as possible.

* The less vulnerable materials, which can be kept in **ambient conditions**, can be packed in cardboard boxes (acid free cardboard if possible) or in polyethylene boxes or crates.

Labels recording the find-spot should be kept with finds at all times.

5. SIGNS OF TROUBLE

In the following table are listed some visual indications that an object is actively deteriorating. If any of these are spotted, or if there is any change generally in the appearance of an object, the storage environment should be adjusted, with advice from a conservator, as soon as possible.

Material	Signs of trouble
Copper alloys:	bright pale green powdery spots, or patches: 'bronze disease'.
Iron:	spots of orange liquid on surface; flaking, cracking, laminating; appearance of bright orange powdery corrosion.
Lead and lead alloys:	appearance of white powdery corrosion.
Ceramics and stone:	whitish crystals – efflorescence – on surface.
Any material (finds or packaging) that is being kept damp or wet:	appearance of: black spots, white fluffy deposits and/or smell of rotten eggs.
Glass:	crazing, flaking, laminating.
Wood, bone, ivory:	shrinkage, warping, cracking.

6. WHAT A MUSEUM IS LIKELY TO DO WITH FINDS BEFORE A CORONER'S INQUEST

In addition to photographing and documenting finds, some conservation and scientific analysis may be undertaken by appropriate museum staff for the purpose of the report to the coroner. Treatment by a conservator could include x-radiography, sufficient preliminary cleaning to clarify identification of the find, 'first aid' to ensure the material is stable and re-packing in the appropriate micro-climate.

7. SOME SOURCES OF CONSERVATION ADVICE

Department of Conservation, British Museum, Great Russell Street, London WC1B 3DG (tel: 0171 636 1555; fax: 0171 323 8636).

National Museums & Galleries of Wales, Cathays Park, Cardiff CF1 3NP (tel: 01222 397951; fax: 01222 373219).

Museum of London, London Wall, London EC2Y 5HN (tel: 0171 600 3699; fax: 0171 600 1058) (can provide advice on finds from the London area).

National Museums and Galleries on Merseyside, The Conservation Centre, Whitechapel, Liverpool L1 6HZ (Tel: 0151 207 0001).

Museums and Galleries Commission (maintains a register of conservators in the private sector), 16 Queen Anne's Gate, London SW1H 9AA (Tel: 0171 233 3683).

United Kingdom Institute for Conservation (Archaeology Section), 6 Whitehorse Mews, Westminster Bridge Road, London SE1 7QD (Tel: 0171 620 3371).

Conservators based in local museums via yellow pages or via Area Museums Councils:

> Area Museum Council for the South west, Hestercombe House, Cheddon Fitzpaine, Taunton TA2 8LQ (Tel: 01823 259696)
>
> South Eastern Museum Service, Ferroners House, Barbican, London EC2Y 8AA (Tel: 0171 600 0219)
>
> West Midlands Museums Service, Hanbury Road, Stoke Prior, Bromsgrove B60 4AD (Tel: 01527 872258)
>
> East Midlands Museums Service, Courtyard Buildings, Wollaton Park, Nottingham NG8 2AE (Tel: 01159 854534)
>
> Yorkshire and Humberside Museums Council, Farnley Hall, Farnley Park, Leeds LS12 5HA (Tel: 0113 2638909)
>
> North West Museums Service, Griffin Lodge, Griffin Park, Cavendish Place, Blackburn BB2 2PN (Tel: 01254 670211)
>
> North of England Museums Service, House of Recovery, Bath Lane, Newcastle upon Tyne NE4 5SQ (Tel: 0191 222 1661)
>
> Council of Museums in Wales, The Courtyard, Letty Street, Cathays, Cardiff CF2 4EL (Tel: 01222 225432)

Finds officers and conservators with local archaeological units from: Institute of Field Archaeologists (Finds Group), c/o IFA University of Manchester, Oxford Road, Manchester M13 9PL (Tel: 0161 275 2304).

English Heritage (London-based as well as regional conservators), Ancient Monuments Laboratory, 23 Savile Row, London W1X 1AB (Tel: 0171 973 3000).

Nautical Archaeology Society, c/o Mary Rose Trust, College Road, H M Naval Base, Portsmouth PO1 3LX (tel: 01705 750521; fax: 01705 870588)

8. BIBLIOGRAPHY

D Watkinson and V Neal, *First Aid for Finds*, Rescue and United Kingdom Institute for Conservation Archaeology Section, 3rd edition, 1997.

K Hunter, *Conservation Guidelines no.1, Excavated Artefacts and Conservation: UK Sites*, United Kingdom Institute for Conservation Archaeology Section, 1988.

Conservation Guidelines no.2. Packing and Storage of Freshly Excavated Artefacts from Archaeological Sites, United Kingdom Institute for Conservation Archaeology Section, 1983.

J Cronyn, *The Elements of Archaeological Conservation*, Routledge, London, 1990.

C Sease, *A Conservation Manual for the Field Archaeologist*, UCLA-IA-Art Volume 4, Los Angeles, 1987.

W Robinson, *First Aid for Marine Finds*, National Maritime Museum, London, 1981.

R Peyton, *The Retrieval of Objects from Archaeological Sites*, Archetype Publications, London, 1992.

K Walker, *Guidelines for the Preparation of Excavation Archives for Long-term Storage*, United Kingdom Institute for Conservation Archaeology Section, 1990.

The Content of Environmental Statements (Schedule 4 to the Town and Country Planning (Environmental Impact Assessment) (England and Wales) Regulations 1999)

Part I

1. Description of the development, including in particular –

(a) a description of the physical characteristics of the whole development and the land-use requirements during the construction and operational phases;
(b) a description of the main characteristics of the production processes, for instance, nature and quantity of the materials used;
(c) an estimate, by type and quantity, of expected residues and emissions (water, air and soil pollution, noise, vibration, light, heat, radiation, etc.) resulting from the operation of the proposed development.

2. An outline of the main alternatives studied by the applicant or appellant and an indication of the main reasons for his choice, taking into account the environmental effects.

3. A description of the aspects of the environment likely to be significantly affected by the development, including, in particular, population, fauna, flora, soil, water, air, climatic factors, material assets, including the architectural and archaeological heritage, landscape and the inter-relationship between the above factors.

4. A description of the likely significant effects of the development on the environment, which should cover the direct effects and any indirect, secondary, cumulative, short, medium and long-term, permanent and temporary, positive and negative effects of the development, resulting from:

(a) the existence of the development;
(b) the use of natural resources;
(c) the emission of pollutants, the creation of nuisances and the elimination of waste,

and the description by the applicant of the forecasting methods used to assess the effects on the environment.

5. A description of the measures envisaged to prevent, reduce and where possible offset any significant adverse effects on the environment.

6. A non-technical summary of the information provided under paragraphs 1 to 5 of this Part.

7. An indication of any difficulties (technical deficiencies or lack of know-how) encountered by the applicant in compiling the required information.

PART II

1. A description of the development comprising information on the site, design and size of the development.

2. A description of the measures envisaged in order to avoid, reduce and, if possible, remedy significant adverse effects.

3. The data required to identify and assess the main effects which the development is likely to have on the environment.

4. An outline of the main alternatives studied by the applicant or appellant and an indication of the main reasons for his choice, taking into account the environmental effects.

5. A non-technical summary of the information provided under paragraphs 1 to 4 of this Part.

Model Planning Condition 25
(form suggested by Secretary of State
for approval of mitigation measures)

No development shall take place until full details of both hard and soft landscape works have been submitted to and approved by the local planning authority and these works shall be carried out as approved. These details shall include [proposed finished levels or contours; means of enclosure; car parking layouts; other vehicle and pedestrian access and circulation areas; hard surfacing materials; minor artefacts and structures (e.g.. furniture, play equipment, refuse or other storage units, signs, lighting etc.); proposed and existing functional services above and below ground (e.g.. drainage, power, communications cables, pipelines etc. indicating lines, manholes, supports etc.); retained historic landscape features and proposals for restoration,* where relevant].

(Source: DOE Circular 11/95; WO Circular 35/95, after Hampshire Local Government Landscape Group)

---

* In many instances the word consolidation or repair will be more appropriate if referring to archaeological sites or monuments. If site restoration as a whole is referred to more explicit wording might be desirable. This condition does not require the approved works to be carried out before development begins; if some tasks are required to be carried out before development commences these should be subject to a specific condition (see chapter 6, planning conditions).

THE ENVIRONMENTAL IMPACT ASSESSMENT REGULATIONS

Town and Country Planning (Environmental Impact Assessment) (England and Wales) Regulations 1999 (S.I.1999, No.293), revoking the Town and Country Planning (Assessment of Environmental Effects) Regulations 1988 and all regulations which amended the 1988 regulations.

Town and Country Planning (General Permitted Development) Order 1995 (S.I.1995, No.418), as amended by regulation 35 of S.I.1999, No.293, which removes most 'schedule 2 development' from the category of permitted development unless the planning authority has adopted a screening opinion to the effect that EIA is not required. S.I.1995, No.417, which prescribed the procedure for obtaining an opinion from the local planning authority is now revoked.

The Town and Country Planning (Environmental Assessment and Unauthorised Development) Regulations 1995 (S.I.1995, No.2258) are now revoked and replaced by regulations 24 and 25 of S.I.1999, No.293.

The Highways (Assessment of Environmental Effects) Regulations 1988 (S.I.1988, No.1241) and S.I.1993, No.1002 which amended them are both revoked by the Highways (Assessment of Environmental Effects) Regulations 1999 (S.I.1999, No.369) which insert a new Part (VA) into the Highways Act 1980.

Land Drainage Improvement Works (Assessment of Environmental Effects) Regulations 1988 (S.I.1988, No.1217).

Environmental Assessment (Forestry) Regulations 1998 (S.I.1998, No.1731).

Environmental Assessment (Salmon Farming in Marine Waters) Regulations 1988 (S.I.1988, No.1218).

Harbour Works (Assessment of Environmental Effects) Regulations 1988 (S.I.1988, No.1336); Harbour Works (Assessment of Environmental Effects) (No.2) Regulations 1989 (S.I.1989, No.424).

Electricity and Pipe-line Works (Assessment of Environmental Effects) Regulations 1990 (S.I.1990, No.442); Electricity and Pipe-line Works (Assessment of Environmental Effects) (Amendment) Regulations 1996 (S.I.1996, No.422).

Transport and Works (Assessment of Environmental Effects) Regulations 1995 (S.I.1995, No.1541); Transport and Works (Assessment of Environmental Effects) Regulations 1998 (S.I.1998, No.2226).

LISTED BUILDINGS AND HISTORIC LANDSCAPES

Planning Policy Guide Note 15:
Planning and the Historic Environment (DOE/DNH) (1994)
[Extracts, omitting contents page, annexes and index]

PART 1

1 PLANNING AND CONSERVATION

1.1 It is fundamental to the Government''s policies for environmental stewardship that there should be effective protection for all aspects of the historic environment. The physical survivals of our past are to be valued and protected for heir own sake, as a central part of our cultural heritage and our sense of national identity. They are an irreplaceable record which contributes, through formal education and in many other ways, to our understanding of both the present and the past. Their presence adds to the quality of our lives, by enhancing the familiar and cherished local scene and sustaining the sense of local distinctiveness which is so important an aspect of the character and appearance of our towns, villages and countryside. The historic environment is also of immense importance for leisure and recreation.

The role of the planning system

1.2 The function of the planning system is to regulate the development and use of land in the public interest. It has to take account of the Government's objective of promoting sustainable economic growth, and make provision for development to meet the economic and social needs of the community. As *PPG 1* makes clear, planning is also an important instrument for protecting and enhancing the environment in town and country, and preserving the built and natural heritage. The objective of planning processes should be to reconcile the need for economic growth with the need to protect the natural and historic environment.

1.3 The Government has committed itself to the concept of sustainable development – of not sacrificing what future generations will value for the sake of short-term and often illusory gains. This approach is set out in *Sustainable Development: The UK Strategy*. It is also a key element of the development plan system, as set out in *PPG 12*. This commitment has particular relevance to the preservation of the historic environment, which by its nature is replaceable. Yet the historic environment of England is all-pervasive, and it cannot in practice be preserved unchanged. We must ensure that the means are available to identify what is special in the historic environment; to define through the development plan system its capacity for change; and, when proposals for new development come forward, to assess their impact on the historic environment and give it full weight, alongside other considerations.

Conservation and economic prosperity

1.4 Though choices sometimes have to be made, conservation and sustainable economic growth are complementary objectives and should not generally be seen as in opposition to one another. Most historic buildings can still be put to good economic use in, for example, commercial or residential occupation. They are a valuable material resource and can contribute to the prosperity of the economy, provided that they are properly maintained: the avoidable loss of fabric through neglect is a waste of economic as well as environmental resources. In return, economic prosperity can secure the continued vitality of conservation areas, and the continued use and maintenance of historic buildings, provided that there is a sufficiently realistic and imaginative approach to their alteration and change of use, to reflect the needs of a rapidly changing world.

1.5 Conservation can itself play a key part in promoting economic prosperity by ensuring that an area offers attractive living and working conditions which will encourage inward investment - environmental quality is increasingly a key factor in many commercial decisions. The historic environment is of particular importance for tourism and leisure, and Government policy encourages the growth and development of tourism in response to the market so long as this is compatible with proper long-term conservation. Further advice on tourist aspects of conservation is given in *PPG 21* and the English Tourist Board's publication *Maintaining the Balance*.

Stewardship : the role of local authorities and others

1.6 The Government urges local authorities to maintain and strengthen their commitment to stewardship of the historic environment, and to reflect it in their policies and their allocation of resources. It is important that, as planning authorities, they adopt suitable policies in their development plans, and give practical effect to them through their development control decisions. As highway authorities too, their policies and activities should reflect the need to protect the historic environment and to promote sustainable economic growth, for roads can have a particular impact at all levels – not only through strategic decisions on the siting of new roads, but also through the more detailed aspects of road building and road maintenance, such as the quality of street furniture and surfaces. Above all, local authorities should ensure that they can call on sufficient specialist conservation advice, whether individually or jointly, to inform their decision-making and to assist owners and other members of the public.

1.7 However, the responsibility of stewardship is shared by everyone – not only by central and local government, but also by business, voluntary bodies, churches, and by individual citizens as owners, users and visitors of historic buildings. The historic environment cannot be preserved unless there is broad public support and understanding, and it is a key element of Government policy for conservation that there should be adequate processes of consultation and education to facilitate this.

2   DEVELOPMENT PLANS AND DEVELOPMENT CONTROL

2.1 The principal Act (as amended) requires development plans to include policies for 'the conservation of the natural beauty and amenity of the land' and for 'the improvement of the physical environment'. The Town & Country Planning (Development Plan) Regulations 1991 require authorities to have regard to environmental considerations in preparing their plan policies and proposals. The protection of the historic environment, whether individual listed buildings, conservation areas, parks and gardens, battlefields or the wider historic landscape, is a key aspect of these wider environmental responsibilities, and will need to be taken fully into account both in the formulation of authorities' planning policies and in development control.

Development plans

2.2 Structure, local, and unitary development plans are the main vehicle for ensuring that conservation policies are coordinated and integrated with other planning policies affecting the historic environment. Imaginative planning policies can not only reduce threats to it, but increase its contribution to local amenity. By including suitable policies in their plans, local authorities can give encouragement to the satisfactory reuse of neglected historic buildings, particularly where major groups of buildings need to be tackled comprehensively, and where other planning factors, such as traffic problems, may be discouraging reuse.

2.3 Section 54A of the principal Act provides that where, in making any determination under the Planning Acts, regard is to be had to the development plan, the determination must be made in accordance with the development plan unless material considerations indicate otherwise. It is therefore important that plans include all the criteria on the basis of which planning decisions will be made. Plans should set out clearly all conservation policies relevant to the exercise of an authority's development control functions, and also policies which are relevant to cases where development and conservation issues are linked and will need to be addressed together.

2.4 The Courts have accepted that section 54A does not apply to decisions on applications for listed building consent or conservation area consent, since in those cases there is no statutory requirement to have regard to the provisions of the development plan. However, authorities should ensure that aspects of conservation policy that are relevant, directly or indirectly, to development control decisions are included - for instance, policies for alterations or extensions to listed buildings that also constitute development (to which section 54A will directly apply). In view of the statutory requirements that authorities should have special regard to the desirability of preserving any listed building or its setting, or any features of special architectural or historic interest which it possesses, and should pay special attention to the desirability of preserving or enhancing the character or appearance of any conservation area in exercising their development control functions, plans should also include policies for works of demolition or alteration which, while not in themselves constituting development, could affect an authority's decision on a related application for planning permission.

2.5 There may be some detailed conservation policies which have no bearing on issues of development control – for instance, policies for the treatment of some internal features of listed buildings where this would not affect consideration of planning applications but might require listed building consent. Other examples may relate to certain types of alteration, repairs, maintenance or decoration. These policies should be presented as supplementary guidance rather than included in the plan itself. Such guidance will carry greater weight to the extent that it has been the subject of public consultation, has been formally adopted by the authority, and is published in a format which gives clear advice and is readily available to the public. Development plans should contain a reference to such policies in the reasoned justification, together with a clear indication of where those policies may be seen in full.

2.6 Full guidance on the preparation of plans is given in *PPG 12*. Structure plans and the first part of unitary development plans provide a statement of the overall strategy for a county, borough or metropolitan district area, and should include conservation of the historic environment as one of their key topics, taking account of any broad strategic objectives or constraints set out in relevant regional planning guidance. The structure plan should provide a broad planning framework, guiding the approach to be adopted in local plans to such issues as the capacity of historic towns to sustain development, the relief of pressure on historic central areas by the identification of opportunities for growth elsewhere, and the provision of transport infrastructure which respects the historic environment.

2.7 Local plans and the second part of unitary development plans should set out more detailed development control policies for an authority's area: they should include both the policies which will apply over the area as a whole, and any policies and proposals which will apply to particular neighbourhoods. Both policies and proposals should be illustrated on the proposals map (see paragraph 7.14 of *PPG 12*).

2.8 Local plans should set out clearly the planning authority's policies for the preservation and enhancement of the historic environment in their area, and the factors which will be taken into account in assessing different types of planning application – for example, proposals for the change of use of particular types of historic building or for new development which would affect their setting. It is important that clear policies are formulated for cases where new development is proposed in order to provide income for the upkeep of historic buildings (see Department of the Environment *Circular 16/91*). Plans should also include a strategy for the economic regeneration of rundown areas, and in particular seek to identify the opportunities which the historic fabric of an area can offer as a focus for regeneration. Excessively detailed or inflexible policies concerning individual buildings or groups of buildings should be avoided.

2.9 Plans should set out authorities' broad criteria for the designation of new conservation areas and for the review of existing conservation area boundaries; and, where possible, which particular areas are in mind for both. The process of assessment, detailed definition or revision of boundaries, and formulation of proposals for individual conservation areas (as required by section 71 of the Act) should involve extensive local consultation and should be pursued separately from the local plan process itself. But the plan should provide a policy framework, making clear to the public how detailed assessment documents and statements of proposals for individual conservation areas relate to the plan, and what weight will be given to them in decisions on applications for planning permission and conservation area consent. (See also paragraphs 4.3-4.7, 4.10 and 4.15.) Designation strategies should take account of the fact that authorities now have general powers to control the demolition of dwelling houses outside conservation areas (see Department of the Environment *Circular 26/92*).

2.10 English Heritage is a statutory consultee on draft plans, but is also able to offer specialist advice at preparation stage. In conjunction with the Countryside Commission and English Nature, it is also issuing guidance on conservation in strategic and local plans. There will often be advantage in consultation at an early stage in plan preparation with other statutory agencies and with the national amenity societies and local conservation bodies, as well as wider public consultation at the formal deposit stage.

Development control

2.11 The Secretary of State attaches particular importance to early consultation with the local planning authority on development proposals which would affect historic sites and structures, whether listed buildings, conservation areas, parks and gardens, battlefields or the wider historic landscape. There is likely to be much more scope for refinement and revision of proposals if consultation takes place before intentions become firm and timescales inflexible. Local planning authorities should indicate their readiness to discuss proposals with developers before formal planning applications are submitted. They should expect developers to assess the likely impact of their proposals on the special interest of the site or structure in question, and to provide such written information or drawings as may be required to understand the significance of a site or structure before an application is determined. The principle of early consultation should extend to English Heritage and the national amenity societies on cases where a formal planning or listed building consent application would be notifiable to them by direction or under the GDO.

2.12 It is generally preferable for both the applicant and the planning authority if related applications for planning permission and for listed building or conservation area consent are considered concurrently. Authorities are required by section 66(1) of the Act, in considering whether to grant planning permission for development which affects a listed building or its setting, to have special regard to the desirability of preserving the building or its setting or any features of architectural or historic interest which it possesses. It is unlikely that they will be able to do so effectively unless the planning application is accompanied by a listed building consent application (where the development in question requires one) or at least contains an equivalent amount of information. If an authority is asked to consider a planning application in isolation, a decision on that application cannot be taken as predetermining the outcome of a subsequent application for listed building consent. Authorities are also required by section 72 of the Act, in the exercise in a conservation area of their powers under the Planning Acts (and Part I of the Historic Buildings and Ancient Monuments Act 1953), to pay special attention to the desirability of preserving or enhancing the character or appearance of that area. In the case of unlisted buildings in conservation areas, the Courts have held that consent for the demolition of a building may involve consideration of what is to take its place (see paragraph 4.27).

2.13 Local planning authorities are urged to ensure that they have appropriately qualified specialist advice on any development which, by its character or location, might be held to have an adverse effect on any sites or structures of the historic environment. The need for environmental assessment of major development proposals affecting historic areas should be considered in the light of the advice given in Department of the Environment *Circular 15/88*. Authorities should ensure that the Royal Fine Art Commission is consulted on all planning applications raising conservation issues of more than local importance, and should take the

RFAC's views fully into account in reaching their decisions.

2.14 The design of new buildings intended to stand alongside historic buildings needs very careful consideration. In general it is better that old buildings are not set apart, but are woven into the fabric of the living and working community. This can be done, provided that the new buildings are carefully designed to respect their setting, follow fundamental architectural principles of scale, height, massing and alignment, and use appropriate materials. This does not mean that new buildings have to copy their older neighbours in detail: some of the most interesting streets in our towns and villages include a variety of building styles, materials, and forms of construction, of many different periods, but together forming a harmonious group. Further general advice on design considerations which are relevant to the exercise of planning controls is given in Annex A to *PPG 1*.

2.15 Some historic buildings are scheduled ancient monuments, and many which are not scheduled are either of intrinsic archaeological interest or stand on ground which contains archaeological remains. It is important in such cases that there should be appropriate assessment of the archaeological implications of development proposals before applications are determined; and that, where permission is to be granted, authorities should consider whether adequate arrangements have been made for recording remains that would be lost in the course of works for which permission is being sought. Further advice on archaeology and planning is given in **PPG 16**.

The setting of listed buildings

2.16 Sections 16 and 66 of the Act require authorities considering applications for planning permission or listed building consent for works which affect a listed building to have special regard to certain matters, including the desirability of preserving the setting of the building. The setting is often an essential part of the building's character, especially if a garden or grounds have been laid out to complement its design or function. Also, the economic viability as well as the character of historic buildings may suffer and they can be robbed of much of their interest, and of the contribution they make to townscape or the countryside, if they become isolated from their surroundings, eg. by new traffic routes, car parks, or other development.

2.17 Local planning authorities are required under section 67 of the Act to publish a notice of all applications they receive for planning permission for any development which, in their opinion, affects the setting of a listed building. This provision should not be interpreted too narrowly: the setting of a building may be limited to obviously ancillary land, but may often include land some distance from it. Even where a building has no ancillary land - for example in a crowded urban street - the setting may encompass a number of other properties. The setting of individual listed buildings very often owes its character to the harmony produced by a particular grouping of buildings (not necessarily all of great individual merit) and to the quality of the spaces created between them. Such areas require careful appraisal when proposals for development are under consideration, even if the redevelopment would only replace a building which is neither itself listed nor immediately adjacent to a listed building. Where a listed building forms an important visual element in a street, it would probably be right to regard any development in the street as being Within the setting of the building. A proposed high or bulky building might also affect the setting of a listed building some distance away, or alter views of a historic skyline. In some cases, setting can only be defined by a historical assessment of a building's surroundings. If there is doubt about the precise extent of a building' setting, it is better to publish a notice.

Changes of use

2.18 New uses may often be the key to a building's or area's preservation, and controls over land use, density, plot ratio, daylighting and other planning matters should be exercised sympathetically where this would enable a historic building or area to be given a new lease of life. The Secretary of State is not generally in favour of tightening development controls over changes of use as a specific instrument of conservation policy. He considers that, in general, the same provisions on change of use should apply to historic buildings as to all others. Patterns of economic activity inevitably change over time, and it would be unrealistic to seek to prevent such change by the use of planning controls.

2.19 Advice on the planning aspects of re-use and adaptation of rural buildings is given in *PPG 7* (paragraph 2.15 and Annex D). English Heritage has also issued guidance entitled *The Conversion of Historic Farm Buildings*. Special considerations apply in Green Belts (see *PPG 2*).

Article 4 directions for listed buildings

2.20 Under article 5 of the GDO, directions under article 4 bringing certain categories of permitted development within planning control can be made by local authorities without the need for approval by the Secretary of State if they relate solely to a listed building or to development within the curtilage of a listed building, provided they do not affect the carrying out of development by a statutory undertaker. Authorities are reminded that permitted development rights should not be restricted without good reason; but there will nevertheless be cases where it will be desirable to invoke this power to ensure that the immediate setting of a listed building is protected when minor development is proposed. For example, farm buildings converted to new uses may otherwise generate curtilage developments - such as garages, fuel tanks or fences - that may not be suitable in an agricultural setting.

Planning controls and other aspects of the historic environment

2.21 Listed buildings and conservation areas are treated in sections 3 and 4 below. Other aspects of the historic environment are considered briefly here.

World Heritage Sites

2.22 Details of World Heritage Sites in England are given in paragraph 6.35. No additional statutory controls follow from the inclusion of a site in the World Heritage list. Inclusion does, however, highlight the outstanding international importance of the site as a key material consideration to be taken into account by local planning authorities in determining planning and listed building consent applications, and by the Secretary of State in determining cases on appeal or following call-in.

2.23 Each local authority concerned, taking account of World Heritage Site designation and other relevant statutory designations, should formulate specific planning policies for protecting these sites and include these policies in their development plans. Policies should reflect the fact that all these sites have been designated for their outstanding universal value, and they should place great weight on the need to protect them for the benefit of future generations as well as our own. Development proposals affecting these sites or their setting may be compatible with this objective, but should always be carefully scrutinised for their likely effect on the site or its setting in the longer term. Significant development proposals affecting World Heritage Sites will generally require formal environmental assessment, to ensure that their immediate impact and their implications for the longer term are fully evaluated (see paragraph 2.13 above).

Historic parks and gardens

2.24 Again no additional statutory controls follow from the inclusion of a site in English Heritage's Register of Parks and Gardens of Special Historic Interest (see paragraph 6.38), but local planning authorities should protect registered parks and gardens in preparing development plans and in determining planning applications. The effect of proposed development on a registered park or garden or its setting is a material consideration in the determination of a planning application. Planning and highway authorities should also safeguard registered parks or gardens when themselves planning new developments or road schemes.

Historic battlefields

2.25 A similar non-statutory Register of Historic Battlefields is being prepared by English Heritage (see paragraph 6.39). This will not entail additional statutory controls, but, when consultation with landowners and others on the content of the Register is complete, it too will need to be taken into account by local planning authorities. The effects of any development on the limited number of registered sites will form a material consideration to be taken into account in determining planning applications.

The wider historic landscape

2.26 Conservation of the wider historic landscape greatly depends on active land management, but there is nevertheless a significant role for local planning authorities. In defining planning policies for the countryside, authorities should take account of the historical dimension of the landscape as a whole rather than concentrate on selected areas. Adequate understanding is an essential preliminary and authorities should assess the wider historic landscape at an early stage in development plan preparation. Plans should protect its most important components and encourage development that is consistent with maintaining its overall historic character. Indeed, policies to strengthen the rural economy through environmentally sensitive diversification may be among the most important for its conservation.

3   LISTED BUILDING CONTROL

3.1 Section 1 of the Act imposes on the Secretary of State for National Heritage a duty to compile or approve lists of buildings of special architectural or historic interest. The Secretary of State's policy for the listing of such buildings is set out in paragraphs 6.10-6.16. Once a building is listed (or is the subject of a building preservation notice), section 7 of the Act provides that consent is normally required for its demolition, in whole or in part, and for any works of alteration or extension which would affect its character as a building of special architectural or historic interest. It is a criminal offence to carry out such works without consent, which should be sought from the local planning authority. This section sets out the main elements of Government policy for listed building controls. Details of the procedures are summarised in Annex B.

3.2 Controls apply to all works, both external and internal, that would affect a building's special interest, whether or not the particular feature concerned is specifically mentioned in the list description. Consent is not normally required for repairs, but, where repairs involve alterations which would affect the character of the listed building, consent is required. Whether repairs actually constitute alterations which require consent is a matter of fact and degree which must be determined in each case. Where painting or repainting the exterior or interior of a listed building would affect the building's character, consent is required. Further detailed guidance on alterations to listed buildings, prepared by English Heritage, is given in Annex C. The Secretaries of State commend this guidance and ask all local planning authorities to take it into account in their exercise of listed building and development controls. Whether proposed works constitute alterations or a demolition is again a matter of fact and degree. Fixtures and curtilage buildings - ie. any object or structure which is fixed to the building, or is within the curtilage and forms part of the land and has done so since before July 1948 - are also treated as part of the building for the purposes of listed building control (see paragraphs 3.30-3.36 below).

3.3 The importance which the Government attaches to the protection of the historic environment was explained in paragraphs 1.1-1.7 above. Once lost, listed buildings cannot be replaced; and they can be robbed of their special interest as surely by unsuitable alteration as by outright demolition. They represent a finite resource and an irreplaceable asset. There should be a general presumption in favour of the preservation of listed buildings, except where a convincing case can be made out, against the criteria set out in this section, for alteration or demolition. While the listing of a building should not be seen as a bar to all future change, the starting point for the exercise of listed building control is the statutory requirement on local planning authorities to 'have special regard to the desirability of preserving the building or its setting or any features of special architectural or historic interest which it possesses' (section 16). This reflects the great importance to society of protecting listed buildings from unnecessary demolition and from unsuitable and insensitive alteration and should be the prime consideration for authorities in determining an application for consent.

3.4 Applicants for listed building consent must be able to justify their proposals. They will need to show why works which would affect the character of a listed building are desirable or necessary. They should provide the local planning authority with full information, to enable them to assess the likely impact of their proposals on the special architectural or historic interest of the building and on its setting.

General criteria

3.5 The issues that are generally relevant to the consideration of all listed building consent applications are:

i.   the importance of the building, its intrinsic architectural and historic interest and rarity, in both national and local terms ('historic interest' is further explained in paragraph 6.11);

ii. the particular physical features of the building (which may include its design, plan, materials or location) which justify its inclusion in the list: list descriptions may draw attention to features of particular interest or value, but they are not exhaustive and other features of importance (eg. interiors) may come to light after the building's inclusion in the list;

iii. the building's setting and its contribution to the local scene, which may be very important, eg. where it forms an element in a group, park, garden or other townscape or landscape, or where it shares particular architectural forms or details with other buildings nearby;

iv. the extent to which the proposed works would bring substantial benefits for the community, in particular by contributing to the economic regeneration of the area or the enhancement of its environment (including other listed buildings).

3.6 The grading of a building in the statutory lists is clearly a material consideration for the exercise of listed building control. Grades I and II* identify the outstanding architectural or historic interest of a small proportion (about 6%) of all listed buildings. These buildings are of particularly great importance to the nation's built heritage: their significance will generally be beyond dispute. But it should be emphasised that the statutory controls apply equally to all listed buildings, irrespective of grade; and since Grade II includes about 94% of all listed buildings, representing a major element in the historic quality of our towns, villages and countryside, failure to give careful scrutiny to proposals for their alteration or demolition could lead to widespread damage to the historic environment.

3.7 The following paragraphs deal first with alterations and extensions and then with demolitions, though considerations relevant to the two types of case to some extent overlap. For instance, some of the considerations set out in paragraph 3.19, in relation to demolitions, may also be relevant to substantial works of alteration or extension which would significantly alter the character of a listed building. Since listed building consent applications will often raise the issue of the most appropriate use for a building, the question of use is also discussed here.

Use

3.8 Generally the best way of securing the upkeep of historic buildings and areas is to keep them in active use. For the great majority this must mean economically viable uses if they are to survive, and new, and even continuing, uses will often necessitate some degree of adaptation. The range and acceptability of possible uses must therefore usually be a major consideration when the future of listed buildings or buildings in conservation areas is in question.

3.9 Judging the best use is one of the most important and sensitive assessments that local planning authorities and other bodies involved in conservation have to make. It requires balancing the economic viability of possible uses against the effect of any changes they entail in the special architectural and historic interest of the building or area in question. In principle the aim should be to identify the optimum viable use that is compatible with the fabric, interior, and setting of the historic building. This may not necessarily be the most profitable use if that would entail more destructive alterations than other viable uses. Where a particular compatible use is to be preferred but restoration for that use is unlikely to be economically viable, grant assistance from the authority, English Heritage or other sources may need to be considered.

3.10 The best use will very often be the use for which the building was originally designed, and the continuation or reinstatement of that use should certainly be the first option when the future of a building is considered. But not all original uses will now be viable or even necessarily appropriate: the nature of uses can change over time, so that in some cases the original use may now be less compatible with the building than an alternative. For example, some business or light industrial uses may now require less damaging alterations to historic farm buildings than some types of modern agricultural operation. Policies for development and listed building controls should recognise the need for flexibility where new uses have to be considered to secure a building's survival.

3.11 If a building is so sensitive that it cannot sustain any alterations to keep it in viable economic use, its future may nevertheless be secured by charitable or community ownership, preserved for its own sake for local people and for the visiting public, where possible with non-destructive opportunity uses such as meeting rooms. Many listed buildings subsist successfully in this way - from the great houses of the National Trust to buildings such as guildhalls, churches and windmills cared for by local authorities or trusts - and this possibility may need to be considered. The Secretaries of State attach particular importance to the activities of the voluntary sector in heritage matters: it is well placed to tap local support, resources and loyalty, and buildings preserved in its care can make a contribution to community life, to local education, and to the local economy.

Alterations and extensions

3.12 Many listed buildings are already in well-established uses, and any changes need be considered only in this context. But where new uses are proposed, it is important to balance the effect of any changes on the special interest of the listed building against the viability of any proposed use and of alternative, and possibly less damaging, uses. In judging the effect of any alteration or extension it is essential to have assessed the elements that make up the special interest of the building in question. They may comprise not only obvious visual features such as a decorative facade or, internally, staircases or decorated plaster ceilings, but the spaces and layout of the building and the archaeological or technological interest of the surviving structure and surfaces. These elements are often just as important in simple vernacular and functional buildings as in grander architecture.

3.13 Many listed buildings can sustain some degree of sensitive alteration or extension to accommodate continuing or new uses. Indeed, cumulative changes reflecting the history of use and ownership are themselves an aspect of the special interest of some buildings, and the merit of some new alterations or additions, especially where they are generated within a secure and committed long-term ownership, should not be discounted. Nevertheless, listed buildings do vary greatly in the extent to which they can accommodate change without loss of special interest. Some may be sensitive even to slight alterations; this is especially true of buildings with important interiors and fittings - not just great houses, but also, for example, chapels with historic fittings or industrial structures with surviving machinery. Some listed buildings are the subject of successive applications for alteration or extension: in such cases it needs to be borne in mind that minor works of indifferent quality, which may seem individually of little importance, can cumulatively be very destructive of a building's special interest.

3.14 As noted above, the listing grade is a material consideration but is not of itself a reliable guide to the sensitivity of a building to alteration or extension. For example, many Grade II buildings are of humble and once common building types and have been listed precisely because they are relatively unaltered examples of a particular building type; so they can as readily have their special interest ruined by unsuitable alteration or extension as can Grade I or II* structures.

3.15 Achieving a proper balance between the special interest of a listed building and proposals for alterations or extensions is demanding and should always be based on specialist expertise; but it is rarely impossible, if reasonable flexibility and imagination are shown by all parties involved. Thus, a better solution may be possible if a local planning authority is prepared to apply normal development control policies flexibly; or if an applicant is willing to exploit unorthodox spaces rather than set a standardized requirement; or if an architect can respect the structural limitations of a building and abandon conventional design solutions in favour of a more imaginative approach. For example, standard commercial office floor-loadings are rarely needed in all parts of a building, and any unusually heavy loads can often be accommodated in stronger areas such as basements. The preservation of facades alone, and the gutting and reconstruction of interiors, is not normally an acceptable approach to the re-use of listed buildings: it can destroy much of a building's special interest and create problems for the long-term stability of the structure.

Demolitions

3.16 While it is an objective of Government policy to secure the preservation of historic buildings, there will very occasionally be cases where demolition is unavoidable. Listed building controls ensure that proposals for demolition are fully scrutinised before any decision is reached. These controls have been successful in recent years in keeping the number of total demolitions very low. The destruction of historic buildings is in fact very seldom necessary for reasons of good planning: more often it is the result of neglect, or of failure to make imaginative efforts to find new uses for them or to incorporate them into new development.

3.17 There are many outstanding buildings for which it is in practice almost inconceivable that consent for demolition would ever be granted. The demolition of any Grade I or Grade II* building should be wholly exceptional and should require the strongest justification. Indeed, the Secretaries of State would not expect consent to be given for the total or substantial demolition of any listed building without clear and convincing evidence that all reasonable efforts have been made to sustain existing uses or find viable new uses, and these efforts have failed; that preservation in some form of charitable or community ownership is not possible or suitable (see paragraph 3.11); or that redevelopment would produce substantial benefits for the community which would decisively outweigh the loss resulting from demolition. The Secretaries of State would not expect consent to demolition to be given simply because redevelopment is economically more attractive to the developer than repair and re-use of a historic building, or because the developer acquired the building at a price that reflected the potential for redevelopment rather than the condition and constraints of the existing historic building.

3.18 Where proposed works would not result in the total or substantial demolition of the listed building or any significant part of it, the Secretaries of State would expect the local planning authority to address the same considerations as it would in relation to an application in respect of alterations or extensions (see paragraphs 3.12 to 3.15 above).

3.19 Where proposed works would result in the total or substantial demolition of the listed building, or any significant part of it, the Secretaries of State would expect the authority, in addition to the general considerations set out in paragraph 3.5 above, to address the following considerations:

    i.   the condition of the building, the cost of repairing and maintaining it in relation to its importance and to the value derived from its continued use. Any such assessment should be based on consistent and long-term assumptions. Less favourable levels of rents and yields cannot automatically be assumed for historic buildings. Also, they may offer proven technical performance, physical attractiveness and functional spaces that, in an age of rapid change, may outlast the short-lived and inflexible technical specifications that have sometimes shaped new developments. Any assessment should also take account of the possibility of tax allowances and exemptions and of grants from public or charitable sources. In the rare cases where it is clear that a building has been deliberately neglected in the hope of obtaining consent for demolition, less weight should be given to the costs of repair;

    ii.   the adequacy of efforts made to retain the building in use. The Secretaries of State would not expect listed building consent to be granted for demolition unless the authority (or where appropriate the Secretary of State himself) is satisfied that real efforts have been made without success to continue the present use or to find compatible alternative uses for the building. This should include the offer of the unrestricted freehold of the building on the open market at a realistic price reflecting the building's condition (the offer of a lease only, or the imposition of restrictive covenants, would normally reduce the chances of finding a new use for the building);

iii. the merits of alternative proposals for the site. Whilst these are a material consideration, the Secretaries of State take the view that subjective claims for the architectural merits of proposed replacement buildings should not in themselves be held to justify the demolition of any listed building. There may very exceptionally be cases where the proposed works would bring substantial benefits for the community which have to be weighed against the arguments in favour of preservation. Even here, it will often be feasible to incorporate listed buildings within new development, and this option should be carefully considered: the challenge presented by retaining listed buildings can be a stimulus to imaginative new design to accommodate them.

Called-in applications

3.20 The Secretary of State may require applications for listed building consent to be referred to him for decision, but this call-in power has only been exercised in a small number of cases per year in recent years. The policy of the Secretary of State is to be very selective about calling in listed building consent cases.

3.21 Cases are likely to be called in where the Secretary of State considers that the proposals raise issues of exceptional significance or controversy. It may also happen that an application for listed building consent is received by a local planning authority when a related matter (eg. a planning appeal, a called-in planning application or a compulsory purchase order) is being considered by the Secretary of State. Unless it is clear that the listed building consent application can reasonably be dealt with separately, such an application will normally be called in.

Recording buildings

3.22 The Royal Commission on the Historical Monuments of England must be notified of all proposals to demolish listed buildings, and allowed access to buildings which it wishes to record before demolition takes place. There are other circumstances where notification may also be appropriate - for instance, where the exterior of a building is likely to be radically changed as a consequence of major repairs, alteration or extension, or where interior work of significance will be lost, affected by subdivision, or substantially rebuilt.

3.23 Local planning authorities should also consider, in all cases of alteration or demolition, whether it would be appropriate to make it a condition of consent that applicants arrange suitable programmes of recording of features that would be destroyed in the course of the works for which consent is being sought. Authorities should not, however, require applicants to finance such programmes in return for the granting of consent. Nor should applicants expect to be granted consent merely because they have arranged suitable programmes. (For recording of archaeological remains see paragraph 2.15.)

3.24 Hidden features of interest are sometimes revealed during works of alteration, especially in older or larger buildings: chimney pieces, fireplaces, early windows and doors, panelling, wattle-and-daub partitions and even wall-paintings may come to light. Applicants for listed building consent should be made aware of this possibility and should seek the advice of the local planning authority when such things are found. If there is any likelihood that hidden features will be revealed, the local planning authority should attach an appropriate condition to the listed building consent to ensure their retention or proper recording, or should require exploratory opening up, with listed building consent as necessary, before considering consent for the main works.

Advice to owners

3.25 Owners of listed buildings should be encouraged to seek expert advice on whether proposed works require listed building consent, and on the best way to carry out any such works to their property. Many will need to obtain professional advice anyway, but the Secretaries of State hope that local planning authorities will give owners informal advice where they can or guide them to other sources where they can get advice for themselves. English Heritage publishes much specialist advice on the care of historic buildings and can sometimes give advice on individual cases, especially where unusual problems are encountered. The national amenity societies are willing to offer advice to individual owners whenever possible. The Royal Commission on the Historical Monuments of England may have a record of a building and its reports and photographs may be available for guidance in understanding the structure and its evolution.

Building and fire legislation; access for disabled people; house renovation grants

3.26 In exercising their responsibilities for the safety of buildings under the building and fire legislation, local planning authorities should deal sympathetically with proposals for the repair or conversion of historic buildings. The Building Regulations should be operated in a way which avoids removal of features which contribute to the character of a listed building and are part of the reason for its being listed. Sufficient flexibility exists within the Building Regulations and Fire Precautions Act systems for authorities to have regard to the possible impact of proposals on the historical or architectural value of a building, and authorities should consult their own conservation officers, or seek expert advice from other sources, when handling difficult situations. It is particularly important that there should be a flexible approach to structural matters, to ensure that any changes are in character with the rest of the building and that there is no unacceptable damage to the fabric. In order to ensure that requirements which are unacceptable in terms of a historic building can be considered as part of a listed building consent application, the precise Building and Fire Regulations requirements should be made explicit *before* an application has been determined. A successful outcome is more likely to be negotiated if the authorities have been consulted from the outset.

3.27 For the longer term, local planning authorities should be aware of the *Report of the Review of the Fire Safety Legislation and Enforcement* which was published on 22 June 1994. The scrutiny was asked to review all legislation for which the Home Office, the Department of the Environment and the Health and Safety Executive have policy responsibility in relation to fire safety; to review the arrangements for enforcing the legislation; and to examine the practicability of bringing policy responsibility for fire safety together in a single department. The

Report makes 61 recommendations, but Ministers are committed to full consultation before any proposals for changing the existing arrangements are made.

3.28 It is important in principle that disabled people should have dignified easy access to and within historic buildings. If it is treated as part of an integrated review of access requirements for all visitors or users, and a flexible and pragmatic approach is taken, it should normally be possible to plan suitable access for disabled people without compromising a building's special interest. Alternative routes or re-organizing the use of spaces may achieve the desired result without the need for damaging alterations.

3.29 Where a local planning authority proposes to grant-aid renovation work to a listed house or a house in a conservation area, care should be taken to ensure that standard grant conditions (eg. for damp proofing or insulation) are not imposed in a way which would be damaging to the historic character of the building. In such cases housing and environmental health departments should consult with the authority's conservation officer or seek expert advice from other sources. Details of grants available are given in the Department of the Environment publication *House Renovation Grants*.

Fixtures and curtilage structures

3.30 It is important to know the extent of a listing, not just to determine whether listed building consent is needed for works, but also to determine the payment of VAT and business rates. List descriptions are for the purposes of identification and are not a comprehensive or exclusive record of all features - see paragraph 6.19. Section 1(5) of the Act sets out the meaning of a listed building for the purposes of the Act: a listed building is one included in a list compiled or approved by the Secretary of State and includes 'any object or structure fixed to the building' and 'any object or structure within the curtilage of the building which, although not fixed to the building, forms part of the land and has done so since before July 1, 1948.' The Courts have considered in a number of cases in this context the meaning of 'any object or structure fixed to the building' and 'curtilage'.

3.31 The listing of a building confers protection not only on the building, but also on any object or structure fixed to the building which is ancillary to the building. The word 'fixed' has the same connotation as in the law of fixtures. These well-known rules provide that any object or structure fixed to a building should be treated as part of it. It is a test therefore of fact in each case as to whether a structure is free-standing or physically fixed to the building. Generally it would be reasonable to expect some degree of physical annexation, together with indications that the annexation was carried out with the intention of making the object an integral part of the land or building. In the light of this test, items such as chimney-pieces, wall panelling and painted or plastered ceilings will normally be found to be part of the building.

3.32 It may be difficult in some individual cases to decide whether a particular object or structure is a fixture or not. Free-standing objects, eg. statues, may be fixtures if they were put in place as part of an overall architectural design; this could include objects specially designed or made to fit in a particular space or room. But works of art which were placed in a building primarily to be enjoyed as objects in their own right, rather than forming part of the land or the building, are not likely to be properly considered as fixtures. Each case must be treated in the light of its own facts, and owners who are contemplating works are advised to contact their local planning authority first.

3.33 The listing of a building confers protection also on any object or structure within its curtilage which forms part of the land and has done so since before I July 1948. Following recent case law, the Secretary of State for National Heritage has attempted to consider individually all the structures and buildings on a site which can be construed as separate buildings and to list those which qualify for listing. There will still be circumstances, however, where a structure or building forms part of land which surrounds or is connected to or serves a listed building, and landowners and local planning authorities will need to consider on the facts of each case whether it forms part of the land and falls within the curtilage of the listed building.

3.34 The principal tests as to whether an object or structure is within the curtilage of a listed building relate to the physical layout of the land surrounding the listed building at the date of the statutory listing and the relationship of the structures on the surrounding land to each other. Changes in ownership, occupation or use after the listing date will not bring about the de-listing of a building which formed part of the principal building at the date of listing. The Courts have held that for a structure or building within the curtilage of a listed building to be part of a listed building it must be ancillary to the principal building, that is it must have served the purposes of the principal building at the date of listing, or at a recent time before the date of listing, in a necessary or reasonably useful way and must not be historically an independent building. Where a self-contained building was fenced or walled-off from the remainder of the site at the date of listing, regardless of the purpose for which it was erected and is occupied, it is likely to be regarded as having a separate curtilage. The structure or building must still form part of the land, and this probably means that there must be some degree of physical annexation to the land.

3.35 Considerations which may assist local planning authorities in forming their own views, or giving advice if requested, include:

- the historical independence of the building;
- the physical layout of the principal building and other buildings;
- the ownership of the buildings now and at the time of listing;
- whether the structure forms part of the land;
- the use and function of the buildings, and whether a building is ancillary or subordinate to the principal building.

3.36 It is always necessary to recognise, however, that the question of whether a building, structure or object is within the curtilage of, or is fixed to, the principal building, unless specifically included in the listing, is in any particular case a matter of fact and ultimately a matter for the Courts. Great caution must, therefore, be exercised in attempting to extrapolate any general principles from recent decisions and this guidance does not purport to be definitive.

Local authority applications

3.37 A county council (where not a local planning authority) is required to make its applications for listed building consent to the relevant district planning authority, which should consider them against the normal criteria. Local planning authorities are normally required to make their own applications to the Secretary of State, whether or not they themselves own the listed building in question. The Secretaries of State ask authorities to deal with their own buildings in ways which will provide examples of good practice to other owners. It is particularly important that every effort should be made to maintain historic buildings in good condition, and to find appropriate new uses for buildings in authority ownership which are no longer in active use. Prompt disposal is important: empty buildings should not be retained on a contingency basis, with all the risk of neglect and disrepair that this can create.

3.38 The Secretary of State will be particularly concerned to ensure that local planning authorities take full account of the policies set out in this PPG, and will not be disposed to grant consent for the demolition of listed buildings in authorities' ownership unless there is clear and convincing evidence that alternative possibilities for new ownership and new uses have been thoroughly explored.

Churches and Crown buildings

3.39 Special provisions apply to ecclesiastical buildings in use for ecclesiastical purposes, which are in some circumstances exempt from listed building and conservation area controls. Details of the arrangements which apply to such buildings are given in section 8.

3.40 The Crown is currently exempt from listed building and conservation area controls; but the Government has undertaken that Crown bodies will normally operate as if these controls did apply (see Department of the Environment *Circular 18/84*). English Heritage should be notified of Crown developments on the same basis as normal applications. Proposals have been published for the removal of Crown exemption in planning and conservation matters; pending the necessary legislation, the arrangements in *Circular 18/84* continue to apply.

3.41 Works by English Heritage on monuments, buildings or land which are owned by or in the care of the Secretary of State for National Heritage and which they are managing on his behalf are treated as Crown development and the procedures in *Circular 18/84* will apply. If English Heritage wishes to carry out works to other listed buildings, or demolish an unlisted building in a conservation area, it must obtain listed building or conservation area consent. The Secretary of State has directed that all such applications should be referred to him. The authority should advertise such applications as they would any other private application and forward any representations received, together with their own comments, to the appropriate regional Government Office.

Listed building consent for works already executed

3.42 Section 8(3) of the Act allows listed building consent to be sought even though the works have already been completed. Applications for consent to retain such works should follow the same procedures as other listed building consent applications and should contain sufficient information (see Annex B paragraph B.3). Local planning authorities should not grant consent merely to recognise a *fait accompli*; they should consider whether they would have granted consent for the works had it been sought before they were carried out, while having regard to any subsequent matters which may be relevant. If the work is not of a suitable type or standard, consent should not normally be given, and the risk of prosecution or enforcement action will remain. If consent is granted, it is not retrospective; the works are authorised only from the date of the consent. A prosecution may still be brought for the initial offence.

Enforcement

3.43 If work is carried out without consent, a local planning authority can issue a listed building enforcement notice (section 38). The notice may (a) require the building to be brought back to its former state; or (b), if that is not reasonably practicable or desirable, require other works specified in the notice to alleviate the effects of the unauthorised works; or (c) require the building to be brought into the state it would have been in if the terms of any listed building consent had been observed. It was held in the case of *Bath City Council v. Secretary of State for the Environment* ([1983] JPL 737) that this provision could not be used to secure an improvement to a listed building compared to its state before the unauthorised works were carried out. There is a right of appeal to the Secretary of State against a notice; the appeal procedures are generally similar to those for enforcement of development control following the Planning and Compensation Act 1991, although there are no provisions equivalent to a planning contravention notice, nor is there any limitation on the period within which a listed building enforcement notice must be issued. If works subject to a listed building enforcement notice are later authorised under section 8(3), the enforcement notice will cease to have effect in relation to those works, although the liability to prosecution for an offence committed before the date of consent remains. Breach of a listed building enforcement notice is itself an offence, with financial penalties parallel to those for a breach of listed building control.

Prosecutions

3.44 It is a criminal offence to execute, or cause to be executed, without first obtaining listed building consent any works for the demolition, in whole or part, of a listed building or any works of alteration or extension which would affect its special interest, or to fail to comply with the terms of any condition attached to a consent (section 9). This includes the theft of architectural fixtures. The current penalty for conviction in a magistrates' court is a fine of up to £20,000 or imprisonment for up to six months (or both), whilst on conviction in the Crown Court an unlimited fine or a prison sentence of up to two years (or both) may be imposed. In determining the amount of any fine, a magistrates' court or the Crown Court must have regard to any financial benefit which has accrued or may accrue from the offence.

3.45 In proceedings for an offence under section 9 it is a defence to prove all of the following matters:

(a)   that works to the building were urgently necessary in the interests of safety or health or for the preservation of the building;

(b)   that it was not practicable to secure safety or health or, as the case may be, to preserve the building by works of repair or works for affording temporary support or shelter;

(c)   that the works carried out were limited to the minimum measures immediately necessary; and

(d)   that notice in writing justifying in detail the carrying out of the works was given to the local planning authority as soon as reasonably practicable.

3.46 Anyone – individuals as well as English Heritage and local planning authorities – can start proceedings. English Heritage and planning authorities can also seek injunctions for breaches of listed building control. A prosecution may also be initiated under section 59 where deliberate damage is caused to a listed building by an owner or his agent, for which financial penalties are provided.

3.47 Local planning authorities will obviously need to consider, when faced with a breach of listed building control, whether to take enforcement action or to prosecute or both. Enforcement may be intrinsically desirable for the benefit of the building in question, while the work entailed by enforcement may also represent a sufficient response to the offence. However, unauthorised work may often destroy historic fabric the special interest of which cannot be restored by enforcement. Moreover, well-publicised successful prosecutions can provide a valuable deterrent to wilful damage to, or destruction of, listed buildings, and it is the Secretary of State's policy to encourage proceedings where it is considered that a good case can be sustained.

3.48 Prosecution and enforcement relate to breaches of listed building control that have already occurred. Where such a breach is continuing or there is good reason to suppose it is about to occur, authorities should consider seeking an injunction to stop or prevent it. Since a breach of listed building control (unlike development control) is itself a criminal offence, there is no need or statutory provision for stop notices. Authorities may, of course, find written warnings useful deterrents. Injunctions can be obtained speedily from the Court even where the actual or expected offender is not present before the Court, or indeed where his or her identity is not known; the essential ingredient is to satisfy the Court that the application is soundly based. In the case of an interim injunction the Court would normally ask the applicant to compensate the restrained party for any costs the latter might incur as a result of the interim injunction if the Court refuse to grant a final injunction. Anyone who refuses to comply with an injunction is in contempt of Court and may be fined or imprisoned (or both).

4   CONSERVATION AREAS

4.1 Section 69 of the Act imposes a duty on local planning authorities to designate as conservation areas any 'areas of special architectural or historic interest the character or appearance of which it is desirable to preserve or enhance'. There are now more than 8,000 conservation areas in England. Whilst listing procedures are focused on the protection of individual buildings, conservation area resignation is the main instrument available to authorities to give effect to conservation policies for a particular neighbourhood or area. Designation introduces a general control over the demolition of unlisted buildings and provides the basis for policies designed to preserve or enhance all the aspects of character or appearance that define an area's special interest.

Assessment and designation of conservation areas

4.2 It is the quality and interest of areas, rather than that of individual buildings, which should be the prime consideration in identifying conservation areas. There has been increasing recognition in recent years that our experience of a historic area depends on much more than the quality of individual buildings – on the historic layout of property boundaries and thoroughfares; on a particular 'mix' of uses; on characteristic materials; on appropriate scaling and detailing of contemporary buildings; on the quality of advertisements, shop fronts, street furniture and hard and soft surfaces; on vistas along streets and between buildings; and on the extent to which traffic intrudes and limits pedestrian use of spaces between buildings. Conservation area designation should be seen as the means of recognising the importance of all these factors and of ensuring that conservation policy addresses the quality of townscape in its broadest sense as well as the protection of individual buildings.

4.3 Local planning authorities also have under section 69 a duty to review their areas from time to time to consider whether further designation of conservation areas is called for. In some districts, areas suitable for designation may have been fully identified already; and in considering further designations authorities should bear in mind that it is important that conservation areas are seen to justify their status and that the concept is not devalued by the designation of areas lacking any special interest. Authorities should seek to establish consistent local standards for their designations and should periodically review existing conservation areas and their boundaries against those standards: cancellation of designation should be considered where an area or part of an area is no longer considered to possess the special interest which led to its original designation.

4.4 The more clearly the special architectural or historic interest that justifies designation is defined and recorded, the sounder will be the basis for local plan policies and development control decisions, as well as for the formulation of proposals for the preservation and enhancement of the character or appearance of an area. The definition of an area's special interest should derive from an assessment of the elements that contribute to (and detract from) it. Conservation areas vary greatly, but certain aspects will almost always form the basis for a coherent assessment: the topography – for example, thoroughfares and property boundaries – and its historical development; the archaeological significance and potential; the prevalent building materials; the character and hierarchy of spaces; the quality and relationship of buildings in the area and also of trees and other green features. The assessment should always note those unlisted buildings which make a positive contribution to the special interest of the area. More detailed advice on assessment and on other aspects of the management of conservation areas is set out in English Heritage's guidance note *Conservation Area Practice.*

4.5 The principal concern of a local planning authority in considering the designation of a conservation area should be to form a judgment on whether the area is of special architectural or historic interest the character or appearance of which it is desirable to preserve or enhance. In deciding whether it is desirable to designate, an authority may take into account the resources likely to be required, not only for the administration of conservation area controls, but also for consultation with local residents and formulation of policies for a new area: without follow-up, designation is unlikely to be effective in itself. An authority's justification for designation, as reflected in its assessment of an area's special interest and its character and appearance, is a factor which the Secretary of State will take into account in considering appeals against refusals of conservation area consent for demolition, and appeals against refusals of planning permission (see also paragraph 2.9).

4.6 Given the nature of conservation area controls – essentially controls over demolition; strengthened controls over minor development; and the protection of trees – designation is not likely to be appropriate as a means of protecting landscape features, except where they form an integral part of the historic built environment and that factor needs to be taken into account in considering any planning applications which would affect them. The Courts have held that it is legitimate in appropriate circumstances to include within a conservation area the setting of buildings that form the heart of that area (*R. v. Canterbury City Council, ex parte David Halford*, February 1992; CO/2794/1991). Designation is clearly not a proper means of controlling activities (eg, agricultural operations) which do not fall within the definition of development. Designation may well, however, be suitable for historic parks or gardens and other areas of historic landscape containing structures that contribute to their special interest and that fall within the categories subject to conservation area controls. Where there are no other reasons for designating a conservation area, trees may instead be protected by means of a tree preservation order.

4.7 There is no statutory requirement to consult prior to designation or cancellation of designation, but it will be highly desirable that there should be consultation with local residents, businesses and other local interests (eg, amenity bodies) over both the identification of areas and the definition of their boundaries. The greater the public support that can be enlisted for designation before it takes place, the more likely it is that policies for the area will be implemented voluntarily and without the need for additional statutory controls. Local planning authorities should advise English Heritage and the appropriate regional Government Office when conservation areas are designated.

4.8 English Heritage and the Secretary of State for National Heritage also have powers to designate conservation areas, but look to local planning authorities in the first instance to consider the case for designation. English Heritage's powers relate to London only, where they are required to consult the London borough council concerned and to obtain the Secretary of State's consent to designation. The Secretary of State must also consult the authorities concerned before using his powers of designation. His policy is to use his own powers only in exceptional cases, for instance where an area is of more than local interest; or where there is evidence to suggest that an authority's ownership of important buildings may have influenced a decision not to use its own powers, and there is a clear threat to the character or appearance of the area. The Secretary of State may also apply such criteria when requested to approve the use of English Heritage's powers.

Policies for conservation areas

4.9 Section 71 of the Act places a duty on local planning authorities to formulate and publish proposals for the preservation and enhancement of conservation areas. It is important that designation is not seen as an end in itself – policies will almost always need to be developed which clearly identify what it is about the character or appearance of the area which should be preserved or enhanced, and set out the means by which that objective is to be pursued. Clear assessment and definition of an area's special interest and the action needed to protect it will help to generate awareness and encourage local property owners to take the right sort of action for themselves.

4.10 The Act requires proposals for the preservation and enhancement of a conservation area to be submitted for consideration to a 'public meeting' in the area, but wider consultation will almost always be desirable, both on the assessment of special interest and on proposals for the area. Consultation should be undertaken not only with local residents and amenity societies but also with chambers of commerce, public utilities, and the highway authority. The character and appearance of many conservation areas is heavily dependent on the treatment of roads, pavements and other public spaces (see paragraphs 5.13-5.18). It is important that conservation policies are fully integrated with other policies for the area, eg. for shopping and traffic management. Account should also be taken of wider policies (eg, for house renovation grants) which may affect the area's character or appearance. The preparation of local plans provides the best opportunity for integrating conservation policies with wider policies for the area, though a local planning authority's detailed statement of proposals for the conservation area should not itself be part of the development plan (see paragraphs 2.9 above and 4.15 below). Carefully targeted grant schemes using the authority's powers under section 57 of the Act to help with repair and enhancement should also be considered as part of the policy for an area. In certain cases English Heritage Conservation Area Partnership funding may be available.

Vacant premises over shops

4.11 Bringing vacant upper floors back into use, particularly residential use, not only provides additional income and security for the shop owner, but also helps to ensure that what are often important townscape buildings are kept in good repair it meets a widespread need for small housing units and helps to sustain activity in town centres after working hours. Local planning authorities are urged to develop policies to secure better use of vacant upper premises, eg, by giving careful consideration to planning applications for shop conversions which would eliminate separate accesses to upper floors; by working with housing associations to secure residential conversions; and through the house renovation grant system.

Local information and consultation

4.12 Once policies for a particular area have been formulated, they should be made available to local residents and businesses in leaflet form, setting out clearly why the area has been designated; what its specially valuable features are; how individual householders can help to protect its character and appearance; and what additional controls and opportunities for assistance designation brings with it. Without such information, the support of local residents is not likely to be realised to the full. (English Heritage's guidance note on conservation areas gives advice on such publicity.)

4.13 Local planning authorities are asked to consider setting up conservation area advisory committees, both to assist in formulating policies for the conservation area (or for several areas in a particular neighbourhood), and also as a continuing source of advice on planning and other applications which could affect an area. Committees should consist mainly of people who are not members of the authority; local residential and business interests should be fully represented. In addition to local historical, civic and amenity societies, and local chambers of commerce, the authority may wish to seek nominations (depending on the character of the area) from national bodies such as the national amenity societies and the Civic Trust. Authorities should consider whether there is scope for the involvement of local people on a voluntary basis in practical work for the enhancement of an area.

Use of planning powers in conservation areas

4.14 Section 72 of the Act requires that special attention shall be paid in the exercise of planning functions to the desirability of preserving or enhancing the character or appearance of a conservation area. This requirement extends to all powers under the Planning Acts, not only those which relate directly to historic buildings. The desirability of preserving or enhancing the area should also, in the Secretary of State's view, be a material consideration in the planning authority's handling of development proposals which are outside the conservation area but would affect its setting, or views into or out of the area. Local planning authorities are required by section 73 to publish a notice of planning applications for development which would in their opinion affect the character or appearance of a conservation area.

4.15 The status now accorded to the development plan by section 54A of the principal Act makes it particularly important that an authority's policies for its conservation areas, insofar as they bear on the exercise of development controls, should be set out in the local plan. There should also be a clear indication of the relationship between the plan itself and detailed assessment documents or statements of proposals for particular conservation areas, making clear that development proposals will be judged for their effect on the character and appearance of the area as identified in the assessment document.

4.16 Many conservation areas include the non-commercial centres of the towns and villages of which they form part. While conservation (whether by preservation or enhancement) of their character or appearance must be a major consideration, this cannot realistically take the form of preventing all new development: the emphasis will generally need to be on controlled and positive management of change. Policies will need to be designed to allow the area to remain alive and prosperous, and to avoid unnecessarily detailed controls over businesses and householders, but at the same time to ensure that any new development accords with the area's special architectural and historic interest.

4.17 Many conservation areas include gap sites, or buildings that make no positive contribution to, or indeed detract from, the character or appearance of the area; their replacement should be a stimulus to imaginative, high quality design, and seen as an opportunity to enhance the area. What is important is not that new buildings should directly imitate earlier styles, but that they should be designed with respect for their context, as part of a larger whole which has a well-established character and appearance of its own.

4.18 Local planning authorities will often need to ask for detailed plans and drawings of proposed new development, including elevations which show the new development in its setting, before considering a planning application. In addition to adopted local plan policies, it may be helpful to prepare design briefs for individually important 'opportunity' sites. Special regard should be had for such matters as scale, height, form, massing, respect for the traditional pattern of frontages, vertical or horizontal emphasis, and detailed design (eg. the scale and spacing of window openings, and the nature and quality of materials). General planning standards should be applied sensitively in the interests of harmonising the new development with its neighbours in the conservation area.

4.19 The Courts have recently confirmed that planning decisions in respect of development proposed to be carried out in a conservation area must give a high priority to the objective of preserving or enhancing the character or appearance of the area. If any proposed development would conflict with that objective, there will be a strong presumption against the grant of planning permission, though in exceptional cases the presumption may be overridden in favour of development which is desirable on the ground of some other public interest.

4.20 As to the precise interpretation of 'preserve or enhance', the Courts have held (*South Lakeland DC v. Secretary of State for the Environment*, [1992] 2 WLR 204) that there is no requirement in the legislation that conservation areas should be protected from all development which does not enhance or positively preserve. Whilst the character and appearance of conservation areas should always be given full weight in planning decisions, the objective of preservation can be achieved either by development which makes a positive contribution to an area's character or appearance, or by development which leaves character and appearance unharmed.

Permitted development in conservation areas

4.21 The GDO requires planning applications for certain types of development in conservation areas which are elsewhere classified as permitted development. These include various types of cladding; the insertion of dormer windows into roof slopes; the erection of satellite dishes on walls, roofs or chimneys fronting a highway; and the installation of radio masts, antennae or radio equipment housing with a volume in excess of two cubic metres (unless the development is carried out in an emergency). The size of house and industrial extensions that may be carried out without specific planning permission is also more restricted.

4.22 On 30 March 1994 the Government announced a new proposal to enable local planning authorities to make directions withdrawing permitted development rights for a prescribed range of development materially affecting some aspects of the external appearance of dwellinghouses, such as doors, windows, roofs and frontages. There would be no requirement to obtain the Secretary of State's approval for such directions, but authorities would have to publicise their proposals in advance and have regard to the views of local people. Further details of these new arrangements will be published by circular shortly.

4.23 The withdrawal of permitted development rights outside these categories will continue to require Article 4 directions for which the Secretary of State's approval is generally needed before they can become effective. The Secretary of State takes the view that permitted development rights should not be withdrawn without clear justification and that, wherever possible, residents in conservation areas should continue to enjoy the same freedom to undertake development as residents elsewhere. He does not consider that the designation of a conservation area in itself automatically justifies making an Article 4 direction. Such directions may, however, have a role to play if they would help to protect features that are key elements of particular conservation areas and do not come within the categories that will be subject to the arrangements set out in paragraph 4.22 above. The Secretary of State will generally be in favour of approving directions in conservation areas where these are backed by a clear assessment of an area's special architectural and historic interest, where the importance to that special interest of the features in question is established, where the local planning authority can demonstrate local support for the direction, and where the direction involves the minimum withdrawal of permitted development rights (in terms of both area and types of development) necessary to achieve its objective.

4.24 Sections 107 and 108 of the principal Act make provision for the payment of compensation in certain circumstances where permitted development rights have been withdrawn by an Article 4 direction or an amendment to the GDO.

Conservation area control over demolition

4.25 Conservation area designation introduces control over the demolition of most buildings within conservation areas (section 74 of the Act); exceptions are specified in section 75 and in the relevant direction. Applications for consent to demolish must be made to the local planning authority or, on appeal or call-in, to the Secretary of State. Procedures are essentially the same as for listed building consent applications.

Authorities' own applications must be made to the Secretary of State. Scheduled ancient monuments are exempt from conservation area control: scheduled monument consent for proposed works must be sought from the Secretary of State for National Heritage (see *PPG 16*).

4.26 In exercising conservation area controls, local planning authorities are required to pay special attention to the desirability of preserving or enhancing the character or appearance of the area in question; and, as with listed building controls, this should be the prime consideration in determining a consent application. In the case of conservation area controls, however, account should clearly be taken of the part played in the architectural or historic interest of the area by the building for which demolition is proposed, and in particular of the wider effects of demolition on the building's surroundings and on the conservation area as a whole.

4.27 The general presumption should be in favour of retaining buildings which make a positive contribution to the character or appearance of a conservation area. The Secretary of State expects that proposals to demolish such buildings should be assessed against the same broad criteria as proposals to demolish listed buildings (paragraphs 3.16-3.19 above). In less clear-cut cases - for instance, where a building makes little or no such contribution - the local planning authority will need to have full information about what is proposed for the site after demolition. Consent for demolition should not be given unless there are acceptable and detailed plans for any redevelopment. It has been held that the decision-maker is entitled to consider the merits of any proposed development in determining whether consent should be given for the demolition of an unlisted building in a conservation area.

4.28 Section 336 of the principal Act states that a building includes 'any part of a building'. The demolition of part of a building should therefore be regarded as falling within the scope of conservation area control. What constitutes a demolition or demolition of part of a building must be a matter of fact and degree, to be decided in the particular case and ultimately by the Courts. Routine works of repair, maintenance or replacement, including work involving such items as doors or windows, would not in the Secretary of State's view normally constitute demolition. Likewise, the removal of internal features, whether replaced or not, would not usually constitute a demolition and for the purposes of conservation area consent would not, in any event, have a material impact on the building's appearance or affect the character or appearance of the area.

4.29 It will often be appropriate to impose on the grant of consent for demolition a condition under section 17(3) of the Act, as applied by section 74(3), to provide that demolition shall not take place until a contract for the carrying out of works of redevelopment has been made and planning permission for those works has been granted. In the past, ugly gaps have sometimes appeared in conservation areas as a result of demolition far in advance of redevelopment.

Leasehold reform

4.30 The extended arrangements for leasehold enfranchisement under the Leasehold Reform, Housing and Urban Development Act 1993 included wider provisions for estate management schemes aimed at maintaining the appearance and amenity of areas currently under a single landlord's control. Schemes can be applied for by landlords or representative bodies such as residents' associations up to October 30, 1995 (in some exceptional cases later with the Secretary of State's agreement) and, when approved, transferred to local planning authorities or specially constituted bodies. Within conservation areas, schemes can by default be promoted by authorities or English Heritage between that deadline and 30 April 1996. The costs of management under such schemes fall to be met by the freeholders. In considering whether to approve a scheme the leasehold valuation tribunal is required to have regard *inter alia* to the past development and present character of the area and to architectural or historical considerations. Moreover, in conservation areas, applicants for schemes are required to notify English Heritage and the local planning authority and invite them to make representations to the tribunal. These provisions should enable authorities in appropriate cases to help maintain the appearance of an architecturally unified estate through regulation of the development, use and appearance of property beyond what can be enforced under the planning system (eg, by regulating external decoration and cleaning), and through being able to require proper maintenance and repair of the structure and external elements of the buildings. Further information is available from English Heritage.

Advertisement control

4.31 All outdoor advertisements affect the appearance of the building or the neighbourhood where they are displayed. The main purpose of the advertisement control system is to help everyone involved in the display of outdoor advertising to contribute positively to the appearance of an attractive and cared-for environment. So it is reasonable to expect that the local planning authority's duty to pay special attention to the desirability of preserving or enhancing the character or appearance of a conservation area will result in practice in applying more exacting standards when the authority consider whether to grant consent for a proposed advertisement in such an area.

4.32 In conservation areas it is important for local planning authorities to be sensitive in the use of their powers under the Town & Country Planning (Control of Advertisements) Regulations 1992, because many areas include retail and commercial premises, ranging from small corner-shops to thriving commercial centres. Outdoor advertising is essential to commercial activity in a free and diverse economy, and the success of local businesses will usually help owners and tenants of commercial premises to maintain buildings in good repair and attractive appearance.

4.33 Local planning authorities may wish to adopt advertisement control policies as part of their duty to formulate and publish proposals for the preservation and enhancement of conservation areas. Such policies can inform prospective advertisers about the type of displays likely to prove acceptable in an area; and they should provide a rational and consistent basis for decision-making on all advertisement control matters, including the serving of discontinuance notices.

4.34 Because of the special interest of most conservation areas, certain categories of 'deemed consent' advertisements which may have a significant visual impact are not permitted for display in a conservation area without the local planning authority's specific consent. But a general prohibition of the display of certain classes of advertisement, or the withdrawal or limitation of those which may be displayed with deemed consent, is not usually justified solely because of designation.

4.35 Attention is drawn to the value of education and co-operation to help prevent unsympathetic advertisements. Local planning authorities may wish to consider mounting programmes, in association with local businesses, to promote advertisement policies by providing advice about the design and siting of suitable displays which respect the character and appearance of an area (either by the publication of design guidelines, the mounting of exhibitions, the setting-up of an advisory service in a Planning Department, or a combination of these approaches).

4.36 Where a local planning authority has pursued this approach, but considers that it has not prevented unsuitable or harmful advertisement displays, the Secretary of State will be prepared to consider making a direction under regulation 7 of the 1992 Regulations referred to above, if the authority can justify it. In seeking such additional control, authorities will be expected to show that they have well-formulated policies for the display of advertisements in the area and that the vigorous use of normal powers of control has proved inadequate. Similarly, when considering whether an advertisement is causing 'substantial injury to amenity', so that its display should be discontinued, the Secretary of State will particularly consider any evidence, on appeal, that the authority have acted in accordance with a well-formulated advertisement control policy.

4.37 Further advice on outdoor advertisement control, including in conservation areas, is given in *PPG 19*.

Trees in conservation areas

4.38 Trees are valued features of our towns and countryside and make an important contribution to the character of the local environment. Under Part VIII of the principal Act, local planning authorities have a power to protect trees and woodlands in the interests of amenity by making tree preservation orders. In addition to this general power, authorities are under a duty to make adequate provision for the preservation and planting of trees when granting planning permission for the development of land. They do this by a combination of planning conditions and tree preservation orders.

4.39 Many trees in conservation areas are the subject of tree preservation orders, which means that the local planning authority's consent must be obtained before they can be cut down, topped or lopped. In addition to these controls, and in view of the contribution that trees can make to the character and appearance of a conservation area, the principal Act makes special provision for trees in conservation areas which are not the subject of tree preservation orders. Under section 21(1), subject to a range of exceptions (including small trees and ones that are dead, dying or dangerous), anyone proposing to cut down, top or lop a tree in a conservation area is required to give six weeks' notice to the local planning authority. The purpose of this requirement is to give the authority an opportunity to consider bringing the tree under their general control by making a tree preservation order in respect of it. Penalties for contravention, which may include a requirement to replant, are similar to those for tree preservation orders. For guidance on these matters see Department of the Environment *Circular 36/78*.

4.40 When considering whether to extend protection to trees in conservation areas, local planning authorities should always take into account the visual, historic and amenity contribution of trees. In some instances new plantings or re-plantings may be desirable where this would be consistent with the character and appearance of the area.

5   TRANSPORT AND TRAFFIC MANAGEMENT

5.1 The Government's commitment to sustainable development entails greater integration of transport with other aspects of land-use planning in order to reduce the need for travel, to moderate future traffic growth, and to minimise the environmental impacts of transport. This may lead to a greater concentration of development on existing centres, including historic towns. In developing policies and projects it is essential, therefore, that local highway and planning authorities take full account of the wider costs of transport choices, including impact on the historic environment.

5.2 Major new transport infrastructure developments can have an especially wide-ranging impact on the historic environment, not just visually and physically, but indirectly, for example, by altering patterns of movement or commerce and generating new development pressures or opportunities in historic areas. Local highway and planning authorities should therefore integrate their activities and should take great care to avoid or minimise impacts on the various elements of the historic environment and their settings.

5.3 The Secretaries of State also attach particular importance to early consultation on traffic management and highway maintenance schemes, and associated development proposals which would affect listed buildings or conservation areas or parks, gardens or battlefields and their settings. Local highway and planning authorities should take great care to assess the impact on existing roads of new projects, eg. for the rerouting of traffic or for pedestrianisation. They are urged to seek the advice of English Heritage, where appropriate, before determining any such proposals.

New traffic routes

5.4 When contemplating a new route, authorities should consider whether the need for it, and any impact on the environment, might be obviated by an alternative package of transport management such as parking and charging policies, park-and-ride schemes, and public transport priority. New roads should not be built just to facilitate more commuting into already congested areas. This is especially true in historic towns where the character and layout cannot easily absorb radical changes such as new roads.

5.5 If a new route is unavoidable, authorities should initially identify any features of the historic environment - including parks, gardens, battlefields and archaeological sites as well as buildings and areas - and evaluate their importance. Wherever possible, new roads (and any other transport infrastructure) should be kept away from listed buildings, conservation areas and other historic sites. However, in each case a suitable balance has to be struck between conservation, other environmental concerns, economics, safety and engineering feasibility. Highway and planning authorities should set common objectives wherever possible and are advised to consult each other about transport proposals affecting historic areas. Such proposals are subject to the same constraints as other major development proposals in areas of protection, and authorities will have to obtain listed building consent or conservation area consent where appropriate. Further advice is given in PPG 13 on how authorities should seek to manage demand and improve the attractiveness of local centres through their transport and planning policies.

5.6 Where work to listed structures or those in conservation areas, such as historic bridges, is needed to meet new national or European requirements, this should be carried out with great care. Many bridges are of considerable age and represent important features of the cultural heritage. Their survival to this day owes a great deal, to the care of past generations, and, where remedial or strengthening works are found to be necessary, proposals should seek to retain the character of these structures for the benefit of future generations. Traditional materials should only be replaced where it can be proved that this is essential in the interests of structural stability. Sympathetic remedial measures, which restore the carrying capacity and extend the life of these structures while retaining their character, are preferable to complete reconstruction, and will normally prove more cost-effective. Authorities are urged to consider sympathetic alterations where necessary to carry heavier traffic, or, where new construction is the only realistic course, to retain and restore the old structure for use by pedestrians and cyclists. Authorities are also urged to exercise flexibility over the design of parapets on historic bridges.

5.7 When the opportunity occurs, the possibility of reusing structures for new transport schemes should always be examined. Disused railway viaducts and bridges provide an environmentally advantageous solution for such schemes, in both rural and urban areas, especially in environmentally sensitive areas. The restoration and conversation of historic structures such as these can be a positive benefit from a transport scheme.

Schemes promoted under the Transport and Works Act 1992

5.8 Since 1 January 1993, when Part I of the Transport and Works Act 1992 came into force, proposals which would have previously been authorised under private Bill procedure have instead had to be authorised by Orders made under that Act. Such proposals include the construction or operation of railways, tramways, trolley vehicle systems, other guided transport systems, inland waterways, and structures interfering with rights of navigation. The Act brings the procedures for authorising such schemes more into line with those which have applied for years to highways projects. If the relevant Secretary of State decides to make an Order under the Act, he may at the same time direct that planning permission be deemed to be granted for the proposal, to the extent to which it involves carrying out any development.

5.9 Where the proposal involves works to a listed building, or demolition of an unlisted building in a conservation area, a separate application must be made to the local planning authority for listed building consent or conservation area consent respectively. The regulations which normally apply to such consent applications are subject to minor modifications so that they may more easily be progressed in parallel with the application for the related order. These changes are set out in the Transport and Works Applications (Listed Buildings, Conservation Areas and Ancient Monuments Procedures) Regulations 1992. An application for listed building or conservation area consent made concurrently with an application for an order under the 1992 Act will automatically be referred by the local planning authority to the Secretary of State for the Environment for his decision, without the need for any specific direction. Where there is need for a public local inquiry, the related applications will be considered at a concurrent inquiry. This means that one Inspector will be able to make mutually compatible recommendations about the different applications.

5.10 A fuller description of these concurrent procedures (together with the procedure for applications under the 1992 Act generally) is set out in the Department of Transport publication *Transport and Works Act 1992: A Guide to Procedures*.

Roads in centres or settlements

5.11 Local highway authorities should take measures to protect the historic environment from the worst effects of traffic. They have powers to create vehicle-restricted areas or pedestrian zones and to introduce traffic-calming measures where appropriate. However, there is increasing recognition that in some historic areas the total exclusion of traffic combined with extensive pedestrianisation can create sterile precincts, particularly at night. In some cases, it may be preferable to consider limited access at selected times for all traffic or particular classes of traffic (eg, buses, trams, service vehicles), or shared streets and other spaces designed to encourage motorists to modify their driving behaviour when mixing with pedestrians. Park-and-ride schemes may also have a part to play in areas where it is desirable to limit car access to historic centres and conservation areas. Advice is available in the English Historic Towns Forum publication *Park and Ride Good Practice Guide*. AU these measures, together with encouraging a variety of uses on the ground floors of developments, can help to increase the attractiveness of town centres, and will also help to meet the policy objectives of *PPG 6* and *PPG 13*, and Department of the Environment *Circular 5/94.*

5.12 Vehicle restrictions and traffic-calming measures can often be effective in reducing the speeds at which people choose to drive. The Department of Transport issues advice on pedestrianisation and a range of traffic-calming features which may be introduced. The Highways (Traffic Calming) Regulations 1993 give authorities the flexibility to use a wide variety of traffic-calming features, in addition to road humps, which can constrain vehicle speeds. These include chicanes, build-outs, pinch points, gateways, rumble devices, islands and overrun areas. However, some designs can be difficult to integrate into an older streetscape and there can be no standard solution. Each feature or device should relate in its design and materials to the overall townscape to ensure that traffic-calming reinforces rather than diminishes local character. Traffic-calming measures using a combination of traditional materials and devices may help to secure the right balance. For instance, the use of traditional cobbles or stone setts may prove effective in keeping down traffic speeds, though they are likely to increase levels of road surface noise; they will also not always find favour with cyclists and disabled people. Authorities should also consult with the emergency services before laying such surfaces to ensure that their response times are not unduly increased. Advice is available to local authorities in the English Historic Towns Forum publication *Traffic Measures in Historic Towns*. Authorities should consider the extent to which these different kinds of traffic-calming measures need to be signed, and ensure that signing is kept to the minimum necessary to ensure safety and comply with legal requirements.

Floorscape and street furniture

5.13 Floorscape and street furniture often make a vital contribution to the appearance of a conservation area. Traditional stone, or in some cases brick, surfaces and layouts should be retained wherever possible, or re-introduced where there is historical evidence for them. In particular, where there is a tradition of rectangular slab paving, small block paviours and arbitrary new patterns should be avoided. In many small towns and villages, rammed earth, hogging or aggregate, in modem times finished with tarmac, was always the traditional surface. Tarmac, preferably dressed with a suitable local aggregate, remains an appropriate and inexpensive finish for many conservation areas. Wherever practical, natural earth, hogging, or aggregate footpaths or drives should be retained and protected for their semi-rural character. If a street is to be pedestrianised, it is important to retain the traditional relationship between footways and carriageway, including kerb lines. Wall-to-wall surfaces are often unsuitable and the scale, texture, colour and laying patterns of any new materials should be sympathetic to the area's appearance.

5.14 In certain circumstances grants may be available from English Heritage towards the cost of street improvement schemes which incorporate the use of traditional paving features. English Heritage's publication *Street Improvements in Historic Areas* offers guidance on the treatment of streets and public open spaces in historic areas, to encourage wider recognition of the important contribution they make to townscape quality. The New Roads and Street Works Act 1991 makes statutory undertakers responsible for carrying out the permanent reinstatement of the highway where they disturb it. They are now required to reinstate the same materials as previously existed, or the closest possible match if the materials cannot be reused. Local authorities play an important role in ensuring that statutory undertakers and their contractors carry out reinstatement to an appropriate specification and timetable.

5.15 Even the smallest towns contain a wealth of street furniture of historic or architectural interest, such as pillar boxes, telephone kiosks, drinking fountains, railings, clocks and many others, often of local distinctiveness. The appearance of historic streets can be improved by preserving or reinstating such items where appropriate (see *Street Improvements in Historic Areas*). Authorities contemplating modern tramway systems should consider the effects that catenary supports and other associated street furniture and electrical equipment may have on historic streetscapes.

5.16 Road signs and markings can also have a significant impact on a street's appearance. These should be of an appropriate character and quality, without unnecessary duplication of signs and posts. Wherever possible signs should be fixed to existing posts or street furniture. Traffic signs are only needed to direct drivers to their desired destinations or to particular facilities, warn them of hazards and indicate mandatory requirements. Signs which do none of these things may not be necessary at all, and much can be done to eliminate sign clutter simply by removing redundant signs, or by combining separate signs onto a single backing board. Regular 'street audits' are valuable and local amenity societies may be able to help with these. Further advice is available in *Traffic Measures in Historic Towns*. Where the Traffic Signs Regulations and the Department of Transport's *Traffic Signs Manual* provide for some degree of flexibility in size, siting and colour, authorities should take advantage of this in historic areas. Parking restriction signs in particular can be sited on buildings where appropriate, thus eliminating the need in many cases for a pole with a single sign. Authorities' attention is drawn to the flexibility permitted in respect of no-waiting lines: a narrower line of a different colour is permitted in environmentally sensitive areas. Consideration should be given to applying waiting restrictions to areas, where appropriate, and removing yellow lines.

5.17 Authorities should seek advice on the selection and positioning of street lighting equipment appropriate to the age and character of the surrounding area. The Department of Transport publication *Road Lighting and the Environment*, for example, provides helpful advice. High pressure sodium lamps (with controlled light spillage) may be preferable in environmentally sensitive areas as they provide a whiter light with a more natural rendition of colour. Off-the-peg 'period' columns and lanterns are not universally appropriate in historic areas. Special designs reflecting established local styles or motifs, or simple modern designs, may be preferable.

5.18 The effects of road works and other transport projects on trees in conservation areas, or trees which form part of the setting of listed buildings, can be particularly damaging. Authorities should stress the need for statutory undertakers and others to take care when excavating, or diverting services, near existing trees in order to avoid damage to roots. Where root damage occurs, this may not show in a tree's health for several years.

PART 2

6   IDENTIFYING AND RECORDING THE HISTORIC ENVIRONMENT

6.1 In its broadest sense, the historic environment embraces all those aspects of the country that reflect the shaping hand of human history. Scarcely any part of England is untouched by the interaction between people and nature which has taken place over thousands of years. Some of the most obvious features of this environment are historic buildings. England is exceptionally rich in these - great churches, houses, and civic buildings – but our understanding of the historic environment now encompasses a much wider range of features, and in particular stresses the relationship between individual buildings, and also the value of historic townscape and landscape as a whole.

6.2 There is growing appreciation not just of the architectural set pieces, but of many more structures, especially industrial, agricultural and other vernacular buildings that, although sometimes individually unassuming, collectively reflect some of the most distinctive and creative aspects of English history. More than this, our understanding and appreciation of the historic environment now stretches beyond buildings to the spaces and semi-natural features which people have also moulded, and which are often inseparable from the buildings themselves. For example, the pattern of roads and open spaces and the views they create within historic townscapes may be as valuable as the buildings. In the countryside, the detailed patterns of fields and farms, of hedgerows and walls, and of hamlets and villages, are among the most highly valued aspects of our environment. England is particularly rich in the designed landscapes of parks and gardens, and the built and natural features they contain: the greatest of these are as important to national, and indeed international, culture as are our greatest buildings.

6.3 Processes of classification are necessary for the practical purposes of identifying and protecting individual sites and areas. This is achieved through the statutory systems for scheduling ancient monuments, listing historic buildings and designating conservation areas. Scheduling and listing are undertaken by the Secretary of State; designation of conservation areas is the responsibility of local planning authorities. In addition, English Heritage compiles registers of parks and gardens of special historic interest, and of historic battlefields. Identified in these ways, the historic environment may be protected through the development control system and, in the case of listed buildings and conservation areas, through the complementary systems of listed building and conservation area control.

6.4 The first part of this PPG explained how these control systems work, and how they relate to the broader planning system for development control. This part of the PPG sets out Government policy for the listing of historic buildings, and for the identification of certain other aspects of the historic environment. It also gives guidance on the upkeep of historic buildings, and on the powers available to local authorities and to the Secretary of State to secure repairs to neglected historic buildings.

6.5 Archaeology plays an essential role in informing and widening our understanding of the historic environment. Many important sites and structures of archaeological interest are identified and protected through the statutory schedule of ancient monuments maintained by the Department of National Heritage. The principles of selection are set out in PPG 16. Other known sites are included in the National Monuments Record of the Royal Commission on the Historical Monuments of England, and in county sites and monuments records.

Historic buildings

6.6 Historic buildings listed by the Secretary of State under section 1 of the Act are placed in one of three grades to give an indication of their relative importance. The current listing position in England is (to the nearest thousand):

List Entries (England, 1993)

Grade I	9,000 (2%)
Grade II*	18,000 (4%)
Grade II	<u>416,000</u> (94%)
	443,000

About 500,000 individual buildings are estimated to be protected: some list entries cover several buildings. Some churches in older lists are still Grades A, B and C (which in the context of planning and listed building consent applications should all be treated in the same way as Grade I and II* buildings). Gradings can be changed following revaluation after damage or alteration, or as more evidence of a building's history comes to light.

Identification of buildings for listing

6.7 Buildings are added to the statutory lists in two main ways:

i.   as a result of systematic resurvey or review of particular areas or building types; or

ii. following proposals from local authorities, amenity societies or other bodies or individuals that particular buildings should be added to the list ('spot listing').

6.8 Before including buildings in the statutory lists the Secretary of State is required to consult English Heritage and such other persons as he may consider appropriate as having special knowledge of, or interest in, buildings of architectural or historic interest. Expert advisers appointed by English Heritage normally visit and report on buildings before they are listed. In the case of systematic resurveys and reviews there will normally be close consultation between English Heritage and the local planning authority before recommendations for listing are submitted to the Secretary of State. Wherever possible the Secretary of State will consider the views of others, but it is not his practice to advertise proposals for new listings.

6.9 The number of listed buildings has increased fourfold since 1970 as a result of 24 years' work to resurvey England's built heritage. Some of the lists deriving from the earlier years of the resurvey are currently being reviewed, but the priority in future will be on more precisely targeted, research-based studies of particular building types which are known to be under- represented in the lists, rather than area surveys.

Principles of selection

6.10 The following are the main criteria which the Secretary of State applies as appropriate in deciding which buildings to include in the statutory lists:

–   **architectural interest**: the lists are meant to include all buildings which are of importance to the nation for the interest of their architectural design, decoration and craftsmanship; also important examples of particular building types and techniques (eg. buildings displaying technological innovation or virtuosity) and significant plan forms;

- **historic interest**: this includes buildings which illustrate important aspects of the nation's social, economic, cultural or military history;
- **close historical association**: with nationally important people or events;
- **group value**, especially where buildings comprise an important architectural or historic unity or a fine example of planning (eg. squares, terraces or model villages).

Not all these criteria will be relevant to every case, but a particular building may qualify for listing under more than one of them.

6.11 Age and rarity are relevant considerations, particularly where buildings are proposed for listing on the strength of their historic interest. The older a building is, and the fewer the surviving examples of its kind, the more likely it is to have historic importance. Thus, all buildings built before 1700 which survive in anything like their original condition are listed; and most buildings of about 1700 to 1840 are listed, though some selection is necessary. After about 1840, because of the greatly increased number of buildings erected and the much larger numbers that have survived, greater selection is necessary to identify the best examples of particular building types, and only buildings of definite quality and character are listed. For the same reasons, only selected buildings from the period after 1914 are normally listed. Buildings which are less than 30 years old are normally listed only if they are of outstanding quality and under threat. Buildings which are less than ten years old are not listed.

6.12 The approach adopted for twentieth century listing is to identify key exemplars for each of a range of building types - industrial, educational, residential, etc. - and to treat these exemplars as broadly defining a standard against which to judge proposals for further additions to the list. This approach has already been successfully applied to the inter-war period, and English Heritage is now engaged on a three-year research programme to extend it to the post-war period (subject to the '30 year rule' mentioned above). Proposals for listings in each building type will be made as each stage of the research is completed.

Selectivity

6.13 Where a building qualifies for listing primarily on the strength of its intrinsic architectural quality or its group value, the fact that there are other buildings of similar quality elsewhere is not likely to be a major consideration. But, as noted above, the listing of buildings primarily for historical reasons is to a greater extent a comparative exercise, and needs to be selective where a substantial number of buildings of a similar type and quality survive. In such cases the Secretary of State's aim will be to list the best examples of the type which are of special historic interest.

Aesthetic merits

6.14 The external appearance of a building - both its intrinsic architectural merit and any group value - is a key consideration in judging listing proposals, but the special interest of a building will not always be reflected in obvious visual quality. Buildings which are important for reasons of technological innovation, or as illustrating particular aspects of social or economic history, may well have little external visual quality.

Historical associations

6.15 Well-documented historical associations of national importance will increase the case for the inclusion of a building in the statutory list. They may justify a higher grading than would otherwise be appropriate, and may occasionally be the deciding factor. But in the Secretary of State's view there should normally be some quality or interest in the physical fabric of the building itself to justify the statutory protection afforded by listing. Either the building should be of some architectural merit in itself, or it should be well preserved in a form which directly illustrates and confirms its historical associations (eg. because of the survival of internal features). Where otherwise unremarkable buildings have historical associations, the Secretary of State's view is that they are normally best commemorated by other means (eg. by a plaque), and that listing will be appropriate only in exceptional cases.

National and local interest

6.16 The emphasis in these criteria is on national significance, though this cannot be defined precisely. For instance, the best examples of local vernacular building types will normally be listed. But many buildings which are valued for their contribution to the local scene, or for local historical associations, will not merit listing. Such buildings will often be protected by conservation area designation (see paragraphs 4.2 ff). It is also open to planning authorities to draw up lists of locally important buildings, and to formulate local plan policies for their protection, through normal development control procedures. But policies should make clear that such buildings do not enjoy the full protection of statutory listing.

Notifying owners and occupiers

6.17 When a building is included in the statutory list, the Department notifies the appropriate local planning authority. That authority must then notify the owner and occupier of the building. As it is a criminal offence to carry out any works (either to the exterior or interior) which would affect the character of a building once it is listed (unless listed building consent has been obtained), notice of listing must be given to the owner as soon as possible. The statutory notice is prescribed in the Planning (Listed Buildings and Conservation Areas) Regulations 1990. Owners and occupiers are also notified by the Department and sent a copy of the Department's leaflet *What Listing Means*.

Public access to the lists

6.18 A complete set of lists for the whole country is kept available for the public to inspect without charge at the National Monuments Record of the Royal Commission on the Historical Monuments of England. Each local authority also keeps available for inspection (without charge) the lists relating to its own area.

List descriptions

6.19 The lists include a description of each building. This is principally to aid identification. While list descriptions will include mention of those features which led English Heritage to recommend listing, they are not intended to provide a comprehensive or exclusive record of all the features of importance, and the amount of information given in descriptions varies considerably. Absence from the list description of any reference to a feature (whether external or internal) does not, therefore, indicate that it is not of interest or that it can be removed or altered without consent. Where there is doubt, the advice of the local planning authority should be sought.

Spot listing

6.20 Requests for individual buildings to be spot listed can be made to the Secretary of State at any time. Where the area in question has recently been the subject of resurvey or review, it is important that requests for spot listing draw attention to any new evidence which may not have been available to English Heritage previously, or otherwise explain why the building's special interest may have been overlooked. The Secretary of State recognises that there may be cases where new evidence justifies reconsideration of a previous decision not to list, but he will not generally be disposed to review earlier decisions unless such evidence is provided.

6.21 Difficulties can arise where proposals for spot listing are made at a very late stage of redevelopment proposals, when buildings are under imminent threat of demolition. Spot listing in such cases can often mean delay, sometimes with serious practical and financial consequences for the developer. The Department will consider all requests for spot listing, but it is preferable from all points of view that buildings should be assessed for possible listing before planning permission has been granted for redevelopment. Local planning authorities should draw the Department's attention at the earliest possible stage to any buildings affected by redevelopment proposals (including their own) which appear to them to merit listing. A building preservation notice served by the authority may be a quicker means of protecting a threatened building than a request for spot listing (see paragraph 6.23 below).

6.22 Requests to list buildings should be sent to the listing Branch, Department of National Heritage, 2-4 Cockspur Street, London SW1Y 5DH. Those sent to English Heritage will be forwarded to the Department. Requests should be accompanied by a justification for adding the building to the list; a location plan (such as an Ordnance Survey map extract) showing, wherever possible, the position of any other listed buildings nearby; clear up-to-date photographic prints of the main elevations of the building; any information about the building (eg. its date); details of specialised function (eg. industrial building); historical associations; the name of the architect (if known); its group value in the street scene; and details of any interior features of interest.

Building preservation notices

6.23 Under Section 3 of the Act district planning authorities and national park authorities have the power to serve building preservation notices in respect of buildings which are not listed, but which they consider are of special architectural or historic interest and are in danger of demolition or alteration in such a way as to affect their character as buildings of such interest. A building preservation notice applies to the building all the provisions of the Act relating to listed buildings (except section 59). It takes effect immediately it is served, and is often a quicker and so more expedient short-term measure than asking the Department to spot list a building.

6.24 A copy of the building preservation notice, a location plan and photographs of the building should be sent to the Department as soon as the notice has been served. The notice remains in force for up to six months, but will lapse if within that period the Department either includes the building in the statutory list or notifies the authority in writing that it does not intend to do so. The authority must notify the owner and occupier if the Department decides not to list the building, and may not serve another building preservation notice in respect of that building within 12 months of the Department's notification.

6.25 In deciding whether to serve a building preservation notice, authorities will realise that they become liable to pay compensation for any loss or damage resulting from the service of a notice which the Secretary of State does not uphold by listing. Neither the Department nor English Heritage can indicate in advance whether the service of a notice in a particular case is likely to result in a listing, though obviously the same general principles of listing, set out above, will apply in these cases as in others. It should not however be assumed that listing will automatically follow the inclusion of a building by English Heritage in a draft list, since that list may be corrected or amended before it is approved.

Requests to de-list buildings

6.26 The Secretary of State is prepared to review listings in the light of new evidence. There is no formal appeal procedure, but owners or others who believe that a listing should be reconsidered should send the evidence to the Department's Listing Branch, together with photographs of the building and a location plan. The evidence must relate to the special architectural or historic interest ascribed to the building: if the objection to listing is (for instance) related to a building's condition and the cost of repairing or maintaining it, or to plans for redevelopment, the appropriate application should be made under the listed building consent procedures described in Annex B. The local authorities concerned and the national amenity societies (listed in Annex A) will be notified by English Heritage of any requests the Department receives to de-list buildings.

6.27 The Secretary of State will not generally entertain an application for de-listing if the building is the subject of an application for listed building consent, or an appeal against refusal of consent, or if action by a local planning authority is in hand because of unauthorised works or neglect. Both listed building consent and enforcement appeal procedures give appellants the right to argue that a building is not of special interest and should be removed from the list. The issue of de-listing should normally be addressed in this way, rather than regarded as a means of avoiding the need for enforcement action.

Certificates of immunity from listing

6.28 Provided that planning permission is being sought or has been obtained, any person may ask the Secretary of State to issue a certificate stating that he does not intend to list the building or buildings involved in the planning application. Once a certificate is issued, the building cannot be listed for five years, nor may the local planning authority serve a building preservation notice during that time. However, if he does not grant a certificate, the Secretary of State will normally add the building to the statutory list, and listed building controls will then apply. This procedure gives greater certainty to developers proposing works which will affect buildings which may be eligible for listing: they will know either that they must seek listed building consent in the normal way, or that they have five years to carry out their development without the possibility of disruption by spot listing.

6.29 Because a certificate of immunity is valid for five years, a building is normally completely reassessed when an application for a certificate is made: an earlier assessment might have been based on a restricted inspection, or new information may have come to light since then. It should not be assumed, therefore, that even a recent decision by the Secretary of State not to list a building necessarily means that he will grant a certificate of immunity.

6.30 Even if a certificate of immunity is granted, a building in a conservation area will still normally need consent for demolition. It is not practicable to extend the certificate procedure to provide immunity from the effects of conservation area designation (but conservation area consent is not required where planning permission was granted prior to designation).

6.31 Applications for certificates of immunity should be made to the Department's Listing Branch. There is no application form and no charge. Applicants should supply a copy of the planning application or planning permission, as well as the information requested for spot listing applications (paragraph 6.22).

6.32 Applicants are required to notify the local planning authority in whose area the building is situated of the application at the same time as it is submitted to the Department. In London, applicants must notify English Heritage as well as the London borough council. Applicants should confirm that they have notified these authorities.

6.33 When a certificate is issued, the Department will notify English Heritage and both the district and county council (in London, the London borough council or, if appropriate, the London Docklands Development Corporation). The existence of a certificate and its expiry date should be disclosed in response to enquiries by prospective purchasers of the building or land, together with other information relating to planning matters.

Relationship between listing and scheduling

6.34 Some buildings are scheduled as ancient monuments as well as listed. These are for the most part unoccupied buildings, such as medieval barns or dovecotes, some bridges, and some urban buildings (eg. guildhalls) and industrial monuments. Some areas of overlap reflect the fact that scheduling pre-dated the listing legislation. Where a building is scheduled and listed, scheduling – which introduces closer controls (eg. over repairs) than does listing – takes priority and listed building controls do not apply. For the future, the policy will be to accord buildings and monuments the type of protection which is most appropriate to them, and where possible to avoid overlaps between listing and scheduling. The overlap is being addressed in the current national survey of archaeological sites (the Monuments Protection Programme) being carried out by English Heritage, to evaluate all known archaeological sites in England, review existing schedulings, and identify further sites and monuments which may be suitable for scheduling.

World Heritage Sites

6.35 The World Heritage Convention (adopted by UNESCO in 1972) was ratified by the United Kingdom in 1984. The Convention provides for the identification, protection, conservation and presentation of cultural and natural sites of outstanding universal value, and requires a World Heritage List to be established under the management of an inter-governmental World Heritage Committee, which is advised by the International Council on Monuments and Sites (ICOMOS) and the World Conservation Union (IUCN). Individual governments are responsible for the nomination of sites, and for ensuring the protection of sites which are inscribed in the list. There are, at present, ten World Heritage Sites in England:

> Durham Cathedral and Castle
> Fountains Abbey, St. Mary's Church and
> Studley Royal Park
> Ironbridge Gorge
> Stonehenge, Avebury and associated sites
> Blenheim Palace and Park
> Palace of Westminster and Westminster Abbey
> City of Bath
> Hadrian's Wall Military Zone
> The Tower of London
> Canterbury Cathedral (with St. Augustine's Abbey and St. Martin's Church).

6.36 Full details of the operation of the World Heritage Convention, including the selection criteria for cultural and natural sites, are contained in the *Operational Guidelines for the Implementation of the World Heritage Convention*.

6.37 The significance of World Heritage designation for local authorities' exercise of planning controls is set out in section 2 (paragraphs 2.22-2.23). Local planning authorities are also encouraged to work with owners and managers of World Heritage Sites in their areas, and with other agencies, to ensure that comprehensive management plans are in place. These plans should:

-     appraise the significance and condition of the site;
-     ensure the physical conservation of the site to the highest standards;
-     protect the site and its setting from damaging development;
-     provide clear policies for tourism as it may affect the site.

ICOMOS can provide advice and assistance in carrying forward this work.

Historic parks and gardens

6.38 The Register of Parks and Gardens of Special Historic Interest in England is maintained by English Heritage, to whom all enquiries about its compilation should be made. Sites of exceptional historic interest are assessed as grade I, those of great historic interest as grade II* and those of special historic interest as grade II. The grading of these sites is independent of the grading of any listed building which falls within the area. The Register is under review, with the aim of extending its coverage of parks and gardens deserving protection. (See also paragraph 2.24.)

Historic battlefields

6.39 English Heritage's draft Register of Historic Battlefields, which will be comparable in status with the Parks and Gardens Register, is shortly to be the subject of public consultation. The proposed Register identifies a limited number of areas of historic significance where important battles are sufficiently documented to be located on the ground. They will not be graded. The Register will be periodically reviewed by English Heritage, to whom all enquiries about compilation and content should be addressed. (See also paragraph 2.25.)

The wider historic landscape

6.40 Suitable approaches to the identification of the components and character of the wider historic landscape are being developed by the Countryside Commission (see its *Landscape Assessment Guidance*) and English Heritage (as part of current research on methodology for historic landscape assessment). Appraisals based on assessment of the historic character of the whole countryside will be more flexible, and more likely to be effectively integrated with the aims of the planning process, than an attempt to define selected areas for additional control. It is unlikely therefore to be feasible to prepare a definitive register at a national level of England's wider historic landscape. The whole of the landscape, to varying degrees and in different ways, is an archaeological and historic artefact, the product of complex historic processes and past land-use. It is also a crucial and defining aspect of biodiversity, to the enhancement of which the Government is committed. Much of its value lies in its complexity, regional diversity and local distinctiveness, qualities which a national register cannot adequately reflect.

7   THE UPKEEP AND REPAIR OF HISTORIC BUILDINGS

7.1 Regular maintenance and repair are the key to the preservation of historic buildings. Modest expenditure on repairs keeps a building weathertight, and routine maintenance (especially roof repairs and the regular clearance of gutters and downpipes) can prevent much more expensive work becoming necessary at a later date. It is a common misunderstanding that historic buildings have a fixed lifespan, and that gradual decay of their fabric is inevitable. On the contrary, unless there are intrinsic defects of design or materials, the lifespan of a historic building may be indefinite provided that timely maintenance, and occasional major repairs such as the renewal of roof coverings and other features, are regularly undertaken. Major problems are very often the result of neglect and, if tackled earlier, can be prevented or reduced in scale. Regular inspection is invaluable.

7.2 The effective use of local planning authorities' controls set out in Part 1 is essential, but it will not of itself prevent historic buildings failing into neglect or disuse. The timely use of urgent works and repairs notice powers, described below, should always be considered, but authorities' resources for conservation will be used to best effect if some are devoted to identifying buildings at risk – from neglect or inappropriate changes – as early as possible and providing advice, encouragement and (where appropriate) grants to owners. Monitoring listed buildings, and unlisted buildings which make a positive contribution to conservation areas, by means of simple, regularly updated condition surveys is a valuable element of this approach. Dated photographs will provide a record of changes (and useful evidence in the event of statutory action being needed). Positive involvement of this kind by authorities will help prevent unnecessary loss of historic fabric, not to mention the probable cost and discord of action at a later stage.

7.3 The theft of architectural features, statuary, monuments and specialist materials has increased in recent years, and local authorities and owners are recommended to take precautions to safeguard them, especially when historic buildings are vacant or being refurbished. This may involve careful removal for safe and secure storage on site. Theft is a criminal offence and adequate records and photographs of vulnerable items will help the police recover them if stolen.

Repair

7.4 There is no specific duty on owners to keep their buildings in a good state of repair (though it will normally be in their interests to do so), but local authorities have powers to take action where a historic building has deteriorated to the extent that its preservation may be at risk. These powers take two forms.

Urgent works

7.5 Section 54 of the Act enables a local authority (or English Heritage in London) to carry out urgent works for the preservation of listed buildings in their area after giving notice to the owner. These powers can be used only in respect of an unoccupied building, or the unused part of a partly occupied building. Section 76 of the Act enables the Secretary of State to direct (after consulting English Heritage) that the powers shall apply to an unlisted building in a conservation area if it appears to him that its preservation is important for maintaining the character or appearance of that area. The Secretary of State will consider sympathetically the making of such a direction in respect of an unlisted building which makes a positive contribution to a conservation area. Authorities or members of the public may ask the Secretary of State to make such a direction; such requests should be supported by evidence confirming the importance of the building.

7.6 The Secretary of State can also exercise these powers himself, but under the terms of the legislation he must authorise English Heritage to give notice and carry out the works on his behalf. His policy is to use his powers only in exceptional cases, for instance where a building is of exceptional interest or is in local authority ownership; or where a conservation area is of more than local interest and either the building in question is so important to the area that failure to carry out urgent works to it would seriously damage the character or appearance of the area, or the building, as well as meeting the basic section 76 criterion, in local authority ownership. In all such cases he would normally only consider the use of his own powers where the local authority concerned has decided not to take action itself.

7.7 Authorities will note that these powers are confined to *urgent* works: in the Secretary of State's view, their use should be restricted to emergency repairs, for example works to keep a building wind- and weather-proof and safe from collapse, or action to prevent vandalism or theft. The steps taken should be the minimum consistent with achieving this objective, and should not involve an owner in great expense. English Heritage has published *Emergency Repairs – A Handbook* which includes advice on methods of temporary repair.

7.8 Local authorities (or English Heritage in London, or the Secretary of State) may recover from owners the cost of urgent works carried out under these provisions, subject to the owner's right to make representations to the Secretary of State. Representations may be made on the grounds that some or all of the works were unnecessary; that temporary arrangements have continued for an unreasonable length of time; or that amounts are unreasonable or their recovery would cause hardship. The Secretary of State will take all such representations into account before determining the amount to be recovered, and will be particularly concerned to establish whether the works carried out were the minimum required to secure the building's preservation and prevent further deterioration. If an authority intends to attempt to recover the cost of the works, the financial circumstances of the owner should be taken into account at the outset and any sums the authority wishes to recover from an owner should not be unreasonable in relation to his or her means.

Repairs notices

7.9 If a local planning authority (or English Heritage in London) considers that a listed building is not being properly preserved, it may serve a repairs notice on the owner (under section 48 of the Act). This notice must specify the works which the authority considers reasonably necessary for the proper preservation of the building, and must explain the relevant provisions of the legislation, which are described briefly below. These powers are not confined to urgent works or to unoccupied buildings, and authorities should consider their use in cases where protracted failure by an owner to keep a listed building in reasonable repair places the building at risk.

7.10 A House of Lords judgment (*Robbins v. Secretary of State for the Environment* ([1989] 1 All E.R. 878) has provided guidance on the nature of the works which may properly be specified in a repairs notice. The judgment held that, while the definition of works reasonably necessary for the proper preservation of the building will always relate to the circumstances of the individual case, and involve judgments about what is reasonable, the word 'preservation' has to be given its ordinary meaning in contrast to 'restoration', and this imposes an objective limitation which must be applied in considering the scope of works to be specified in a notice. The judgment also made clear that a notice can include works for the preservation of a building having regard to its condition at the date when it was listed: in other words, where a building has suffered damage or disrepair since being listed, the repairs notice procedure can be used to secure the building's preservation as at the date of listing, but should not be used to restore other features. If, however, repairs are necessary to preserve what remains of the rest of the building – for example, to a roof that was defective at the time of listing – it is legitimate, in the Secretary of State's view, to include them in a repairs notice.

7.11 Repairs notice powers may also be exercised by the Secretary of State, but, as with urgent works, his policy is to treat these powers essentially as reserve powers, and to use them only in exceptional circumstances. It is not open to the Secretary of State to authorise the use of repairs notices in respect of unlisted buildings in conservation areas.

Compulsory acquisition of listed buildings in need of repair

7.12 If at least two months have elapsed following the service of a repairs notice, and it appears to the body who served the notice that reasonable steps are not being taken for the proper preservation of the building, they may begin compulsory purchase proceedings. Compulsory purchase orders (CPOs) made by a local planning authority or by English Heritage require the Secretary of State's confirmation, and the Secretary of State must consult English Heritage before making an order himself or confirming an authority's order. In making or confirming an order, the Secretary of State must be satisfied that it is expedient to make provision for the preservation of the building and to authorise its compulsory acquisition for that purpose. The Secretary of State will also need to be satisfied that the means and the resources necessary for securing the buildings repair will be available. A listed building CPO may also include land which an authority wishes to acquire for the purposes of access, amenity or management in connection with the building ('relevant land' in the Act).

7.13 The Secretary of State considers that privately owned historic buildings should, wherever possible, remain in the private sector. Local planning authorities are encouraged to identify a private individual or body, such as a building preservation trust, which has access to funds to carry out the necessary repairs and to which the building will be sold on as quickly as possible. Suitable covenants should be negotiated to ensure that repairs will be carried out by a purchaser. Authorities should be aware that where they wish to acquire a listed building and pass it on, 'back to back' deals are possible. These are explained in Department of the Environment *Circular 11/90* and are set out in regulation 15 of the Local Authorities (Capital Finance) Regulations 1990 as amended. Authorities are reminded that where a historic building is disposed of (either by freehold sale or long lease) within two years of its acquisition (or, where disposal was contracted for, but not implemented, in that period, within three years of acquisition), and the price received on resale is no more than the price paid, use of the capital receipt is unrestricted. Acquisitions under arrangements for immediate onward sale should, therefore, have no adverse financial implications for the authority, though there will clearly be other resource costs involved in securing confirmation of a CPO.

7.14 Any person who has an interest in a listed building which a local planning authority wishes to acquire compulsorily, and who has been served with a notice under the Acquisition of Land Act 1981, may apply to a magistrates' court for an order staying further proceedings on the compulsory purchase order. If an applicant is aggrieved by the decision of the magistrates' court, he or she may appeal to the Crown Court. Authorities should also be aware that where a compulsory purchase order is objected to, and a local public inquiry held (and also where representations against the recovery of expenses for works carried out under section 54 are heard as part of a related planning matter), the Secretary of State may make an order as to the costs of the parties at the inquiry (see Department of the Environment *Circular 8/93*).

General considerations

7.15 The possible need to follow up with a CPO is clearly something which local planning authorities should take into account when contemplating repairs notice action. But the following are also relevant considerations:

- a recent study (*Listed Building Repairs Notices*) has shown that in over 60% of cases authorisation or formal service of a notice was itself sufficient to prompt owners either to begin repairs or to sell the building in question on to a third party: in only 13% of cases did the matter reach a CPO inquiry;
- the purpose of compulsory purchase is to ensure that reasonable steps are taken for properly preserving a listed building: it is not a requirement that the local authority should itself carry out the repairs or pay for them. Indeed in the Secretary of State's view it is preferable, as stated in paragraph 7.13 above, for the authority to obtain a firm commitment from a private purchaser to repair the building and meet the costs (perhaps with the assistance of any relevant grant-aid available);
- the Act contains provisions for minimum compensation where an owner has deliberately allowed a building to fall into disrepair in order to justify its demolition and secure permission for redevelopment of the site (section 50 of the Act); minimum compensation should however be sought only where there is clear evidence of such an intention;
- where the minimum compensation provisions do not apply, normal market value rules apply (as laid down in the Land Compensation Act 1961); but even here, high costs of repair, combined with limited possibilities for development, may indicate a very low or even nominal value.

Authorities also have powers under section 52 of the Act to acquire land and buildings by agreement.

8 CHURCHES AND THE ECCLESIASTICAL EXEMPTION

8.1 Ecclesiastical buildings are fully subject to planning control, but ecclesiastical buildings which are for the time being used for ecclesiastical purposes are exempt from listed building and conservation area controls, except in so far as the Secretary of State provides otherwise by Order under section 60(5) and 75(7) of the Act. Ecclesiastical exemption does not apply to the residences of ministers of religion (section 60(3)).

8.2 The context of the exemption is provided by an undertaking by the Church of England that its historic buildings would be subject to a separate Church system of control which took account of the historical and architectural importance of churches. This system, known as faculty jurisdiction, has developed over time, in particular in a series of ecclesiastical measures passed by the General Synod and approved by Parliament, and in subordinate arrangements approved by the General Synod; a separate system covers Church of England cathedrals[1]. The exemption has, however, extended to ecclesiastical buildings of all denominations, not just those of the Church of England.

8.3 Following public consultation in 1992 the Secretary of State, in conjunction with the Secretary of State for Wales, announced that an Order would be made to provide that the exemption would in future apply only to the Church of England and to other denominations and faiths which set up acceptable internal systems of control embodying the principles set out in the Government's code of practice. The Ecclesiastical Exemption (Listed Buildings and Conservation Areas) Order 1994 has now been made and is due to come into force on 1 October 1994.

---

1. The Faculty Jurisdiction Measure 1964, the *Care of Churches and Ecclesiastical Jurisdiction Measure 1991*, the Faculty Jurisdiction Rules 1992, and the Faculty Jurisdiction (Injunctions and Restoration Orders) Rules 1992; and, for cathedrals, the Care of Cathedrals Measure 1990, the Care of Cathedrals (Supplementary Provisions) Measure 1994, and the Care of Cathedrals Rules 1990.

Code of practice for denominations' internal control systems

8.4 The Government's code comprises the following points:

1. proposals for relevant works² should be submitted by the local congregation or minister for the approval of a body independent of them;

2. that body should include, or have arrangements for obtaining advice from, people with expert knowledge of historic church buildings;

3. the decision-making process should provide for:

   (a) consultation with the local planning authority, English Heritage and national amenity societies, allowing them (except in cases of emergency) 28 days to comment;

   (b) the display for the same 28-day period of a notice in a prominent position outside the building describing the proposed works and similarly inviting comments;

   (c) the publication of a similar notice in a local newspaper;

   (d) in cases of demolition, notification of the Royal Commission on the Historical Monuments of England (see also paragraph 3.22).

4. the decision-making body should be required, in considering proposals submitted to it, to take into account any representations made and, along with other factors, the desirability of preserving historic church buildings and the importance of protecting features of architectural merit and historic interest (including fixtures – see paragraphs 3.13 and 8.11);

5. there should be a clear and fair procedure for settling all disputes between the local congregation or minister and the decision-making body as to whether proposals should proceed;

6. there should be procedures for dealing with any breach of the control system, including provision for reinstatement where works to historic church buildings have been carried out without consent;

---

2. ie. works for the demolition of a listed ecclesiastical building or for its alteration or extension in any manner which would affect its character as a building of special architectural or historic interest; or works for the demolition of an unlisted ecclesiastical building in a conservation area.

7. there should be arrangements for recording how the above procedures were implemented in each case and the nature of the decision taken; for making such records available for public inspection during reasonable hours; and for notifying the decision to the above consultees;
8. there should be arrangements to ensure the proper maintenance of historic church buildings including thorough inspections on a fixed cycle of not more than five years.

So far as a denomination's circumstances permit, these points should be incorporated in legally binding procedures.

8.5 In considering proposals for such works, any effects on the archaeological importance of the church or archaeological remains existing within it or its curtilage should be taken into account along with other relevant factors. Where works of repair or alteration are to be carried out which would affect the fabric of listed churches or churches in conservation areas, denominations should attach any necessary conditions for proper recording in accordance with the principles set out in paragraphs 3.22-3.24 and, in respect of archaeological remains, in paragraph 2.15.

Future scope of the exemption

8.6 For those denominations and faiths which retain the exemption, its scope is reduced by the Order to the following:

– any church building;
– any object or structure within a church building;
– any object or structure fixed to the exterior of a church building, unless ,the object or structure is itself a listed building;
– any object or structure within the curtilage of a church building which, although not fixed to that building, forms part of the land, unless the object or structure is itself a listed building.

('Church building' is defined as a building whose primary use is as a place of worship.)

8.7 The Order provides continued exemption on this reduced basis (to the extent specified in it) for the Church of England and also for the Church in Wales, the Roman Catholic Church, the Methodist Church, the Baptist

Union of Great Britain, the Baptist Union of Wales and the United Reformed Church. Ecclesiastical buildings of these denominations are covered by acceptable internal systems of control broadly conforming to the principles in the Government's code of practice. It is intended to monitor these arrangements and review them after two years. (Further Orders can be made if any other denominations or faiths are subsequently accepted as qualifying.)

8.8 Details of these denominations' arrangements will be published in a separate leaflet circulated to all local authorities. This will include the special arrangements made for Church of England cathedrals where all buildings, objects or structures within an area designated by the Secretary of State for National Heritage, after consulting the Cathedrals Fabric Commission for England, and places of worship and unlisted tombstones and other monuments elsewhere within the cathedral precinct, are exempt. A list of addresses for the denominations concerned, and related bodies, is included in Annex A.

8.9 The Order also provides continued exemption for ecclesiastical buildings of these denominations in various categories where insufficient information is currently available (eg. buildings of Church of England 'peculiars', viz those outside the faculty jurisdiction system; Church of England and Roman Catholic religious communities; and school and other institutional chapels). The intention is that by the end of a limited period all buildings within these categories will either become subject to the normal local authority controls or be included within the scope of an exempted denomination's internal system of control. The bodies concerned have been notified of the Order and invited to consider what future arrangements would be appropriate for them.

Exercise of controls over non-exempt church buildings

8.10 For denominations, faiths and independent congregations not listed in the Order, their places of worship will be fully subject to listed building and conservation area control from October 1, 1994. For non-exempt denominations, works begun or contracted for before October 1, 1994 are exempt. Conservation area control will extend to memorials, monuments and tombstones of whatever size erected prior to 1925, in order to bring authorities' controls into alignment with those which will be operated by the denominations listed in the Order; this will be done by a direction made under section 75(2) by the Secretary of State.

8.11 Much of the architectural character and historic interest of places of worship lies in the arrangement and furnishing of their interiors. The great majority of furnishings are likely to be fixed and so form part of the listed building (paragraphs 3.30-3.32), and their architectural coherence and quality will need to be taken into account when considering any proposals for re-ordering. It is probable that some changes have taken place in the past, and before considering further alterations the chronology and completeness of the existing arrangements should be carefully assessed. It is particularly important to identify, and where possible retain, the spatial arrangements and fixtures that belong to the principal period of building. When considering proposals for creating cleared areas for multi-purpose use, the possibility of making fixed seating capable of being dismantled or moved should be investigated. Proper recording in accordance with the principles set out in paragraphs 3.22-3.24 and, in respect of archaeological remains, paragraph 2.15, should always be considered. Where extensive re-ordering takes place, some examples of the replaced furnishings should be retained wherever possible and, where appropriate, materials such as panelling should be re-used within the building or offered for re-use in a similar context, rather than destroyed.

8.12 In considering applications for consent relating to buildings used for worship authorities are advised that, in addition to the general considerations set out in section 3, the following matters (mainly relating to interiors) should be given due weight as material considerations, viz whether the changes proposed:

  i.   are necessitated by a change in the worship needs of the congregation;
  ii.   are necessitated by an increase or a reduction in congregation size;
  iii. are directed at accommodating other activities within the building to help ensure its continued viability primarily as a place of worship;
  iv.   would involve substantial structural changes, eg, subdivision of important existing spaces;
  v.   would involve the removal or destruction of important fixtures and fittings, or are more in the nature of a reversible re-ordering

of internal features;
vi. would involve disturbance of archaeologically important remains below ground.

8.13 English Heritage has published guidance entitled *New Works to Historic Churches* which local planning authorities may find useful in respect of buildings of all denominations. The Church of England has published a *Code of Practice on the Care of Churches and Ecclesiastical Jurisdiction Measure* which gives detailed guidance on many of the procedures to be followed and recommended practice under its own system of control (other than for cathedrals).

8.14 The Secretary of State will continue to have the power to bring within normal listed building or conservation area controls by a further Order any individual ecclesiastical building where it seems likely that potentially damaging works will be carried out without the necessary authorisation having been obtained under an exempt denomination's procedures, and without legal sanctions being available to the denomination internally.

Buildings no longer in ecclesiastical use

8.15 In the case of the Church of England total or partial demolitions of a redundant building in pursuance of a pastoral or redundancy scheme under the Pastoral Measure 1983 are exempt from listed building control by virtue of section 60(7) of the Act, and from conservation area control by a direction under section 75(2). The Church Commissioners have, however, agreed to ask the Secretary of State for the Environment whether he wishes to hold a non-statutory public local inquiry into any such proposal for total or partial demolition (which would otherwise fall within the scope of those controls) where English Heritage, the Advisory Board for Redundant Churches, the local planning authority or a national amenity society have lodged reasoned objections. The Church Commissioners have also undertaken to accept a recommendation from the Secretary of State for the Environment following such an inquiry that the church is of sufficient importance to be vested in the Churches Conservation Trust (formerly the Redundant Churches Fund) or, in cases where the recommendation was not that the building should go to the Trust, to make further efforts to find an alternative use and to engage in further consultation with the Secretary of State for the Environment before using the Pastoral Measure powers to demolish. In considering what recommendation he will make, following a non-statutory inquiry, the Secretary of State for the Environment will take into account the financial implications of retaining a church building as well – as the architectural and historic interest of the church and other planning and social factors, and will consult the Secretary of State for National Heritage.

8.16 Total demolition by faculty is not exempt but would require listed building and conservation area consent in the normal way, as would total demolition by exempt denominations other than the Church of England. This is because the exemption only applies to a building in ecclesiastical use, and the view of the Courts has been that a building cannot be considered to be in such use if it is being totally demolished. Denominations have been asked to notify the local authority concerned when a church building covered by the exemption ceases to be used primarily for worship. Where total demolition is proposed, denominations may find it useful, before applying to the local planning authority for consent, to see that the proposal has been scrutinised through their normal procedures where these apply.

8.17 Except as mentioned above, Church of England buildings which are no longer in regular ecclesiastical use are fully subject to the normal listed building and conservation area controls once a declaration of redundancy under the Pastoral Measure comes into operation. These controls also cover buildings vested in the Churches Conservation Trust, in most of which church services are still held on an occasional basis. During the waiting period between a declaration of redundancy under the Pastoral Measure and the coming into operation of a redundancy scheme authorities are advised to discuss the application of the controls with the diocesan or parish bodies concerned where the authority is considering taking action under the urgent works provisions of section 54 of the Act or where the diocesan board of finance considers it necessary to remove fixtures for safe keeping under section 49(2) of the Pastoral Measure.

8.18 Many churches, of all denominations, when no longer required for worship may nevertheless have a continuing and valuable contribution to make to the community in terms of architecture, art, social and local or national history. They often occupy central and convenient positions in villages and towns and can, therefore, offer suitable venues for a variety of social and community purposes, such as meetings, concerts, exhibitions, indoor sports and evening classes. Even where the building itself is not worthy of individual listing as of architectural or historic interest, it may nevertheless be a familiar and important feature of an urban or rural landscape - while a surrounding churchyard may possess considerable ecological interest. It is important that once a church becomes redundant no unnecessary delay should occur in finding an alternative use for it. Conversion to another use which preserves the most interesting elements, internal and external, is to be preferred to demolition.

Welsh Office Circular 61/96
Planning and the Historic Environment:
Historic Buildings and Conservation Areas
[Extracts, omitting annexes]

Introduction

1. *Planning Guidance (Wales): Planning Policy* sets out the Government's land-use planning policies as they apply in Wales. It lists relevant legislation, sets out general principles including sustainable development and the role of the planning system, and at paragraphs 114 to 140 sets out policy guidance of specific relevance to the historic environment. This Circular, which sets out advice on legislation and procedures relating to historic buildings and conservation areas and conveys certain Directions which the Secretary of State has made, supplements that guidance. Together with Planning Guidance (Wales): Planning Policy it should be taken into account by local planning authorities in the preparation of development plans. The combined guidance may be material to decisions on individual planning applications and should always be taken into account in the exercise of listed building and conservation area controls. It will be taken into account by the Secretary of State and his Inspectors in the determination of called-in applications and planning appeals in Wales.

2. Cadw: Welsh Historic Monuments is the Executive Agency within the Welsh Office which discharges the Secretary of State for Wales's responsibilities for the built heritage. Cadw will be included in internal consultations on all aspects of the Secretary of State's responsibilities affecting the historic environment. A brief guide to the legislation and the main heritage bodies together with the address of key bodies and organisations is set out at Annex A.

3. This Circular has an introduction followed by six parts and six Annexes. The contents fall into the following sections:

Introduction [paragraphs 1-3] and Annex A:
Welsh Office Planning Guide - the role of this Circular and of Cadw.

Part 1 [paragraphs 4-16] and Annex B:
The Planning Framework:

Development Plans and control; the setting of listed buildings; World Heritage Sites and historic parks and gardens.

Part 2 [paragraphs 17-44]:
Conservation Areas:
The designation procedures; importance of assessment and information; conservation area consent.

Part 3 [paragraphs 45-129] and Annexes C-F:
Listing and Listed Building Controls:
How buildings are selected for inclusion in the list; building preservation notices, certificates of immunity from listing. Listed building control, consideration of applications for listed building consent, enforcement and prosecutions.

Part 4 [paragraphs 130-141]:
Historic Buildings in Need of Repair:
Urgent works, repairs notices and compulsory acquisition.

Part 5 [paragraphs 142-143]:
Ecclesiastical Exemption:
Church bodies with continued exemption; handling of proposals for alterations.

Part 6 [paragraph 144]:
Cancellation:
Cancellation of Welsh Office Circular 61/81.

List of Annexes
Annex A   *Brief Guide to Legislation and Heritage Bodies**
Annex B   *Historic Parks and Gardens**
Annex C   *Listed Buildings - Principles of Selection**
Annex D   *Alterations to Listed Buildings - General Principles**
Annex E   *Listed Building Consent - Procedures**
Annex F   *Listed Building Consent - Conditions**

*   not reproduced in this appendix

PART 1: THE PLANNING FRAMEWORK

Development Plans

4. Development plans should ensure that conservation policies are coordinated and integrated with other planning policies affecting the historic environment. Imaginative planning policies can reduce threats to the historic environment and increase its contribution to local amenity. Plans should set out clearly the conservation policies relevant to the exercise of the authority's development control functions and policies relevant to cases where development and conservation issues are linked and need to be addressed together.

5. Section 54A of the Town and Country Planning Act 1990 provides that where, in making any determination under the Planning Acts, regard is to be had to the Development Plan the determination must be made in accordance with the Plan unless material considerations indicate otherwise. However, the Courts have accepted that this does not apply to decisions on applications for listed building consent or conservation area consent, since in those cases there is no statutory requirement to have regard to the provisions of the Plan.

Development Control

6. The Secretary of State attaches particular importance to early consultation, by developers and authorities, on development proposals which would affect historic sites and structures, whether listed buildings, conservation areas, parks and gardens or historic landscapes. There is likely to be more scope for refinement and revision of proposals if consultation takes place before intentions become firm and timescales inflexible. Local planning authorities should indicate their readiness to discuss proposals with developers before formal planning applications are submitted. They should expect developers to assess the likely impact of their proposals on the special interest of the site or structure in question, and to discuss them directly with other owners and interest groups including amenity societies. Developers should provide information sufficient to inform understanding of a site's/structure's special interest.

7. Local planning authorities are required by sections 67 and 73 of the

Planning (Listed Buildings and Conservation Areas) Act 1990 to publish a notice of planning applications for development which in their opinion affects the setting of a listed building, or the character or appearance of a conservation area; this requirement should not be interpreted narrowly.

8. It is generally preferable for both the applicant and the planning authority if related applications for planning permission and for listed building or conservation area consent are considered concurrently. Authorities are required by section 66(l) of the Act (throughout this Circular 'the Act' refers to the Planning (Listed Buildings and Conservation Areas) Act 1990) in considering whether to grant planning permission for development which affects a listed building or its setting, to have special regard to the desirability of preserving the building or its setting or any features of architectural or historic interest which it possesses. It is unlikely that they will be able to do so effectively unless the planning application is accompanied by a listed building consent application (where the development in question requires one) or at least contains an equivalent amount of information. If an authority is asked to consider a planning application in isolation, a decision on that application cannot be taken as predetermining the outcome of a subsequent application for listed building consent. Authorities are also required by section 72 of the Act, in the exercise in a conservation area of their powers under the Planning Acts, to pay special attention to the desirability of preserving or enhancing the character or appearance of that area. In the case of unlisted buildings in conservation areas, the Courts have held that consent for the demolition of a building may involve consideration of what is to take its place (see paragraph 33).

9. Authorities should ensure that they have appropriately qualified specialist advice on any development which, by its character or location, might be held to have an effect on any sites or structures of the historic environment. The need for an environmental assessment of major development proposals affecting historic areas should be considered in the light of the advice given in Welsh Office Circular 23/88. The advice of the Royal Fine Art Commission should be sought on planning applications raising conservation issues of more than local importance and should be taken fully into account.

10. Some historic buildings are scheduled ancient monuments (see

paragraph 65), and many which are not scheduled are either of intrinsic archaeological interest or stand on ground which contains archaeological remains. It is important in such cases that there should be appropriate assessment of the archaeological implications of development proposals before applications are determined and that, where permission is to be granted, authorities consider whether adequate arrangements have been made for recording remains that would be lost in the course of works to which permission will relate. Further advice on archaeology is given in Welsh Office Circular 60/96.

The Setting of Listed Buildings

11. Sections 16 and 66 of the Act require authorities considering applications for planning permission or listed building consent for works which affect a listed building to have special regard to certain matters, including the desirability of preserving the setting of the building. The setting is often an essential part of a building's character especially if a park, garden or grounds have been laid out to complement its design or function. Also, the economic viability as well as the character of historic buildings may suffer and they can be robbed of much of their interest and of the contribution they make to townscape or the countryside if they become isolated from their surroundings, e.g. by new traffic routes, car parks, or other development.

Changes of Use

12. New uses may be the key to the preservation of a building or area and controls over land use, density, plot ratio, daylighting and other planning matters should be exercised sympathetically where this would enable an historic building or area to be given a new lease of life. The Secretary of State is not in favour of tighter development controls over changes of use of historic buildings as a specific instrument of conservation policy; generally the same provisions on change of use should apply to historic buildings as apply to others.

World Heritage Sites

13. The World Heritage Convention (adopted by UNESCO in 1972) was ratified by the United Kingdom in 1984. The Convention provides for the

identification, protection, conservation and presentation of cultural and natural Sites of outstanding universal value, and requires a World Heritage List to be established under the management of an inter-governmental World Heritage Committee. This is advised by the International Council on Monuments and Sites (ICOMOS) and the World Conservation Union (IUCN). Individual governments are responsible for the nomination of sites, and for ensuring the protection of sites listed. There is one World Heritage entry for Wales comprising the castles and town walls of King Edward I in North Wales:

*   Caernarfon Castle and Town Walls;
*   Conwy Castle and Town Walls;
*   Harlech Castle; and
*   Beaumaris Castle.

14. No additional national planning restrictions follow from the inclusion of a site in the World Heritage List. Inclusion does, however, highlight the outstanding national and international importance of the site as a material consideration to be taken into account by local planning authorities in determining planning and listed building consent applications, and by the Secretary of State in determining cases on appeal or following call-in.

15. It is for each local authority, taking account of World Heritage Site designation and other relevant statutory designations, to formulate planning policies for these sites and to include these policies in their development plans. Different policies will be appropriate for different sites. Policies should, however, reflect the fact that all these sites have been designated for their pre-eminence and local planning authorities should place great weight on the need to protect them for the benefit of future generations as well as our own. Development proposals affecting these sites or their setting may be compatible with this objective, but should always be carefully scrutinised for their likely effect on the site in the longer term. ICOMOS can provide advice and assistance in considering issues relating to World Heritage Sites.

Historic Landscapes, Parks and Gardens

16. Cadw, in collaboration with ICOMOS and the Countryside Council for Wales is preparing a Register of Landscapes, Parks and Gardens of Special Historic Interest in Wales. The Register is being prepared in two parts. The first, covering Historic Parks and Gardens, is being produced in a series of county-by-county (former county council areas) volumes whilst the Historic Landscapes section has been issued for consultation. No additional statutory controls follow from the inclusion of a site in the Register. Local planning authorities are asked to take it into account in preparing local plans and in determining planning applications, especially those concerning road schemes, which would affect registered parks and gardens and their settings (see also Welsh Office Circular 29/95 Appendix B) or where the proposed development is of a sufficient scale to have more than local impact on the historic landscape. As the county volumes of historic parks and gardens are produced, planning authorities are asked to consult Cadw on planning applications in respect of Grade I and II* sites and the Garden History Society on all parks and gardens on the Register. For further information, see Annex B.

PART 2: CONSERVATION AREAS

17. Planning Guidance (Wales): Planning Policy 1996 (paragraphs 122-133) sets out the Secretary of State's policy for Conservation Areas including the restriction of permitted development rights (Article 4 Directions) and should be read alongside this guidance.

Assessment and Designation of Conservation Areas

18. Section 69 of the Act imposes a duty on local authorities and National Park Authorities to review their areas from time to time and to consider whether further designation of conservation areas is called for. The Secretary of State also has powers to designate conservation areas. His policy is to use his own powers only in exceptional cases, for instance where an area is of more than local interest, or where there is evidence to suggest that an authority's ownership of important buildings may have influenced a decision not to use its own powers, and there is a clear threat to the character or appearance of the area. The Secretary of State would

consult the authority concerned before using his powers.

19. Whilst listing procedures are focused on the protection of individual buildings, conservation area designation provides the basis for policies designed to preserve or enhance all the aspects of character or appearance that define an area's special interest.

20. Quality of place should be the prime consideration in identifying conservation areas. This depends on more than individual buildings. It is recognised that the special character of a place may derive from many factors, including: the grouping of buildings; their scale and relationship with outdoor spaces; the network of routes and nodal spaces; the mix and relative importance of focus and background buildings; vistas and visual compositions; hierarchies of public and private space; materials used in buildings and other surfaces (pavements, roads, garden walls, railings, ...); architectural detailing (of windows, doors, eaves, gates, kerbs, ...); patterns of use; colours; hard and soft landscaping; street furniture; and so on. Conservation area designation should be seen as the prime means of recognising, protecting and enhancing the identity of places with special character; local conservation policy should be sensitive to quality of place (townscape) in the broadest sense. Authorities should seek to establish consistent criteria against which they should periodically review existing conservation areas and their boundaries. Cancellation of designation should be considered where an area or part of an area is no longer considered to possess the special interest which led to its designation.

Assessment and Proposals

21. The legislation requires that local authorities publish proposals for the preservation and enhancement of conservation areas. Preparation of these proposals should include an appraisal of strategies for the future and relate these to an appraisal of the area's special interest, including those unlisted buildings which make a positive contribution to the special interest of the area. An assessment of the effectiveness of current planning controls in the area and the need for supplementary protection, including Article 4 Directions also should be included. Local plan policies and development control decisions which relate to a conservation area will have a sounder basis, and make more positive contributions to long term aims, if the character of each conservation area is defined and policies for

its enhancement set out in detail. Proposals need to take account of the Government's objective of, wherever possible, keeping to the necessary minimum control over businesses and householders.

22. Bringing vacant upper floors back into use, particularly residential use, not only provides additional income and security for the shop owner, but also helps to ensure that what are often important townscape buildings are kept in good repair. It meets a widespread need for small housing units and helps to sustain activity in town centres after working hours. Local planning authorities are urged to develop policies to secure better use of vacant upper premises, e.g. by giving careful consideration to planning applications for shop conversions which would eliminate separate accesses to upper floors; by working with housing associations to secure residential conversion; and through the house renovation grant system.

23. Authorities should take into account the resources likely to be required for the administration of conservation area controls, for consultation with local residents and formulation of policies for a new area. An authority's justification for designation, as reflected in its assessment of an area's special interest and its character and appearance, is a factor which the Secretary of State will take into account in considering appeals against refusals of conservation area consent for demolition, and appeals against refusal of planning permission.

24. Given the nature of conservation area controls (which are essentially controls over demolition, plus strengthened controls over minor development and the protection of trees) designation is not likely to be appropriate as a means of protecting landscape features, except where they form an integral part of the historic built environment. This needs to be taken into account in considering any planning applications that would affect them. Designation is not a means of controlling activities (e.g. agricultural operations) which do not fall within the definition of development. Trees are best protected by means of a tree preservation order.

Local Information and Consultation

25. Whilst there is no statutory requirement to consult prior to designation

or cancellation of designation, there should be consultation with local residents, businesses and other local interests (eg, amenity bodies) both over the identification of areas and the definition of their boundaries. The greater the public support that can be enlisted for designation before it takes place, the more likely it is that policies for the area will be implemented voluntarily and without the need for additional statutory controls.

26. Section 71(2) of the Act requires proposals for the preservation or enhancement of a conservation area to be submitted for consideration to a public meeting in the area; but wider consultation will always be desirable. Consultation should be undertaken with local residents and amenity societies, and with chambers of commerce, public utilities, and the highway authority. The character and appearance of many conservation areas is heavily dependent on the treatment of roads, pavements and other public spaces. It is important that conservation policies are fully integrated with other policies for the area, e.g. for shopping and traffic management. Account should also be taken of wider policies (e.g. for house renovation grants) which may affect the area's character or appearance.

27. Once policies for an area have been formulated, they should be made available to local residents and businesses in leaflet form, setting out clearly why the area has been designated; what its specially valuable features are; how individual householders can help to protect its character and appearance; and what additional controls and opportunities for assistance designation brings with it.

Advisory Committees

28. Authorities are asked to consider setting up conservation area advisory committees, both to assist in formulating policies for the conservation area (or for several areas in a particular neighbourhood), and as a continuing source of advice on planning and other applications which could affect an area. Committees should include local residential and business interests, local historical, civic and amenity societies, and local chambers of commerce and the authority may wish to seek nominations (depending on the character of the area) from national bodies such as the national amenity societies and the Civic Trust for

Wales. Authorities should consider whether there is scope for the involvement of local people on a voluntary basis in practical work for the enhancement of the area.

General Planning Control in Conservation Areas

29. The status now accorded to the development plan by Section 54A of the Town and Country Planning Act 1990 makes it particularly important that an authority's policies for its conservation areas, insofar as they bear on the exercise of development controls, should be in the plan. There should be a clear indication of the relationship between the plan itself and detailed assessment documents or statements of proposals for particular conservation areas, making clear that development proposals will be judged against their effect on the character and appearance of the area as identified in the assessment and proposal document.

30. Many conservation areas include the commercial centres of towns and villages and generally there will need to be an emphasis on controlled and positive management of change, to allow the area to remain alive and prosperous, and ensure that any new development accords with the area' special architectural and historic qualities. Many conservation areas include gap sites, or buildings that make no positive contribution to, or indeed detract from, the character or appearance of the area; and their replacement should be a stimulus to imaginative, high quality design, and an opportunity to enhance the area. What is important is not that new buildings should directly imitate earlier styles, but that they should be designed with respect for their context, as part of a larger whole which has a well-established character and appearance of its own.

Conservation Area Control Over Demolition

31. Conservation area designation introduces control over the demolition of most buildings within conservation areas (Section 74 of the Act) and this is discussed here. Exceptions to conservation area control over demolition are specified in Section 75 of the Act and in the following Direction:

Direction – Conservation area consent

Consent is not needed under Section 74 for the demolition of listed buildings, buildings protected under ancient monuments legislation, or for the partial demolition of ecclesiastical buildings and the Secretary of State may direct that the section shall not apply to certain other types of buildings. **In pursuance of his powers under** Section 75 of the Act, the **Secretary of State** hereby directs that **Section 74 shall not apply to the following descriptions of buildings:**

(a) any building with a total cubic content not exceeding 115 cubic metres or any part of such a building;

(b) any gates, wall, fence or railing which is less than 1 metre high where abutting on a highway (including a public footpath or bridleway) or public open space, or less than 2 metres high in any other case;

(c) any building erected since January 1, 1914 and used, or last used, for the purposes of agriculture or forestry;

(d) any part of a building used, or last used, for an industrial process, provided that such part (taken with any other part which may have been demolished) does not exceed 10%, of the cubic content of the original building (as ascertained by external measurements) or 500 metres^2 of floor space, whichever is the greater;

(e) any buildings required to be demolished by virtue of a discontinuance order made under Sections 102 and 103 of the Town and Country Planning Act 1990;

(f) any building required to be demolished by virtue of any provision of an agreement made under Section 106 of the Town and Country Planning Act 1990; (g) any building in respect of which the provisions of an enforcement notice served under Section 172 of the Town and Country Planning Act 1990 or Section 38 of the Planning (Listed Buildings and Conservation Areas) Act 1990 require its demolition, in whole or in part, however expressed;

(h) any building required to be demolished by virtue of a condition of planning permission granted under Section 70 or 71 of the Town and Country Planning Act 1990;

(i) any building included in an operative clearance order or compulsory purchase order made under Part III of the Housing Act 1988 or to which a demolition order made under Part II of that Act applies;

(j) any building purchased by a local authority by agreement where Part III of the Housing Act 1988 applies to that building;

(k) a redundant building (within the meaning of the Pastoral Measure 1983) or part of such a building where the demolition is in pursuance of a pastoral or redundancy scheme (within the meaning of that Measure).

Notes

(1) In this Direction, except in paragraph 31 (a) above 'building' has the meaning assigned to it by Section 91 of the Act.

(2) Paragraph 31(b) of the Direction means that consent is not required for the demolition of buildings of the type described whenever erected, if the re-erection of what has been demolished would be permitted development under the specified classes of the General Development Order, e.g. any wall less than 1 metre high abutting a highway or 2 metres elsewhere.

(3) Authorities are not required to notify the Secretary of State before granting consent to applications for the demolition of an unlisted building in a conservation area but their own applications are required to be made to the Secretary of State.

32. Applications for consent to demolish must be made to the local planning authority or, on appeal or call-in, to the Secretary of State. Procedures are essentially the same as for listed building consent applications (see Part 3). Authorities' own applications (for buildings in their own areas) must be made to the Secretary of State. Scheduled ancient monuments are exempt from conservation area control: scheduled monument consent for proposed works must be sought from the Secretary of State. See Annex I of Welsh Office Circular 60/96.

33. The general presumption should be in favour of retaining buildings which make a positive contribution to the character or appearance of a conservation area. Proposals to demolish such buildings should be assessed against the same broad criteria as proposals to demolish listed buildings. In cases where a building makes little or no such contribution the authority will normally need to have full information about what is

proposed for the site after demolition. Consent for demolition should not be given unless there are acceptable and detailed plans for redevelopment. It has been held that the decision-maker is entitled to consider the merits of any proposed development in determining whether consent should be given for the demolition of an unlisted building in a conservation area.

34. It will be appropriate to impose on the grant of consent for demolition a condition under Section 17(3) of the Act – as applied by Section 74(3), that demolition shall not take place until a contract for carrying out development work has been made and planning permission granted.

35. Section 336 of the Town and County Planning Act 1990 states that a building includes "any part of a building". The demolition of part of a building should therefore be regarded as falling within the scope of conservation area control. What constitutes a demolition or demolition of part of a building must be a matter of fact and degree, to be decided in the particular case and ultimately by the Courts. Routine works of repair, maintenance or replacement, including work involving such items as doors or windows, would not in the Secretary of State's view normally constitute demolition. Likewise, the removal of internal features, whether replaced or not, would not usually constitute a demolition and for the purposes of conservation area consent would not, in any event, have a material impact on the building's appearance or affect the character or appearance of the area.

Advertisement Control

36. All outdoor advertisements affect the appearance of the building or the neighbourhood where they are displayed. One of the purposes of the advertisement control system is to encourage the display of outdoor advertisements which make a positive contribution to the appearance of an attractive environment. So it is reasonable to expect that the local planning authority's duty to pay special attention to the desirability of preserving or enhancing the character or appearance of a conservation area will result, in practice, in more exacting standards when the authority consider whether to grant consent for a proposed advertisement in such an area.

37. In conservation areas it is important for local planning authorities to be flexible in their use of the powers under the Town and Country Planning (Control of Advertisements) Regulations 1992, because many areas include retail and commercial premises ranging from small corner-shops to thriving commercial centres. Outdoor advertising is essential to commercial activity in a free and diverse economy, and the success of local businesses will usually help owners and tenants of commercial premises to maintain buildings in good repair and attractive appearance.

38. Local planning authorities may wish to adopt advertisement control policies as part of their duty to formulate and publish proposals for the preservation and enhancement of conservation areas. Such policies can inform prospective advertisers about the type of displays likely to prove acceptable in an area; and they should provide a rational and consistent basis for decision-making on all advertisement control matters, including the serving of discontinuance notices.

39. Because of the special interest of most conservation areas, certain categories of 'deemed consent' advertisements which may have a significant visual impact are not permitted for display in a conservation area without the local planning authority's consent. But a general prohibition of the display of certain classes of advertisement, or the withdrawal or limitation of those which may be displayed with deemed consent, is not usually justified solely because of designation.

40. Authorities may wish to consider mounting programmes, in association with local businesses, to promote advertisement policies by providing advice about the design and siting of displays which respect the character and appearance of an area.

41. Where an authority has pursued this approach, but considers that it has not prevented unsuitable or harmful advertisement displays, the Secretary of State will be prepared to consider making a Direction under Regulation 7 of the 1992 Regulations, where an authority can show it is justified. In seeking a Direction to control the display of particular classes of advertisement, displayed with deemed consent, authorities will be expected to show that it would improve visual amenity and that the vigorous use of normal powers of control has proved inadequate.

Similarly, when considering whether an advertisement is causing 'substantial injury to amenity', so that its display should be discontinued, the Secretary of State may take into account any evidence, on appeal, that the authority has acted in the light of with a well-formulated advertisement control policy.

Trees in Conservation Areas

42. Trees are valued features of our towns and countryside and make an important contribution to the character of the local environment. Under Part VIII of the Town and Country Planning Act 1990, local planning authorities have a power to protect trees and woodlands in the interests of amenity by making tree preservation orders. In addition to this general power, authorities are under a duty where appropriate to make adequate provision for the preservation and planting of trees when granting planning permission for the development of land. They do this by a combination of planning conditions and tree preservation orders.

43. When considering whether to extend protection to trees in conservation areas, local planning authorities should always take into account the visual, historic and amenity contribution of trees. In some instances new plantings or re-plantings may be desirable where this would be consistent with the character and appearance of the area.

44. Many trees in conservation areas are the subject of tree preservation orders, which means that the local planning authority's consent must be obtained before they can be cut down, topped or lopped. In addition to these controls, and in view of the contribution that trees can make to the character and appearance of a conservation area, there is special provision for trees in conservation areas which are not the subject of tree preservation orders. Under Section 211, subject to a range of exceptions (including small trees and ones that are dead, dying or dangerous), anyone proposing to cut down, top or lop a tree in a conservation area is required to give six weeks' notice to the local planning authority. The purpose of this requirement is to give the authority an opportunity of considering bringing the tree under their general control by making a tree preservation order in respect of it. Penalties for contravention, which may include a requirement to replant, are similar to those for tree preservation orders. For guidance on these matters see Welsh Office Circular 64/78.

PART 3: LISTING AND LISTED BUILDING CONTROLS

45. Planning Guidance (Wales): Planning Policy 1996 (paragraphs 116-121) sets out the Secretary of State's policy for listing buildings of special architectural or historic interest and for addressing the subsequent control of works.

46. Section 1 of the Act requires the Secretary of State to compile a list of buildings of special architectural or historic interest with a view to the guidance of local planning authorities in the performance of their functions under the Act. The purpose of listing is to ensure that a building's special architectural or historic interest is fully recognised and that any works for the demolition of a listed building, or for its alteration or extension in any way which would affect its character as a listed building, are brought within statutory control.

47. Buildings are listed in three grades which reflect their relative importance. The current listing position in Wales is:

List Entries (Wales: September 1996)

Grade	Nos
I	329 (1.7%)
II*	1,045 (5.6%)
II	16,845 (89.7%)
Old grades (churches)	569 (3.0%)
	18,788

Identification of Buildings for Listing

48. The main criteria which the Secretary of State applies in deciding which buildings to include in the statutory lists are set out at Annex C. The emphasis in these criteria is on national significance, though this cannot be defined precisely. For instance, the best examples of local vernacular building types will normally be listed. But many buildings which are valued for their contribution to the local scene, or for local historical associations, will not merit listing. Such buildings will often be protected by conservation area designation (see Part 2). It is also open to planning authorities to draw up lists of locally important buildings, and to formulate policies for their protection through development control

procedures. Policies should make clear that such buildings do not enjoy the full protection of statutory listing. Buildings are added to the statutory lists in two main ways:

    (i) as a result of a systematic resurvey of particular areas or building types; or

   (ii) following proposals from local authorities, amenity societies or other bodies or individuals that particular buildings should be added to the lists ('spot listing').

49. Before including buildings in the statutory lists the Secretary of State is required to consult such other persons as he may consider appropriate as having special knowledge of, or interest in, buildings of special architectural or historic interest. Expert advisers usually visit and report on buildings before they are listed. In all cases – resurveys and spot listing – there will normally be close consultation between Cadw and the local planning authority. The Secretary of State will consider the views of others, **but his decision must be based on the special architectural or historic interest of the building**. It is not his practice to advertise proposals for new listings.

Notification of Owners and Occupiers

50. When a building is included in the statutory list, Cadw notifies the appropriate local planning authority. That authority must then notify the owner and occupier of the building. As it is a criminal offence to carry out any works (either to the exterior or interior) which would affect the character of a building once it is listed (unless listed building consent has been obtained), notice of listing **must be given to the owner as soon as possible**. The statutory notice is prescribed in the 1990 Regulations. In addition, Cadw aims to send an informal notification to the occupier of the building at the point of listing.

Public Access to the List

51. The lists for Wales are available for free public inspection at Cadw's offices in Cardiff and at the Royal Commission on the Ancient and Historical Monuments of Wales (RCAHMW) in Aberystwyth. Each local planning authority has available the lists relating to its own area.

List Descriptions

52. The lists include a description of each building. This is principally to aid identification. It has no statutory force. List descriptions will include mention of those features which led to the listing, but they are not intended to provide a comprehensive or exclusive record of all the features of importance, and the amount of information given in descriptions varies considerably. Absence from the list description of any reference to a feature (whether external or internal) does not, therefore, indicate that it is not of interest or that it can be removed or altered without consent. Where there is doubt, the advice of the local planning authority should be sought.

Spot Listing

53. Requests for individual buildings to be spot listed can be made to the Secretary of State at any time and will be considered by Cadw. Where the area in question has recently been the subject of resurvey or review, it is important that requests for spot listing draw attention to any new evidence which may not have been available to Cadw previously, or otherwise explain why the building's special interest may have been overlooked. The Secretary of State recognises that there may be cases where new evidence justifies reconsideration of a previous decision not to list, but generally he will not be disposed to review earlier decisions unless such evidence is provided.

54. Difficulties can arise where proposals for spot listing are made when buildings are under imminent threat of alteration or demolition. Spot listing in such cases can often mean delay, sometimes with serious practical and financial consequences for the developer. All requests for spot listing are considered, but it is preferable from all points of view that buildings should be assessed for possible listing before planning permission has been granted for redevelopment. Local planning authorities should draw to Cadw's attention at the earliest possible stage any buildings affected by redevelopment proposals (including their own) which appear to them to merit listing. A building preservation notice served by the authority may be a quicker means of protecting a threatened building than a request for spot listing (see paragraph 56).

55. Requests to list buildings should be sent to Cadw's Listing Branch, Crown Building, Cathays Park, Cardiff CF1 3NQ. They should be accompanied by a justification for adding the building to the list; a location plan (such as an Ordnance Survey map extract) showing, wherever possible, the position of any other listed buildings nearby; clear up-to-date photographic prints of the main elevations of the building; any information about the building (e.g. its date); details of specialised function (e.g. industrial building); historical associations; the name of the architect (if known); its group value in the street scene; and details of any interior features of interest.

Building Preservation Notices

56. Under Section 3 of the Act, local planning authorities have the power to serve building preservation notices in respect of buildings which are not listed, but which they consider are of special architectural or historic interest and in danger of demolition or alteration in such a way as to affect their character as buildings of such interest. A building preservation notice applies all the provisions of the Act relating to listed buildings (except Section 59) to the building concerned. It takes effect immediately it is served, and is often a quicker and so more expedient short-term measure than asking Cadw to spot list a building. A copy of the building preservation notice, a location plan and photographs of the building should be sent to Cadw as soon as the notice has been served. The notice remains in force for up to six months, but will lapse if within that period the Secretary of State either includes the building in the statutory list or notifies the authority in writing that it does not intend to do so. The authority must notify the owner and occupier if Cadw indicates it has been decided not to list the building, and may not serve another building preservation notice in respect of that building within twelve months of Cadw's notification.

57. In considering whether to serve a building preservation notice, authorities will appreciate that they become liable to pay compensation for any loss or damage resulting from the service of a notice which the Secretary of State does not uphold by listing. Cadw cannot indicate in advance whether the service of a notice in a particular case subsequently will result in listing. The same general principles of listing, set out above, will apply in these cases as in others. It should not however be assumed

that listing will automatically follow the inclusion of a building by Cadw in a draft list sent to a local planning authority for consultation purposes, since that list may be amended before it is approved.

Requests to De-List Buildings

58. The Secretary of State is prepared to review listings in the light of new evidence. There is no formal appeal procedure, but owners or others who believe that a listing should be reconsidered should send the evidence to Cadw's Listing Branch, together with photographs of the building and a location plan. The evidence must relate to the special architectural or historic interest ascribed to the building: if the objection to listing is (for instance) related to a building's condition and the cost of repairing or maintaining it, or to plans for redevelopment, the appropriate application should be made under the listed building consent procedures. The local authority concerned will be notified by Cadw of any requests received to de-list buildings.

59. The Secretary of State will not generally entertain an application for de-listing if the building is the subject of an application for listed building consent, or an appeal against refusal of consent, or if action by a local planning authority is in hand because of unauthorised works or neglect. Both listed building consent and enforcement appeal procedures give appellants the right to argue that a building is not of special interest and should be removed from the list. The issue of de-listing should normally be addressed in this way, rather than regarded as a means of avoiding the need for enforcement action.

Certificates of Immunity from Listing

60. Currently, provided that planning permission is being sought or has been obtained, any person may ask the Secretary of State to issue a certificate stating that he does not intend to list the building or buildings involved in the planning application. Once a certificate is issued, the building cannot be listed for five years, nor may the local planning authority serve a building preservation notice during that time. However, if he does not grant a certificate, the Secretary of State will normally add the building to the statutory list, and listed building controls will then apply. This procedure gives greater certainty to developers proposing

works which will affect buildings which may be eligible for listing: they will know either that they must seek listed building consent in the normal way, or that they have five years to carry out their development without the possibility of disruption by spot listing.

61. As a certificate of immunity is valid for five years, a building is normally completely reassessed when an application for a certificate is made because new information may have come to light. It should not be assumed, therefore, that even a recent decision by the Secretary of State not to list a building necessarily means that he will grant a certificate of immunity.

62. Even if a certificate of immunity is granted, a building in a conservation area will still normally need consent for demolition (see Part 2). It is not practicable to extend the certificate procedure to provide immunity from the effects of conservation area designation (but conservation area consent is not required where planning permission was granted prior to designation).

63. Applications for certificates of immunity should be made to Cadws' Listing Branch. There is no application form and no charge. Applicants should supply a copy of the planning application or planning permission, as well as the information requested for spot listing applications (paragraph 55). Applicants are required to notify the local planning authority in whose area the building is situated of the application at the same time as it is submitted to Cadw. Applicants should confirm that they have notified these authorities.

64. When a certificate is issued, Cadw will notify the relevant local authority. The existence of a certificate and its expiry date should be disclosed in response to enquiries by prospective purchasers of the building or land, together with other information relating to planning matters.

Relationship Between Listing and Scheduling

65. Cadw maintains a schedule of ancient monuments of national importance. Most scheduled monuments are archaeological sites, ruins, or buildings for which there is little prospect of an economic use. The

principles of selection are set out in Annex 3 of Welsh Office Circular 60/96. Where a building is both scheduled and listed, scheduling – which introduces closer controls than does listing – takes priority and listed building controls do not apply.

Listed Building Control – General

66. Once a building is listed (or is the subject of a Building Preservation Notice) under Section 1 of the Act, Section 7 provides that consent is normally required for its demolition, in whole or in part, and for any works of alteration or extension which would affect its character as a building of special architectural or historic interest. It is a criminal offence to carry out such works without consent, which should be sought from the local planning authority.

67. Controls apply to works, both external and internal, that would affect a building's special interest, whether or not the particular feature concerned is specifically mentioned in the list description. Consent is required where painting or repainting the exterior or interior of a listed building would affect the building's character. Consent is not normally required for repairs, but, where repairs involve alterations which would affect the character of the listed building, consent is required. Whether repairs actually constitute alterations which require consent and whether proposed works constitute alterations or demolition is a matter of fact and degree which must be determined in each case. Fixtures and curtilage buildings – i.e. any object or structure which is fixed to the building, or which is within the curtilage and forms part of the land and has done so since before July 1, 1948 – are also treated as part of the building for the purposes of listed building control.

68. While the listing of a building should not be seen as a bar to all future change, the starting point for the exercise of listed building control is the statutory requirement on local planning authorities to "have special regard to the desirability of preserving the building or its setting or any features of special architectural or historic interest which it possesses" (Section 66 of the Act).

69. Applicants for listed building consent must be able to justify their proposals. They will need to show why works which would affect the

character of a listed building are desirable or necessary. They must provide the local planning authority with full information, to enable them to assess the likely impact of their proposals on the special architectural or historic interest of the building and on its setting.

General Criteria

70. The issues that are generally relevant to the consideration of all listed building consent applications are:

   (i)   the importance of the building, its intrinsic architectural and historic interest and rarity, in both national and local terms (further explained in Annex C);
   (ii) the particular physical features of the building (which may include its design, plan, materials or location) which justify its inclusion in the list: list descriptions may draw attention to features of particular interest or value, but they are not exhaustive and other features of importance (e.g. interiors) may come to light after the building' inclusion in the list;
   (iii) the building's setting and its contribution to the local scene, which may be very important, e.g. where it forms an element in a group, park, garden or other townscape or landscape, or where it shares particular architectural forms or details with other buildings nearby; and
   (iv) the extent to which the proposed works would bring substantial benefits for the community, in particular by contributing to the economic regeneration of the area or the enhancement of its environment (including other listed buildings).

71. The grading of a building in the statutory lists is clearly a material consideration for the exercise of listed building control. Grades I and II* identify the exceptional architectural or historic interest of a small proportion (7-8%) of all listed buildings. These buildings are of particularly great importance to the nation's built heritage: their significance will generally be beyond dispute. But it should be emphasised that the statutory controls apply equally to all listed buildings, irrespective of grade; and since Grade II includes some 90% of all listed buildings, representing a major element in the historic quality of our towns, villages, and countryside, failure to give careful scrutiny to

proposals for their alteration or demolition could lead to widespread damage to the historic environment. Detailed technical guidance on the consideration of listed building consent applications is provided in Annex D. The Secretary of State commends this guidance and asks all planning authorities to take it into account in their exercise of listed building and development controls.

Secretary of State's Directions

72. This Part sets out the requirements for notification of applications for listed building consent. The following Directions are in force:

A **Direction – Notification to Cadw of listed building consent applications**
Section 13 of the Planning (Listed Buildings and Conservation Areas) Act 1990 requires the local planning authority to notify the Secretary of State of any application for listed building consent which they propose to grant. So far as applications to alter listed buildings are concerned, the Secretary of State is empowered under Section 15(l) of the Act to direct that notification shall not apply to specified descriptions of building. **He hereby directs that Section 13 shall not apply to applications for listed building consent for the carrying out of work affecting the interior only of a Grade II (unstarred) building, other than applications for consent for the carrying out of works to buildings in respect of which he has made a grant under Section 4 of the Historic Buildings and Ancient Monuments Act 1953, or in respect of which an application for grant under that section has been made but not yet decided.** Notification must still be given of any application which involves demolition, or affects either the interior or exterior of a Grade I or II* building, the exterior of a Grade 11 (unstarred) building, or any listed building grant-aided under the 1953 Act.

B **Direction – Notification to other interested parties of applications for listed building consent**
The Secretary of State has power under Section 15(5) of the Act to direct local planning authorities to notify specified persons of any applications for listed building consent and the decisions taken by the authority on them. **The Secretary of State hereby directs that**

notice of all applications for consent to demolish (including partial demolition) a listed building and of the decisions taken thereon should be given to the following bodies: the Ancient Monuments Society, the Council for British Archaeology, the Georgian Group, the Society for the Protection of Ancient Buildings, the Victorian Society and the Royal Commission on the Ancient and Historical Monuments of Wales. The addresses of these bodies are given below. Except in the case of the Royal Commission, the notifications of the applications should be accompanied by the relevant extract from the list describing the building*. Any representations received in response to these notifications should be taken into account when the application is being considered.

Notifications

73. These bodies are required to be notified under the terms of the Direction:

The Ancient Monuments Society
St Ann's Vestry Hall, 2 Church Entry
London EC4V 5HB

The Council for British Archaeology
Crud y Ser, 15 Church Meadow
Rhydymwyn, Mold CH7 5HX

The Royal Commission on the
Ancient and Historical Monuments
of Wales
Crown Building, Plas Crug
Aberystwyth SY23 1NJ

The Georgian Group
6 Fitzroy Square
London W1P 6DX

The Victorian Society
(South and West Wales Area)
2 Nant yr Adar
Llantwit Major CF62 9TW

The Victorian Society
(North Wales and Mid-Wales Area)
Environmental Institute
Bolton Road, Swinton
Manchester M27 2UX

The Society for the Protection of
Ancient Buildings
37 Spital Square
London E1 6DY

* Consultation arrangements have been shown to work best where sufficient information is provided both to identify the building and the extent of work proposed.

Departmental Evaluation and Determination Processes

74. All private applications for listed building consent to which local authorities are minded to grant consent (other than applications for works to the interior only of Grade II listed buildings which have not been grant-aided under the Historic Buildings and Ancient Monuments Act 1953) are formally notified to the Secretary of State under Section 13 of the Act before they may be determined.

75. The initial evaluation of an application for listed building consent notified to the Secretary of State is made by Cadw. Cadw's professional officers provide an expert assessment of the application on the basis of the effect of the proposals on the special architectural or historic interest of the building in question and, if appropriate, on the character and appearance of the conservation area. Where, having taken account of the professional assessment, any representations received, the guidance in Planning Guidance (Wales): Planning Policy 1996 and in this Circular, it is considered that the application may be determined by the local authority Cadw will advise accordingly. Where necessary Cadw will notify the local planning authority that the Secretary of State needs further time, beyond the 28 day statutory period, in which to consider whether call-in under Section 12 of the Act is required. Once notified that an application may be determined, it is for the local planning authority to issue the decision, a copy of which must be sent to Cadw.

Called-in Applications

76. The Secretary of State may require applications for listed building consent to be referred to him for decision, but this call-in power has been exercised only in a small number of cases per year in recent years. The policy of the Secretary of State is to be very selective about calling in listed building consent cases.

77. Cases are likely to be called in where the Secretary of State considers that the proposals raise issues of exceptional significance or controversy. It may also happen that an application for listed building consent is received by a local planning authority when a related matter (e.g. a planning appeal, a called-in planning application or a compulsory purchase order) is being considered by the Secretary of State. Unless it is

clear that the listed building consent application can reasonably be dealt with separately, such an application will normally be called in.

78. Where a private application for listed building consent is called in, a written assessment by Cadw's professional officer offering an expert opinion on the merits of the application will be made available to interested parties.

Local Authority Applications

79. Local authority applications for listed building consent are referred to the Secretary of State under Section 12 of the Act. Applications by a local authority for conservation area consent are determined by the Secretary of State under the provisions of Section 74(2) (a) of the Act. All applications by local authorities should be made to Cadw. Cadw's professional assessment will be sent to the applicant authority if the subsequent evaluation and determination of the application is undertaken by further written representations or public inquiry procedures.

Advice to Owners

80. Owners of listed buildings should be encouraged to seek expert advice on whether proposed works require listed building consent, and on the best way to carry out any such works to their property. Many will need to obtain professional advice anyway, but the Secretary of State hopes that local planning authorities will give owners informal advice where they can or guide them to other sources where they can get advice for themselves. Much specialist advice is published on the care of historic buildings and Cadw can sometimes give advice on individual cases, especially where unusual problems are encountered. The national amenity societies are willing to offer advice to individual owners whenever possible. The RCAHMW may have a record of a building and its reports and photographs may be available for guidance in understanding the structure and its evolution.

Recording Buildings

81. The RCAHMW must be notified of all proposals to demolish listed buildings, and allowed access to buildings which it wishes to record

before demolition takes place. There are other circumstances where notification may be appropriate – for instance, where the exterior of a building is likely to be radically changed as a consequence of major repairs, alteration or extension, or where interior work of significance will be lost, affected by subdivision, or substantially rebuilt.

82. Local planning authorities should consider, in all cases of alteration or demolition, whether it would be appropriate to make it a condition of consent that applicants arrange suitable programmes of recording of features that would be destroyed in the course of the works for which consent is being sought. Authorities should not, however, require applicants to finance such programmes in return for the granting of consent. Nor should applicants expect to be granted consent merely because they have arranged suitable programmes. (For recording of archaeological remains see paragraph 10.)

83. Hidden features of interest may be revealed during works of alteration, especially in older or larger buildings: chimney pieces, fireplaces, early windows and doors, panelling, wattle-and-daub partitions and even wall paintings may come to light. Applicants for listed building consent should be made aware of this possibility and should seek the advice of the local planning authority when such things are found. If there is any likelihood that hidden features will be revealed, the local planning authority should attach an appropriate condition to the listed building consent to ensure their retention or proper recording, or should require exploratory opening up, with listed building consent as necessary, before considering consent for the main works.

Fixtures and Curtilage Structures

84. It is important to know the extent of a listing, not just to determine whether listed building consent is needed for works, but also to determine the payment of VAT and business rates. Section 1(5) of the Act sets out the meaning of a listed building for the purposes of the Act: a listed building is one included in a list compiled or approved by the Secretary of State and includes 'any object or structure fixed to the building' and 'any object or structure within the curtilage of the building which, although not fixed to the building, forms part of the land and has done so since before 1 July 1948.' The Courts have considered in a number of cases in this context the

meaning of 'any object or structure fixed to the building' and 'curtilage'.

85. The listing of a building confers protection not only on the building, but also on any object or structure fixed to the building which is ancillary to the building. The word 'fixed' has the same connotation as in the law of fixtures. These rules provide that any object or structure fixed to a building should be treated as part of it. It is a test therefore of fact in each case as to whether a structure is free-standing or physically fixed to the building. Generally it would be reasonable to expect some degree of physical annexation, together with indications that the annexation was carried out with the intention of making the object an integral part of the land or building. In the light of this test, items such as chimney-pieces, wall panelling and painted or plastered ceilings will normally be found to be part of the building.

86. It may be difficult in some individual cases to decide whether a particular object or structure is a fixture or not. Free-standing objects, e.g. statues, may be fixtures if they were put in place as part of an overall architectural design; this could include objects specially designed or made to fit in a particular space or room. But works of art which were placed in a building primarily to be enjoyed as objects in their own right, rather than forming part of the land or the building, are not likely to be properly considered as fixtures. Each case must be treated in the light of its own facts, and owners who are contemplating works are advised to contact their local planning authority first.

87. The listing of a building confers protection on any object or structure within its curtilage which forms part of the land and has done so since before July 1, 1948. Following recent case law, the Secretary of State's policy is to consider individually all the structures and buildings on a site which can be construed as separate buildings and to list those which qualify for listing. There will still be circumstances, however, where a structure or building forms part of land which surrounds or is connected to or serves a listed building, and landowners and local planning authorities will need to consider on the facts of each case whether it forms part of the land and falls within the curtilage of the listed building.

88. The principal tests as to whether an object or structure is within the curtilage of a listed building relate to the physical layout of the land

surrounding the listed building at the date of the statutory listing and the relationship of the structures on the surrounding land to each other. Changes in ownership, occupation or use after the listing date will not bring about the de-listing of a building which formed part of the principal building at the date of listing. The Courts have held that for a structure or building within the curtilage of a listed building to be part of a listed building it must be ancillary to the principal building, that it must have served the purposes of the principal building at the date of listing, or at a recent time before the date of listing, in a necessary or reasonably useful way and must not be, historically an independent building. Where a self-contained building was fenced or walled-off from the remainder of the site at the date of listing, regardless of the purpose for which it was erected and is occupied, it is likely to be regarded as having a separate curtilage. The structure or building must still form part of the land, and this probably means that there must be some degree of physical annexation to the land.

89. Considerations which may assist local planning authorities in forming their own views, or giving advice if requested, include:

*   the historical independence of the building;
*   the physical layout of the principal building and other buildings;
*   the ownership of the buildings now and at the time of listing; whether the structure forms part of the land;
*   the use and function of the buildings, and whether a building is ancillary or subordinate to the principal building.

90. It is always necessary to recognise that the question of whether a building, structure or object is within the curtilage of, or is fixed to, the principal building, unless specifically included in the listing, is in any particular case a matter of fact and ultimately a matter for the Courts. Great caution must be exercised, therefore, in attempting to extrapolate any general principles from recent decisions and this guidance does not purport to be definitive.

Demolition of Listed Buildings

91. There are outstanding buildings for which it is in practice almost

inconceivable that consent for demolition would ever be granted. The demolition of any Grade I or Grade II* building should be wholly exceptional and require the strongest justification. The Secretary of State would not expect consent to be given for the total or substantial demolition of any listed building without convincing evidence that all reasonable efforts have been made to sustain existing uses or find viable new uses, and these efforts have failed; that preservation in some form of charitable or community ownership is not possible or suitable; or that redevelopment would produce substantial benefits for the community which would decisively outweigh the loss resulting from demolition. The Secretary of State would not expect consent for demolition to be given simply because redevelopment is economically more attractive to the developer than repair and re-use of a historic building, or because the developer acquired the building at a price that reflected the potential for redevelopment rather than the condition and constraints of the existing historic building.

92. The Secretary of State would expect authorities to address the following considerations in determining applications where the proposed works would result in the total or substantial demolition of the listed building, or any significant part of it:

(i) the condition of the building, the cost of repairing and maintaining it in relation to its importance and to the value derived from its continued use. Less favourable levels of rents and yields cannot automatically be assumed. Any assessment should also take account of the possibility of tax allowances and exemptions and of grants from public or charitable sources. In those cases where it is clear that a building has been deliberately neglected, less weight should be given to the costs of repair;

(ii) the adequacy of efforts made to retain the building in use. This should include the offer of the unrestricted freehold of the building on the open market at a price reflecting the building's condition (the offer of a lease would normally reduce the chances of finding a new use for the building); and

(iii) the merits of alternative proposals for the site. Whilst these are a material consideration, the Secretary of State takes the view that subjective claims for the architectural merits of proposed replacement buildings should not in themselves be held to justify the demolition of any listed building. Even where it is thought that the proposed works would bring substantial benefits for the community, it will often be feasible to incorporate listed buildings within the new development, and this option should be carefully considered: the challenge presented by retaining listed buildings can be a stimulus to imaginative new design.

Alterations and Extensions to Listed Buildings

93. The listing of a building confers protection not only on the building but also on any object or structure fixed to the building and which is ancillary to it and, if built before July 1, 1948, within its curtilage.

94. Many listed buildings are already in well-established uses, and any changes need be considered only in this context. But where new uses are proposed, it is important to balance the effect of any changes on the special interest of the listed building against the viability of any proposed use and of alternative, and possibly less damaging, uses. In judging the effect of any alteration or extension it is essential to have assessed the elements that make up the special interest of the building in question. They may comprise obvious visual features such as a decorative facade or, internally, staircases or decorated plaster ceilings, and the spaces and layout of the building and the archaeological or technological interest of the surviving structure and surfaces. These elements are often just as important in simple vernacular and functional buildings as in grander architecture.

95. Many listed buildings can sustain a degree of sensitive alteration or extension to accommodate continuing or new uses. Indeed, cumulative changes reflecting the history of use and ownership are themselves an aspect of the special interest of some buildings, and the merit of new alterations or additions, especially where they are generated within a secure and committed long-term ownership, should not be discounted. Nevertheless, listed buildings do vary greatly in the extent to which they can accommodate change without loss of special interest. Some may be sensitive even to slight alterations; this is especially true of buildings with important interiors and fittings - not just great houses, but also, for example, chapels with historic fittings or industrial structures with surviving machinery. Some listed buildings are the subject of successive

applications for alteration or extension: in such cases it needs to be borne in mind that minor works of indifferent quality, which may seem individually of little importance, can cumulatively be very destructive of a building's special interest.

96. The listing grade is a material consideration, but is not in itself a reliable guide to the sensitivity of a building to alteration or extension. For example, many Grade II buildings are humble, once common building types which have been listed precisely because they are relatively unaltered examples of their sort. They can have their special interest ruined by unsuitable alteration or extension as readily as can Grade I or II* structures.

97. Achieving a proper balance between the special interest of a listed building and proposals for alterations or extensions is demanding and should always be based on specialist expertise; but it is rarely impossible, if reasonable flexibility and imagination are shown by all parties involved. Thus, a better solution may be possible if a local authority is prepared to apply normal development control policies flexibly; or if an applicant is willing to exploit unorthodox spaces rather than set a standardised requirement; or if an architect can respect the structural limitations of a building and abandon conventional design solutions in favour of a more imaginative approach. For example, standard commercial office floor-loadings are rarely needed in all parts of a building, and any unusually heavy loads can often be accommodated in stronger areas such as basements.

98. The preservation of facades alone, and the gutting and reconstruction of interiors, is not normally an acceptable approach to the reuse of listed buildings: it can destroy much of a building's special interest and create problems for the long- term stability of the structure.

99. Local authorities are reminded that they have the power to relax certain requirements of the Building Regulations where their strict application would be unreasonable in a particular case and sympathetic consideration should be given to applications for relaxation in respect of work to listed buildings. Often, it will be possible to meet the requirements of the Building Regulations in a way which does little or no damage to the appearance of the building. Authorities should seek expert

advice in endeavouring to strike a balance.

Advice from Cadw

100. As Cadw is an Executive Agency within the Welsh Office, the Agency's professional officers are permitted only to offer their informal advice to applicants and local planning authorities on proposals (which are, or may become, the subject of an application for listed building consent) where this can be done without prejudice to the Secretary of State's position in the planning process. The principle which governs their conduct lies in their position as officials of the Secretary of State. Their purpose in entering into discussions is to provide professional guidance to inform the development of proposals or their consideration and to inform the applicant's proposals from a specialist viewpoint. In this context, the advice given is not binding on consideration of an application for consent.

101. Cadw's professional officers are not permitted to undertake informal discussions once:

Private LBC Applications
(a) the owner or developer has made an application for LBC unless the local planning authority is present at the discussions;
(b) (with either the applicant or the local planning authority) a case for call-in is being considered; and

Local Authority Applications
(c) the authority has made an application for LBC.

102. Cadw's professional officers will not have bilateral discussions with an applicant, rather the local planning authority is expected to be party to discussions.

Applications

103. The various steps relevant to authorities' handling of listed building consent applications are summarised at Annex E. Every application for listed building consent should be accompanied by adequate scaled

drawings. These should normally show the building as existing and the full extent of the proposed alterations, together with details of the materials and proprietary products to be used. In some cases sectional drawings will be required. Drawings are the principal record of changes to historic buildings and the foundation of proper control. They will also make the consultation procedure more effective. Local planning authorities should not accept applications with inadequate drawings.

104. Applications for listed building consent must be made in duplicate on a form issued by the local planning authority. Section 10(2) of the Act requires that they include sufficient particulars, including a plan, to identify the building in question and such other plans and drawings as are necessary to describe the works for which consent is sought. For all but the simplest work this should normally mean measured drawings of all floor plans and external or internal elevations affected by the work proposed. There should be two sets of such drawings, showing the structure before work and the altered structure or new development to replace it after the proposed work. The Act also empowers an authority to seek such other particulars as it requires and, in the case of complex proposals, an authority should be prepared to require sufficient particulars to ensure that it has a full understanding of the impact of the proposals on the character of the building in question.

Granting of Consents

105. Section 8(1)-(2) of the Act requires that the RCAHMW be allowed at least one month to record a listed building before demolition takes place (unless they indicate that they do not wish to record it). Authorities should make sure that applicants are aware of this requirement. It is helpful if authorities can draw attention to the provisions of the relevant sections in their application forms for listed building consent. All decisions granting consent for demolition should draw attention to the provisions of Sections 8 (1) and (2), and enclose form RCAHMW for applicants to use to notify the Commission of their proposals (copies are available from RCAHMW): the decision must also be copied to RCAHMW at Plas Crug, Aberystwyth SY23 1NJ.

106. Local authorities should not authorise demolition to make way for new development unless it is certain that the new development will

proceed. This can be done by imposing a condition on the grant of consent providing that demolition shall not take place before a contract for carrying out works of redevelopment on the site has been made and planning permission has been granted for the redevelopment for which the contract provides.

107. Listed buildings acquired for demolition and development, whether by private owners or local authorities, should be kept in use for as long as possible, or at least kept wind, weather and vandal-proof until work actually starts. If plans subsequently change, urgent action should be taken to ensure that the building is put into good repair and brought back into suitable use.

108. Granting of consent for demolition does not always mean that it will be implemented. When local authorities know that total demolition has taken place, they should notify Cadw's Listing Branch so that the building can be removed from the list.

Conditions

109. The power to impose conditions on a listed building consent is wide, but the Act specifically empowers certain types of condition (Section 17). All conditions should be necessary, relevant, enforceable, precise and reasonable. Some examples of conditions which may be appropriate are set out at Annex F.

110. A listed building consent shall always be granted subject to a condition that the work to which it relates must be begun not later than five years (or whatever longer or shorter period is considered appropriate in a particular case) from the date on which the consent is granted (Section 18). If any consent is granted without a time limit, the five year period will automatically apply. Conditions requiring the preservation of particular features, or making good damage caused by works, or reconstruction of the building (with the use of original materials so far as practicable) may also be imposed. A listed building consent will normally operate for the benefit of the building regardless of ownership, but, where appropriate, a condition limiting the benefit of the consent to a specified person or persons may be imposed. See also the condition restricting premature demolition in paragraph 34 above.

Later approval of details

111. The authority must always be satisfied that it has adequate information to assess the effect of proposed works on the listed building before granting consent: the extent of the work, the method to be used, and the materials involved are all important. However, Section 17 (2) of the Act permits authorities to impose conditions requiring the subsequent approval of specified details of the works (whether or not these had been set out in the application). This does not provide in any sense an outline listed building consent: it is simply intended to speed up the consideration of applications. It avoids the need for an authority to refuse consent if it is satisfied that the remaining details can safely be left for subsequent approval but it should never be used unless authorities are satisfied that they have enough details to assess the impact of the proposals on the building as a whole.

Applications for the discharge or variation of a condition

112. Conditions should not be varied or discharged lightly. Frequently consent would not be given without conditions to safeguard the treatment of the building or to require works to be carried out in a certain way. Nevertheless, occasionally it may become clear that a condition is no longer appropriate (e.g. because genuine structural problems arise, or better solutions for the treatment of the building are devised, or other features of interest are revealed once work has started). Section 19 of the Act therefore enables an application to be made by persons with a legal interest in the building which simply seeks a change in the conditions without reopening the entire question of whether consent should have been granted. In dealing with such an application it is also open to the authority (or the Secretary of State) to add consequential new conditions to the consent.

Appeals

113. The procedure for appeals broadly follows that for ordinary planning appeals. There is, however, provision for one special ground of appeal, namely that the building does not merit its listed status (Section 21 (4)). Where this argument is advanced Cadw will be consulted.

Purchase Notices

114. When listed building consent is refused or granted subject to conditions, any owner of the land may serve a listed building purchase notice on the local authority requiring it to purchase the interest in the land if the owner can establish that because of the refusal or conditions the land has become "incapable of reasonably beneficial use" (Sections 32-37). The authority must respond within three months; where it proposes not to accept such a notice it must first refer it to the Secretary of State who must give the parties the opportunity of being heard and may then confirm the notice or take other action. (See Welsh Office Circular 22/83 for more detailed advice.)

Revocation of Listed Building Consent

115. An authority may make an order revoking or modifying a listed building consent if it appears expedient to do so, having regard to the development plan and any other material considerations (Sections 24-26). Such an order must be advertised and the owner and occupier of the land and all persons who, in the authority's opinion, will be affected by the order must be notified. If all those persons notify the authority in writing that they do not object to the order, it can take effect (unless it relates to a consent granted by the Secretary of State); but in all other circumstances the order must be sent to the Secretary of State for confirmation. The Secretary of State also has default powers to make such orders. Compensation may be payable for abortive expenditure or other loss or damage caused by the order (Section 28).

Prosecutions

116. It is an offence to execute, or cause to be executed without first obtaining listed building consent, any works for the demolition, alteration or extension of a listed building in any manner affecting its character or to fail to comply with the terms of any condition attached to a consent (Section 9). The current penalty for conviction in a Magistrates' Court is a fine of up to £20,000 or imprisonment for up to six months (or both). Whilst on conviction in the Crown Court, an unlimited fine or a prison sentence of up to two years (or both) may be imposed in determining the amount of any fine, the Magistrates Court or Crown Court must have

regard to any financial benefit accruing from the offence.

117. In proceedings for an offence under Section 9 it is a defence to prove the following matters:

(a) that works to the building were urgently necessary in the interests of safety or health or for the preservation of the building;

(b) that it was not practicable to secure safety or health or, as the case may be, to preserve the building by works of repair or works for affording temporary support or shelter;

(c) that the works carried out were limited to the minimum measures immediately necessary; and

(d) that notice in writing justifying in detail the carrying out of the works was given to the local planning authority as soon as reasonably practicable.

118. Private individuals as well as local authorities can start proceedings. The Secretary of State can initiate prosecution proceedings or seek injunctions for breaches of listed building control. A prosecution may be made under Section 59 for deliberate damage to a listed building.

Listed Building Consent for Works Already Executed

119. Section 8(3) of the Act allows listed building consent to be sought even though the works have already been completed. Applications for consent to retain such works should follow the same procedures as other listed building consent applications. Authorities should not grant consent without considering the merits of the case as they would if consent for the works had been sought before they were carried out. If the work is not of a suitable type or standard, normally consent should not be given, and the risk of prosecution or enforcement action will remain. If consent is granted, it is not retrospective; the works are authorised only from the date of the consent. A prosecution may still be brought for the offence of undertaking work without consent.

Enforcement

120. If work is carried out without consent local planning authorities can

issue a listed building enforcement notice (Section 38). The notice may require the building to be brought to its former state; or, if that is not reasonably practicable or desirable, require such other works specified in the notice to alleviate the effects of the unauthorised works; or require the building to be brought into the state it would have been in if the terms of any listed building consent had been observed. It was held in the case of *Bath City Council v. Secretary of State for the Environment* (1983 JPL 737) that this provision could not be used to secure an improvement to a listed building compared to its state before the unauthorised works were carried out. There is a right of appeal to the Secretary of State against a notice; the appeal procedures are generally similar to those for enforcement of planning controls following the Planning and Compensation Act 1991, although there are no provisions equivalent to a planning contravention notice, nor is there any limitation on the period within which a listed building enforcement notice must be issued. If works subject to a listed building enforcement notice are later authorised under Section 8 (3), the enforcement notice will cease to have effect in relation to those works, although the liability to prosecution for an offence committed before the date of consent remains. Breach of a listed building enforcement notice is in itself an offence, with **financial** penalties parallel to those for a breach of listed building control.

121. Local planning authorities will need to consider, when faced with a breach of listed building control, whether to take enforcement action or to prosecute or both. Enforcement may be desirable for the benefit of the building in question, while the work entailed by enforcement may represent a sufficient response to the offence. Unauthorised work may often destroy historic fabric, the special interest of which cannot be regained by enforcement. Well-publicised, successful prosecutions can provide a valuable deterrent to the wilful damage or destruction of listed buildings.

Compulsory Purchase Orders Which Include Listed Buildings in Conservation Areas

122. Welsh Office Circular 1/90 gives general guidance on the submission of compulsory purchase orders which include listed buildings or buildings in conservation areas. Welsh Office Circular 2/93 summarises the provisions on compulsory purchase orders made under Housing Act

powers.

Dangerous Structures

123. Local planning authorities may not consider making a dangerous structures order for listed buildings, buildings subject to building preservation notices and buildings in conservation areas unless they have considered, as an alternative, whether to exercise their powers under Sections 47, 48 or 54 of the Act relating to repairs (Section 56). Even when they consider that a dangerous structures order is appropriate, the works specified in such an order relating to such buildings still require listed building consent. Authorities making dangerous structures orders should remind owners of the need to obtain listed building consent – or fulfil the requirements of Section 9 (3) which provides a defence against prosecution.

Building and Fire Regulations

124. In exercising their responsibilities for the safety of buildings under the building regulations and fire legislation, local authorities should deal sympathetically with proposals for the repair or conversion of historic buildings. Authorities should seek expert advice in endeavouring to strike a balance.

Access for Disabled People

125. It is important in principle that disabled people should have dignified easy access to and within historic buildings. If it is treated as part of an integrated review of access requirements for all visitors or users, and a flexible and pragmatic approach is taken, it should normally be possible to plan suitable access for disabled people without compromising a building's special interest. Alternative routes or organising the use of spaces may achieve the desired results without the need for damaging alterations. Local authorities should take account of the requirements of the Disability Discrimination Act 1995.

House Renovation Grants

126. Where an authority proposes to grant aid renovation work to a listed house or a house in a conservation area, care should be taken to ensure that standard grant conditions (e.g. for damp proofing or insulation) are not imposed in a way which would be damaging to the historic character of the building. In such cases housing and environmental health departments should consult the authority's conservation officer or seek expert advice from other sources.

Local Authorities' Own Buildings

127. Local authorities are normally required to make their own listed building consent applications to the Secretary of State, whether or not they themselves own the listed building in question. The Secretary of State asks authorities to deal with their own buildings in ways which will provide examples of good practice to other owners. It is particularly important that every effort should be made to maintain historic buildings in good condition, and to find appropriate new uses for buildings in authority ownership which are no longer in active use. Prompt disposal is important: empty buildings should not be retained on a contingency basis, with all the risk of neglect and disrepair that this can create. The Secretary of State will not be disposed to grant consent for the demolition of a listed building in an authority's ownership unless there is clear and convincing evidence that alternative possibilities for new ownership and new uses have been thoroughly explored.

Churches and Crown Buildings

128. Special provisions apply to ecclesiastical buildings in use for ecclesiastical purposes, which are in some circumstances exempt from listed building and conservation area controls (see Part 5).

129. The Crown is exempt from listed building and conservation area controls; but the Government has undertaken that Crown bodies will normally operate as if the controls apply (see Welsh Office Circular 37/84). Proposals have been published for the removal of Crown exemption in planning and conservation matters, but pending the necessary legislation these arrangements continue to apply.

PART 4: HISTORIC BUILDINGS IN NEED OF REPAIR

Urgent Works

130. Section 54 of the Act enables a local authority to carry out urgent works for the preservation of listed buildings in its area. These powers can be used only in respect of an unoccupied building, or the unused part of a partly occupied building. The Act enables the Secretary of State to direct that the powers shall apply to an unlisted building in a conservation area if it appears to him that its preservation is important for maintaining the character or appearance of that area. Local authorities or members of the public may ask the Secretary of State to make such a Direction; such requests should be supported by evidence confirming the importance of the building in question.

131. The Secretary of State can also exercise these powers himself. His policy is to use the powers only in exceptional cases, for instance where a building is of exceptional interest or is in local authority ownership; or where a conservation area is of more than local interest and either the building in question is so important to the area that failure to carry out urgent works to it would seriously damage the character or appearance of the area or the building as well as meeting the basic Section 76 criterion, or is in local authority ownership. In all such cases he would consider the use of his own powers only where the local authorities concerned had decided not to take action themselves.

132. Authorities will note that these powers are confined to urgent works: in the Secretary of State's view, their use should be restricted to emergency repairs, for example works to keep a building wind and weather-proof and safe from collapse, or action to prevent vandalism or theft. The steps taken should be the minimum consistent with achieving this objective.

133. Local authorities may recover from owners the cost of urgent works carried out under these provisions, subject to the owner's right to make representations to the Secretary of State (Section 55 of the Act). Representations may be made on the grounds that some or all of the works were unnecessary; that temporary arrangements have continued for an unreasonable length of time; or that amounts are unreasonable or

their recovery would cause hardship. The Secretary of State will take all such representations into account before determining the amount to be recovered, and will be particularly concerned to establish whether the works carried out were the minimum required to secure the building's preservation and prevent further deterioration.

Repairs Notices

134. If a local authority or National Park Authority considers that a listed building is not being property preserved, it may serve on the owner a Repairs Notice (Section 48 of the Act). This notice must specify the works which the authority considers reasonably necessary for the proper preservation of the building, and must explain the relevant provisions of the legislation, which are described briefly below. These powers are not confined to urgent works or to unoccupied buildings, and authorities should consider their use in cases where protracted failure by an owner to keep a listed building in reasonable repair places the building at risk.

135. Repairs Notice powers may also be exercised by the Secretary of State, but, as with urgent works, his policy is to treat these powers essentially as reserve powers, and to use them only in exceptional circumstances. It is not open to the Secretary of State to authorise the use of Repairs Notices in respect of unlisted buildings in conservation areas.

Compulsory Acquisition of Listed Buildings in Need of Repair

136. If at least 2 months have elapsed following the service of a Repairs Notice, and it appears to the body who served the Notice that reasonable steps are not being taken for the proper preservation of the building, they may begin compulsory purchase proceedings. Orders made by a local authority require the Secretary of State's confirmation. In making or confirming a compulsory purchase order (CPO), the Secretary of State must be satisfied that it is expedient to make provision for the preservation of the building and to authorise its compulsory acquisition for that purpose. The Secretary of State will need to be satisfied that the means and the resources necessary for securing the building's repair will be available.

137. The Secretary of State considers that privately owned historic buildings should, wherever possible, remain in the private sector. Every effort should be made to identify a private individual or body, such as a building preservation trust, which has access to funds to carry out the necessary repairs and to which the building will be sold as quickly as possible. Suitable covenants should be negotiated to ensure that repairs will be carried out by a purchaser.

Extent of Repairs

138. A House of Lords judgment (*Robbins v. Secretary of State for the Environment* (1989 1 All. E.R.878)) has provided guidance on the nature of the works which may properly be specified in a Repairs Notice. The judgment held that, while the definition of works reasonably necessary for the proper preservation of the building will always relate to the circumstances of the individual case, and involve judgments about what is reasonable, the word 'preservation' has to be given its ordinary meaning in contrast to 'restoration', and this imposes an objective limitation which must be applied in considering the scope of works to be specified in a Notice. The judgment also made clear that a Notice can include works for the preservation of a building having regard to its condition at the date when it was listed: in other words, where a building has suffered damage or disrepair since being listed, the Repairs Notice procedure can be used to secure the building's preservation as at the date of listing but should not be used to restore other features.

General Considerations

139. The possible need to follow-up with a CPO is something which local authorities should take into account when contemplating Repairs Notice action. A recent study in England* has shown that in over 80% of cases, authorisation or formal service of a Notice was itself sufficient to prompt owners either to begin repairs or to sell the building in question to a third party: in only 16% of cases did the matter reach a CPO inquiry.

The following too are relevant considerations:

– the purpose of compulsory purchase is to ensure that reasonable steps are taken to properly preserve a listed building: it is not a requirement that the local authority should itself carry out the repairs or pay for them. Indeed in the Secretary of State's view it is preferable, as stated in para 8 above, for the local authority to obtain a firm commitment from a private purchaser to repair the building and meet the costs (perhaps with the assistance of grant-aid);

– the Act contains provisions for minimum compensation where an owner has deliberately allowed a building to fall into disrepair in order to justify its demolition and secure permission for redevelopment of the site (Section 50 of the Act); minimum compensation should however be sought only where there is clear evidence of such an intention;

– where the minimum compensation provisions do not apply, normal market value rules apply (as laid down in the Land Compensation Act); but even here, high costs of repair, combined with limited possibilities for development, may indicate a very low or even nominal value.

* *Listed Building Repairs Notices; Bob Kindred, for the Association of Conservation Officers, 1992.*

Authorities have powers under Section 52 of the Act to acquire land and buildings by agreement.

140. Authorities are reminded that where a historic building is disposed of (either by freehold sale or long lease) within 2 years of its acquisition, and the price received on resale is no more than the price paid, the capital receipt is unrestricted. Acquisitions under arrangements for immediate onward sale to e.g. a building preservation trust should, therefore, have no adverse financial implications for the authority, though there will clearly be other resource costs involved in securing confirmation of a CPO.

141. Grant assistance is available from Cadw: Welsh Historic Monuments towards the cost of repair of buildings of outstanding historic or architectural interest and towards the cost of works (usually to historic buildings) which significantly enhance a conservation area. Increasingly, this assistance is channelled through Town Schemes in partnership with

local authorities. The Historic Buildings Council for Wales is the statutory advisory body on historic buildings grants. Additionally, grants may be available from the Heritage Lottery Fund.

PART 5: ECCLESIASTICAL BUILDINGS – LISTED BUILDING CONTROL

142. Since the Ecclesiastical Exemption (Listed Buildings and Conservation Areas) Order 1994 came into force on October 1, 1994 the exemption of ecclesiastical buildings from listed building and conservation area control under Section 60 of the 1990 Act applies in Wales only to those denominations and faiths who have set up internal systems of control which embody the following principles, and have been approved by the Secretary of State:

(a) proposals for relevant works (i.e. works for the demolition of a listed ecclesiastical building or for its alteration or extension in any manner which would affect its character as a building of special architectural or historic interest; works for the demolition of an unlisted ecclesiastical building in a conservation area; or works which would affect the archaeological importance of an ecclesiastical building or archaeological remains within it or its curtilage) should be submitted by the local congregation for the approval of a body independent of them;

(b) that body should include, or have arrangements for obtaining advice from, people with expert knowledge of historic church buildings;

(c) the decision-making process should provide for:

    (i) consultation with the local planning authority and national amenity societies, allowing them (except in cases of emergency) 28 days to comment;

    (ii) the display of a notice in a prominent position outside the building describing the proposed works and inviting comments within the same 28 day period;

    (iii) the publication of a similar notice in a local newspaper circulating in the locality; and

    (iv) in cases of demolition, notification to RCAHMW;

(d) the decision-making body should be required, in considering proposals for relevant works, to take into account any representations made and, along with other factors, the desirability of preserving historic ecclesiastical buildings and the importance of protecting features of architectural merit and historic interest;

(e) there should be a clear and fair procedure for settling all disputes between the local congregation and the decision- making body as to whether proposals should proceed;

(f) there should be procedures for dealing with any breach of the control system including provision for reinstatement where works to historic ecclesiastical buildings have been carried out without consent;

(g) there should be arrangements for recording in the case of each proposal for works how the above procedures were implemented and the nature of the decision taken, and for notifying the decision to those who made representations;

(h) for those denominations and faiths with an approved internal system of control on these lines the exemption should be redefined as covering buildings primarily used as places of worship and possibly some curtilage structures as well; and

(i) **the denominations and faiths which have been accepted as having an internal system of control qualifying for the exemption are the Church of England, the Church in Wales, the Roman Catholic Church, the Methodist Church, the Baptist Union of Great Britain and the Baptist Union of Wales, and the United Reformed Church.**

143. For denominations and faiths and independent congregations not listed, all relevant works will be subject to the secular systems of listed building and conservation area control. In considering applications for consent relating to the interiors of buildings used for worship, local planning authorities are advised that liturgical requirements should be given due weight as a material consideration. Among the matters which should be taken into account are:

(i) whether the changes proposed are a requirement of the liturgical authority of the relevant denomination, or are discretionary changes put forward by the local congregation;

(ii) whether they are necessitated by a reduction in congregation size and are directed at accommodating other activities within the building to help ensure its continued viability;

(iii) whether they would involve substantial structural changes, e.g. subdivision of important, existing spaces;

(iv) whether they would involve removal and destruction of important fixtures and fittings, or are more in the nature of a reversible re-ordering of internal features; and

(v) whether proposed changes would involve disturbance of archaeologically important remains below ground.

PART 6: CANCELLATION

144. The advice contained in this Circular replaces that in Welsh Office Circular 61/81 which is hereby cancelled.

Unitary Authorities)

National Parks   ) in Wales

T J Cassidy

Chief Executive

Cadw: Welsh Historic Monuments

Archaeological Contracts

Archaeological work is unlikely to be catered for sufficiently in construction contracts or other, commonly encountered works contracts. Standard form building and engineering contracts usually refer to archaeological remains but only to the extent necessary to spell out what is to happen if unexpected finds are made. The *JCT Standard Form of Building Contract (1980): Private with Quantities* deals with 'Antiquities' at clause 34. The contractor must not disturb any remains discovered and must inform the supervising architect who, under the contract, is able to issue instructions about how the finds are to be dealt with. As between the parties to the contract finds become the property of the employer, i.e. the person who engaged the contractor. Losses suffered by the contractor due to the issue of instructions by the architect will be met by an additional payment added to the 'contract sum'. The *JCT Standard Form of Building Contract (1981): With Contractor's Design* contains similar provisions, except the employer, not the architect, is responsible for issuing instructions. The *ICE Conditions of Contract (6th Edition)* covers archaeological remains at clause 32, under the heading 'fossils'. The employer must pay the contractor to deal with archaeological remains. Under both the JCT and the ICE conditions third parties admitted to the site to excavate or carry out other archaeological investigations will be the responsibility of the employer and not the contractor. Even the *JCT Standard form of Management Contract (1987)* provides that the management contractor is not responsible for such third parties. 'Rescue' archaeologists, therefore, are unlikely to be sub-contracted.

Unexpected finds cause delays and may increase employers' costs significantly. Where archaeological remains are suspected it may, at the outset, be possible to agree amendments to the standard wording so that there is contractual provision for a period of, say, three months for carrying out archaeological work on a part of the site. The better solution, however, is always to properly assess the extent of archaeological remains so that construction works can be phased to take account of them. Phased development will also increase costs but usually to a lesser degree than unforeseen delays. General delay is unlikely to satisfy anybody.

Where archaeological provision is known to be necessary before development commences archaeological contractors will need to be part of the construction team, like any other specialist contractor. Given the sensitive nature of archaeological work it is still not uncommon for the employer, not his contractor, to contract directly with the archaeologists. Sole negotiation is still the norm although some selective tendering occurs.

Whether directly employed or sub-contracted the essential parts of the contract are the specification to which the archaeologists will work, and the payment provisions. In a specially drawn contract both may appear in the same document, the specification as a schedule, the payment provisions in the main body of the agreement; however, the specification may stand alone and be incorporated into the agreement by reference. Provided that a specification sets out matters clearly and explicitly and distinguishes the mandatory from the merely declaratory, there can be savings in legal drafting time if lawyers are able to incorporate the technical details by cross-referencing. Of course, special care must be exercised when incorporating documents, as one mistake is likely to have significant adverse impact on interpretation. Incorporation of a specification into a separate contractual document is more likely to be adopted when work is put out to tender.

The specification is not the same as the project brief. An archaeological project brief should outline the nature of the archaeological remains and indicate what works will be required to deal with them in the context of the development proposal, but the brief does not provide for a measurable standard of work or a detailed timetable. The latter are features of a specification (in some excavations extending over many digging seasons, a hybrid *project design* may be the relevant document). A specification should address the following matters:

1. short description (with map) of the development proposal and the archaeological remains affected (stipulating their legal status where appropriate);
2. the expected geological and archaeological conditions on site (referring to plans and sections where necessary);
3. detailed aims of the archaeological investigation required (including timetable);
4. the desired archaeological methodology (including recording and sampling strategies);
5. restrictions and directions on working;
6. staffing and management on site;
7. non-staffing resources to be employed;
8. preparation and deposition of site archive.

Additional matters such as health and safety, hours of working, site security, monitoring, copyright, ownership of finds etc. may be mentioned in the specification but it is usually more convenient to address these general issues in the main contract document if there is one. Under the Copyright, Designs and Patents Act 1988 copyright rests with the person producing reports/surveys etc., and not the person funding their production. An express contractual term may be required to deal with this presumption. If post-excavation work is also to be contracted for, a separate specification may be produced; alternatively, the relevant requirements may be placed in a subsidiary part of the main specification as long as this does not underestimate the equally complex nature of the post-excavation phase.

The main contract will define the legal context of the specification. It will formalise the obligations and liabilities of the parties and, in particular, it is the place where provisions relating to payment, variation of works, force majeure, damages and contingencies, property matters, indemnity, warranty and arbitration of disputes are usually found. Where contracts are let on tender, payment should be distinguished from pricing. Tender documents will sometimes comprise an additional 'pricing document' which the tenderer must complete so that the employer is able to compare rival bids easily. The pricing document becomes the document which provides how much the successful tenderer will receive for carrying out each specified task but it does not provide for how and when the payments will be made. Useful forays into the area of model contracts have been made by the Standing Conference of Archaeological Unit Managers/The British Property Federation (1989) and by the IFA. The latter model (Darvill and Atkins (1991)) is the better starting point, though a true standard form of agreement such as is seen in the construction industry is still to be achieved. Circumstances vary so greatly that a large proportion of archaeological contracts are still drafted largely from scratch. As long as archaeology is conceived of as a multi-disciplinary endeavour, leaning against technical segmentation, this is likely to remain the case. Most archaeological contracts will require drafting by persons with legal expertise; although model forms are available, the complexity of archaeological work means that the background law must be properly understood if the contract is to perform as the parties expect. The production of briefs and specifications is facilitated by a number of advisory/regulatory publications. The Association of County Archaeological Officers (ACAO) has published a paper on *Model Briefs and Specifications for Archaeological Assessments and Field Evaluations* (1993), which provides generalised frameworks for the drafting of project briefs and briefs with specifications. The IFA has also issued standards and guidance *inter alia* for field evaluations (1994), for excavations (1994) and for the investigation and recording of standing buildings and structures (1996). The IFA documents in particular are an essential tool for those drafting specifications and aim at a consistency of terminology in archaeological contracting.

Planning Obligation (By Agreement)

This Agreement is made the   day of   199[ ]

Between:

(1) [Council] of [
                                          ] ('the Council')
(2) [   ] of [
                                          ] ('the Developer')
[(3) [   ] of [
                                          ] ('the Landowner')] and
[(3)] [(4)] [   ] of [
                                          ]('the Mortgagee')

Whereas:

1. The Council is the local planning authority for the area within which the Land is situated and by whom the planning obligations contained in this deed are enforceable.

2. The Developer [The Landowner (*where the Developer does not own the site*)] is the owner in fee simple absolute in possession of the Land [subject to the Mortgage but otherwise] free from encumbrances.

3. The Developer has applied to the Council by the Application for planning permission to develop the Land and to ensure (a) that the development of the Land in a manner which properly preserves by record archaeological remains on the Land and (b) that sufficient financial resources are available to complete a satisfactory programme of archaeological work the parties have agreed to enter this deed.

Now this deed witnesses as follows:

1. Definitions and Interpretation

1.1 A reference to any party to this agreement includes unless a contrary intention is expressed the successors in title and/or the assigns of that party and the expression 'the Developer' means any person who develops the Land or any part thereof under the Planning Permission.

1.2 The schedules to this agreement are part of this agreement and unless expressly indicated to the contrary reference to a schedule or a paragraph is a reference to a schedule or paragraph of this agreement.

1.3 Reference to any gender includes all genders and reference to the singular includes the plural and vice versa.

1.4 Any obligation expressed to be the obligation of more than one party shall unless expressly indicated to the contrary be a joint and several obligation of those parties.

1.5 Reference in this agreement to the giving of any consent or approval of a matter by any of the parties shall be read as if the giving of such consent or approval by such a party shall not be unreasonably withheld or delayed.

1.6 Reference to an Act of Parliament or regulation, order or rule is reference to that Act of Parliament, regulation, order or rule at the date of this agreement.

1.7 The following words shall have the following meanings:

'the Act': the Town and Country Planning Act 1990
'the Application': the application for [outline] planning permission submitted by the Developer to the Council under application reference number [   ] for the development and use of the Land as [   ]
'the Development': development of the Land in accordance with the Planning Permission
'the Land': the land shown for the purpose of identification only edged red on the Plan
'the Mortgage': the mortgage dated [   ] made between the [*Developer or Landowner*] (1) and the Mortgagee (2)
'the Plan': the plan annexed to this agreement at schedule one
'the Planning Permission': planning permission granted on the Application by the Council or otherwise

'Statutory Undertakers': such bodies as fall within the definition of statutory undertaker in section 262 of the Act.

2. This agreement is made pursuant to section 106 of the Act and is a planning obligation to the extent that the obligations are within section 106(1) of the Act and otherwise in pursuance of section 111 of the Local Government Act 1972, section 33 of the Local Government (Miscellaneous Provisions) Act 1982 and all other enabling powers.

3. The obligations and covenants in this deed are conditional on and shall only come into effect upon the [granting of the Planning Permission] [*or insert date earlier than disturbance of the Land*] [the commencing on the Land of any operations which disturb the surface of the Land (including demolition of buildings or the removal or installation of equipment or services by any Statutory Undertaker or other person but excluding the sinking of boreholes or the use of remote sensing apparatus) and which are carried out in order either to implement or prepare for the implementation of the Planning Permission (*)].

* Conditional wording such as this should be approached with caution as it introduces uncertainty into the effectiveness of the obligation. The 'five year clock' for discharge or modification also starts to run from the date of the obligation not the date when conditions precedent are satisfied. In some circumstances it may be preferable to hold an executed agreement in escrow until it is to come into operation.

4. Archaeological Work

4.1 The Developer shall carry out and complete the programme of archaeological work contained in the first part of the second schedule in relation to the area of archaeological interest defined in that part.

4.2 The programme of archaeological work shall be carried out and completed in accordance with the methodology standards timetable reporting and other requirements of the specification contained in the second part of the second schedule and where that specification does not in its terms impose an obligation or requirement to do any thing in relation to any matter or thing stipulated therein the Developer agrees that (save where expressly provided otherwise) it shall be an obligation of the Developer to ensure that such matter or thing occurs or is complied with.

[4.3 Before any operations which disturb the surface of the Land (including demolition of buildings or the removal or installation of equipment or services by any Statutory Undertaker or other person but excluding the sinking of boreholes or the use of remote sensing apparatus) are carried out in order either to implement or prepare for the implementation of the Planning Permission the Developer shall furnish the Council with such evidence (including copies of written agreements or deeds binding on the Developer certified by a solicitor as true copies thereof) as the Council shall reasonably require that the Developer has (a) contracted for the provision of archaeological services sufficient to complete the archaeological work required by this clause and (b) has paid or has secured the payment (by way of bond trust charge or other security acceptable to the Council) of the sum of [   ] pounds to [   ] for [*all payments due under that contract*] [*all payments due under the contract or other arrangement which provides for [   ]*]].

4.4 [4.3] The Developer shall comply with the restrictions contained in the third schedule and in particular shall not implement the Planning Permission in the area of archaeological interest or any part or parts thereof until such time as the Council notifies the Developer in writing that the programme of archaeological work required to be carried out on the Land under this agreement has been completed.

5. The Landowner and the Mortgagee severally consent to this agreement and each separately covenants with the Council that each of their respective interests in the Land shall be bound by the terms of this agreement and the obligations and restrictions contained within it as if this agreement had been completed and registered as a local land charge immediately before the vesting of the title to the Land in the Landowner and (in the case of the Mortgagee) immediately before the creation of the Mortgage.

6. It is agreed and declared as follows:

6.1 No person shall be liable for a breach of any covenant restriction or obligation in this deed after he has parted with all interest (including all equitable interest) in the Land or the part or parts thereof in respect of which such a breach occurs but without prejudice to his liability for any subsisting breach of covenant restriction or obligation which occurs prior to his parting with such interest.

6.2 This agreement is and shall be registered as a local land charge.

6.3 This agreement shall be void and of no further effect if either of the following occurs:

- the Planning Permission is revoked or is quashed
- the Planning Permission expires.

In witness whereof the parties have executed this agreement as a deed on the day and year first written above

[Usual forms of execution of each of the parties]

Planning Policy Guidance Note 16:
Archaeology and Planning
November 1990
[Extracts, omitting annexes]

Introduction

1. This guidance is for planning authorities in England, property owners, developers, archaeologists, amenity societies and the general public. It sets out the Secretary of State's policy on archaeological remains on land, and how they should be preserved or recorded both in an urban setting and in the countryside. It gives advice on the handling of archaeological remains and discoveries under the development plan and control systems, including the weight to be given to them in planning decisions and the use of planning conditions. (Separate controls exist for scheduled monuments - see Annex 3.) The guidance pulls together and expands existing advice, within the existing legislative framework. It places no new duties on local authorities, and should not place any significant additional burden on local authorities.

2. The guidance is arranged as follows:

A – **The importance of archaeology**: a general introduction (paragraphs 3-14)

B – **Advice on the handling of archaeological matters in the planning process:**

- Development plans (paragraphs 15-16)
- Sites and Monuments Records – SMRs (paragraph 17)
- Planning applications (paragraphs 18-26)
- Planning decisions (paragraphs 27-28)
- Planning conditions (paragraphs 29-30)
- Discovery of archaeological remains during development (paragraph 31)

[Annex 1 – *Key bodies and organisations**

Annex 2 – *Contact Addresses for County Archaeological Officers and SMRs**

Annex 3 – *Legislative arrangements: scheduling of ancient monuments, control of scheduled monuments and their management; Offences, Metal Detectors; Areas of Archaeological Importance (AAIs); Environmental Assessment; Simplified Planning Zones (SPZs)**

Annex 4 – *Secretary of State' criteria for scheduling**
Annex 5 – *Ancient Monuments (Class Consent) Order 1981*]*

*   not reproduced in this Appendix.

A: THE IMPORTANCE OF ARCHAEOLOGY

3. Archaeological remains are irreplaceable. They are evidence - for prehistoric periods, the only evidence - of the past development of our civilization.

4. Today's archaeological landscape is the product of human activity over thousands of years. It ranges through settlements and remains of every period, from the camps of the early hunter gathers 400,000 years ago to remains of early 20th century activities. It includes places of worship, defence installations, burial grounds, farms and fields, and sites of manufacture.

5. These remains vary enormously in their state of preservation and in the extent of their appeal to the public. "Upstanding" remains are familiar enough - the great stone circles, the castle and abbey ruins of the Middle Ages or abandoned coastal defence systems. But less obvious archaeological remains, such as ancient settlements and field systems, are also to be found across large parts of the country. Some prehistoric sites in wetland areas contain important wood and organic remains. Many buildings in older towns lie on top of Roman, Anglo-Saxon or medieval structures.

6. **Archaeological remains should be seen as a finite, and non-renewable resource, in many cases highly fragile and vulnerable to damage and destruction. Appropriate management is therefore essential to ensure that they survive in good condition. In particular, care must be taken to ensure that archaeological remains are not needlessly or thoughtlessly destroyed. They can contain irreplaceable information about our past and the potential for an increase in future knowledge. They are part of our sense of national identity and are valuable both for their own sake and for their role in education, leisure and tourism.**

7. The present century has been a period of striking environmental

change. Some changes, like the erosion of coastal areas, have occurred naturally. But much archaeological heritage has been destroyed by human activity - for example, by modern construction methods in urban development and expansion of the road network, by modern agricultural techniques (in particular deep ploughing or drainage of wetlands), and by mineral extraction.

8. With the many demands of modern society, it is not always feasible to save all archaeological remains. The key question is where and how to strike the right balance. **Where nationally important archaeological remains, whether scheduled or not, and their settings, are affected by proposed development there should be a presumption in favour of their physical preservation**. Cases involving archaeological remains of lesser importance will not always be so clear cut and planning authorities will need to weigh the relative importance of archaeology against other factors including the need for the proposed development (see also paragraph 27). Regardless of the circumstances, taking decisions is much easier if any archaeological aspects of a development site can be considered early on in the planning and development control process. This is discussed in Section B.

9. Archaeological records for England currently contain around 600,000 sites and monuments. Some 13,000 nationally important cases enjoy special protection as "scheduled monuments", under the Ancient Monuments and Archaeological Areas Act 1979. English Heritage have embarked on a survey programme which is expected to result in significant additional numbers being given this statutory protection (see Annex 3).

10. Scheduling archaeological remains ensures that the case for preservation is fully considered given any proposals for development or other work which might damage the monument. The planning system, as paragraph 18 emphasizes, is equally in a position to consider the desirability of preserving archaeological remains, and the various options open to planning authorities for dealing with archaeological remains are considered in Section B. Much can be achieved within the wider planning process when developers are prepared to enter into discussions with archaeologists and consider fully the needs of archaeology. This voluntary approach to considering the needs of archaeology is a well-established and growing practice and has been formalized in Codes of Practice by the

'British Archaeologists' and Developers' Liaison Group (BADLG) (see paragraph 26; also Annex 1, paragraph 9), and the Confederation of British Industry (CBI) Code for Mineral Operators.

11. Archaeological issues are often important in minerals planning, particularly in the extraction of sand and gravel. River valleys have provided an attractive place for man to settle but at the same time these areas often contain valuable sand and gravel resources. Minerals can clearly only be worked where they are found so they often differ from other forms of development in that there is not the same flexibility of choice of location. The CBI's revised Code of Practice for Mineral Operators on archaeological investigations provides advice on how minerals operators should consult archaeological interests in formulating planning applications, to ensure that archaeological factors are fully taken into account in the planning decision process.

12. The key to informed and reasonable planning decisions, as emphasized in paragraphs 19 and 20, is for consideration to be given early, before formal planning applications are made, to the question of whether archaeological remains exist on a site where development is planned and the implications for the development proposal. When important remains are known to exist or when archaeologists have good reason to believe that important remains exist, developers will be able to help by preparing sympathetic designs using, for example, foundations which avoid disturbing the remains altogether or minimise damage by raising ground levels under a proposed new structure, or by the careful siting of landscaped or open areas. There are techniques available for sealing archaeological remains underneath buildings or landscaping, thus securing their preservation for the future even though they remain inaccessible for the time being.

13. If physical preservation *in situ* is not feasible, an archaeological excavation for the purposes of 'preservation by record', may be an acceptable alternative (see also paragraphs 24 and 25). From the archaeological point of view this should be regarded as a second best option. The science of archaeology is developing rapidly. Excavation means the total destruction of evidence (apart from removable artefacts) from which future techniques could almost certainly extract more information than is currently possible. Excavation is also expensive and time-consuming, and discoveries may have to be evaluated in a hurry

against an inadequate research framework. The preservation *in situ* of important archaeological remains is therefore nearly always to be preferred.

14. Positive planning and management can help to bring about sensible solutions to the treatment of sites with archaeological remains and reduce the areas of potential conflict between development and preservation. Both central government and English Heritage have important roles to play (see Annex 1). **But the key to the future of the great majority of archaeological sites and historic landscapes lies with local authorities, acting within the framework set by central government, in their various capacities as planning, education and recreational authorities, as well as with the owners of sites themselves. Appropriate planning policies in development plans and their implementation through development control will be especially important.**

B: ADVICE ON THE HANDLING OF ARCHAEOLOGICAL MATTERS IN THE PLANNING PROCESS

Development Plans

15. Development plans should reconcile the need for development with the interests of conservation including archaeology. Detailed development plans (i.e. local plans and unitary development plans) should include policies for the protection, enhancement and preservation of sites of archaeological interest and of their settings. The proposals map should define the areas and sites to which the policies and proposals apply. These policies will provide an important part of the framework for the consideration of individual proposals for development which affect archaeological remains and they will help guide developers preparing planning applications.

16. Although the surviving numbers of archaeological remains are finite and irreplaceable, obviously not all of them are of equal importance. Planning authorities may therefore wish to base their detailed development plan policies and proposals on an evaluation of the archaeological remains in their area. **Archaeological remains identified and scheduled as being of national importance should normally be earmarked in development plans for preservation. Authorities should**

bear in mind that not all nationally important remains meriting preservation will necessarily be scheduled; such remains and, in appropriate circumstances, other unscheduled archaeological remains of more local importance, may also be identified in development plans as particularly worthy of preservation.

Sites and Monuments Records - SMRs

17. All shire counties now maintain Sites and Monuments Records (SMRS) staffed by at least one professional officer, usually employed by the County Council. In London the SMR is maintained by English Heritage. In ex-Metropolitan county areas centralised SMRs are jointly maintained by Metropolitan Boroughs. An increasing number of non-metropolitan District Councils now employ archaeological staff within their planning departments. **All planning authorities should make full use of the expertise of County Archaeological Officers or their equivalents** (see Annex 1 paragraphs 4-6). English Heritage is ready to advise on the archaeological policies proposed for inclusion in draft plans. Consultation with English Heritage, as suggested by DOE Circular 22/84 (Annex C, paragraph 1), may be of particular help in urban areas where important archaeological remains may not be adequately identified by scheduling.

Planning Applications

18. **The desirability of preserving an ancient monument and its setting is a material consideration in determining planning applications whether that monument is scheduled or unscheduled.** Developers and local authorities should take into account archaeological considerations and deal with them from the beginning of the development control process. Where local planning authorities are aware of a real and specific threat to a known archaeological site as a result of the potential exercise of permitted development rights (as set out in Schedule 2 to the Town and Country Planning General Development Order 1988) they may wish to consider the use of their powers under Article 4 of that Order to withdraw those rights and to require specific planning permission to be obtained before development can proceed. Most such directions require the Secretary of State's approval, either before they come into effect or within six months of being made, unless they relate solely to a listed building. Further advice on the use of Article 4 Directions is given in Appendix D to DOE Circular 22/88.

(a) The First Step: Early Consultations between Developers and Planning Authorities

19. The needs of archaeology and development can be reconciled, and potential conflict very much reduced, if developers discuss their preliminary plans for development with the planning authority at an early stage. Once detailed designs have been prepared and finance lined up, flexibility becomes much more difficult and expensive to achieve. In their own interests, therefore, prospective developers should in all cases include as part of their research into the development potential of a site, which they undertake before making a planning application, an initial assessment of whether the site is known or likely to contain archaeological remains. The first step will be to contact the County Archaeological Officer or equivalent who holds the SMR, or English Heritage in London. The SMR provides information about the locations where archaeological remains are known or thought likely to exist. Where important remains are known to exist or where the indications are that the remains are likely to prove important, English Heritage are also ready to join in early discussions and provide expert advice. Special notification requirements apply in designated Areas of Archaeological Importance – see Annex 3, paragraphs 19-20.

20. These consultations will help to provide prospective developers with advance warning of the archaeological sensitivity of a site. As a result they may wish to commission their own archaeological assessment by a professionally qualified archaeological Organisation or consultant. This need not involve fieldwork. Assessment normally involves desk-based evaluation of existing information: it can make effective use of records of previous discoveries, including any historic maps held by the County archive and local museums and record offices, or of geophysical survey techniques.

(b) Field Evaluations

21. Where early discussions with local planning authorities or the developer' own research indicate that important archaeological remains may exist, it is reasonable for the planning authority to request the prospective developer to arrange for an archaeological field evaluation to be carried out before any decision on the planning application is taken. This sort of evaluation is quite distinct from full archaeological excavation.

It is normally a rapid and inexpensive operation, involving ground survey and small-scale trial trenching, but it should be carried out by a professionally qualified archaeological organisation or archaeologist. The Institute of Field Archaeologists (see Annex I for address), publishes a Directory of members, which developers may wish to consult. Evaluations of this kind help to define the character and extent of the archaeological remains that exist in the area of a proposed development, and thus indicate the weight which ought to be attached to their preservation. They also provide information useful for identifying potential options for minimising or avoiding damage. On this basis, an informed and reasonable planning decision can be taken.

22. Local planning authorities can expect developers to provide the results of such assessments and evaluations as part of their application for sites where there is good reason to believe there are remains of archaeological importance. If developers are not prepared to do so voluntarily, the planning authority may wish to consider whether it would be appropriate to direct the applicant to supply further information under the provisions of Regulation 4 of the Town and Country Planning (Applications) Regulations 1988 and if necessary authorities will need to consider refusing permission for proposals which are inadequately documented. In some circumstances a formal Environmental Assessment may be necessary. For further details see Annex 3, paragraphs 21 and 22.

(c) Consultations by Planning Authorities

23. When planning applications are made without prior discussion with the local planning authorities, the authorities should seek to identify those applications which have archaeological implications, and to assess their likely archaeological impact by consulting the County Archaeological Officer or equivalent and the County Sites and Monuments Record. When it is evident that a particular development proposal is likely to affect archaeological remains, applicants may need to be asked to provide more detailed information about their scheme - for example, the type of foundations to be used - or they may be asked to carry out an evaluation. Planning authorities should also ensure that they are fully informed about the nature and importance of the archaeological site and its setting. They should therefore seek archaeological advice, normally from the County Archaeological Officer or equivalent who in turn may wish to consult locally based museums and archaeological units and societies. In the case

of a development proposal that is likely to affect the site of a scheduled ancient monument Article 18(1) of the Town and Country Planning General Development Order 1988, requires local planning authorities to consult English Heritage. Local planning authorities may find it helpful to consult more generally with English Heritage on applications for development that affect non-scheduled sites. Existing information about a site is often sufficient to allow authorities to make planning decisions which take into account all material considerations.

(d) Arrangements For Preservation By Record Including Funding

24. The Secretary of State recognises that the extent to which remains can or should be preserved will depend upon a number of factors, including the intrinsic importance of the remains. Where it is not feasible to preserve remains, an acceptable alternative may be to arrange prior excavation, during which the archaeological evidence is recorded.

25. **Planning authorities should not include in their development plans policies requiring developers to finance archaeological works in return for the grant of planning permission.** By the same token developers should not expect to obtain planning permission for archaeologically damaging development merely because they arrange for the recording of sites whose physical preservation *in situ* is both desirable (because of their level of importance) and feasible. **Where planning authorities decide that the physical preservation in situ of archaeological remains is not justified in the circumstances of the case and that development resulting in the destruction of the archaeological remains should proceed, it would be entirely reasonable for the planning authority to satisfy itself before granting planning permission, that the developer has made appropriate and satisfactory provision for the excavation and recording of the remains. Such excavation and recording should be carried out before development commences, working to a project brief prepared by the planning authority and taking advice from archaeological consultants. This can be achieved through agreements reached between the developer, the archaeologist and the planning authority (see following paragraph). Such agreements should also provide for the subsequent publication of the results of the excavation. In the absence of such agreements planning authorities can secure excavation and recording by imposing conditions (see paragraphs 29 and 30).** In particular cases where the developer is a non-profit making

community body, such as a charitable trust or housing association, which is unable to raise the funds to provide for excavation and subsequent recording without undue hardship, or in the case of an individual who similarly does not have the means to fund such work, an application for financial assistance may be made to English Heritage.

26. Agreements covering excavation, recording and the publication of the results may take different forms. For example, developers or their archaeological consultants and local planning authorities may wish to conclude a voluntary planning agreement under section 106 of the Town and Country Planning Act 1990 or other similar powers. The Secretary of State is pleased to note the increasing number of agreements being reached within the terms and spirit of the British Archaeologists' and Developers' Code of Practice. Model agreements between developers and the appropriate archaeological body regulating archaeological site investigations and excavations can be obtained from the British Property Federation. These agreements can provide for the excavation and recording of sites before development work starts. Voluntary agreements are likely to provide more flexibility and be of greater mutual benefit to all the parties than could be provided for by alternative statutory means. They have the advantage of setting out clearly the extent of the developer's commitment, thereby reducing both uncertainty over the financial implications of having to accommodate any archaeological constraints and the possibility of unforeseen delays to the construction programme.

Planning Decisions

27. Once the planning authority has sufficient information, there is a range of options for the determination of planning applications affecting archaeological remains and their settings. As stated in paragraph 8, where nationally important archaeological remains, whether scheduled or not, and their settings, are affected by proposed development there should be a presumption in favour of their physical preservation *in situ* i.e., a presumption against proposals which would involve significant alteration or cause damage, or which would have a significant impact on the setting of visible remains. **The case for the preservation of archaeological remains must however be assessed on the individual merits of each case, taking into account the archaeological policies in detailed**

development plans, together with all other relevant policies and material considerations, including the intrinsic importance of the remains and weighing these against the need for the proposed development.

28. There will no doubt be occasions, particularly where remains of lesser importance are involved, when planning authorities may decide that the significance of the archaeological remains is not sufficient when weighed against all other material considerations, including the need for development, to justify their physical preservation *in situ*, and that the proposed development should proceed. As paragraph 25 explains, planning authorities will, in such cases, need to satisfy themselves that the developer has made appropriate and satisfactory arrangements for the excavation and recording of the archaeological remains and the publication of the results. If this has not already been secured through some form of voluntary agreement, planning authorities can consider granting planning permission subject to conditions which provide for the excavation and recording of the remains before development takes place (see following section). Local planning authorities may, as a matter of last resort, need to consider refusing planning permission where developers do not seek to accommodate important remains.

Planning Conditions

29. **Planning authorities should seek to ensure that potential conflicts are resolved and agreements with developers concluded before planning permission is granted. Where the use of planning conditions is necessary, authorities should ensure that, in accordance with DOE Circular 1/85, they are fair, reasonable and practicable.** It is however open to the local planning authority to impose conditions designed to protect a monument and to ensure that reasonable access is given to a nominated archaeologist - either to hold a "watching brief" during the construction period or specifically to carry out archaeological investigation and recording in the course of the permitted operations on site. Conditions on these lines help to ensure that if remains of archaeological significance are disturbed in the course of the work, they can be recorded and, if necessary, emergency salvage undertaken.

30. In cases when planning authorities have decided that planning permission may be granted but wish to secure the provision of archaeological excavation and the subsequent recording of the remains, it is open to them to do so by the use of a negative condition i.e. a condition prohibiting the carrying out of development until such time as works or other action, e.g. an excavation, have been carried out by a third party. In such cases the following model is suggested:

> "No development shall take place within the area indicated (this would be the area of archaeological interest) until the applicant has secured the implementation of a programme of archaeological work in accordance with a written scheme of investigation which has been submitted by the applicant and approved by the Planning Authority." (Developers will wish to ensure that in drawing up a scheme, the timetable for the investigation is included within the details of the agreed scheme).

The use of this model is also advocated in the CBI Code of Practice for Mineral Operators. The advice on the use of the above condition should be regarded as supplementary to that contained in DOE Circular 1/85 relating to archaeology.

Discovery of Archaeological Remains during Development

31. The preceding guidance (paragraphs 19 and 20 in particular) has been framed to minimise occasions when totally unexpected problems arise while development is in progress. Nevertheless, and in spite of the best pre-planning application research, there may be occasions when the presence of archaeological remains only becomes apparent once development has commenced. Developers may wish to consider insuring themselves against the risk of a substantial loss while safeguarding the interest of historic remains unexpectedly discovered on the site. Conflicts that may otherwise arise between developers and archaeologists may not be easy to solve although English Heritage, who have a great deal of experience in handling these situations, are ready to offer practical advice, as is the British Archaeologists' and Developers' Liaison Group. Where fresh archaeological discoveries are deemed by the Secretary of State, on English Heritage's advice, to be of national importance, in accordance with his published criteria (see Annex 4), the Secretary of State for National Heritage has power to schedule the remains. In that event

developers would need to seek separate scheduled monument consent before they continue work. It is also open to a planning authority or the Secretary of State to revoke a planning permission if deemed necessary, in which case there is provision for compensation. In the majority of cases, however, it should prove possible for the parties to resolve their differences through voluntary discussion and for a satisfactory compromise to be reached.

Welsh Office Circular 60/96:
Planning and the Historic Environment: Archaeology
[Extracts, omitting annexes 2-4]

Introduction

1. *Planning Guidance (Wales): Planning Policy* sets out the Government's land-use planning policies as they apply in Wales. It lists relevant legislation, sets out general principles including sustainable development and the role of the planning system, and at paragraphs 114 to 140 sets out policy guidance of specific relevance to the historic environment. This Circular sets out advice on legislation and procedures relating to archaeological remains and supplements that guidance. Together with *Planning Guidance (Wales): Planning Policy*, it should be taken into account by local planning authorities in the preparation of development plans. The combined guidance may be material to decisions on individual planning applications and will be taken into account by the Secretary of State and his Inspectors in the determination of called-in applications and planning appeals in Wales.

2. This Circular is arranged as follows:

A   The importance of archaeology (paras.3-7)
B   Advice on the handling of archaeological matters in the planning process (paras.8-25)
C   Cancellation of PPG 16 (Wales)
Annex 1   Legislative arrangements
[Annex 2   Key bodies, Organisations and Sites and Monuments Records*
Annex 3   Secretary of State's criteria for scheduling ancient monuments*
Annex 4   Ancient Monuments (Class Consents) Order 1994*]

*   not reproduced in this appendix.

The documents listed under the Reference column in the margin of this Circular provide more detailed information which should be read in conjunction with the Circular.

© Crown Copyright 1996
First published in 1996

ISBN 1 85760 092 4

A: THE IMPORTANCE OF ARCHAEOLOGY

3. Archaeological remains are a finite, and non-renewable resource, in many cases highly fragile and vulnerable to damage and destruction. They are the product of human activity over thousands of years and may vary enormously in their state of preservation and in their appeal to the public. Their importance, as evidence of the past development of our civilisation and as part of our sense of national identity, is not necessarily related to their size or popularity. Some remains are small or barely visible while others form parts of large and complex historic landscapes. Much has been destroyed by human activity - for example, by modern construction methods in urban development and expansion of the road network, by modern agricultural techniques (in particular deep ploughing or drainage of wetlands), and by mineral extraction. Appropriate management is essential to ensure that archaeological remains survive in good condition. In particular, care must be taken to ensure that they are not needlessly or thoughtlessly destroyed. They are part of our cultural heritage not least in terms of the information they provide about the past, valuable both for their own sake, and for their role in education, leisure and tourism.

4. Archaeological records for Wales contain around 75,000 sites and monuments. Nearly 3,000 nationally important sites enjoy special protection as 'scheduled ancient monuments'. Cadw: Welsh Historic Monuments Executive Agency is engaged upon a survey programme which is expected to result in significant additions to this category of site.

Reference: Ancient Monuments and Archaeological Areas Act 1979.

See Annex 1.

5. Scheduling archaeological remains ensures that the case for preservation is fully considered given any proposals for development or other work which might damage the monument. The planning system is equally in a position to consider the desirability of preserving archaeological remains and the various options open to planning authorities for dealing with archaeological remains are considered in Section B. Much can be achieved when developers are prepared to enter into discussions with archaeologists and consider fully the needs of archaeology as early as possible in the development process. This voluntary approach to considering the needs of archaeology is

well-established and has been formalised in various Codes of Practice.

Reference: Planning Guidance (Wales): Planning Policy 1996, para.140.

See Annexes 1 and 2.

6. Archaeological issues are often important in minerals planning, particularly in the quarrying of stone, the extraction of sand and gravel and in opencast coal working. Minerals can only be worked where they are found so they often differ from other forms of development in that there is not the same flexibility of choice of location.

Reference: The CBI's revised Code of Practice for Mineral Operators on archaeological investigations provides advice on how minerals operators should consult archaeological interests in formulating planning applications, to ensure that archaeological factors are fully taken into account.

7. Positive planning and management can help to bring about sensible solutions to the treatment of sites with archaeological remains and reduce the areas of potential conflict between development and preservation. **While the Welsh Office (through Cadw) has an important role to play, the key to the future of the great majority of archaeological sites and historic landscapes lies with local authorities, acting within the framework set by central government, in their various capacities as planning, highways, education and recreational authorities, as well as with the owners and occupiers of sites themselves. Appropriate planning policies in development plans and their implementation through development control will be especially important.**

B: ADVICE ON THE HANDLING OF ARCHAEOLOGICAL MATTERS IN THE PLANNING PROCESS

Development Plans

8. **Development plans should reconcile the need for development with the interests of conservation including archaeology. They should include policies for the protection, enhancement and preservation of sites of archaeological interest and their settings.** Although the surviving numbers of archaeological remains are finite and irreplaceable, obviously not all are of equal importance. Planning authorities will

therefore wish to base their development plan policies and proposals on an assessment of the archaeological remains in their area. **These policies will provide an important part of the framework for the consideration of individual proposals for development which affects archaeological remains and will help guide developers in preparing planning applications. The proposals map should define the areas and sites to which the policies and proposals apply.** Cadw is ready to advise on the archaeological content of policies proposed for inclusion in draft plans and should be consulted early in their preparation. This may be of particular help in urban areas where important archaeological remains may not be adequately identified by scheduling.

Reference: Planning Guidance (Wales): Planning Policy 1996, paras.135 and 137.

Sites and Monuments Records - SMR

9. A small number of planning authorities have their own archaeological staff and sites and monuments records. Those without this in-house provision are advised to make full use of the expertise of the Welsh Archaeological Trusts in development control and planning advice, preferably by formally adopting the regional Sites and Monuments Records (SMR) maintained by the Trusts.

Reference: See Annex 2 paras.10-12.

Planning Applications

10. **The desirability of preserving an ancient monument and its setting is a material consideration in determining a planning application whether that monument is scheduled or unscheduled.** Developers and local authorities should take into account archaeological considerations and deal with them from the beginning of the development control process. Where local planning authorities are aware of a real and specific threat to a known archaeological site as a result of the potential exercise of permitted development rights, they may wish to consider the use of their powers to withdraw those rights and require that planning permission be obtained before the development can proceed. The majority of such directions require the Secretary of State's approval, either before they come into effect or within six months of being made.

Reference: Planning Guidance (Wales): Planning Policy 1996, para.134.

Permitted development rights are set out in Schedule 2 to the Town and Country Planning (General Permitted Development) Order 1995. Powers to withdraw those rights exist under Article 4 of that Order.

Further advice on the use of Article 4 Directions is given in Appendix D to Welsh Office Circular 29/95.

(a) The First Step: Early Consultations between Developers and Planning Authorities

11. Developers should discuss their preliminary plans with the planning authorities at an early stage. Once detailed designs have been prepared and finance arranged, flexibility becomes more difficult and expensive. In their own interests, therefore, prospective developers should in all cases include as part of their research into the development potential of a site, which they undertake before making a planning application, an initial appraisal of whether the site is known or likely to contain archaeological remains. The first step will be to consult the regional SMR (whether held by the local authority or the regional Welsh Archaeological Trust). The SMR will provide information about the locations where archaeological remains are known or thought likely to exist and on their relative significance.

Reference: Planning Guidance (Wales): Planning Policy 1996, para.136.

(b) Archaeological Assessments

12. These consultations will help to provide prospective developers with advance warning of the archaeological sensitivity of a site. As a result they may wish to commission their own archaeological assessment by a professionally qualified archaeological organisation or consultant. This need not involve fieldwork. Assessment normally involves desk-based evaluation of existing information: it can make effective use of records of previous discoveries, including any historic maps held by the local authority archive and local museums and record offices, or of geophysical survey techniques. In some circumstances a formal Environmental Assessment may be necessary.

Reference: See Annex 1, paras.22 and 23.

(c) Field Evaluations

13. Where early discussions with local planning authorities or the developer's own research indicate that important archaeological remains may exist, the planning authority should request the prospective developer to arrange for an archaeological field evaluation to be carried out before any decision on the planning application is taken. Such an evaluation, normally a rapid and inexpensive operation involving ground survey and/or small-scale trial trenching, is quite distinct from full archaeological excavation but it should be carried out by a professionally qualified archaeological organisation or archaeologist. Evaluations of this kind help to define the character and extent of the archaeological remains that exist in the area of a proposed development, and indicate the weight which ought to be attached to their preservation. They also provide information useful for identifying potential options for minimising or avoiding damage.

Reference: The Institute of Field Archaeologists (see Annex 2, para.7) publishes a directory of members (both individuals and archaeological organisations) which developers may wish to consult.

14. Local planning authorities should expect developers to provide the results of such appraisals, assessments and/or evaluations as part of their application for sites where there is a good reason to believe there are remains of archaeological importance. If developers are not prepared to do so voluntarily, the planning authority may wish to consider whether it would be appropriate to direct the applicant to supply further information. Authorities will need to consider refusing permission for proposals which are inadequately documented.

Reference: Regulation 4 of the Town and Country Planning (Applications) Regulations 1988.

(d) Consultations by Planning Authorities

15. When planning applications are made without prior discussion with the local planning authorities, the authorities should seek to identify those applications which have archaeological implications, and to assess their likely archaeological impact by consulting the local authority Archaeological Officer, National Park Archaeologist or regional Welsh Archaeological Trust. When it is evident that a particular development

proposal is likely to affect archaeological remains, applicants may need to be asked to provide more detailed information about their scheme - for example, the type of foundations to be used - or they may be asked to carry out an evaluation. Planning authorities should be fully informed about the nature and importance of the archaeological site and its setting. They should therefore seek archaeological advice. In the case of a development proposal that is likely to affect the site of a scheduled ancient monument, local planning authorities are required to consult the Secretary of State (Cadw). In exceptional cases, where issues of more than local importance are raised, applications may be called in for determination by the Secretary of State.

Reference: Article 10(1)(n) of the Town and Country Planning (General Development Procedure) Order 1995.

Planning Decisions

16. **The Secretary of State recognises that the extent to which archaeological remains can or should be preserved will depend upon a number of factors. The case for the preservation of archaeological remains must be assessed on the individual merits of each case, taking into account the archaeological policies in development plans, together with all other relevant policies and material considerations, including the intrinsic importance of the remains and weighing these against the need for the proposed development.**

Reference: Planning Guidance (Wales): Planning Policy 1996, para.134.

(a) Preservation of Archaeological Remains *in situ*

17. Once the planning authority has sufficient information, there is a range of options for the determination of planning applications affecting archaeological remains and their settings. Where nationally important archaeological remains, whether scheduled or not, and their settings, are affected by proposed development there should be a presumption in favour of their physical preservation *in situ* i.e., a presumption against proposals which would involve significant alteration or cause damage, or which would have a significant impact on the setting of visible remains. In certain circumstances, it may be possible to preserve important archaeological remains where developers prepare sympathetic designs

using, for example, foundations which avoid disturbing the remains altogether or minimise damage by raising ground levels under a proposed new structure or by careful siting of landscaped or open areas. There are techniques available for sealing archaeological remains underneath buildings or landscaping, thus securing their preservation for the future even though they remain inaccessible for the time being.

Reference: Planning Guidance (Wales): Planning Policy 1996, paras.134 and 137.

(b) Preservation of Archaeological Remains by Record

18. There will be occasions, particularly where remains of lesser importance are involved, when planning authorities may decide that the significance of the archaeological remains is not sufficient when weighed against all other material considerations, including the need for development, to justify their physical preservation *in situ*, and that the proposed development should proceed. Planning authorities will, in such cases, need to satisfy themselves that the developer has made appropriate and satisfactory arrangements for the excavation and recording, or other investigation, of the archaeological remains and the publication of the results. If this has not already been secured through some form of voluntary agreement, planning authorities should consider granting planning permission subject to conditions which provide for the excavation and recording of the remains before development takes place. Local planning authorities may, as a matter of last resort, need to consider refusing planning permission where developers do not seek to accommodate important remains.

Reference: Planning Guidance (Wales): Planning Policy 1996, para.138.

19. From the archaeological point of view excavation should be regarded as a second best option. The science of archaeology is developing rapidly. Excavation means the total destruction of evidence (apart from removable artefacts) from which future techniques could almost certainly extract more information than is currently possible. Excavation can be expensive and time-consuming, and discoveries may have to be evaluated in a hurry against an inadequate research framework. The preservation *in situ* of important archaeological remains is therefore to be preferred.

(c) Arrangements for the Investigation of Archaeological Remains Including Funding

20. Archaeological investigations, such as excavation and recording should be carried out before development commences, working to a project brief prepared by the planning authority (with reference to their archaeological advisers). Investigation can be achieved through agreements reached between the developer, the archaeologist and the planning authority. Such agreements should secure and implement an appropriate scheme of archaeological investigation, to an agreed timetable, and provide for the subsequent publication of its results. In particular cases where the developer is a non-profit making community body, such as a charitable trust or housing association, which is unable to raise the funds to provide for excavation and subsequent recording without undue hardship, or in the case of an individual who similarly does not have the means to fund such work, an application for financial assistance may be made to the Secretary of State.

21. Agreements covering archaeological investigations, the publication of their results and deposition of records in a designated public archive may take different forms. For example, the developers or their archaeological consultants and local planning authorities may wish to conclude a voluntary planning agreement. These agreements can provide for the excavation and recording of sites before development work starts. Voluntary agreements are likely to provide more flexibility and be of greater mutual benefit to all the parties than could be provided for by alternative statutory means. They have the advantage of setting out clearly the extent of the developer's commitment, thereby reducing both uncertainty over the financial implications of having to accommodate any archaeological constraints and the possibility of unforeseen delays to the construction programme.

Section 106 of the Town and Country Planning Act 1990 which contains statutory powers dealing with planning obligations and other similar statutory powers.

Model agreements between developers and the appropriate archaeological body regulating archaeological site investigations and excavation can be obtained from the Institute of Field Archaeologists (see Annex 2, para.7).

Planning Conditions

22. Planning authorities should seek to ensure that potential conflicts are resolved and agreements with developers concluded before planning permission is granted. Where the use of planning conditions is necessary, authorities should ensure that they are fair, reasonable and practicable. It is open to the local planning authority to impose conditions designed to protect a monument and to require that an archaeological watching brief is carried out (either intensively or intermittently) during the construction period by a suitably qualified archaeologist. Conditions on these lines help to ensure that if remains of archaeological significance are disturbed in the course of work, they can be excavated, recorded and reported.

Reference: Welsh Office Circular 35/95, para.81.

Planning Guidance (Wales): Planning Policy 1996, para.137.

23. In cases when planning authorities have decided that planning permission may be granted but on the basis of a negative condition, the following model is suggested:

"No development shall take place within the area indicated [this would be the area of archaeological interest] until the applicant, or their agents or successors in title, has secured the implementation of a programme of archaeological work in accordance with a written scheme of investigation which has been submitted by the applicant and approved in writing by the local planning authority." (Developers will wish to ensure that in drawing up a scheme, the timetable for the investigation is included within the details of the agreed scheme).

Welsh Office Circular 35/95, Appendix A model condition 55.

Planning Guidance (Wales): Planning Policy 1996, para.139.

Discovery of Archaeological Remains During Development

24. The preceding advice has been framed to minimise occasions when totally unexpected problems arise while development is in progress. Nevertheless, and in spite of the best pre-planning application research, there may be occasions when the presence of archaeological remains only becomes apparent once development has commenced. Developers may

wish to consider insuring themselves against the risk of substantial loss while safeguarding the interest of historic remains unexpectedly discovered on the site. Conflicts that may otherwise arise between developers and archaeologists may not always be easy to resolve. Where fresh archaeological discoveries are deemed by the Secretary of State to be of national importance, in accordance with published criteria, he has the power to schedule the remains. In the event of scheduling, developers would need to seek separate scheduled monument consent before they continue work. It is also open to a planning authority or the Secretary of State to revoke a planning permission if deemed necessary, in which case there is provision for compensation. In the majority of cases, however, it should prove possible for the parties to resolve the issues through voluntary discussion and for arrangements satisfactory to both parties to be reached.

Reference: See Annexes 1 and 3.

C: CANCELLATION PPG 16 (WALES)

25. The advice contained in this Circular replaces that in PPG16 (Wales) which is hereby cancelled.

Unitary Authorities)	**T J Cassidy**
National Parks) In Wales	Chief Executive
	Cadw: Welsh Historic Monuments

ANNEX 1

LEGISLATIVE ARRANGEMENTS

Scheduling of Ancient Monuments of National Importance

1. Under the Ancient Monuments and Archaeological Areas Act 1979 (the 1979 Act) the Secretary of State has a duty to compile and maintain a schedule of monuments; monuments on the schedule have statutory protection. Inclusion of monuments on the schedule is at the Secretary of State's discretion although monuments added to it must be of national importance. The non-statutory criteria for scheduling published in 1983 (and restated in 1990) are set out in Annex 3. The Inspectorate of Ancient Monuments is responsible for advising on which monuments should be considered for scheduling and on whether a monument

should be de-scheduled or the entry or protected area revised. In practice, many of the recommendations arise from suggestions made to the Inspectorate from fieldworkers in the Royal Commission on the Ancient and Historical Monuments of Wales (RCAHMW), Welsh Archaeological Trusts, local authorities or national parks. Occupied dwellings and churches in use for ecclesiastical purposes cannot be scheduled.

2. Owners are normally consulted before sites are added to the schedule, although this is not a statutory requirement and there may not always be time in cases where development is impending. Scheduled sites are registered as a charge in the Local Land Charges Register and notified to the regional Sites and Monuments Record. Cadw publishes lists of scheduled monuments. Enquiries concerning these lists should be directed to Ancient Monuments Administration, Cadw: Welsh Historic Monuments, Crown Building, Cathays Park, Cardiff CFI 3NQ, Telephone 01222 500200.

3. The present schedule of nearly 3,000 sites has been compiled over a period of more than a hundred years, since statutory protection for monuments was first introduced in 1882. However it is recognised to contain an inadequate sample of the extensive archaeological remains now known to survive in Wales. Cadw has, therefore, embarked upon a programme to evaluate all known archaeological remains in Wales to identify those which may be suitable for scheduling. This exercise is being carried out in close liaison with archaeological interests and is expected to result in a significant increase in the number of scheduled monuments. But even so, the stringent criteria for scheduling means that large numbers of identified sites are likely to remain unscheduled. Whether or not they are preserved will depend upon the value of the remains, the commitment of owners and of the public and the policies of local authorities.

4. As a selective example of the nation's archaeology the schedule differs from the more comprehensive lists of buildings of special architectural or historic interest compiled under Section 1 of the Planning (Listed Buildings and Conservation Areas) Act 1990. But, broadly speaking, scheduled monuments rank in importance with Grade I or Grade II* listed buildings. Where buildings are both scheduled and listed, ancient monuments' legislation takes precedence, and scheduled monument consent rather than listed building consent is required for works.

Control of Work to Scheduled Monuments

5. Once a monument has been scheduled, the consent of the Secretary of State is required before any works are carried out which would have the effect of demolishing, destroying, damaging, removing, repairing, altering, adding to, flooding or covering up the monument. The scope of the control is therefore both more extensive and more detailed than that applied to listed buildings. Consent

can be granted only for detailed proposals and unlike planning permission there is no provision for the granting of outline consent. There are however ten class consents currently in force which enable owners to proceed with certain specified types of work - they are listed at Annex 4. The Secretary of State has power to revoke or modify a consent (whether granted following an application or deemed to have been granted by class consent).

6. Although monuments on Crown land may be scheduled (Section 50 of the 1979 Act), works by or on behalf of the Government on such land currently enjoy exemption from scheduled monument consent controls. However, they remain subject to a non-statutory procedure known as scheduled monument clearance which follows similar procedures to scheduled monument consent.

7. The form of application for scheduled monument consent is laid down in Regulations [The Ancient Monuments (Applications for Scheduled Monument Consent) Regulations 1981] and forms may be obtained from Cadw.

8. Where appropriate, the Secretary of State will consult the Royal Commission on the Ancient and Historical Monuments of Wales, the Council for British Archaeology, the regional Welsh Archaeological Trust and the relevant local authority on applications for scheduled monument consent. Other archaeological or relevant interests may be consulted, too, as the need arises.

9. Paragraph 3(2) of Part 1 to Schedule 1 of the 1979 Act requires the Secretary of State to cause a local inquiry to be held or afford an applicant for scheduled monument consent the opportunity of a hearing before an application is determined. As a general rule, it is his policy to hold a public inquiry, in the absence of a request from an applicant, only in cases where a related matter is formally before him for determination and is due to be heard at a public inquiry, e.g. an appeal against the refusal of planning permission.

10. To assist an applicant to decide whether he/she wishes to exercise his/her right to a hearing, it is the Secretary of State's practice to extend the invitation in a letter setting out a provisional decision on an application based on the evidence submitted with it, any representations made by consultees or interested parties and the advice put forward by the regional Inspector of Ancient Monuments. The regional Inspector will, where necessary, have visited the site and resolved any doubts or ambiguities as to the nature of the proposed works before submitting his/her detailed recommendation including a list of conditions proposed to be attached to the terms of any consent. Site discussions can inform applications but are entirely without prejudice to the Secretary of State's consideration of an application for scheduled monument consent.

Secretary of State's Policy

11. The Secretary of State regards the main purpose of scheduling as ensuring the

preservation of ancient monuments thus there should be a presumption in favour of their physical preservation when considering applications for consent to undertake works to them, i.e. a presumption against proposals which would involve significant alteration or cause damage, or which would have a significant impact on the setting of visible remains. In considering applications for scheduled monument consent, therefore, the Secretary of State will expect applicants (particularly where underground pipelines, cables or sewers are intended to be laid), to demonstrate that no practicable alternative route or location, avoiding the monument, exists and that the need to undertake the works outweighs the presumption in favour of the protection of a monument of national importance.

12. Where a building is both listed and scheduled, Section 61 of the Planning (Listed Buildings and Conservation Areas) Act 1990 provides that application to demolish, alter or extend the structure, need only be made under the provisions of. Section 2 of the 1979 Act since that is deemed to take precedence. In determining an application for work to such a building, the Secretary of State will continue to have regard to his published policies relating to listed buildings particularly with regard to the need to explore alternative uses, where demolition is proposed, and to retain important features where it is proposed to undertake alterations.

Offences Relating to Scheduled Ancient Monuments

13. The 1979 Act created a number of offences relating to ancient monuments. Well publicised successful prosecutions of those who carry out unauthorised work to, or damage, scheduled monuments can provide a valuable deterrent to the wilful damage or destruction of monuments, and it is Welsh Office policy to initiate proceedings where it is considered a good case can be sustained. The Act provides a number of defences including genuine and reasonable ignorance of the scheduled status of the site, and the need to undertake urgently necessary work in the interests of health and safety.

14. Section 28 of the 1979 Act makes it an offence to destroy or damage a protected monument - defined as a scheduled ancient monument or any monument under the ownership or guardianship of the Secretary of State or a local authority by virtue of the 1979 Act. The power to initiate prosecution proceedings is not limited to the Secretary of State. Local authorities and the police can also initiate prosecutions when offences have been discovered by them.

15. Because the majority of local authorities in Wales do not have in-house archaeological expertise, the Secretary of State (through Cadw) will continue to take the lead in the investigation and prosecution of offences arising from damage to scheduled ancient monuments when incidents are reported to, or discovered by, him. In the case of a scheduled ancient monument owned by, or in the guardianship of, a local authority, he would normally expect the local

authority to be responsible for the prosecution of offenders though archaeological advice (including the provision of an expert witness) will be made available by Cadw if required. It is suggested, therefore, that before undertaking prosecutions, local authorities should consult Cadw. Local authorities will continue to be solely responsible for prosecutions arising from damage to unscheduled, protected monuments.

Metal Detectors

16. Most metal detector users act responsibly. However, illegal metal detecting can cause serious damage to ancient monuments - not only to the fabric of the monument, but also to its interpretation and understanding once artefacts have been removed from their archaeological context. It is an offence under Section 42 of the 1979 Act to use metal detectors in a protected place (any place which is either the site of a scheduled monument or any monument in the ownership or care of the Secretary of State or a local authority) without prior consent from the Secretary of State to whom written application will need to be made. Consent is not normally given except for bona fide, non destructive, research purposes or for the recovery of valuable items of lost property, e.g. rings and watches.

Monument Management

17. Statutory protection may not of itself secure the future preservation of a monument. In most cases it is essential to develop a management plan and to carry out regular maintenance to prevent progressive decay of the building or site. Ruins, as much as buildings in use, need constant minor repair to prevent their deterioration. Grassed field monuments can be seriously damaged by neglect which allows pests and shrubs or trees to proliferate, or by unsuitable farming regimes. While the responsibility for repairing and maintaining monuments rests with the owner, Cadw can provide advice and financial assistance of two main kinds for the preservation of important sites.

18. Grants under Section 24 of the 1979 Act are provided by the Secretary of State principally towards the costs of the preservation, maintenance and management of monuments and, more rarely, they may be given towards the purchase of monuments which are at risk of damage or destruction.

19. Management agreements made under Section 17 of the 1979 Act either by the Secretary of State or local authorities provide financial assistance to occupiers of land to encourage the beneficial management of usually field monuments through such work as pest and weed control and control of stocking levels. Such agreements extend over a number of years and can include an initial payment to cover the cost of any capital works, such as fencing.

20. Cadw provides advice on the management of ancient monuments, principally

through the Inspectorate of Ancient Monuments but also through a network of Field Monument Wardens assigned to individual areas. The Wardens in particular inspect scheduled monuments on a regular basis, reporting on their condition and are available to discuss with both owners/occupiers and local authorities measures for the improved management of sites.

Preservation by Record

21. The Secretary of State can offer financial assistance under Section 45 of the 1979 Act for preservation by record. In terms of quality, sites must be of national importance measured against the published criteria (Annex 3). Their excavation must accord with current academic priorities. The present emphasis is increasingly on projects which can illuminate important research questions and fill gaps in our knowledge. Funds will not normally be made available unless the site is under threat.

Environmental Assessment

22. For certain types of development (listed in Schedules 1 and 2 to the Town and Country Planning (Assessment of Environmental Effects) Regulations 1988, as amended) formal environmental assessment (EA) may be necessary. Where EA is required, the developer must provide an environmental statement setting out the information specified in Schedule 3 to the Regulations about the site and the likely significant effects of the proposed development on the environment. This should include information relating to any significant effects on material assets and the cultural heritage, such as archaeological features and other human artefacts, and the measures envisaged to avoid, reduce or remedy adverse effects.

23. Where development requiring EA affects the site of a scheduled ancient monument, the Secretary of State must be consulted on the submitted environmental statement and he may be able (although not required to do so) to provide information to assist in the preparation of the statement. Further information about the EA procedures may be found in Welsh Office Circular 23/88 and the booklet *Environmental Assessment - A Guide to the Procedures* published by HMSO.

Simplified Planning Zones (SPZs)

24. The provisions relating to SPZs are set out at sections 82 to 87 of, and Schedule 7 to, the Town and Country Planning Act 1990, as amended by the Planning and Compensation Act 1991. SPZs have the effect of granting planning permission for specified types of development within the scheme. Where archaeological remains lie within the area of a proposed SPZ, it may be necessary to tailor the scheme to accommodate them. Scheduled monuments within SPZs remain subject to scheduled monument consent.

Cylchlythyr 60/96 y Swyddfa Gymreig
Cynllunio a'r Amgylchedd Hanesyddol: Archaeoleg
[Extracts]

Cyflwyniad

1. Mae *Canllawiau Cynllunio (Cymru): Polisi Cynllunio* yn nodi polisïau'r Llywodraeth ar ddefnyddio tir fel y maent yn gymwys yng Nghymru. Maent yn rhestru'r ddeddfwriaeth berthnasol, yn nodi egwyddorion cyffredinol gan gynnwys datblygiad cynaliadwy a swyddogaeth y system gynllunio, ac ym mharagraffau 114-140 nodir canllawiau polisi sy'n berthnasol yn benodol i'r amgylchedd hanesyddol. Yn y Cylchlythyr hwn nodir cyngor ar ddeddfwriaeth a gweithdrefnau ynglyn â gweddillion archaeolegol a chydategir y canllawiau hynny. Dylai'r awdurdodau cynllunio yng Nghymru ei gymryd i ystyriaeth, ynghyd â *Canllawiau Cynllunio (Cymru): Polisi Cynllunio*, wrth baratoi cynlluniau datblygu. Gall y canllawiau cyfun fod yn berthnasol i benderfyniadau ar geisiadau cynllunio unigol a chânt eu cymryd i ystyriaeth gan yr Ysgrifennydd Gwladol a'i Arolygwyr wrth benderfynu ar geisiadau wedi'u galw i mewn ac apelau cynllunio yng Nghymru.

2. Mae'r Cylchlythyr hwn wedi'i drefnu fel a ganlyn:

A Pwysigrwydd archaeoleg (paragraffau 3-7)
B Cyngor ar drafod materion archaeolegol yn y broses gynllunio (paragraffau 8-25)
C Dileu PPG 16 (Cymru)

Atodiad 1 Trefniadau deddfwriaethol
[Atodiad 2 Cyrff a mudiadau allweddol, a chofnodion safleoedd a henebion*
Atodiad 3 Meini prawf yr Ysgrifennydd Gwladol ar gyfer cofrestru henebion*
Atodiad 4 Gorchymyn Henebion (Caniatadau Dosbarth) 1994*]

* not reproduced in this Atodiad.

Mae'r dogfennau a restrir yn y golofn Cyfeiriad yn ymyl y Cylchlythyr hwn yn cynnig gwybodaeth fanylach a ddylai gael ei darllen ar y cyd â'r Cylchlythyr.

ISBN 1 85760 092 4

A: PWYSIGRWYDD ARCHAEOLEG

3. Mae gweddillion archaeolegol yn adnoddau meidrol na ellir eu hadnewyddu, ac mewn llawer o achosion maent yn fregus iawn ac yn hawdd i'w difrodi a'u dinistrio. Maent yn deillio o weithgarwch pobl dros filoedd o flynyddoedd a gallant amrywio'n fawr o ran eu cyflwr a'u hapêl i'r cyhoedd. Nid yw eu pwysigrwydd, fel tystiolaeth o ddatblygiad ein gwareiddiad yn y gorffennol ac fel rhan o'n hymwybyddiaeth o'n cenedligrwydd, yn gysylltiedig o reidrwydd â'u maint nac â'u poblogrwydd. Mae rhai gweddillion yn fach neu'n anodd eu gweld ac eraill yn rhan o dirluniau hanesyddol mawr a chymhleth. Mae llawer wedi'i ddinistrio trwy weithgarwch pobl – er enghraifft, trwy ddulliau adeiladu modern mewn datblygu trefol ac ehangu'r rhwydwaith ffyrdd, trwy dechnegau amaethyddol modern (yn arbennig aredig dwfn neu draenio tir gwlyb), a thrwy gloddio mwynau. Mae rheolaeth briodol yn hanfodol i sicrhau bod gweddillion archaeolegol yn goroesi mewn cyflwr da. Dylid cymryd gofal, yn benodol, i sicrhau na chânt eu dinistrio'n ddiangen neu'n ddifeddwl. Maent yn rhan o'n treftadaeth ddiwylliannol, nid lleiaf yn nhermau'r wybodaeth a gynigiant am y gorffennol, sy'n werthfawr ynddynt eu hunain ac am eu rôl mewn addysg, hamdden a thwristiaeth.

4. Mae cofnodion archaeolegol Cymru yn cynnwys tua 75,000 o safleoedd a henebion. Mae bron 3,000 o safleoedd cenedlaethol pwysig o dan warchodaeth arbennig fel 'henebion cofrestredig'. Mae Asiantaeth Weithredol Cadw: Henebion Cymru wrthi'n cynnal rhaglen o arolygon y disgwylir iddi esgor ar nifer sylweddol o ychwanegiadau at y categori hwn o safleoedd.

Cyfeiriad: Deddf Mannau Archaeolgol a Henebion 1979.

Gweler Atodiad 1.

5. Mae cofrestru gweddillion archaeolegol yn sicrhau bod yr achos dros

gadwraeth yn cael ystyriaeth lawn mewn unrhyw gynigion i ddatblygu neu i wneud gwaith arall a allai ddifrodi'r heneb. Mae'r system gynllunio mewn sefyllfa hefyd i ystyried dymunoldeb cadw gweddillion archaeolegol, a chaiff yr amrywiol ddewisiadau sydd ar gael i'r awdurdodau cynllunio ar gyfer ymdrin â gweddillion archaeolegol eu hystyried yn Adran B. Gellir cyflawni llawer pan fydd datblygwyr yn fodlon trafod gydag archaeolegwyr ac ystyried anghenion archaeoleg yn llawn mor gynnar â phosibl yn y broses ddatblygu. Mae'r ymagwedd wirfoddol hon at ystyried anghenion archaeoleg wedi'i hen sefydlu, ac mae wedi'i ffurfioli mewn amrywiol Godau Ymarfer.

Cyfeiriad: Canllawiau Cynllunio (Cymru): Polisi Cynllunio 1996, paragraff 140.

Gweler Atodiadau 1 a 2.

6. Mae materion archaeolegol yn aml yn bwysig wrth gynllunio ynglyn â mwynau, yn enwedig wrth chwarela am garreg, cloddio am dywod a graean, a chloddio am lo brig. Ni ellir gweithio mwynau ond lle y cânt eu darganfod felly maent yn aml yn wahanol i fathau eraill o ddatblygu gan nad oes yr un hyblygrwydd yn y dewis o leoliad.

Cyfeiriad: Mae Cod Ymarfer diwygiedig y CBI ar gyfer Gweithredwyr Mwynau ynghylch ymchwiliadau archaeolegol yn cynnig cyngor ar sut y dylai gweithredwyr mwynau ymgynghori â buddiannau archaeolegol wrth lunio ceisiadau cynllunio, er mwyn sicrhau y caiff ffactorau archaeolegol eu cymryd i ystyriaeth yn llawn.

7. Gall cynllunio a rheoli cadarnhaol fod yn gymorth i sicrhau atebion synhwyrol ynghylch triniaeth safleoedd â gweddillion archaeolegol a lleihau'r gwrthdaro posibl rhwng datblygu a chadwraeth. **Er bod gan y Swyddfa Gymreig (trwy Cadw) ran bwysig i'w chwarac, mae'r allwedd i ddyfodol y** mwyafrif mawr o safleoedd archaeolegol a thirluniau hanesyddol yn nwylo'r awdurdodau lleol, yn gweithredu o fewn y fframwaith a osodwyd gan y llywodraeth ganolog, yn eu hamrywiol swyddogaethau fel awdurdodau cynllunio, priffyrdd, addysg a hamdden, yn ogystal ag yn nwylo perchnogion a deiliaid y safleoedd eu hunain. Bydd polisïau cynllunio priodol mewn cynlluniau datblygu a gweithredu'r polisïau hyn trwy reoli datblygu yn arbennig o bwysig.

B: CYNGOR AR DRAFOD MATERION ARCHAEOLEGOL YN Y BROSES GYNLLUNIO

Cynlluniau Datblygu

8. **Dylai cynlluniau datblygu gysoni'r angen i ddatblygu â buddiannau cadwraeth, gan gynnwys archaeoleg. Dylent gynnwys polisïau ar gyfer diogelu, gwella a chadw safleoedd o ddiddordeb archaeolegol a'u cefndir.** Er bod nifer y gweddillion archaeolegot sydd wedi goroesi yn feidrol ac er na all dim gymryd eu lle, mae'n amlwg nad yw pob un o bwysigrwydd cyfartal. Bydd yr awdurdodau cynllunio felly yn dymuno seilio'u polisïau a'u cynigion yn eu cynlluniau datblygu ar werthusiad o'r gweddillion archaeolegol yn eu hardal. **Bydd y polisïau hyn yn rhan bwysig o'r fframwaith ar gyfer ystyried cynigion unigol ar gyfer datblygu sy'n effeithio ar weddillion archaeolegol ac yn helpu i arwain datblygwyr sy'n paratoi ceisiadau cynllunio. Dylai'r map cynigion ddiffinio'r ardaloedd a'r safleoedd y mae'r polisïau a'r cynigion yn gymwys iddynt.** Mae Cadw yn barod i roi cyngor ar gynnwys archaeolegol polisïau y cynigir eu cynnwys mewn cynlluniau drafft a dylid ymgynghori â hwy yn gynnar wrth eu paratoi. Gall hyn fod o gymorth penodol mewn ardaloedd trefol am ei bod yn bosibl nad yw'r gweddillion archaeolegol pwysig yno wedi'u nodi'n ddigonol drwy gyfrwng eu cofrestru.

Cyfeiriad: Canllawiau Cynllunio (Cymru): Polisi Cynllunio 1996, paragraffau 135 a 137.

Cofnodion Safleoedd a Henebion - SMR

9. Mae gan nifer fach o awdurdodau cynllunio lleol eu staff archaeolegol eu hunain a'u cofnodion safleoedd a henebion eu hunain. Cynghorir yr awdurdodau nad oes ganddynt ddarpariaeth fewnol fel hyn i ddefnyddio arbenigedd yr Ymddiriedolaethau Archaeolegol Cymreig, ym maes rheoli datblygu a chyngor archaeolegol, i'r eithaf a hynny, os oes modd, drwy fabwysiadu yn ffurfiol y Cofnodion Safleoedd a Henebion (SMR) a gedwir gan yr Ymddiriedolaethau.

Cyfeiriad: Gweler Atodiad 2 paragraffau 10-12.

Ceisiadau Cynllunio

10. **Mae dymunoldeb cadw heneb a'i gefndir yn ystyriaeth berthnasol wrth benderfynu ar gais cynllunio boed yr heneb hwnnw wedi'i**

gofrestru ai peidio. Dylai datblygwyr ac awdurdodau lleol roi sylw i ystyriaethau archaeolegol ac ymdrin â hwy o ddechrau'r broses o reoli datblygu. Lle mae'r awdurdodau cynllunio lleol yn ymwybodol o fygythiad real a phenodol i safle archaeolegol hysbys o ganlyniad i'r posibilrwydd y caiff hawliau datblygu a ganiateir eu hymarfer, gall y byddant yn dymuno ystyried defnyddio'u pwerau i dynnu'r hawliau hynny yn ôl a'i gwneud yn ofynnol bod caniatâd cynllunio penodol yn cael ei sicrhau cyn y gall y datblygiad fynd rhagddo. Rhaid sicrhau cymeradwyaeth yr Ysgrifennydd Gwladol i'r mwyafrif o gyfarwyddiadau o'r fath, naill ai cyn iddynt ddod i rym neu o fewn chwe mis o'u gwneud.

Cyfeiriad: Canllawiau Cynllunio (Cymru): Polisi Cynllunio 1996, paragraff 134.

Nodir hawliau datblygu a ganiateir yn Atodlen 2'or Gorchymyn Cynllunio Gwlad a Thref (Datblygu Cyffredinol a Ganiateir) 1995. Ceir pwerau i dynnu'r hawliau hynny'n ôl o dan Erthygl 4 o'r Gorchymyn hwnnw.

Ceir cyngor pellach ar ddefnyddio Cyfarwyddiadau Erthygl 4 yn Atodiad D o Gylchlythyr 29/95 y Swyddfa Gymreig.

(a) Y Cam Cyntaf: Ymgynghori Cynnar rhwng Datblygwyr ac Awdurdodau Cynllunio

11. Dylai datblygwyr drafod eu cynlluniau rhagarweiniol gyda'r awdurdodau cynllunio yn gynnar. Pan fydd cynlluniau manwl wedi'u paratoi ac arian wedi'i drefnu, mae hyblygrwydd yn llawer anos a drutach. Er eu lles eu hunain felly, dylai darpar-ddatblygwyr ym mhob achos gynnwys gwerthusiad cychwynnol, fel rhan o'u hymchwil i botensial datblygu safle, sef ymchwil y byddant yn ei chynnal cyn gwneud cais cynllunio, i weld a yw'n hysbys bod y safle yn cynnwys, neu'n debygol o gynnwys, gweddillion archaeolegol. Y cam cyntaf fydd cyfeirio at yr SMR rhanbarthol (p'un ai'r awdurdod lleol neu'r Ymddiriedolaeth Archaeolegol ranbarthol sy'n ei gadw). Bydd yr SMR yn darparu gwybodaeth am y lleoliadau lle mae'n hysbys bod gweddillion archaeolegol yn bodoli, neu'n debygol o fodoli, ac am eu harwyddocâd cymharol.

Cyfeiriad: Canllawiau Cynllunio (Cymru): Polisi Cynllunio 1996, paragraff 136.

(b) Asesiadau Archaeolegol

12. Bydd yr ymgynghori hwn yn helpu i roi rhybudd ymlaen llaw i

ddarpar-ddatblygwyr ynghylch sensitifrwydd archaeolegol safle. O ganlyniad gallent ddymuno comisiynu eu hasesiad archaeolegol eu hunain gan gorff neu ymgynghorydd archaeolegol a chymwysterau proffesiynol. Nid oes rhaid i hyn gynnwys gwaith maes. Fel rheol mae'r asesiad yn golygu gwerthusiad desg o'r wybodaeth sy'n bodoli: gall wneud defnydd effeithiol o gofnodion darganfyddiadau blaenorol, gan gynnwys unrhyw fapiau hanesyddol a gedwir yn archifau'r awdurdod lleol ac mewn amgueddfeydd a swyddfeydd cofnodion lleol, neu o dechnegau arolygu geoffisegol. O dan rai amgylchiadau, gall fod angen Asesiad Amgylcheddol ffurfiol.

Cyfeiriad: Gweler Atodiad 1, paragraffau 22 a 23.

(c) Gwerthusiadau Maes

13. Lle mae trafodaethau cynnar gyda'r awdurdodau cynllunio lleol neu ymchwil y datblygwr ei hun yn dangos y gall gweddillion archaeolegol pwysig fodoli, dylai'r awdurdod cynllunio ofyn i'r darpar-ddatblygwr drefnu bod gwerthusiad archaeolegol yn cael ei gynnal yn y maes cyn i unrhyw benderfyniad ar y cais cynllunio gael ei wneud. Mae gwerthusiad o'r fath yn hollol wahanol i gloddiad archaeolegot llawn. Fel rheol mae'n weithred gyflym a rhad, sy'n cynnwys arolygu'r tir a/neu agor ffosydd ar raddfa fach, ond corff archaeolegol neu archaeolegydd â chymwysterau proffesiynol a ddylai wneud y gwaith. Mae gwerthusiadau fel hyn yn helpu i ddiffinio cymeriad a graddfa'r gweddillion archaeolegol sy'n bodoli yn ardal y datblygiad arfaethedig, ac felly nodi'r pwysau y dylid eu rhoi ar eu cadw. Mae hefyd yn darparu gwybodaeth ddefnyddiol ar gyfer adnabod dewisiadau posibl ar gyfer lleihau neu osgoi difrod.

Cyfeiriad: Mae Sefydliad yr Archaeolegwyr Maes (gweler Atodiad 2, paragraff 7) yn cyhoeddi cyfeirlyfr o aelodau (unigolion a chyrff archaeolegol) y gall datblygwyr ddymuno cysylltu â hwy.

14. Dylai'r awdurdodau cynllunio lleol ddisgwyl i ddatblygwyr ddarparu canlyniadau asesiadau a/neu werthusiadau o'r fath fel rhan o'u cais ar gyfer safleoedd lie ceir rheswm da dros gredu bod gweddillion o bwysigrwydd archaeolegol yn bodoli. Os nad yw'r datblygwyr yn fodlon gwneud hynny o'u gwirfodd, gall yr awdurdod cynllunio ddymuno ystyried a fyddai'n briodol cyfarwyddo'r ceisydd i roi rhagor o

wybodaeth. Bydd angen i'r awdurdodau ystyried gwrthod caniatâd i gynigion nad ydynt wedi'u dogfennu'n ddigonol.

Cyfeiriad: Rheoliad 4 o'r Rheoliadau Cynllunio Gwlad a Thref (Ceisiadau) 1988.

(d) Ymgynghori gan yr Awdurdodau Cynllunio

15. Pan gaiff ceisiadau cynllunio eu gwneud heb drafod ymlaen llaw gyda'r awdurdodau cynllunio lleol, dylai'r awdurdodau geisio nodi'r ceisiadau hynny sydd â goblygiadau archaeolegol, ac asesu eu heffaith archaeolegol debygol trwy ymgynghori â Swyddog Archaeolegol yr awdurdod lleol, Archaeolegydd Parc Cenedlaethol neu'r Ymddiriedolaeth Archaeolegol ranbarthol. Pan welir bod cynnig datblygu penodol yn debygol o effeithio ar weddillion archaeolegol, gall fod angen gofyn i geiswyr ddarparu gwybodaeth fanylach ynghylch eu cynllun – er enghraifft, y math o seiliau sydd i'w defnyddio - neu gellir gofyn iddynt wneud gwerthusiad. Dylai'r awdurdodau cynllunio sicrhau hefyd fod ganddynt wybodaeth gyflawn am natur a phwysigrwydd y safle archaeolegol a'i gefndir. Dylent ofyn felly am gyngor archaeolegol. Yn achos cynnig datblygu sy'n debygol o effeithio ar safle heneb cofrestredig, mae'n ofynnol i'r awdurdodau cynllunio lleol ymgynghori â'r Ysgrifennydd Gwladol (Cadw). Mewn achosion eithriadol, lle codir materion o fwy na phwysigrwydd lleol, gellir galw ceisiadau i mewn i'w penderfynu gan yr Ysgrifennydd Gwladol.

Cyfeiriad: Erthygl 10(1)(n) o'r Gorchymyn Cynllunio Gwlad a Thref (Gweithdrefn Ddatblygu Gyffredinol) 1995.

Penderfyniadau Cynllunio

16. Mae'r Ysgrifennydd Gwladol yn cydnabod y bydd i ba raddau y gellir neu y dylid cadw gweddillion archaeolegol yn dibynnu ar nifer o ffactorau. Rhaid asesu'r achos dros gadw gweddillion archaeolegol ar ragoriaethau unigol pob achos, gan gymryd i ystyriaeth y polisïau archaeolegol mewn cynlluniau datblygu, ynghyd â phob polisi ac ystyriaeth berthnasol arall, gan gynnwys pwysigrwydd cynhenid y gweddillion, a mesur y rhain yn erbyn yr angen am y datblygiad arfaethedig.

Cyfeiriad: Canllawiau Cynllunio (Cymru): Polisi Cynllunio 1996, paragraff 134.

(a) Cadw Gweddillion Archaeolegol in-situ

17. Pan fydd gan yr awdurdod cynllunio ddigon o wybodaeth, mae yna amrediad o ddewisiadau ar gyfer penderfynu ar geisiadau cynllunio sy'n effeithio ar weddillion archaeolegol a'u cefndir. Lle bydd datblygiad arfaethedig yn effeithio ar weddillion archaeolegol o bwysigrwydd cenedlaethol, boed y rheiny wedi'u cofrestru ai peidio, a'u cefndir, dylai fod rhagdybiaeth o blaid eu cadwraeth ffisegol in situ h.y., rhagdybiaeth yn erbyn cynigion a fyddai'n golygu eu haddasu'n sylweddol neu'n peri difrod, neu a fyddai'n creu effaith sylweddol ar gefndir y gweddillion gweladwy. 0 dan rai amgylchiadau, gall fod yn bosibl cadw gweddillion archaeolegol pwysig lle mae datblygwyr yn paratoi cynlluniau cydymdeimladol drwy ddefnyddio, er enghraifft, sylfeini sy'n osgoi tarfu ar y gweddillion yn gyfan gwbl neu sy'n lleihau'r difrod trwy godi lefelau'r tir o dan strwythur nevrydd arfaethedig neu drwy leoli llecynnau wedi'u tirfunio neu fannau agored yn ofalus. Mae technegau ar gael i selio gweddillion archaeolegol o dan adeilad neu'r tirlun, gan sicrhau felly y cânt eu cadw at y dyfodol er nad oes modd eu cyrraedd am y tro.

Cyfeiriad: Canllawiau Cynllunio (Cymru): Polisi Cynllunio 1996, paragraffau 134 a 137.

(b) Cadw Gweddillion Archaeolegol drwy Gofnodi

18. Bydd yna achlysuron, yn enwedig lle mae gweddillion o bwysigrwydd llai o dan sylw, lle y gall yr awdurdodau cynllunio benderfynu nad yw arwyddocâd y gweddillion archaeolegol yn ddigonol o'i fesur yn erbyn yr holl ystyriaethau perthnasol eraill, gan gynnwys yr angen am ddatblygu, i gyfiawnhau eu cadwraeth ffisegol in situ, ac y dylai'r datblygiad arfaethedig fynd rhagddo. Mewn achosion o'r fath, bydd angen i'r awdurdodau cynllunio eu bodloni eu hunain fod y datblygwr wedi gwneud trefniadau priodol a boddhaol ar gyfer cloddio a chofnodi'r gweddillion archaeolegol a chyhoeddi'r canlyniadau. Os nad yw hyn eisoes wedi'i sicrhau trwy ryw fath o gytundeb gwirfoddol, dylai'r awdurdodau cynllunio ystyried rhoi caniatâd cynllunio o dan amodau sy'n darparu ar gyfer cloddio a chofnodi'r gweddillion cyn i'r datblygu ddechrau. Gall fod angen, fel y cam eithaf, i'r awdurdodau cynllunio lleol ystyried gwrthod caniatâd cynllunio lle nad yw'r datblygwyr yn ceisio darparu ar gyfer gweddittion pwysig.

Cyfeiriad: Canllawiau Cynllunio (Cymru): Polisi Cynllunio 1996, paragraff 138.

19. O safbwynt archaeolegol, fel y dewis ail orau y dylid trin gwaith cloddio. Mae gwyddor archaeoleg yn datblygu'n gyflym. Mae cloddio'n golygu dinistr llwyr i dystiolaeth (heblaw'r arteffactau a all gael eu symud) y mae bron yn sicr y gallai technegau'r dyfodol dynnu mwy o wybodaeth ohoni nag sy'n bosibl ar hyn o bryd. Gall gwaith cloddio lyncu arian ac amser, a gall y bydd rhaid pwyso a mesur y darganfyddiadau ar frys yn erbyn fframwaith ymchwil annigonol. Gwell felly yw cadw gweddillion archaeolegol pwysig in situ.

(c) Trefniadau ar gyfer Ymchwilio i Weddillion Archaeolegol, gan gynnwys Cyllid

20. **Dylid cyflawni gwaith ymchwil archaeolegol, megis cloddio a chofnodi, cyn i'r datblygiad ddechrau, gan weithio yn ôl briff a baratowyd gan yr awdurdod cynllunio (gan gyfeirio at eu hymgynghorwyr archaeolegol). Gellir ymchwilio trwy gytundebau a wneir rhwng y datblygwr, yr archaeolegydd a'r awdurdod cynllunio. Dylai cytundebau o'r fath sicrhau a gweithredu cynllun priodol o ymchwilio archaeolegol, yn ôl amserlen gytûn, a darparu ar gyfer cyhoeddi canlyniadau'r gwaith cloddio wedyn.** Mewn achosion penodol pan fo'r datblygwr yn gorff cymunedol dielw, megis ymddiriedolaeth elusennol neu gymdeithas tai, sy'n methu â chodi arian i ddarparu ar gyfer cloddio a chofnodi dilynol heb galedi amhriodol, neu yn achos unigolyn sydd yn yr un ffordd heb fodd i ariannu gwaith o'r fath, gellir gwneud cais i'r Ysgrifennydd Gwladol am gymorth ariannol.

21. Gall cytundebau ar gyfer ymchwiliadau archaeolegol, cyhoeddi canlyniadau a'u hadneuo mewn archifdy cyhoeddus dynodedig fod ar sawl gwahanol ffurf. Er enghraifft, hwyrach y bydd y datblygwyr neu eu hymgynghorwyr archaeolegol a'r awdurdodau cynllunio lleol yn dymuno gwneud cytundeb cynllunio gwirfoddol. Gall y cytundebau hyn ddarparu ar gyfer cloddio a chofnodi safleoedd cyn i waith datblygu ddechrau. Mae cytundebau gwirfoddol yn debygol o ddarparu mwy o hyblygrwydd a budd i'r holl bartïon nag y gellid ei ddarparu trwy ddulliau statudol eraill. Mae ganddynt y fantais o nodi'n eglur raddau ymrwymiad y datblygwr ac felly maent yn lleihau ansicrwydd ynghylch goblygiadau ariannol gorfod ildio i unrhyw gyfyngiadau archaeolegol a phosibilrwydd oedi annisgwyl yn y rhaglen adeiladu.

Cyfeiriad: Adran 106 o Ddeddf Cynllunio Gwlad a Thref 1990 sy'n cynnwys pwerau statudol ynglyn â rhwymedigaethau cynllunio a phwerau statudol tebyg eraill.

Gellir cael cytundebau enghreifftiol rhwng dablygwyr a'r corff archaeolegol priodol sy'n rheoleiddio ymchwiliadau a chloddiadau safleoedd archaelegol oddi wrth Sefydliad yr Archaeolegwyr Maes (gweler Atodiad 2, paragraff 7).

Amodau Cynllunio

22. **Dylai'r awdurdodau cynllunio geisio sicrhau y caiff gwrthdrawiadau posibl eu datrys a chytundebau gyda datblygwyr eu cwblhau cyn rhoi caniatâd cynilunio.** Lle bo'n rhaid defnyddio amodau cynllunio, dylai'r awdurdodau sicrhau eu bod yn deg, yn rhesymol ac yn ymarferol. Mae'n agored i'r awdurdod cynllunio lleol osod amodau wedi'u cynllunio i ddiogelu heneb ac i sicrhau bod briff gwylio yn cael ei gadw (naill ai'n barhaus neu o bryd i'w gilydd) yn ystod y cyfnod adeiladu gan archaeolegydd â chymwysterau addas. Mae amodau ar y llinellau hyn yn gymorth i sicrhau y gellir eu cloddio, eu cofnodi ac adrodd arnynt os caiff gweddillion o arwyddocâd archaeolegol eu tarfu yn ystod y gwaith.

Cyfeiriad: Cylchlythyr 35/95 y Swyddfa Gymreig, paragraff 81.

Canllawiau Cynllunio (Cymru) Polisi Cynllunio 1996, paragraff 137.

23. **Mewn achosion lle mae'r awdurdodau cynllunio wedi penderfynu y gellir rhoi caniatâd cynllunio, ond ar sail amod negyddol, awgrymir y model canlynol:**

"Ni chaiff yr un datblygiad ddigwydd o fewn yr ardal a nodir [sef yr ardal o ddiddordeb archaeolegol] nes bod y ceisydd, neu eu hasiantau neu eu holynwyr mewn teitl, wedi sicrhau bod rhaglen o waith archaeolegol wedi'i gweithredu yn unol â chynllun ymchwilio ysgrifenedig sydd wedi'i gyflwyno gan y ceisydd ac wedi'i gymeradwyo gan yr awdurdod cynllunio lleol." (Bydd datblygwyr yn dymuno sicrhau, wrth lunio cynilun, fod amserlen ar gyfer yr archwiliad wedi'i gynnwys o fewn manylion y cynllun cytûn).

Cyfeiriad: Cylchlythyr 35/95 y Swyddfa Gymreig, Atodiad A, amod enghreifftiol 55.

Canllawiau Cynllunio (Cymru): Polisi Cynllunio 1996, paragraff 139.

Darganfod Gweddillion Archaeolegol yn Ystod Gwaith Datblygu

24. Diben y canllawiau uchod yw lleihau'r achlysuron lle Mae problemau cwbl annisgwyl yn codi yn ystod gwaith datblygu. Er hynny, ac er gwaethaf yr ymchwil orau cyn cais cynllunio, gall fod adegau pan na ddaw presenoldeb gweddillion archaeolegol i'r golwg ond pan fydd y datblygu wedi dechrau. Gall datblygwyr ddymuno ystyried eu hyswirio'u hunain yn erbyn y perygl o golled sylweddol tra'n diogelu diddordeb gweddillion hanesyddol a ddarganfyddir yn annisgwyl ar y safle. Nid yw gwrthdrawiadau a all ddigwydd fel arall rhwng datblygwyr ac archaeolegwyr bob amser yn hawdd i'w datrys. Lle bernir bod darganfyddiadau archaeolegol newydd o ddiddordeb cenedlaethol gan yr Ysgrifennydd Gwladol, yn unol â'r meini prawf y mae wedi'u cyhoeddi, mae gan yr Ysgrifennydd Gwladol bŵer i gofrestru'r gweddillion. Os felly, byddai angen i'r datblygwyr geisio caniatâd heneb cofrestredig ar wahân cyn iddynt barhau â'r gwaith. Mae hefyd yn agored i'r awdurdod cynllunio neu i'r Ysgrifennydd Gwladol dynnu caniatâd cynllunio yn ôl os bernir bod hynny'n angenrheidiol, ac mewn achos o'r fath mae yna ddarpariaeth ar gyfer iawndal. Ond, ran amlaf, dylai fod yn bosibl i'r partïon ddatrys y materion trwy drafodaeth wirfoddol a gwneud trefniadau sy'n foddhaol i'r ddau barti.

Cyfeiriad: Gweler Atodiadau 1 a 3.

C: DILEU PPG 16 (CYMRU)

25. Mae'r cyngor yn y Cylchlythyr hwn yn disodli'r cyngor yn **PPG16 (Cymru)** sydd drwy hyn wedi'i ddileu.

Awdurdodau Unedol   )   **T J Cassidy**
Parciau Cenedlaethol   ) Cymru   Prif Weithredwr
                                                Cadw: Henebion Cymru

ATODIAD 1

TREFNIADAU DEDDFWRIAETHOL

Cofrestru Henebion o Bwysigrwydd Cenedlaethol

1. O dan Ddeddf Mannau Archaeolegol a Henebion 1979 (Deddf 1979) mae'n ddyletswydd ar yr Ysgrifennydd Gwladol i lunio a chadw cofrestr o henebion;

mae gan yr henebion ar y gofrestr ddiogelwch statudol. Dewis yr Ysgrifennydd Gwladol yw cynnwys henebion ar y gofrestr er bod rhaid i henebion a ychwanegir fod o bwysigrwydd cenedlaethol. Nodir y meini prawf anstatudol ar gyfer cofrestru a gyhoeddwyd ym 1983 (a'u hailddatgan ym 1990) yn Atodiad 3. Mae'r Arolygiaeth Henebion yn gyfrifol am roi cyngor ynghylch pa henebion y dylid eu hystyried ar gyfer cofrestru ac a ddylid dadgofrestru heneb neu a ddylid adolygu'r cofnod neu'r ardal sydd wedi'i diogelu. Yn ymarferol, mae llawer o'r argymhellion yn deillio o awgrymiadau a wneir i'r Arolygiaeth gan weithwyr maes Comisiwn Brenhinol Henebion Cymru (RCAHMW), Ymddiriedolaethau Archaeoleg Cymru, awdurdodau lleol neu barciau cenedlaethol. Ni ellir cofrestru anheddau a feddiannir nac eglwysi a ddefnyddir at ddibenion eglwysig.

2. Fel rheol ymgynghorir â pherchnogion cyn ychwanegu safleoedd at y gofrestr, er nad yw hyn yn ofyniad statudol a'i bod yn bosibl na fydd amser bob tro mewn achosion lle mae'r datblygu ar fin cychwyn. Caiff safleoedd cofrestredig eu cofrestru fel pridiant yn y Gofrestrfa Pridiannau Tir Leol a'u hysbysu i'r Cofnod Safleoedd a Henebion. Mae Cadw'n cyhoeddi rhestrau o henebion cofrestredig. Dylid cyfeirio ymholiadau ynghylch y rhestrau hyn at yr Adran Gweinyddu Henebion, Cadw: Henebion Cymru, Adeilad y Goron, Parc Cathays, Caerdydd CFI 3NQ. Ffôn 01222 500200.

3. Mae'r gofrestr bresennol o bron 3,000 o safleoedd wedi'i llunio dros gyfnod o fwy na chan mlynedd, ers cyflwyno'r diogelwch statudol cyntaf i henebion ym 1882. Ond, cydnabyddir nad yw'n cynnwys sampl ddigonol o'r gweddillion archaeolegol helaeth y gwyddys eu bod wedi goroesi yng Nghymru. Mae Cadw felly wedi dechrau rhaglen i werthuso'r holl weddillion archaeolegol hysbys yng Nghymru ac i nodi'r rhai a all fod yn addas i'w cofrestru. Mae'r ymarfer hwn yn cael ei gynnal mewn ymgynghoriad agos â buddiannau archaeolegol a disgwylir cynnydd sylweddol yn y nifer o henebion o ganlyniad i'r ymarfer. Ond hyd yn oed wedyn, oherwydd y meini prawf llym ar gyfer cofrestru, mae nifer fawr o safleoedd sydd wedi'u nodi'n debygol o barhau heb eu cofrestru. Bydd a gânt eu cofrestru ai peidio yn dibynnu ar werth y gweddillion, ymrwymiad perchnogion yr henebion a'r cyhoedd a pholisïau'r awdurdodau lleol.

4. Fel enghraifft ddethol o archaeoleg y genedl, mae'r gofrestr yn wahanol i'r rhestr fwy cynhwysfawr o adeiladau o ddiddordeb pensaernïol neu hanesyddol arbennig a lunnir o dan Adran I o Ddeddf Cynllunio (Adeiladau Rhestredig ac Ardaloedd Cadwraeth) 1990. Ond yn fras, mae henebion cofrestredig yn cymharu o ran eu pwysigrwydd ag adeiladau rhestredig Gradd 1 neu Radd II*. Lle mae adeiladau wedi'u rhestru ac wedi'u cofrestru, y ddeddfwriaeth henebion sy'n cael blaenoriaeth ac mae angen caniatâd heneb cofrestredig yn hytrach na chaniatâd adeilad rhestredig ar gyfer gwaith.

Rheoli Gwaith ar Henebion Cofrestredig

5. Pan fydd heneb wedi'i gofrestru, mae angen caniatâd yr Ysgrifennydd Gwladol cyn gwneud unrhyw waith a fyddai'n golygu dymchwel, dinistrio, difrodi, symud, trwsio, addasu, ychwanegu at, boddi neu orchuddio'r heneb. Mae cwmpas y rheolaeth felly'n fwy helaeth a mwy manwl na'r rheolaeth a gymhwysir at adeiladau rhestredig. Dim ond ar gyfer cynigion manwl y gelfir rhoi caniatâd ac yn wahanol i ganiatâd cynllunio nid oes darpariaeth ar gyfer rhoi caniatâd amlinellol. Er hynny mae yna ddeg caniatâd dosbarth mewn grym ar hyn o bryd sy'n galluogi perchnogion i fynd ymlaen â rhai mathau penodol o waith – cânt eu rhestru yn Atodiad 4. Mae gan yr Ysgrifennydd Gwladol bŵer i ddiddymu neu ddiwygio caniatâd (boed wedi'i ganiatáu yn dilyn cais neu wedi'i ganiatáu yn dybiedig trwy ganiatâd dosbarth).

6. Er y gall henebion ar dir y Goron gael eu cofrestru (Adran 50 o Ddeddf 1979), mae gwaith gan neu ar ran y Llywodraeth ar dir o'r fath wedi'i esemptio o reolau caniatâd henebion statudol ar hyn o bryd. Er hynny, mae'n dal i ddod o dan y weithdrefn anstatudol a adnabyddir fel cliriad heneb cofrestredig sy'n dilyn gweithdrefnau tebyg i ganiatâd heneb cofrestredig.

7. Nodir ffurflen gais am ganiatâd heneb cofretredig mewn Rheoliadau [Rheoliadau Henebion (Ceisiadau am Ganiatâd Heneb Cofrestredig) 1981] a gellir cael ffurflenni oddi wrth Cadw.

8. Lle bo'n briodol, bydd yr Ysgrifennydd Gwladol yn ymgynghori â Chomisiwn Brenhinol ar Henebion Cymru, Cyngor Archaeoleg Prydain, yr Ymddiriedolaeth Archaeolegol Gymreig ranbarthol a'r awdurdod lleol perthnasol ynghylch ceisiadau am ganiatâd heneb cofrestredig. Gellir ymgynghori â buddiannau archaeolegol neu berthnasol eraill hefyd, yn ôl yr angen.

9. Mae'n ofynnol o dan baragraff 3(2) o Ran 1 o Atodlen 1 o Ddeddf 1979 i'r Ysgrifennydd Gwladol gynnal ymchwiliad lleol neu roi cyfle i'r ceisydd am ganiatâd heneb cofrestredig gael gwrandawiad cyn gwneud penderfyniad ar gais. Fel rheol gyffredinol, dim ond yn yr achosion hynny lle mae mater cysylltiedig ger ei fron yn ffurfiol ar gyfer penderfyniad ac i fod i gael gwrandawiad mewn ymchwiliad cyhoeddus, e.e. apêl yn erbyn gwrthod caniatâd cynllunio, y mae'n bolisi ganddo cynnal ymchwiliad cyhoeddus, yn niffyg cais oddi wrth y ceisydd.

10. I helpu ceisydd i benderfynu a yw'n dymuno ymarfer ei hawl i gael gwrandawiad, arfer yr Ysgrifennydd Gwladol yw rhoi'r gwahoddiad mewn llythyr yn nodi penderfyniad dros dro ar gais ar sail y dystiolaeth a gyflwynwyd gydag ef, unrhyw sylwadau a wnaethpwyd gan y rhai yr ymgynghorwyd â hwy neu bartïon sydd â diddordeb a'r cyngor a roddwyd gan yr Arolygydd Rhanbarthol He-nebion. Bydd yr Arolygydd rhanbarthol wedi ymweld â'r safle, lle mae hynny'n angenrheidiol, ac wedi datrys unrhyw amheuon neu amwysedd

ynghylch natur y gwaith arfaethedig cyn cyflwyno'i argymhelliad manwl gan gynnwys rhestr o amodau i'w hatodi i delerau unrhyw ganiatâd. Gall trafodaethau safle roi gwybodaeth am geisiadau ond maent yn gyfan gwbl heb ragfarn i ystyriaeth yr Ysgrifennydd Gwladol ar gais am ganiatâd heneb cofrestredig.

Polisi'r Ysgrifennydd Gwladol

11. Mae'r Ysgrifennydd Gwladol o'r farn mai cadw henebion yw prif ddiben cofrestru ac felly y dylai fod yna ragdybiaeth o blaid eu cadwraeth ffisegol wrth ystyried ceisiadau am ganiatâd i wneud gwaith iddynt hy rhagdybiaeth yn erbyn cynigion a fyddai'n golygu eu haddasu'n sylweddol neu achosi difrod iddynt, neu a fyddai'n cael effaith sylweddol ar gefndir gweddillion gweladwy. Wrth ystyried ceisiadau am ganiatâd heneb cofrestredig felly, bydd yr Ysgrifennydd Gwladol yn disgwyl i'r ceiswyr (yn enwedig lle bwriedir gosod piblinellau, ceblau neu garthffosydd o dan y ddaear), ddangos nad oes llwybr na lleoliad ymarferol arall yn bodoli, sy'n osgoi'r heneb, a bod yr angen i wneud y gwaith yn fwy na'r rhagdybiaeth o blaid diogelu heneb o bwysigrwydd cenedlaethol.

12. Lle mae adeilad wedi'i restru ac wedi'i gofrestru, mae Adran 61 o Ddeddf Cynllunio (Adeiladau Rhestredig ac Ardaloedd Cadwraeth) 1990 yn darparu nad oes angen gwneud cais am ddymchwel, addasu neu ymestyn y strwythur ond o dan ddarpariaethau Adran 2 o Ddeddf 1979 gan y tybir bod y ddeddfwriaeth honno'n cael blaenoriaeth. Wrth benderfynu ar gais am waith ar adeilad o'r fath, bydd yr Ysgrifennydd Gwladol yn parhau i roi sylw i'w bolisïau cyhoeddedig ynghylch adeiladau rhestredig yn enwedig ynglyn â'r angen i archwilio dibenion eraill, lle caiff dymchwel ei gynnig, ac i gadw nodweddion pwysig lle caiff addasiadau eu cynnig.

Troseddau yn Gysylltiedig â Henebion Cofrestredig

13. Creodd Deddf 1979 nifer o droseddau'n gysylltiedig â henebion. Gall erlyniadau llwyddiannus gyda chyhoeddusrwydd da yn erbyn y rhai sy'n gwneud gwaith diawdurdod i henebion, neu'n difrodi henebion, fod yn ataliad gwerthfawr i ddifrod neu ddinistr bwriadol ar henebion, a pholisi'r Swyddfa Gymreig yw dechrau achos lle bernir y gellir cynnal achos da. Mae'r Ddeddf yn darparu nifer o amddiffyniadau gan gynnwys anwybodaeth wirioneddol a rhesymol o statws cofrestredig y safle, a'r angen am waith at ddibenion iechyd a diogelwch.

14. Mae Adran 28 o Ddeddf 1979 yn ei gwneud yn drosedd dinistrio neu ddifrodi heneb sydd wedi'i ddiogelu – a ddiffinnir fel heneb cofrestredig neu unrhyw heneb o dan berchnogaeth neu warchodaeth yr Ysgrifennydd Gwladol neu awdurdod lleol yn rhinwedd Deddf 1979. Nid yw'r pŵer i erlyn troseddwyr wedi'i gyfyngu i'r Ysgrifennydd Gwladol. Gall awdurdodau lleol a'r Heddlu

hefyd ddechrau erlyniadau pan ydynt hwy wedi darganfod troseddau.

15. Am nad oes gan y mwyafrif o'r awdurdodau lleol yng Nghymru arbenigedd archaeolegol mewnol, bydd yr Ysgrifennydd Gwladol (trwy Cadw) yn parhau i gymryd yr awenau wrth ymchwilio ac erlyn troseddau sy'n deillio o ddifrod i henebion cofrestredig pan gaiff digwyddiadau eu hadrodd iddo, neu eu darganfod ganddo. Yn achos heneb cofrestredig sy'n perthyn i awdurdod lleol, neu o dan warchodaeth awdurdod lleol, byddai fel rheol yn disgwyl i'r awdurdod lleol fod yn gyfrifol am erlyn troseddwyr er y bydd cyngor archaeolegol ar gael oddi wrth Cadw os oes ei angen (gan gynnwys darparu tyst arbenigol). Awgrymir felly y dylai'r awdurdodau lleol gysylltu â Cadw cyn erlyn. Bydd yr awdurdodau lleol yn parhau yn gyfan gwbl gyfrifol am erlyniadau sy'n deillio o ddifrod i henebion sydd wedi'u diogelu ond heb eu cofrestru.

Canfodyddion Metalau

16. Mae'r mwyafrif o ddefnyddwyr canfodyddion metal yn ymddwyn yn gyfrifol. Er hynny, gall defnyddio canfodyddion metalau yn anghyfreithlon greu difrod difrifol i henebion - nid yn unig i ffabrig yr heneb, ond hefyd i'w ddehongliad a'i ddealltwriaeth pan fydd arteffactau wedi'u symud o'u cyd-destun archaeolegol. O dan Adran 42 o Ddeddf 1979 mae'n drosedd defnyddio canfodyddion metalau mewn man wedi'i ddiogelu (unrhyw le sydd naill ai'n safle heneb cofrestredig neu'n heneb sy'n perthyn i'r Ysgrifennydd Gwladol, neu yng ngofal yr Ysgrifennydd Gwladol, neu awdurdod lleol) heb ganiatâd ymlaen llaw gan yr Ysgrifennydd Gwladol y bydd angen gwneud cais ysgrifenedig iddo. Ni chaiff caniatâd ei roi fel rheol ac eithrio at ddibenion ymchwil bona fide, di-ddinistr neu i adfer eitemau gwerthfawr o eiddo sydd wedi'u colli, e.e. modrwyon ac oriaduron.

Rheoli Henebion

17. Ni all diogelwch statudol ynddo'i hun sicrhau cadwraeth heneb yn y dyfodol. Ran amlaf mae'n hanfodol datblygu cynllun rheoli a gwneud gwaith cynnal-a-chadw rheolaidd i rwystro dirywiad graddol adeilad neu safle. Mae ar ddadfeilion, yn gymaint ag adeiladau a ddefnyddir, angen mân waith trwsio cyson i rwystro'u dirywiad. Gall henebion mewn caeau glas gael eu difrodi'n ddifrifol yn sgil esgeulustod sy'n gadael i blâu a llwyni neu goed gynyddu, neu oherwydd arferion ffermio anaddas. Er mai'r perchennog biau'r cyfrifoldeb am drwsio a chynnal henebion, gall Cadw ddarparu cyngor a chymorth ariannol o ddau brif fath ar gyfer cadw safleoedd pwysig.

18. Rhoir grantiau o dan Adran 24 o Ddeddf 1979 gan yr Ysgrifennydd Gwladol yn bennaf tuag at gostau cadw, cynnal a rheoli henebion, ac yn llai cyffredin felly eu rhoi tuag at brynu henebion sydd mewn perygl o gael eu difrodi neu eu

dinistrio.

19. Gall cytundebau rheoli a wneir o dan Adran 17 o Ddeddf 1979 naill ai gan yr Ysgrifennydd Gwladol neu gan yr awdurdodau lleol roi cymorth ariannol i ddeiliaid y tir er mwyn hybu rheolaeth fanteisiol ar henebion mewn caeau fel arfer, drwy waith megis rheoli plâu a chwyn a rheoli lefelau stocio. Mae'r cytundebau'n rhedeg am nifer o flynyddoedd a gallant gynnwys taliad cychwynnol i dalu costau unrhyw waith cyfalaf, megis ffensio.

20. Mae Cadw'n darparu cyngor ar reoli henebion, yn bennaf trwy'r Arolygiaeth Henebion ond hefyd trwy rwydwaith o Wardeniaid Henebion Maes sydd wedi'u neilltuo i ardaloedd unigol. Mae'r Wardeniaid yn arbennig yn archwilio henebion ar sail reolaidd, gan adrodd ar eu cyflwr ac maent ar gael i drafod mesurau gyda pherchnogion/deiliaid ac awdurdodau lleol ar gyfer gwell rheolaeth ar safleoedd.

Cadw Drwy Gofnodion

21. 0 dan adran 45 o Ddeddf 1979, gall yr Ysgrifennydd Gwiadol gynnig cymorth ariannol ar gyfer cadw drwy gofnodi. Yn nhermau ansawdd, rhaid i'r safleoedd fod o bwysigrwydd cenedlaethol wedi'u mesur yn erbyn y meini prawf cyhoeddedig (Atodiad 3). Rhaid i'r gwaith cloddio gyd-fynd â blaenoriaethau academaidd cyfredol. Mae'r pwyslais presennol yn fwy ac yn fwy ar brojectau a all fwrw goleuni ar gwestiynau ymchwil pwysig a llenwi bylchau yn ein gwybodaeth. Ni threfnir bod arian ar gael fel rheol oni bai bod y safle o dan fygythiad.

Asesiad Amgylcheddol

22. Ar gyfer rhai mathau o ddatblygiad (wed''u rhestru yn Atodienni 1 a 2 o Reoliadau Cynllunio Gwlad a Thref (Asesu Effeithiau Amgylcheddol) 1988, fel y'u diwygiwyd) gall asesiad amgylcheddol (AA) ffurfiol fod yn angenrheidiol. Lie mae AA yn ofynnol, rhaid i'r datblygwr ddarparu datganiad amgylcheddol yn nodi'r wybodaeth a bennir yn Atodlen 3 o'r Rheoliadau ynghylch y safle ac effeithiau sylweddol tebygol y datblygiad arfaethedig ar yr amgylchedd. Dylai hyn gynnwys gwybodaeth am unrhyw effeithiau sylweddol ar asedau perthnasol a'r dreftadaeth ddiwylliannol, megis nodweddion archaeolegol ac arteffactau dynol eraill, a'r mesurau a ragwelir i osgoi, lleihau neu adfer effeithiau andwyol.

23. Lle mae datblygiad y mae angen AA ar ei gyfer yn effeithio ar safle heneb cofrestredig, rhaid ymgynghori â'r Ysgrifennydd Gwladol ynghylch y datganiad amgylcheddol a gyflwynir ac fe all ef ddarparu gwybodaeth i helpu i baratoi'r datganiad (er nad yw'n ofynnol iddo wneud hynny). Gwelir rhagor o wybodaeth am weithdrefnau AA yng Nghylchlythyr 23/88 y Swyddfa Gymreig ac yn y llyfryn *Environmental Assessment - A Guide to the Procedures* a gyhoeddwyd gan

Wasg Ei Mawrhydi.

Parthau Cynllunio Syml (PCS)

24. Nodir y darpariaethau ynglyn â PCs yn adrannau 82 i 87 ac Atodlen 7 o Ddeddf Cynllunio Gwlad a Thref 1990 fel y'i diwygiwyd gan Ddeddf Cynllunio ac lawndal 1991. Effaith PCS yw rhoi caniatâd cynllunio i fathau penodol o ddatblygiad o fewn y cynllun. Lle mae gweddillion archaeolegol yn gorwedd o fewn ardal y PCS arfaethedig, gall fod yn angenrheidiol teilwra'r cynllun i ddarparu ar eu cyfer. Mae henebion o fewn PCS yn dal yn destun caniatâd heneb cofrestredig.

Planning Guidance (Wales) Planning Policy
[Extract]

Archaeology

134. Where nationally important archaeological remains, whether scheduled or not, and their settings are affected by proposed development, there should be a presumption in favour of their physical preservation. Cases involving lesser archaeological remains will not always be so clear cut and planning authorities will need to weigh the relative importance of archaeology against other factors including the need for the proposed development.

135. Archaeological remains identified and scheduled as being of national importance should normally be earmarked in development plans for preservation. Authorities should bear in mind that not all nationally important remains meriting preservation will necessarily be scheduled; such remains and, in appropriate circumstances, other unscheduled archaeological remains of more than local importance, may also be identified in development plans as particularly worthy of preservation.

136. The needs of archaeology and development can be reconciled, and potential conflict very much reduced, if developers discuss their preliminary plans for development with the planning authority at an early stage. In certain circumstances, this may involve the developer in commissioning an archaeological assessment (sometimes as part of a wider environmental assessment) before submitting a planning application. If important remains are thought to exist at the development site, it is reasonable for the planning authority to request the prospective developer to arrange for an archaeological field evaluation to be carried out before any decision on the planning application is taken.

137. Planning authorities should not include in their development plans policies requiring developers to finance archaeological works in return for the grant of planning permission. By the same token, developers should not expect to obtain planning permission for archaeologically damaging development merely because they arrange for the recording of sites whose physical preservation *in situ* is both desirable (because of their level of importance) and feasible.

138. Where planning authorities decide that physical preservation *in situ* of archaeological remains is not justified in the circumstances of the case and that development resulting in the destruction of the archaeological remains should proceed, it would be entirely reasonable for the planning authority to satisfy itself, before granting planning

permission, that the developer has made appropriate and satisfactory provision for the excavation and recording of the remains and the publication of the results of that work.

139. In cases when planning authorities have decided that planning permission may be granted but wish to secure the provision of archaeological excavation and the subsequent recording of the remains, it is open to them to do so by use of a negative condition, i.e., a condition prohibiting the carrying out of the development until such time as works or other action, e.g., an excavation, have been carried out by a third party.

140. Scheduled ancient monuments are exempt from conservation area control; Scheduled Monument Consent for proposed works to a scheduled ancient monument must be sought from the Secretary of State. Planning permission alone is not sufficient to authorise the works.

BIBLIOGRAPHY

Biddle, Martin (1994). *What Future for British Archaeology?* (Opening address to the Eighth Annual Conference of the IFA). Oxford, Oxbow.

Cleere, H. F. (1984). *Approaches to the Archaeological Heritage.* Cambridge, C.U.P.

Colcutt, Simon (1997). *Archaeological Works and Development Control: A Case Study in Approval of Funding,* J.P.L., 797-814.

Darvill, Timothy (1996). Review of McGill (1995), in *The Field Archaeologist,* No.25, 21-22. Manchester, IFA.

Darvill, T., Saunders, A., and Startin, B. (1987). *A Question of National Importance: Approaches to the Evaluation of Ancient Monuments for the Monuments Protection Programme in England,* Antiquity 61, 393-408.

Darvill, Timothy and Atkins, Meryl (1991). *Regulating Archaeological Work by Contract.* IFA TP 8. Birmingham, IFA.

Evans, D. Morgan, Pugh-Smith, John and Samuels, John (1994). *World Heritage Sites: Beauty Contest or Planning Constraint?* J.P.L., 503-508.

Garratt-Frost, S., Harrison, G., and Logie, J.G. (1992). *The Law and Burial Archaeology.* IFA TP 11. Birmingham, IFA.

Hunter, John and Ralston, Ian (1993). *Archaeological Resource Management in the U.K: An Introduction.* Stroud, Alan Sutton.

Jewkes, P. (1993). *Protecting the Historic Built Environment,* J.P.L., 417-422.

Lambrick, G. (1993). *Environmental Assessment and the Cultural Heritage: Principles and Practice* in Ralston, Ian and Thomas, Roger ed. Environmental Assessment and Archaeology. IFA OP 5, 9-20. Birmingham, IFA.

869

Manley, John (1987). *Archaeology and Planning: A Welsh Perspective (Pt. I and Pt. II)*, J.P.L., 466-484; 552-563.

McGill, Greg (1995). *Building on the Past: A Guide to Archaeology and the Development Process*. London, E. & F.N. Spon.

Mynors, Charles (1993). *The Extent of Listing*, J.P.L., 99-111.

Mynors, Charles (1995). *Listed buildings and Conservation Areas*. London, Longman.

O'Keefe, P.J. (1993). *The European Convention on the Protection of the Archaeological Heritage*, Antiquity 67, 406-413.

Pugh-Smith, John and Samuels, John (1993). *PPG16: Two years on*, J.P.L., 203-210.

Pugh-Smith, John and Samuels, John (1996). *Archaeology in Law*. London, Sweet & Maxwell.

Ross, M. (1991). *Planning and the Heritage*. London, E. and F.N. Spon.

Scarse, T. (1991). *Archaeology and Planning - a Case for Full Integration*, J.P.L., 1103-1112.

Suddards, Roger W. (1988). *Listed Buildings: the Law and Practice of Historic Buildings, Ancient Monuments and Conservation Areas*. London, Sweet & Maxwell. 2nd edn.

Suddards, Roger W. and Hargreaves, June M. (1996). *Listed Buildings: the Law and Practice of Listed Buildings, Ancient Monuments and Conservation Areas*. London, Sweet and Maxwell.

INDEX

abandonment of objects 226
access 31, 184-6, 472-4, 530, 546, 830
  AAIs 125-6, 133, 186
  adjacent land 183
  English Heritage 25
  Europe (EA) 285, 287
  grants and grant aid 188
  listed buildings 341, 369, 391, 397, 707, 709, 802
  management agreements 191
  NHMF 37-8
  offences 80, 158, 185-6
  RCHM(e) records 29, 30
  restriction 173
  scheduled monuments 77-80, 97, 105, 119-21, 184-6
  treasure 238, 239, 629
  upkeep and repair 751
  Wales 788, 802
Accounts Directive and Financial Memorandum (EH) 13, 15
acknowledgement payments 64
acquisition by agreement 15, 65, 179, 183
adjacent land 16, 121, 183, 329, 545, 751
advertisements
  AAIs 128
  control 726-7, 774-6
  ecclesiastical exemption 358
  listed buildings 319, 342, 352-3
  scheduled monuments 99
advice 18-20, 22, 24-5, 29, 194-6, 680-2
  Wales 195-6, 770-1, 835-42

Advisory Board for Redundant Churches 758
aerial archaeology 32, 55, 59, 69, 287
aftercare works 120
agriculture 402, 407, 544, 553, 697
  AAIs 131
  class consents 85-6, 89, 92-3
  compensation 198
  Europe 263-4, 275, 277
  hedgerows 327-8
  management agreements 192
  operations notice exemption 595
  scheduled monuments 120
  Wales 772, 834, 847
Alton Building Preservation Trust 396
analysis 26, 40, 48, 55, 469
Ancient Monuments Board for England 11
Ancient Monuments Society 355, 786
animus revertendi 230-1, 233, 241
annexation 310, 315, 710-11
  Wales 790-1
appeals 8-9, 371-3, 428-9, 486-97, 697, 798
  AAIs 128
  AMAA (1979) 549-51, 560-1
  authorisation of development 401, 427-30
  compulsory purchase 751-2
  conservation areas 717, 723, 769, 773
  conservation policy 525-6
  de-listing 743

enforcement procedures 374,
376-9, 427-30, 713, 801
Europe (EA) 280, 285-6
fines for damage to scheduled
monument 168
hedgerows 331
listed buildings 304, 309, 320,
334, 340, 347, 370-3, 376-9,
706, 713
control 706, 713
enforcement notices 374,
376-9, 713, 801
repairs notices 395
Wales 781, 787, 798, 801
parks and gardens 325
planning considerations 434,
439, 442, 466, 468, 471,
474-5, 477, 483, 486-97
scheduled monument consent
100, 113-14, 148
scheduling of monuments 76,
93, 845
securing archaeological
facilities 499-503, 511,
516, 518, 521, 524
Wales 761, 766, 833, 845
conservation areas 769, 773
listed buildings 781, 787,
798, 801
appointments to heritage
organisations 8, 11-12, 29-30,
33
archaeological assessments and
evaluations 826-7, 837-8
AAIs 127, 139-40
applications for SMC 99, 104
consultants 51
Europe (EA) 288-90, 292-3
IFA 58

planning 438, 452-3, 466-70,
475, 477-9, 481-2, 484, 826-7
scheduled monument consent
84, 88, 89-90, 103, 105,
118-19
securing facilities 500-3, 514
treasure 229, 233, 247-8
Wales 836, 837-8, 839, 840,
866
see also desk-based assessments
archaeological facilities 400,
497-524
archaeological investigation 51,
71, 80, 530, 549, 553-4
advice and assistance 194-6
AAIs 126, 132-40
authorisation of development
410, 420
contracts 811-12, 814
English Heritage 19-20, 22,
25, 26
Europe 301
facilities 498, 500-1, 504-5,
516-18
listed buildings 369
local authorities 38, 42, 44,
46-8
NHMF 36-7
operations notices 594
parks and gardens 324
planning 400, 444, 451-3,
462-4, 469-70, 472-4,
477, 481-6, 829-31
scheduled monuments 68
consent 96-7, 103, 109,
112-13, 118, 120-2
Wales 840, 841, 842
Area Inspector of Ancient
Monuments 189

Areas of Archaeological
  Importance (AAIs) 7, 125-40
  access 125-6, 133, 186
  authorisation of development
    409, 422
  compensation 136, 204
  English Heritage 23, 127-8,
    132, 133, 135-6, 138-9
  injunctions 137, 156
  landscapes 333
  legislation 530, 547, 551
  metal detectors 138, 139, 174
  offences 158, 173, 174
  planning 126-7, 139, 409, 422,
    444, 826
  portable antiquities 206
  RCHM(e) 31, 130, 136
  regulations 586-94
  revocation or variation 128,
    141
  scheduled monuments 80, 83,
    91, 127-8, 132, 139
Areas of Archaeological Priority
  500
Areas of Outstanding Natural
  Beauty 276, 331, 405, 409, 455
artefacts and objects 27, 42,
    206-56, 257, 472
  English Heritage 16
  Europe 263, 289
  NHMF 34-5, 38
  return 263, 295-7
  temporary custody 80, 136
  see also portable antiquities;
    treasure
Association of County
  Archaeological Officers
  (ACAO) 40, 813

Association of District
  Archaeological Officers
  (ADAO) 40
Association for Industrial
  Archaeology 48
Association of Local
  Government Archaeological
  Officers (ALGAO) 40
Association of Museum
  Archaeologists 40

Banqueting House 9
Baptist Union of Great Britain
  358, 755, 809
Baptist Union of Wales 358, 755,
  809
battlefields 323, 325-6, 746
  Europe (EA) 294
  identifying and recording
    735, 746
  landscapes 325, 332
  planning 325-6, 441, 449, 690,
    693, 729, 735, 746
Bell Street, Romsey, Hants 390
Board of Trade 253
bona vacantia 226
bonds 52, 507-8
boundaries 69, 311-12, 329, 402
breach of condition notices 423,
  430, 463
British Academy 59
British Archaeologists and
  Developers Liaison Group
  (BADLG) 40, 823, 829, 831
British Museum 48, 61, 671, 680
  exports of antiquities 255
  treasure 233, 235, 245, 604,
    640
British Property Federation 829

British Waterways Board 85, 87
Broads Authority 127, 352
building and fire regulations
    402, 708
    Wales 794, 802
building preservation notices
    741-2, 780-1
    English Heritage 24
    listed buildings 310, 312,
        334-8, 396
        planning guidelines 699,
            741-2, 743
    Wales 762, 779, 780-1, 783,
        802
burial grounds 82, 207-29, 600,
    821
    assignment of rights in
        treasure 602-3
    form of notice 597-9
    listed buildings 213, 363
    Treasure Act (1996) 604-82
    treasure trove declaration 601
bushes 83, 86, 402

cables 402, 416
Cadw (Welsh Historic
    Monuments) 1-2, 4, 64, 795,
    834-6, 839
    advice and assistance 195-6
    AAIs 132
    authorisation of development
        421
    compensation 199, 202, 204,
        205, 583
    ecclesiastical exemption 358
    English Heritage 11, 23, 26
    Europe (EA) 284, 297
    grants and grant aid 188-90
    hedgerows 327

injunctions 157
landscapes 333
listed buildings 304, 333-4,
    338, 354-5, 388, 761, 767,
    778-82, 785-8, 795-8, 807
management agreements
    191, 193
parks and gardens 322, 324
planning 26, 458, 466
scheduled monuments 81, 90,
    844, 845, 846-7
territorial waters 74
Calke Abbey, Derbyshire 35
call-ins 8-9, 442, 697, 706, 787-8
    authorisation of development
        401, 405, 416
    conservation areas 723, 773
    conservation policy 525-6
    Europe (EA) 286
    listed buildings 353, 372, 706,
        787-8, 795
    Wales 761, 766, 773, 787-8,
        795, 833
canals 85, 87
Canterbury 50, 138
Canterbury Archaeological
    Trust 50
capital gains tax 17, 34
car parking 120-1, 462, 476, 515,
    532
    English Heritage 15, 21
castles 62
catering 15, 21, 532
cathedrals 13, 753, 756, 758
    listed building exemption
        356-7, 360-1
Cathedrals Fabric Commission
    360-1, 756
caves 62, 65

Central Archaeology Service 22
certificates of ownership 95
certificates of removal of
    remains 222
certiorari writs 152, 155-6
changes of use 696, 701-3
    authorisation of development
        402, 403, 413, 426
    redundant churches 760
    Wales 765, 793
charges 44-5, 47, 109, 186, 352,
    403
    advice and assistance 194
    English Heritage 19, 20, 24,
        25
    museums 47
    removal of human remains
        211-12
charities 16-17, 34, 50-1, 59, 61,
    62
chattels 27, 203, 206, 310, 344
    see also artefacts and objects;
    portable antiquities
Cherwell District Council 453
Chester 138
Church Commissioners 9
Church of England 61
    burial grounds 209-10, 214,
        215-18, 223-5
    ecclesiastical exemption
        356-60, 363-4, 753, 755-6,
        758-9, 809
    treasure 244, 611
Church in Wales 358, 755, 809
churches and churchyards 9, 59,
    690, 712, 753-60, 803
    burial grounds 207-9, 214-19,
        223-5
    conservation policy 526

demolition 9
form of notice 597-9
identifying and recording
    736
listed buildings 313, 356-64,
    702, 712
scheduled monuments 72-3
Wales 762, 777, 803, 808-10
see also ecclesiastical buildings
Churches Conservation Trust
    758-9
Civic Trust for Wales 770-1
class consents 84-93
    AAIs 132
    compensation 201
    English Heritage 23, 26
    grants and grant aid 88-9, 90,
        190
    intentional or reckless
        damage 172
    not for utilities 94
    RCHM(e) 32, 89, 90
    SMC conditions 118-20
    unauthorised works 160,
        164-5
    Wales 845
coal board 85, 86-7
coastal protection works 270
coins 229-30, 242-4
    Treasure Act 607-8, 610, 615,
        624-6, 635, 638, 671-3
compensation 9, 196-205, 534,
    543-5, 577-85
    AAIs 136, 204
    building preservation notices
        742, 780
    burial rights 220, 222
    conservation areas 723
    conservation policy 526

enforcement procedures 427-8
listed buildings 336, 715, 742,
 780
 compulsory acquisition
 394-5, 397, 807
 revocation of consent 799
 upkeep and repair 752
planning 197-9, 203, 435, 479,
 715
remains discovered during
 development 832, 843
scheduled monuments 63-4,
 67, 75, 76, 79, 196-205
 compulsory acquisition
 179, 196-7, 202-3, 204
 consent 82, 93, 97, 125,
 196-202, 577-85
 unauthorised works 170
Wales 780, 799, 807
compulsory acquisition and
 purchase orders 6-7, 391-7,
 799, 801-2, 805-6
AAIs 130
adjacent land 183
authorisation of development
 413, 420
burial grounds 209, 224
compensation 179, 196-7,
 202-3, 204,
 listed buildings 394-5, 397,
 807
easements 183
ecclesiastical exemption 356
English Heritage 15, 27
listed buildings 312, 387-8,
 391-7, 706, 750-2, 807
management agreements 193
scheduled monuments 77,
 178-80, 196-7, 202-4

Wales 762, 773, 787, 799,
 801-2, 805-6, 807
conditions to conservation area
 consent 725, 727
conditions to LBC 364-9, 371-2,
 381, 398, 707, 714
 enforcement notices 373-4,
 378-9
 Wales 789, 797, 798, 799
conditions to planning 458-86,
 487, 492, 495, 685, 830-1
 appeals 487, 492, 495
 archaeological facilities
 499-500, 502, 508-12, 517, 521
 authorisation of development
 405, 407, 410, 414, 422-4
 breach notices 423, 430, 463
 Wales 776, 840, 841-2, 867
conditions to SMC 105-23, 368,
 540, 575-6
 applications 97, 102-4
 breach 105-6
 compensation 196, 197-201
 metal detectors 175, 177
 unauthorised works 159, 163
 Wales 845
confidentiality in planning 510
consecrated ground
 human remains 207-10, 214,
 215-16, 225
 listed buildings 363
 treasure 244, 611, 628
 see also churches and
 churchyards
conservation and conservation
 areas 4-9, 22-7, 688-90,
 715-28, 767-76
 burial grounds 213
 CBA 60

ecclesiastical buildings 362,
526, 753-60, 808-9
English Heritage 10, 12 16-18,
22-7, 525-7, 717-20, 725
Europe 260-3, 265, 294
hedgerows 326-8
IFA 53, 55-6, 58
landscapes 331-2, 716-17
listed buildings 303-4, 314,
321, 348, 350-1, 356-7
planning 702, 708, 709, 712
Wales 777, 782, 787, 788,
801-5
local authorities 38-40, 46, 48,
526, 689-90, 715-28, 767-71,
773-6
NHA (1983) 528-31
NT 61
parks and gardens 323, 717
planning 399, 688-90, 715-28,
767-76
archaeology as con-
siderations 435, 440-1, 445,
449, 454-5, 457, 477, 493
authorisation of
development 404-5, 412,
420-2
development control 690-9
ecclesiastical exemption
753-60
identifying and recording
735, 739, 744-6
listed buildings 702, 708,
709, 712
securing archaeological
facilities 500, 523
transport and traffic
management 729-33
upkeep and repair 747-50

RCHM(e) 29, 31, 32, 525
responsibility for policy
525-7
scheduled monuments 82, 99,
100, 102, 180, 525, 724, 773
sources of advice 680-2
Wales 761-2, 763-4, 767-76,
835, 867
ecclesiastical buildings
808-9
listed buildings 777, 782,
787, 788, 801-5
consistory courts 359-62
consultants 2, 46, 51-3, 89
CBA 60
IFA 54, 55, 57
planning 485-6, 828-9
SMC applications 100
Wales 841
contracts and contractors 2,
51-3, 89, 485-6, 811-14
archaeological trusts 49-51
CBA 61
IFA 55, 57, 813-14
local authorities 39-41, 43,
46-8
NHMF 37
RCHM(e) 32
securing archaeological
facilities 498, 506-8, 515,
522
conversion 228, 252
coroners 644-62
treasure 177, 232-4, 236-7,
243-7, 601
Act 637, 640-1, 680
code of practice 604-6, 610,
613-15, 619-28, 635-6
corporation tax 17

corporations and unauthorised
works 166-7
costs 496-7, 504-8
AAIs 138
advice and assistance 195-6
archaeological investigation
549
class consent 88-9
Europe (EA) 288-9
grants and grant aid 188-90
injunctions 430, 715
inquiries 102, 125, 563
listed buildings 389-91, 396
appeals 372, 377
offences 383, 385
local authorities 41-3, 45
management agreements 191
planning appeals 488, 491
planning considerations 466,
468, 476-7, 486, 488, 491,
496-7
remedying planning non-
compliance 426
repairs and urgent works
389-91, 396, 749, 752, 804-7
scheduled monuments
acquisition 180
scheduled monuments
consent 96, 102, 125
securing archaeological
facilities 498, 501, 503,
504-8, 511, 515-18, 522, 524
unauthorised works 161, 163,
168-9
unexpected finds 811
see also charges
Cotswold District Council
449-50

Council for British Archaeology
1-2, 40, 58-61, 355
ecclesiastical exemption
359-60
Wales 60, 786, 845
Council for Scottish
Archaeology 59
Countryside Agency 284, 448
Countryside Commission 693,
746
Countryside Council for Wales
284, 767
Covent Garden opera house 434
Crown and Crown land 3, 9, 14,
226, 532, 712
AAIs 131
English Heritage 14, 26
Europe 269, 270
listed buildings 314, 351, 389,
712
planning 416-17, 418, 522
scheduled monuments 73,
93-4, 146, 161, 179, 314
treasure 80, 229-32, 235-7,
240, 242, 245, 247, 251
Act 637, 639-42
code of practice 601, 605,
609, 612, 623, 626
Wales 803, 845
wrecks 251
Crown Prosecution Service
161-2, 172
Cultural Heritage Committee
(EC) 298
curtilage 315-19, 789-91, 808
ecclesiastical buildings 357,
359, 362, 755, 808
hedgerows 328

listed buildings 305, 311-12,
313-19, 323, 339, 354
conditions 368-9
enforcement notices 379
planning control 699,
709-11
Wales 783, 789-91, 793
planning 402, 405, 412-13,
434, 697, 699, 709-11, 755
damage to scheduled monu-
ments 66, 77, 83, 146, 170-4
consent conditions 103
unauthorised works 159-60,
162-3, 165-9
dangerous structures 397, 802
defences to offences
AAIs 137-8
breach of planning 427
human remains 208
listed buildings 375-6, 381-3,
386, 714, 802
metal detectors 176, 548
scheduled monuments 159,
163-4, 173, 541, 846
treasure 244-5
de-listing 308, 334, 396, 710,
742-3
Wales 781, 791
demolition 7, 9, 344-51, 704-6,
723-5, 771-4, 791-3
AAIs 129
authorisation of development
402, 407, 410-11, 412, 419
building preservation notices
741-2
class consents 86, 93
conservation areas 99, 717,
723-5, 744, 769, 771-4
dangerous buildings 397

development plans and
control 693, 694
ecclesiastical buildings 9, 357,
364, 526, 754, 758-60, 808
listed buildings 338, 340-1,
343, 344-51, 353-5, 380,
390, 704-6
compulsory purchases
394-7
conditions 365, 367-9
control 699-701, 704-6, 707,
712, 714
enforcement notices 379
offences 381, 383-5
Wales 777, 779-80, 782-3,
785-6, 788-9, 791-3,
796-7, 799, 803, 807
planning considerations 434,
440, 460, 462
planning obligations 817-18
RCHM(e) 31
scheduled monuments 82-3,
346, 350, 539, 544
acquisition 179
compensation 198, 203
spot listing 741
transport and traffic
management 730-1
upkeep and repair 752
Wales 764
conservation areas 769,
771-4
ecclesiastical buildings 808
listed buildings 777, 779-80
782-3, 785-6, 788-9, 791-3,
796-7, 799, 803, 807
Department for Culture, Media
and Sport (DCMS) 6-8, 31,
100, 336

see also Secretary of State for
Culture, Media and
Sports (SSCMS)
Department of the Environment
(DOE) 1, 4, 5, 8, 10, 13
AAIs 126, 139
Europe 297
planning policy guide
688-760
responsibilities for
conservation policy 525-7
treasure 240
see also Secretary of State for
the Environment
Department of Environment,
Transport and the Regions
(DETR) 3, 8-9, 281, 377
see also Secretary of State for
the Environment, Transport
and the Regions (SSETR)
Department of National
Heritage 1, 3, 4-6, 422, 671
class consent 92
listed buildings 304
planning policy guide
688-760
responsibilities for
conservation policy 525-7
treasure 236
see also Secretary of State for
National Heritage
depth of works and soil
disturbance 120, 131-2, 595-6
class consents 85-6, 89, 92-3
designation orders 128-9, 138,
142, 143, 145-6
desk-based assessments 58,
467-8, 503, 826, 837

developer funding 122, 133,
437-8
development benefits 346,
349-50
development plans 8, 403-22,
442-58, 690-3, 763, 824-5,
835-6
advice and assistance 195
archaeology as consideration
400, 431-5, 438-41, 442-58,
468, 471-2, 477, 489, 495
authorisation 403-22, 425
conservation areas 719, 771
conservation policy 526
Europe (EA) 286
planning policy guidelines
690-3, 719, 820, 824-5,
828, 830
Wales 761-2, 763, 771, 799,
833, 835-6, 839, 866
Diocesan Advisory Committee
(DAC) 359-60
disabled people 709, 802
Downe Hall, Bridport 348
drainage works 268, 407, 408,
416, 596
AAIs 131
class consents 85-6
Ducks Walk, Twickenham 500,
501
dual listing 312, 321, 387-8,
744-5
Wales 782-3, 844, 846

easements 15, 183-4, 197, 202-3
ecclesiastical buildings 7,
356-64, 753-60, 803
exemption 356-64, 526, 554,
753-60, 808-10

grants 189
listed buildings 313, 350, 351,
  356-64, 389
scheduled monuments 72-3,
  313
Wales 762, 772, 803, 808-10
see also cathedrals; churches
  and churchyards
educational facilities 36, 39, 54,
  59, 528
English Heritage 16, 17, 27
electricity generation 415-16
endowments 16, 27, 33
enforcement 422-31, 526, 800-1
  authorisation of development
    422-31
  listed buildings 303, 713,
    714-15, 762, 800-1
  planning conditions 461, 463
  planning considerations 438,
    461, 463, 496
  Wales 762, 800-1
enforcement notices 9, 373-9,
  424-7, 713
  ecclesiastical exemption 357
  injunctions 380
  listed buildings 170, 311, 344,
    370-1, 373-9, 387-8, 713
    authorisation of
      development 425
    conditions 366
    repairs notices 392
  planning 401, 423, 424-7,
    428-30, 463, 713
  Wales 772, 801
English Heritage 10-27, 87, 822,
  824-6, 828-9, 831
  AAIs 23, 127-8, 132, 133,
    135-6, 138-9

advice and assistance 194-6
AMAA (1979) 536-49, 551,
  555, 558-60
authorisation of development
  407-8, 410, 417, 421, 422,
  424, 429
battlefields 325, 698
commissioners 11-14,
  19, 26
compensation 199, 201-2,
  204-5, 578, 581-2, 583-5
conservation areas 10, 12,
  16-18, 22-7, 717-20, 725
conservation policy 525-7
development plans 693-4,
  696, 698
easements 183-4
ecclesiastical exemption 358,
  361, 754, 758
Europe (EA) 284, 289, 297
grants and grant aid 12-13,
  22, 26-7, 187-90
guardianship 15, 22, 25-6,
  180-1
hedgerows 327, 330
heritage organisations 1-27,
  52, 61
  IFA 55
  local authorities 40, 48
  NHMF 36
  RCHM(e) 29, 30-1
identifying and recording
  735, 737-8, 740-6
injunctions 157, 379
judicial review 147, 150, 154
landscapes 333
listed buildings 313, 322-3,
  333-4, 336, 338, 348, 352,
  354-5

control 699, 702, 708, 712, 714
enforcement notices 375
repairs notices 392
urgent works 388
management agreements 190-3
NHA (1983) 528-35
operations notices 586, 593-4
parks and gardens 322-5, 698
planning considerations 441, 446-8, 455, 458, 466, 469, 477
scheduled monuments 11, 15-17, 64-8, 70, 72-9, 124, 143, 321
access 185
acquisition 178-80
applications 95, 98-100, 102-4
class consents 85, 87, 88-93
conditions 105, 109, 114, 116, 119-20, 123
consent 81, 83, 84, 94, 124
guardianship 180-1
guidance notes on excavations 572-6
intentional or reckless damage 170, 172, 173
metal detectors 174-5
public facilities 186
unauthorised works 159-65, 169-70
securing archaeological facilities 503, 506
transport and traffic management 729, 733
upkeep and repair 748-9, 751
English Nature 61, 448, 693

Environment Agency 10, 284, 421
environmental archaeology 55
environmental assessments and environmental impact assessments 399, 683-4, 686-7, 694, 698, 827, 848
authorisation of development 415-16
consultants 51
Europe 261-3, 266-71, 272-95, 299, 301
planning considerations 475
treasure 250
Wales 764, 837, 848, 866
World Heritage Sites 258-9
Environmental Grant Fund 526
environmental matters 3, 100, 399, 821-2
authorisation of development 403
conservation 688-9
development plans 690
Europe 260, 262, 266-71, 272-95, 297-9, 301
hedgerows 326-8
identifying and recording 734-47
information regulations 263, 297-8
planning considerations 435, 453-4, 470, 475, 488
planning obligations 523
transport and traffic management 728-30
World Heritage Sites 258-9
environmental statements 267, 270-1, 281-95, 466
content 683-4

Wales 848
Environmentally Sensitive Areas
61, 263-6, 331
transport and traffic
management 730, 734
Eton College 481
Europe 257, 260-301, 683-7, 729
export of antiquities 254, 256,
263, 296
excavations 49, 65, 540
AAIs 130, 133-5, 137,
139-40
advice and assistance 194-6
authorisation of development
406-8, 426, 430
compensation 204
contracts 812, 814
Europe 294, 296, 299
guardianship 182
human remains 207, 210, 212,
223
IFA 55, 58
listed buildings 369
local authorities 38, 40, 42
NHMF 35, 37
operations notices 592-4
planning considerations 437,
444, 471-4, 476-82
planning guidelines 823,
828-31
powers of entry 80
scheduled monuments 65, 80,
84, 572-6
consent applications 97,
102-4
consent conditions 103,
105, 113, 117-19, 122
securing archaeological
facilities 504-5, 507, 512

treasure 236, 246, 251-2, 624,
628, 632
unauthorised works 426
Wales 838, 840-2, 848, 867
wrecks 251
expert evidence 100, 493-4
export of antiquities 207, 253-6,
257, 624
Europe 254, 256, 263, 296

faculties and faculty jurisdiction
356-7, 359-63, 753, 759
human remains 208-9, 214-17
fees see charges; costs
fences 86, 192, 194, 470
authorisation of development
402, 410-12, 423
Field Monument Wardens
847-8
field-walking 288, 467
finders of objects 226, 232-3,
235-9, 244-9, 613-23
Treasure Act 604-8, 610-11,
613-26, 628-35, 640-2
fines 534, 541, 547-8, 558
access 186
breach of planning control
426, 428, 430
export of antiquities 253-4
hedgerows 327
intentional or reckless
damage 168, 172, 173-4
listed buildings 383-6, 387,
714-15, 799
enforcement notices 375-6
metal detectors 176
treasure 240, 251, 614, 640
unauthorised works 160,
167-9

Wales 799
wrecks 251
fish farming 268, 270
Flecknoe, Warwickshire 503
flooding 83, 129, 160, 539, 552,
    553
forestry 117, 402, 407,
    544, 553
    AAIs 131
    class consents 85-6, 92
    compensation 198
    Europe 267, 268, 269-70, 275
    hedgerows 328
    operations notices exemption
        595
    Wales 772
Forestry Commission 269-70,
    275
franchise holders for treasure
    231-2, 235, 236, 245
    Treasure Act 612-13, 627, 637,
        639, 642
funding 8, 395, 828
    AAIs 133, 136, 139
    advice and assistance 194-5
    archaeological investigation
        420, 841
    CBA 59-60
    English Heritage 12-14
    environmentally sensitive
        areas 263
    scheduled monument consent
        97, 575
    conditions 108-9, 112, 122
    securing archaeological
        facilities 505-6, 514-15,
        517-18
    Wales 841
    see also grants and grant aid

Garden History Society 324
gardens and gardening *see*
    parks and gardens
Georgian Group 355, 786
Glamorgan and Gwent
    Archaeological Trust 50
gold 229-31, 233, 240-4, 249
    Treasure Act 605, 607-8, 622,
        638, 671-3, 674-5
grants and grant aid 5, 187-90,
    193, 526, 529, 803
    AAIs 135
    advice and assistance 195-6
    CBA 59-60
    class consents 88-9, 90, 190
    conservation areas 719, 769
    English Heritage 12-13, 22,
        26-7, 187-90
    environmentally sensitive
        areas 265
    Europe 265, 270, 275
    IFA 58
    listed buildings 189, 345, 354,
        702, 705, 709
    Wales 785, 787, 792, 803,
        807-8
    local authorities and
        universities 40, 48, 188-90
    NHMF 33-8
    RCHM(e) 32
    scheduled monuments 97,
        178, 187-90
    consent conditions 113
    Wales 847, 848
    securing archaeological
        facilities 506-7, 513
    transport and traffic
        management 733
    upkeep and repairs 752

Wales 187-90, 769, 803
  listed buildings 785, 787, 792, 803, 807-8
  scheduled monuments 847, 848
grave goods 225-9, 231, 237, 252
green belts 434, 437, 696
groups and group value 71, 321-2
  listed buildings 306, 321-2, 337, 343, 701, 738
guarantees 14-15, 21, 532
guardianship 66, 170, 180-2, 529, 552, 553
  access 184-6
  adjacent land 183
  authorisation of development 410, 422
  easements 184
  English Heritage 15, 22, 25-6, 180-1
  grants and grant aid 187
  local authorities 43
  metal detectors 174
  powers of entry 79, 80, 182
  public facilities 186-7

ha-has 311, 316
Hampshire Buildings Preservation Trust 396
Hampton Court 9
harbour works 268, 270
Hazel Farm, Ledbury 466
health and safety 87, 541
  AAIs 138
  access 185
  advice and assistance 196
  authorisation of development 411

class consents 85, 87, 89, 91
IFA 57
listed buildings 346, 377, 382, 397, 708-9, 714
  Wales 800, 802
public facilities 187
unauthorised works 164-5
Wales 800, 802, 812, 846
hearings 6, 558-9, 561
  listed buildings 353, 372, 380
  planning considerations 487-8, 496
  scheduled monument consent 98-100, 102, 140, 143
  conditions 105
  judicial review 151, 154-6
  revocation or modification 125
  Wales 845
hedges and hedgerows 85-6, 326-31
heirlooms 227
Henbury Hall, Dorset 434, 475
Heritage Lottery Fund (HLF) 2, 36, 808
Heritage Projects (Management) Ltd 50
Historic Buildings Council for England 11
Historic Buildings Council for Wales 421, 808
Historic Buildings and Monuments Commission for England *see* English Heritage
Historic Royal Palaces (HRP) 1-2, 4, 9-10
Historic Royal Palaces Agency (HRPA) 4, 10
Historic Scotland 11

Home Office 209-14, 215, 218, 221, 225, 598-9
House of Commons National Heritage Committee 12, 14
House of Commons Environment Committee 12
human remains 207-29, 252, 363, 597-9
  battlefields 326

immunity from listing 7, 334-5, 336-7, 743-4
  Wales 762, 781-2
imports 253-4, 256, 257
income generation 10, 13-14, 19
indemnification 136, 196, 336
inheritance tax 17
injunctions 156-7, 379-80, 429-31
  AAIs 137, 156
  authorisation of development 423, 429-31
  interlocutory 151, 429-30
  listed buildings 366, 379-81, 714-15, 800
  planning 156-7, 380, 522
  scheduled monuments 146, 151, 156-7, 158
inquiries 6, 31, 60, 558-9, 561, 563
  authorisation of development 414, 415
  compulsory purchase 394, 752
  demolition of churches 758
  landscapes 333
  listed buildings 303, 353, 372
  planning considerations 442, 487-96

scheduled monument consent 98-103, 140, 142-4, 845
  conditions 105
  judicial review 152-3
  revocation or modification 125
  transport and traffic management 731
inspections 31, 42, 78, 116-17
  AAIs 134, 136, 139-40
Institute of Field Archaeologists (IFA) 1, 2, 40, 52, 53-8, 61, 827
  contracts 55, 57, 813-14
  planning considerations 438, 467, 485
  Wales 838
insurance 52, 54
International Charter on Archaeological Heritage Management (ICAHM) 300, 301
International Council on Monuments and Sites (ICOMOS) 300, 745-6, 766, 767
interim preservation notices 64, 81
Isle of Man 59

judicial review 146-56, 468, 524
  Europe (EA) 279, 281, 285
  exports of antiquities 256
  listed buildings 152, 373, 376
  scheduled monuments 141, 146-56
  treasure 248, 249, 626, 635

Kensington Palace 9
Kew Palace 9

King's Road, Brentwood, Essex 474-5

Lake District 401
land acquisition 525-6, 530
  heritage organisations 7, 15-16, 34, 62
landowners 226, 227, 415, 520-1, 698, 710
  environmentally sensitive areas 265
  hedgerows 327
  planning considerations 433, 434-5
  planning obligations 815, 818
  treasure 235-9, 245-6, 248-9, 252, 605-6, 618, 622, 624-6, 629-34, 641
  Wales 844, 847-8
Lands Tribunal 523, 534, 547
landscapes 30, 331-3, 746-7, 767
  battlefields 325, 332
  conservation areas 331-2, 716-17
  development plans 690, 694, 698-9
  Europe (EA) 261, 267, 276, 287, 292, 294
  hedgerows 327, 329-30
  identifying and recording 735, 746-7
  listed buildings 331-3, 338, 343
  parks and gardens 324, 332-3
  planning considerations 434, 441, 449, 464, 470
  planning policy guide 688-760, 821, 823, 824
  Wales 763, 767, 769, 784, 840

leasehold reform 725
Leighton Hall, Welshpool 311
limitations to planning permission 405, 407, 410-11, 414, 424
limitations to scheduled monument consent 106, 120-1
listed buildings 144, 158, 203, 302-98, 530
  AAIs 139
  authorisation of development 402, 405, 409, 412-13, 415, 418-19, 425, 429
  battlefields 325-6
  breach of condition 105
  burial grounds 213, 363
  class consents 91
  consent 351-6, 364-9, 370-3, 799
    conditions 364-9
  conservation 688-90, 767-76
    areas 715-28, 767-76
    policy 525-7
  constraints 339-41
  control 699-715
  demolition 344-51
  development plans 690-9
  ecclesiastical exemption 356-64, 753-60
    Wales 808-10
  enforcement notices 373-9
  Europe (EA) 277-8, 293-4
  grants and grant aid 189, 345, 354, 702, 705, 709
    Wales 785, 787, 792, 803, 807-8
  hedgerows 326-31
  heritage organisations 3-4, 6-9, 17, 22-4, 27, 31-2, 35-6, 60

identifying and recording
734-47
injunctions 366, 379-81,
714-15, 800
judicial review 152, 373, 376
landscapes 331-3, 338, 343
local authorities 337-8
parks and gardens 322-5, 343,
352
planning considerations 434,
440-2, 457, 461
planning policy guide
688-760, 825
portable antiquities 206
procedures 333-7
purchase notices 9, 398, 526,
799
repairs notices 77, 374, 387-97
scheduled monuments 72, 77,
81
consent 82, 84, 94, 96, 100,
102
statutory and policy context
302-22
transport and traffic
management 728-34
unauthorised works 164-5,
169-70, 366, 370, 375-6,
381-8
uncertainties in definition 69
upkeep and repair 747-53,
804-8
Wales 761-810, 844, 846
conservation areas 767-76
controls 777-803
ecclesiastical exemption
808-10
planning 763-7
repairs 394, 804-8

World Heritage Sites 259
local authorities 2, 38-48, 65, 66,
337-8, 662-71, 711-12, 788,
803, 826, 827-8
AAIs 126-30, 132-3, 136-8
access 185
advice and assistance 195,
770-1, 835-42
AMAA (1979) 537, 539,
545-7, 549, 552, 555, 563
antiquities at sea 250
authorisation of development
400-19, 422-30
battlefields 325-6
burial grounds 224
CBA 61
challenge 143
class consents 90
compensation 199
compulsory acquisition 27,
179-80, 391, 395, 398
conservation 38-40, 46, 48,
526, 689-90
conservation areas 715-28,
767-71, 773-6
consultants 52
development plans 691-8
ecclesiastical exemption
358-9, 363, 754, 756,
758-9, 808-9
English Heritage 23-4
Europe (EA) 261-2, 270,
274-5, 278-89, 291-2, 297
grants and grant aid 40, 48,
188-90
hedgerows 327-8, 330-1
identifying and recording
735-7, 739-45
injunctions 156-7, 379

landscapes 332
listed buildings 311, 319-25, 332-9, 342, 348-56, 371-2
  compulsory purchase 391, 395, 398
  conditions 365-6, 368
  control 699-700, 702, 704-15
  dangerous structures orders 397
  enforcement notices 375, 377, 379
  offences 382-4
  urgent works 388-90
  Wales 777-85, 787, 788, 789-93
management agreements 191-3
operations notices 586-7
parks and gardens 39, 322-5
planning considerations 431-51, 455, 458-9, 461-90, 495-7
planning obligations 815-16
planning policy guidelines 820, 822, 824-32
powers of entry 79-80
scheduled monuments 42, 43, 75-6, 79, 844-8
  acquisition 179-80
  consent applications 99
  consent conditions 106, 109, 123
  easements 183
  guardianship 180
  intentional or reckless damage 170, 173
  metal detectors 174
  registration 75
  unauthorised works 159, 161-3

securing archaeological facilities 497-524
transport and traffic management 728-34
treasure 617, 619-21, 623
upkeep and repair 747-52
Wales 761, 763-71, 773-6, 833-4, 866-7
  advice 770-1, 835-42
  conservation areas 767-71, 773-6
  ecclesiastical buildings 808-9
  listed buildings 777-85, 787, 788, 789-803
  repairs 804-8
  scheduled monuments 844-8
World Heritage Sites 259
local land charges 338, 522, 819
  AAIs 128
  burial grounds 218-19
  compensation 201
  easements 184
  guardianship 181
  management agreements 192
  scheduled monuments 75, 81, 538, 844
local plans 403-4, 690, 692, 721, 824
  archaeology as considerations 432, 439, 442-3, 446, 454, 489
  Wales 767, 768
Lombard Street, Birmingham 366
London 30, 47-8, 400, 552, 744, 825, 826
  AAIs 127-8

conservation areas 718
English Heritage 12, 22, 23-4
hedgerows 330
listed buildings 336, 353,
    388-9, 397
planning considerations 475
scheduled monuments 67
treasure 235, 612-13, 627
upkeep and repair 748-9

Macclesfield 452
machinery 72, 85, 87, 554
listed buildings 309, 311, 703
management agreements 25,
    187, 190-3, 422, 518, 545-7
class consents 88, 90
grants and grant aid 189
scheduled monuments 97,
    113, 123, 190-3
Wales 847-8
mandamus writs 146, 151, 152,
    155, 297
marine archaeology 6, 73, 250-1
    see also wrecks
Maritime Greenwich 258
material considerations 433
archaeology 431-41, 456-7,
    472
authorisation of development
    405
conservation areas 720
development plans 697
listed buildings 701
securing archaeological
    facilities 509
Wales 763, 766, 784, 794, 799,
    825, 830
advice 836, 839-40

metal detectors 25, 76, 206,
    547-8
AAIs 138, 139, 174
class consents 90
offences 158, 174-7, 548
treasure 177, 233, 240, 246,
    249, 250, 643
code of practice 606,
    615-18, 621, 633
Wales 847
Methodist Church 358, 755, 809
minerals and mining 111, 401,
    408-10, 822, 823
AAIs 131
authorisation of development
    406, 407, 408-10
operations notices exemption
    596
Wales 834, 835
Ministry of Agriculture,
    Fisheries and Food 61, 265,
    326, 422
Ministry of Defence 94, 417
Ministry of Transport 269
mitigation 685
Europe 286, 287-8, 291-2, 294
listed buildings 373, 385
planning considerations 469,
    471-2, 475, 477, 483, 491,
    493
scheduled monuments 76,
    96-7, 101, 103
securing archaeological
    facilities 498, 518, 522
unauthorised works 159, 164
moats 311, 320
modification of consent 23, 124,
    542-3, 550, 559-63
compensation 196, 201-2

Monkspath Hall, Solihull 383
monuments defined 65
  criteria for classification
    69-77
Monuments Protection
  Programme (MPP) 25, 72,
  312, 455, 744
Moss Fen Lodge 308
motorway service areas 270
Museum of London 47, 477
Museum of London
  Archaeological Service 477
museums 2, 38-49, 113, 251-3,
  367, 826, 827
  exports of antiquities 255
  NHMF 35, 37
  securing archaeological
    facilities 504-5, 514
  treasure 177, 233, 235, 245-8,
    251-3
    Act 604-6, 610, 613-14, 618-
      31, 634-5, 641-2, 644, 680
  Wales 837
  see also British Museum;
    National Museums and
    Galleries of Wales

national amenity societies 694
  conservation areas 719-20
  conservation policy 526-7
  ecclesiastical exemption
    358-9, 361, 754, 758, 808
  identifying and recording
    737, 743
  listed buildings 334, 342, 355,
    708
  transport and traffic
    management 734
  Wales 770, 778, 788, 808

National Archaeological Record
  (NAR) 29, 32
National Heritage Memorial
  Fund (NHMF) 2, 4, 6, 33-8,
  525
National Land Fund 33
National Monuments Record 28
  RCHM(e) 29, 30, 32, 736, 740
National Museums and
  Galleries of Wales 48, 671,
  680
  exports of antiquities 255
  treasure 233, 235, 245, 604,
    640
National Parks Authorities
  authorisation of development
    400-1, 405, 409, 422
  building preservation notices
    741-2
  Wales 767, 805, 838, 844
National Rivers Authority
  (NRA) 10, 421
National Trust 2, 27, 35, 61-2,
  702
natural justice 101-2, 144
Nature Conservancy Council
  284
necessity of planning conditions
  461
necessity of planning obligations
  514
newspapers 282, 285, 353, 808
  burial grounds 211-12,
    217-19
nominated archaeologists 498-9
Norfolk Broads 406, 409
Normanby Street, Alton, Hants
  396
Northern Ireland 59, 64

treasure 604, 606, 609, 637, 642-3
Nostell Priory, West Yorkshire 35
notices and notification 76, 282, 285, 696
  AAIs 156
  burial grounds 211-12, 217-18, 219-21, 225
  conservation areas 720, 769-70
  ecclesiastical exemption 754-5, 808
  listed buildings 319, 342, 352-3, 355,
    Wales 778, 785-6, 799
nuclear fuel reprocessing 152

objects *see* artefacts and objects
offences 136-8, 157-74, 381-6, 387, 714-15, 799-800
  access 80, 158, 185-6
  AMAA (1979) 136-8, 540-1, 547-8, 557-8
  breaches of conditions 366
  breaches of planning 424-30
  ecclesiastical exemption 357
  enforcement notices 375-7
  exports 253-4
  false certificates 158, 174
  false information 75-6, 95, 130-1, 158, 173
  hedgerows 327-8, 331
  human remains 208, 212
  injunctions 156
  intentional or reckless damage 170-4, 233, 387
  late implementation of SMC 107

listed buildings 158, 312, 338, 366, 370, 381-8, 740
  control 699, 713, 714-15
  unauthorised works 366, 370, 375, 381-5, 387-8
  upkeep and repair 748
  Wales 778, 783, 799-800, 801
metal detectors 158, 174-7
NHA (1983) 534
obstruction 80, 158, 174
operations notices 158, 160, 173, 174
portable antiquities 206
scheduled monuments 81, 94, 105-6, 125, 135, 137, 157-8, 159-70, 173, 233, 541, 846-7
treasure 232-3, 244-5, 251
  Act 614, 630, 632-3, 640
wrecks 251
see also theft
onerous or unjustifiable burdens 461, 465, 483
operations notices 586-94, 595-6
  AAIs 127, 129-34, 136, 139
  compensation 204
  offences 158, 160, 173, 174
Ordnance Survey 32
outline permission 478-9
outstanding universal value 258-9

Painswick, Gloucestershire 501
Park Lane, Croydon 477, 479
parks and gardens 2, 79, 322-5, 326, 331, 669-70, 698, 746, 767
  AAIs 127, 131
  advice and assistance 195

authorisation of development
400-1, 405, 409, 422
building preservation notices
336, 741-2
conservation areas 323, 717
development plans 690, 693,
695, 698
domestic works 86, 93, 131
English Heritage 16, 21, 24,
27
Europe 276, 294
grants and grant aid 188
guardianship 180
identifying and recording
735, 746
judicial review 150
landscapes 324, 332-3
listed building 322-5, 343, 352
local authorities 39, 322-5
management agreements 191
planning considerations 441,
449
transport and traffic
management 729
Wales 322, 324, 670-1, 763,
765, 767, 784, 805, 838, 844
parliamentary authority 407-8,
413-14
Peak District 401
perjury 234
permitted development 405-6,
722-3, 767, 825, 836
persons aggrieved 141, 151
perversity 143-4
piling 102-3, 476, 478, 500-1
Pitchford Hall 14
planning 8, 399-524
AAIs 126-7, 139, 409, 422,
444, 826

AMAA (1979) 543-4
archaeological contracts
811-14
archaeology as consideration
431-97
authorisation of development
400-31
battlefields 325-6, 441, 449,
690, 693, 729, 735, 746
burial grounds 213, 224
challenge 143-5
compensation 197-9, 203, 435,
479, 715
conservation 688-90
areas 715-28, 767-76
policy 525
court supervision 140
development control
690-9
ecclesiastical buildings 358-9,
363, 753-60
Europe 261-2, 265-6, 268-75,
277-95, 299
gardens 24
injunctions 156-7, 380, 522
inquiries 140
judicial review 150, 152
landscapes 332-3
listed buildings 319-21, 332,
335, 337-42, 348-55
appeals 371-3
conditions 365-9
control 699-715
intentional damage 386
repairs notices 392
Wales 777-803
obligations 815-19
parks and gardens 323-4, 441,
449

policy guidelines 688-760,
820-32
scheduled monuments 82, 84,
91, 94, 126
consent 95-102
consent conditions 105-12,
114-15, 121-3
securing archaeological
facilities 497-524
setting of scheduled
monuments 319, 321
transport and traffic
management 728-34
unauthorised works 169
Wales 761-810, 833-65,
866-7
advice 835-43
conservation areas 767-76
framework 763-7
importance of archaeology
834-5
listed buildings 777-803
World Heritage Sites 258-9
see also local authorities
planning agreements 508, 510,
512
planning benefits and gains
434, 443, 513-17, 523
planning contravention notices
423
Planning Inspectorate 6, 99, 487,
489-90
planning obligations 320,
508-24, 815-19
archaeology as consideration
434
authorisation of development
417
Europe 292

scheduled monuments
consent 97, 123
securing archaeological
facilities 497, 507-24
pollution 167, 171, 266, 278,
297-8
portable antiquities 49, 61,
206-56, 600
assignment of rights in
treasure 602-3
battlefields 326
burial grounds 597-9
Europe 295-7, 300
Treasure Act (1996) 604-82
treasure trove declaration 601
see also artefacts
and objects
post-excavation work 504-5,
517-18, 574, 813
power stations 416
powers of entry 77-80, 194, 426,
522, 533-4
AAIs 130, 133-6
compensation 197, 203-4
English Heritage 24
guardianship 79, 80, 182
offences 158, 174
scheduled monuments
consent conditions 117-19
preciseness in planning
conditions 461, 464
Prehistoric Society 48
prerogative writs 146, 155
preservation 528, 546
access 185
authorisation of development
404
conservation areas 716,
718-22, 724, 768, 770

development plans 692,
694-6, 835
ecclesiastical buildings 362,
809
English Heritage 18, 26-7
Europe 301
grants and grant aid 187-8
guardianship 182
landscapes 332
listed buildings 305, 310, 338,
342-3, 350-1, 382
conditions 364, 367
control 700, 702, 704, 706,
714
enforcement notices 377
repairs notices 391-6
urgent works 388
Wales 783, 792, 797, 800,
804-7
local authorities 38, 42
management agreements 191
National Trust 62
NHMF 35, 36-7
objects 80
offences 158
parks and gardens 323-5
planning considerations 348,
440, 444, 446-9, 452-3,
457-8, 471, 476
planning policy 820-5, 827-9
RCHM(e) 28
scheduled monuments 65,
67-8, 71, 77-8, 80
acquisition 178, 180
class consent 88
consent 81, 95-7
judicial review 152
Wales 844, 845-7, 866
transport and traffic

management 733
upkeep and repair 747-53
Wales 764, 765, 834-5
advice 836, 839
conservation areas
768, 770
development plans 835
ecclesiastical buildings 809
listed buildings 783, 792,
797, 800, 804-7
scheduled monuments 844,
845-7, 866
preservation by avoidance
476-8, 483
preservation by record 291, 294,
823, 828, 840, 848
listed buildings 369
planning considerations 437,
471, 476-7, 479, 481
planning obligation 815
scheduled monuments 97,
113, 123
securing archaeological
facilities 505, 514-15, 517,
519
preservation *in situ* 823-4, 828,
829-30
Europe 299
planning considerations
448-9, 453, 471, 477, 481
scheduled monuments 95, 97,
103, 111, 123
securing archaeological
facilities 500, 515, 519
Wales 839-40, 866
preservation orders 8, 64
prohibition writs 146, 155, 156
proofs of evidence 490, 491,
492-6

public facilities 120-1, 183,
    186-7, 191, 532
public interest 554, 555
    English Heritage 16, 20
    grants and grant aid 188
    judicial review 147
    listed buildings 394
    metal detectors 175
    planning considerations 433
    scheduled monuments 66, 72,
        178
    treasure 235
publications 80, 128, 532
    CBA 59, 60
    English Heritage 21, 26
    scheduled monuments 74-5,
        113, 575
    securing archaeological
        facilities 504, 512
purchase notices 9, 398, 526, 799

railways 408, 413, 414, 730
reasonableness 465-8
    judicial review 149
    listed buildings 320
    planning appeals 496
    planning conditions 460, 461,
        463, 465-8
    planning obligations 513,
        515, 524
    scheduled monument consent
        108, 111-12, 143-4
records 554, 707, 734-47, 788-9
    AAIs 126, 133-4, 136
    advice and assistance 194,
        837, 840-2
    authorisation of development
        409-10
    compensation 204

contracts 812-14
ecclesiastical buildings 362,
    809
    English Heritage 18-19, 25
    Europe 287, 294, 301
    grants and grant aid 190
    hedgerows 330
    IFA 55-6, 58
    listed buildings 308, 322, 341,
        367-9, 707, 708
        Wales 788-9, 796
    local authorities 41, 42
    NHA (1983) 529, 533-4
    NHMF 37-8
    parks and gardens 322
    planning considerations 449,
        451, 453, 468-9, 471-5, 480-3
    planning policy 820, 822, 826,
        828-31
    RCHM(e) 28-33
    scheduled monuments 78-80,
        117, 574-5
        criteria for classification 71
    securing archaeological
        facilities 504-5, 512, 514,
        518
    treasure 252
    Wales 834, 867
        advice 837, 840-2
        listed buildings 788-9, 796
    see also preservation by
        record; Sites and
        Monuments Record (SMR)
registration
    AAIs 128
    burial grounds 218
    compensation 201
    easements 184
    guardianship 181

listed buildings 338
  management agreements 192
  planning obligations 522
  scheduled monuments 75, 81
relevance 144, 149, 461-3
remote sensing 69, 289, 463
removal of scheduled
  monument 83, 159-60, 163,
    179, 539
repair and maintenance 410,
  747-53
  access 185
  adjacent land 183
  easements 183
  ecclesiastical buildings 362
  English Heritage 24, 26
  guardianship 181
  listed buildings 345-6, 349,
    747-53, 806-7
  management agreements
    190, 191
  scheduled monuments 83,
    181, 183, 185, 191
    grants and grant aid 188-9
  Wales 847
  unauthorised works 159-60,
    163, 167
repairs notices 391-7, 747,
  749-50, 752, 805
  conservation policy 525
  ecclesiastical exemption 357
  English Heritage 24
  listed buildings 77, 374,
    387-97
  Wales 762, 805, 806-7
Replacement Berkshire
  Structure Plan 445
reporting treasure 229, 232, 233,
  236, 240, 244-6, 248

rescue archaeology 40, 126, 811
RESCUE: The British
  Archaeological Trust 48
research 47, 49, 51, 529
  CBA 59, 60
  English Heritage 18, 19, 25,
    26-7
  human remains 208
  IFA 55
  listed buildings 308, 323
  NHMF 36
  RCHM(e) 29
  scheduled monuments 97,
    104, 113
reserved matters 365, 478
retrospective consent 371
revocation 23
  AAIs 128, 141
  listed building consent 9, 799
  scheduled monument consent
    124-5, 142
    compensation 196, 201-2
rewards 631-5, 641
  treasure 229, 235-7, 240,
    245-6, 248-9
    Act 612-13, 617, 622, 624,
      627-35, 637, 641
roads and highways 271-2, 275,
  476, 505, 728-34
  AAIs 131
  authorisation of development
    402, 414, 415
  conditions 110, 121
  conservation 690
  conservation areas 719, 770
  development plans 698
  identifying and recording 735
  operations notices exemption
    596

Wales 767, 770, 834
Roman Catholic Church 358, 755, 756, 809
Royal Archaeological Institute 48
Royal Armouries 4
Royal Commission on the Ancient and Historical Monuments of Scotland (RCAHM(s)) 28
Royal Commission on the Ancient and Historical Monuments of Wales (RCAHM(w)) 2, 28, 32, 99, 297, 844-5
  class consents 89, 90
  ecclesiastical buildings 808
  listed buildings 334, 341, 355, 369, 778, 786, 788, 796
Royal Commission on the Historical Monuments of England (RCHM(e)) 1-2, 6, 27-33, 99, 297
  AAIs 31, 130, 136
  authorisation of development 417
  CBA 60
  class consents 32, 89, 90
  commissioners 29-30
  compensation 204
  conservation policy 525
  ecclesiastical buildings 361, 754
  identifying and recording 736, 740
  listed buildings 334, 341, 355, 369, 707, 708
Royal Fine Art Commission (RFAC) 525, 694-5, 764

Royal Opera House, Covent Garden 349

St Albans Abbey 103, 471
scheduled monument clearance 73, 94
scheduled monument consent (SMC) 81-4, 105-23, 124-5, 197-201, 321, 556-63, 564-71
  AAIs 132
  acquisition 180
  advice and assistance 194-5
  AMAA (1979) 540-5, 547, 550-2, 556-63
  applications 95-104, 564-71
  authorisation of development 415, 418
  burial grounds 213
  challenge 141-6
  charges 352
  class 84-93
  compensation 63-4, 76, 82, 93, 97, 125, 196-202, 577-85
  conditions 105-23, 368, 540, 575-6
  conservation areas 724
  conservation policy 525
  Crown 73, 93-4, 314
  demolition 350
  Europe (EA) 278
  excavation guidance notes 572-6
  grants and grant aid 97, 113, 178, 188-90
  intentional or reckless damage 172, 174
  management agreements 193
  matters to be considered 68
  metal detectors 175, 177

NHA (1983) 530
objections 124-5
planning considerations
  459-60, 470-1, 489
powers of entry 77-8
remains discovered during
  development 832, 843
revocation or modification
  124-5
supervision by court 140-1
unauthorised works 159-61,
  163-4, 166, 169
Wales 843, 845-6, 848, 867
scheduled monuments 6, 49, 63,
  64-8, 387-8, 399, 530
AAIs 80, 83, 91, 127-8, 139
access 77-80, 97, 105, 119-21,
  184-6
acquisition 77, 178-80, 182,
  187, 196-7, 202-4
adjacent land 183
advice and assistance 194-6,
  836, 839, 843
AMAA (1979) 536-48, 550-63
authorisation of development
  409, 412-13, 418-19, 425
CBA 60, 61
class consents 84-93
compensation 67, 75, 79, 170,
  179, 196-205
conservation areas 724, 773
conservation policy 525
criteria for classification
  69-77
defined 66-7
development plans 695
easements 183-4
ecclesiastical buildings 72-3,
  361, 363

English Heritage 11, 15-27
Europe (EA) 276-8, 284
grants and grant aid 97, 113,
  178, 187-90, 847-8
guardianship 180-2
hedgerows 329
identifying and recording
  735-6, 744-5
injunctions 146, 151, 156-7,
  158
intentional or reckless
  damage 170-4, 233, 386
judicial review 141, 146-56
listed buildings 304-6, 309,
  311-14, 319, 321, 332, 336-8,
  342, 346-7, 352, 356, 370,
  387-9, 782-3
local authorities 42, 43, 75-6,
  79, 844-8
management agreement 97,
  113, 123, 190-3
metal detectors 174-7
NHMF 35, 37
offences 81, 94, 105-6, 125,
  135, 137, 157-8, 159-70, 173,
  233, 541, 846-7
parks and gardens 323
planning considerations
  435-6, 438, 443, 445-7,
  450-2, 455-6, 458-60, 462,
  466, 471, 479
planning policy 820-1, 822,
  824-5, 829, 831-2
portable antiquities 206-7
powers of entry 77-80, 117-19
public facilities 186-7
RCHM(e) 28-9, 31, 32
securing archaeological
  facilities 506, 523

supervision by the courts
140-1
territorial waters 250
unauthorised works 81, 94,
105-6, 125, 135, 137, 157-8,
159-70, 173, 233, 541, 846-7
Wales 764-5, 773, 782-3, 834,
843-8, 866-7
advice 836, 839, 843
World Heritage Sites 258
see also scheduled monument
consent (SMC)
Scotland 11, 59, 64, 226
screening 275, 276-7, 280
sealing 476-7, 481, 823, 840
Secretary of State for Culture,
Media and Sport (SSCMS) 1,
2-9
AAIs 127-8, 130-3, 135-6, 138
access 185
advice and assistance 194
CBA 59-60
compensation 197-205
easements 183-4
English Heritage 10-17,
19-21, 23-6
exports of antiquities 254-6
grants and grant aid 187, 189
injunctions 157
intentional or reckless
damage 170, 173
judicial review 147-9, 152,
155
listed buildings 303-4, 340,
356
management agreements
191-3
metal detectors 174-5
NHMF 33-5

operations notices 589, 593
RCHM(e) 27, 30
scheduled monuments 64-8,
70, 72-80, 356
acquisition 178-80
class consents 84, 87-93
consent 81, 95-104, 140,
141-6, 570, 581, 585
consent conditions 105,
108-10, 112-23
guardianship 180-1
revocation or modification
of consent 124-5
unauthorised works 159,
164-5, 169-70
wrecks 251
see also Department of
Culture, Media and Sport
Secretary of State for Defence
94, 417
Secretary of State for the
Environment AMAA
(1979) 536-60
conservation policy 525
demolition of churches 758-9
listed buildings 303-4
NHA (1983) 530-1, 534
scheduled monument consent
564, 569
compensation 578, 581, 585
conditions 575-6
transport and traffic
management 731
see also Department of the
Environment (DOE)
Secretary of State for the
Environment, Transport and
the Regions (SSETR) 1, 2-9
appeals 486

authorisation of development
401, 404-5, 409, 412, 414-16,
423, 427
ecclesiastical exemption 358-9
Europe 275
hedgerows 326
listed buildings 303-10, 322,
333-42, 344-6, 351-6
appeals 371-3
compulsory purchase
391-2, 394-7
enforcement notices 375-7
urgent works 388-90
planning considerations 432,
435, 438-40, 442, 445, 450,
452, 465, 468, 473, 479,
486-9, 495-6
securing archaeological
facilities 499, 511, 513,
516, 518-19, 523-4
see also Department for the
Environment, Transport
and the Regions (DETR)
Secretary of State for Health 417
Secretary of State for the Home
Office 598-9
see also Home Office
Secretary of State for National
Heritage (SSNH) 1, 2,
235, 242, 243-5, 248-50
conservation areas 717-18,
720, 723-5, 727
conservation policy 525
ecclesiastical exemption 756,
758
discovery of remains during
development 831-2
identifying and recording
735-7, 739, 741-4

listed buildings 303-4, 699,
702, 704-7, 709-15
scheduled monument consent
724
transport and traffic
management 730
treasure 638, 640-4
code of practice 604-6, 612,
617, 620, 623-36
upkeep and repair 748-52
see also Department of
National Heritage (DNH)
Secretary of State for Trade and
Industry 275, 416, 418-19
Secretary of State for Wales 3,
23
compensation 583
ecclesiastical exemption 753
injunctions 157
listed buildings 304
operations notices 587, 589,
593-4
planning policy 761-810,
833-65
scheduled monument consent
564, 569
see also Welsh Office
set-aside 192, 265
setting 319-21, 695-6, 765
authorisation of development
409, 413, 418-19
conservation areas 717
development control 694-6,
697-8
ecclesiastical buildings 360
listed buildings 319-21, 332,
338, 343, 355, 700-1, 783-4
planning considerations
437-8, 446, 457, 466, 470

planning policy 822, 824, 825, 827, 829
scheduled monuments 319, 321, 332, 846, 866
  consent conditions 121, 123
  transport and traffic management 729, 734
  unauthorised works 169
  Wales 762, 764, 765, 767, 783-4, 836, 839, 846, 866
  World Heritage Sites 258
sewers 402, 407, 408, 846
shrubs and shrub roots 83, 86, 402
silver 229-31, 233, 240-4, 249
  Treasure Act 605, 607-8, 622, 638, 671-3, 674-5
Simplified Planning Zones (SPZs) 848
site clearance 129, 130, 134, 135, 136-7, 589
Sites and Monuments Record (SMR) 50, 662-71, 825, 836
  authorisation of development 410, 420-1, 424
  environmentally sensitive areas 265
  Europe 284, 287
  hedgerows 329-30
  listed buildings 338
  local authorities 46
  NHMF 37
  planning considerations 438, 450, 466, 475, 484
  planning policy 820, 825, 826, 827
  RCHM(e) 29, 32, 33
  treasure 177, 611, 617-18, 620, 622, 624

Wales 670, 836, 837, 844
Sites of Special Scientific Interest 276, 409
smuggling 257
Special Grants Programme 526
spot-listing 334, 337, 737, 741, 742, 743-4
  Wales 778, 779-80, 782
Society of Antiquaries of London 48, 52
Society for Medieval Archaeology 48
Society for the Promotion of Roman Studies 48
Society for the Protection of Ancient Buildings 355, 384, 786
souvenirs 21, 532
staffing 8, 11-12, 39, 42
stamp duty 16
Standing Conference of Archaeological Unit Managers (SCAUM) 40
statements of case 490-2
statutory undertakers 417-22, 553, 697, 733, 817-18
  authorisation of development 402, 407-8, 412, 415-16, 417-22
Steadman, Baroness 126
stop notices 423, 427-8, 429, 430, 715
storage 504-5
Stotford Water Mill 309
structure plans 403-4, 442-5, 489, 690, 692
supervision 24, 29, 33, 53
  AAIs 133
  advice and assistance 194-5

by court 140-1
evaluation 88, 90
grants and grant aid 190
judicial review 146
listed buildings 367, 383
Surrey Archaeological Society
241
surveys 43, 49, 406, 420, 503,
827
compensation 204
Europe 289-90, 294
grants and grant aid 190
IFA 55
listed buildings 334, 335
RCHM(e) 28-9, 30, 32
scheduled monuments 79, 89,
90-1
consent conditions 117-19
Wales 837-8
wrecks 251
Sussex Archaeological Society
49

taxation 14, 16-17, 513
listed buildings 319, 345, 705,
792
territorial waters 27, 73-4, 250-1,
254, 549
Europe 270, 299
theft 177, 206, 748, 749, 804
grave goods 228-9
treasure 232, 237
Thremhall Priory, Essex 320
time-limits 150-4
judicial review 147-8, 150-4
scheduled monument consent
124
tipping 83, 129, 160, 539, 552,
553

class consents 86, 92
tombstones and memorials
218-29, 252, 363, 597-9, 756
Tower of London 9
transfer of land or property
16-17, 510-11
treasure 49, 80, 229-53
Act (1996) 637-43
assignment of rights 602-3
care of finds 673-82
coins commonly found 671-3
coroners 644-62
form of declaration 601
metal detectors 177, 233, 240,
246, 249, 250, 606,
615-18, 621, 633, 643
portable antiquities 206, 207,
226, 227
recording of finds 643-4
SMRs 662-71
sources of advice 644-71
statutory code of practice
604-36
treasure trove 229-40
Treasury 12, 14-15, 33
tree preservation orders 718,
727-8
Wales 769, 776
trees in conservation areas 718,
727-8, 734
Wales 769, 776
trespass 130, 157, 177, 206, 228
treasure 238-40, 249, 615, 622,
633
trial trenching 84, 289, 827, 838
Trundle, West Sussex 471

uncertainty in planning
conditions 460

underwater archaeology 55, 504
Europe 294, 296, 299, 300
see also territorial waters
unitary development plans
(UDPs) 404, 439, 442, 444,
446, 454
planning appeals 489
planning policy 690, 692, 824
securing archaeological
facilities 500
United Reformed Church 358,
755-6, 809
universities 2, 31, 38-48
Urban Development Areas
(UDAs) 30, 401
Urban Development
Corporation (UDC) 401
urgent works 7, 25, 388-91,
748-9, 804-5
AAIs 138
authorisation of development
411, 418
listed buildings 312, 377, 382,
714
notices 387, 388-91, 396
Wales 800, 804-5
notices 387, 388-91, 396, 525
scheduled monuments 68, 78,
87, 91, 846
unauthorised 164, 170
upkeep and repair 747, 748-9,
750
Wales 762, 800, 804-5, 846
utilities 93-4, 131, 400, 719
authorisation of development
402, 407-8, 415-18, 420
operations notices exemption
596
Wales 770

value added tax 141, 142, 189,
319, 709, 789
Victorian Society 355, 786
visitor centres *see* public
facilities
votive deposits 610

Wales 49-50, 64, 258, 400,
761-810, 833-65, 866-7
AAIs 130, 132, 333
authorisation of development
421
battlefields 326
CBA 60, 786, 845
coroners 660-2
ecclesiastical exemption 358,
753, 808-10
environmentally sensitive
areas 263, 264
Europe 263-4, 268, 281, 284
grants and grant aid 187-90,
769, 803
listed buildings 785, 787,
792, 803, 807-8
hedgerows 326
heritage organisations 3-4, 7
landscapes 333
listed buildings 303-5, 342,
350, 352, 354, 355, 761-810
conservation areas 767-76
controls 777-803
repairs 394, 804-8
urgent works 388, 390-1
parks and gardens 322, 324,
670-1, 763, 765, 767, 784,
805, 838, 844
planning considerations 437,
438, 440, 443, 445

securing archaeological
facilities 502
SMRs and local authority
archaeologists 670, 836,
837, 844
territorial waters 74
treasure 233, 245, 250-1, 640,
642
code of practice 604,
606-7, 609, 618, 620
see also Cadw
watching brief 469, 473, 475,
830, 842
IFA 58
scheduled monument consent
conditions 117-18
Waverley criteria for exports
255-6
Wednesbury grounds 274, 320-1,
427, 460, 465, 499
scheduled monument consent
conditions 107-8, 110
Welby Almshouses,
Lincolnshire 384
Welsh Archaeological Trusts
836, 837, 838, 844, 845
Welsh Assembly 3, 64, 188
listed buildings 304, 372, 388

Welsh Office 11, 60, 132, 281,
336
see also Secretary of State for
Wales
Winckley Square, Preston
373
wind generators 270
works already executed
713, 800
World Conservation Union
(IUCN) 745, 766
World Heritage Sites 258-60,
331-2, 441, 450, 697-8, 745-6,
765-6
wrecks 7, 72-3, 244, 250-1, 252,
526, 555
treasure 609, 611, 639
written representation appeals
488, 496

York Archaeological Trust
(YAT) 50, 132
York Development and
Archaeological Study
(YDAS) 476
Yorkshire Archaeological
Society 49